University-Community Collaborations for the Twenty-First Century

Michigan State University Series on Children, Youth, and Families
(Vol. 4)
Garland Reference Library of Social Science
(Vol. 1119)

MICHIGAN STATE UNIVERSITY SERIES ON CHILDREN, YOUTH, AND FAMILIES

John Paul McKinney, *Senior Editor*
Lawrence B. Schiamberg, *Advisory Editor*
Amy B. Slonim and Linda Spence, *Associate Editors*

Child Maltreatment and Optimal Caregiving in Social Contexts
by Diana Baumrind

Adolescent Parenthood and Education
Exploring Alternative Programs
by Mary Pilat

Adolescents, Cultures, and Conflicts
Growing Up in Contemporary Europe
by Jari-Erik Nurmi

University-Community Collaborations for the Twenty-First Century
Outreach Scholarship for Youth and Families
edited by Richard M. Lerner and Lou Anna K. Simon

University-Community Collaborations for the Twenty-First Century
Outreach Scholarship for Youth and Families

edited by
Richard M. Lerner
Lou Anna K. Simon

GARLAND PUBLISHING, INC.
A MEMBER OF THE TAYLOR & FRANCIS GROUP
New York & London
1998

Library of Congress Cataloging-in-Publication Data

University-community collaborations for the twenty-first century : outreach scholarship for youth and families / edited by Richard M. Lerner, Lou Anna K.
Simon.

        p.   cm. — (Michigan State University series on children, youth,
and families ; vol. 4) (Garland reference library of social science ; vol. 1119)
    Includes bibliographical references and index.
    ISBN 0-8153-2445-6 (alk. paper)
    1. Community and college—United States. 2. Education, Higher—Social
aspects—United States.   I. Lerner, Richard M.   II. Simon, Lou Anna Kimsey.
III. Series: Michigan State University series on children, youth, and families ;
v. 4.   IV. Series: Garland reference library of social science ; v. 1119.
LC238.U547   1998
378.1'03'0973—dc21   97-30385
                                            CIP

Printed on acid-free, 250-year-life paper
Manufactured in the United States of America

Contents

Series Preface
Outreach Scholarship for
Children, Youth, and Families

The publication of Richard M. Lerner and Lou Anna K. Simon's volume, *University-Community Collaborations for the Twenty-First Century: Outreach Scholarship for Youth and Families,* signals the continued prominence and success of the Michigan State University Series on Children, Youth, and Families. The authors' scholarly work, accompanied by the insightful foreword by Peter Magrath, is a prime example of the creative emphasis on cutting-edge scholarship which the MSU Series represents—a focus on issues of social policy, program design and delivery, and evaluation—which addresses the needs of a diversity of children, youth, families, and communities. In particular, this book promises to be a seminal and landmark volume in rethinking the role of the American university in fostering, enhancing, and building university-community partnerships in the service of children, youth, and families.

Furthermore, the Lerner/Simon volume is a clear illustration of the goals of the Institute for Children, Youth, and Families (ICYF). It serves as an example of the relationship of outreach scholarship to essential issues of policy and program development which, in turn, has the potential for enhancing the lives of children, youth, and families in the diverse communities which the Institute serves. Likewise, the publication of this challenging and most impressive volume provides evidence that the MSU Series, initiated by ICYF and well served by the commitment and intellectual leadership of Senior Editor John Paul McKinney with the able guidance of Marie Ellen Larcada of Garland Publishing, serves as a compendium of scholarly work reflecting the very best scholarship aimed at enhancing the life experiences of a diversity of children, youth, and families. As such, both the Lerner/Simon volume and the MSU Series demonstrate the importance and feasibility of the mission of ICYF in integrating research and outreach.

The mission of the Institute for Children, Youth, and Families at MSU is based on a vision of the nature of a land-grant university as an academic institution with a responsibility for addressing the welfare of children, youth, and families in communities. More specifically, the mission of ICYF is shaped by an ecological perspective that places the life-span development of human beings in the context of the significant settings of human experience, including community, family, work, and peer networks (Lerner et al., 1994; Schiamberg, 1985, 1988). Historically, the ecological perspective has both been associated with, and a guiding frame for, colleges of home economics or, as they are more recently termed, colleges of human development, human ecology, or family and consumer sciences (Miller & Lerner, 1994). Using the ecology of human development as a conceptual framework, the Institute for Children, Youth, and Families continues to develop programs that integrate the critical notion of development in context with the attempt, indeed the necessity, of creating connections between such scholarship and social policy, program design, delivery, and evaluation.

The MSU Series is a unique collection of books, designed to provide a vehicle for the publication and transmission of research/outreach efforts characterized by the collaborative relationship (and potential relationship) between university expertise and the community. Lerner and Simon's book represents the careful and visionary thinking of authors who have worked, first hand, with university-community partnerships and collaborations which reflect both successful and "best practice" efforts in the service of enhancing the life prospects of children, youth, and families in community settings. As universities begin to respond to continuing social pressures to apply their resources to address a variety of critical social problems, there is a compelling need for such careful scholarship and for best practice in helping universities and communities to frame joint programs addressing the needs of the diverse groups of children and families that both serve. The Michigan State University Series on Children, Youth, and Families is, itself, an example of the outreach scholarship which reflects the contextual and practical policy focus of the ICYF research program. The MSU Series publishes reference and professional books, including monographs and edited volumes, which appeal to a wide audience in communities as well as in universities, including such constituencies as scholars, practitioners, service deliverers, child and family advocates, business leaders, and policymakers. As illustrated by the superb scholarly effort of Lerner and Simon, the MSU Series has substantial import and appeal to these constituencies primarily because of its focus on the integration of research and outreach and, as well, an emphasis on collaborative relationships between universities and communities.

The unique role and perspective of both ICYF and the MSU Series can be further appreciated in light of the ongoing trends for both university accountability and social contribution. In particular, the various university stakeholders, including business, government, and community leadership, are increasingly urging universities to use their research and scholarly resources to address problems of social, political, and technological relevance (Boyer, 1990; Votruba, 1992). Thus, communities are seeking a greater involvement in outreach on the part of their universities. Both ICYF and Michigan State University are committed to integrating outreach into the full fabric of university responsibility (Provost's Committee on University Outreach, 1993).

The volume by Lerner and Simon represents an outstanding contribution to this emerging outreach/research focus. The MSU Series editors, including John Paul McKinney, Amy B. Slonim, Linda Spence, and Lawrence B. Schiamberg, as well as the staff editor of the Institute for Children, Youth, and Families at MSU, Linda Chapel Jackson, are proud and grateful to have this path-breaking book on the emerging issues and patterns of university partnerships with the diverse communities of America as part of the MSU Series.

Lawrence B. Schiamberg
Series Editor, MSU Series on Children, Youth, and Families

References

Boyer, E.L. *Scholarship reconsidered: Priorities of the professoriate.* Princeton, NJ: The Carnegie Foundation for the Advancement of Teaching.

Lerner, R.M., Miller, J.R., Knott, J.H., Corey, K.E. Bynum, T.S., Hoopfer, L.C., McKinney, M.H., Abrams, L.A., Hula, R.C., & Terry, P.A. (1994). Integrating scholarship and outreach in human development research, policy, and service: A developmental contextual perspective. In D.L. Featherman, R.M. Lerner, & M. Perlmutter (Eds.), *Life-span development and behavior, Vol. 12* (pp. 249–273). Hillsdale, NJ: Erlbaum.

Miller, J.R., & Lerner, R.M. (1994). Integrating research and outreach: Developmental contextualism and the human ecological perspective. *Home Economics Forum, 7,* 21–28.

Provost's Committee on University Outreach. (1993). *University outreach at Michigan State University: Extending knowledge to serve society.* East Lansing: Michigan State University.

Schiamberg, L.B. (1985). *Human development* (2nd ed.), New York: Macmillan.

———. (1988). *Child and adolescent development* (2nd ed.). New York: Macmillan.

Votruba, J.C. (1992). Promoting the extension of knowledge in service to society. *Metropolitan Universities, 3* (3), 72–80.

Foreword
Creating the New Outreach University

Richard M. Lerner and Lou Anna K. Simon have assembled—and contributed to—an important book. It is far more than a series of isolated, interesting case studies on how colleges and universities must adapt themselves to serve society's interest in the new century just ahead. There are case studies in this book, but in its totality and the sweep of its conceptual and descriptive essays, *University-Community Collaborations for the Twenty-First Century* presents a lively demonstration of some of the most critical issues facing our society—and how colleges and universities can help meet these needs.

Put another way, this book provides both a theoretical and a practical primer, with rich illustrations, on how colleges and universities must become even more society-serving. The message is implicitly and explicitly clear: our colleges and universities, wonderful as they are, must change and reform themselves so as to serve the needs of contemporary America. We are a nation of great accomplishments and potential, but we are also riven with huge problems in our communities: alcohol and drug abuse, crime, inadequate schooling, families (or, perhaps more accurately, nonfamilies), and the reality and growing threat of a lost, wasted generation of youth—which, in turn, has massive implications for the economic competitiveness of the United States.

America's colleges and universities are still, as those of us who have labored within them love to say, "the envy of the world." The American research university has been incredibly successful in helping to identify and solve countless problems through its research in agriculture, medicine, and the sciences. Just as important, America's colleges and universities have performed excellently in helping to educate millions of Americans every year with the insights and skills essential to being effective human beings in a complex, technological world. A fair question then might be,

"Why should our colleges and universities change?" The answer is simple: because the world has changed.

A little history is instructive. Half a century ago, World War II ended and American higher education quickly confronted three monumental challenges. First, education-hungry war veterans populated our colleges and universities—and these institutions responded effectively. Second, the long and hard Cold War began and our universities were called upon to develop a world-class research capability heavily geared to our nation's security—and these institutions responded effectively. And third, tens of millions of Americans, especially minorities and women and people of modest means, yearned for the tools provided by higher education—and colleges and universities responded effectively.

This is a great success story, one in which America's public colleges and universities played the leading role. But that was then, and this is now. Now America faces new and even more monumental challenges. The Cold War is over, but the world is still an unsafe place, and international economic competitiveness is critical to our nation's security.

Moreover, we confront difficult, riveting, domestic challenges: a troubled health and welfare security system, a seemingly uncontrollable crime and corrections problem, a large population of men, women, and children, many of them minorities, who are economically and socially disenfranchised, and an elementary and secondary school system that in too many cases fails our society. And all of these challenges compete against a national consensus that public deficits and government spending must be curbed.

What does this mean for America's colleges and universities? The answer is, a great deal—in effect a monumental challenge at least as critical as that of the Cold War era. Because universities are indispensable generators of intellectual and economic creativity, they are essential to America's social and economic well-being in the century before us, just as two- and four-year colleges are also vital contributors to the talent pool of our society in their work of educating students who, ideally, become lifelong learners.

But to meet this challenge successfully, our universities, especially, must adapt and change. Yesterday's good works are inadequate for tomorrow's needs. We must recognize the new realities of diminished public resources while facing our shortcomings forthrightly. Clearly, these include our need to use faculty time more productively, our obligation to pay more attention to undergraduate students and to become full-time collaborators with public schools, and our duty to link research discoveries and educational insights with our states and communities in partnerships that strengthen our economy and society. And we dare not be afraid to use the new technologies—most of them spawned in our universities—to improve how we teach, learn, and communicate in a world not defined by campus boundaries or restricted by towers built of ivory.

This challenge, the challenge of adapting to change and, indeed, leading it, is really the thesis—the prescription—of this volume's description of the rich possibilities inherent in the new outreach university. This is a university, whether public or private, collaborating with community and liberal-arts colleges of all kinds, not only in their important traditional missions of educating students on campuses and producing life-saving research, but a university focused on community partnerships and collaborations that address the crisis afflicting much too much of America's youth. The exciting truth is that the kinds of practical educational-outreach programs called for by the contributors of this volume can be done. They are not just theory, but models that are being put in place—even though there are not enough of them to meet our society's needs.

The fulfillment of this challenge to meet the need for new outreach universities, building on their rich historic traditions, is one of the central challenges facing our universities. William C. Richardson, the president of the W.K. Kellogg Foundation, who has himself led major research universities, has stated the issue correctly and precisely:

One of the critical challenges for higher education is to redirect our knowledge and our resources in the service of rural communities and urban neighborhoods. In fact, it may be these investments that prove the true test and value of our research and outreach programs. Can we, for example, make a difference in the lives of people where they live, in the towns and communities of America? Can we build the capacity of people to play a central role in finding their own solutions? And, can we impact public policy that creates both economic and social opportunities for people to improve their quality of life? (Richardson, 1996)

Richardson, in a speech to university presidents, goes on to quote Dr. Donald Schön, Ford Professor Emeritus at MIT, who suggests that we should stop thinking about "practice" (outreach, if you will) as simply a kind of laboratory setting for the application of knowledge. Instead, Schön makes the fundamental point that practice leads also to the generation of knowledge; as he puts it, "we should ask not only how practitioners can better apply the results of academic research, but what kinds of knowing are already embedded in competent practice" (Schön, 1995). For those who care, as all of us should, about the future of research universities and their need for adequate funding, here is the solution. By doing what is needed, our universities will not only generate a climate of political support that will help with their funding needs, but they will also be generating insights and new knowledge from their outreach practices, from their literal "doings," which in turn stimulate and nourish the critical research function.

The essays in this book illustrate this point dramatically, even as they provide excellent descriptive models of ongoing outreach programs, whether at Penn State, Kent State, Virginia Tech, or smaller colleges such as Goucher. There are conventional and strong academic preju-dices about university-community outreach programs, and they are well described in the chapter about the University of Pittsburgh experience with its Office of Child Development. And yet the point is that the programs of that university have not only proven their value both to the community and to the university, but that undoubtedly they have in-formed the engaged faculty with new academic insights and understand-ings with regard to the complex challenges involving children, youth, and families in our modern society.

Indeed, the issue of research and scholarly relevance, so vital to our universities, is well explained and cogently argued by Stephen A. Small and Karen Bogenschneider in chapter 12, describing models of scholar-ship and relevance at the University of Wisconsin at Madison. The out-reach youth and family programs of the University of Wisconsin clearly demonstrate that scholarship can be relevant in outreach work. Moreover, these projects lead to genuine results—actual implementation in commu-nities—where they can make a difference in people's lives. But beyond this, this chapter provides compelling evidence that the scholarship of rel-evance and practice can meet the high scholarly expectations of academia. As the authors note, "each of the outreach projects cited in this paper and many described throughout this book have been published in refereed journals or presented at scholarly meetings."

Unfortunately, as the authors and contributors to this volume full well know, it's difficult to sell the idea of revitalizing America's universities so that outreach activities become as mainstream and valued within the academy as is currently true for the research function and the traditional ways of teaching students. As the contributors to the chapter on "Chang-ing the Culture of the University to Engage in Outreach Scholarship" write in concluding their chapter:

Our institutional mission and values provide a context essential for our ongo-ing commitment to the work. However, we know that it will take a cultural sea change to accomplish our goals. Time will tell if our sustained efforts will be integrated into the broader fabric of Boston College and become, as Fullan and Steigelbauer wrote . . . "a new way of life, not just another project."

The academic culture and faculty-reward system is one of the key underlying issues that must be addressed and modified if outreach is to become a truly mainstream part of our colleges and universities. All of us who deal with these issues and work for change recognize that this is one of the toughest, but not insuperable, challenges we face. To again quote Bill Richardson in his speech to university presidents, he argues that the "research-as-king mindset has shaped the academic culture and hierarchy of most American universities." He goes on to suggest that we must change the status quo on this issue if we are to meet the true challenges faced by higher education. There is of course no magic formula, but there is a need for a rebalancing of university efforts involving the teaching and learning of undergraduate and other students, the role of research, and the applica-tion of research in many forms—including outreach needed and relevant to our nation's communities.

It is because of this commitment to significant change and adapta-tion, and the opportunity for our colleges and universities to lead and direct change—as opposed to being driven haphazardly by the new envi-ronment confronting higher education in this post–Cold War era—that the Kellogg Foundation has stepped in. It supported the establishment of the Kellogg Commission on the Future of State and Land-Grant Univer-sities, intended to provide direction and leadership in dealing with some of the most critical challenges before higher education. The Commission has already concluded that these challenges revolve primarily around the student experience and can be placed at the heart of institutional con-cerns; addressed the question of access to our nation's colleges and univer-sities as a priority, despite financial and political pressures; advocated the creation of a learning society that encourages learning throughout life; advocated the reform of the campus culture so that excellence is redefined through the new agenda of social needs that are so obvious; and—espe-cially relevant to the thesis of this book—promoted the idea of "engaged institutions," those that go beyond traditional extension programs in or-der to become more productively involved with our communities.

No book, and certainly no single commission of university presidents, can presume to identify all of the issues and challenges before us, much less to solve them in some kind of a neat package. But this volume clearly identifies one of the most critical agendas before the house of American higher education: how our colleges and universities can reach out to communities and encourage communities to "reach in" to them, so that old collaborations can be strengthened and new ones developed and nurtured for the sake of addressing our nation's future—its youth. There are so many excellent essays and chapters in this book that one hesitates to single any one out; they are all on the right message of university-community involvement and the land-grant mission of serving public needs.

But it is not inappropriate to cite the essay on "Boldness for Our Times," written by the chairman emeritus of the Kellogg Foundation, Russell G. Mawby, for its insistence that our universities must, far more than they have and in new and imaginative ways, engage with education. This means not only the vital sector of K–12 education, but equally that which addresses the developmental process of youngsters from pre-birth through adolescence and into young adulthood. Mawby's thesis is that universities have to, in an integrated fashion, address and collaborate with communities in order to address the needs of the family and the local community and its schools. As he writes in his concluding paragraphs, our society urgently needs outreach scholarship that links the intellectual resources of institutions of higher education with communities and their needs, and he goes on to make this essential point:

> . . . *the multiplicity of problems confronting and confounding America's youth . . . provides the venue for this enhanced outreach initiative, building on higher education's oldest tradition of public service. America simply must do a better job of preparing its coming generations for the responsibilities they will assume and the lives they will lead. The richness of the intellectual resources of higher education must be mobilized to this end.*

One of the dangers facing American higher education is the erosion of public understanding and support, joined to an ideology that regards higher education as primarily serving private and selfish interests. In fact, our colleges and universities are primarily and overwhelmingly in public service. Their work of educating students, undertaking research, and fostering its application is essentially a public good, not a private benefit. The historic record demonstrates that higher education, while appropriately benefiting individuals, has fundamentally been a benefit—indeed a critical resource—serving the public good. If the colleges and universities of America consider and take to heart the insights, and then implement the practices, from this volume put together by Richard M. Lerner and Lou Anna K. Simon, both our society and its universities will be richly rewarded.

C. Peter Magrath
President
National Association of State Universities and Land-Grant Colleges

References

Richardson, W.C. (1996, January). Coming in from the Cold War: A peace time mission for higher education. Speech presented at the Kellogg Commission.

Schön, D.A. (1995, November/December). The new scholarship requires a new epistemology. *Change*, 27–34.

Preface

America's youth and families face an historically unprecedented set of problems, involving health and health care, economic opportunity and employment, educational and school failures, poverty, physical and social ecological deterioration, crime, inadequate social-service systems, and a set of behavioral risks (e.g., drug and alcohol use and abuse, violence, and unsafe sex) that engage increasingly broader segments of our citizenry. At the same time, America's universities are being challenged to become directly involved in addressing these problems. They are being pressed to reorient their missions to conduct teaching, research, and service in manners that help the communities beset by these problems address them—in ways defined by these communities as meaningful and useful. This reorientation involves the conduct of outreach scholarship and the creation of outreach universities.

Simply, then, universities are being challenged to work, in partnerships with communities, to use their abilities to generate, transmit, preserve, and apply knowledge in ways that improve the life chances of the individuals and families of the communities with which they are involved. This volume illustrates how these challenges are being met productively and successfully. It brings university administrators and faculty leaders from state, land-grant, and private colleges and universities together with leaders from several sectors of the community, from nongovernmental organizations, from state government, and from foundations supporting youth and family programming in order to: (1) present their views about issues pertinent to the problems facing America's universities and communities; and, most important, (2) to describe their actions aimed at creating community-collaborative, outreach universities. These are institutions that, in partnership with communities, integrate research, teaching, and service in order to effectively address the vital community and national concerns we have noted.

We believe that this volume gives unique voice to the solutions that universities and communities are currently forging for these problems. The chapters in this book make clear that there remain several important issues to address in order to continue to pursue these efforts; these issues involve both the university (for example, changing the system by which faculty are rewarded, so that community collaboration is both encouraged and sustained) and the community (overcoming, for example, the perhaps deserved skepticism that exists about the commitment of universities to work, as full partners, with communities). In addition, there exist issues that pertain to the collaborative system created by university and community partnerships, including issues involving placing the sustainability of the collaboration and the empowerment of citizens above concerns for the independent benefits to the partners. Nevertheless, the chapters attest to the fact that successful community-university collaborations can be developed and maintained; they also underscore the view that, if the programs described in this book are used as sample cases or models of what might be accomplished, there is reason for great optimism about the role that universities—as community-collaborative institutions—can play in promoting the positive development of our nation's youth and families.

There are numerous people we wish to thank for their collegiality and collaboration during the preparation of this book. Most of all, we wish to thank all the contributors to this volume. As the authors of the chapters of this book, these colleagues brought life and force to our vision of the potential that the creation of outreach universities has for enhancing opportunities for America's youth and families. We want to thank especially Dr. C. Peter Magrath, President, National Association of State Universities and Land-Grant Colleges, for encouraging the efforts of all contributors to the volume and for writing an insightful and supportive foreword.

Linda Chapel Jackson, Editor at the Institute for Children, Youth, and Families at Michigan State University, and her assistant, Adrienne E. Wile, provided expert professional editorial contributions to the entire volume. Their commitment and productivity are greatly appreciated. We also wish to express our gratitude to Dr. Lawrence B. Schiamberg, Senior Editor of the MSU Series on Children, Youth, and Families, for his sponsorship of the volume and for his helpful scholarly advice throughout the process of the book's development. We are grateful as well to the staff of Garland Publishing for their expert guidance throughout the production process.

Finally, we want to express our deep and abiding affection for our respective families—to whom this book is dedicated. It is their love and support that continue to motivate us to merge our professional abilities and our personal values in order to advance the institutions we most cherish—family, community, and university—in manners that enhance the lives of all citizens of our nation.

Richard M. Lerner
Lou Anna K. Simon

Section I

Creating Community-
Collaborative Universities

A View of the Issues

Chapter 1
The New American Outreach University
Challenges and Options

Richard M. Lerner   *Lou Anna K. Simon*
Boston College   *Michigan State University*

Too many of our faculty, in all of our disciplines, are far too insulated, too isolated, and in fact and perception seen as indifferent to worlds other than their own Our traditional faculty culture, which is built around every faculty person as an entrepreneur, a free thinker, and a free doer, has much to commend itself. But it also has much to condemn itself when that individual freedom is divorced from social reality and the needs and aspirations of America's citizens and voters. (C. Peter Magrath, President, National Association of State Universities and Land-Grant Colleges, 1993, p. 4).

America, and the communities that comprise it, face a set of problems of historically unprecedented scope and severity. Issues of economic development, environmental quality, health and health-care delivery, and—ultimately—of people, of children, youth, and families, challenge the current resources and future viability of our nation.

Indeed, across the communities of our nation, children and adolescents are dying—from violence; from drug and alcohol use and abuse; from unsafe sex; from poor nutrition; and from the sequelae of persistent and pervasive poverty (Dryfoos, 1990; Hamburg, 1992; Hernandez, 1993; Huston, 1991; Lerner, 1993a, 1993b, 1995; McKinney, Abrams, Terry, & Lerner, 1994; Schorr, 1988; Wilson, 1987). And, if our youth are not dying, their life chances are being squandered—by school failure, underachievement, and dropout; by crime; by teenage pregnancy and parenting; by lack of job preparedness; by prolonged welfare dependency; by challenges to their health (e.g., lack of immunizations, inadequate screening for disabilities, insufficient prenatal care, and lack of sufficient infant and childhood medical services); and by the feelings of despair and hopelessness that pervade the lives of children whose parents have lived in poverty and who see themselves as having little opportunity to do better, that is, to have a life marked by societal respect, achievement, and opportunity (Dryfoos, 1990; Huston, 1991; Huston, McLoyd, & Coll, 1994).

Numerous sectors of society have worked, and continue to work, to address these issues. However, although the sum total of these efforts affords a "comprehensive" approach, the whole has been less than the sum of its parts. Current efforts often involve different agencies and organizations competing for "turf," or "ownership" of a problem, and duplicating services that are delivered independent of input from program recipients; such an orientation to service provision is quite typically coupled with a deficit view of communities, families, and individuals and, as a consequence, few instances exist of community-wide, integrative collaboration. As such, most existing efforts do not build on community assets and do not create the capacity for communities to sustain effective programs.

A vision for such community empowerment exists, however. This vision seeks to create caring communities through broad, multi-institutional and citizen collaborations, and acts to envision, implement, and evaluate community-based programs; to engage policy; and to build a new generation of community leaders (e.g., see Dryfoos, 1990, 1994; Hamburg, 1992; Lerner, 1995; Lerner, Ostrom, & Freel, 1995, 1997; Ostrom, Lerner, & Freel, 1995; Schorr, 1988; Weiss & Greene, 1992).

Universities have a critical role to pay in such collaborations. They can act as agents of technical assistance, knowledge development, demonstration, training, and dissemination. However, to make such contributions, universities must change from their currently perceived (and, in several respects, actual) status as enclaves for ethereal elitism (Bonnen, 1986, 1992; Lerner, 1996) and become agents in community engagement and empowerment. To produce this change, a revised view of the scholarly functions of universities is needed, one that creates "outreach universities," that is, universities that generate, transmit, preserve, or apply knowledge to address societal problems, as these problems are defined in concert with community collaborators. To reach such collaborative definitions, a "co-learning" model, that is, a model involving a merger of expertise in communities with expertise in universities, must be developed.

Illustrations exist of productive university-based initiatives consistent with the promotion of such community-collaborative outreach scholarship. A key purpose of this volume is to present these examples of "systems change," that is, of alterations in the way universities function in and with the communities they serve and of the issues of academic restructuring that need to be addressed in order to enhance and sustain outreach scholarship pertinent to the youth and families of these communities. In turn, perspectives from key community stakeholders—from foundations, from nongovernmental organizations (NGOs), and from governmental bodies also involved in promoting the positive and healthy development of our nation's youth, families, and communities—are included in order to underscore the need for, and significance of, these university systems changes.

The presentation of these university and community illustrations is predicated on the belief that if the university and the society served by its efforts are to survive and prosper into the next century, collaborations that build and maintain such programs will have to be supported. However, and despite the productivity of the examples of outreach presented in this book, it is still the case that such initiatives are not modal in American society. Accordingly, it is important to understand the academic and societal context within which these systems changes are occurring. This context both promotes the need for such changes and, as well, constrains the possibility that they will occur.

The Context for Creating Outreach Universities:
Academic and Community Opportunities and Constraints

The American university has been dominated by an emphasis on the development of the disciplines (Bok, 1992; Bonnen, 1986, 1992; Boyer, 1990; Votruba, 1992). American universities have been modeled after the nineteenth-century German university—wherein community-disengaged, independently working scholars pursued "ethereal" knowledge, that is, knowledge that was not contingent on the extant sociocultural context pertinent at a given historical moment (Lynton & Elman, 1987). Historically, the more decontextualized the knowledge, the higher its value (Bonnen, 1986, 1992).

Contemporary intellectual and societal forces are challenging this value. University scholars—whether they are in the role of teacher, researcher, and/or administrator—are currently engaged in discussions about the existence or validity of decontextualized knowledge, and about the legitimacy of the disciplinary and sociocultural isolation associated with such knowledge.

These issues have been discussed in fields as seemingly disparate as:

- the physical sciences—involving concepts such as quantum mechanics (Zukav, 1979), chaos (Gleick, 1987), and dissipative systems and entropy (Prigogine, 1978);

- evolutionary biology—involving concepts such as exaptation (Gould & Vrba, 1982), self-selection (Lewontin & Levins, 1978), and behavioral neophenotypes (Gottlieb, 1992);
- the social and behavioral sciences—involving concepts such as individual-environment dialectics (Riegel, 1975, 1976); the ecology of human development (Bronfenbrenner, 1977, 1979; Bronfenbrenner & Morris, 1998); developmental systems (Ford & Lerner, 1992; Lerner, 1997; Sameroff, 1983; Thelen & Smith, 1998) and contextualism (Lerner, 1986, 1991, 1992, 1995); the home economics/human ecology vision of integrative (community-collaborative, multidisciplinary, and multiprofessional) scholarship (Lerner & Miller, 1993; Lerner et al., 1994; Lerner, Miller, & Ostrom, 1995; Miller & Lerner, 1994); and applied developmental science (Fisher et al., 1993; Lerner & Fisher, 1994).

Together, these concepts have fostered a challenge to prior conceptions of the nature of the world. The idea that all knowledge is related to its context has promoted a change in the typical "philosophy of being" (the ontology) within the academy; that is, a focus on "relationism" has helped advance the view that all existence is contingent—on the specifics of the physical and social cultural conditions that exist at a particular moment of history (Pepper, 1942). As a consequence, changes in epistemology have been associated with this revision in ontology: Contingent knowledge can only be understood if relationships are studied (Schön, 1995). Accordingly, any instance of knowledge (e.g., the core knowledge of a given discipline) must be integrated with knowledge of the context surrounding it, *and of the relation* between knowledge and context. Part of this context is the community. As such, one key implication of these philosophical changes for outreach scholarship is that the university scholar's knowledge must be integrated with the knowledge that exists in the communities within which universities are embedded.

From Multidisciplinary Knowledge to
Community-Collaborative Universities

The philosophical ideas associated with the emerging interest in relational knowledge result in an increased emphasis among scholars on integrating knowledge across multiple dimensions (i.e., across multiple disciplines and multiple professions). As such, the interest in relationism and integration constitute a set of internal pressures within the academy for multidisciplinary scholarship. Moreover, these contemporary intellectual emphases converge with external pressures on the academy that, in effect, provide a corresponding press for integrative, multidisciplinary knowledge. That is, coupled with pressures stemming from academic philosophical and scholarly revisions, external pressure is being placed on the academy to use its knowledge to address the problems of the community. Thus, the relationism being promoted by academic/scholarly changes converges with a relationism fostered by interest in the community to have universities apply their knowledge to community problems—as the community defines these problems.

Therefore, since these community problems—involving issues of employment and economic development, of health and health services, of environmental quality, of crime, of a severely challenged educational system, of poverty, and ultimately of the quality of life of individuals, families, and communities—are not arrayed in insulated disciplinary compartments, this appeal constitutes a press for multidisciplinary knowledge that is integrated with the needs of the community (Lerner et al., 1997; Miller & Lerner, 1994). Thus, these pressures involve calls for universities to be accountable for helping address, in a sustained manner, the social and cultural problems of the diverse proximal and distal communities in which they are embedded.

Such efforts by universities are not distinct from traditional activities pursued by, in particular, land-grant institutions. Indeed, the pressure by the community for the university to use its knowledge to address community-defined problems, that is, the demand for outreach scholarship (Lerner, 1995; Lerner et al., 1994; Miller & Lerner, 1994), pertinent to the quality of life of youth and families, is a demand consistent with one of the three foundational foci of land-grant institutions (Bonnen, 1986, 1992). That is, a concern with improving people's lives has been, along with concerns for providing access to information and for promoting economic development, a core focus of the land-grant mission. However, the pressures for sustained university contributions to the enhancement of the lives of individuals and families are not placed today only on land-grant institutions. All state universities, and indeed all institutions of higher learning, in both the public and private arenas, receive such pressures—and this is why this range of public and private institutions is represented in this volume.

Moreover, these pressures—rather than being able to be interpreted as a brief discontinuity in expectations maintained about universities—promise to be of such scope that institutions of higher education will have to develop a long-term strategy for response, one that will require not the compartmentalization (or, in some cases, marginalization) of such responses within one section or unit of the university (e.g., cooperative extension); rather, such responses will require action across the entire fabric of the university. The implementation of such responses will necessitate changes in the academic system that extend well into the next century and will involve major revisions in the mission and structure of the American university. Indeed, as Magrath has observed:

First and foremost our universities, all of them, both those that are technically land-grant and those that are not technically land-grant, are in the people-serving business. That is why they exist, and indeed all of them really are in the spirit of the land-grant tradition of serving society and being responsive to social needs in collaborative partnerships with our community and its legitimate interests. . . . But above all else public service means that all of our universities, from the most prestigious research-intensive universities to those that are smaller and may be more focused, have a fundamental, irreducible, obligation to recognize that we serve not our interest, but our state and national interests as defined, not just by us clever professionals, though we have contributions to make; but as defined by the people who pay taxes and who provide the tuition, and who make contributions that enable us to be blessed with fulfilling and well-paying jobs that gives us much. It is therefore not only appropriate, but morally right, that much be expected of us. (Magrath, 1993, pp. 5–6)

In sum, then, converging intellectual and societal pressures are acting as an important impetus for the emergence of a university system wherein knowledge integration—across disciplines, across professions, and across the borders that may divide the university from the diverse communities it serves—may become both intellectually and ethically normative. That is, we believe that contemporary societal pressures serve to reinforce the direction of change involved in the above-noted philosophical issues: Both sets of pressures will require universities to integrate their abilities to generate, transmit, preserve, and apply knowledge (Boyer, 1990) with the needs of the community.

Of course, American universities and the pressing social issues facing the nation have always been interrelated (Bonnen, 1986, 1992; Boyer, 1994). Leaders of our nation's institutions of higher education and of the nation itself have traditionally linked academic scholarship and the "practical" needs of America. Indeed, Boyer (1994) describes the history of the links between higher educational teaching and research and service to the nation, a history that involved both private and public institutions, and which began during the colonial period, extended through the American Revolution and the 1862 and 1890 Morrill acts, and included the National Defense Education Act of 1958. Indeed, as Boyer (1994) notes, the very title of this latter act illustrates the essential link between higher education and a very vital societal issue: the security of our nation.

Nevertheless, today in America this historical association between the scholarship of our universities and the problems of our nation has weakened. From outside of the university there is, as Boyer observes, a general belief that:

The overall efforts of the academy are not considered to be at the vital center of the nation's work. And [there] is the growing feeling in this country that higher education is a private *benefit, not a public good. (emphasis in original) (Boyer, 1994, p. 48)*

Although there is controversy within the academy about the necessity of any association between the scholarly agenda of the professorate and the critical issues facing our nation, it is our view that the pressures on universities by the diverse communities of our nation will foster increased reliance on an integrative vision for the future of American universities, for example, as found in the view of scholarship embodied in the perspective labeled "applied developmental science" (Fisher et al., 1993; Lerner & Fisher, 1994), or the home economics/human ecology and development perspective forwarded by Miller and Lerner (1994) and by Lerner, Ostrom, and Freel (1997). Such integrative views promote collaborative approaches to working across units, disciplines, and professions, and with communities.

Indeed, the problems facing our nation as we move to the twenty-first century, and, as such, the problems within which universities find themselves embedded, are so profound that such integrative visions must be developed and sustained. It is important, then, to consider the pressures for integration now facing American universities and the social and cultural problems that have led to these pressures.

Sociocultural Pressures and Youth and Family Problems Confronting American Universities

The remainder of this decade will be a period of profound challenge for American universities. To address adequately the focal pressure to improve the quality of life of America's youth and families, universities will have to respond to an historically unprecedented set of problems confronting the people of our nation's communities.

For example, consider just some of the high-risk behaviors that, as noted above, pervade the lives of America's youth: drug and alcohol use; crimes, often of a violent nature; school failure and dropout; and unsafe sex and teenage pregnancy and parenting. In America, there are approximately 28 million children and adolescents between the ages of 10 and 17 years. About 50% of these youth engage in *two or more* of the above-noted categories of risk behaviors (Dryfoos, 1990). Moreover, 10% of our nation's youth engage in *all* of the four categories of risk behaviors (Dryfoos, 1990).

These data regarding the prevalence of risk behaviors indicate that the current status of American youth is exceedingly problematic. Indeed, these data suggest that nothing short of a "generational time bomb" (Lerner, 1993a, 1995) is confronting American society. With so many of our nation's youth beset with so many instances of behavioral risk, America is on the verge of shortly losing much of its next generation, that is, the human capital upon which the future of our nation relies (Hamburg, 1992; Lerner, 1993a, 1993b, 1995). Moreover, poverty exacerbates the risk behaviors of youth and, in fact, Schorr (1988) notes that poverty is the single best predictor of "rotten outcomes" of youth development. Quite unfortunately, then, poverty is a growing problem for America's youth and families (Huston, 1991; Lerner, 1993a, 1995). By the end of the 1980s approximately 20% of America's children and adolescents were poor (Huston, 1991; Huston, 1994; Simons, Finlay, & Yang, 1991). Moreover, data in the 1992 *Kids Count Data Book* indicate that across the 1980s the percentage of youth living in poverty in the United States increased by 22%. Indeed, this national trend was present in forty states, and continues to increase across the nation (Huston, 1991). Furthermore, of the 12 million American children under the age of three years, 25% live in poor families (Carnegie Corporation of New York, 1994). In addition, whereas the number of children under age six years decreased by 10% between 1971 and 1991, the number of poor children in this age group *increased by 60%* (Carnegie Corporation of New York, 1994).

As a means to summarize the costs—not only to youth but to all of America—of pervasive youth and family poverty, as well as of the risk behaviors associated with it, we may note Hamburg's view that:

Not only are many more children growing up in poverty than was the case a decade or two ago, but many more are mired in persistent, intractable poverty with no realistic hope of escape. They are profoundly lacking in constructively oriented social-support networks to promote their education and health. They have very few models of competence. They are bereft of visible economic opportunity. The fate of these young people is not merely a tragedy for them, but for the entire nation: A growing fraction of our potential work force consists of seriously disadvantaged people who will have little if any prospect of acquiring the necessary competence to revitalize the economy. If we cannot bring ourselves to feel compassion for these young people on a personal level, we must at least recognize that our economy and our society will suffer along with them. Their loss is our loss. (Hamburg, 1992, p.10)

In sum, then, given the number of youth and families that today are at such profound levels of risk, we are faced as a society with a crisis so broad that the entire fabric of American society is in serious jeopardy (Lerner, 1995; Simons, Finlay, & Yang, 1991). With so many of our nation's communities facing the likelihood of losing much of their next generation to one or more of the several high-risk behaviors increasingly present among our nation's youth, all of our children, whether or not they themselves engage in given risk behaviors, nevertheless in effect live in risk—of experiencing the adverse economic and employment conditions associated with living in a nation that is increasingly globally uncompetitive, has a diminished pool of future leaders, offers lowered standards of living, requires lower expectations about life chances and, in fact, provides fewer and fewer opportunities for healthy and wholesome development (Lerner, 1993a).

Put simply, America is wasting its most precious resource: the human capital represented by its youth (Hamburg, 1992; Lerner, 1993a, 1993b, 1995; Lerner & Miller, 1993). And this destruction of human capital is a problem that cuts across race, ethnicity, gender, and rural or urban environments (Center for the Study of Social Policy, 1992, 1993; Simons, Finlay, & Yang, 1991). Accordingly, all of us, all Americans, and certainly all of our children and adolescents, are now and for the foreseeable future confronted by this crisis of youth and family development. The breadth of the problems affecting our nation's youth and families requires that we see the issues we face as pertaining to all of us, and not to only a segment or a subgroup of America. All of our nation's institutions—and certainly its universities—must participate in finding solutions to (in bringing knowledge to bear on) these issues critical to the quality of life in our nation. The responses to this historically unparalleled challenge will influence not only the structure of much of higher education in the twenty-first century, but will determine whether these, and possibly all public and private universities are viable institutions into the next century. Indeed, as Sheldon Hackney noted, in his May 21, 1991 commencement address at the University of Pennsylvania:

... *as the university has become more important to society, it is losing the special place it once held in the scheme of things. Knowledge has become much more central to society and to the economy, yet universities are increasingly pictured as just another snout at the public trough.*

Thus, research universities, whether public or private, are being asked to address pressing societal problems and are being held accountable for their performance in these areas.

After several decades in which the nation has made a massive commitment of resources to public research universities, the mood has changed. The public, government, and governing boards are beginning to question the raison d'etre of the public research universities. As a result of this point of view, the Pew Higher Education Research Program (1991) has predicted:

... *an end to the public perception of the collegiate campus as a place of sanctuary, a place where values other than the purely financial might prevail, where commitment to the freedom of expression and truly unfettered inquiry guarantees a standard of conduct exceeding that observed by the population at large. The message is that whatever their claims to a special calling, these institutions are no different, no better, no longer exempt from public scrutiny and caricature. . . . The practical consequence is that institutions of higher education can expect less of the public purse and more of public intervention.*

To maintain or to increase funding, the public and private donors must perceive that the agenda of these institutions is pertinent to the needs of the diverse proximate and distal governmental, business, and "grass roots" communities within which universities are embedded, and upon which universities rely for their financial and political support. If such pertinence is not demonstrable, then support will be eroded, if not completely withdrawn (Bok, 1992).

We believe, then, that all American universities will be asked increasingly to provide knowledge that is relevant to the needs of the youth and families of the communities within which they are embedded. Such relevance is the mandate of the American land-grant university; and at this time in the history of our nation, the necessity for land-grant universities and, as well, state universities and public and private colleges, to provide leadership for such relevance is inescapable (Magrath, 1993).

Furthermore, it seems clear that relevance will be defined and evaluated from the vantage point of these communities and not from the perspective of the universities themselves (Bok, 1992; Boyer, 1994). It would be sheer folly to "hunker down and ride out the storm." As the Pew Higher Education Research Program notes in response to the question "Why not hold our breath and wait out the next turn?":

Our answer is simple: This time, those who hold their breath are likely to turn blue before higher education again feels secure in its claim to public support and trust. Already there has been a steady and marked decline in the proportion of financial support that state legislatures provide their colleges and universities. Indeed, legislatures began according higher education a smaller share of their budgets more than a decade ago, well before the financial crunch that dramatically reduced the size of everyone's pie. States tend to increasingly regard higher education as a mature industry, and the monies they accord to colleges and universities have become a prime source of "flexible" funds capable of redirection without adverse political consequence. (Pew Higher Education Research Program, 1992)

Thus, it is important that colleges and universities, led, we believe, by land-grant institutions, become "part of the solution" rather than "part of the problem" (Cleaver, 1967). The problems confronting communities require that the academy be open to input from, and available to be influenced by, communities and by the diverse youth and families within them. If universities are not accessible and responsive to the diverse communities within which they are embedded, the universities' contribution to solving community-defined problems will be, at best, haphazard. If universities do not pay attention to communities and provide avenues of communication, they will not be able to learn about the pressing issues of the day.

What is called for then, is nothing short of a cultural change in the role that universities play in contributing to the critical issues facing society (Boyer, 1990, 1994; Lynton & Elman, 1987). In Boyer's (1990) terminology, universities are being challenged to view their scholarship from a problem-focused rather than a discipline-based perspective. Problems such as pervasive and persistent poverty, economic development and competitiveness, health, environmental quality, and youth development do not fall neatly into a single disciplinary category. Solutions to such problems require integrative scholarship (Brown, 1987).

Integrative scholarship will lead to closer collaborations between universities and the communities within which they are embedded. The creation of such community-collaborative relationships is the core intellectual issue around which discussion of changes in the American university system reside (Boyer, 1994; Lynton & Elman, 1987; Magrath, 1993). We believe that the needed reorientation can be achieved by synthesizing the missions of the university around the concept of "outreach."

Features of an Outreach University

Recently, a provost-empaneled committee of faculty and administrators at Michigan State University completed a report on how the university might extend knowledge to serve society (Provost's Committee on University Outreach, 1993). The Committee emphasized that the key missions of the academy—teaching, research, and service—are all different manifestations of a scholar's core concern, that is, knowledge, and its generation, transmission, application, and preservation (Boyer, 1990). Outreach, the Committee emphasized, is a form of scholarship that involves one or more of the teaching, research, and service missions. That is, outreach involves the generation, transmission, application, or preservation of knowledge in manners consistent with university and unit views of these missions. However, these activities are carried out to directly benefit audiences external to the university—and are to be defined by these diverse community groups, in concert with universities. In other words, then, outreach is a cross-cutting activity; it involves all instances of the above-noted knowledge functions and, as such, can engage all facets of unit and university missions in a community-collaborative, co-learning approach to scholarship.

Accordingly, successful outreach is predicated on accountability and access. Universities can provide few benefits to external audiences if they are disconnected from these groups: Among the myriad issues upon which university faculty might focus their scholarship, only a subset, and perhaps a small one, might be important to the communities in which they are embedded. Thus, once again, universities will not be successfully accountable in addressing the needs of communities if there is no access by the community to the scholarly agendas of the academy, if there is not collaboration between university and community, if there is no co-learning. Accordingly, outreach, which integrates the knowledge, functions, and missions of the university, also involves the integration of accountability and access into the core of the university.

Moreover, to promote and sustain a commitment to outreach into the breadth and depth of the university, other issues, core to the functioning of academic institutions, must be engaged integratively, that is, in a manner that promotes systems change. These issues include:

- restructuring of the tenure system;
- changing the faculty reward (review) system;
- addressing the pressures from funding sources;
- fostering outreach as a major feature of university and unit missions;
- fostering balance across the other functions of the university;
- promoting multidimensional excellence;
- framing outreach as a feature of institutional adaptive capacity (an issue integrally related to accountability);
- indexing and evaluating productivity;
- revisions in graduate education;
- undergraduate education and service learning.

Accordingly, an integrative approach to knowledge, and to academic system change in the service of fostering outreach, can lead universities to become institutions *for* the communities within which they exist, that is, institutions for the people they seek to both understand and systematically enhance. Such "outreach scholarship" can, then, be an effective means through which the knowledge functions of America's universities (i.e., knowledge generation, transmission, application, and preservation) can meet the needs of communities and thus of our society (Boyer, 1990, 1994; Votruba, 1992). This approach to integrative research and outreach can help create—in actuality and in the perceptions of the public—an academy that is socially useful and relevant, an institution that, consistent with the land-grant mission (Enarson, 1989), truly employs knowledge to address the "practical" problems of life. Moreover, when this orientation is used as a frame for educating future generations of university faculty, then a means will be created for sustaining an "outreach university," an institution wherein research, teaching, and community collaboration are synthesized.

Reorganizing Higher Education Institutions around the Concept of "Outreach"

It is clear that internal economic challenges and societal pressures converge. Government, business, and "grass roots" constituents demand that the resources society allocates to both "public" and "private" universities be spent on activities that are relevant to the needs of the constituents—as the constituents, and not the professorate, conceive of and define these needs (Boyer, 1990; Lynton & Elman, 1987). Accordingly, internal reorganization and external reorientation of American state and land-grant universities of the next century will be produced by a recognition that a revised approach to the knowledge functions of the academy will be required if scholarship is to be used to address key and pervasive problems confronting society.

As we have emphasized, integrative responses by American universities to the economic and societal pressures facing our nation may be especially important at this point in our history. Indeed, providing a frame for such integration may be a special contribution that state and land-grant universities can make to society. This role for such universities is brought to the fore because, as we have noted, the issues associated with the key youth and family problems confronting society cross domains of scholarship, involve the public, business, private, and political sectors of society, and occur in distinct ways in diverse community settings. Accordingly, to address these problems in ecologically valid ways, academics must join in both multidisciplinary and multiprofessional collaborations, associations that require knowledge of, and the participation by, the youth and families of the specific communities one is attempting both to understand and to serve (Lerner & Miller, 1993; Miller & Lerner, 1994).

One way of representing the import of the federal acts that created the combined teaching, research, and service missions of the land-grant system is to depict such an institution as the university *for* the people of the state. That is, the land-grant university's functions of knowledge generation (research), knowledge transmission (teaching), and knowledge utilization (outreach) exist to improve the lives of the people of its state *as they live in their communities.* Moreover, the vision of the tripartite, land-grant mission was that research, teaching, and service (or outreach) should be viewed as integrated, or synthetic, activities. Teaching about, or research conducted within, the ecologically valid settings within which children and families live their lives (that is, within their homes and within their communities), is predicated on an understanding of the needs, values, and interests of the specific people and particular community the land-grant institution is trying to serve.

Accordingly, when knowledge generation or transmission occurs in a context wherein the community values and sees "practical" significance for these facets of knowledge, the application of this knowledge by the specific communities becomes more likely. At least three specific scholarly foci challenge the academy to move in directions that have not been traditional within institutions of higher education.

Implementing the Vision: Promoting Changes in American Universities and Colleges

First, to obtain an adequate understanding of the problems of the youth and families of our communities, we should pursue multidisciplinary research efforts that focus on the richness and diversity of the people, settings, and potential of human life. Our research efforts should not only synthesize ideas and methods from multiple disciplines in an integrative manner, they should be conducted by and with youth and families of as wide a range of ethnic, racial, physical ability, family, community, and sociocultural backgrounds as possible. Only through an emphasis on such diversity can integrated knowledge be fully extended to the range of problems, and of possibilities, involving the people of our communities.

Second, it is clear that such scholarship will not succeed unless the youth and families from within these diverse settings are engaged cooperatively in the endeavor. Scholarship must be seen as relevant and important by the youth, families, and communities about whom we wish to learn; such research, then, should be seen as returning, or providing, something of value to these groups. Accordingly, techniques that give voice to the community need to be employed in order to activate this university-community collaboration and to remain accountable to the people it serves.

Finally, a third challenge brings us full circle to the issues confronting higher education in the 1990s; it involves the developmental systems view (Ford & Lerner, 1992; Thelen & Smith, 1998) that we, as scholars, are not disconnected from the people and society we study and serve. As parts of the same system it is entirely appropriate that we discuss—within the framework of our model of integration—what changes need to be developed in scholars and in scholarly institutions in order to best implement (or test) our vision of integrated knowledge.

One change involves having established scholars reorient their own work. In addition, leaders of graduate education programs should begin to train their students differently (Birkel, Lerner, & Smyer, 1989; Fisher et al., 1993). An appreciation of integrated knowledge, systematic change, context, and human relationships should be the cornerstone of graduate education. This is a central point stressed in the growing attention being paid among scholarly societies and universities to the importance of training in applied developmental science for future scholars and professionals in fields associated with human development and education (Fisher et al., 1993). We should instill in these future "outreach scholars and professionals" a greater appreciation of the importance of knowledge integration, of community-collaboration, of human diversity and of the contextual variation that is both a product and a producer of it (Fisher, Jackson, & Villarruel, 1998; Lerner, 1982; Lerner & Busch-Rossnagel, 1981; Lerner & Miller, 1993; Miller & Lerner, 1994).

Furthermore, it is important to add that university tenure and promotion committees evaluating the new outreach scholar must be urged to begin to consider the relative value of multidisciplinary collaborative, and hence, multiauthored, publications, in comparison to within-discipline, single-authored products. We must also consider the nature of the reception given by university review committees to the sort of contextual and collaborative research we are furthering (Votruba, 1992, 1996). The issue to be debated here is whether we can train future cohorts of applied developmental scientists to engage productively in the multidisciplinary, multiprofessional, and community collaborations requisite for advancing integrated knowledge and then not reward and value them for successfully doing so (Votruba, 1992, 1996).

In essence, we must engage in a debate about changing the reward system within our universities. If we follow an integrative perspective that leads to the synthesis of science and service (e.g., Lerner, Ostrom, & Freel, 1997; Miller & Lerner, 1994), then it would seem that we must devise means to assign value to, and reward, an array of integrative, collaborative, multidisciplinary, and multiprofessional activities.

The key challenge for American colleges and universities as they move into the twenty-first century is to integrate knowledge across multiple academic disciplines *and* multiple professional activities, with the youth and families of the community. This integration must be achieved while providing access to the diverse communities served by the university and while remaining accountable for contributing to effective solutions to the problems identified through such access.

If we are to help foster such a university through pursuing the vision of integrative scholarship, we must act soon (Bok, 1992; Boyer, 1994). Our communities cannot wait for American universities to contribute in thorough, sustained, and effective ways to the problems they face. It may very well be that nothing less than the future of the academy and, more important, the quality of life in our nation, is pending on the adequacy of our actions. Accordingly, discussions must be engaged, and action plans formulated, among the leaders of American universities and colleges.

The Plan of This Book

The purpose of this book is to move this agenda forward—not merely by detailing the academic and institutional issues that must be confronted, since these have been well articulated in several important essays (e.g., Bok, 1992; Bonnen, 1986, 1992; Boyer, 1990, 1994; Lynton & Elman, 1987; Millard, 1991; Votruba, 1996; Walshok, 1995)—but by discussing the ways these issues are being integratively addressed by universities and by the communities within which they are embedded. That is, we seek to help further the creation of outreach universities by focusing this volume on current attempts at systems change, that is, on what is being done to work within the array of interrelated issues that confront leaders acting to create outreach universities. Thus, this book will not be an attempt to redefine the land-grant mission. Rather, the book will illustrate ways to achieve a foundational goal of universities, and particularly land-grant universities; that is, to improve the quality of life of the youth, families, and communities served by the university. This is achieved through outreach, community collaboration based on co-learning, a redefinition of research, and the synthesis of the (higher) educational enterprise with the social issues faced by the youth and families of our nation's communities.

In order for higher education institutions to provide leadership in the creation of such "outreach universities," that is, universities wherein integrative, community-collaborative, multidisciplinary, and multiprofessional knowledge is normatively pursued and rewarded, this book will discuss also the several arenas of the academy that must undergo qualitative change. For example, as illustrated in several of the chapters in this volume, changes must occur in the roles of the disciplines, in systems of faculty rewards, in graduate and undergraduate education, in community access, in faculty and administrative unit accountability for excellence across the breadth of the university's mission, and in administrative vision and leadership. The organization and implementation of such changes involves both scholarly creativity, intellectual vision, and—frankly—administrative courage. The importance of these attributes for promoting systems change is represented across the sections of this book.

Section 1 has two chapters. In addition to the present, introductory chapter, the second chapter in this section discusses the history of the idea of "knowledge-social application" synthesis. This concept is at the heart of the land-grant vision and, now, is at the core of both societal and academic pressures promoting university-community collaborations across the range of America's universities.

The second section of the book contains chapters describing the agendas of systems change being pursued—at land-grant universities, at state universities, and at selected large and small private institutions—to create and sustain outreach universities enhancing the lives of youth and families in America's communities. The chapters in this section present the ongoing efforts of university and college presidents, provosts, deans, and faculty leaders to promote the systems changes requisite to meet this challenge.

The third part of the book includes chapters from sections of the community with which universities do (or at least should) collaborate and/or from organizations (foundations, governmental bodies) that have an interest in promoting such collaborations. Accordingly, these chapters are written by NGO leaders, foundation leaders, and leaders of governmental bodies.

The last section of the book contains a chapter that draws conclusions and addresses their implications. Here we derive common features of, and principles for, the systems changes illustrated in section 2 and discussed, as well, in section 3 of the book. We also identify the obstacles facing these agents of systems change. Last, we indicate the recommendations for further change, and for evaluation of the efficacy and outcomes of the change process, which we see as both reasonable and feasible. The chapter ends with a specification of academic and social policy changes that need to be pursued to implement our recommendations.

In sum, this volume includes the perspectives of the several sectors of society that must collaborate in the creation of outreach universities for America's youth, families, and communities: university administrators and faculty leaders, NGO leaders, foundation officers, and government officials. By including and integrating these perspectives, we believe that this book gives voice to the ways in which issues of knowledge integration and community collaboration currently challenging American universities are being actively addressed in America. Across its chapters, then, our hope is that this book will promote a vision for the further development of initiatives in American higher education to create a university system predicated on the integration of cutting-edge scholarship with the needs and problems of the people of the community. In this way, then, this book may both enlighten our present and provide a productive path for our future.

References

Birkel, R., Lerner, R. M., & Smyer, M. A. (1989). Applied developmental psychology as an implementation of a life-span view of human development. *Journal of Applied Developmental Psychology, 10,* 425–445.

Bok, D. (1992). Reclaiming the public trust. *Change,* 13–19.

Bonnen, J. T. (1986). A century of science in agriculture: Lessons for science policy. *American Journal of Agricultural Economics, 68,* 1065–1080.

Bonnen, J. T. (1992). Changing roles of agricultural economists and their institutions. *American Journal of Agricultural Economics, 74,* 1260–1261.

Boyer, E. L. (1990). *Scholarship reconsidered: Priorities of the professorate.* Princeton, NJ: The Carnegie Foundation for the Advancement of Teaching.

Boyer, E. L. (1994, March 9). Creating the new American college [Point of View column]. *The Chronicle of Higher Education* (p. A48).

Bronfenbrenner, U. (1977). Toward an experimental ecology of human development. *American Psychologist, 32,* 513–531.

———. (1979). *The ecology of human development.* Cambridge, MA: Harvard University Press.

Bronfenbrenner, U., & Morris, P. A. (1998). The ecology of developmental processes. In R. M. Lerner (Ed.), *Theoretical models of human development.* Volume 1 of the *Handbook of Child Psychology* (5th ed. pp. 993–1028), Editor-in-Chief: William Damon. New York: Wiley.

Brown, N. A. (1987). *Youth development in the land-grant university* (McDowell Series Lecture). University Park: The Pennsylvania State University.

Carnegie Corporation of New York. (1994, April). *Starting points: Meeting the needs of our youngest children.* Available from Carnegie Corporation of New York, PO Box 753, Waldorf, MD 20604.

Center for the Study of Social Policy (1992). *1992 Kids Count data book: State profiles of child well-being.* Available from the Center for the Study of Social Policy, Suite 503, 1250 Eye Street NW, Washington DC 20005.

——— (1993). 1993 *Kids Count data book: State profiles of child well-being.* Available from the Center for the Study of Social Policy, Suite 503, 1250 Eye Street NW, Washington DC 20005.

Cleaver, E. (1967). *Soul on ice.* New York: McGraw-Hill.

Dryfoos, J. G. (1990). *Adolescents at risk: Prevalence and prevention.* New York: Oxford University.

———. (1994). *Full service schools: A revolution in health and social services of children, youth and families.* San Francisco: Jossey-Bass.

Enarson, H. L. (1989). *Revitalizing the landgrant mission.* Blacksburg, VA: Virginia Polytechnic Institute and State University.

Fisher, C. B., Jackson, J. F., & Villarruel, F. A. (1998). The study of African American and Latin American children and youth. In R. M. Lerner (Ed.), *Theoretical models of human development.* Volume 1 of the *Handbook of Child Psychology* (5th ed. pp. 1145–1207), Editor-in-Chief: William Damon. New York: Wiley.

Fisher, C. B., Murray, J. P., Dill, J. R., Hagen, J. W., Hogan, M. J., Lerner, R. M., Robok, G. W., Sigel, I., Sostek, A. M., Smyer, M. A., Spencer, M. B., & Wilcox, B. (1993). The national conference on graduate education in the applications of developmental science across the life span. *Journal of Applied Developmental Psychology, 14,* 1–10.

Ford, D. L., & Lerner, R. M. (1992). *Developmental systems theory: An integrative approach.* Newbury Park, CA: Sage.

Gleick, J. (1987). *Chaos: Making a new science.* New York: Viking.

Gottlieb, G. (1992). *Individual development and evolution: The genesis of novel behavior.* New York: Oxford.

Gould, S., & Vrba, E. (1982). Exaptation: A missing term in the science of form. *Paleobiology, 8,* 4–15.

Hackney, S. (1991). *Commencement address.* Philadelphia: University of Pennsylvania.

Hamburg, D. A. (1992). *Today's children: Creating a future for a generation in crisis.* New York: Time Books.

Hernandez, D. J. (1993). *America's children: Resources from family, government, and the economy.* New York: Russell Sage Foundation.

Huston, A. C. (1991). Children in poverty: Developmental and policy issues. In A. C. Huston (Ed.), *Children in poverty: Child development and public policy* (pp. 1–22). Cambridge: Cambridge University Press.

Huston, A. C., McLoyd, V. C., & Garcia Coll, C. T. (1994). Children and poverty: Issues in contemporary research. *Child Development, 65,* 275–282.

Lerner, R. M. (1982). Children and adolescents as producers of their own development. *Developmental Review, 2,* 342–370.

———. (1986). *Concepts and theories of human development* (2nd ed.). New York: Random House.

———. (1991). Changing organism-context relations as the basic process of development: A developmental contextual perspective. *Developmental Psychology, 27,* 27–32.

———. (1992). *Final solutions: Biology, prejudice, and genocide.* University Park: The Pennsylvania State University.

———. (1993a). Early adolescence: Toward an agenda for the integration of research, policy, and intervention. In R. M. Lerner (Ed.), *Early adolescence: Perspectives on research, policy, and intervention* (pp. 1–13). Hillsdale, NJ: Erlbaum.

———. (1993b). Investment in youth: The role of home economics in enhancing the life chances of America's children. *AHEA Monograph Series, 1,* 5–34.

———. (1995). *America's youth in crisis: Challenges and options for programs and policies.* Thousand Oaks, CA: Sage.

———. (1996). Creating caring communities: Building university-community partnerships to enhance youth and family development. *Conversations, 3* (1–2), pp. 8–12. [newsletter of the National Center for Social Work and Education Collaboration]. Bronx, NY: Fordham University.

———. (1997). Theories of human development: Contemporary perspectives. In R. M. Lerner (Ed.), *Theoretical models of human development.* Volume 1 of the *Handbook of Child Psychology* (5th ed. pp. 1–24), Editor-in-Chief: William Damon. New York: Wiley.

Lerner, R. M., & Busch-Rossnagel, N. (1981). Individuals as producers of their development: Conceptual and empirical bases. In R. M. Lerner & N. A. Busch-Rossnagel (Eds.), *Individuals as producers of their development: A life-span perspective* (pp. 1–36). New York: Academic.

Lerner, R. M., & Fisher, C. B. (1994). From applied developmental psychology to applied developmental science: Community coalitions and collaborative careers. In C. B. Fisher & R. M. Lerner (Eds.), *Applied developmental psychology* (pp. 505–522). New York: McGraw-Hill.

Lerner, R. M., & Miller, J. R. (1993). Integrating human development research and intervention for America's children: The Michigan State University model. *Journal of Applied Developmental Psychology, 14,* 347–364.

Lerner, R. M., Miller, J. R., Knott, J. H., Corey, K. E., Bynum, T. S., Hoopfer, L. C., McKinney, M. H., Abrams, L. A., Hula, R. C., & Terry, P. A. (1994). Integrating scholarship and outreach in human development research, policy, and service: A developmental contextual perspective. In D. L. Featherman, R. M. Lerner, & M. Perlmutter (Eds.), *Life-span development and behavior* (Vol. 12, pp. 249–273). Hillsdale, NJ: Erlbaum.

Lerner, R. M., Miller, J. R., & Ostrom, C. W. (1995, Spring). Integrative knowledge, accountability, access, and the American university of the twenty-first century: A family and consumer sciences vision of the future of higher education. *Kappa Omicron Nu FORUM, 8*(1), 11–27.

Lerner, R. M., Ostrom, C. W., & Freel, M. A. (1995). Promoting positive youth and community development through outreach scholarship: Comments on Zeldon and Peterson. *Journal of Adolescent Research, 10,* 486–502.

———. (1997). Preventing health compromising behaviors among youth and promoting their positive development: A developmental-contextual perspective. In J. Schulenberg, J. L. Maggs, & K. Hurrelmann (Eds.), *Health risks and developmental transitions during adolescence* (pp. 498–521). New York: Cambridge University Press.

Lewontin, R. C., & Levins, R. (1978). Evolution. In *Encyclopedia Einaudi, 5*. Turin: Einaudi.

Lynton, E. A., & Elman, S. E. (1987). *New priorities for the university: Meeting society's needs for applied knowledge and competent individuals.* San Francisco: Jossey-Bass.

Magrath, C. P. (1993). *Comments to the Board on Home Economics on November 12, 1993.* Washington, DC: National Association of State Universities and Land-Grant Colleges.

McKinney, M., Abrams, L. A., Terry, P. A., & Lerner, R. M. (1994). Child development research and the poor children of America: A call for a developmental contextual approach to research and outreach. *Family and Consumer Sciences Research Journal, 23*, 26–42.

Millard, R. M. (1991). *Today's myths and tomorrow's realities: Overcoming obstacles to academic leadership in the 21st century.* San Francisco: Jossey-Bass.

Miller, J. R., & Lerner, R. M. (1994). Integrating research and outreach: Developmental contextualism and the human ecological perspective. *Home Economics Forum, 7*, 21–28.

Ostrom, C. W., Lerner, R. M., & Freel, M. A. (1995). Building the capacity of youth and families through university-community collaborations: The development-in-context evaluation (DICE) model. *Journal of Adolescent Research, 10*, 427–448.

Pepper, S. C. (1942). *World hypotheses.* Berkeley: University of California.

Pew Higher Education Research Program (1991). *Policy Perspectives, 3* (4).

Pew Higher Education Research Program (1992). *Policy Perspectives, 4* (3).

Prigogine, I. I. (1978). Time, structure, and fluctuation. *Science, 201*, 777–785.

Provost's Committee on University Outreach (1993). *University outreach at Michigan State University: Extending knowledge to serve society: A report by the Provost's Committee on University Outreach.* East Lansing: Michigan State University.

Riegel, K. F. (1975). Toward a dialectical theory of development. *Human Development, 18*, 50–64.

Riegel, K. F. (1976). The dialectics of human development. *American Psychologist, 31*, 689–700.

Sameroff, A. J. (1983). Developmental systems: Contexts and evolution. In W. Kessen (Ed.), *Handbook of Child Psychology: Vol. 1. History, theory, and methods, 1* (pp. 237–294). New York: Wiley.

Schön, D. A. (1995). The new scholarship requires a new epistemology. *Change, 27* (9), 27–34.

Schorr, L. B. (1988). *Within our reach: Breaking the cycle of disadvantage.* New York: Doubleday.

Simons, J. M., Finlay, B., & Yang, A. (1991). *The adolescent and young adult fact book.* Washington, DC: Children's Defense Fund.

Thelen, E., & Smith, L. B. (1998). Dynamic systems theories. In R. M. Lerner (Ed.), *Theoretical models of human development.* Volume 1 of the *Handbook of Child Psychology* (5th ed. pp. 563–634), Editor-in-Chief: William Damon. New York: Wiley.

Votruba, J. C. (1992). Promoting the extension of knowledge in service to society. *Metropolitan Universities, 3* (3), 72–80.

Votruba, J. C. (1996). Strengthening the university's alignment with society: Challenges and strategies. *Journal of Public Service & Outreach, 1* (1), 29–36.

Walshok, M. L. (1995). *Knowledge without boundaries: What America's research universities can do for the economy, the workplace, and the community.* San Francisco: Jossey-Bass.

Weiss, H. B., & Greene, J. C. (1992). An empowerment partnership for family support and education programs and evaluations. *Family Science Review, 5*, 131–148.

Wilson, W. J. (1987). *The truly disadvantaged: The inner city, the underclass, and public policy.* Chicago: University of Chicago.

Zukav, G. (1979). *The dancing Wu Li masters.* New York: Bantam.

Chapter 2
The Land-Grant Idea and the Evolving Outreach University

James T. Bonnen
Michigan State University

I used to believe that neither society nor university faculty understood the land-grant idea. But today I am convinced that it is worse than that. It is the university as an historical institution that is not understood—even by faculty. Remarkably, the reason is that academics, for all of their intellectual and analytic capacities, never reflect on it or study it—or few do. Rather, we faculty mostly take the university for granted and believe it has pretty much always had the same roles and functions, as when we entered it. In addition most faculty believe that it has only the "harmoniously integrated" roles that each of us plays within the university. In short, many of us behave as if the university was created in our "own image and likeness."

In fact, different faculty play very different roles. Their beliefs are in stark contrast to the complex reality of diverse, often conflicting, roles actually being performed across a large university, the management of which is far more difficult than most faculty appreciate. Nor are these multiple roles a recent phenomenon. Many are in fact ancient.

The basic argument of this chapter has been made before but is not well understood by most academics: The university has survived for nearly a millennium by creating new roles and adapting its mix of roles to fundamental changes in the nature of society and its practical needs. Society is changing in radical ways again and we in the university are in a mode of adaptation that appears to be creating deeper involvement in society's efforts to resolve its practical problems. Today's evolving "outreach university" had its origin in a unique nineteenth-century American educational innovation, the land-grant college. The land-grant tradition introduced "service to society" as a function of U.S. higher education. However, we still have difficulty defining and agreeing on what outreach, extension, or service should involve as a legitimate university function. The existence of such a variety of terms is indicative of our lack of consensus about the nature of this century-old function of the American university.

This chapter first addresses the historical development of the university and the accumulating roles in which the university has served society over the centuries. It then turns to the impact of science on the modern American university and its societal context, and to a review of the challenges facing U.S. universities today, including the rise of a knowledge-centered society. The last half of the chapter is devoted to a survey of the growing direct involvement of U.S. universities in addressing societal problems, an attempt to define this more direct involvement, which we call "university outreach," and finally an assessment of the risks and limitations of outreach as a major role of the university.

Evolution of the University and Its Social Roles

The modern university has many roles. These have accumulated over the centuries, generally without dropping earlier ones. The university was a medieval creation of the eleventh and twelfth centuries (Rashdall, 1929; Rudy, 1984, pp. 14–26). Before it was anything else, the medieval university was a professional school that taught theology and provided the vocational training of priests—some of whom constituted the society's only educated elite (Deanesly & Bateson, 1926). Training in law and medicine developed in the Middle Ages as functions of the university (Mullinger, 1911). These schools conserved and transmitted knowledge for future generations. An organized liberal-arts curriculum (the trivium and quadrivium) developed as a formal preparation for law and especially medicine. All of these roles were responses to medieval societal needs for civil and ecclesiastical leadership, lawyers, and medical doctors (Rudy, 1984, p. 31; Mullinger, 1911, p. 751).

With the rise of the renaissance university in the fourteenth and fifteenth centuries, education of a lay elite for societal leadership first evolved as a significant role. Humanistic studies and scholarship developed very slowly, initially outside the university, driven by the growing revival of classical Greek and Roman learning, first in Renaissance Italy and then in Europe. However, the medieval roles remained the dominant university functions in the Renaissance. Thus, the renaissance university continued to be motivated by society's perceived practical needs. (Rudy, 1984, p. 40)

The pursuit of knowledge for its own sake, rather than for God, or in the Renaissance, man's sake, did not become a major force in European scholarship until well into the seventeenth and eighteenth centuries. Until this time, all scholarly study tended to be devoted to religion, vocational, and other perceived practical needs of society.

The "Scientific Revolution" began a fundamental transformation of society and its institutions in the nineteenth and twentieth centuries. While modern science as an enterprise runs back into the seventeenth century, it did not have a major presence in the university until the nineteenth century (Ashby, 1974, pp. 1–15). The university as a social organization resists and only slowly adopts new roles. The constraint of tradition on innovation explains much of the history of the university.

American higher education was established during the seventeenth and eighteenth centuries, borrowed from the British Oxford and Cambridge version of the liberal arts as conceived in the renaissance university (Newman, 1976). Initially these were church-sponsored colleges or seminaries for undergraduates. University graduate education and science research were introduced in the nineteenth century, an innovation modeled on the German university that evolved out of Wilhelm von Humbolt's reforms of German higher education. This is the model for the modern research university, which in the U.S. was imposed on top of the undergraduate college. These two ideas of the university involve very different goals and values, and thus social roles that often conflict. Today some faculty are devoted to one, some to the other, some to both (Brubacher and Rudy, 1968, pp. 171–201).

It is difficult today to imagine the complexity of the conflict over the nature and purpose of the university that occurred during the early decades of this century. A confusing combat of beliefs and values drove a great diversity of views within the academy over the appropriate role of higher education in U.S. society (Veysey, 1965, pp. 439–444). Today we face a new configuration of equally complex conflicts and confusions, some new, but many ancient (Brubacher, 1977; Ashby, 1974, pp. 73–149).

The Land-Grant Idea

But what of the land-grant university, its "service to society," and origins? Some decades ago, I wondered, "What do senior faculty mean by their endless appeals to the land-grant mission or land-grant philosophy?" I never got a satisfactory answer. The definitions proved too general or did not encompass many things going on around me.

I came to the College of Agriculture at Michigan State University from graduate work at Duke and then Harvard and was the first member of my department who did not have a farm background. Baffled by my environment, I started reading histories of land-grant colleges and the autobiographies and biographies of early pioneers such as Liberty Hyde Bailey and Isaac Roberts. What I learned surprised me. Contrary to the beliefs of many faculty:

1. The land-grant system of colleges did not spring into existence as a coherent idea or set of institutions in one decade or even one generation of leadership. The land-grant college evolved as an idea and then as an institution and a national system over the seven decades between 1850 and 1920. There was a lot of trial and much error, and it was not clear before the turn of this century whether the idea would be even a partial success (Roberts, 1946, p. 136).

2. The land-grant idea was not conceived solely for agriculture. It is not any specific set of organizations, such as the trilogy of the experiment station, the extension service, and on-campus or resident instruction. These were designed specifically to address agriculture.

3. The land-grant idea is not just access to higher education for those with limited resources. It is not just good science. It is not just science applied to practical problems. It is not just extension education for people of the state who have practical problems to solve. It was all of this and more.

So what is the land-grant idea? It is, indeed, an idea. *It is a set of beliefs about the social role of the university*. What then are the beliefs that have defined the social role of the land-grant university? And what gave rise to this set of beliefs?

The history of the last half of the nineteenth century shows that the land-grant university arose out of an industrializing society's increasingly complex problems and deficiencies (Brubacher & Rudy, 1968, pp. 64–66). There was a growing need for more highly trained professionals, especially in the new science-based fields necessary to address the requirements of an industrial society—in engineering, public health, agriculture, forestry, nursing, etc. Many of the professional schools of the modern university were needed but did not exist. Secondly, it arose out of an industrializing society's frustration with an unresponsive set of mostly private colleges providing a classical or "literary" education for a wealthy elite of less than 1% of the population. U.S. colleges of the day were generally church-sponsored, and higher education was viewed as a religious responsibility. With few exceptions these institutions were unwilling to sully their hands addressing society's common but real needs. This was not their role. Thirdly, it arose out of middle-class concern for the "American dream" of unlimited opportunities that was being threatened by industrialization. This was creating great wealth for some, but also a large, disadvantaged working-class population of poor farmers and industrial workers with no prospect of access to the skills and practical education necessary for a better life. It was, they believed, creating a trapped underclass of potential peasants and workers. This concern was not only for equality of opportunity for a disadvantaged population, from which many in the middle class had come, but arose as well from their fear that democratic institutions and individual liberty, and thus survival of the middle class, were at stake in a society of growing economic inequality. (Morrill, 1961; Eddy, 1957, pp. 1–45; Brubacher & Rudy, 1968, pp. 64–66).

In partial response, a new kind of college or university was created: The land-grant university or college, the unique part of the nineteenth-century public university movement (Nevins, 1962). The Morrill Act of 1862 founded the land-grant colleges around an explicit commitment to education and service for the broader society. The land-grant university in its mature form was devoted to science and education in the service of society by:

1. Educating and training the professional cadres of an industrial, increasingly urban, society;
2. providing broad access to higher education, irrespective of wealth or social status;
3. working to improve the welfare and social status of the largest groups in society, who at that time were among the most disadvantaged—farmers and industrial workers, the latter called "mechanics" in the nineteenth century.

Justin Morrill, the congressional sponsor of the act establishing the land-grant university system, was primarily concerned for broader, more democratic access to higher education to strengthen political democracy.

The Land-Grant colleges were founded on the idea that a higher and broader education should be placed in every State within reach of those whose destiny assigns them to, or who may have the courage to choose industrial vocations where the wealth of nations is produced. . . . It would be a mistake to suppose it was intended that every student should become either a farmer or a mechanic when the design comprehended not only instruction for those who may hold a plow or follow a trade, but such instruction as any person might need . . . and without the exclusion of those who might prefer to adhere to the classics. *(emphasis added) (Morrill, 1961)*

By the turn of this century, these were a well-formed set of U.S. beliefs about the social role of the university. This is the land-grant idea. And it has, within the limits of society's resources, been generously supported by society for successfully pursuing these goals. Arnold Toynbee, the British historian, once observed that the land-grant idea is the one original contribution of American higher education. Today the land-grant university, along with other public and some private universities, appears to be evolving toward a twenty-first century "outreach university."

In pursuing these social goals, the most visible, early success of the land-grant university occurred in agriculture, where these beliefs were translated into the organizations of the experiment stations (a national system), the extension service (despite appearances, really only state systems)—plus an ever-changing set of research and extension programs. The improved welfare of the potential underclasses of the nineteenth century was achieved through improved productivity and the wider distribution of its benefits through more equitable access to the opportunities in life. Open access and low tuition were long a general feature of the land-grant and other public universities, and have provided opportunity for upward mobility in society irrespective of background or wealth.

The Multiple Roles of the Modern University

From its earliest days the university has inherited several, very different roles: The scholarly pursuit of knowledge for God and man's sake; general or liberal education of clerical, and later, lay elites; and from the very beginning, professional and vocational training. These constitute responses to major needs of medieval and renaissance society and thus primary social roles of the university. Scholarship contributed to the cultural capacity and knowledge of the society and kept the university intellectually vital. It was valued then as today more by academics than by the supporting society, although an increasingly better-educated but small elite, lay and clerical, did share in and sponsor these values. Academics have frequently demonstrated considerable innocence in denying or denigrating the legitimacy of these historical roles.

Stout denials to the contrary notwithstanding, vocational training has always been a function of the university (Paulsen, 1906, pp. 111–114). How else does one view the medieval and renaissance university training of priests, medical doctors, and lawyers? It does no good to argue that these are professions and thus different. The university took them as vocations and professionalized them. They are no less vocations for it.

It is quite clear historically that the university has served society in every epoch by training and professionalizing those vocations that society judged critical to its functioning. This stabilizes training, establishes common standards of professional performance, and bestows an enlarged social status upon the vocation, increasing its access in and capacity to serve society while enabling the profession to attract talented individuals. The university continues to this day to professionalize those vocations that the ordering of society makes essential, as for example not only in engineering and agriculture, but also primary and secondary education, journalism, social work, public administration, dentistry, architecture, business, hotel and restaurant management, industrial relations, police administration, and on and on.

Interestingly enough, over recent centuries there has been resentment within the university that this vocational and professionalizing role should exist. This attitude arises out of academic values that honor the pursuit of intellectually pure over applied knowledge—for that which has no obvious value in immediate material and practical use, whatever its intellectual meaning. This belief arises from the seventeenth and eighteenth century European ethic of the leisured, land-owning, aristocrat turned gentleman scientist or academic, further reinforced by aristocratic resentment of the growing social and economic power of the material and practical-minded, rising commercial middle class.

The primary values of the academic vocation are determinedly intellectual. Sustaining the integrity of these values against the everyday pressures of the world and from outside meddling in the affairs of the university has never been an easy task—as a personal or an institutional matter. In defense of its interior intellectual life, the university tends to produce a culture that in its extreme form rejects as inappropriate all direct involvement in the affairs of the world, which leads some individuals even to deny that the university as an institution has any social role. This, of course, is wishful but hardly clear thought. Some balance of these multiple roles is necessary, along with respect for those who pursue the roles of the university that one does not oneself pursue. This makes the governance of the university a complex challenge.

All academic protests to the contrary do not change the historical fact that any institution that has survived for nearly a millennia is inevitably a social institution. Society has secured its survival simply because of the university's utility in society, that is, its social roles. In fact, the university from its inception has been preeminently a social institution, a creature of its society and time (Paulsen, 1906, pp. 111–114). To deny this is to deny the history of every epoch of the university's existence. The real question is one of defining or redefining the social role of the university for each age and society so that legitimate needs are met while the university's intellectual integrity (and therefore, its long-run vitality as a social institution) is protected from external encroachment and compromise. Sir Eric Ashby concluded that, "What has survived and is significant is the social purpose of the university, its independence from church and state, and its peculiar method of internal government" (1959, p. 2). Not only is the social role of the university one of its preeminent dimensions, but it is a role that by nature is in slow but continuous evolution. The social role of the medieval university was somewhat different from that of the great renaissance university, and further still from that of the modern university, which was formed in the crucible of the scientific revolution of the nineteenth century. As the nature of the society that sustains the university changes in fundamental ways, the social role of the university will very slowly undergo change in response to that new social reality.

This keeps many academics thoroughly confused, for just as they begin to grasp the reality of their environment, it changes. This is especially the case in an organization with multiple roles in which any one academic's experience may extend to only one or a few of those roles. There is a predictable response. Reaching out for what they know, academics will use their bit of academic "turf" as a model of "the university," substituting the values and norms of their own activities for those of the university as a whole. Thus, the individual from the humanities, for example, or one whose commitment lies primarily in undergraduate teaching, will argue the primacy of the humanistic and scholarly values of the late-renaissance university. The bench scientist and the graduate and professional school-teacher will often assert the exclusive claim of the values of the nineteenth-century German university model, even when unaware of their historical origin. This idea of the university is devoted all but exclusively to the creation of knowledge of the material world and to graduate education rooted in that search for new knowledge. Both the humanistic idea of the renaissance university and the German or research-university idea are inherently elitist in intellectual terms, which, in twentieth-century practice, can and does deteriorate into a social elitism that is antidemocratic.

The research (or German) university idea and the land-grant college were introduced in the U.S. in the nineteenth century. Both were merged in the land-grant university, creating a constructive tension between knowledge creation and its use in society and between the intellectually elitist values of a scholarly life and the egalitarian values of a democratic society.

The land-grant idea at its best is determinedly democratic in a social sense, while intellectually elitist. It requires a commitment to first-class science and excellent scholarship—to an intellectual elitism. But the land-grant university is also committed to apply that science and scholarship to the practical problems of society. This combines intellectual excellence with equality of access to scientific and scholarly knowledge, which is socially democratic or egalitarian both in research and education. Involved is an inherent tension that must be understood, accepted, and managed.

The science beliefs of the land-grant idea were put well almost six decades ago by the philosopher Alfred North Whitehead. Speaking at Harvard's tercentenary celebration of its founding, he said:

In the process of learning there should be present, in some sense or other, a subordinate activity of application. In fact, the applications are part of the knowledge. For the very meaning of things known is wrapped up in the relationships beyond themselves. Thus, unapplied knowledge is knowledge shorn of its meaning. Careful shielding of a university from the activities of the world around is the best way to chill interest and to defeat progress. (Whitehead, 1936, p. 267)

The Impact of Modern Science

Science has probably been the single greatest force molding the culture of the modern age. It has transformed a traditional society into an industrial and now an information age in which vastly different technologies and organizations and a radically different view of human life and of the world prevail. This is quite as fundamental a transformation as occurred between the Middle Ages and the Renaissance. Its philosophical and organizational impact on the university is still being assimilated.

"The scientific method" (in actuality a variety of methods that are in some degree positivistic) became the dominant, and in most environments, the only or at least the most, acceptable and respected approach to knowledge. Positivism was a reaction to and rejection of the Aristotelian idea that understanding the world required a teleological explanation—that is, the belief that purpose determines the character of the natural world that man experiences. Consequently, the purpose of any entity must be divined before it is possible to explain its nature. Positivism sought to limit claims of explanation to the more proximate causes of phenomena, to observable dimensions of causation, while avoiding metaphysical inquiry or unnecessary value judgments. A logical positivist view of science (an extreme now generally rejected in philosophy) accepts as scientifically meaningful only those propositions implied by a scientific theory (a group of scientifically meaningful propositions) or those propositions that are capable of being defined precisely and quantitatively measured. This logical positivism excludes from scientific knowledge, as best it can, all normative and subjective matters. The contribution of a theory-based, empirical science to the understanding of the material world and to the wealth of society has been immense. But positivistic rules of evidence of whatever degree, when accorded the role of *the sole means to knowledge*, have disordered and eroded the society's and the university's commitment to the celebration of human values and culture, even, to some extent, in the modern humanities. "Hard scientists" often talk of science as involving a logical positivistic method devoid of subjectivity, but for many practical reasons they practice a "softer" less rigorous positivism in research. This hard-science talk intimidates the "softer" social scientists and humanists of the academy. Thus, the great renaissance university, that marriage of faith in reason with human values, has unnecessarily but inexorably all but dissolved in the early positivism of the age of science. This and the progressive secularization of society have left education and society with a moral void and a different concept of man.

We have replaced the renaissance ideal of the whole man with that of man the research specialist—the expert, the technocrat. This is the ideal to which our education has aspired, the prototype of man most valued in society. Like most cultural evolution, for the most part this has not been a conscious change. We have become what we set before ourselves as valued, although we now seem to be struggling to escape the cultural trap we have created.

The great demonstrated power of science has been so generally admired in society and in the university that the ethos and methods of science are mimicked in most, even if not all, matters. Science derives much of its intellectual power from two things. It concentrates on matters of positive knowledge (relatively "value-free knowledge") to the most careful exclusion or impounding of questions of normative knowledge (values) in order to obtain singular answers on which, after empirical tests, scientists can reach consensus. In addition, science pushes its intellectual frontiers further and further into the unknown by factoring positive knowledge into progressively smaller, more specialized categories in order to make operational the empirical tests of underlying conceptual hypotheses. Despite a certain illogic, the old gag definition of an expert—as a person who knows more and more about less and less until he knows all there is to know about nothing—has an increasingly poignant, if not painful, ring.

The societal and university response to science has done several things to man's view of himself and his world. The philosophic distinction between positive and normative knowledge, that is, between relatively value-free and value knowledge, has been powerful and useful. However, as MIT's 1970 review of its educational enterprise observed, "the adulation of scientific method has acted to prevent a synthesis of the humanistic and scientific perspectives by casting doubt on the need for any but the scientific mode of thought" (*Creative Renewal*, p. 75). This "scientific mode of thought" has led educated man to depreciate human values and their study and has contributed to a progressive dehumanization of society and to a degradation of wisdom derived from the human condition and experience. If God was the measure of all things in the Middle Ages, and man was the measure in the Renaissance, today man-made technology is that measure—despite some growing dissent.

The decline in the celebration of human values has lead to the treatment of mankind as an object, as a part of the technology that science has made possible. In such a society the eternal search of the individual for meaning in life has little significance if human life itself has no transcendental or humanistic value, but is constrained to material, technocratic ends. Thus, if the past foretells anything, the promise of Western civilization may likely end in the technologically efficient but lobotomized man of Walden II (Skinner, 1948), or in an extreme ideological and an authoritarian fundamentalist revolt against any material understanding of man as only instrumental to technological and economic ends. One must hope not.

The effect of this on educational ideals has been disastrous. In describing the pre-1940 German university and its faculty, Lilge concludes:

. . . their reduction of the human person to a thoroughly determined mechanism constitutes an emphatic denial that education is a moral problem at all. For them it has, in fact, become a branch of technology. (Lilge, 1948, pp. 82–83)

That is the point. It is as if we had to make man a machine in order to accommodate our technologies.

Until early in the twentieth century, higher education had at its center the formation of a moral human being to sustain a moral society. The growing hollowness of Western civilization (along with other problems) was explored early in this century by Thomas Mann in his novel, *The Magic Mountain.* Today, at the end of the century, the same endemic failing is a central theme of the thought of Vaclav Havel, poet, playwright, anticommunist dissenter and the first postcommunist president of Czechoslovakia. Havel faults not just totalitarian societies but all Western civilization, and indeed, the world, for an erosion of the human spirit, for destruction of man's humaneness and his metaphysical certainty. Modern man's search for certitude, for a moral compass, is evident in the growth of both fundamentalist sects and terrorist organizations associated with Christianity, Islam, and other religions. However, some of these sects and all terrorist groups are intolerant totalitarians. They are themselves symptoms of the moral collapse to which Mann, Havel, and other traditional humanists testify. Make no mistake. Science did not do this; man did—in the ideals celebrated, in what has been valued.

Another factor that complicates this problem and structures modern man's view of himself and his world is the progressively more intense specialization that tends to fracture knowledge. Man's activities and social organization have also become more specialized and fragmented, leading to greater human isolation and alienation. To give meaning and coherence, to synthesize, is today a heroic task. But the effort is rarely made, for we now celebrate not holistic man, nor the educated generalist nor the traditional philosopher, but the technical expert.

A rather basic dilemma arises from the social response to the great accomplishments of science. In reaping the benefits of a modern scientific and technological civilization, how do you "prevent the separation of technical power from moral responsibility?" (Lilge, 1948 p. 69). This perhaps is the real question that lies behind the distress in American society today over such diverse issues as censorship of pornography, the impact of corporate downsizing on employment, environmental pollution, and the political alienation from and decline in legitimacy of government and, indeed, of the university and of science. We seem to have difficulty in bringing into an effective, common focus both the technological (or economic) alternatives and human values that are inevitably involved in any decision, large or small. Because the technological capacity to wage war at great remove exists, or because we can produce our nation's industrial output more cheaply by promiscuous dumping of byproduct wastes, it does not follow that this is what should be done. Yet it almost seems that this is what happens all too frequently in modern society, whether democratic or totalitarian.

There is a world of difference between *is* and *ought*. In every decision of man, both the relatively value-free positive knowledge of what is and what can be done is unavoidably combined with normative value criteria of what is "good" or "bad," and processed through the social and political decision rules of society to produce something very different—a prescriptive statement of what "ought" or "should" be done that is either "right" or "wrong." There is no such thing as a value-free decision. Positive knowledge we are generally able to bring to bear with expert skill, but normative knowledge is too often handled without rigor and in a manner accidental and unconscious. Needless to say, this frequently leads to flawed or sloppy, if not immoral, social decision-making. We have become a nation of experts in specialized positive knowledge, but we are often inept and unconscious where application of normative knowledge is concerned. We leave ourselves vulnerable to the ideologues who, with or without moral vision, stir man's passions. It constitutes a moral time bomb at the very center of modern scientific-technological culture.

It is clear at this juncture that the real source of our difficulty lies in the specific furniture of man's mind, the epistemologies and configuration of factual and value beliefs, which, in collaboration with a few other institutions, is education's primary responsibility. Thus, this ticking time bomb is embedded in the curriculum as well as the research and outreach activities of the modern university. How the university handles this is perhaps its greatest challenge today.

The Current Environment of the University and Its Challenges

Over the last century and a half, as society and its expectations of the university have changed, the university has evolved by adapting to society's needs. The period since World War II has been one of unprecedented growth in the scale and scope of higher education. Despite an expected future expansion of the student-age cohort, university capacities are now constrained by limited and even declining real or inflation-adjusted resources. From these changes in society and the university, many of our current problems flow. It is in this changing context that the outreach role of the university is now evolving.

In most of the fifty states the great growth of universities since the 1950s has created more activities (and institutions) than today's resources can support. The question in today's resource-limited world is where and how will cuts be made. How should individual institutions address this problem? As a national system, what values and strategy should American universities pursue? For surely we will sink or swim together as well as individually.

Low levels of economic growth since the mid-1970s, plus national budget deficits, inflation, and now the end of the Cold War defense budgets, have eroded the real-dollar support of universities by both federal and many state governments. At the same time, the cost of running large public (and private) universities has increased faster than the per-capita income of society. This is at least partly due to the competitive effort of each institution to create an outstanding research and scholarly presence in all the expanding number of major fields of intellectual endeavor. Governments have compounded this problem by imposing more and more regulation and oversight on universities. Among the several consequences are growth in university overhead costs and in nonacademic staffs, constrained research budgets, and rising student tuition. Much of the increase in oversight and regulation arises out of a widening belief in society that the university is failing in its traditional responsibility to police itself.

While the scale of higher education was expanding after World War II, progressive specialization in science and scholarship shattered the intellectual enterprise of academia into myriad activities and organizations frequently isolated from each other and from society, leading some academics to believe they have little or no obligation to society. Matching this fragmentation of our enterprise is a set of specialized journals and professional associations that now tend to dominate the tenure and promotion decisions of universities. This has pushed tenure criteria toward national-level activities and toward research, while pulling institutions away from their state and regional missions and from any emphasis on teaching, outreach, and service obligations. This trend is reinforced by the growth since World War II of multiple, external funding sources that have increasingly dominated university priorities and faculty incentives, making it difficult to pursue coherent institutional obligations and compounding problems of university governance. Internal governance of most universities has grown more structured, with multiple levels of faculty and administrative councils and committees greatly increasing the transaction costs of making internal governance decisions. As a consequence, the university has trouble today getting its act together, both as an individual institution and as a system of national higher education.

At the same time, for more than a decade the society has been saying that it is not satisfied with our performance. This is made confusing by the fact that society is experiencing fundamental conflict over many of the values that govern its own behaviors, and these inevitably spill into the university and into supporting institutions such as state legislatures, the Congress, private foundations, the National Science Foundation, the National Institutes of Health, etc. We are caught in the middle of, and are often a forum for, these conflicts. Compounding the university's problem in many cases are rising expectations of university participation in, and even leadership for, state and local problem-solving and economic development. As the federal government has cascaded its budget deficits down onto the states (by mandating state functions, but not financing them), the governors and state legislatures have slowly realized that by default the economic development and conservation of state resources as well as other roles have become a state responsibility.

Many governors and state legislatures have turned to their state universities, expecting to get help and even leadership. Very few have gotten what they wanted from "their university." No doubt some of these expectations were unrealistic, but disillusionment has seriously eroded support for the university. When Derek Bok, president of Harvard, lectures his peers in private institutions about their accountability to society and their obligation to help society solve its most urgent problems, it is time for the public institutions, especially the land-grant universities, to ask themselves "How well are we performing our obligations to the society that sustains us?" (Bok, 1982, 1990, p. 105).

We must face the fact that the covenant that has governed the university's relationship with society since World War II has dissolved. During World War II, a unique relationship developed between U.S. universities, its science community, and the federal government. Scientific and engineering resources were combined in a major mission to unleash the energy of the atom and beat the Nazi's to the atomic bomb. Statisticians, language scholars, social scientists, and other academics deciphered codes, encrypted intelligence, and performed unique feats of analysis based on probability theory. During and since World War II, university scientists have worked on a wide range of weaponry and national defense problems. Department of Defense, National Aeronautics and Space Administration, and Atomic Energy Commission-Department of Energy research funding have made major demands upon the university, but also built much of the current university basic physical-science research capacity— from which it is now withdrawing. The creation of the National Science Foundation and the investment of other government resources to sustain basic science after the war was, in a sense, the *quid pro quo* in the institution-alization of university science in the service of national interest. Thus, society's covenant with the university and with science was born in the crucible of war and continued in an act of faith by society that in peace science would contribute to the greater economic strength and welfare of the nation. Such a direct university-government relationship has raised questions about the independence and the intellectual integrity of the university.

Today society is in the midst of respecifying that covenant, both in Congress and state legislatures, and in other legitimating and funding sources. The university needs to participate vigorously in the debate over the design of any new covenant, since its complex, multidimensional na-ture is so poorly understood, even within the university, to say nothing of elsewhere in society.

At the same time the conflict over national science policy suggests that the post–World War II covenant between science and society has also unraveled. Since so much of science takes place in the university, the uni-versity and its science faculties have a great stake in the outcome and must inform themselves and participate fully in this debate. The decline in the legitimacy of science has undermined the university's legitimacy in society as well. Too many scientists still think the only problem is one of funding: It is not! Renewing these covenants is both a matter for individual institu-tions in their immediate environment and for the society-wide system or systems of higher education.

G. Edward Schuh, Dean of the Humphrey School of Public Affairs at the University of Minnesota, points out, "Society will let the university contemplate its navel if that is what we want to do, but it does not have to pay for it" (1991, p. 4). University administration, faculty, student bodies, and governing boards must recognize this fundamental problem that all U.S. universities face today, and respond in a coherent, unified manner on the issues essential to the survival of the university as an effective social institution. In doing so it is imperative that within the university each of us respect the other's views and grant each other the dignity we expect from others. Without ethical standards and civility, which are declining in society and the university, neither intellectual community nor intellectual integrity is possible.

Many public university faculty follow careers focused almost entirely on basic research and on national or international problems. This adds to the stature of their institution as a national and international research university. But these faculty must respect and support others in their college and departments who, in many instances, literally make the existence of national and international faculty activity possible. Without a large endowment, no public university can survive solely on its national or international activity and reputation. The keystone in the arch of a public university's existence are its state and local sources of support. A national university cannot be great without national and international dimensions, but with few exceptions the public university would be quite weak or not even exist without its state support for educating the state's young and for addressing state and local problems. Public universities forget, at their peril, that they are creatures of their states. That said, however, in an increasingly global and interdependent world, it is also true that to be effective in state and local problem solving and in undergraduate education, the university must develop national and international knowledge and involvement.

We need to put our house in better order not only in identifying clearly and making more consistent our department, college, and university priorities, but in very consciously cutting the cloth of our activities to match our available resources, which are going to be limited for the foreseeable future. In doing so, we also need to pay closer attention to those who provide us support and those whom that support is intended to serve. In every speech to the faculty of Michigan State University, President John A. Hannah used to state, "Our first obligation is to the sons and daughters of the taxpayers of the State of Michigan—to our students." It still is. The public university must also respond, within its relevant capacities, to the expressed needs of the state, especially in the research and development obligations financed by the state. It must perform well the outreach obligations financed by the state and by state and local institutions (public and private). Finally, many public universities also have major national and international obligations in teaching, research and development, and outreach. If faculty do not serve their state well in the first three of these obligations, they will not long have the resource base and capacity necessary to attract the resources to serve their national and international clientele. The alarm bells are ringing for American universities. Yet many faculty and some administrators and trustees do not seem to hear. Some hear, but are in deep denial of their problem. Others see only that their specialized interest is threatened.

The land-grant university has a unique niche in the structure of higher education. Such institutions need to understand and strengthen what is strong and unique about their role. I despair of colleagues and administrators who compare their land-grant university to Harvard, Princeton, Berkeley, and other "elite" private and near-private institutions, and insist their institution become like them.

From community colleges, through regional four-year colleges, to Ph.D. granting universities, to the mostly private, national research universities, everyone is in a mode of emulation and envy, trying to climb the ladder to become another Chicago, Stanford, or Harvard. As a Harvard product, I honor Harvard for its contributions to scholarship and to this society. But society will be poorly served if every college and university is a Harvard clone.

To prosper in an era of limited resources, the individual public institution must differentiate its product—play to its strengths and unique role in its environment or societal niche. That niche will determine most of the demands made on an institution. The question each institution needs to answer is, "What is our niche?" What are our strengths and how do we build on our strengths? How do we match our strengths to current and future opportunities? In what direction does our future lie?

Society is demanding greater accountability for its investment in universities. We are being asked to change our performance and mix of activities undertaken at society's behest, since society's needs are changing. There is nothing new in this. The university faces these challenges periodically. But we are also being asked, in this process, to share the resource-limitation burdens of society. This makes our choices more difficult, especially since newly developed, competing institutions now undermine the uniqueness of the university in society.

As university educators and intellectuals we are an especially privileged group in society—and with that privilege comes special obligations, which perhaps we have not tended to all that well in recent times. In any case, we now face the task of relegitimizing the university after several decades of growing criticism and erosion in credibility—some of which is justified, much not. We appear to have exhausted most of the moral credit conferred on the university in the past.

We need to explain ourselves better. Many critics of the university, right and left, are just plain wrong, or with the help of the media greatly exaggerate the incidence of that about which they complain. Legislators in some states, for example, and the public, by and large, have never understood how much time good teaching takes, requiring many hours outside of class if it is to be done well. While there are only so many hours in the day, it is the university reward system, the faculty culture at individual universities, and the mind-set and behavior of individual faculty that makes research either highly competitive or highly complementary with teaching. Without involvement in scholarship or research, teaching can easily become stale and even isolated from developments in a field, while student interaction with faculty in class and in the lab often contributes to or stimulates ideas for research.

The Rise of the Knowledge-Centered Society

Man, with the help of science, has transformed the role of knowledge in society. In the early stages of industrialization in the eighteenth and early-nineteenth century, society's man-made capital was increasingly embodied in machines, but as the industrialization process matured and as the scientific revolution began to have a significant impact on society, this has changed. Increasingly, the largest and most strategic investment is that made in the human resources and organization that are devoted to problem-solving and innovation in the production process (Boulding, 1953). "Today, the economically significant industrial property is not the machine, but the design, and not so much the design as the capacity to innovate design in process and product. This is scarcely property at all, but is rather a capacity inhering in an organization." (Piel, 1961, pp. 274–275) It is the organization of human knowledge and the human capacity to create new knowledge that is driving the information revolution. This has been clear for some decades.

Knowledge has become a highly valued input in the production processes of society, largely as a consequence of the application of science to the activities of man. Whereas university education had previously been viewed in the U.S. primarily as a cultural or a consumer good that might advantage an individual, it now tends also to be viewed as a producer's good that is necessary to the functioning of society. This change has given rise to research and development activities in universities and in industry that early on in the information revolution were termed "the knowledge industry" (Machlup, 1962; Slichter, 1958, pp. 1610–1613). The systematic application of science leads to an increase in the rate at which material knowledge accumulates and thus also in the rate at which the existing stock of earlier knowledge grows obsolete.

Historically, the university has been a primary knowledge center of society. However, as society becomes more dependent upon scientific knowledge for its continued growth and vitality, its focus on knowledge shifts in emphasis from the conservation, retrieval, and communication of existing knowledge to place in a strategic role the process by which knowledge is created and moved into productive use. The capacity for creating and transmitting knowledge has made the university even more important to society as society becomes progressively more dependent on the creation of new knowledge for its continued growth. At the same time other institutions have developed, which now complement or compete with the university. The university no longer has, if it ever did, a monopoly on the creation of scientific and scholarly knowledge.

The Social Organization of the Knowledge-Centered Society

Applied science, particularly through communication and transportation technologies, has transformed a traditional nineteenth century society of many small localized decision systems, organizations, and communities that were viable and reasonably self-sufficient, into a modern society of functionally specialized, large-scale, and therefore bureaucratic organizations, which are frequently managed from a regional, national, or international level of decision making. Many of these specialized decision systems transcend the scale of even the largest city or nation. Since such decision systems are usually focused around a single specialized function such as international finance or national highway building, they function effectively in a vertical sense but are not often coordinated well across society with other functions and decision systems. These functional systems do not respond easily to broad, complex, social problems requiring integrated cooperation of multiple decision systems. Vertically specialized systems thus are not responsive to multidimensional developmental goals or to more general public or community needs.

Under the impact of the changing scale and intense specialization of organization and decision making, there has been a breakdown in effective community, both local and national. More recent globalization of markets and growing international interdependence compound the problem. Immense flows of capital move with electronic speed back and forth from one national economy to another, undermining the capacity for any effective national monetary policy. In fact, the concepts of national sovereignty and community self-sufficiency may well be themselves obsolescent ideas at this point. Many traditional functions of national governance appear to be moving in two directions, some back down to state and local levels, while other strategic elements of policy-making have passed beyond the immediate control of national governments to international organizations. Private transnational organizations increasingly seem little constrained by the policies and power of government at either national or international levels. There is a pervasive feeling in American society and elsewhere in the world that, despite the great technological power with which we live, we lack the power to control our own future. The sense of community and individual identity decays and with that decay the potential for democratic governance also erodes. At the same time historical ethnic and regional separatism is threatening to fragment current nation-states into even smaller entities in Spain, Canada, Eastern Europe, and the Balkans, as well as in the Middle East and the sovereign republics of the former Soviet Union (Guéhenno, 1995; Sandel, 1996; Elshtain, 1995).

America and other parts of the world face a rising incidence of social pathologies generating problems of civil disorder, crime, poverty, unemployment, pollution, inadequate education, housing, transportation, medical and health services, and justice. In the U.S., a society that has long been committed to the optimistic belief that the application of positive knowledge can solve all difficulties, these problems create great pressures to involve the university in addressing them.

The University's Involvement in Societal Problems

The American university, through some of its parts, has long worked on societal problems. Over the years its most visible commitments have variously been termed "university extension," "outreach," or "public service." It is not a new commitment. But it is still poorly defined and focused, and thus not well internalized in the value system and incentive structure of the modern university. What is new is the growing pressure of an increasingly complex society for commitment by the university to assist in a wider range of society's problem-solving efforts. Pressure is now felt in private as well as public institutions, community colleges as well as large universities, and in the arts and science colleges of a university as well as in its professional schools. The responses vary greatly. Higher education, however, seems to be slowly evolving toward the creation of an outreach mission or extension of education and research on a par with its social commitment to on-campus teaching and research. The land-grant idea is the kernel from which much of this grew and certainly one of the most highly developed and successful examples. Nevertheless, it must be observed that the land-grant university, the large state universities and even the private research universities are now increasingly alike in their functions and societal roles.

Some think of university involvement in society's problems as simply the service part of the classical rhetoric about university functions—teaching, research, and service. However, most extension or outreach activities involve not just service but teaching and/or research as well. The teaching of urban planners and sanitary engineers, for example, can be regarded as both teaching and a service to the society. University research to find a means of ridding humanity of cancer or controlling environmental pollution is both research and a public service. Such applied problem solving in the past also required or led to contributions to basic scientific knowledge. University outreach commitments are complex combinations that usually exhibit some mixture of teaching and research, but with a clear purpose that serves society much more directly than disciplinary education and basic research.

Almost all public universities have long performed public-service roles for society in the sense of professional training of the new vocations of an industrial society. The explicit commitment of the land-grant colleges to education and public service for the broader society, in the Morrill Act of 1862, was made concrete primarily in the university's application of science and involvement in social action to improve the productivity, material well-being, and social status of the two largest components of the laboring classes of the nineteenth century, farmers and industrial workers. Large parts of this rural and urban working class achieved upward social mobility through democratic access to college education (Nevins, 1962). The land-grant college and the associated institutions that it helped to build in rural life have transformed the productivity, welfare, and social class of today's successful commercial farmer to an extent that would astonish its early founders. The consequent lower relative cost of food has contributed to the welfare of all laboring people and to the more rapid development of the American economy. In terms of deliberate national commitment, the Morrill Act was certainly the beginning, but only the beginning, of higher education's mission in outreach or extension (Eddy, 1957, pp. 78–79; Bonnen, 1990).

The "land-grant tradition" has generated organizational arrangements that constitute one major historical model of university outreach. Basic and applied research activities developed around the federal and state funded problem-solving focus of the experiment stations established nationally by the Hatch Act of 1887. In the effort to move knowledge more effectively from the university campus to the farm and rural user, the Cooperative Extension Service was created by the Smith Lever Act of 1914. This organization, financed from federal, state, and local sources, provides for on-campus specialists and for a field staff in local communities both of which together attempt to relate the campus to the community, providing a means for facilitating community problem identification and the direction of university knowledge toward the problems selected for university action. While the informal educational activities of the land-grant college of agriculture have more recently broadened their scope even in some states with strong agricultural sectors, these organizations were designed to serve agriculture.[1] However, a mistaken idea persists that because of their success the organizational structure of the colleges of agriculture are a model that can be transferred without modification to other parts of the university and to entirely different problem areas.

Even before the development of agricultural extension, some public and private universities were creating general extension programs for continuing adult education. General extension has tended to focus on formal classroom teaching, but in the evening hours or on weekends and frequently in locations removed from the university campus. The needs served have ranged from training adults in technical skills (e.g., secretarial, accounting, etc.) to refresher and continuing education for various professional groups (e.g., engineers, lawyers) to general cultural enrichment (Ziegler, 1964, pp. 1162–1183). In a few cases, general extension programs, for example at Syracuse University, developed around the informal educational approach characteristic of agricultural extension and similarly focused on the decision needs of the community and its leadership. It is also worth noting that well before the Morrill Act, engineers were trained at West Point and at Rensselaer Polytechnic Institute, a private institution in Troy, New York, that spent the first decade after its founding (in 1825) providing training for farmers.

Many university outreach-like activities take place outside the context of the university's different extension frameworks, and some of these were in existence before either agricultural or general extension. This is because some outreach activities evolved as a logical extension of the regular teaching or research activity of the university's many professional schools, which in both public and private universities have long independently carried on quite varied activities in problem-solving research and for the continuing education of their own professional and related groups. Some more recent on-campus teaching programs attempt to expose students and their values to learning situations in the world outside the university classroom by putting them into public-service or social-action situations that have also been described by some as a form of outreach. In other cases, graduate research programs collaborate in the U.S. and abroad with communities or societal organizations that constitute a laboratory in which the university provides problem-solving research and education.

In a few states, unique relationships were forged between the university and state government, creating a partnership in which the university trained some professional cadres of state government, led or worked in the planning of state economic development, provided analysis of state problems, and on occasion, participated in the design of legislation in a broad range of areas. This happened, for example, in Wisconsin and California. One of the products of this type of collaboration are the many university institutes of government or government research that have existed for decades. In an often closely related process, public administration developed as an academic field and as a profession. These policy-oriented university efforts occurred early in private as well as public universities. Today some of the most distinguished schools of public administration (or public policy) are in private institutions such as Syracuse, Harvard, and Princeton, to name just three.

Individual universities have often developed unique relationships to specific industries where such industries constitute a major and strategic element in the well-being of the region or state. For example, the University of Minnesota early committed resources to research on the technology of mining and, in past decades, mounted research on the utilization of low-grade iron ore in an attempt to offset the decline in economic activity and employment that occurred in Minnesota as the high-grade ores of the Mesabi range were exhausted. North Carolina State University has long invested in the research and education that sustains the state's major textile industry. There is, in fact, a general national pattern of specialized public-service commitments that have developed from geographic location and the nature of the economic base of the state served by a given institution.

In the period since World War II one of the most distinctive public-service missions developed by American universities has been in international programs. Both public and private higher education in the United States have become increasingly involved in activities ranging from cultural exchange to helping build various institutions abroad, particularly research and educational institutions, to a major involvement in various types of foreign economic development. This has included development planning activities and applied research programs for the improvement of the technologies and institutions of agriculture, industry, and other sectors of developing nations.

In a complex and rapidly changing knowledge-centered world, to invest only in research is rarely sufficient to assure that new knowledge thus created will be most effectively utilized or make the greatest contribution to society. If new knowledge is to produce the greatest social value, research on R&D demonstrates that it must be moved into use as rapidly as possible. This normally requires some institutional interconnection between the research process and society. Some of these outreach arrangements are operated by the university, some by commercial users of knowledge, and others by agencies of the state. Some are combinations. Most are the consequence of a pragmatic tailoring of institutional form and function to specific purpose.

The university is often directly involved today in the affairs of the society (Price, 1965; Bazelon, 1967). Since World War II, universities have acquired access to primary instruments of power in this society through a complex of private, professional, and governmental organizations, ranging from foundations and the National Academy of Sciences and the National Science Foundation to the President's Council of Economic Advisors and the Office of Science and Technology Policy. Eminent members of university faculties, particularly in the physical, biological, and social sciences, now exercise direct influence in private-sector resource and public-policy decisions far beyond the wildest academic dreams of fifty years ago. Formal institutional arrangements and long-term contracts now link private firms and universities in complementary and common endeavors. Most major universities now employ national and state lobbyists, something they would not do if they were not able and did not feel a need to influence public policy.

University Outreach: Imperatives and Constraints

The diverse nature of these involvements raises questions about the appropriateness of some university activities and their impact on the nature and integrity of the university as an institution. The post–World War II expansion of higher education, which is at least partly responsible for this diverse involvement, has ended. It is time to rethink and to clarify the social role of the university. We need more precise definition and articulation of the appropriate roles of the university for today's and tomorrow's society, if that society is to understand us and renew its covenant with the university. The current financial "downsizing" of almost all major public and private institutions creates a window of opportunity for that purpose. Unfortunately it has been accompanied by financially opportunistic privatizing of some university academic functions, which further confuses the primary public-good purpose of higher education.

Adding to the confusion is a current focus on unethical behavior in science, and the university generally, testifying to an apparent erosion of academic values and integrity as competition for resources and advancement has become intense in a resource-constrained era. With this rising level of visible influence of the university in society comes greater pressure for accountability and a growing volume of criticism of the university. No one needs reminding of Lord Acton's dictum about power corrupting (Price, 1965). Small wonder that some faculty wish to retreat from society's embrace to an academic "ivory tower."

The outreach role of the university arises as society is confronted by problems for which the university is a highly competent and relevant source of knowledge. In the knowledge-centered society this involves a growing range of problems. In some fashion, society will be served in its most urgent needs. When the university has the knowledge and expertise needed in society's problem-solving efforts, particularly where there is no good alternative source of this knowledge, the university must have convincing reasons if it refuses to respond to the most important of society's needs. Refusal, without adequate reason, will lead to further withdrawal of societal support and to the creation of even more substitutes for the university.

The university's social responsibility has long been to give society what it needs, not necessarily what it wants. There is often a difference. Thus, the university's responsibility as a social critic is a most serious one. Society, through its many public and private organizations, often asks of the university things that would serve society poorly or not at all. Some simply attempt to "use" the university for political or private gain. Similarly, many real social needs tend to go long unrecognized in society. The university's public responsibility is to exercise its role of social critic as persuasively as possible, in identifying genuine social needs, establishing university priorities as best it can, and responding with its knowledge whether it has been asked to do so or not. The problem for the university is not really whether it should act but what it should do and how, as well as when. The real problem for the university is one of appropriate choices and timing.

Values are unavoidably embedded in all choices or decisions to act. Value judgments are as important to the success or failure of societal efforts to solve problems as is any positive knowledge with which these values are combined. Responsible decision making involves understanding the implications of the value choices involved, accepting responsibility for a decision, and educating one's partners in outreach and the people affected as to the likely consequences of the proposed action or outreach activity (Castle, 1971, p. 553).

Often the university is asked to involve itself in commitments for which it has little capacity or for which other institutions are better prepared and, thus, in which it probably has little legitimate role. Consulting firms and other private and public organizations are often better equipped today to handle some needs than is a university. Other requests would make the university an agent of partisan interests, perhaps embroiling it in political conflict and impairing its capacity and reputation for objectivity. Such activities are inconsistent with the true nature and limits of a university. The university must be careful to commit its limited resources to outreach activities that are legitimate for a university and are of major social significance.

But the question remains, what is legitimate? What has major social significance? By what criteria is such a question answered? Indeed, what is meant by the very term "university outreach"? How is it to be defined so that we know what we are talking about, can manage it intelligently, and can communicate its meaning to others? Out of the almost infinite range of activities that are sometimes described as university outreach or public service activities of the university, what is legitimately included in its outreach role?

What Is Outreach?

The term "outreach" is slowly but increasingly replacing those of "extension" and "public affairs."[2] The traditional view of university outreach identifies this role as the third member of that long-revered trinity—teaching, research, and service. This view persists, apparently, for its simplicity. Its logic is clearly deficient. Any careful examination of what universities do under this rubric leads to the conclusion that outreach activities are some combination of teaching, research, and service.

One does not need to talk very long with faculty and administrators in different institutions to realize that the range of activities that they collectively would include in outreach is so diverse that little a university does would be excluded. This is not very helpful. It signifies only that university people believe that practically all their activities have a direct public value—a belief that is not fully shared by the public or state legislatures these days.

What Do Faculty and Administrators Include in the Definition of Outreach?

Generally, no one suggests basic or pure research be included in the definition. But the varieties of mission-oriented research that are seen as outreach are extensive. A distinction is made by some between research done at the researcher's initiative on general funds at the university and the applied research contracted for with an outside financing source. In the latter case, a distinction is also often made between research contracts with government and those with private firms. Some who would include contract research with private firms distinguish between research having a public or scientific value and research having only a private value to the firm. Closely related is the distinction between classified research, whether for government or a private firm, and that which is public. Finally, many also distinguish between applied research contracts entered into by the university or contracts to which the university is a party, and those in which only an individual professor is involved. Some of these categories are not only excluded by many faculty from university public affairs, but also are described as not legitimate for the university or its faculty to undertake—for example, research with only classified or private and proprietary benefits.

Another set of questions arises in considering the entrepreneurial enterprises of faculty outside of their on-campus teaching and research activities. Many faculty in the sciences and engineering are involved with corporations spun off from the research generated in university laboratories. Their involvement ranges from minor commitments to situations in which a predominant portion of a faculty member's research time is devoted to the firm. Many are shareholders or participating partners in such firms. In some cases these activities are the result of conscious university policy aimed at state economic development; in other cases they are tolerated in order to hold strong faculty.

Some faculty spend considerable time consulting. Much of it is for proprietary firms, but not too many faculty see this as a university outreach activity. On the other hand, the equally large volume of consultation with governmental bodies is often regarded as outreach.

The same distinction is often drawn between the activities of university professors when on leave to government service or private firms. The distinction is not always clear-cut, for some consulting and service in private firms may carry a substantial element of public interest, while work with some governmental activities may be of dubious public value.

Faculty generally do not see their individual involvement in local community activities and public service as any part of university outreach. A few distinguish between those situations in which faculty members serve because of professional competence and situations in which they serve as a citizen.

A third set of questions concern the university's corporate involvement in the local community and broader society. A distinct subset is the university's unavoidable corporate responsibility as a citizen in a specific community setting. Student and faculty activists have brought this area of previously vague responsibilities into sharper focus. Different, higher, and more distinct standards of behavior have been imposed on the university and on many other corporate entities. This accountability ultimately takes the form of federal, state, or local government regulations. Thus, university policies in land acquisition and management, housing, investing, employment, etc., are now evaluated and managed, not just for their effect on the university, but for their impact on the university's various external communities.

Beyond responsibility for the effects of its day-to-day operations on the community, the university has also undertaken a broad range of voluntary, university corporate commitments in the problem-solving activities of society. These range from programs that are aimed at improvement of productivity in various industrial or business sectors to improvement of critical public services in health and education. These activities all exhibit some effort to build long-term, organized linkages into the society from an academic unit or units of the university. Thus, the activities of such diverse organizational forms as university-associated laboratories, research institutes, policy institutes, general or university extension, and cooperative extension can all be appropriately included in this category. In general terms, these activities of the university are direct corporate responses to societal needs in human and cultural development, community and resource development, and economic development.

A fourth general set of activities, which faculty often include as university outreach, involves manpower training and leadership education. Many faculty distinguish between training for professional or vocational roles from the education that develops general human capabilities. Both can be seen in the undergraduate and postgraduate preparation for high-priority social roles in leadership and in the complex technologies and organizations necessary in modern society. In the case of postgraduate training and education, university research activities are often an intimate part of the process.

Ordering the Universe of Possibilities

How does one impose conceptual order on this wide array of activities? Is there such a thing as a clearly definable outreach role for the university? If there is, at this point it is obvious that it is not a pure category such as teaching or research. The one common dimension is that of social response or responsibility. An approach that orders but reflects many of the differences between university activities is presented in figure 2.1. While it is not totally satisfactory, it does provide an initial ordering of the problem.

At least three dimensions seem essential to any university and to a definition of outreach: the university as a socially responsible organization (Area 1), as a researcher (Area 2), and as a teacher (Area 3). Research and teaching are primary university functions and cannot per se be considered outreach, even though it is possible for faculty to extend their research and teaching into the outreach milieu.

Several perspectives develop from this approach. A series of three university activities are often seen as elements of outreach, but in themselves may also be viewed as distinct roles of the university. These are found in Areas 4, 5, and 6 of the figure. Area 4, which is common to research and social responsibility, incorporates mission-oriented research and consulting. Area 5 represents a parallel, but slightly different, interface between research and teaching that includes the university's activities of self-renewal through research inputs into teaching and the education of the next generation of university and other public- and private-sector researchers. Area 6, which is unique to teaching and social responsibility, includes primarily manpower training and some, mostly masters'-level, professional and graduate education. In addition, a useful distinction can be made between the university's activities as a responsible corporate citizen whose normal day-to-day operations have an impact on society (Area 1) and those activities (Areas 4, 6, and 7) that comprise the university's more volitional response to a broad set of societal problems. Nevertheless, as one analyzes specific cases, there often seems to be no hard, clear line between these categories. Rather, for example, the manpower and applied research activities of Areas 4 and 6 overlap or blend into Area 7 in cases where they

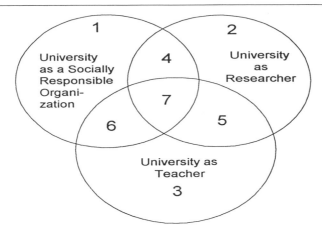

1. Behavior while managing its day-to-day operations that is undertaken by the university as a responsible corporate citizen of its immediate specific communities.

2. Disciplinary research plus multidisciplinary, subject-matter research.

3. Undergraduate education.

4. Mission-oriented research to serve society.

5. Renewal of the university and of society's research capacity—through research inputs to teaching and the education of the next generation of researchers.

6. Manpower training and master's-level professional and graduate education.

7. Corporate commitments of the university in extension or outreach that involve problem solving, the processes of development and conservation of human and natural resources, delivery systems, and institution building.

Figure 2.1

are part of an organized corporate commitment of some part of the university devoted to a clear societal need.

The logic of this approach suggests that the heartland of university outreach lies in that area which alone is common to all three fundamental dimensions of the university, in Area 7; but it is also something more. Thus, an examination of the many examples of university corporate commitment to society suggests that at the heart of university outreach is an implied synergism generally characterized by:

1. developmental processes;
2. institution building;
3. an interactive linkage into society for the explicit purpose of societal problem solving.

Most substantive outreach commitments appear to involve the university in some developmental process in society, human and cultural development, community and resource development, or economic development. When the university activity is not part of a societal developmental process, the university may be performing some valuable function in society, but it probably is not a full example of university outreach.

As the university extends its resources and expertise to society, it cooperates with numerous societal agencies and organizations already in existence. In major outreach efforts, however, the university and these agencies inevitably encounter situations demanding the creation of new organizations and institutions to facilitate their problem-solving effort either because existing societal arrangements are incomplete, anachronistic, or missing. When this occurs, the university occasionally builds new organizations and institutions directly, but more often finds itself in a collaborative or catalytic role with its societal partners in such endeavors.

Since both development and organization or institution building are innovative roles, they demand considerable creativity and experimentation from the university. The university is not the exclusive agent for these creative processes, but it is often better prepared to work on a high-risk, knowledge-intensive public goal than are proprietary or political institutions. The university is one of only a few institutions having much of the necessary expertise for such endeavors. Finally, since its primary motivation for involvement is neither political nor proprietary, it should be easier for the university to disengage itself once the organization or institution-building and the development process is self-sustaining. If the university outreach role is to remain innovative, it must eventually disengage from the programs and organizations it helps to create. Otherwise, it will find its outreach role weighed down with increasing numbers of bureaucratic operating responsibilities and eventually becomes little different from the action agencies of government.

The final element of this tripartite conception of outreach is some form of interactive, two-way linkage into society. Since problem solving is a process that implies working *with* rather than *for* other segments of society, the university must operationalize its knowledge, skills, and expertise through an outreach structure that is capable of providing external linkages for the university to institutions in society, and also reciprocating linkages back into the university. The concept of institutional linkage is not meant to imply that the university already has the solution, but rather that it *participates* or *collaborates* in the problem-solving processes of society. Its organized linkage to society enhances university access to societal experience, and thus its capacity to help identify problems as well as tap needed societal resources more effectively.

A Proposed Definition

One must go beyond the tripartite approach in figure 2.1 to achieve a definition that considers the other distinctions and dimensions discussed above. Outreach can be defined as:

The corporate *activities of a university, beyond its immediate civic responsibilities, which involve* conscious commitment *by academic units of the university to some role in the* problem-solving efforts *of society, and which are focused on the* developing *of human, national, and community resources. It involves* a purposive extension or linkage of the university's special competence *and resources to organizations and individuals outside the university.*

This outreach effort will usually lead to participation in the creation of new organizations or institutions to facilitate problem solving. University outreach is the response of the university to what it perceives to be primary local, state, regional, national, or international needs. Thus, it is university teaching, research, and service that are combined in problem-solving missions, conceived in the *public interest*, and ordered by the university's understanding of the priorities of social need, but within the constraints of the university's special competencies, resources, and societal environment.

What are some of the implications of such a definition? By virtue of limiting university outreach to those activities sponsored and sustained by one or more of the academic units of the university, the private activities of individual faculty are excluded. Also excluded are activities associated with such things as university land acquisition, capital investment, and employment. These activities arise as a consequence of the university's responsibility as a corporate citizen whose operations have an important effect on its immediate communities. Thus, this definition limits outreach to Areas 4, 6, and 7 of figure 2.1.

By limiting university outreach to conscious, direct commitments to societal problem solving, one excludes from university outreach the incidental services delivered in the execution of some other university functions. An example of the latter might be the medical services provided a local community as a by-product of its clinical curriculum.

Since we have defined university outreach as a role in society's problem-solving processes, those activities that are not mission-oriented are
excluded. This does not mean that university involvement in outreach is
always itself directly a problem-solving activity. In some cases it may be
only a partial input into one of society's well institutionalized problem-
solving processes. But it is a corporate commitment of the university, whose
ultimate social value lies in societal problem solving.

University outreach involves the creation of socially useful knowledge
and services, plus conscious effort to extend this knowledge and service to
problem areas in society. This is more than the effort of individual faculty
to propagate their ideas. Rather it presumes a corporate effort by the university or one or more of its academic units to design and maintain linkage
into society that runs well beyond the university's general public information or research publication activities. It is seen in its most highly organized form in the university's various interactive outreach structures such
as extension and the policy and practical problem-oriented applied institutes and laboratories.

University outreach is also limited to responses involving societal
problems in which there is a major public interest component. Those
matters that are solely or predominately of private or proprietary interest are excluded.

Finally, the university is an institution of finite resources and competence. It is not a surrogate for society. It has neither the resources nor the
expertise to do all things well or safely. Its role in outreach is limited to
specific areas in which it has a unique or at least a comparative advantage.

Everything imaginable in the way of university interventions in society have been described as outreach at one time or another by faculty or
administrators. Some fall within what we have described as the heartland
of public affairs (Area 7 above); others do not. The somewhat broader
definition provided here includes Areas 4 and 6 as well. Greater order is
imposed by a definition that distinguishes between different types of university interaction with society, and limits outreach to a subset with specific, definable characteristics. However, an important question remains.

The university is a unique social institution whose relationship to
society, like any institution, has limits. The university serves society by
creating, preserving, and transmitting knowledge, and by playing the role
of social critic. In the U.S. at least, it also serves as a handmaiden in societal problem solving. Both the roles of societal problem solving and social
critic are risky and can involve conflicts over strongly held political and

value beliefs. Society grants the university the freedom to perform these roles on the condition that it limit its corporate intervention to knowledge-based persuasion and its corporate participation to that of handmaiden. In short, the university as a corporate entity may not substitute itself or attempt to act for society. As an organization it may serve one or all societal combatants in a policy debate but it must maintain a careful corporate neutrality in society's political wars. Despite its profound engagement with society, the university is not a surrogate for society. Faculty are free within the law to take any position or action they wish in political or social conflicts, but the price paid for academic freedom of faculty is the corporate neutrality of the university. This is a constraint on outreach as a corporate activity of the university. Since outreach involves an intimate embrace with society, a tension exists in which there are risks for the university and its perceived legitimacy.

The Risks of University Intervention in Society
University involvement in society's affairs can be categorized in terms of a risk continuum of varying degrees, which rests at one end close to the conventional teaching and research activities of the university and at the other extreme in a deep involvement in the making of societal decisions and in the risks of public advocacy. Thus, these strategies range from very low to high in visibility and in risk. In all cases we are concerned with the university's corporate commitments and exclude the activity of faculty as individuals.

1. There is a "low silhouette" involvement that consciously avoids conflict. In this case the university extends research, education, and service on demand and pretty much in the form in which it is requested. There is little independent university initiative in problem identification. Also there is very little effort, except as requested, in applied problem solving. In short, the balance between problem solving and the delivery of services is focused toward the delivery of services on demand. Generally, the groups served are elements of the existing political establishment rather than groups not empowered by society.
2. The next level of risk is exemplified by programs that focus on the processes of problem evaluation, identification of possible alternative solutions, and an evaluation of the consequences of following any one alternative. In this approach, it is relatively easy to maintain the scholar's objective stance and yet work on societal problems. Depending on

how conflict-ridden and controversial the problem is, this approach will produce more or less controversy.

These first two levels of risk involve activities that are normally no more difficult to defend than the university's conventional role in teaching and research. Level two does entail a slightly higher amount of risk, since it involves the direct evaluation of the consequences of alternative policies or solutions that some groups will not wish to hear or have others hear, especially when cloaked in the authority of the university.

3. Risk level three is level two plus organized interaction with, or outreach to, the decision makers and influentials in society associated with the particular problem upon which one is focused. In effect, this approach carries the academic capacities of problem identification and alternative evaluation directly into the society's decision processes. The decision makers in this case are those highly legitimized ones who dominate the existing social system. Despite deep involvement in the decision process, you do not in this case put yourself in the position of attempting to tell decision makers what they ought to do. You still hold to the scholar's position of providing objective analysis and evaluation of consequences.

4. The next level is similar to risk level three but this case involves the university with participants who are in direct political contest over the problems being addressed. One example might be the university programs that work with poorly legitimized or stigmatized and disenfranchised groups. These groups, such as minorities and the poor, are not generally part of the existing power structure. Depending upon the nature of the university's program, the minority group's political activities, and its acceptance in the society, this will be a more or less risky program area. The tricky part of it is that you are working with the often fractious leadership elements of minority groups in an attempt to wire them into the overall decision processes of society, while simultaneously dealing with other groups antagonistic to your program goals. Maintaining credibility in the midst of this can be difficult, but usually necessary to success.

A different situation might involve intense conflict for high stakes between well-legitimized groups in society. In the 1980s, for example, the electrical power industry of a midwestern state proposed to expand capacity to meet expected demand by building nuclear power plants. Well-financed and politically strong environmental and other groups adamantly opposed this form of energy, and the beginnings of a long, high-cost political conflict spilled into state politics. The land-grant university was asked by a beleaguered governor to help resolve the conflict, which it did in a few years of consensus building between the parties. The effort was begun on the neutral ground of the university and constructed around a program of research agreed to by all parties to establish a common factual base. This was followed then by a complex educational effort ending in a compromise negotiated in private by the leadership of the contending groups—well away from the university and the unstable waters of state politics. It was a dangerous undertaking which, if not managed astutely, could have injured the university's reputation for objectivity. On the other hand, to have refused the governor's request might have impaired the university's state support.

5. An even higher level of risk involves a major break from the educational posture of avoiding advocacy. In this case, one takes the additional initiative of privately and informally advocating specific solutions to problems with influentials and decision makers of various power structures. Since this outreach effort would already be involved in activities characterized by risk levels three and four, it would have highly developed informal relationships with the influential role players in the decision system. One becomes an advocate but only in an informal and personal manner, away from public exposure. This does not put the politician, decision maker, or outreach personnel on the spot politically. As with level four this takes very skilled practitioners of outreach, who are themselves politically astute.

6. Risk level six, besides providing analysis and evaluation of alternatives and other knowledge for various decision systems, adds the dimension of university involvement in building new organizations and institutions. When attempting actually to solve problems in society, one almost invariably finds that the design of the solution requires some alteration in the fabric of society. That is, there is not in place an adequate set of arrangements for implementing an appropriate solution. Thus, before one can insure genuine resolution of the problem, new organizations, new rules, new roles in society need to be created. In this approach the university participates in the creation of that new arrangement in the fabric of society.

For example, when one needs to change the values of central city youth in order to do something about a social pathology, it will

be necessary to build community centers or youth clubs, or some
new institutional arrangement to reach them and to involve them
in an educational and socialization process. The university's involvement can vary from creation and direct management of a project to
rather indirect collaboration with other organizations or community groups.

7. The highest level of risk involves the ultimate step to public advocacy
    of a particular position in the policy process. There are very few ex-
    amples of universities taking corporate stands involving public advo-
    cacy. These few exceptions involved universities in their roles as cor-
    porate citizens (where the university's interests were at stake), and also
    a few situations in which there was such great consensus in the com-
    munity over the program goals and actions that the risk associated
    with public advocacy was nil. Indeed, often the university only ap-
    pears to be supporting an already highly legitimized community ac-
    tion. There are also the blessedly rare cases in which faculty senates
    and presidents, speaking for the university, have injudiciously taken
    stands in the past on inflamed public issues such as the Vietnam War
    and the draft. Generally, this would appear to be the sort of action
    that is unnecessary and carries with it the very highest risks. Indi-
    vidual members of the university's board of trustees, if they have highly
    visible and legitimized standing outside the university, may have more
    freedom to be advocates, but even this is usually limited to defending
    the integrity or interests of the university. The faculty as individuals
    and in groups that do not represent the university are free to take such
    stands, but the university as a corporate entity and those who speak
    for it do not—or not without the risk of severe political costs.

One thing is clear. Beyond the obligation to protect its existence and
integrity, ideally the university should not be involved in corporate advocacy at all. In rare instances universities can find themselves in situations
that appear to dictate the necessity of advocacy. As we have seen this can
occur when a social consensus is so great that risk of advocacy is practically
nil. In some cases failure to participate as an advocate in one problem
might preclude the university from working on subsequent problems as a
consequence of having injured its relations with the community. But such
situations are extremely rare.

Thus, as a rule public advocacy should not be undertaken at all and
informal advocacy only under very special circumstances. Too much is

risked, and corporate advocacy is fundamentally inconsistent with the maintenance of academic freedom.

These different levels of risk do not constitute separable strategies, but levels of risk associated with varying degrees of intervention. It does not appear possible to sort out from university experience any distinctly different general strategies of university intervention—only differing levels of risk. The design of organizational strategies is too dependent on the specific capacities and environment of the university, and on the nature of the problem and sector of society with which the university is collaborating in some problem-solving effort.

Other Considerations

A few other dimensions appear to be important to successful intervention. Some are contextual, others are organizational, a few are process variables associated with the dynamics of problem solving, and finally there appear to be some general action or behavioral principles that are important to understand.

Both the degree of risk and the probability of success in design and institutionalization of a program strategy depend to a considerable extent upon the degree of consensus that prevails in the community over both the objectives as well as the means of implementation. The higher the level of consensus, the less risk and the higher the probability of success. As pointed out above, in some cases consensus can be so high that universities are induced or forced to become public advocates.

In most cases outreach participants describe a need for the creation and organization of clientele to support new programs. It would appear that this is a concomitant of program success, especially when there is little consensus in the community concerning the program goals and means. If the community and its major organizations agree that the objectives should be pursued, there is far less need to develop specific clientele organizations. On the other hand, if you are developing programs for embattled minorities or unorganized groups, it is quite clear that the program will encounter difficulty becoming self-sustaining until effectively organized clientele actively support the program politically. Innovators can often sustain programs initially, but in the long run, if their efforts are to be institutionalized, some kind of clientele relationship and organization will usually be necessary.

When developing new university outreach programs, one frequently encounters difficulty in establishing the legitimacy and credibility needed to gain access to the groups and individuals essential to the program. New programs normally involve entirely new groups of people, so that the university frequently finds itself starting from scratch. Several obvious resources are at hand. One generally is offering new and often critical resources to the community and this combines with the neutral ground and credibility of the university as an objective and relatively disinterested actor to cause people to listen and often invite the university into their problem-solving efforts.

There are other less obvious considerations. In developing entry one must always proceed with a non-threatening approach. That is, one must proceed in a manner that does not threaten or challenge any of those groups with whom one must have cooperative relationships. This means that as a matter of initial strategy it is necessary to practice a most careful public organizational neutrality. Later one will have more freedom with the same groups of people, but not initially while lacking full credibility.

It is also true that as a matter of timing initially one should not engage in any organization or institution building. The creation of new organizations or rules invariably threatens someone in the existing structure. In the initial stages of developing a program and establishing credibility with new groups in the community, institutional and organizational innovations should be entered into only under conditions of high consensus.

Another important strategic consideration is that of responding to the felt needs of the various groups in the community with whom one is trying to develop relationships, even when these make little sense in terms of the problem at hand. In the early stages of entry into a problem situation, before any research or educational work has been done, groups often have inaccurate perceptions of their problems and will focus on factors and needs that in reality are low priority, if not sometimes counterproductive. The university must respond to some, if it is to gain the confidence of the other actors. It is this practice that regularly gets university-outreach organizations ridiculed for having published or done something apparently frivolous or wasteful for a university, but which is specific to some "perceived need" of the community or a group in that community.

Another strategic factor that is very important in establishing the credibility necessary for setting up new programs is that of being very careful to take no credit for program accomplishments but rather to let those with whom one is working take credit. University attempts to claim credit for accomplishments in the community are usually counterproductive and in the early stages of program development often fatal. Let the leaders of the community give you credit, if they will.

After the institutionalization of a program is well under way, a natural human instinct frequently destroys its potential. This is the desire to eliminate all ambiguity from organizational relationships and role definitions. This must be resisted. While it may complicate management, it is ambiguity that most often provides the freedom for initiative and creativity on the part of individuals as well as organizations. If the purpose of outreach is creative innovation, an outreach organization that has become an efficient command and control bureaucracy has lost all ambiguity and is dead.

In building new institutional or organizational arrangements in society, one often encounters a difficulty analogous to that in medical transplants in the human body—rejection by the host environment. Such change usually implies new values, but in order to succeed one must include enough of the old to make the new arrangement palatable. Revolutionary changes or major social inventions will usually require great consensus or a major crisis to allow the mobilization of sufficient strategically placed political and organizational power to make the change effective. There must be some degree of readiness for change in the society. There is only a finite degree of freedom for manipulation and facilitation of the process. A university acts in this process not so much as a leader but as a catalyst for change. It does not have the capacity or authority to act for society.

One human characteristic seems to run through all successful university-outreach activities. It permeates the personalities of the leadership that operate successful programs. Not so surprisingly, this is the trait of pragmatism. It is seen in the design, implementation, and management of outreach. Pragmatic behavior, of course, is necessary for survival in most social and political processes. This is worth remarking on since it is a trait not commonly admired nor cultivated in academic life.

A strategic dimension of great importance is that of the difference between intervention at the informal level of organization versus the formal. This is the primary distinction between risk-level 5 and 7 described above. In both cases, one becomes an advocate of some specific policy position. University-outreach organizations have proceeded well into the stage of advocacy without incurring excessive risks by keeping their intervention private, staying out of any public debate. This is to say that they worked informally to persuade the critical decision makers and influentials of the society, but stayed entirely away from advocacy in public forums. One can find a few cases in which great arguments took place privately over protracted periods of time without apparent injury either to the program or the university. Even informally, pushing very specific action programs with community leaders obviously takes some skill, if one is to avoid injuring personal relationships. If done ineptly it can be destructive of both university and program relationships, and at the level of personal as well as political relationships.

There are many societal problems the solutions to which a university may have some capacity to contribute, but there are many more to which it does not. One of the clearest reasons why university outreach organizations fail is that they do not command enough knowledge of the problem addressed. It is a mistake to construct a university-outreach effort without linking it to or developing a relevant research base within the university. Corporate university commitments to outreach must establish their foundation in the knowledge base of one or more academic units of the university. If the problem is not amenable to a knowledge-intensive educational effort, or if the university does not command the needed knowledge, it has no business becoming involved. Some early urban-affairs efforts of universities failed for having mounted outreach structures without a research base. A related knowledge failure occurs when university-outreach organizations apply their accumulated research knowledge without having developed adequate understanding of factors within individual communities that might influence the applicability of knowledge from the research base. It is also a fact that research is not available or capable of dealing with all of society's problems. Some must be dealt with using the best judgment of society—not necessarily that of university faculty.

However, it must be recognized that the knowledge base for outreach differs in nature from that of the core disciplines of the university. It requires a different way of knowing—a different epistemology—because it faces not the clear and carefully defined questions of science, but the ill-defined and often large and messy problems of society, only small pieces of which may be amenable to the quantitative rigor of science. Rather, the large, highly relevant problems of society must be addressed from the perspective of eclectically combined subject matters and analytic methods, some no more than accurate descriptions that allow one to think more clearly about societal options for action and their potential impact on some specific problem. Addressing the relevant question is paramount. The business of outreach involves producing knowledge for decisions to act: this cannot be delayed or debated until full or precise knowledge is available from the academy. In fact, much of the knowledge needed must come from the decision processes of society rather than the university.

Professor Donald Schön of MIT argues that the epistemology of knowing and learning for both teaching and research is fundamentally different for the professional schools and outreach activities of the university that address society's problems than for the science disciplines of the university. Science, he says, produces fundamental knowledge under high standards of rigor (reductionism?) focused on "manageable" (well-defined) or "technical problems" with no practical relevance to individuals or society. On the other hand, professional practice deals mostly with the messy, practical problems of society and individuals, problems most of which are "incapable of technical solution." Solutions to these practical problems require combinations of diverse elements produced and combined at a much lower level of rigor. This results not in fundamental knowledge but highly judgmental knowledge and experiential learning. Professor Schön calls this "knowing-in-action," which "makes up the great bulk of what we know how to do in everyday and in professional life. It is what gets us through the day." It should be noted that his epistemology readily admits values into its calculus. This very different epistemology must be recognized as legitimate and respected in academe, if outreach is to become an effective, university-wide function.(Schön, 1995)

Also before such success is achieved, the internal university incentives and reward system—what the university values—must be modified to sustain outreach as a systematic function of the university. Even in many professional schools this is still not the case.

Finally, the university cannot overlook the challenge it faces to educate its societal partners in outreach about the character and limitations of the university's participation in society's affairs. The partners in outreach must learn as a condition of collaboration to respect the university's need to protect its institutional neutrality in partisan political issues, to protect its reputation for objectivity and for consensus building, as well as its commitment to public over private interest. Above all it must be recognized that any university's knowledge base has limits and that knowledge is not the universal solvent for all problems. Failing most of this, the direct collaboration in society's affairs that outreach entails becomes a danger to the university, not an additional strength.

The dangers in university outreach arise in part out of the paradox of a growing societal ambivalence in wanting more knowledge to solve problems (*vide* outreach), while simultaneously fearing knowledge because of concern over how it might be used. Clearly the traditional optimistic

American belief in the inevitability of progress and in human improvement through knowledge, beliefs of the Enlightenment that spawned the land-grant idea, have lost much of their hold on society. Thus, the construction of university outreach takes place today in a very different and more challenging societal environment.

Conclusions

Some of the strategic dimensions of university intervention have been described. The evidence suggests that the design of successful intervention structures and behavior are specific to particular institutions, environments, and missions, and must be worked out in a pragmatic and experimental manner. Thus, it would appear that while one may discover general principles that guide intervention, such as those above, the organizational form and strategies of university outreach remain specific to each university, its various academic organizations and their competencies, and the social and political environment of the problem addressed. University leadership should give up the search for a standard organizational solution for university-wide outreach.

Universities have assumed many roles in society's problem-solving processes. As a consequence, some difficult questions are inevitably posed: "In helping society solve its problems can the university participate as an action-taking decision maker?" "How far can the university go toward such a role?" How far can it go without endangering the integrity of the traditional functions of teaching and research and thus the intellectual life of the university?" This is not a question about mere involvement in the action process. The American university has been so deeply involved in society and its problems since the public university and land-grant movement of the last century that it is no longer worth debating whether the university legitimately should be involved. It is. Sir Eric Ashby put it well two decades ago.

Today universities everywhere face a common peril: the peril of success. Formerly each was a detached organism, assimilating and growing in accordance with its own internal laws. Now universities have become absolutely essential to the economy and to the very survival of nations. . . . They are living through one of the classical dilemmas of systems in evolution: they must adapt themselves to the consequences of success or they will be discarded by society: they must do so without shattering their integrity or they will fail in duty to society. (Ashby, 1974, p. 7)

The only real question is the nature and degree of that involvement and its legitimacy and clarity. Two and half decades ago, one of the most astute scholars of higher education, Martin Trow, identified the central danger.

It is a matter of continual amazement that an institution so deeply involved in public service in so many ways has been able to preserve its autonomy and its critical and scholarly and research functions. The question is whether its new commitments to public service, on campus and off, will seriously endanger that autonomy and the disinterested and critical intellectual life it allows. One answer, very tentatively, is: that depends on how it performs these new services. The issue is very much in doubt. But if the autonomous functions of the great state universities are threatened and then crippled by the political pressures arising out of their commitments to service, then those functions, at their highest levels of performance, will be confined to the private universities or forced outside the university altogether. (Trow, 1970, pp. 39–40)

The viability and social significance of the outreach university turns on the answer to Trow's question.

Notes

The chapter author is indebted to Ed Bishop, Emery N. Castle, Kenneth R. Farrell, James C. Hite, Elmer W. Learn, Richard M. Lerner, James H. Meyer, Lester V. Manderscheid, Paul A. Miller, and Bruce Poulton for thoughtful critiques of this chapter.

1. It is also true that in their early decades, the land-grant colleges offered a very broad scope of off-campus education. They pioneered in areas ranging from personal and public health, nutrition education, clothing design and production, design of indoor plumbing and water supply systems, to youth programs—all aimed at improving the health, human capacities, and welfare of the population served. Success and economic development have brought most of this to an end.

2. The title "public affairs" has eroded as a descriptor for outreach, in part because it has been appropriated for the office that lobbies for the university and manages its public relations. The term "extended education" has also been used in a few cases, usually where education is defined to include both research and teaching.

References

Ashby, Sir E. (1959). *Technology and the academics: an essay on universities and the scientific revolution.* London: Macmillan.

———. (1974). *Adapting universities to a technological society.* San Francisco, CA: Jossey-Bass.

Bazelon, D. T. (1967). *Power in America: The politics of the new class.* New York: New American Library.

Bok, D. (1982). *Beyond the ivory tower: Social responsibilities of the modern university.* Cambridge, MA: Harvard University Press.

———. (1990). *Universities and the future of America.* Durham, NC: Duke University Press.

Bonnen, J. T. (1990). Agricultural development: transforming human capital, technology, and institutions. In C. K. Eicher and J. M. Staatz (Eds.), *Agricultural development in the third world.* 2nd Edition. Baltimore, MD: Johns Hopkins University Press.

Boulding, K. (1953). *The organizational revolution*. New York: Harper and Brothers.

Brubacher, J. S. (1977). *On the philosophy of higher education*. San Francisco: Jossey-Bass.

Brubacher, J. S. & Rudy, W. (1968). *Higher education in transition: A history of American colleges and universities, 1638–1968*. New York: Harper and Row.

Castle, E. N. (1971). The university in contemporary society. *American Journal of Agricultural Economics, 53*, No. 4. p. 553.

Creative renewal in a time of crisis: Report of the commission on MIT education (1970, November). Cambridge: MIT.

Deanesly, M. & Bateson, M. (1926). Medieval schools to c. 1300. In J. K. Tanner, C. W. Previté-Orton and Z. N. Brooke, (Eds.), Ch. XXII, *The Cambridge medieval history*, Vol. V. Cambridge: Cambridge University Press.

Eddy, Jr., E. D. (1957). *Colleges for our land and time*. New York: Harper and Brothers.

Elshtain, J. B. (1995). *Democracy on Trial*. New York: Basic Books.

Guéhenno, J. M. (1995). *The end of the nation state*. Minneapolis: University of Minnesota Press.

Havel, V. (1990). *Disturbing the peace: A conversation with Kavel Hvizdala*. New York: Alfred E. Knopf.

Lilge, F. (1948). *The abuse of learning: The failure of the German university*. New York: Macmillan.

Machlup, F. (1962). *The production and distribution of knowledge in the United States*. Princeton: Princeton University Press.

Mann, T. (1927). *The magic mountain*. New York: Alfred Knopf.

Morrill, J. S. (1961). "I would have higher education more widely disseminated." Address delivered at the Massachusetts Agricultural College, 1887. Reprinted, Amherst, MA: University of Massachusetts Centennial Committee.

Mullinger, J. B. (1911). Universities. In *Encyclopaedia Britannica*, 11th ed. (Vol. 27, pp. 749–776). New York: The Encyclopaedia Britannica Co.

Nevins, A. (1962). *The state universities and democracy*. Urbana: University of Illinois Press.

Newman, Cardinal J. H. (1976). *The idea of the university*. Oxford: Clarendon Press.

Paulsen, F. (1906). *The German universities and university study*. New York: Schribner's and Sons.

Piel, G. (1961). *Science in the cause of man*. New York: Knopf.

Price, D. K. (1965). *The scientific estate*. Cambridge: Harvard University Press.

Rashdall, H. (1929) The Medieval Universities. In J. R. Tanner, C. W. Previté-Orton & Z. N. Brooke (Eds.). *The Cambridge medieval history*, Vol. 6. (pp. 562–585). Cambridge: Cambridge University Press.

Roberts, I. P. (1946). *Autobiography of a farm boy*. Ithaca, NY: Cornell University Press. p. 136.

Rudy, W. (1984). *The universities of Europe, 1100–1914*. Cranbury, NJ: Associated University Presses.

Sandel, M. J. (1996). *Democracy's Discontent*. Cambridge: Harvard University Press.

Schön, D. A. (1995). Knowing in action: the new scholarship requires a new epistemology. *Change*, November/December, pp. 27–34.

Schuh, G. E. (1991). Political and social trends affecting the 1860 land grant institutions. Paper presented at the U.S. Agricultural Information Network National Conference, University of Minnesota, Minneapolis, MN, October 14–16, p. 4.

Skinner, B. F. (1948). *Walden II*. New York: Macmillan.

Slichter, S. H. (1958). The industry of discovery. *Science, 128* (3339) 1610–1613.

Trow, M. (1970). Reflections on the transition from mass to universal higher education. *Daedalus, 99*, (1) 1–42.

Veysey, L. R. (1965). *The emergence of the American university*. Chicago: University of Chicago Press.

Whitehead, A. N. (1936). Harvard: The future. *Atlantic Monthly*, (September), 267.

Zeigler, J. M. (1964). Continuing education in the university. *Daedalus, 93*, (4), 1162–1183.

Section II

Creating Outreach Universities
Contemporary Efforts

Chapter 3
Marshaling the Forces of the Land-Grant University to Promote Human Development

Graham B. Spanier and Mary Beth Crowe
The Pennsylvania State University

In the shifting sands of societal needs, the challenges of youth, families, and communities are increasingly emerging as critical to our nation's future. Other broad challenges, such as defense-related concerns, have abated to some extent, and still others, including economic competitiveness, remain a priority although the context for addressing them now is vastly different than in the past. Institutions of higher education must be responsive to such changes to sustain their special leadership for society.

New paradigms for teaching and learning that bring colleges and universities closer to the public they serve can enhance this leadership for the future. Promoting human development, in contrast to the longstanding emphasis on economic development held by much of higher education, is one such framework that invites new perspectives on the core functions of teaching, research, and service, and accompanying changes in institutional culture and practice responsive to contemporary societal needs. The integration of teaching, research, and service is a closely related approach that, although also supportive of economic development, broadens the active learning community and thereby enlarges higher education's impact on people's lives.

This chapter explores the theme of human development as a focal point for the contributions of land-grant universities to society. We take an institution-wide look at some of the ways The Pennsylvania State University promotes human development, with a special focus on programs and activities that support the development of families and youth and integrate the teaching, research, and service missions. Drawing on several in-depth Penn State examples, we identify issues that influence the land-grant university's ability to address the human problems and needs of the people they serve.

Changing the Paradigm

The contribution of America's land-grant universities to economic development is widely recognized as one of the great success stories of higher education. Created from a vision of access, relevance, and service to society, the land-grant institutions from their beginning embraced the needs of agriculture and industry, first through promoting "the liberal and practical education of the industrial classes in the several pursuits and professions of life" (Morrill Act, 1862), and subsequently, with the articulation of research and extension as necessary components of their work if knowledge were indeed to be useful and widely used. The resulting tripartite mission of teaching, research, and service proved highly effective in supporting the progress of an agrarian and industrial society (see Bonnen, chapter 2, this volume). It continues to serve well in the knowledge and technology-driven marketplace of the global society of today.

The development of the land-grant universities as agents of economic progress has influenced substantially their internal culture and external support. These institutions have a strong orientation to science and technology and substantial research expertise; many are among the leading universities nationwide in science and engineering research and development. This activity is important institutionally not only as a matter of mission (some would say disproportionately so in its emphasis on research), but also in terms of the income it generates through external grants and contracts. It also supports a major argument for the investment of public funds—federal, state, and local—in higher education that is based on the economic fruits of research and related technology transfer.

The capacity of the land-grant universities to contribute to economic development is clearly linked to their livelihood. The impetus for an active economic development role has only grown stronger in recent decades in the wake of recent troubling challenges to the nation's competitiveness that have preoccupied so much of the public agenda. Responding to these real and urgent needs, the land-grant commitment to economic development has been significant and appropriate but sometimes overshadowing or even derailing other important concerns.

In addition to their role in economic development, the land-grant universities also have a capacity, responsibility, and tradition for promoting human development that can be brought to the fore. The teaching, research, and service missions that evolved to serve marketplace needs are an equally powerful model for meeting the human side of society's challenges. Marshaling the forces of the land-grant university to address these challenges in human development is a compelling expression of relevance and service in higher education and a necessary complement to economic development in supporting society's ultimate success. The most compelling problems of our nation are the problems of its people: crime, drug abuse, teen pregnancy, divorce, homelessness, hunger, illiteracy, and other human concerns that divert substantial economic resources, detract from economic competitiveness, and deeply affect individual and collective quality of life.

Within the traditions that have shaped the land-grant universities, there is a well-established commitment to the development of individuals, communities, families, and youth on which to build a stronger future for society. This commitment takes many forms. It is inherent in an abiding concern for access that first opened personal doors for members of the working class, and has expanded to support opportunity for others who have been underrepresented in higher education, including women, minorities, and so-called nontraditional students. It is the heart of the teaching mission, particularly undergraduate education, that seeks to provide a lifetime foundation of broad understanding and skills rather than narrow job training.

The land-grant commitment to human development may be seen in a long history of extension work with families and youth that is no longer limited to rural areas but is active in urban communities as well. It can also be traced through the evolution of the departments, schools, and colleges of home economics that are closely identified with the land-grant movement. It is further reflected in the contributions of the social sciences and humanities to the academic community.

At Penn State, a concern for human development also is expressed through a system of twenty-three campuses that bring the University's resources within thirty miles of more than 90% of Pennsylvania's citizens. This local presence in communities across the state and through the Penn State Cooperative Extension county offices makes possible many of the specific initiatives cited below.

The Penn State projects and programs we share here are but a few examples that collectively bring the many forces of the land-grant university to bear on human development. They were selected to represent a variety of administrative homes and academic fields as well as to illustrate how each of the University's missions can be especially responsive to the challenges of families and youth when expressed in concert with one or both of the other missions. We look at a classic example of grassroots outreach through cooperative extension, a community-based program in support of the teaching mission, and some examples of community-collaborative research.

The Grassroots Tradition

The establishment of the Cooperative Extension Service by the federal Smith-Lever legislation in 1914 formalized the public-service mission of the land-grant universities and created a model for university/community collaboration that remains in place today. The mission of Penn State Cooperative Extension was and is to extend research-based information to the citizens of the Commonwealth. Extension's reach is considerable. More than one in six Pennsylvania households are touched by Penn State Extension each year.

Children, youth, and families are an important focus within this tradition. For example, 4-H annually serves approximately 114,000 Pennsylvanians nineteen years of age and younger, and involves some 12,000 adult volunteers. Philadelphia has one of the nation's largest 4-H programs.

Penn State Cooperative Extension programs serving children, youth, and families are wide-ranging. In addition to the diverse activities within 4-H, some examples include:

- Community-based coalitions to address tobacco control issues, a collaborative effort of Penn State Cooperative Extension and the Fox Chase Cancer Center.
- The Penn State Urban Gardening Program that, working with Philadelphia community food gardens and backyard gardeners, grew more than $1.9 million in produce in 1994–1995; 86% of the growers donated a portion of their produce to food cupboards, local churches, neighbors, and families.
- Visits With You and Your Baby, a two-year, age-graded statewide program that reaches 25,000 limited-literacy and teen parents or parents to be. The program focuses on nutrition, health, and safety in child development.
- The Better Kid Care Program trains child-care providers and parents about quality child care. In 1994–1995, more than 48,000 credit units of workshops and course training were provided by extension family-living agents to 12,000 child-care givers in Pennsylvania, and about 6,000 providers enrolled in a learn-at-home program.
- More than 100 different coalitions in 40 counties to provide education programs for at-risk youth. These coalitions link extension with

the schools, human service groups, public housing authorities, youth corrections institutions, and community centers.

The Expanded Food and Nutrition Education Program (EFNEP) operated by Penn State Cooperative Extension since 1969 is a long-lived example of grassroots university outreach that improves the quality of life for families. EFNEP brings together faculty expertise, an extensive network of community-based educators, community organizations, and a variety of program objectives and approaches to make a demonstrable difference in the nutrition of low-income families.

Pennsylvania's EFNEP is part of a national program funded by the United States Department of Agriculture. Participating counties contribute office space and clerical staff. Local agencies such as United Way provide additional funding. Professional staffing comes from Penn State Cooperative Extension.

EFNEP's five educational objectives are: (1) enable low-income families, youth, and pregnant teens to make life-skill decisions about food choices for themselves and their families based on dietary guidelines; (2) raise awareness of pregnant women and teens regarding the need for an adequate weight gain during pregnancy; (3) raise awareness of pregnant women and teens regarding the benefits of breastfeeding; (4) raise awareness among low-income families, youth, and pregnant teens of health risks associated with obesity, and help them to learn a lifestyle approach to changes in eating behaviors; and (5) raise awareness of low-income families, youth, and pregnant teens so that they can manage resources to facilitate appropriate food choices for themselves and their families.

Using a nationally standardized curriculum revised and updated by Penn State faculty and extension staff, Pennsylvania's EFNEP teaches low-income families, particularly those with young children, how to have a healthful diet on limited financial resources. Topics include stretching food dollars; planning and preparing tasty, healthy meals; feeding babies and children; food safety; reading food labels; and using food stamps and other resources effectively. A special Pennsylvania curriculum, Eating for a Better Start, which was developed by Penn State's Center for Nutrition Education in the College of Health and Human Development, targets pregnant teens. EFNEP also includes a Peer Breastfeeding Educator Program operated in twelve Pennsylvania counties.

In addition, EFNEP plays a key role in SuperCupboards, a community-owned program created to reach chronic users of emergency food systems. The SuperCupboard model brings public, private, and nonprofit groups together within local communities to provide nutrition education and teach parenting and life skills that enable participants to break their cycle of dependency and move toward self-reliance. The nutrition segment is taught by EFNEP nutrition education advisors or extension home economists. EFNEP staff also contribute to the continuing development of SuperCupboards in conjunction with the Pennsylvania Coalition of Foods and Nutrition, for example, recently revising the SuperCupboard manual and conducting a statewide conference on how to organize and deliver the program. A recent survey of SuperCupboards, conducted by EFNEP in collaboration with Penn State's Department of Food Science, indicated that the program helps to instill positive attitudes about meal preparation and also encourages self-esteem and self-reliance.

Participants in all EFNEP programs are referred by various community agencies and programs such as WIC, foods stamps, and Headstart. They are taught in small groups or individually by program paraprofessionals, meeting in community centers, housing developments, schools, churches, or homes. The paraprofessionals, called nutrition education advisors, are hired from within the community, and trained and supervised by extension staff. Last year, there were seventy-six full-time-equivalent paraprofessionals and just over nine full-time-equivalent professional staff. More than 2,800 volunteers contributed over 33,000 hours of assistance with program activities.

In-service training of professional and paraprofessional staff is provided periodically by a College of Agricultural Sciences food and nutrition faculty specialist and other extension faculty members. The food and nutrition specialist also reviews and revises curricular materials for scientific accuracy and answers nutrition-related questions from the field.

In fiscal year 1995, EFNEP served 5,867 adults and 10,749 youth. Upon entering the program, 29% of the adult participants reported diets that contained foods from the five food groups and fewer than 3% met Food Guide Pyramid recommendations. By program completion, within six months for 62% of the participants, more than 69% reported diets containing all food groups and more than 19% met Food Guide Pyramid recommendations. The consumption of fruit increased 80%; of vegetables, 39%; of milk, 47%; of breads and cereals, 25%; and of meat, 16%.

EFNEP nutrition education advisors report that many of the program's clients and their families also become better connected to a wide variety of other support systems including food stamps, job training, GED classes, and other extension programs, and eventually gain greater self-sufficiency.

EFNEP's success rests on many factors. Its community bases bring important local support, foster program awareness, and facilitate referrals, all of which enable EFNEP to reach large numbers of clients annually. The community-based paraprofessional nutrition education advisors also play a significant role. They are peer educators who are easily accepted by program participants and who provide an important measure of cost efficiency in program delivery.

At the same time, the paraprofessionals are limited in what they can teach. Required to stay within the parameters of the basic nutrition lessons included in the EFNEP curricula, they do not address issues of parenting, financial management, or specialized diets, which can impact substantially on good nutrition behavior. Yet EFNEP, more broadly speaking, is responsive to such issues through referrals to extension specialists and faculty with appropriate expertise. EFNEP's university base also is vital in assuring that the nutrition information provided is accurate, up-to-date, and communicated effectively. In bringing the university and local community members together, EFNEP also creates opportunities for policy-related research. For example, based on questions from the field about microwaving baby formula, the Penn State food and nutrition specialist involved with the program worked with a university food engineer to develop guidelines for this heating method.

The Extension of Teaching

In this age of lifelong learning, the teaching mission of the university is rapidly expanding to embrace more fully what once were considered non-traditional learners and marginal educational activities. Part-time students, returning adults, and continuing-education participants have become important constituents whose enrollments contribute substantially to institutional activity. Accommodating these individuals through work- and family-sensitive schedules, localized and distance learning opportunities, specially tailored programs, and other arrangements is one way Penn State and many universities are recasting their teaching mission to promote the ongoing educational development of the public.

At the same time, we are reaching downward into the educational pipeline to ensure an adequate, broad-based foundation for such continuing higher learning. Every academic college at Penn State offers programs targeted to pre-college students that provide special assistance and encouragement for educationally disadvantaged students and a variety of academic enrichment opportunities. These efforts offer yet another perspective on fulfilling our teaching mission, not only in terms of the instruction provided but also in regard to the contributions they make to the recruitment of future students at Penn State and elsewhere. Among these precollege initiatives, the Penn State Educational Partnership Program (PEPP) illustrates a particularly rich interplay of teaching and outreach activities.

PEPP seeks to increase the number of disadvantaged students in Pennsylvania who attend some form of higher education. The program, targeted to average- and above-average-ability middle and high-school students, builds self-esteem, strengthens academic performance, and promotes the value of education and academic excellence for students and their families.

Initially created to address pipeline concerns that influence access to higher education and that have an impact on the diversity of the University community and the educational experience of all students, PEPP is broadly supportive of Penn State's teaching mission while also fulfilling a public-service role. Staffed with Penn State undergraduate volunteers and student teachers, PEPP also supports the teaching mission directly by providing service learning opportunities and preservice teacher practicum experiences.

PEPP programs have been established in several Pennsylvania communities served by Penn State campuses. The first partnership was created in 1989 in Reading, Pennsylvania, through the collaboration of the Penn State Berks Campus, the Reading School District, and Reading New Futures Project, Inc., a community-development organization. The following year the program was expanded through the partnership of the Penn State McKeesport Campus, the McKeesport Area School District, and the Mon Valley Education Consortium. In 1991, a PEPP partnership was added at Penn State Erie with the Erie School District. In addition, the Penn State Wilkes-Barre and Beaver Campuses have informal partnerships with local school districts involving many of PEPP's components. A PEPP program in Philadelphia, in conjunction with Penn State Cooperative Extension, is in the early stages of development.

All of the formal partnership programs are administered by Penn State program directors under the auspices of the College of Education, with the exception of the Erie program, which is administered by Penn State Erie. Program funds are provided primarily by corporate and community sponsors and government grants. Various PEPP activities are described in detail in Light and Daniels (1995) and Nicely (1995).

In McKeesport and Reading, PEPP runs two after-school study programs. PEPP Academy serves middle-school students in Grades 5 through 8 three days per week. PEPP Institute enrolls high-school students in Grades 9 through 12 two days per week. The PEPP after-school programs provide homework assistance, teach study skills, and offer career awareness and educational enhancement opportunities such as field trips, guest speakers, and visits to nearby colleges. Volunteer tutor/mentors from the local Penn State campus and student teachers from University Park staff the after-school programs with supervision from a school-district teacher employed by PEPP.

Students enrolled in these extended-day programs also participate in summer enrichment opportunities. Students who complete the program are guaranteed admission to Penn State. The empowerment of parents to reinforce partnership efforts in the home is encouraged through special parent workshops. Professional development activities for schoolteachers and administrators are offered through the College of Education. The Erie PEPP program has similar components but also calls on student volunteer tutors from other nearby institutions of higher education in addition to those from Penn State, and incorporates an extensive mentoring program using volunteers from area businesses.

PEPP is popular with both students and parents; participants show improvement in grades, and although numbers are still small, there is a good track record of graduates going on to college. Surveys administered at parent empowerment workshops indicated that more than 90% of the parents participating felt that the strategies presented were beneficial; 28% reported they had adopted the strategies at home. Another indicator of the program's success is its emulation by others.

The first PEPP McKeesport cohort to begin the program in middle school graduated in 1995. All of the sixteen seniors in the program that year went on to college, six of them to Penn State. Ten of the seniors graduated with honors. In 1994, six out of seven PEPP graduates went to college; in 1993, nine of eleven did so.

PEPP McKeesport now serves 195 students; the Reading program enrolled 144 students last year. As the program has grown, opportunities for Penn State students have increased. McKeesport employed sixty-four learning assistants in 1994–1995; forty-five assistants worked in Reading that year. Among them were student teachers who had worked for PEPP previously and wanted to return to the PEPP schools. As part of the PEPP initiative, a multicultural early field experience course in the teacher preparation program was developed and offered at the Penn State McKeesport and Beaver campuses. Most of the students enrolled in this course reported that the experience had a positive impact on their comfort in multicultural settings and their willingness to consider working in urban communities.

In addition to its impact on students, PEPP generates significant goodwill toward Penn State in the local community. The PEPP model also has attracted the interest of community organizations and other educational institutions. In McKeesport, for example, the Altrusa Club and the YMCA have implemented similar after-school programs with assistance from PEPP. Other school districts and colleges interested in developing similar partnership programs have visited the McKeesport PEPP.

The long-term commitment of PEPP to its communities is emphasized by the program director as critical to its success. With the established partnerships now six or more years old, communities, schools, and parents count on Penn State to be there, and the resultant trust and track record generate important community support.

Yet PEPP has learned from experience and evolved over the years. The early program in Reading emphasized teacher workshops whose impact was curtailed by teaching-staff turnover. Although teacher professional-development activities are still made available, the main focus of PEPP now is on student intervention. PEPP also has found that realistic expectations are an important framework for success. This is reflected in the selection process for PEPP students. Initially, program referrals for "at-risk" students were obtained from school counselors. This tended to identify students whose behavioral and emotional problems were greater than an academic intervention program could handle. Rather than continuing to target these students, the program redefined its audience as students with demonstrated academic ability but who were not performing up to their full potential, relying on teacher recommendations to select appropriate program participants.

The PEPP program began as an affirmative-action effort and reported organizationally within that area of the university. PEPP's move to the College of Education has strengthened the program's connection to the academic mission, particularly as a natural laboratory for preservice teacher-education clinical experiences. The college has administratively consolidated outreach efforts, including PEPP and continuing education, with preservice teaching experiences. This organizational structure is supportive of a new College of Education initiative, the Schools for SUCCESS

Network, which comprises ongoing partnerships between the college and schools throughout the state. These partnership efforts may include PEPP, continuing education, research, internship experiences, and for all schools involved, the placement of student teachers. The network is intended to expand collaborative efforts among school personnel, university faculty, parents, and community representatives to improve school effectiveness and improve teacher education.

Community-Collaborative Research

While the full continuum of research from basic to applied contributes to the land-grant university's capacity to promote human development, needs assessments, demonstration projects, program evaluations, intervention studies, and policy analyses provide critical validation of this role. These applied efforts, which fuse research and practice, of necessity involve the individuals and groups whose concerns they address.

Many are collaborative relationships that make external interest groups active partners in university research-based initiatives. Such partnerships create rich opportunities for the expansion and application of knowledge, but at the same time pose special challenges to all parties involved. We present two examples of such university-community collaborative research initiatives currently under way at Penn State. These are a series of program demonstration and evaluation projects with Boys & Girls Clubs of America, focusing on youth-drug prevention education, and Project PRIDE, the Penn State project "Policy, Research, and Intervention for Enhancing Development in Early Adolescence."

In the first of these efforts, researchers from Penn State's Institute for Policy Research and Evaluation have been working with Boys & Girls Clubs of America over the last ten years to evaluate and enhance the Stay SMART drug-education programming provided by the clubs. Stay SMART, a component of the national prevention program of Boys & Girls Clubs, teaches youth a variety of social and personal competence skills to help them resist pressures to use alcohol, cigarettes, and marijuana, and engage in early sexual activity.

This series of projects began with an evaluation of prevention programming at a single Boys & Girls Club in Broward County, Florida. Three larger-scale evaluation projects funded by the Office for Substance Abuse Prevention of the United States Public Health Service have followed, over time integrating additional components into the prevention programming, expanding the age-range of youth served, and introducing more rigorous evaluation methodology. These developments have been made possible by the ongoing, mutually supportive relationship between the Penn State researchers and Boys & Girls Club staff.

The first of the large-scale evaluation projects studied the impact on thirteen-year olds of the Stay SMART program and a two-year follow-up booster program developed by the Penn State researchers (St. Pierre, Kaltreider, Mark, Aikin, 1992; St. Pierre, Mark, Kaltreider, Aikin, 1995). Fourteen Boys & Girls Clubs across the United States located in economically disadvantaged areas with high crime rates and drug use participated in the twenty-seven-month project. The study showed positive results for the Stay SMART program alone and for the booster program for marijuana, cigarette, alcohol, and overall drug-related behavior. The booster program had additional positive effects on attitudes toward alcohol and marijuana after each of the two years of the booster program. In addition, the Stay SMART program had a positive impact on sexual attitudes and behavior of nonvirgin participants.

A second project added family involvement to the Stay SMART prevention programming. This component, the Family Advocacy Network, or FAN Club, was designed to strengthen high-risk families by bringing youth and their families together in a variety of activities, reducing maternal isolation, and providing social and educational support. A three-year evaluation of program impact on at-risk eleven-year olds, conducted at sixteen club sites, suggested that offering the youth drug-prevention program with additional monthly youth activities and the FAN Club experience would be beneficial for community youth organizations with adequate staff and high commitment to program implementation, and that offering one of the program variations would be more beneficial than providing no drug-prevention programs at all (St. Pierre, Mark, Kaltreider, Aikin, 1997).

The third study, now in the second of five years, expands on the previous work to offer prevention programming to second- and third-grade high-risk students and their parents, in cooperation with selected club sites and local school districts. Three Boys & Girls Clubs, those in Bethlehem, Pennsylvania; Broward County, Florida; and North Little Rock, Arkansas, are participating in this program. Project components include SMART Kids, a drug-prevention program designed by Boys & Girls Clubs for youths ages six through nine; SMART Parents, which offers parenting sessions and opportunities for parents to help with youth program sessions and after-school activities; regular parent-teacher meetings and family social activities; and frequent contact between teachers, parents, and club prevention coordinators concerning the youths' progress. In contrast to the two previous studies, which used quasi-experimental research designs, this project is a randomized experiment, the rigors of which, the researchers point out, would not be attainable without the positive on-site relationships that have been developed over the years.

Frequent communication, in the form of program training, site visits, and weekly process interviews by phone have been essential to establishing and maintaining a common vision that helps all parties involved respect the interests and work within the constraints of the various organizations. The weekly phone calls are an especially important link that provide technical assistance in program implementation, resolve conflicts, collect qualitative data, and provide a gateway for Boys & Girls Club staff to call on Penn State expertise in other areas of their work where questions and problems occur.

The Boys & Girls Clubs have come to view their association with Penn State more broadly than the prevention programming projects alone, calling on this relationship for support and to help establish credibility in their communities. For the Penn State researchers, the close working relationships have proved an important source of insight into the development and implementation of drug-prevention programs by community youth-serving organizations (Kaltreider & St. Pierre, 1995).

The second university-community collaborative initiative we describe is Project PRIDE, whose goal is to build collaborative relationships among researchers in Penn State's College of Health and Human Development who study adolescent development, Penn State Cooperative Extension Service staff, and local community members, to promote healthy development of area youth (McHale et al., 1996). Funded by the Carnegie Corporation of New York, Project PRIDE's activities have included needs assessments and the design, implementation, and evaluation of intervention programs.

The project has worked with three Pennsylvania communities: Allentown, Middleburg, and Wilkes-Barre. Wilkes-Barre, the oldest and most extensive Project PRIDE site, is illustrative of the approaches, activities, and challenges associated with this initiative. In Wilkes-Barre, as in all sites, the local Cooperative Extension youth specialist provided an introduction for the College of Health and Human Development researchers to the community, and serves in a key linkage role for project activities.

A needs assessment collected survey data from almost 1,000 Wilkes-

Barre fifth through eighth graders and fourth through twelfth grade teachers. Discussions involving the university, the community youth partnership, and the school district also contributed to the development of a multifaceted intervention plan. Resulting programs were directed at parents, teachers, and youth workers, and special long-term activities were targeted to sixth and seventh graders in schools located in the most ethnically diverse and disadvantaged neighborhoods. One of the main programs was a teacher-advisor program for seventh graders aimed at helping these students adjust to the transition to a large junior/senior high school. This effort included weekly meetings between teachers and their advisees, regular meetings of the teacher-advisors to share experiences, and workshops for teachers on adolescent development. Initial evaluation results suggest a positive impact for this program. Project PRIDE activities also include the dissemination of evaluation data, work with school staff to expand on and modify programs and, in conjunction with community groups, the development of grant proposals to secure additional project funding.

Among the challenges of university-community collaborations, Project PRIDE faculty and staff emphasize the considerable time necessary to establish and maintain community relationships. They note the need to overcome community distrust of academic researchers and to negotiate constantly around competing agendas. Here the credibility and efforts of the Cooperative Extension agent and the interpersonal relationships that were developed among all parties were of great help.

Methodological challenges from the program evaluation perspective centered on the lack of control over program implementation, making process evaluation especially important. The university researchers and staff also report that project activities taught them that the diverse needs and resources of Pennsylvania's communities affect the design and implementation of programs for adolescents.

In addition to university-community collaborations to promote adolescent development, a secondary focus of Project PRIDE was to influence a broader audience and impact youth-related policy. This goal was addressed through a series of educational seminars about early adolescence for state and local policymakers. There is evidence, including the addition of a position for adolescent health in the Pennsylvania Department of Maternal and Child Health, that this effort has helped to give greater attention to adolescent issues on state and local agendas. The Project PRIDE researchers underscore the viability of such policy seminars for extending the university's teaching mission to important audiences.

Enhancing the Land-Grant's Capacity
to Promote Human Development

There are many more programs and activities throughout the University that improve the quality of life for individuals, families, and communities. Penn State's College of Health and Human Development fully embraces this goal through its focus on health, disease prevention, and life-span issues. The college's research activities, education programs that prepare students for a wide variety of human-service careers, and outreach to professionals and the general public in such areas as nursing, nutrition, biobehavioral health, institutional management, child care, adolescent development, gerontology, and communication disorders, among others, are responsive to important societal trends and human needs.

The College of Education has a broad range of research and instructional programs, continuing and distance education activities, and outreach services in such areas as elementary and secondary education and counseling and rehabilitation that promote human development. In the College of the Liberal Arts, psychology, sociology, and anthropology, for example, long have addressed human problems and concerns not only through research and undergraduate and graduate education programs, but also through outreach units such as the Psychology Clinic and the Child Study Center in the Department of Psychology that address the teaching, research, and service missions in concert. The College of Agricultural Sciences, through its linkages with Penn State Cooperative Extension, is an active promoter of human development. Penn State's College of Medicine is a leader as well in humanizing medicine, having been the first among the nation's medical schools to establish a department of humanities and the first to establish a department of family and community medicine to promote a holistic, integrated view of patients and their needs.

Among the dozens of examples to be found in these fields, the few discussed in depth above were selected to highlight factors that expand and enhance the university's impact on the quality of life for families and youth. Outreach is an important theme throughout all of these examples. The direct involvement of people and their communities creates important opportunities for learning, both within the university community and for those the university serves.

The examples we have cited show the added complexity that outreach adds to the fulfillment of the university's teaching, research, and service missions. These projects and programs support multiple missions and call for multiple roles for the university and community members involved.

Not just teachers, researchers, and learners, but community activists and co-learners, the faculty, staff, and students participating in these projects have a far-reaching impact. Importantly, their projects have an impact on them as well, as these efforts raise new questions, provide new insights, and give new visibility to the university's capacity to make a difference in people's lives.

Partnerships, coalitions, and collaborative efforts are critical to these efforts. Such relationships open doors to communities and their residents, help to build credibility and cooperation, bring the strength of many perspectives, and pool important resources. Community partnerships themselves may be a source of project funding, or they may provide added, valuable weight to grant requests to funding agencies.

Intra-university collaboration and cooperation also are needed to focus institutional resources efficiently and effectively. For example, linkages between faculty and program delivery staff both stimulate and support outreach. Collaboration among similar interests and units located in different parts of the university can encourage participation and at the same time avoid duplication of effort. Interdisciplinary teams are an important focus of intra-institutional cooperation as well.

The integration of teaching, research, and service; engagement in external partnerships; and collaboration across units within the university are wonderful sources of opportunity for the land-grant university to promote human development. But they also present special challenges to the academic community. Outreach activities can require an exceptional investment of faculty time and a long-term commitment to make a visible and lasting difference in the lives of people, families, and communities. Such faculty involvement can compete for attention with more traditionally rewarded activities. The problem-focused approach of interdisciplinary collaborations, in contrast to discipline-based work, also challenges traditional academic values and reward structures, and poses organizational issues in bringing together people and resources from different parts of the university. The difficulties in obtaining federal funding for the social and behavioral sciences add considerably to the challenges of promoting human development in the university.

The initiatives we have described here suggest that these challenges can be met, but clearly more can be done to elevate the promotion of human development to a status equal to the economic-development role of the land-grant universities. There is a tremendous depth of academic experience to be directed toward this goal, compelling societal reasons to do so, and, in the long run, issues of institutional viability that will be determined by the quality of higher education's contributions in this regard. Marshaling the forces of the land-grant university to promote human development surely will be a predominant theme for our future.

References

College of Agricultural Sciences. (1995). Fiscal Year 1995 Accomplishments, Adult and Youth EFNEP in Pennsylvania. Unpublished report, The Pennsylvania State University.

Kaltreider, D. L. & St. Pierre, T. L. (1995). Beyond the schools: Strategies for implementing successful drug prevention programs in community youth-serving organizations. *Drug Education,* 25 (3), 223–237.

Light, R. W. & Daniels, D. (October 1995). Penn State educational partnership programs. Final report for school year 1994–1995. Penn State Erie, The Behrend College, unpublished report.

Morrill Act. (1862). The United States Congress.

McHale, S. M., Crouter, A. C., Fennelly, K., Tomascik, C. A., Updegraff, K. A., Graham, J. E., Baker, A. E., Dreisbach, L. Ferry, N. Manlove, E. E., McGroder, S. M., Mulkeen, P. & Obeidalla, D. A. (1996). Community based interventions for young adolescents: The Penn State PRIDE project. *Journal of Research on Adolescence,* 6 (1), 23–36.

Nicely, R. F. Jr. (1995). The Pennsylvania State University Penn State Educational Partnership Program (PEPP). Final Report to the Howard Heinz Endowment. College of Education, The Pennsylvania State University, unpublished report.

St. Pierre, T. L., Kaltreider, D. L., Mark, M. M., & Aikin, K. (1992). Drug prevention in a community setting: A longitudinal study of the relative effectiveness of a three-year primary prevention program in Boys & Girls Clubs across the nation. *American Journal of Community Psychology,* 20 (6), 673–706.

St. Pierre, T. L., Mark, M. M., Kaltreider, D. L. & Aikin, K. J. (1995). A 27-month evaluation of a sexual activity prevention program in Boys & Girls Clubs across the nation. *Family Relations,* 44, 69–77.

———. (1997). Involving parents of high-risk youths in drug prevention: A three-year longitudinal study in Boys & Girls Clubs. *Journal of Early Adolescence,* 17 (1), 21–50.

Chapter 4
Toward a New Century of Service
Community Collaborative Programs
at Kent State University

Carol A. Cartwright

> *Kent State University is committed to being a catalyst in finding solutions to the social, economic, and cultural challenges facing society.*
> *—Kent State University Strategic Plan*
> *(Committee for University-wide Strategic Planning, 1994)*

Given the scope of ills and issues confronting children, families, communities, and the whole of society at the close of the twentieth century, and the compounding demands of a "knowledge society" in which knowledge and the ability to apply knowledge supersede all other economic resources (Drucker, 1994), America and Americans stand to reap enormous benefits from the achievement of an optimum level of integration between university scholarship in all its forms and community needs, problems, and issues. Walshok (1995, p. 277) refers to such a synthesis as "knowledge without boundaries" and predicts, "In the university of the 21st century, it is likely that the functions connected with serving the economic, workplace, and civic knowledge needs of the public will be as central as those connected with research, undergraduate, graduate and professional education today."

The antecedent of such a reconceptualized system of higher education must be a transformation in the prevailing academic culture from the status quo under which research, instruction and outreach stand separate and unequal, with research eclipsing other academic functions in terms of centrality to promotion, tenure, and professional prestige, to a culture in which scholarly pursuits are reviewed critically for their quality and rewarded accordingly. Herein lies one of the great leadership challenges in contemporary higher education. From presidents to department chairs, administrative leaders must convince faculty that they support new ways of fulfilling all components of university missions. Moreover, administrative leaders must demonstrate that faculty may pursue nonresearch-centered scholarship not only with professional impunity, but with appropriate rewards.

The challenge of transforming an entrenched and unidimensional view of scholarship does not stem from a lack of interest among faculty in activities other than research. Research scholarship is the predominant basis for rewards because widespread acceptance exists for determining the quality of research through peer reviews of proposals for research funding and of manuscripts for publication. Despite the difficulties inherent in defining quality in nonresearch activities, there is no valid reason why all scholarly pursuits should not be critically reviewed to the same degree as research or why the higher-education community cannot develop compacts about what constitutes quality for each type of scholarship. For example, in the draft manuscript of a monograph on reassessing scholarship, the sequel to "Scholarship Reconsidered: Priorities of the Professorate" (Boyer, 1990), Boyer (1994) advances six plausible standards of faculty performance that apply across the disciplines: knowledge of field; clarity of goals; use of appropriate methodology; effective use of resources; quality of communication; and significance of results.

Through higher-education organizations such as the American Association for Higher Education and the National Association of State Universities and Land-Grant Colleges, disciplinary and professional associations, academic alliances such as the Committee on Institutional Cooperation, and individual campus experiments from clinical professorships to tenured, part-time appointments, administrative and faculty leaders at universities nationwide have demonstrated a willingness to address the relative status of research, instruction, and scholarly outreach, and to re-align mission and faculty roles to meet community needs in the twenty-first century.

A Vision for Community Collaboration at Kent State University

At Kent State University, a Research University II institution serving approximately 30,000 students at the flagship Kent Campus and seven regional campuses, the leadership challenge is being addressed in an ongoing, public process of revising mission and academic policies, re-evaluating scholarship and faculty roles, and identifying institutional values.

The process began in 1991 with the formation of the University's first broad-based, presidential advisory committee focused on planning and budget matters. The faculty, administrators, academic and nonacademic staff members, and students of the University Priorities and Budget Advisory Committee (UPBAC) were charged with representing the overall university community, as opposed to their respective units. The group's initial assignments were to recommend revisions in the university mission statement and to draft a companion document, the Kent Institutional Characteristics Statement (University Priorities and Budget Advisory Committee, 1993a), to guide annual and long-term planning efforts.

With the completion of these defining documents, a solid platform for long-range planning and decision making about related resource issues was in place, and a university-wide strategic planning effort was launched. The two-year process was overseen by the provost and the Committee for University-wide Strategic Planning (CUSP) comprising UPBAC and a number of other faculty and administrative leaders, including the chair of the Faculty Senate.

Throughout these interrelated processes of re-evaluating university mission and reaching a consensus on values and goals emanating from mission, the immediate leadership challenge was to foster an atmosphere in which discussions could be inclusive and open to a diversity of viewpoints. The strategic-planning process was designed to incorporate an unprecedented degree of campus participation, with written analyses from every school and college solicited from and considered by CUSP.

In each of the aforementioned documents, scholarly outreach was re-affirmed as among the University's primary missions for the remainder of the 1990s and beyond.

During the strategic-planning process, Kent State University was one of thirty institutions nationwide invited to form a campus roundtable under the auspices of the Pew Higher Education Roundtable program, and the Faculty Senate began a discussion of Boyer's (1990) pivotal monograph. These discussions were enhanced by dissemination of results of a pilot study of faculty work (Kent State University Managing for the Future Task Force, 1992). The study, which yielded striking proof of the diversity of scholarly activities across disciplines, was part of a response to a state-mandated review of institutional efficiency and effectiveness.

These synchronous developments fostered a sense of permission among faculty members and administrators to engage in open dialogue about scholarship in general and scholarship at Kent State University in particular. The dialogue continues through such vehicles as regular, public Pew Roundtable forums. A significant result of the dialogue has been the development by Kent's Faculty Senate of a set of principles for evaluating and rewarding scholarship (Faculty Senate Commission on Scholarship, 1992) that incorporates all aspects of scholarship.

Six years after the process of reassessing university mission and goals was introduced, there is ever-increasing acceptance among the Kent State University faculty that each of the various forms of scholarship is essential to fulfilling mission. Further, an expanding core group of faculty recognizes that outreach scholarship is a valuable and valid means of generating, testing, and applying knowledge, and that adding an outreach dimension to their work will not have a negative impact on tenure and promotion. In fact, a common response from faculty members engaged in the community-collaborative projects described in this chapter is that a new dynamism imbues their research and teaching.

In addition, the larger community is gaining a greater understanding of the Kent State University mission, and the centrality of outreach to that mission, via articles in the weekly faculty-staff newsletter, and regular, presidential progress reports about university goals that are disseminated to all employees.

The changes taking hold, including the gradual realization that the University's leadership endorses a revitalized view of scholarship, are manifested in an array of community-collaborative projects, from units—colleges, departments, and department-based centers—with a history of engagement in outreach activities as well as those not traditionally associated with outreach. As the faculty culture evolves to embrace a broader view of scholarship and a deeper regard for community collaboration, a number of programs with active outreach components are being modified to be more responsive to the authentic needs of families, children, and communities, and to elevate the scholarly expectations associated with outreach efforts.

The Kent Educational Network for Tomorrow

A new initiative of the College and Graduate School of Education, whose community connections extend to the University's 1910 origin as a teacher-training college, points to such an "outreach metamorphosis." The Kent Educational Network for Tomorrow (KENT) is a reconfiguration of earlier projects that stresses scholarship in education and teacher education, and focuses on educational needs expressed by communities.

With the strong advocacy of the dean of the college, the KENT network of nine school districts, seven social-service agencies, and Kent faculty and staff was created in 1994 to improve support services for children and families through joint problem solving and the sharing of ideas and resources. The principal objectives of the KENT partnership are the preparation of new educators in schools and agencies; the lifelong professional development of educators; a commitment to continuous engagement in inquiry about how to improve practice; and the simultaneous improvement of professional practice in the university, schools, and agencies ("An Introduction to KENT," 1995).

Encompassing a four-county area comprising rural, suburban, and urban school districts, network partners serve approximately 100,000 children and families. Each member has agreed to make the partnership a high priority within its own institution, and has signed a formal agreement with the College of Education to share an agenda of collaborative professional education and research (Kent Educational Network for Tomorrow, 1995).

The interactive foundation of the KENT partnership is a departure from a traditional collaborative model under which faculty serve primarily as consultants to school districts. The project is designed to be fluid and dynamic, with needs, interests, and related goals identified by the Partnership Council, consisting of the chief administrators of all partners. The council meets regularly to set and evaluate direction and policies, and identify funding strategies. Projects are implemented by task forces focusing on specific aspects of the network's mission: staff development; clinical training in field settings: collaboration between schools and agencies; technology; and inquiry/action research. Parents and students are encouraged to participate.

To date, KENT's largest partner is the Columbiana County Center for Rural Teaching, a consortium of the College of Education, Kent State University's Salem and East Liverpool regional campuses, the Columbiana County Educational Service Center, eleven school districts, and Columbiana County social-service agencies. Professionals from these institutions collaborate with the goal of developing a cadre of teachers with skills to teach at all levels in rural areas, and of expanding learning opportunities for the county's children. Schools in Columbiana County, which is part of the Appalachian region, tend to be small, isolated, and financially distressed, with many children facing the additional obstacles of poverty (*Introduction to CCRT*, 1995).

With a focus on the real problems of teachers, administrators, and other county personnel, comprehensive professional-development programs are being researched and designed for students coming from rural schools who want to become teachers; teachers who intend to teach in rural areas; teachers who teach in rural areas; administrators in the field of teacher education; and faculty members who teach rural students.

KENT partners have identified several long-term outcomes, including the production of instructional cases focusing on families and children, leadership, and teacher education, and tailored to the development of rural, suburban, and urban partnerships. In addition, models of collaborative professional development will be developed, with accompanying materials, evaluation plans, and curriculum. Resulting monographs, video case studies, curricula, brochures, and other materials will be made available statewide as a portfolio for each initiative. Ultimately, partners will be able to archive information electronically at the University and share it with social-service agencies and other school districts statewide.

The Center for Applied Conflict Management (CACM)

Another unit that is broadening the scope and interactivity of its outreach activities is the Political Science Department's Center for Applied Conflict Management (CACM). Originally the Center for Peaceful Change, the CACM was founded by the faculty in 1971 as a living memorial to the 1970 shootings on the Kent Campus. In addition to offering an undergraduate major and graduate study in conflict management and dispute resolution, the CACM applies conflict-management theory to public and private education, business, government, law, and human services through research, training, and consultation in conflict intervention.

The CACM is engaging increasingly in collaborative, as opposed to prescriptive, approaches to community concerns. For example, a five-year project began recently with Cleveland's urban housing complexes, where such problems as gang violence and unemployment affect the quality of life for residents from children to senior citizens.

The CACM is serving as Technical Assistant Partner with the Cleveland Technical Assistance Organization (TAO), one of seven U.S. Department of Housing and Urban Development national demonstration projects. CACM faculty and staff, with faculty from Kent's departments of Sociology, Pan-African Studies, and Adult, Counseling, Health and Vocational Education, will provide education and training in conflict management to enhance the ability of TAO, Progressive Action Council, local advisory council boards, and building, block, floor, and courtyard captains of Cleveland Metropolitan Housing Authority complexes to peacefully resolve interpersonal, group, and community conflicts. The overall goal of this effort is to empower residents to participate in decision making and community building, as opposed to becoming more dependent on the service of experts, and to build job skills (Maxwell, 1995). Throughout the project, faculty researchers will examine the effectiveness of various types of adult education and conflict management and mediation training, including such variables as training style, trainer gender, and cross-cultural settings.

Approximately 2,400 residents will be served through community organizing and leadership/conflict management programming in all five years, more than doubling the number of residents participating in leadership roles and serving as role models.

As part of the project, a continuing series of seminars will address residents' needs related to career exploration, job interviews, attending college as an adult student, and parenting. Kent faculty will work closely with residents to evaluate the effectiveness of the seminars in providing real-world skills and in meeting goals identified by the community.

Community empowerment and violence prevention are the focus of another CACM project emanating from prior faculty research indicating a critical need for new approaches to addressing violence, particularly among youth (Maxwell, 1989). To this end, CACM faculty and staff collaborated with community agencies to develop a pilot project in the juvenile justice system and the schools. Project EMPOWER (Experiential Model Program on Win-Enabling Responses) is designed to increase participants' ability to control aggressive responses and to employ socially acceptable methods of conflict management. A Project EMPOWER aftercare program is conducted for felony youth offenders through the Ohio Department of Youth Services in Cleveland (Maxwell, 1995), as is a camp at which young felons engage in team-building, trust-building, and aggression-control activities. Project EMPOWER is evaluated and redesigned continually to meet the needs of the participants (e.g., programming was added on Saturdays because more young people could attend).

Preventing Violence

Ameliorating the growing problem of juvenile crime is at the heart of a number of community-collaborative projects conducted by faculty in Kent State University's Department of Criminal Justice Studies. Working closely with local communities and with local, regional, and state law-enforcement agencies, department faculty also focus on the often interrelated societal problems of gang violence (Kratcoski & Kratcoski, 1996), family violence (Kratcoski, 1988), violence against women (Tontodonato & Crew, 1992), and child abuse (Erez & Tontodonato, 1989).

Recent collaborations have taken faculty to neighborhoods and communities throughout northeast Ohio, for projects ranging from an evaluation of thirty-eight Cleveland neighborhoods where police ministations operate as crime deterrents, to a study of crime victims in northeast Ohio (Tontodonato & Kratcoski, 1995), to an assessment of state victim-assistance programs (Kratcoski & Tontodonato, 1993).

A new project will provide critical information about the effectiveness of the state's Disproportionate Minority Confinement Pilot projects in Akron and Cleveland to reduce the number of minority youth offenders in confinement in Ohio's juvenile justice facilities. Faculty researchers will track the progress of these youths, concentrating activity on the family and school, to examine the degree to which they are subsequently able to develop attachments to society, secure and hold jobs, establish relationships, and assume community responsibilities (Kessler & Kratcoski, 1995).

Addressing Urban Problems

As the aforementioned projects demonstrate, Kent State University's proximity to urban centers in Cleveland and Akron, Ohio, makes urban problems a natural focus of outreach efforts. A number of community-collaborative efforts focused on urban needs have emerged from the Urban Design Center (UDC), an interinstitutional venture of northeast Ohio's four public universities that is based in Kent's School of Architecture and Environmental Design. UDC faculty analyze urban-planning problems, conduct detailed research, and develop creative design solutions in concert with community leaders, neighborhood groups, developers, design review boards, historical societies, and professional architects. Projects are supported by the Ohio Board of Regents through the Ohio Urban Universities Program.

UDC faculty frequently initiate real-world experiences for students enrolled in design studio classes. For example, sixty-five students worked on an intensive project to revitalize the neighborhood at East Fifty-fifth Street and Euclid Avenue in Cleveland by creating a mixed-use district of residences, entertainment facilities, and businesses. This unique opportunity was generated by the UDC's relationship with the Cleveland Neighborhood Development Corporation and other civic organizations. Many students characterized the project as the most challenging and relevant work they had performed during their academic careers ("Kent's Urban Design Center," 1995).

A design philosophy emphasizing economic and social factors is also evidenced in the school's Environmental Technology course. In a recent project, students designed and built prototypical homeless shelters made of castoffs ranging from plastic cartons to shopping carts, and then occupied them for a day to test their resistance to the elements.

Programs in Health and Behavioral Science

Just as Kent's location makes urban problems a natural target of outreach scholarship, its proximity to several major medical facilities has been the impetus for a variety of programs in the health and behavioral sciences. The University is a partner with the Northeastern Ohio Universities College of Medicine (NEOUCOM), a consortium including the University of Akron and Youngstown State University, located minutes from the Kent Campus. Kent students may pursue medical education through the Integrated Life Sciences program, a six-year, combined program leading to bachelor of science and doctor of medicine degrees. Kent also offers a Ph.D. program in biomedical sciences through its School of Biomedical Sciences. The school's faculty represent thirteen departments, NEOUCOM, and the University of Akron.

The education of physicians who will practice medicine, particularly primary care, on the community level is central to NEOUCOM's mission. To this end, the medical school is constructing a $1.7 million Clinical Competency and Teaching and Assessment Center. The facility is based on the established effectiveness of assessing clinical and diagnostic skills by observing students' treatment of "standardized patients" (actors trained to assume the role of patients with well-defined symptoms and conditions). Through its strong community links, NEOUCOM has developed an extensive pool of approximately 250 standardized patients representing the communities the college serves. The patients also are used to train and assess medical students and residents at eighteen associated community hospitals.

A number of health-related programs focusing on children and families have evolved as the result of a collaboration between Kent State University's School of Speech Pathology and Audiology, the College and Graduate School of Education, and Children's Hospital of Akron through the Family Child Learning Center (FCLC). The FCLC is distinctive regionally for its treatment of infants and children with disabilities by multidisciplinary teams of speech pathologists, special-education specialists, psychologists, physical therapists, and occupational therapists.

The management team at the FCLC, which is located minutes from the Kent Campus, is composed of University faculty members and Children's Hospital staff. The executive director serves as an adjunct faculty member at Kent State University.

The FCLC's Early Childhood Services Program provides intervention services to approximately fifty infants, toddlers, and their families each semester. Faculty and students in the departments of Early Childhood Special Education, Speech/Language Pathology, Audiology, and Educational Psychology evaluate child and family strengths and needs, and design intervention plans in close cooperation with families.

The Hearing-Impaired Infants, Toddlers and Families Program is a new initiative under which faculty from Kent's audiology program and Children's Hospital staff provide infants and toddlers with intensive, communication-based educational experiences; facilitate the transition of children with hearing impairments into preschool programs; and provide family-centered intervention services that assist families in dealing with the unique stresses and demands associated with caring for young children with hearing impairments. The program emphasizes community-based services in settings that allow infants and toddlers with normal hearing to interact with infants and toddlers with hearing loss (Family Child Learning Center, 1995).

Training activities at the FCLC involve master's- and doctoral-degree candidates from academic units including Speech Pathology, Audiology, Psychology, Special Education, School Psychology, and Education of the Hearing Impaired. Master's-degree students receive practicum experiences as members of early intervention teams that work with caseloads of ten to twelve families that have young children with disabilities. Advanced master's and doctoral candidates gain practical experience in supervisory positions, or in one of several research projects being conducted through the center on topics including early motor intervention procedures, family-focused intervention, developmentally appropriate assistive technology for young children with disabilities, services to foster-care families of infants and toddlers exposed to drugs prenatally, and infant communication development. Support groups for families and workshops involving caregivers and families as experts are held at the FCLC, with more than 1,500 parents and professionals participating in workshops annually.

Family and community health problems also have become a focus of Kent's Applied Psychology Center (APC), a unit within the Department of Psychology designed to match faculty skills and research with local, state, and national community groups, including education and health-care systems, government organizations, businesses, and human-services programs in need of expert help. Since its inception in 1988, the APC has embodied the concept of "outreach research" that is being promoted at Michigan State University (Provost's Committee on University Outreach, 1993).

APC researchers are collaborating with Kent faculty from the Department of Sociology and the College of Education, the Obstetrics Division of Summa Health System of Akron, Ohio, the Akron Health Department, and Planned Parenthood of Summit County in pursuit of a self-empowerment–based, culturally sensitive approach to AIDS prevention among women, especially those subject to the stresses of inner-city life.

The team is coaching 800 women ages 16–40, including single, pregnant women and women seeking medical care for other sexually transmitted diseases, to increase awareness of what is needed to protect their health, bolster self-esteem, and to build skills needed to respond assertively to situations that put them at risk for exposure to AIDS. The approach is novel in its inclusion of participants' social networks (i.e., boyfriends, other family members and friends) as change agents who can help women incorporate safer-sex behaviors into their lives.

Six months after participating in the project, women who received the AIDS-prevention intervention changed their knowledge, attitudes, and behavior, despite an environment that encourages risky sexual behavior (Hobfoll, Jackson, Lavin, Britton, & Shepherd, 1994). The results attracted the immediate interest of AIDS policymakers and led to testimony about the findings before the U.S. Congressional Committee on Families and Children, and meetings by APC researchers with representatives of the Surgeon General's Office and the Center for Disease Control.

Many APC projects are related directly to family issues. For example, faculty involved in the Women's Multiple Roles Study are exploring the dynamics of caregiving, particularly among the growing ranks of "women in the middle," who simultaneously occupy the roles of wife, mother, and caregiver to an impaired parent or parent-in-law (Stephens, Franks, & Townsend, 1994). Work through the APC also focuses on family and community stress, including stress related to war and other traumatic events (Hobfoll & de Vries, 1995). For example, after the Persian Gulf War, the APC initiated and cosponsored with the American Psychological Association a task force to develop strategies for helping returning service person-

nel, their families, and their communities deal with the negative psychological consequences that often ensue from the stress of war and family
disruption. Special attention was given to children's reactions and needs
(Hobfoll et al., 1991). In addition to presenting their recommendations
to Congress, the task force's report was given to the chiefs of psychological
services of each branch of the military, a version was made available to
mental health and allied health professionals likely to be dealing with the
treatment and care of war veterans, and a companion guide was sent to all
Gulf War families (American Psychological Association-Kent State University Applied Psychology Center Task Force on War-Related Stress, 1991).

Arts and Humanities Outreach Programs

Departments such as Psychology and Criminal Justice Studies and professional schools such as Speech Pathology and Architecture have natural
links to the problems and needs of communities, families, and children.
The community-collaborative momentum that is building at Kent State
University is not limited to traditional outreach disciplines. It also extends
to areas such as the arts and humanities.

For example, the School of Art's Enameling Outreach Program, which
offers workshops and special programs for adults and young people, has
enhanced town-gown relations and received a great deal of positive attention in the city of Kent and surrounding communities. A recent collaboration among the Enamel Outreach Program, Theodore Roosevelt High
School, and Kent City Council resulted in the creation and installation of
an eight-panel mural depicting historical images of Kent in the new City
Hall building (Shinn, 1995).

At the suggestion of faculty members in the enamel program and the
high school's art instructor, the mayor organized a mural competition committee that included the dean of Kent's School of Fine and Professional
Arts and a representative of the Ferro Corporation of Cleveland. The company donated the enamel for the project as a result of a long-standing
relationship with the School of Art. More than 150 high-school art students submitted mural designs after School of Art faculty visited the high
school to demonstrate enameling techniques. After the selection of the
winning design, work moved to the University's large-scale enamel studio,
where the project was completed using a rare, gradient furnace donated to
the University by Ferro in 1989. In a similar effort, local high-school students were involved in the creation of a mural for the young people's treatment center of Cleveland Metro Health Center.

High-school students also are the focus of a new outreach initiative of Kent's School of Journalism and Mass Communication. The outreach imperative in the University's strategic plan provided the incentive for faculty and administrators to expand a long-standing commitment to hosting the Northeastern Ohio Scholastic Press Association Press Day. As a result, the school is about to launch a two-year pilot for a Scholastic Media Center that will serve high schools throughout Ohio.

The Center was conceived as a way to incorporate state-of-the-art technology into the region's high-school journalism programs, play a role in the University's distributed-learning initiatives, and to join ongoing efforts to provide outreach to communities served by Kent's Regional Campus System. In addition, the Center will provide fertile ground for researching the effectiveness of new instructional and communications technology, and for increasing the visibility of and, ultimately, enrollment in, the journalism program (Bowen, 1995).

Plans for the Center include interdisciplinary summer workshops, weekend short courses, programs at selected media sites and regional campuses, an on-line news service, and programs that explore new communications technologies and innovative instructional methods. The Center is designed to be highly responsive to the needs of high-school journalists and their advisers, 100% of whom, when contacted for a feasibility study (Bowen, 1995), reported a need or desire for such programming and for university support. For example, center faculty will work with the growing ranks of secondary students who write for popular "teen pages" in daily newspapers, and expect to create a World Wide Web page to serve as a clearinghouse for students' articles.

Using the University's Technological Assets

The University's resources in the realm of computer and networking technologies will be a major component of the center. In fact, new technologies can be of immeasurable use in virtually all outreach efforts, offering user-friendly vehicles for providing academic and consulting services far beyond campus boundaries. Among the most innovative technology outreach efforts at Kent State University is the multidisciplinary "Science and Math on the Net" (SAM-Net), a successful fusion of outreach scholarship and basic science. The science education networking project is offered through Kent's National Science Foundation Center for Advanced Liquid Crystalline Optical Materials (ALCOM). The University's internationally respected Liquid Crystal Institute serves as the hub of the

ALCOM, a consortium with Cleveland's Case Western Reserve University and the University of Akron.

SAM-Net was created in 1993 as a joint project of ALCOM, the Libraries and Media Services Department, and the Department of Mathematics and Computer Science in response to the outreach component in ALCOM's mission.

The program features a series of intensive Saturday workshops based on the physics and chemistry of liquid crystals. Workshops are conducted in Kent State University's Electronic Classroom, a state-of-the-art teaching facility equipped with thirty computers connected to the Internet. The program already has reached every middle and high school in Portage County, and has since been extended to surrounding counties. Workshops are conducted by ALCOM scientists and faculty from Libraries and Media Services and the Department of Mathematics and Computer Science. Not only are workshops taught by interdisciplinary faculty teams, they are presented to teams consisting of a science teacher, a math teacher, a librarian, and students. As teams learn firsthand about how scientific research is conducted, the electronic classroom provides a prototype for science education reform (Bartolo & Palffy-Muhoray, 1996).

ALCOM researchers collaborate with the teams to develop hands-on experiments and lesson plans that integrate physical sciences, mathematics, and information management. The results are made available to teachers and students worldwide via the Internet. During the school year, ALCOM scientists visit participating schools and students make trips to the Liquid Crystal Institute. In addition, students present their liquid crystal–based research projects at an annual symposium on the Kent Campus.

To build comfort with computers and promote learning through direct experience, each school involved in SAM-Net is given a computer account linking students and teachers to the Internet, and, thus, to myriad electronic reference tools. SAM-Net also allows teachers and students anywhere in the world to interact with ALCOM researchers through the "Ask a Scientist" program, in which ALCOM scientists respond directly to students and teachers who pose questions electronically. This component of SAM-Net also connects students to peers at other schools who have similar scientific interests.

Not only does SAM-Net strengthen understanding of and enthusiasm for science, by teachers as well as students, it provides educational opportunities for schools that may be isolated geographically and/or economically.

Programs such as SAM-Net demonstrate the power of the Internet and the vast array of computer and networking technologies to facilitate new levels of university outreach. It is therefore not coincidental that technology was a variable in virtually all aspects of Kent's strategic-planning process.

The use of technology to advance outreach and maximize access to higher education is related directly to Kent State University's multiple-campus structure. The University's seven regional campuses throughout northeast Ohio offer a variety of two- and four-year degree programs, many of which have been developed in response to community-specific needs voiced by the educational and business sectors.

The regional campus system serves about 9,000 students, many of whom have full-time jobs and families, and are thus "placebound." Given such geographic and demographic considerations, the University is eager to take advantage of new technologies for connecting its campuses. The issue of regional access to higher education and technical training has led to the University's pursuit of a distributed-learning model (Cartwright, 1995) that makes time as irrelevant to communication as location, and that allows outreach to businesses, hospitals, schools, and others in the larger community.

The advent of powerful new academic technologies presents a number of leadership imperatives, chief among them is an obligation to provide faculty with ongoing technical training and professional development opportunities. As distributed- and distance-learning technologies become commonplace on campuses, the boundaries between knowledge and practice will blur, and the role of classroom lecturer will be supplanted by that of learning consultant. Administrative leaders must be prepared to support approaches to faculty assignments, unit structures, and evaluation and reward systems that recognize these inevitable shifts. For example, the appointment of faculty to clinical ranks in fields such as nursing, psychology, and architecture could be extended to other academic areas; faculty in a department might interact much the same as partners in a law firm, setting individual and collective goals and criteria for evaluation; and departments could be empowered to negotiate mission-specific, individual faculty contracts or short-term contracts for mission-directed outreach.

Conclusions

The outcome of such changes should be campus cultures in which faculty and administrative roles are integrated, categories of scholarship are less important, while quality and excellence of a variety of contributions are paramount, and in which the formation of effective problem-solving teams is a priority. This vision is beginning to take shape in the community-collaborative projects described here. However, as promising as early efforts at Kent and universities nationwide have been, significant barriers to systems change exist, ranging from a natural resistance to cultural change on the part of many faculty and administrators, to the challenge of funding collaborations with schools, social-service agencies, and other community entities that have equally limited resources.

To realize the goal of institutionalizing outreach scholarship, administrative and faculty leaders must continue to champion changes that upgrade the status of outreach from a peripheral activity; that loosen the stranglehold of a "publish or perish" culture; that permit flexible approaches to faculty roles and rewards; and that allow colleges and universities to fully integrate outreach into academic life for a new century of service.

References

American Psychological Association-Kent State University Applied Psychology Center Task Force on War-Related Stress (1991). *A Guide to Help Families and Communities Find Peace after War*. (Available from Applied Psychology Center, Kent State University, P.O. Box 5190, Kent, OH 44242-0001).

Bartolo, L., & Palffy-Muhoray, P. (1996, March). *SAM-Net: Connecting Students and Teachers to Scientific Research through Scientific Communication and Electronic Networking.* Paper accepted for presentation at the annual Technology and Teacher Education Conference of the Association for the Advancement of Computing in Education, Phoenix, AZ.

Bowen, C. P. (1995). Scholastic media center: A feasibility study. (Available from School of Journalism and Mass Communication, Kent State University, P.O. Box 5190, Kent, OH 44242-0001).

Boyer, E. L. (1990). Scholarship reconsidered: Priorities of the professorate. Princeton, NJ: The Carnegie Foundation for the Advancement of Teaching.

———. (1994). *Scholarship assessed.* Speech delivered to the 2nd Annual Conference on Faculty Roles and Rewards, American Association for Higher Education Conference.

Cartwright, C. A. (1995). High technology in higher education: A presidential perspective. *Educators' Tech Exchange, 3,* 6–13.

Committee for University-wide Strategic Planning. (1994). Kent State University Strategic Plan. (Available from Office of of the Provost, Kent State University, P.O. Box 5190, Kent, OH 44242-0001).

Drucker, P. F. (1994). The age of social transformation. *The Atlantic Monthly, 274,* 53–80.

Erez, E., & Tontodonato, P. (1989). Patterns of reported parent-child abuse and police response. *Journal of Family Violence, 4,* 143–159.

Faculty Senate Commission on Scholarship (1992). Principles for the Evaluation and Reward of Faculty Scholarship. Kent State University.

Family Child Learning Center (1995). *Hearing-Impaired Toddlers, Infants, Families*. (Brochure). (Available from the Family Child Learning Center, 143 Northwest Avenue, Building A, Tallmadge, OH 44278).

Hobfoll, S. E., Jackson, A. P., Lavin, J. P., Britton, P.J., & Shepherd, J. P. (1994). Reducing inner-city women's AIDS risk activities: A study of single, pregnant women. *Health Psychology, 13,* 397–403.

Hobfoll, S. E., Spielberger, C. D., Breznitz, S., Figley, C., Folkman, S., Lepper-Green, B., Meichenbaum, D., Milgram, N. E., Sandler, I., Sarason, I., & van der Kolk, B. (1991). War-related stress: Addressing the stress of war and other traumatic events. *American Psychologist, 46,* 848–855.

Hobfoll, S. E., & de Vries, M. W. (Eds.) (1995). Extreme stress and communities: Impact and intervention. Norwell, MA: Kluwer Academic Publishers.

Introduction to CCRT. (1995). (Brochure). (Available from the Columbiana County Center for Rural Teaching, Kent State University, Salem Campus, 2491 St. Rt. 45, Salem, OH 44460).

An introduction to KENT. (1995, October). *KENT Newsletter, 1,* 1.

Kent Educational Network for Tomorrow (1995). Proposal for Goals 2000: Grants for School/ University Partnerships, Ohio Department of Education.

Kent State University Managing for the Future Task Force (1992). *Report.*

Kent's urban design center: A real-world resource for communities and students. (1995, October 2). Inside Kent, 15, 3.

Kessler, D. A., & Kratcoski, P. C. (1995). Evaluation of Ohio's minority youth over-representation pilot project: A concept paper. (Available from the Department of Criminal Justice Studies, P.O. Box 5190. Kent, OH 44242 0001).

Kratcoski, P. C. (1988). Families who kill. In F. E. Hagan & M. B. Sussman (Eds.), *Deviance and the Family* (pp. 47—70). New York, NY: Haworth Press.

Kratcoski, P. C., & Kratcoski, L. D. (1996). Gang delinquency and violence. In P. C. Kratcoski & L. D. Kratcoski (Eds.), *Juvenile Delinquency* (pp. 86–123). Upper Saddle River, NJ: Prentice Hall.

Kratcoski, P.C., & Tontodonato, P. (1993). *Assessment of victim assistance programs: Final research report for the governor's office of criminal justice services.* Kent, OH: Kent State University, Department of Criminal Justice Studies.

Maxwell, J. P. (1989). Mediation in the schools: Self-regulation, self-esteem, and self-discipline. *Mediation Quarterly, 7,* 149–155.

———. (1995). Center for applied conflict management annual planning report. (Available from the Center for Applied Conflict Management, Department of Political Science, P.O. Box 5190, Kent, OH 44242-0001).

Provost's Committee on University Outreach. (1993). University outreach at Michigan State University: Extending knowledge to serve society. A report by the Provost's Committee on University Outreach, Michigan State University.

Shinn, D. (1995, December 3). Mural for Kent city hall reflects cooperative effort. *Akron Beacon Journal,* p. B1.

Stephens, M. A., Franks, M. A., & Townsend, A. L. (1994). Stress and rewards in women's multiple roles: The case of women in the middle. *Psychology and Aging, 9,* 45–52.

Tontodonato, P., & Crew, K. (1992). Dating violence, social learning theory, and gender: A multivariate analysis. *Violence and Victims, 7,* 3–14.

Tontodonato, P., & Kratcoski, P. (1995). *Crime victims' utilization of services: Final research report for the governor's office of criminal justice services.* Kent, Ohio: Kent State University, Department of Criminal Justice Studies.

University Priorities and Budget Advisory Committee. (1993a). Kent Institutional Characteristics Statement.

———. (1993b). The role and mission of Kent State University.

Walshok, M. L. (1995). *Knowledge without boundaries: What America's research universities can do for the economy, the workplace, and the community.* San Francisco: Jossey-Bass.

Chapter 5
Community Collaboration Programs at Goucher College
A Commitment to Connect

Judy Jolley Mohraz and Carol Weinberg
Goucher College

Goucher College's commitment to respond to critical needs in contemporary society is most appropriate, considering the impulses that led to the founding of the college in 1885. Baltimore leaders, led by the Reverend John Goucher, established the Women's College of Baltimore City in response to the "urgent demand" for collegiate education and equal opportunities for women (Knipp and Thomas, 1938, p. 6). Advocates of the proposed college proclaimed, "Not that we love our sons less or our daughters more, but let us give them equal advantages in the business of life" (Knipp and Thomas, 1938, p. 10). This conviction, which fueled the very founding of women's colleges in the nineteenth century, is important to recall at the end of the twentieth century as we renew our commitment to civic engagement among universities and colleges. Just as visionaries such as Justin Morrill created land-grant universities to serve community needs, the founders of the women's colleges also responded to social conditions that prevented half of the population from access to higher education. In fact, the cornerstones of the majority of private and public institutions established in the nineteenth century in this nation were laid in response to urgent social concerns, whether it was abolition, women's rights, the needs of the freedman, a "heathen frontier," or a burgeoning industrial nation.

Throughout the eleven decades since its founding, Goucher has committed itself to reaching out and becoming engaged with community and national concerns. During World War II, for example, select Goucher students were secretly trained on campus to decode messages intercepted from the German navy. In the sixties, students and faculty signed an open letter to President Kennedy decrying his emphasis on civil defense shelters, and marched on Washington, precursors of the campus spirit that would ultimately produce a multidisciplinary Peace Studies major at Goucher in the 1990s. Not content with remaining separated from the nearby suburb of

Towson, in 1961 students marched into Towson to sit in and desegregate a local restaurant.

Prompted by one of the oldest internship programs in the nation, students for seventy-five years have fanned out through Baltimore City, the state capital of Annapolis, and Washington, D.C. to serve internships in government, not-for-profit community organizations, as well as the private sector. Because of the conviction that a Goucher education must transcend the world of an idyllic, secluded campus, all students are required to undertake an off-campus experience, either through study abroad or an internship. In fact, the melding of a strong liberal arts curriculum with outreach and connections to the larger community has served as a hallmark of Goucher College throughout its history.

The tradition of community outreach imprinted generation after generation of students and graduates who have chosen in disproportionate numbers careers in social work, legal reform, political action, and community service. When the college celebrated its centennial, one Baltimore civic leader applauded Goucher as "a shining example of the way an institution of higher education can relate to the community," and stated further that the college "has consistently tried to avoid an ivory tower approach by providing an atmosphere that encourages the students' intellectual pursuits to have real meaning in the community beyond the immediate campus" (Abelson, 1984, p. 40).

Alumni continue to see community service as a high priority, not only for the individual but also as a shared endeavor with other Goucher graduates that cuts across generational lines. Currently, regional Goucher alumni associations throughout the nation are determining which of several national volunteer efforts alumni should support through collective effort. They envision, for example, sporting T-shirts in Atlanta, Philadelphia, San Francisco, and other cities proclaiming "Goucher for Habitat for Humanity" as they head off to construction sites.

Because historic celebrations of a college or university emphasize core institutional values, we wanted to ensure that the inauguration of a new president in 1994 reflected truly representative values of Goucher. We chose the theme, "Citizenship, Scholarship, Leadership." Two events that inaugural week recognized the importance of a civically engaged institution. The first event was a panel of Goucher alumni who work tirelessly from local to national levels for the benefit of others. The second event was one afternoon dedicated to service. Students were joined by faculty, staff, alumni, trustees, and parents on projects such as house construction for Habitat for Humanity, serving at a city soup kitchen, and participating in a Special Olympics soccer tournament held on campus.

A culture of community engagement is fostered not only by a historic institutional legacy and the values students have embraced before arrival, but also by the very structure and size of a small residential college. Indeed, such an environment can foster the necessary sensibility for community outreach: the belief that individuals make a difference. Throughout students' years at Goucher they encounter the reality that individuals make a difference—in small classes oriented around discussion, in student organizations that can literally rise or fall by individual effort, and in volunteer outreach beyond the campus walls. The strong sense of community on campus also appears to transfer to a shared sense of connection that cuts across faculty, staff, and student lines.

One project last year is instructive. Several members of the housekeeping and physical plant staff expressed interest in obtaining their GEDs. Staff and students volunteered to tutor them in a GED training course held on campus after their work day. The program continues this year. Community outreach also creates other connections between different constituencies on campus. A physical plant driver who was scheduled to drive students to a soup kitchen where they would prepare and serve food for the homeless asked if he could participate as well. He did, and our students enjoyed working side by side with him.

Goucher today educates over 1,000 undergraduates each year, now both women and men, and 200 graduate students. Given the college's historic orientation, it is not surprising that Goucher attracts a type of student who is already committed to community service. Last year the nationally administered Cooperative Institutional Research Program Freshman Survey (CIRP) indicated that over 52% of the Goucher freshmen expected to be engaged in volunteer community service in college, compared with an average 28.8% of freshmen at other selective liberal arts institutions. Recent graduates sustain their commitment to community outreach. Studies show that 75% of our graduates who are five years out of college are active in volunteer work.

How We're Making the Connections Today at Goucher: A Case Study
Building on Our Strengths

At Goucher College we have been building on our strengths—a strong base of interest in service, an environment where faculty and staff are involved and accessible, our proximity to Baltimore—to include more members of the campus community in service and to weave the service ethic into the total life of the institution. For example, our new student orientation includes a half-day devoted to community service. All incoming students are required to sign up for one of ten sites. We then send out all new students, in vans and busses with one or two upperclass students, to do several hours of service. Projects have included: painting a homeless shelter; doing clean-up work in local state parks and streams; planting organic fruits and vegetables at a farm that donates its harvest to the soup kitchens, shelters, and food banks of Baltimore City and county; performing needed jobs at an agency that provides safe houses for women and children who are homeless as a result of domestic violence; and cleaning the kitchen and sorting food supplies at a site that prepares and delivers meals to people who are homebound with AIDS. This activity involves the entire freshman class and sends out the message, from day one, that service is an integral part of the Goucher experience.

While Goucher students usually head out into the community to perform service, we also host a number of programs here on campus. One of the advantages of being a small institution with a commitment to a liberal arts education is that there is a great willingness to share that love of learning with others. In that spirit, much of the campus generously offers both facilities and personal attention to community members who come on campus as part of programs we sponsor. The efforts of many constituencies were shown throughout Goucher's seven-year commitment to Project RAISE. Over this period, approximately 100–125 students, faculty, and staff mentored a group of students beginning in the sixth grade and following them through their middle and high-school years until their high-school graduation in 1995. The Baltimore County Special Olympics also practices on the Goucher campus several times a week, with Goucher students serving as assistant coaches. Other young people come to campus as part of the Choice Middle Schools Tutoring Program (for at-risk middle-schoolers) and through the Middle River Mentorship Program (for talented fifth graders who could benefit from additional support). They not only meet with an assigned Goucher tutor/mentor, but they also make use of the library, computer labs, physical-education facilities, and recreational space.

The academic curriculum has incorporated service through a long-standing off-campus experience requirement that is often fulfilled through service-related internships. Our education department includes field placements in many courses and the Peace Studies Program offers a three-credit course called *Community Service Agencies: Building a Just and Peaceful World*. This class, taught by the college chaplain, combines supervised work in a community agency with weekly group reflection and discussion. Our biology and chemistry departments also oversee a program in which Goucher science students mentor high-school students in Baltimore City.

Goucher's academic program offers students the opportunity to study both traditional liberal arts subjects and to explore the implications of theory and research for today's world. Students here learn to take the initiative to ask questions, think creatively and critically, and put their knowledge into action. One example of how this progression occurs can be seen in a student-initiated project that is just beginning. The words of one student, in a letter sent to the principal of a nearby middle school, eloquently describe the connections they are making:

I am a senior at Goucher College and one of the co-presidents of the Women's Issues Group on campus. We are interested in establishing a mentorship program with your school, in which Goucher women could mentor some of the girls at your school. Last semester, a number of Goucher students participated in a developmental psychology seminar that focused on gender and girls' education. The course was taught by Professor Rick Pringle, who has been researching these issues since 1985. He would be the faculty sponsor of the mentorship program. . . .

Throughout the semester, we reflected both personally and as a class on our own experiences. We made connections between the choices we had made growing up and the sometimes rigid stereotyping that we had witnessed. . . . As we learned about girl's development and discussed our own experiences, we often wished that someone had been there to guide us along some of the rocky terrain. We wished that someone had been there to tell us that we were not alone and that we really could make it through. We wished there had been more support available for young, capable women.

Unlike the usual college model of studying issues in theory and never moving on to real situations, we decided that we wanted to share what we had learned. Goucher is building a strong tradition by encouraging what we call "service-learning." So committed to the idea of reaching out to middle school girls were we that the Women's Issues Group petitioned the Student Government Association for funds to help us make this idea a reality. We did receive a small grant with which to begin a mentorship program. Additionally, there are several Goucher men who would be interested in mentoring middle school boys. (E. Hottenstein, personal communication, September 15, 1995)

The student-driven quality of this program, with its roots in an academic course and the support of faculty and staff, is the type of initiative common at a small liberal arts college such as Goucher. The programs described below reflect the range of efforts that are presently underway.

The Masters in Education Program

Goucher's M.Ed. program, which has received national recognition, is an innovative graduate program grounded in community needs. Established in 1991, it provides teachers with skills to understand the needs and motivation of students at risk of school failure, and assist them in overcoming obstacles to learning. One of the program's major concentrations addresses the particular educational challenges found working with at-risk students, and offers specialized training seldom found in most master's level education programs.

Goucher's M.Ed. program was developed in collaboration with Sheppard Pratt Hospital, a medical center recognized for more than a century for innovative mental health services. The M.Ed. program integrates theoretical and practical coursework to help practicing teachers understand the psychological and social forces affecting student development. The program offers five areas of concentration: Education of the At-Risk Student, School Mediation, Urban Education, Middle School Education, and School Improvement Leadership. What is particularly distinctive about this program is the requirement of all degree candidates to complete an action research project that applies theory to address practical problems in schools and classrooms.

Action research contrasts with traditional education research in that it grows out of teachers' classroom experience and is designed to answer specific instructional questions. The action research projects that teachers enrolled in the M.Ed. program have completed offer practical strategies and valuable insights into the problems presented by teaching today's diverse, complex, and demanding students. For example, a Baltimore-area elementary-school teacher last year designed and tested a variety of techniques to keep at-risk students focused and "on task." Another candidate demonstrated the effectiveness of cooperative group learning to improve students' math skills. Another crafted a curriculum to raise students' self-esteem and dramatically cut the attrition rate among at-risk 15-year-old males. The fact that the M.Ed. program has mushroomed from twenty students in 1991 to more than two hundred today reflects the felt need of teachers for this type of orientation.

A special project currently underway involves the training of twenty Baltimore-area school teams in mediation skills. The project, funded by a FIPSE grant, provides teachers, administrators, and counselors the requisite information needed to establish a series of different mediation programs.

The Service Credit Option

Our most extensive efforts at integrating service into the undergraduate curriculum have come through the development of a service credit option program. First offered in the fall of 1994, this program encourages faculty members to give students in a course the opportunity to take an additional credit (usually a fourth credit for a three-credit course), graded pass/ no pass, for doing thirty hours of community service at a site relevant to the content of that course. Students also complete required academic assignments in order to integrate that experience into the class. The purpose of the service credit option is to give students real-life experiences that can bring to life what they're studying, and also to give them an academic context in which to reflect upon those experiences. One student, for example, did the service credit option for a history course called "Baltimore as Town and City" by working at Habitat for Humanity in Baltimore's Sandtown neighborhood, which is currently the focus of a major empowerment zone revitalization effort. The student describes her integrative experience as follows:

I felt the opportunity to see a more complete picture of the city of Baltimore as the city developed and racial segregation became the norm—the process related well to Professor Baker's course structure. During the course we studied the migration of subpopulations within the city which caused both ethnic and racial segregation. This process led to the development of the rich and very vital African American culture in the Sandtown neighborhood. I was surprised that even in the midst of the current decay, traces of those better days were still visible in the richness of the architecture. (B. Lilly, personal communication, May 1995)

The service credit option has been offered in an increasing range of courses. We began with mostly social science courses—political science, peace studies, sociology, women's studies, psychology—and have expanded to include classes in the arts—photography, art, English, theater. Feed-back about the service credit option has been mostly positive from all sides:

I think that we, as college students, often become so focused on textbook data that we forget about the "real world." The service option was a great way to enhance our studies with a hands-on experience. It also reminded me that instinct is sometimes more important than knowledge, and that getting an "A" on a paper isn't the only reason to be happy. (E. Raskin, student, personal communication, May 1995)

I can honestly say that I learned more about issues concerning the elderly than I would have in 30 hours of lectures. . . . I would not normally get to experi-ence interacting with someone with dementia, and it took me out of my com-fort zone and brought classroom knowledge to life. . . . It put faces and person-alities on all the theories and numbers. (H. Santos, student, personal communication, May 10, 1995)

Actively engaging students in community organizations creates an affective connection to the class material that is seldom reproduced in other forms of learning and enhances students' understanding of the issues at hand. In my domestic violence class, many students identify violence as a phenomenon that happens to certain kinds of people, not to women like themselves. The service-learning component helps move students from their cultural starting blocks by breaching the line between us and them, and provides an opportu-nity for students to learn firsthand about the causes and consequences of domestic violence. (J. Shope, professor, personal communication, November 30, 1995)

With the help of Goucher volunteers, we were able to develop and implement a psychosocial history tool, as well as a program evaluation survey. These im-portant additions would not have been possible without the help of the very capable and enthusiastic volunteers. (J. Langdon, nonprofit agency staff, per-sonal communication, December 1994)

The most difficult and challenging aspect of the service credit option program has been finding effective methods for faculty to integrate service experiences into their courses. Samples of techniques used by faculty at other institutions have been shared, and comprehensive training work-shops could provide even greater assistance.

Partnerships

Our most beneficial and effective programs have been those in which we develop working partnerships—with our peer institutions, with community agencies, with schools, and with other institutions and organizations.

The Shriver Center

The purpose of the Shriver Center Higher Education Consortium is to link ten colleges and universities in the Baltimore area in order to engage our students in academically based community service work in four key issue areas: human needs, education, environment, and public safety. The consortium approach allows a small liberal arts college like Goucher to join forces with other institutions as diverse as the University of Maryland at Baltimore County, Loyola College, Towson University, the College of Notre Dame, Morgan State University, Johns Hopkins University, the University of Baltimore, Villa Julie College, and Coppin State University. We can share information about service sites, training and placement processes, and program development on all of our campuses. Representatives from two community agencies (Parents Anonymous and the United Way) and several of the service organizations in Maryland (the Governor's Commission on Service, the Maryland Student Service Alliance) also sit on the Consortium. The Shriver Center has provided summer planning grants to encourage faculty at each institution to develop new courses that incorporate service-learning approaches, and runs several training workshops for faculty members.

Each year, with the help of our students, we also plan an annual "superconference," which brings together students from all ten institutions, representatives of various service agencies, and staff and some faculty from consortium member institutions. Our first superconference was held at Goucher in 1995 with Kathleen Kennedy Townsend, Maryland's lieutenant governor, as keynote speaker.

Our partnership within the Shriver Center Consortium allows Goucher to provide far more for its students than we could if we worked solely on our own. While a few institutions in the consortium have community-service offices with several staff members, most of us function with a single person in charge of the service program. The opportunity to know colleagues at the other schools and meet with one another monthly allows us to feel less isolated in our work and encourages us to feel like part of a larger team effort. The Shriver Center Higher Education Consortium has, during its first two years, been partially funded through a Learn and Serve

America Higher Education grant from the Corporation for National and Community Serve.

The Choice Middle Schools Program

In the spring of 1994 Goucher tried to implement a big-brother/big-sister type of program, on our own, with a grassroots community group in Baltimore City. It was not as successful as we had hoped. As we evaluated the reasons why we fell short of our goals, the Goucher volunteers all suggested that perhaps we could do better by working within a more comprehensive structure, such as a school. This made sense, as we had very limited staff at our end to plan and oversee a structured program, and the grassroots organization we had worked with was likewise stretched too thin to provide the needed supervision and structure.

During our first conversation with the Shriver Center, in the summer of 1994, we discovered that while we were looking for a structure to be a part of, they were seeking additional college tutoring centers for a program already in place—the Choice Middle Schools Program. One of the program's satellites was located in a low-income area of Baltimore County about a half hour from Goucher. We made plans to set up a one-on-one tutoring component within their ongoing program, and began this collaboration fall semester, 1994. The program has evolved each subsequent semester based on regular feedback from the Choice staff, the Choice students, the Goucher volunteers, and the coordinator of community service at Goucher.

The success of this partnership is a result of a mutual commitment and complementary skills and strengths. Goucher's coordinator of community service oversees all the logistics and arrangements on campus. She also attends most of the tutoring/activity sessions. The Choice Middle Schools Program staff transports between twenty and thirty middle-school students to Goucher each week (half come every Monday and half every Wednesday) for tutoring and activities. The Choice educational coordinators and caseworkers communicate regularly with parents and teachers at the students' schools. They bring with them material that can help in the tutoring sessions as students work on homework assignments for their classes. They also monitor student school attendance and grades.

Tutor training is a shared responsibility between the Choice staff and the coordinator of community service at Goucher. In addition, the chair of Goucher's education department has conducted sessions on tutoring both reading and math. Her contribution has been invaluable. Goucher team leaders recruit tutors from the student population and tutors commit to come once a week for a full semester. Each Goucher tutor works with one Choice student for eight weeks. Tutor/student pairs can go over to the library or the computer center with a Choice staff member, in order to use the resources there to work on a project or assignment. It is hoped that the experience of getting to know a college campus will enable these middle-schoolers to consider additional alternatives for their lives after high school.

This program has proven highly successful for all involved. Statistics gathered during the first full year of the program show an average grade point average increase of 25% for those who attended one semester of tutoring at Goucher and an increase of 31% for those who attended both semesters. Improvement was more marked among seventh and eighth graders than for the sixth graders who participated. Goucher tutors enjoyed their experiences and approximately one-third of the tutors each semester were people who had tutored in the program before.

The Middle River Mentorship Program

This partnership involves the community service office, the education department at Goucher, the Baltimore County Public Schools' central office, and two elementary schools in a low-income area of the county. The idea began with the director of elementary schools in the northeast area of Baltimore County and the specialist in the county's gifted and talented office (who happened to be an alumna of Goucher). They contacted us about the possibility of beginning a mentorship program that would pair Goucher students with fifth graders who had been identified as having potential but not performing up to that potential in class. Teachers and guidance counselors believed that these students could benefit from some additional support and attention—the kind of support and attention a one-on-one relationship with a college-student mentor could provide. This eight-week program pairs Goucher students with fifth graders. The fifth graders decide on topics they want to explore and do a project about one they select. The Goucher students help them develop their topic, narrow their focus, plan their research, and use the library resources at both their own school and on the Goucher campus to accomplish their goals. The end result is a project that gets presented back at their home school, often to the rest of their class. Half of the sessions are scheduled at the elementary schools with the Goucher students traveling there, and the other half are held on Goucher's campus, with the elementary school's assistant principal or guidance counselor transporting the students to Goucher. One definite by-product of this dual-site approach is the opportunity for these fifth graders to see more of a college campus and perhaps begin to seriously think about college as a possibility in their own futures.

The execution of this program is also a highly collaborative effort. Goucher's coordinator of community service and the chair of the education department handle the planning and supervision of the program from the college end. The two central office administrators from Baltimore County Public Schools work with the two elementary schools involved. All four, plus the principals, guidance counselors, and fifth-grade teachers from the schools meet at the end of each semester to review feedback from all involved and incorporate any changes that could improve the program the next semester. The gifted and talented specialist runs the training session for the Goucher mentors, focusing on creative problem-solving approaches that mentors can use with the students.

This program has been a great success. Feedback from the fifth graders, their teachers, their parents, and the Goucher mentors has all been excellent. Teachers report seeing positive changes in these students' participation in class and approach to their schoolwork. Counselors have heard students in the program begin to talk about college as a future goal.

ACTS

The Active Coalition for Transitional Services, Inc. (ACTS), is a Baltimore County agency that provides transitional housing, case management, and other support services to women with young children who are all homeless as a result of domestic violence. The partnership with ACTS has been an exciting one for Goucher at many levels. First, our student community service organization, CAUSE (Community Auxiliary for Service) has, for the past year, sent a team of students to ACTS one night a week to do activities with the children while their mothers are attending different types of meetings. In addition, ACTS has been a very successful placement for students in several courses offering the service credit option, particularly one sociology seminar on domestic violence.

Our first experience placing students from that seminar at ACTS in the fall of 1994 was extraordinarily successful from both sides. The students seeking placements were seniors who had already experienced three years of a rigorous Goucher education. ACTS' approach to working with volunteers is to interview them and discover what their interests, skills, and experience are and then to develop a service experience for them that uses their talents to meet a real need at ACTS. When ACTS learned that several students had taken a research methods course, they made use of this skill. Two of the Goucher volunteers spent time with a number of the women living in ACTS transitional housing and developed two instruments—a psychosocial history tool and a program evaluation survey—to help ACTS assess the impact of their services and programs. These tools have since become an integral part of the work of the agency. When asked how these would have been developed otherwise, the executive director said simply, "They wouldn't have. That's why we love having Goucher volunteers."

One of these volunteers was so thrilled with her experience at ACTS (and they were so thrilled with what she brought to their agency), that her service-credit option experience served as a steppingstone to a three-credit internship there during spring semester, 1995. This in turn was so successful that ACTS offered her a full-time job when she graduated. Although she wound up taking a graduate school fellowship instead, she referred a friend to ACTS for a summer internship and that also worked out well.

In fall 1995, four students taking the domestic violence seminar did their placements at ACTS. At Goucher, one student had been responsible for starting a publication called *Hear My Voice*, an outlet for Goucher students to speak out about sexual assault, battering, incest, and abuse. The student brought the publication's faculty advisor to ACTS to run some poetry-writing workshops with the residents. The result of this will likely be a similar publication to be shared within the ACTS program. Two other students researched programs for children coming from violent homes, and one of those students will continue on in a full internship at ACTS to implement the program they developed through their service-credit option work.

The coordinator of community service meets several times a semester with the executive and associate directors at ACTS in order to assess how things are going and also to consider future possibilities. Much of the success of this partnership is due to the willingness of both sides to work together, explore new possibilities, and deal with any obstacles that arise. This exploration of possibilities also includes faculty resources. Dr. Janet Shope, a sociology professor who teaches the domestic violence seminar, has a strong research interest in domestic violence. She also participated in the Shriver Center workshops for faculty and was very open to the idea of becoming involved with the service site.

In the summer of 1995, Dr. Shope and the coordinator of community service sat down with the executive and associate directors of ACTS to brainstorm ideas for how they all might connect with one another. Some exciting possibilities came out of this process. The professor extended an invitation to have some of the ACTS staff and residents come to sessions of her seminar that fall. The ACTS staff talked about how they really wished they had someone who knew research who could help them create and use a database of the information they were gathering (using the psychosocial history tool developed by last year's Goucher volunteers!) to better understand their population and evaluate their services. Dr. Shope had done similar work for a shelter in New York and she offered to help ACTS with their database. Since that meeting at ACTS, she has been working with them on this project. While she is helping them, she also credits the experience with opening her own eyes still further to the issues facing those who work directly, on a day-to-day basis, with the survivors of domestic violence. This type of mutual give and take and the creativity of the group process is the kind of problem solving approach that far surpasses what one institution or agency can accomplish on its own.

What We Have Learned from Our Experiences

We have discovered that it is more effective to cultivate ongoing relationships with a limited number of organizations and to place some students at these same sites every semester rather than spread out our students at many different sites. Good service-learning partnerships are like good marriages. There needs to be a mutual attraction and an equality of effort to make it work. We have learned to concentrate on those partnerships that feel two-sided, where both parties give and gain, where both parties want to be involved with one another, where both are willing to work at it being successful.

It is also important to be responsive to student interests. Unless an issue draws students in, it can become hard to recruit volunteers. Those service sites that relate to courses that offer service credit options, and those that respond to continuing student interests tend to succeed. Goucher College has a long and proud history as a former women's college, and domestic violence is an issue that engages the hearts and minds of Goucher women. Working with children to excite them about their educational possibilities is another arena that has consistently drawn Goucher volunteers. These are the kinds of partnerships we can safely make commitments to because we can be sure of getting student volunteers from semester to semester. Sites benefit most from an ongoing commitment and we need to provide that to them.

We have also learned to look for partnerships with places that are willing to share the responsibility for making the experience work and for developing the necessary training and ongoing support. Open communication has been important, and so is the willingness to provide students with service experiences that challenge them and use the skills and experiences they bring with them. The most exciting and productive partnerships are those that always feel "in process"—where we are both constantly thinking about what we can do better, what we can do differently, and how we can do that together.

What Is Essential to Make Service-Learning Collaborations Work

Certainly the interest and energy of student volunteers is important to make any community service program work. A truly comprehensive service-learning program that engages the entire campus community, however, requires a lot more. Faculty must be receptive to the idea and willing to put creative energy into rethinking appropriate courses. They must accept that integrative service does have a place in the academic structure of the liberal arts. This is not always easy to achieve, and the support of allies among the faculty who can help articulate the argument is crucial.

It is also essential that there be a community service coordinator to serve as an advocate for the infusion of service into the bloodstream of the institution, to create new initiatives, to develop and nurture collaborative relationships with community agencies, and to manage the logistics of the efforts. This way students can concentrate on doing the service and reflecting on it, faculty can concentrate on integrating the service into their courses, and service sites can concentrate on providing service. What we initially saw at Goucher was much interest in service learning, but a hesitancy on the part of faculty to undertake the time-consuming "legwork" necessary to arrange potential sites and verify that the necessary number of hours of service are performed. Once the community service office was created, it undertook that aspect of the program and proposed a coherent plan for implementing the service credit option. Approval and implementation followed quickly.

First and foremost, it is necessary that the institution recognize and support service as a core value of the institution. This means funding a community service office and seeking to make it a part of ongoing programs and the day-to-day life of the college. Community service could also be considered in the reward structure that determines merit salary increases and other forms of recognition. This would be a major change for most institutions and would likely require widespread discussion and debate.

Next Steps for Goucher

Campus/community collaborations are always growing and changing. We need to evaluate each semester's service credit option offerings and our success in integrating these experiences into various courses. We also plan to expand the scope of courses offering service credit options, and particularly hope to make progress in the arts and natural sciences as well as in the social sciences.

Faculty-service site connections, such as the one developing between Goucher's sociology professor and ACTS, will be explored in hopes of identifying additional collaborations that can be mutually beneficial. We will also seek to expand the ways we weave the service experience into a longitudinal path that includes future internships, career possibilities, and the development of a service ethic that already extends well into our students' lives after they leave Goucher.

We should also look at additional ways the college and our community partners can educate one another. Perhaps the college could offer the opportunity for staff and/or participants at our partner agencies to take some classes here. Perhaps agency staff and/or the populations they serve would be valuable resources for assisting in the instruction of some courses.

We would also like to use the service context to increase cooperative efforts among various constituencies on our campus who may not have a lot of contact with one another at present. For example, students in our post-baccalaureate premedical program have limited, if any, interaction with traditional-age undergraduates and faculty and staff outside their field. Projects that involve mixed groups could be instrumental in helping to break down some of the barriers that exist. In addition, our being able to refer these graduates, many of whom have extensive experience and interests, to service sites could provide the sites with volunteers having a wider range of skills, experience, and knowledge than much of the traditional undergraduate population.

Finally, an exciting possibility emerged when we had representatives from five service sites come together to speak about what their agency does and what they would like volunteers to do. Site representatives were fascinated to hear what others were doing, and found many common links among their services. Moveable Feast, which prepares and delivers meals to those who are homebound with AIDS, for example, realized that they receive some of the organic fruits and vegetables grown at Garden Harvest. When Heart's Place Shelter described their need for a clothing drive, Moveable Feast readily offered to send over to them the clothing they had received but could not use. ACTS, whose clients are chiefly women and children, offered to send donated men's clothing to Heart's Place. As this process unfolded, the potential for the college to play some future role in bringing together several agencies in a new type of partnership began to take shape. This is a direction we wish to pursue.

For our program to continue to work, grow, and be beneficial to both the college and the community agencies, we need to do several things. First and foremost we must maintain and nurture the connections that should always be our focus—the needs of the community and the interests of students, faculty, and staff. All have to be considered. The service partnerships developed must meet the needs of the service sites in order to make collaborative effort worthwhile for them. The sites we form partnerships with should be able to provide sufficient training and support for our volunteers to perform up to the standards necessary.

These partnerships must also make a difference to Goucher and be consistent with our academic mission and priorities. If they do not, it will be difficult to maintain institutional interest and commitment. When integrating service with the curriculum, we have to maintain a healthy balance between the academic context and theory and the practical service experience. Faculty members need to be able to meaningfully integrate the experiences into their academic courses and research agenda, and there should be time for reflection and to help students put their service experiences into perspective, both academically and personally.

We have to recognize our limits, especially during these times when federal funding and support for many social services is in jeopardy. We cannot spread ourselves too thin among too many partnerships, but we also need to not become so focused that we fail to recognize changing times, needs, and interests, or the emergence of potential new partnerships.

Conclusion

We are striving to solidify community service as a valued and integral part of the Goucher experience for students, staff, faculty, and alumni. We are seeking to create community partnerships that will add rigorous practical experience to complement the rigorous academic program. With true collaborative efforts, the potential for unique educational experiences for our students and significant service for the community is vast. The expertise of our faculty and staff can both contribute to the needs of the community and also be enlightened and broadened by working with it. It is our hope that members of the Goucher community will recognize why service to the surrounding community is important; will experience the benefits for themselves and others; will carve out for themselves an education that transcends the front gates of the college campus; and will choose to commit themselves, as many of our graduates have already done, to service throughout their lives. This goal of sustained civic engagement for our graduates is, we believe, nothing short of an essential facet of the mission of a liberal-arts institution.

References

Abelson, J. (1984). The first hundred years. *Goucher Quarterly*, LXII, 40.

Knipp, A. & Thomas, T. (1938). *The History of Goucher College*. Baltimore: Goucher College.

Chapter 6
Outreach for the Twenty-First Century
The Virginia Tech Approach

Peggy S. Meszaros

Virginia Polytechnic Institute and State University

> *The difficulty lies not in new ideas, but in escaping from old ones.*
> —*J.M. Keynes*

A new era for American universities is emerging as we end one century and begin another. Major indicators for this new era in higher education include increased public scrutiny and accountability for both human and financial resources. This in turn, has resulted in restructuring and refocusing the services of higher education generally, and at Virginia Tech specifically, to better meet the needs of the public. Societal demand to reshape the academy to better meet the needs of citizens is being felt in every state, through legislative actions and policy initiatives from state higher-education coordinating bodies. The state of Virginia, responding in the early 1990s to severe reductions in support to higher education, led the way in mandating restructuring efforts.

Long before the mandate to restructure, Virginia Tech launched its own plan to restructure itself in internal initiatives known as Phase I and Phase II. These early efforts to reflect decreased state revenues and increased pressures to refocus the university culminated in an intense study by all units on the campus, and a report, *Restructuring Virginia Tech* (Virginia Polytechnic Institute and State University, 1994), which was submitted to the Secretary of Education in August 1994. The report concludes with a considerable challenge in the section "Our Vision for the Future: The Model Land-Grant University for the 21st Century." The report emphasizes that "we can only become the model land-grant university for the future if we fulfill our mission of *service* to the Commonwealth and the nation." Thus, the challenge to more fully develop our service dimension was launched.

Need and Issues Nationally and in Virginia

The challenge to restructure the service or outreach mission to better meet the needs of citizens is not unique to Virginia Tech. For example, since 1990, Michigan State University, the University of Minnesota, Oregon State University, Colorado State University, the University of Georgia, and others have engaged in major study and revival of their outreach missions. Albert C. Yates, president of Colorado State University, characterized this national "renaissance of outreach in the land-grant tradition" in his 1994 Seaman A. Knapp Memorial Lecture by stating that, "Conceived as a practical and political construct, the uniqueness of the land-grant university is derived from the special interplay of teaching, research and public service in extending knowledge to a broad public constituency." He further stated that, "Perhaps our greatest opportunities to enhance our importance and regain the public trust rest in the pursuit of our outreach agenda—that is, how we extend ourselves beyond the campus and service to our many external clientele. Real success, however, in this defining piece of the land-grant mission requires that we raise the level of importance of outreach as a university function—embracing it as a scholarly activity equivalent in status and distinction to teaching and research and cutting across all areas of knowledge." He continued, "Every faculty member should be regarded as a specialist whose skills may be brought to bear in developing and delivering programs." (Yates, 1994)

Ernest L. Boyer, former president of the Carnegie Foundation for the Advancement of Teaching, also articulated the importance of outreach scholarship in his book, *Scholarship Reconsidered: Priorities of the Professoriate*. He stated that knowledge is acquired through research, through synthesis, through practice, and through teaching. Boyer saw the work of the university, of the professorate, as having four separate yet overlapping functions: the scholarship of discovery (basic disciplinary research), the scholarship of integration (applied interdisciplinary research), the scholarship of application (outreach and practice), and the scholarship of teaching (education and instruction). Boyer further believes that the scholarship of application, which includes outreach and practice, stands equal in importance to the traditional missions of teaching and research. (Boyer, 1990)

Given that respected academicians such as Yates and Boyer have called nationally for recognition and expansion of the outreach mission, we might question why we are just now hearing these voices? Perhaps the answer lies in both understanding the origins of public-service and current pressures on universities from external constituents. Steven Schomberg and James

Farmer (1994) describe the evolving concept of public-service outreach in land-grant and state universities as encompassing a variety of faculty activities and different views of service and its reward structure for faculty. Historically, one question has dominated the debate over what constitutes public service: Is public service a separate function of the university or a special case of teaching and research? The prevailing view on a growing number of campuses is the separate function/mission view. It is a popularly accepted belief that the idea of public service originated with the Morrill Act of 1862. However, Elden L. Johnson describes how the realization of the idea of outreach came later, and was dependent both on "the generation of knowledge to apply (to problems) and the development of staff to share (the knowledge)" (Johnson, 1989, p. 217). Therefore, public service, or outreach, was the last of the three major functions of the land-grant universities to evolve. In many universities, including Virginia Tech, it continues to be fraught with definitional problems, lack of proper recognition within the academy, and lack of a clearly articulated tie to faculty rewards such as promotion and tenure. However, resolving these problems and more clearly defining the outreach mission is where we find ourselves today.

What are the external pressures driving our elevation of concerns with outreach? Two recent studies, one national, *What the Public Wants from Higher Education: Workforce Implications from a 1995 National Survey* (Dillman, Christenson, Salant and Warner, 1995) and a Virginia study, *Public Opinion Regarding Higher Education in Virginia* (Virginia Commonwealth University Survey Research Lab, 1995), provide evidence of growing public concern for outreach. The national survey found strong public support for universities, and land-grants in particular, to do more than educate 18–22-year-old undergraduates. Asked how they would distribute $100 of taxpayer money among the priorities of teaching students on-campus, off-campus education and technical help, and doing research, respondents said they would spend the most for teaching students on-campus ($45), followed by off-campus education and technical help ($30), and doing research ($25). Taxpayers in this national study expressed their support for lifelong learning in both formal and nonformal formats. Further, they wanted education brought to them rather than always traveling to a college campus. Distance-education strategies were favored as well as tailored educational services to truly meet the pressures of working in a knowledge-based economy. Finally, respondents wanted to be partners with universities in planning services they need. New policy measures such as training vouchers allowing flexibility to individual learners in choice of lifelong learning options were suggested by the respondents and would release one of the barriers to learning for people with lower incomes. They would also give lifelong learners a stronger voice as courses and services are planned. Voice and access are priorities for our public and potential partners as we develop lifelong educational services.

The Public Opinion Regarding Higher Education in Virginia Survey (1995) found Virginians generally supportive of several activities of public higher education beyond its traditional mission of teaching. Seventy-two percent of those interviewed said that working with primary and secondary schools to improve K–12 education was a very important activity. Over half (58%) of the respondents felt that generating new knowledge by conducting research was very important. Helping with economic development by providing support to local government and business was very important to 45% of the public surveyed. Providing cultural and intellectual events for the public was seen as a very important activity by 34%. Thus, Virginia respondents recognized and supported dimensions of outreach, particularly work to improve K–12 schools, economic development, and cultural and intellectual events.

In summary, the recent interest in outreach activities and services in Virginia grows out of the pressing need Virginians feel to continue to learn, to be lifelong learners in a society increasingly knowledge dependent. Interest also grows out of the need for universities to be increasingly accountable for outcomes the public seeks. Extending the services of the university through a new focus on the outreach mission is clearly where we stand at Virginia Tech. This new definition and implementation of outreach must be comprehensive, focused on meeting the needs of the public, accountable for measurable outcomes and a partnership venture with citizens in their communities statewide. As we work to refocus outreach on our campus, we must reconnect with our communities and their needs. Becoming the "new American college" or the "model land-grant of the twenty-first century" demands that we recognize the needs and issues pertinent to the creation of community-collaborative universities and that we promote large-scale systems change to bring about this new model university.

The Virginia Tech Vision

At Virginia Tech, systems change began in August 1994 as the senior vice president and provost appointed a task force of fifteen faculty, representing all facets of the university, to review the current outreach mission and offer recommendations for the future.

Specifically their charge was:

- to define, characterize, and describe outreach at Virginia Tech;
- to articulate a future vision and mission statement for outreach to be considered by the president and the provost;
- to suggest options by which that vision can be realized, including organizational structure, program emphasis, resource generation and allocation, integration with academic units, and faculty rewards.

The task force held eighteen meetings from September through April, which focused on both internal assessment and external scanning, with a final report completed in July 1995. Concurrently, the New Century Council, a citizen-led group of 1,100 individuals from the region including many university faculty and staff, were also engaged in a broad and intensive study focused on revitalization of the region. Fifty nine of the one-hundred-fifty recommendations directly involved collaborations with the university. The top five priorities from this list have now been identified and considered for implementation along with the fourteen recommendations from the on-campus task force. This process of intensive internal study of outreach combined with the community-collaborative New Century Council study provided the first step in assuring that community problems of employment and economic development, health and health services, environmental quality, crime, poverty, access to education and, ultimately, the quality of life of individuals, families, and communities, will be addressed. The next steps to be taken by the university as we reconceptualize outreach for the twenty-first century require a long-term strategy for response and action across the entire fabric of the university. The appointment of an Outreach Implementation Task Force in 1995, and work to formulate a new mission statement for outreach which clearly speaks to partnerships with and empowerment of communities were our next steps. The new mission statement now reads:

The faculty and staff at Virginia Tech enrich the lives of the citizens of the Commonwealth of Virginia through activities which:

- *generate and transfer new knowledge between the institution and society;*

- *assist and create mutually beneficial relationships with individuals, families, communities, agencies, and businesses;*
- *identify and meet needs important to the economic and social vitality of the Commonwealth;*
- *extend the University's resources throughout the Commonwealth and beyond.*

The vision statement for outreach provides further evidence of the commitment to serve communities directly:

To achieve its outreach mission, Virginia Tech will become fully integrated throughout the Commonwealth via its graduate and continuing education centers and extension offices to provide points of local access to the resources of the institution, thereby establishing Virginia Tech as the outreach university in Virginia.

The importance of outreach as a university priority in the coming century is also highlighted in the University Plan Update for 1996–2001. One of the six strategic directions reads:

We will position the university as the leading provider of outreach services in the Commonwealth by reconceptualizing and restructuring the service component of our land-grant mission.

Promoting systems change at Virginia Tech has been broadly approached with two task forces, wide university participation, discussion and initial "buy-in" from key faculty and staff. The 1996 report of the implementation group has been organized in a matrix format showing the original recommendations, implementation strategies, responsible parties, timetable, and costs/funding sources. Decisions have been reached on each recommendation and implementation action by the president, provost, and executive vice president. Initial meetings have been held with each responsible party to begin work on the strategies agreed upon and monthly progress checks have been instituted. A complete review of accomplishments were held in June 1997.

Changing the culture systematically involves five broad categories of change: leadership, organization structure, resources and faculty involvement, academic integration and access. Our agenda for implementation action is an aggressive one:

1. Leadership

Recommendations in this section focus on issues of leadership, direction, and focus for outreach activities in university.

1A. Develop strategies to more fully operationalize the outreach mission at Virginia Tech, starting with the new University Plan.

1B. Develop and promote a more holistic description of the benefits achieved from outreach activities to all constituencies and member of the University community.

1C. Develop a taxonomy of outreach-related terms and integrate their daily use into major university communications channels, including speeches by senior administrators, *Spectrum*, advertising, alumni publications, university style manual, and other communications tools.

1D. Enhance outreach visibility by instructing the deans and Director of University Relations to give comparable attention to outreach as with instruction and research in all university publications and communication tools.

2. Organizational Structure

Recommendations in this section focus on organizational structure, positions, and reporting relationships for outreach activities in the university.

2A. Establish the position of Vice Provost for Outreach and Extension as recommended in the original Outreach Task Force Report and implement an organizational structure as proposed in the attached organizational chart.

2B. Create the position of Director of Distance Learning, reporting to the Vice Provost for Outreach (and Extension), to support and coordinate the University's alternative delivery systems.

2C. Petition the Commission on Public Service and Extension to change its name to the Commission on Outreach and Extension.

2D. Install the Provost, until the VPOE is appointed, as the chair of the 229 Division Council. Membership will include the deans of Forestry and Wildlife Resources, Human Resources and Education, Agriculture and Life Sciences and Veterinary Medicine.

2E. Establish an Outreach Administrative Council, including directors of the Virginia Cooperative Extension Service, Continuing Education, Public Service, Distance Learning, Associate Deans for Outreach from the colleges, and representatives from the Library, Information Systems, and Research and Graduate Studies (VPOE as chair).

2F. & 2G. Change the reporting structure of the Director of Cooperative
Extension from the Dean of the College of Agriculture and Life Sciences to the Vice Provost for Outreach (and Extension). If this recommendation is not accepted for prompt implementation, make
this change in the reporting relationship as soon as is feasible, but not
later than July 1, 1999.

3. Resources and Faculty Involvement

Recommendations in this section focus on strategies for enhancing faculty
involvement in outreach activities and in establishing levels of resources
and rewards sufficient to "balance" efforts among the three missions of the
University.

3A. Establish evaluation standards of quality and productivity for outreach, including off-campus research negotiated among department,
colleges, and the provost's office that would be used as a basis for
rewards (merit increases; promotion and tenure).

3B. Establish agreements between the provost and deans on the respective
college contributions to each area of the triple mission, including outreach, and link resource-allocation (e.g. faculty positions, merit increases, graduate assistantships) to productivity in each area.

3C. Negotiate agreements between deans and department heads that define expectations in each area of the triple mission and include the
allocation of resources and measurable outcomes.

3D. Negotiate an annual activity plan between department heads and individual faculty members that includes outreach activities, and use it
as a basis for annual evaluation and rewards (merit increases; promotion and tenure.)

3E. Establish a fund, by directing 15% of profits from noncredit continuing-
education events and business seminars, to provide "seed" moneys for
grants to develop targeted marketing materials and for subsidizing
appropriate programs; a working model of this approach is the Capital Appropriations Account in the Research Division funded by a 13%
allocation from research overhead funds.

4. Academic Integration

Recommendations in this section focus on the integration of learning
processes and services to ensure that the University will be able to re-

spond appropriately to the needs of a variety of customers in the years ahead.

4A. Create a Learning Transformation Center to complement information systems and the Center for Excellence in Undergraduate Teaching activities.

4B. Develop a proposal to create a lifelong learning compact with VT students to provide for learning experiences that meets their needs for up-to-date professional and personal information. In accordance with item C, this commitment should include updated "learning packages" to meet a variety of needs in a number of alternative delivery formats.

4C. Conduct a statewide marketing assessment of programming needs (both credit and noncredit) identifying potential markets, developing marketing strategies and implementation plans that build on traditional on- and off-campus delivery systems as well as new initiatives such as asynchronous learning, ATM network-based course, satellite and compressed video, etc.

4D. Develop a plan to exploit collaboration with other universities, to establish partnerships with the private sector and governmental agencies (e.g., by participating in the National Learning Infrastructure Initiative) and to explore the creation of and participation in global networks of universities through extended-learning capabilities.

4E. Establish a Credit and Curriculum Options Task Force.

4F. Initiate a systematic review of all University policy leading to revisions in academic policy statements that will accommodate a variety of emerging issues including but not limited to transfer-credit policies, credit banking, time-to-degree, residency, credit and noncredit students simultaneously enrolled in a course, and other nontraditional student issues.

4G. Develop a cohesive, comprehensive outreach plan in each college that describes the college's focus and specific actions. Deans will review progress in quarterly face-to-face meetings with the provost. To facilitate the development of these plans, the provost should convene a seminar with college deans, the provost's staff, and other appropriate unit leaders to define format and content expectations of college outreach reports.

4H. Assign an individual in each college with administrative responsibility for outreach at the associate/assistant dean or director level.

4I. Create incentive structures and find ways to build bridges to further integrate outreach and extension activities by VCE and non-VCE faculty (e.g. through the development of a Memorandum of Understanding) that can help to ensure appropriate recognition of all efforts and sharing of revenues.

4J. Develop and implement partnership agreements between VCE and CE to provide educational services for industry and community support in addition to agricultural support.

5. Access

Recommendations in this section focus on strategies for enhancing and ensuring access to the University's outreach programs and service in the Commonwealth and beyond.

5A. Establish a network of distance-learning centers throughout the state using modern technology.

5B. Examine current access difficulties and develop strategies, in collaboration with BEV, for ensuring greater access to networked University information and services.

5C. Expand the role and scope of Electronic Villages consulting services.

5D. Develop strategies for taking greater advantage of existing University facilities around the state as a point of information and reference to Virginia Tech. Such strategies might include access to programs, courses, admission, registration, and related functions for credit, noncredit, extension, public service, and other university-sponsored activities.

Implementing the Vision

The task ahead for Virginia Tech is a massive one but one essential to us if we intend to become the model land-grant of the twenty-first century. The implementation strategies will create a culture emphasizing community-collaborative learning and integration of knowledge. We will be teaching undergraduate and graduate students differently as they participate in service-learning projects that place them squarely in communities and make them keenly aware of knowledge integration to solve the problems of real people. Further, we will have changed the reward system for faculty with a more explicit understanding of the expectations of outreach scholarship and greater value thus placed on its reward.

The ultimate success of this major restructuring of outreach at Virginia Tech will be the improvement of the quality of life of the youth, families, and communities served by the university. The indicators of success will be defined and redefined collaboratively with citizens over the coming years. The University's motto, "Ut Prosim", (to serve), will take on even greater meaning as faculty, staff, and students live out their service to one another and the broader community.

References

Boyer, E. L. (1990). *Scholarship reconsidered: Priorities of the professorate.* Princeton, NJ: The Carnegie Foundation for the Advancement of Teaching.

———. (1994). Creating the new American college. [Point of View column]. *The Chronical of Higher Education,* A48.

Dillman, D., Christenson, J., Salant, P., and Warner, P. (1995). *What the public wants from higher education: Work force implications from a 1995 national survey.* Available from the Social and Economic Sciences Research Center, Washington State University, Pullman, WA 99164–4014.

Implementation Task Force on University Outreach (1996). *Outreach at Virginia Tech: Toward the model land-grant university of the 21st century.* Available from the Provost's Office, 210 Burruss Hall, Blacksburg, VA 24061–0132.

Johnson, E. L. (1989). *Misconceptions about the early land-grant colleges.* In L. F. Goodchild and H. S. Mechsler (Eds.), *ASHE Reader on the History of Higher Education* (pp 211–225). Medham Heights, MA: Ginn Press. (Original article published in *Journal of Higher Education,* 52 (4), 1981).

Schomberg, S., and Farmer, J. (1994). The evolving concept of public service implications for rewarding faculty. *The Journal of the National University Continuing Education Association,* 58 (3), 122–140.

Virginia Commonwealth University Survey Research Laboratory. (1995). *Public Opinion Regarding Higher Education in Virginia.* October 1995 Commonwealth Poll.

Virginia Polytechnic Institute and State University. (1994). *Restructuring Virginia Tech.* Report submitted to the Secretary of Education, Richmond, VA.

Yates, Albert C. (1994). *1994 Seaman A. Knapp Memorial Lecture: The renaissance of outreach in the land-grant tradition.* USDA: Cooperative Extension System.

Chapter 7
Building University System Collaboration
The Florida Inter-University Center
for Child, Family and Community Studies

Lionel J. Beaulieu   *Ann K. Mullis and Ronald L. Mullis*
Southern Rural Development Center   *Florida State University*

Introduction

Florida is currently the fourth-most populous state in the nation, with nearly 14 million residents. More than one in five Floridians (21%) are children under the age of eighteen years old. Recent predictions are that Florida's population will increase by a total of 2.5 million residents over the course of the current decade (1990–2000), and more than 74% of that growth will be linked to net migration. While Florida's population is predominantly white (84.5%), it is emerging as a highly heterogeneous, culturally diverse state. Over 14% of Florida's population is comprised of African Americans, and approximately 12% are of Hispanic descent. In fact, the state's Hispanic population has increased dramatically, rising by 81% over the past decade (Israel, 1995). This expanding and increasingly diversified population is expected to make significant and ever-increasing demands on the state's human and health service infrastructure. These trends suggest that Florida lawmakers and human service agency representatives are being faced, and will continue to be faced, with arduous (sometimes impossible) decisions about how the finite economic resources of the state are to be allocated to meet the critical needs of its citizens.

Of the three million children currently residing in the state of Florida, many are immersed in at-risk environments as an outgrowth of poverty, abuse, neglect, inadequate health care, or education. In fact, recent data contained in the *Kids Count Data Book* (Annie E. Casey Foundation, 1996) offer a disturbing portrait of Florida's children and families. Based on an assessment of ten benchmark statistics related to child well-being, Florida ranks among the nation's worst states, placing forty-eighth among the country's fifty states. Among the key indicators contributing to this low ranking are the large proportion of births to single teens, high juvenile violent-crime rates, sizable percentages of high-school dropouts, high numbers of children in poverty, and a large proportion of children living in single-parent households.

It is a well-accepted fact that single parenthood often creates severe economic hardships for the family (Bianchi, 1995; U.S. Department of Commerce, 1993b). Approximately 81% of single-parent families with related children under eighteen years old are headed by a female in Florida. Nearly two of every five of these families fall below the poverty line. For African American female-headed households with children under eighteen, the number living in poverty approaches the 54% mark (U.S. Department of Commerce, 1993b). The estimated average cost of raising a child in the urban South from conception to age seventeen in a husband-and-wife family is nearly $91,920 (American Demographics, 1992). With such a high percentage of single parents who are impoverished, single parents—especially single mothers—are at a severe disadvantage in their capacities to meet the economic, psychological, and social needs of their children.

While the needs of many of Florida's children and families remain largely unmet, the reality is that Florida is a rich state, ranking nineteenth in the country on per capita income. But the current political climate is one of fiscal conservatism and, as a result, few substantive investments in children and families are being made. Among the few exceptions are legislative activities that have sought to embrace high-profile solutions. For instance, to combat the increasing crime rate among adolescents and adults in the state, Florida legislators funded "juvenile boot camps" to address the problem of adolescent offenders, and invested sizable amounts of the state's resources to construct more prisons to house the state's burgeoning population of adult offenders. Unfortunately, these strategies have failed to give due consideration to the underlying reasons as to why crime and rates of recidivism continue to spiral upward.

These diverse and very complex issues are reflective of the tough decisions that await the leaders and citizens of Florida, whether they are at the state or local levels. Finding appropriate and viable solutions will require careful, conscious, and deliberate study of the knowledge base. What science tells us about these issues can be of critical importance in helping shape policies and programs that genuinely address the core elements of these concerns.

Without question, the university system constitutes a valuable resource for providing guidance on children and family issues. Contained in the university enterprise is a talented pool of faculty who are actively engaged in knowledge generation and transfer. Ironically, the very individuals who are positioned to provide valuable insight and guidance to the leaders and citizens of the state on children and family concerns are disconnected, more often than not, from these key policy and programmatic activities. Equally disconcerting is the relative scarcity of strong, ongoing working relationships among faculty, with complementary interests and expertise on children and family issues, who are located at different institutions of higher education across a state.

This chapter showcases one of the important initiatives that has been undertaken by the university system in Florida to bring the talents and resources of the faculty to bear on the substantive problems impacting the well-being of children and families in the state. This effort has been designed to demonstrate the commitment of the academic community to work in partnership with state and local leaders, agency representatives, and other interested individuals, to address the real-life concerns that face families and children in the state. Specifically, this chapter offers an overview of the Florida Inter-University Center for Child, Family and Community Studies (IUC), a unique applied social sciences entity recently established within the state's university system. Next, it highlights a subset of recent center activities that are demonstrative of its unique capacity to mobilize the expertise of a multidisciplinary team of faculty from across the state to respond, in an efficient and effective manner, to the call for assistance by state legislative leaders. The final section of the chapter presents what are viewed as the essential building blocks for bringing to fruition an inter-university center within any given state, one that is dedicated to outreach activities on behalf of children and families.

The Birth of the Florida Inter-University Center

The seed for the establishment of an inter-university center, committed to addressing the myriad issues impacting children and families in the state, was planted in the spring of 1993. During a meeting involving a small cadre of faculty and administrators from Florida A & M University, Florida State University, and the University of Florida, the idea of creating a mechanism for facilitating collaborative research and outreach activities was put forth. The University of Florida representative was asked to take a lead role in exploring the feasibility of bringing this idea to fruition. With the assistance of selected faculty from the three institutions, an invitation was extended to faculty from the respective universities to take part in a meeting to more fully explore the proposed collaborative effort. While only a handful of individuals were involved in this initial meeting, the interest of faculty intensified as the idea of an inter-university center began to take shape. Holding several meetings over the period of the next thirty months, the group was successful in producing an important document that not only proposed a name for the center, but also outlined its mission and objectives. This product proved vital in communicating with state agencies, organizations, legislators, and university administrators and faculty about the principal purpose and substantive focus areas of the center. Over this period of time, interest in the center's work slowly spread among other state universities and as a result, two new university partners joined in the center's efforts, the University of South Florida (in early 1995) and the University of Miami (in the spring of 1996). Thus, five of Florida's major universities are now actively engaged in the work of the inter-university center. While the IUC has been in full operation for over a year, its official status as an approved State University System Board of Regents "Center" will commence July 1, 1996.

Statement of Mission and Rationale

The mission of the Florida Inter-University Center for Child, Family and Community Studies is to develop and support family and community effectiveness in meeting the needs of children at all stages of development. The center is a multidisciplinary team of faculty from the five institutions of higher education focusing their energies on research, education, policy, and outreach activities that are designed to improve the well-being of families and children in Florida.

The Inter-University Center for Child, Family and Community Studies is serving as an important conduit for integrating the unique skills and capabilities offered by each of the five universities. For example, Florida A & M University and the University of Florida function as the 1890 and 1862 land-grant institutions of the state, respectively. While both have a strong commitment to meeting the needs of Florida's families and children via their Cooperative Extension Service activities, neither have in place a strong cadre of applied researchers or policy analysts who are actively engaged in the generation of new knowledge regarding families and children. These activities are largely the province of Florida State University, the University of Miami, and the University of South Florida. Thus, the center has strengthened the link between research and outreach.

Furthermore, the host of problems facing children and families are not uniform across the state. For one, research has offered ample proof that issues such as family structure, poverty, juvenile violence, education, child care, and human-service delivery differ across space (Beaulieu and Mulkey, 1995; Flora and Christenson, 1991; Fuguitt, Brown, & Beal, 1989; Garbarino, 1992; Marotz-Baden, Hennon, & Brubaker, 1988; O'Hare, 1988; Wilkinson et al., 1982). It is clear that the problems and capacities of urban Florida communities are not the same as those facing the state's rural localities. The University of Miami and the University of South Florida (located in Tampa) offer an appreciation and understanding of urban issues, while Florida A & M and the University of Florida have a long history of addressing problems in rural Florida. Moreover, as noted earlier, Florida is a culturally diverse state. Florida A & M University's history of excellence in addressing the needs of rural minorities, coupled with the University of Miami's strong focus on the problems of urban minorities, bring to the inter-university center a genuine understanding of the multicultural elements associated with child and family well-being.

The Center's Objectives

The activities of the Florida Inter-University Center for Child, Family and Community Studies are directed at understanding the factors that contribute to positive outcomes for children and families. It does so with full appreciation of the diversity of contexts in which these individuals are embedded. The specific objectives of the center are to:

- Conduct applied research that is designed to advance scientific knowledge of forces influencing the capacity of families and communities to create healthy environments for child and family development;
- Use research-based information to guide and inform state and local policies formulated to impact child and family well-being, and to critically evaluate the outcomes of current and proposed policies on children and families;
- Design and deliver educational programs that empower families and communities to foster the optimal development of children and families.

General Activities of the Center

The activities of the IUC are determined, in part, by the faculty having formal linkage to the center as associates. To date, some thirty-five faculty have become center associates and have offered their expertise in delineating priority child and family issues in the state. Advice and counsel is also secured from key public- and private-sector agencies and organizations having an interest in the work of the center. As a means of facilitating ongoing dialogue with these individuals and groups, a formal Lay Leaders Advisory Board is being established. The hope is that this board will become an active player in helping shape the work of the center and keeping faculty associates attuned to the priority needs of children and families in Florida.

The current and proposed activities of the IUC include the following: (1) identifying, exploring, and applying for extramural grants that relate directly to the expertise of center associates and to the priority children and family issues in the state; (2) keeping state policymakers, agency representatives, educators, and other interested citizens aware of new research and policy strategies on children, youth, families, and communities through newsletters, conferences, and policy briefs; and (3) designing educational curricula to be incorporated in the activities of the formal school system, the Florida Cooperative Extension Service system, and other important delivery outlets in the state.

Administrative and Organizational Structure

Given the inter-university aspect of the center's work, the Florida Inter-University Center for Child, Family and Community Studies has an important presence on all five university campuses. The director of the center is located at the University of Florida, the primary host for the center. In addition, an associate director is housed at each of the remaining four universities—Florida A & M University, Florida State University, University of Miami, and the University of South Florida. The director and the four associate directors provide overall coordination to the center's activities.

The "associates" of the center represent nationally recognized faculty from the five institutions who have indicated a desire to be part of the research and applied activities of the center. These individuals are drawn from a variety of academic units, including departments in the Institute of Food and Agricultural Sciences, College of Medicine, and College of Liberal Arts and Sciences at the University of Florida; Florida A & M University College of Agriculture and College of Education; College of Human Sciences and College of Social Work, Florida State University; Florida Mental Health Institute, College of Education, College of Public Health, and College of Arts and Sciences at the University of South Florida, and the College of Medicine located at the University of Miami (see the organizational chart presented in figure 7.1).

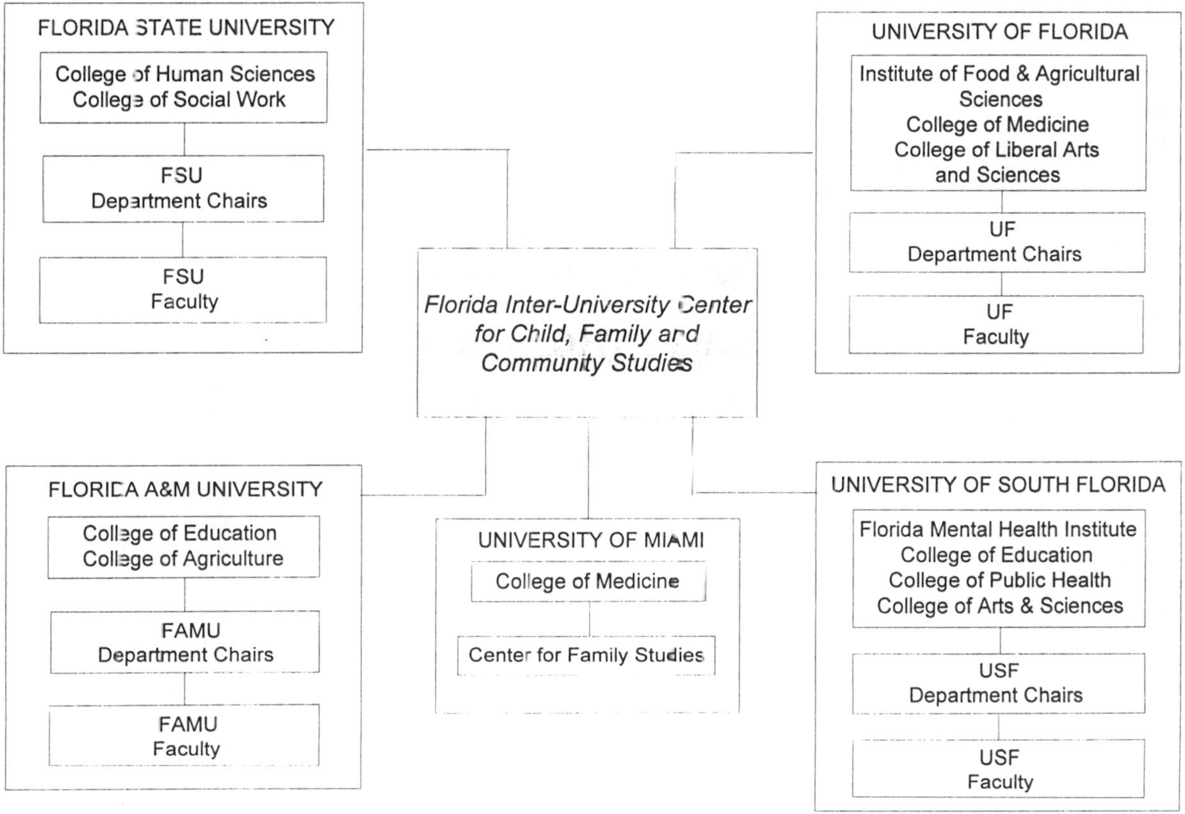

Figure 7.1. Organizational Structure of the Florida Inter-University Center for Child, Family and Community Studies

The Inter-University Center in Action: Case Examples

As noted earlier, the faculty associates of the Florida Inter-University Center for Child, Family and Community Studies represent expertise and experience in diverse disciplines. Furthermore, they share a commitment to interdisciplinary and collaborative work designed to support family and community effectiveness in meeting the needs of children and families at all stages of development. The IUC focuses on several topical areas, including: resiliency in children, families, and communities; early intervention programs with high-risk children and their families; quality child care; lifespan nutrition and health; violence and violence prevention; school preparedness, school-to-work transition issues, and family/community investments in schools.

Although the IUC's subject matter areas are a reflection of the varied interests of faculty associates, they are not the sole determinants of work conducted by the IUC. The benefit of inter-university, multidisciplinary collaboration is the ability to quickly assemble faculty having the capacity to meet stated and emerging needs of constituencies at the state and local levels. This collaboration also provides faculty with ready access to a variety of statewide data resources maintained by various IUC institutions—such as the Kid's Count and state agency data—that can be employed to enlarge the knowledge base from which applied research and outreach programs can be developed.

The director and associate directors of the IUC take an active role in helping organize work groups from the pool of individuals serving as faculty associates. Some work groups evolve from a shared interest in pursuing a particular issue, while others are formed based on the needs or interests of an outside group, such as state legislative committees or foundations. Work group membership is initiated through a review of faculty associate interests and expertise. This core group has at least two initial functions: (1) to clarify and define the issue to be examined; and (2) to collaborate with others in identifying experts from agencies, organizations, and other university units who might participate in the work group.

Developing resources to support the work of IUC working groups and the maintenance of the IUC organization has been a challenge. Upon joining the IUC, each institution provides local faculty associates with seed funds. These funds are to be used in support of IUC activities, but may be accessed only by faculty from that member university. Faculty associates have used funds to travel to IUC meetings, support graduate students working on an IUC project, prepare materials requested by legislative committees, and communicate with faculty associates from other units. Faculty associates have relied on collaborative grant writing to support activities of specific working groups. For example, IUC associates have collaborated on a proposal that resulted in funding the Early Childhood Development Project to improve child-care quality in rural north Florida communities. Similar IUC collaborations have continued to result in grant proposals funded by a variety of state, federal, and private sources, including proposals on family violence, workforce preparation, and human capital resource issues in rural areas. Overhead funds from these grants are used to maintain IUC infrastructure and to facilitate development of new focus areas for pursuit by faculty associates.

Case Study: Legislative Initiative on Family Violence and Child Maltreatment

Although the IUC is a relatively new organization, it has participated in activities designed to bring statewide attention to families and children issues. At Florida State University's Family Institute Conference, "Florida Families in the Twenty-First Century," the 1995 Tyner Eminent Scholar in Human Sciences, Richard M. Lerner, offered participants an important keynote address titled "Contemporary Crises of America's Diverse Youth and Families." This address, coupled with the leadership roles carried out by IUC faculty associates during the conference in articulating the need for consistent and positive family and child policy activities, helped establish the IUC as a source of expertise on child, family, and community issues.

The conference participation and the ongoing involvement of the eminent scholar was instrumental in creating new opportunities for the the IUC organization. Several months following the conference, an important "Connect the Dots" conference was held in Florida's capital city (Tallahassee). The purpose of this meeting was to engage state agency staff and legislative staff in a discussion of overlaps and gaps in services to families, and share information about successful programs for children and families. Of particular interest to legislators was discerning the long-term impact of child abuse and exposure to family violence on outcomes for those children. Richard Lerner, the FSU eminent scholar was in attendance and was able to sensitize participants to the relative dearth of scientific, research-based, longitudinal studies that could document the long-term impacts of domestic violence on children.

This initial comment had immediate impact on the work of the IUC. The co-chairs of the Florida House of Representatives Select Committee on Child Abuse and Neglect, who were actively represented at the "Connect the Dots" conference, called a meeting with representatives of IUC. Included in this group were faculty associates from three of the five IUC participating universities. IUC representatives provided an overview of the current state of knowledge concerning long-term impacts associated with child abuse, as well as a synopsis of the methodological difficulties associated with many of these research studies. As an outgrowth of these presentations, the House Select Committee leadership asked IUC representatives to offer their thoughts about what research design would offer the best hope of enriching the knowledge base regarding the long-term consequences of child abuse on its victims, and what costs might be associated with a project of this magnitude. In the hour-long meeting, a project was outlined, a preliminary budget suggested, and proviso language written. A week later, the Florida House and Senate passed legislation with this amendment incorporated into the budget. In a unique demonstration of collaboration, university lobbyists from four of the participating IUC schools joined together in support of this budget amendment. Two months later, after several related line items were vetoed, the Governor signed the budget with this project in place.

While waiting for the budget to move through its various levels of approval, members of the IUC met for strategic and organizational planning. During these meetings, agreement was reached on an administrative framework and the leadership roles and responsibilities of various working group members. An initial draft of a proposal, including a time line and a more extensive budget, were developed. Internal organization and communication among members of the IUC and working group members continued in a highly collaborative and positive manner.

Despite these initial successes, communication gaps with other partners led to some early problems. For example, funds for this project were channeled through the state social service agency, known as the Florida Department of Health and Rehabilitative Services (HRS), an agency that had suffered severe cuts in the recently approved legislative budget. There were feelings among some HRS administrators and staff that the resources dedicated to the IUC study could be better utilized to support those agency programs that had been subjected to severe reductions as a product of the recent legislative session. However, given that the project appeared in specific proviso language, and the intense interest demonstrated by the House Select Committee in the anticipated product of the IUC study, returning the money was simply not an option.

Also at issue was a sense of uncertainty that agency representatives may have had about the ability of the IUC to carry out the legislatively mandated activities. Of course, with the IUC's entre into five major universities, tapping faculty who have expertise in the areas of domestic violence and child maltreatment was not a very difficult task. But what became quite clear was that more in-depth interactions with agency personnel were required to help build their confidence in the capabilities of the IUC faculty. So, open ongoing communications between key state agency representatives and the IUC became a matter of high priority. These interactions facilitated the delineation of a clearer set of IUC activities, deliverables, and timetables that would effectively respond to the needs of the legislature and the state agency.

The time period from the signing of the state budget to the actual transfer of resources to the IUC to begin project work has been a slow process. It has taken several iterations of the proposal to reach an agreement with the state agency (HRS). Fortunately, these delays did not halt IUC activities completely. Members of the project working group met frequently to outline work that could go on in support of the project. The faculty associates from the University of South Florida completed a review of literature and presented this during one of the IUC's working conferences. The University of South Florida supported two research interns from Florida A & M University to assist faculty associates working in the child abuse and family violence project.

Nearly a year after the initial meeting with the House Select Committee co-chairs was held, agreement between IUC and HRS was finally reached regarding the desired project outcomes. The project went into full gear in summer/fall 1996 and was successfully completed December 1996. One of the concrete products that materialized from this project was a scientifically rigorous research plan for carrying out a longitudinal study of family violence and child maltreatment, including what effects these incidences may have had on young victims over time. The intent is to seek either legislative or foundation financial support to put this comprehensive longitudinal plan into action.

Other Current Inter-University Center Initiatives

Partnering with a state agency and the legislature has proven to be both an opportunity and a challenge. Despite the best intentions of all involved parties, progress has been painfully slow, and thus the potential for community outreach and involvement in a broad sense has been limited. However, it is our belief that the Florida Inter-University Center for Child, Family and Community Studies is gaining increased recognition and credibility in the eyes of state legislative and agency officials. Furthermore, with the increasing interest being shown by state legislators and agencies in the IUC, university administrators are displaying greater interest in the IUC and its capabilities in promoting collaborative efforts in the state.

The following are examples of recent child and family legislative activities that the Florida Inter-University Center also played a leadership or facilitative role in bringing to fruition:

- The House Select Committee on Child Abuse and Neglect, during its 1996 legislative session, asked the IUC to present testimony on noncustodial parental involvement in the lives of children. The concern of the committee was that far too many fathers (since they are most often the noncustodial parent in divorce or separation cases) were not actively engaged in the lives of their children. A team of IUC faculty associates offered expert testimony in three areas: defining the problem in Florida; examining long-term goals for strengthening families; and community programs and resources that work. As an outgrowth of that testimony, the IUC team was asked to assist the Select Committee staff in writing a legislative bill that would call for the creation of a Commission on Responsible Fatherhood. That commission would be charged with the responsibility of: (1) compiling information on the extent and implications of the absence of responsible fathers from families; (2) identifying barriers, in both the public and private sectors, to responsible fatherhood and making recommendations that pursue the elimination of those barriers; (3) delineating successful strategies that encourage responsible fatherhood and recommend and promote those that should be recognized, expanded, and replicated; and (4) identifying how existing state and community resources can be used to encourage responsible fatherhood. The bill was passed by both the Florida House and Senate in May 1996.

- The IUC served as the principal entré for communications by the House Select Committee on Child Abuse and Neglect with the University of Florida's Cooperative Extension Service (CES). The committee was interested in seeing expansion of "supervised visitation centers" in the state. These centers are designed to facilitate contact between a noncustodial parent and one or more children in the presence of a third person responsible for observing and ensuring the safety of those involved. Given the presence of CES offices in every county in the state, the House Select Committee sought to explore the feasibility of locating these centers in a select number of the Extension facilities. IUC members, in concert with UF/CES administrators, assisted the committee staff in writing the proviso language for a legislative bill that would provide support for the creation of a "Florida Family Visitation Network." The bill called for CES to establish, within its resource capabilities, supervised visitation projects in communities in the state. Furthermore, CES would be actively involved in the design and delivery of educational programs that would seek to strengthen parenting and communication skills of those parties taking part in the supervised visitation program. The bill was ratified by the Florida House and Senate during its 1996 legislative session.

Establishing an Inter-University Center: The Essential Building Blocks

The process of creating the Florida Inter-University Center for Child, Family and Community Studies has been a long, arduous process. All along, our challenge has been rooted in the fact that new ground was being broken at every turn. In essence, no "models" for creating an inter-university center, with special focus on children and family well-being, could be found in any university system across the nation. As a result, we were constantly delving into uncharted waters.

The past three years have allowed the IUC team to gain a significant amount of knowledge and experience regarding the process of creating an inter-university entity. This section offers what we believe to be the essential building blocks for creating a viable inter-university center within an academic setting—one dedicated to directing the talents of university system faculty in helping solve problems impacting children and families.

• *A Receptive and Visionary Administrative Leadership:* The creation of an inter-university center is dependent, in no small way, on the presence of an administrative leadership that embraces creative institutional approaches for utilizing the talents of the university system in affecting the lives of children and families in the state. These administrators must, as well, feel comfortable and confident operating in an environment where their administrative responsibilities are carried out in concert with administrative colleagues located at the other participating universities.

- *Desire to Reject Turfism:* In times of tight resources, it is not unusual for universities to seek a competitive edge over other sister institutions of higher education in the funding game. For the IUC to operate effectively, it is essential that "turf wars" be abandoned. Universities must work with one another in a true spirit of collaboration.

- *Faculty Driven:* The IUC's capacity to be responsive to the needs of the families and children at both the state and local levels requires the commitment of a talented pool of faculty with diverse disciplinary perspectives. Faculty bring to the table an understanding of the scientific literature that can prove invaluable when exploring effective strategies for addressing such important needs. These individuals must be given an important voice in helping give shape to part of the substantive activities of the IUC.

- *Active Involvement of Local and State Users:* An important aspect of the IUC mission is to link the resources of universities with the needs of children and families throughout the state. One of the effective means for doing so is by having user groups be full partners in the center as lay advisory committee members. Membership could be drawn from a broad-based group of stakeholders who have a good pulse on the needs of children, families, and communities in the state. Their active involvement would help ensure that the work of the IUC is relevant to the needs of people at the state and local levels.

- *A Flexible Project Agenda:* One of the ongoing criticisms leveled against universities is their inability to be responsive, in a timely fashion, to the needs of state organizations or local communities. An effective IUC requires a cadre of faculty who are highly adaptable, people who are able to mobilize themselves in quick fashion to be responsive to the urgent needs expressed by national, state, or local entities. As an example, in recent months, the Florida Inter-University Center received materials seeking proposals to examine domestic violence issues among military families, as well as one that would incorporate child-care training as part of a job preparatory program for non–college-bound youth. Both necessitated quick turnaround times in order to comply with deadline dates. In short order, appropriate teams of faculty from the pool of IUC associates were tapped to work on each proposal, and both documents were submitted to the funding agencies within the required time period.

- *Keep Communications Alive and Well:* A successful IUC requires ongoing communication, both internally and externally. Internally, given that only a portion of the faculty associates are directly engaged in the work of the IUC at any given time, keeping all associates fully apprised of the current and emerging activities of the center is crucial. This is facilitated, in part, through semiannual meetings of all faculty associates, as well as electronic mail messages and internal newsletters. The internal information-sharing activities, however, should extend beyond those formally linked to the IUC. It should include interactions with appropriate administrators, department chairs, faculty, and sponsored research personnel at each university campus who are not directly tied to the IUC. If these individuals are made knowledgeable of the ongoing foci of the IUC, they then can alert the IUC to opportunities that they see for IUC involvement. Furthermore, they could serve as an important conduit for locating other university faculty whose expertise could enhance the work of the IUC.

As for external activities, maintaining good links with current and potential users should be pursued along a number of different lines. First, periodic, face-to-face meetings should be held with key state legislative committees, agencies, and organizations having an interest in family and child welfare (such as state and local agencies involved in family and child services, education, juvenile justice, and community affairs). These meetings would serve as important vehicles for keeping these groups apprised of the work of the IUC, as well as helping the IUC be attuned to the current and emerging needs of these legislative committees, agencies, and organizations. A second element of the external communication effort should include the preparation and distribution of brochures and booklets that would broaden the awareness by individuals and organizations of the existence, mission, objectives, and work of the IUC. Third, well-written newsletters, policy briefs, and research reports, focusing on a variety of timely issues, should be released by the IUC and distributed to individuals and organizations in the state having an interest in children and family issues. And fourth, in this age of information technology, creating an IUC home page should be given serious consideration. The home page could contain information about the IUC, names and biographical sketches of all faculty associates, list of current activities, electronic versions of IUC newsletters and research reports, and links to sites containing excellent data and resources on children and family issues. The home page could also include up-to-date information on current legislation being considered by the state legislature having implications for children and family well-being, as well as listings of educational outreach programs and services that IUC faculty are able to offer to communities and/or organizations.

- *Maintain Scientific Integrity.* The one notable asset that universities typically bring to the table is a reputation for conducting scientifically sound, objective work. This is a major strength that sets universities apart from many other entities. Scientific integrity is an element that must remain an essential part of the work of the IUC. The integrity of the IUC rests on its capacity to address critical and, at times, controversial issues. These necessitate IUC's employment of the best science at hand in the examination of these matters. For example, if certain punitive policies are being considered to address juvenile crime, but the research clearly indicates that such policies are highly ineffective, it is incumbent upon the IUC to inform appropriate legislative leaders and staff of these findings. Coupling this information with a list of scientifically supported options for addressing the juvenile-crime problem would further strengthen IUC's role as a valuable and rich resource for reliable information on key matters affecting children and family well-being.

- *Sponsored Research Program Officials with a "Can Do" Attitude.* The establishment of an IUC can create much havoc among sponsored research program officials situated at each of the IUC member universities. In many instances, the management of extramural funds is not handled in a common fashion. For example, overhead cost rates, fringe benefits for personnel, and graduate student stipends often differ among institutions. These disparities can prove quite complex given that IUC-secured grants generally involve faculty from various universities. It is essential, therefore, that meetings be held of sponsored research representatives from each of the IUC member institutions to help work out the protocol regarding grants administration by the IUC. In many cases, facilitating the grant activities of the IUC will necessitate the establishment of new ways to do business, but a "can do" attitude on the part of sponsored research program individuals can ensure that the IUC will be able to administer extramural grants with a minimal number of impediments.

- *Need for Seed and Base Funding.* The transition of an IUC from the stage of "idea" to "reality" requires resources. Seed funding is essential in the early phases of the development of the IUC to facilitate frequent interactions among interested faculty located at various institutions of higher education in a state. Moreover, as the concept of the IUC begins to take shape, meetings with potential users, be they state legislative committees, or state or local agencies or organizations, are necessary to help sharpen the focus of the IUC. Beyond these initial resources, ongoing base funding for the IUC is needed to ensure that a core set of activities can be consistently carried out by the IUC faculty. These efforts include: (1) the preparation and dissemination of newsletters, policy briefs, and research reports/updates; (2) the development and management of a statewide database containing key data on children and families; (3) the generation of educational resources, dealing with important child or family issues, for use in formal and nonformal settings; (4) the creation of a clearinghouse for materials and other resources addressing myriad important child and family topics; and (5) the sponsorship of an annual statewide conference devoted to addressing high-priority family and children's issues in the state.

- *Faculty Reward System:* Within traditional university settings, faculty who devote a sizable amount of time to applied, customer-oriented activities often subject themselves to much risk. These initiatives are not perceived as the common ingredients for securing good salary adjustments or for strengthening one's prospects for tenure and promotion. In order for an IUC to realize its full potential, it must be embedded in a university climate in which faculty investment in applied research and outreach activities of relevance to state and community stakeholders are acknowledged, appreciated, and rewarded. Unfortunately, the "publish or perish" syndrome has denied individuals and organizations at state and local levels access to the rich pool of talent that is commonplace within universities. The mind-set as to what constitutes valued work of university faculty must be modified to ensure that efforts along the line of an IUC are given unequivocal support among those associated with the IUC-member universities.

Conclusion

In today's climate, it is not unusual for the activities of public-assisted university systems to be the subject of intense interest on the part of state legislative committees and taxpayers. Unfortunately, there are no magical walls that surround universities that can shield them from external attacks. The reality is that stakeholders are no longer content to know that cutting-edge research is being conducted at their institutions of higher learning. They want to know how these investments are making a real difference in the lives of people in the state.

The Florida Inter-University Center constitutes one model that five major universities in the state have embraced for intensifying faculty involvement in bettering the lives of families and children in the state. While the IUC is a relatively young entity in the university system, early signs indicate that its activities are having an impact in guiding the state's family and child agenda. In time, the hope is that the Florida Inter-University Center for Child, Family and Community Studies will become a shining example of the truly valuable role that universities perform in improving family and child well-being in the state.

References

American Demographics. (1992, Spring). *Hoover Newsletter.*

Annie E. Casey Foundation. (1996). *Kids Count Data Book: State Profiles of Child Well-Being.* Available from the Annie E. Casey Foundation, 701 St. Paul St., Baltimore, MD 21202.

Beaulieu, L. J., & Mulkey, D. (1995). *Investing in People: The Human Capital Needs of Rural America.* Boulder, CO: Westview Press Rural Studies Series.

Bianchi, S. M. (1995). The changing demographics and socioeconomic characteristics of single parent families. In S. M. H. Hanson, M. L. Heims, D. J. Julian, M. B. Sussman (Eds.), *Single Parent Families: Diversity, Myths and Realities* (pp. 71–97). New York: Hearth Press.

Flora, C. B., & Christenson, J. A. (1991). *Rural Policies for the 1990s.* Boulder, CO: Westview Press Rural Studies Series.

Fuguitt, G. V., Brown, D. L., & Beale, C. L. (1989). *Rural and Small Town America.* New York: Russell Sage Foundation.

Garbarino, J. (1992). *Children and Families in the Social Environment.* 2nd ed. New York: Aldine De Gruyter.

Israel, G. D. (1995). *Population and Agriculture in Florida: An Update on Trends and Characteristics.* Gainesville: Institute of Food and Agricultural Sciences, University of Florida.

Marotz-Baden, R., Hennon, C. B., & Brubaker, T. H. (1988). *Families in Rural America: Stress, Adaptation and Revitalization.* St. Paul, MN: National Council on Family Relations.

O'Hare, W. P. (1988). *The Rise of Poverty in Rural America.* Population Trends and Public Policy No. 15. Washington, DC: Population Reference Bureau.

U.S. Department of Commerce. (1993a, September). *Social and Economic Characteristics: Florida.* 1990CP-2-11. Economics and Statistics Administration. Bureau of the Census.

U.S. Department of Commerce. (1993b, September). *We the American . . . Children.* Bureau of Census, Economics and Statistics Administration.

Wilkinson, K. P., Thompson, J. G., Reynolds, Jr., R. R., & Ostresh, L. M. (1982). Local social disruption and western energy development. *Pacific Sociological Review, 25* (3), 275–295.

Chapter 8
Educating the Applied Developmental Psychologist for University-Community Partnerships
The Fordham Model

Ann Higgins-D'Alessandro, Celia B. Fisher, and Mimi G. Hamilton
Fordham University

The latter part of the twentieth century has been marked by public anxiety about myriad social problems, some old, some new, affecting the lives of vulnerable children, adolescents, older adults, and their families. While poverty, child abuse, adolescent pregnancy, discriminatory practices, educational underachievement, health-related problems of later life, and crime have had an unfortunate tradition in American communities, recognition that action must be taken to stem the growing tide of conditions threatening the development of our younger and older generations has been slow to develop in both academic and public-policy arenas. The sea change in the way in which social scientists have begun to reconceptualize their roles and responsibilities to society is no greater evidenced than in the emergence of the new field of applied developmental psychology. Long a laboratory-based discipline devoted to uncovering "universal" aspects of development by stripping away contextual influences (Hagen, 1996; Youniss, 1990), in some universities the mission and methods of developmental psychology are being transformed into an *applied* developmental psychology devoted to discovering diverse developmental patterns by examining individuals within the multiply embedded contexts in which they live (Fisher & Brennan, 1992; Fisher & Lerner, 1994; Fisher & Murray, 1996; Horowitz & O'Brien, 1989; Morrison, Lord, & Keating, 1984; Power, Higgins, & Kohlberg, 1989; Sigel, 1985).

Sensitivity to the contextual nature of human development and the need to apply the knowledge and methods of developmental psychology to practical problems facing our young and our old have fostered increased attention to the need to not only understand the influence of communities on psychological welfare, but to actively engage community members as partners in forging a new knowledge base and new ways of conducting the science and practice of psychology (Fisher & Fyrberg, 1994; Fisher, Higgins-D'Alessandro, Rau, Kuther, & Belanger, 1996; Lerner, 1995; Lerner et al., 1996; Lerner & Fisher, 1994; Melton, Levine, Koocher, Rosenthal, & Thompson,1988). To adequately address issues intimately tied to the hopes and dreams that individuals hold for themselves and their families, applied developmental psychologists seek to collaborate with community members in understanding the forces that shape their development and to work with policymakers to ensure that community goals can be achieved (Fisher & Murray, 1996; Lerner & Fisher, 1994).

The hopes for the survival and optimal development of vulnerable citizens of all ages depend in large part on our ability to train a new generation of scientist-professionals who can integrate the developmental psychology knowledge and methodological base into successful strategies for helping communities help themselves. Fordham University's doctoral specialization in applied developmental psychology has been at the forefront in facing this challenge (Fisher, Rau, & Colapietro, 1993; Kuther, 1996). The Fordham Model for Graduate Training in Applied Developmental Psychology recognizes that the responsibility to use methodologically sound and reliable research methods goes hand and hand with the need to integrate the perspectives and concerns of community members into the very fabric of scientific discovery. Fordham's goal is to produce scientist-professionals who can create research and program designs that ensure that the relationship between data and conclusions have both scientific and social validity and who are able to optimize human development through helping individuals and communities toward positive change and growth.

The goal of this chapter is to illustrate how the Fordham ADP model attempts to operationalize in its curriculum and put into practice in its research the multifaceted idea of university-community partnerships. Part one articulates the Fordham model's mission and goals; part two describes their implementation in the ADP academic curriculum; and part three describes their expression in practica field experiences and internships for advanced students. Figure 8.1 illustrates the relationships between these three aspects of the Fordham model. To conclude the chapter, we offer the idea of "good enough" practices to be used in conjunction with the idea of best practices for filling in, and reconceptualizing, the proverbial gaps between research and practice.

Figure 8.1. Educating the Applied Developmental Psychologist for University-Community Collaboration: The Fordham Model

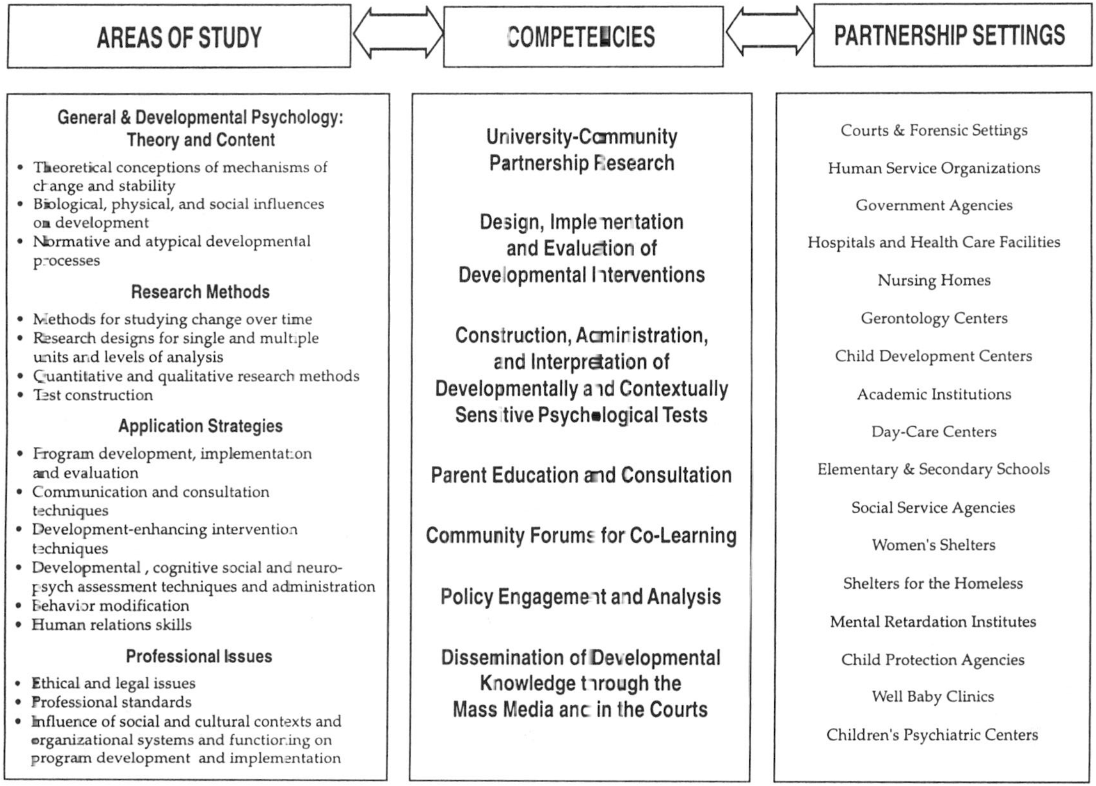

AREAS OF STUDY

General & Developmental Psychology: Theory and Content

- Theoretical conceptions of mechanisms of change and stability
- Biological, physical, and social influences on development
- Normative and atypical developmental processes

Research Methods

- Methods for studying change over time
- Research designs for single and multiple units and levels of analysis
- Quantitative and qualitative research methods
- Test construction

Application Strategies

- Program development, implementation and evaluation
- Communication and consultation techniques
- Development-enhancing intervention techniques
- Developmental, cognitive social and neuro-psych assessment techniques and administration
- Behavior modification
- Human relations skills

Professional Issues

- Ethical and legal issues
- Professional standards
- Influence of social and cultural contexts and organizational systems and functioning on program development and implementation

COMPETENCIES

University-Community Partnership Research

Design, Implementation and Evaluation of Developmental Interventions

Construction, Administration, and Interpretation of Developmentally and Contextually Sensitive Psychological Tests

Parent Education and Consultation

Community Forums for Co-Learning

Policy Engagement and Analysis

Dissemination of Developmental Knowledge through the Mass Media and in the Courts

PARTNERSHIP SETTINGS

Courts & Forensic Settings

Human Service Organizations

Government Agencies

Hospitals and Health Care Facilities

Nursing Homes

Gerontology Centers

Child Development Centers

Academic Institutions

Day-Care Centers

Elementary & Secondary Schools

Social Service Agencies

Women's Shelters

Shelters for the Homeless

Mental Retardation Institutes

Child Protection Agencies

Well Baby Clinics

Children's Psychiatric Centers

Part One: Teaching Applied Developmental Psychologists to Assist Individuals-in-Communities

Fordham University's doctoral specialization in applied developmental psychology was formally initiated in the fall of 1989 following several years of study and planning. The initial impetus for establishing an applied specialization emerged from a core ethical concern that as traditionally trained developmental psychologists were increasingly being called upon to act as problem solvers outside the laboratory, they were unprepared to grapple with the practical challenges associated with studying and working with individuals within the daily contexts of their lives (Fisher & Rosendahl, 1990; Fisher & Tryon, 1988, 1990). To competently serve communities, the ability to engage the community as a partner in any applied developmental psychology endeavor must be woven into a student's research and practical skills. To assure that applied developmental psychologists are adequately trained to understand and assist individuals in communities, our mission is to educate Fordham students not only in developmental theory and research design, but also in the practical skills essential to helping directly promote individual and community development.

Many issues of central concern to communities can be addressed by the field of applied developmental psychology. They are issues about how to create environments and systems that optimize human development; how to support families and other institutions that care for the vulnerable—children, elderly, and people with special needs; and how to assess the readiness of individuals to benefit from programs and interventions designed to enhance their welfare. The fields of education, mental health, and social service delivery systems are asking vital questions that can be addressed by students trained in applied developmental psychology (McCall, 1996; Talley & Short, 1996). For instance, in order to operate effectively and efficiently, service-providing institutions need to be able to predict who will use which of their services and delivery systems. Thus, one specific goal is to train applied developmental psychology students to design assessment batteries and surveys for individuals and groups that help accurately predict who needs services, who will be able to easily enter a system to obtain services, and who are likely to be left unserved without outreach programs.

Creating change defines the applied nature of ADP and moves developmental psychologists into high-risk and high-profile endeavors. As applied developmental psychologists helping to change individuals in communities, Fordham's faculty and students work with individuals in families, in schools and universities, in clinics and hospitals, and in residential and nursing homes. We seek and offer advice, assess the need for and develop programs and interventions. Our research addresses and integrates evaluative concerns with basic scientific questions, an approach shared with other developmental psychologists (Lerner et al., 1994). We recognize that any work designed to help individuals in communities is value-laden, even value-driven, as well as scientific. In short, having an applied focus means that our mission is to recognize, respect, understand, and work in partnership with the communities in which we conduct research, administer assessments, evaluate programs, and disseminate knowledge.

Working with Students to Cultivate and Sustain University-Community Partnerships

To implement this mission, Fordham faculty and students seek extensive and sustainable ties with communities-of-interest, that is, communities in our geographic area, communities that want relationships with us, and communities with whom we initiate relationships. We recognize that if university-community partnerships are to be of value to the academy and to agencies and the clients they serve, they must be built carefully, sensitively, and incrementally. Some university-community partnerships described in this volume are based in funded centers that were established with specific missions; others have grown out of the extension services and teaching of land-grant universities. Both of these models have many strengths, which several chapters illustrate. Those chapter authors also point out weaknesses inherent in these models. The funded center model is vulnerable to shifts in funding priorities, which makes long-range planning difficult and the sustainability of relationships tenuous. Both university and community partners often hedge their bets and thus, their commitments, in such situations. The extension model sometimes means that there is too great a distance between the work in the field and the work in the university if all or most of the extension faculty do not also hold positions teaching in the main university and if most faculty have no direct connection with field work. By incorporating community outreach into the curriculum, the Fordham model has tried to build in strengths that address, although they cannot eliminate, the above vulnerabilities.

To reach the goal of sustainability, our ADP-training model tries to teach students how to decrease the intellectual and social distance between basic and field research and between science and application. Although it is important for ADP students to become competent and sensitive liaisons between the university and social agencies (and often between social agencies and community members), we teach an ADP perspective that emphasizes the responsibility of the university and of psychology as a discipline to be part of and to serve the public. There are both substantive and practical implications when the role of community is taken seriously in the training of the applied developmental psychologist. Students learn to integrate knowledge of biological, ecological, and cultural influences on development into an awareness of how these factors operate and are perceived by community members. As scientist-professionals, the ADP students must be alert to the impact (both positive and negative) that she or he can make in the lives of those that become involved in knowledge generation and application. Thus, we seek to reach this second goal by bringing to the community a broader perspective with which to understand their lives. The questions asked and the methods used must have a relevance to the community that can empower its members to participate in knowledge acquisition and program implementations that will vest them with a sense of project ownership and promote optimal development in their lives.

At times, the psychologist initiates contact with the community to conduct research to acquire empirical data to describe or explain a community's problems, or to create interventions to test the ecological validity of a developmental theory and, hopefully, to maximize community strengths. At other times, the applied development psychologist is invited into the community to provide assistance in identifying factors underlying perceived problems in development or creating a program to foster positive change (e.g., Higgins-D'Alessandro & Hamilton, 1996). Therefore, a critical component of ADP training is teaching students how to: (1) work with agency and community members to identify concerns and goals through needs assessments and community focus groups; (2) provide the technical support for developmental screening, assessment, and program evaluation that are sensitive to cohort, socioeconomic, and cultural differences; (3) share data with community stakeholders and listen to their concerns; (4) discuss alternative evaluation ideas and strategies and, if desired; and (5) help community members develop and carry out a new plan of action. This last component often entails discussions of future projects, ideas for funding, and planning for further collaboration and cooperation between the university and the community or agency.

Ethical Responsibilities

The third goal embodied in our mission is to educate Fordham students to the ethical responsibilities that go hand and hand with applied developmental work (Fisher, 1993; Fisher & Brennan, 1992; Fisher & Rosendahl, 1990; Fisher & Tryon, 1988, 1990). They are required to spend time educating and informing community members of their rights, interests, and potential risks of participating in a research, assessment, or intervention programs. In addition, we interweave appropriate service-referral activities into all projects that have the potential to tap sources of pathology, disability, abuse, or health compromising behaviors that require attention beyond that provided by the specific applied developmental project (Fisher, 1993, 1994; Fisher, Higgins-D'Alessandro, Rau, Kuther, & Belanger, 1996).

In many instances, applied developmental psychologists leave a site after a specific research project, evaluation, or intervention has ended. Fordham students are trained to consider how formal mechanisms can be incorporated into a project that empower communities-of-interest to continue activities on their own or with continuing but altered university support. This may take the form of training community members at the outset to be part of an intervention team, assisting a community in fundraising to continue a project, and planning formal post-project consultation visits to assist continued implementation by the community. The Fordham model also assures sustainability of several university-community partnerships through it Practicum Field Experience course, described in part three.

Teaching Applied Developmental Psychologists to Form Viable Partnerships in an Ever-Shifting Urban Landscape

To create and sustain partnerships with communities, applied developmental psychologists, especially those who wish to work in large urban settings, must be trained to work within the shifting landscape of the multiple communities that the university serves. Fordham University, like other urban universities in large cosmopolitan cities, faces a unique set of challenges when trying to develop sustained relationships with the multilayered, diverse, sophisticated, and sometimes even cynical communities with whom we share the urban landscape. First, large urban communities have a dynamic quality marked by rapid changes in the ethnic, cultural, and economic characteristics of community members, in funding for health and human services, and in personnel in administrative positions. It is not uncommon to spend a year establishing a working relationship with an educational, health, or social-service institution to address a problem faced by their consumers, only to find that during the next year the population to be served has changed in its economic or language needs, that funding has been cut from the programs to be designed or evaluated, or that the administrative contact has left the institution. No amount of didactic classroom experience will prepare students for the challenges of working in such dynamic communities. To adequately train our students, the Fordham model immediately plunges them into community involvement through first-year research apprenticeships and keeps them involved through advanced-year practica and internships.

Second, in large urban cultural centers like New York City, several universities may be interested in serving the same school system or hospital network, creating turf issues and feelings of divided loyalties or confusion. For example, it is not uncommon to attend a meeting on school change at the behest of a principal or local board of education member only to meet representatives from other universities, who were similarly invited. From the viewpoint of the school, the more input and ideas they can gather the better; however, even among gracious academics practical issues of responsibility must be worked out and it is more common that other more personal and political issues must be worked out as well. The usual result is that all but one university withdraws or that all decrease their commitment and their enthusiasm, thereby disappointing the school and furthering the view that academics do not really help. Relatedly, communities and institutions in large urban settings become jaded as over the years university people come and go, bringing in research and programs that are not sustainable once the grant has run out or the data have been collected. From their perspective, which we believe is a valid one, academics are interested in communities as research pools rather than research partners; and thus community leaders begin to greet new ideas with cynicism, disappointing enthusiastic academics.

This set of issues points to the need to train students to educate communities and agencies about universities—about what we really can do and what we cannot. Most of us cannot easily share grants, graduate students, and support staff, employing them in projects not grounded in our own university. In complex urban communities, it is crucial that all the stakeholders should be engaged in framing an endeavor and specifying the goals and objectives that will indicate success to all, not just some, of the stakeholders. Much community cynicism about joining with universities seems to stem from the inability of the different partners to understand or accept the objectives of the others (Groark & McCall, 1996). For example, community partners often want programs that produce immediate, dramatic, and permanent change, and university partners are often unwilling to dampen community enthusiasm with a realistic appraisal of what can be expected. Moreover, community partners are reluctant to accept "objective" measures of program success or failure when it is inconsistent with their perceptions, and university partners are reluctant to recognize that quantitative measures may not fully reflect the qualitative changes experienced by participants. These misunderstandings lead to university partners evaluating outcomes that they can reliably measure, but that miss the mark of validity from the point of view of the community partners, who in turn are reluctant to accept the constraints and structure necessary in data collection and measurement choice to meet the goals of scientific validity and generalizability.

To help future professionals avoid these university-community partnership pitfalls, students in Fordham's ADP program are introduced to a highly contextualized process of developing research questions and intervention strategies, which, at its best, means building from mutually agreed upon premises and goals. The Fordham model includes comprehensive training in: (1) conceptualizing service-delivery systems to include the goals and competencies of service providers and service recipients; (2) taking into account the cultures, languages, and norms of community members and the regulations and missions of the agencies and institutions that serve them; (3) negotiating and crossing bureaucratic boundaries; and (4) becoming legitimate and integral members of the communities in which they work.

Part Two: Collaborating with University "Communities-of-Interest" in Curriculum Planning and Implementation

The concept of community has played an integral role in the evolution of the Fordham ADP doctoral training model. Early in the program and curriculum planning process, the developmental faculty recognized that our students, our colleagues in the clinical psychology and psychometric programs, university administrators, and other university programs comprised communities-of-interest with which we needed to form partnerships to insure a valid and sustainable applied developmental psychology specialization. Thus a major component of program planning was the exploration and articulation of the needs, resources, and perspectives of our university stakeholders. This included: (1) discussions with students about their career goals and the competencies required to attain such goals; (2) meetings with faculty to ascertain the types of expertise they could bring to an applied developmental psychology program, how such a program could contribute to faculty development, and how applied developmental psychology at Fordham could be distinguished from and complement traditional applied psychology specializations; and (3) ongoing dialogue with university administrators and directors of other university programs to discuss how a new ADP doctoral specialization could contribute to the mission of the university and strengthen interprogram collaborations. Our next step was to conduct a survey of the needs and resources of community institutions surrounding the university to determine what types of field experiential training we could and should provide students.

Once we had determined our university and neighborhood community stakeholders' goals for and potential contributions to the program, we proceeded to design a curriculum that could meet these goals within the framework of (1) educational standards for training in the discipline of psychology (APA, 1987); (2) the knowledge base and methodologies of life-span, ecological, and contextual approaches to developmental psychology (e.g., Baltes, Reese, & Lipsitt, 1980; Bronfenbrenner, 1977; Lerner, 1986, 1984); (3) the practical skills necessary to apply the developmental knowledge base to real-world problems (Fisher, Murray, et al., 1993; Power, Higgins, & Kohlberg, 1989); and (4) the ethical and professional competencies needed to transform developmental science activities into applied developmental psychology activities (e.g., APA, 1992; Fisher, 1993; Fisher & Tryon, 1988, 1990).

Professional Identification with the Discipline of Psychology and Licensure Qualifying Education

One of the most salient insights emerging from our communities-of-interest planning process was the consensus that our students should be educated, first and foremost, as psychologists. We believed that the basic goals of psychology—to describe, explain, predict, and change behavior—aptly describe the spectrum of activities that our students would need to directly address the developmental challenges facing individuals and their families in the settings in which they lived. Thus the Fordham model trains students for a new configuration of competencies based upon complementing the scientific and theoretical orientation, the knowledge base, and the research methods of traditional developmental psychology with the assessment skills, intervention techniques, and ethical standards of professional psychology. We merge the contextual, life-span, temporal orientation championed by the field of developmental psychology with the mental-health promoting orientation of professional psychology into the new configuration of applied developmental psychology: *The application of psychological principles to promote normative human development and prevent developmental problems through synthesis of theory, basic research knowledge, and assessment and intervention techniques.*

To insure that students graduating from our program would have the qualifications to obtain employment in community-based settings and perform competently and ethically in mental health and social service agencies, we decided it is important to provide them with the training experiences to qualify for state licensure as a psychologist. As developmental psychologists move out of laboratory and other educational settings into health care and social service agencies, professional licensure becomes important from both an ethical and economic perspective (Fisher & Koocher, 1990; Koocher, 1990; Scarr, 1990). Increasingly, the services of applied developmental psychologists impact the lives of individuals (Fisher & Koocher, 1990; Fisher & Lerner, 1994). The influence may be indirect through curriculum development for interventions aimed at preventing adolescent substance use, research on children's competence as legal witnesses, or position papers to inform social policy directed at children of HIV-positive parents. Applied developmental psychologists often interact directly with individuals through assessments of developmentally delayed children, parenting classes for adolescent mothers, or expert testimony in custody hearings. In many states direct delivery of psychological services to individuals can only be legally conducted by those holding state licensure in psychology.

The purpose of professional licensure in psychology is to assure the public that individuals who are engaged in psychological activities possess minimal levels of professional competencies (as defined by coursework, supervised field experience, and examination) and to protect the public from professional misconduct by requiring licensees to abide by specific standards of professional conduct (and to subject licensees to disciplinary proceedings if these standards are violated). The protections of licensure are seen as necessary when a psychologist's activities directly impact individuals, for example, through assessments leading to a diagnosis or through interventions designed to promote psychological change.

Applied developmental psychologists utilizing psychometrically valid assessment instruments to examine developmental processes or to evaluate the outcome of a developmental intervention often have the opportunity, and in many cases the responsibility, to use the results of these assessments to identify participants that may be in need of additional services, and for consultation with families or practitioners. Since such services directly impact the lives of child and adult participants, the applied developmental psychologist engaged in such work is ethically, and in many states, legally required to obtain a license.

From an economic perspective, even when applied developmental psychologists are conducting research or administrative work that does not directly impact individuals, when such work occurs in a hospital, health care, or social service setting, professional status, rank, and salary are often contingent upon professional licensure. Thus professional licensure enables applied developmental psychologists to qualify for a wider variety of employment opportunities and receive compensation on a par with graduates of other applied psychology programs (Fisher & Koocher, 1990). The Fordham model insures both a breadth of employment opportunities for graduates of our applied developmental psychology specialization and adequate public protection by having taken a curriculum that meets the educational criteria for licensure in psychology in New York State.

The Applied Developmental Psychology Curriculum

The Fordham model of graduate education in applied developmental psychology is designed to produce a scientist-professional whose competencies and identity reflect a new configuration of knowledge and techniques traditionally associated with the discipline of psychology, the field of human development, and the activities of extension and outreach-research. Our applied developmental psychology specialization provides students with the competencies to: (1) investigate the causes, consequences, and correlates of developmental strengths, vulnerabilities, and problems; (2) construct, administer, and interpret developmental assessments; (3) design, implement, and evaluate development-enhancing and problem-prevention interventions; and (4) formulate and evaluate legal decisions and social policies impacting individual and family development. Students learn to implement these tasks within a value framework that emphasizes: the importance of participant/community perspectives on project planning, implementation, evaluation, and dissemination, and the bidirectional relationship between science and application, in which research and theory guide intervention strategies, and the evaluation of interventions and policies provides the bases for reformulating theory, future research, and applications (Fisher & Murray, 1996; Fisher, Murray, et al., 1993).

Fordham's applied developmental psychology curriculum is composed of both coursework and field experiences designed to provide students with the scientific and professional foundations of the discipline of psychology, the knowledge base and methods of developmental psychology, and the skills and ethical considerations inherent in the new configuration of applied developmental psychology. The curriculum gives equal weight to both scientific and applied skills training to produce a scientist-professional who can appreciate the practical implications of his or her research findings, the theoretical implications of developmental assessments and intervention outcomes, and the importance of engaging and empowering community members as partners in such endeavors.

Drawing upon the Expertise and Resources of Our University Communities-of-Interest

The thread of community is woven through the entire fabric of the Fordham graduate student's education. Coursework in the foundations of psychology is intradisciplinary within the department of psychology; developmental students take classes with graduate students in the psychometric and clinical programs taught by professors from all three programs (psychometrics, clinical, and developmental psychology). The collegial relationships established with both faculty and peers from the three programs within the department provide a template for later intra- and interdisciplinary collaboration at the practicum site and in professional settings.

Additionally, two multidisciplinary agencies on the Fordham campus provide research and training experiences for graduate students. The Hispanic Research Center (HRC) conducts collaborative research with anthropologists, sociologists, and psychologists to study and intervene in the lives of Hispanic children, families, and older adults with the aim of enhancing the mental health of the Hispanic communities in New York City and throughout the United States (Hispanic Research Center, 1994). The nationally recognized Third Age Center conducts applied research and services for mature and elderly adults. Ethicists, psychologists, and sociologists implement programs for well and frail older adults, develop survey instruments and outreach programs for caregivers of the elderly, inform social policy at a variety of levels, and study the ethical implications of care for the elderly in nursing homes. Psychologists from both the HRC and the Third Age Center teach courses in ADP that directly reflect their practical experience and address issues of applied interest, including Psychological Services for Ethnic Minorities and Aging and Social Policy.

Students also benefit from the expertise and field placements in research and application provided by the Westchester Institute for Human Development (WIHD) and the Lighthouse for the Blind. At WIHD, Fordham students interested in careers designed to promote the psychological and social trajectories of children with developmental disabilities or children in foster care gain invaluable experience designing and evaluating developmental interventions, assessing child and family strengths and vulnerabilities, investigating the systemic nature of foster care, and consulting with parents, social workers, and administrators on policies and practices that can enhance development and prevent developmental problems. At the Lighthouse, students interested in careers in gerontology have the opportunity to conduct research on individual and contextual factors associated with adaptation to vision loss and to create and evaluate programs designed to increase compliance with health regimens and psychological well-being.

The Core Curriculum

The General Psychology Core. Fordham students are expected to become familiar with the knowledge base and ethical standards of the discipline of psychology. For example, in a course on history and systems in psychology, students learn about: the evolution of psychology as a science-based discipline; the contextual and value-laden nature of theory building and testing; how to identify implicit theoretical and cultural assumptions in research design and psychological practice; the historical and contemporary relationship of psychology to other disciplines such as philosophy, theology, physiology, and medicine—and how these relationships have impacted the scope and limitations of psychological theory and activities; and the historic and ongoing nature of psychological inquiry in science and practice. Students also acquire breadth of knowledge in biological, cognitive, and social bases of behavior.

Ethical and professional standards in science, teaching, and practice are also core elements of the curriculum (APA, 1992). For example, students are taught how to design and obtain adequate participant informed consent for research, assessment, and intervention. They are also taught how to respect human differences, how to avoid exploitative or harmful relationships with those with whom they work, and how to insure that they meet ethical standards when presenting information in the media, consulting, or providing expert testimony in the courts. They are sensitized to the need for appropriate debriefing and dissemination procedures when a research project is concluded. They are educated to engage a community in developing questions that should be asked in the research, and to report back to the community at the completion of the project—information that can be useful to their own development and the development of those they love and care for. Specific ethical considerations for protecting the rights and welfare of younger, older, and other at-risk populations are also addressed (Fisher, 1993; Fisher & Tryon, 1990).

To prepare for field experience and later licensure, the students attend a seminar on the identification and reporting of child abuse. This seminar provides an opportunity to learn about the applied developmental psychologist's responsibilities when confronted with a case of potential child abuse, including the ethical considerations and legal steps that must be taken in its reporting (see Liss, 1994 for extended discussion of this issue).

The Developmental Psychology Core. A core assumption of the applied developmental perspective is the importance of understanding the practical problems faced by individuals and families within the context of normative and atypical developmental patterns (Fisher & Lerner, 1994; Fisher & Murray, 1996; Fisher, Murray, et al., 1993). Thus coursework includes coverage of basic and culturally distinct developmental biological, cognitive, and social processes and atypical patterns including developmental disabilities and developmental psychopathology across the lifespan. Recognition of the needs of the multiethnic and lower socioeconomic communities-of-interest in the New York metropolitan area has led to an emphasis on cultural, economic, and political-legal influences on development. Collaborations with Fordham's Hispanic Research Center, courses in psychological services to ethnic minorities, social policy, and psychology and law assure that students have the skills and sensitivity to work with diverse populations and to assist legal and public institutions in decisions that promote positive growth and development.

The Research Methods Core. From the beginning of their graduate education, Fordham students are involved in a four-year sequence of community-based research experiences that is designed to increase in complexity, application, and responsibility to match the student's increasing expertise (Fisher, Rau & Colapietro, 1993; Kuther, 1996). As a complement to the hands-on research experience, students take courses in multivariate statistical analyses, qualitative analyses, and research methodologies that can measure change over time, the bidirectional influences of person and context, and the multiple variables that are part of the real-life issues raised in their research.

The research methods core teaches students that there are both substantive and practical implications of the role of community in the training of the applied developmental psychologist. Through theoretical emphasis on ecological and sociocultural contextualism in the coursework (Fisher, Rau & Colapietro, 1993), students develop a sensitivity to and awareness of the relationships between the individual and the many contextual levels in which he/she develops (Bronfenbrenner, 1977; Lerner, 1984). This orientation informs the practice of applied developmental psychologists who as scientist-practitioners are cognizant of the impact they make in the lives of those they study and the communities in which they reside. As a corollary, the research conducted by applied developmental psychologists brings to community members a broader perspective with which to understand their lives.

The ADP educational process is designed to empower both our own students and communities-of-interest to have greater investment in the research enterprise. Students are taught that the first step in conducting research or developing an intervention is to develop a relationship with the institution—the schools, hospitals, community centers, and nursing homes— and with those within the institution, the different stakeholders—administrators, staff, and participants who become partners with the researcher.

The Applied Skills Core. In the applied skills core, students start with basic psychology courses in cognitive and personality assessment, focusing on psychometric characteristics and appropriate administration of reliable and valid psychological tests. They then move to a specialized course in developmental assessment, focusing on issues of test construction and the selection of measurement equivalent and contextually sensitive tests for different developmental periods and the administration of specific instruments (e.g., the Bayley Tests of Infant Development, the McCarthy Scales of Mental Ability, the Home Observation for Measurement of the Environment, the Child Behavior Checklist, the Issues Checklist for adolescents and their families, and the Older Adult Rating Survey). Courses in test construction, multicultural assessment, child neuropsychology, and biological bases of aging provide additional breadth in the construction, administration, and interpretation of developmentally sensitive psychological instruments.

Program design, implementation, and evaluation are the cornerstones of our community partnerships and core components of applied developmental psychology training at Fordham. Students are educated in the techniques of needs assessment, community empowerment, cost-benefit and cost-effective analyses, formative and summative evaluations, and interpretation, communication, and dissemination of outcome measurement. Communication and consultation strategies with community partners are explicit aspects of instruction and field experiences so that our students develop competency in techniques that can lead to successful community-based developmental interventions.

Transforming community members into partners in program design, implementation, and evaluation is reflected in the methods and techniques we teach. Students spend time developing needs assessments, listening to the participants in focus groups or interviews in which they can help to define issues and ask questions, creating culturally sensitive instruments, educating and informing participants of their rights and interests in participating in outcome research, and providing referrals for those participants found to be experiencing difficulties beyond the scope of the researcher's purview. Students are also sensitized to the inherent ethical issues associated with starting a community project that cannot sustain itself after the applied developmental psychologist moves on to other work. Consequently, from their first contact with a school, agency, parents group, psychiatric center, or nursing home, students explore with community members the mechanisms necessary to allow the community to continue the program without the applied developmental consultant.

The Fordham model also recognizes that applied developmental psychologists must have the knowledge base and skills to consult with families who want to tailor their parenting techniques to the needs of their children, and with family and formal caregivers who want to further the life adaptation skills of the developmentally disabled or elderly. Consequently, students are trained in behavior modification and consultation techniques. Courses in social policy, psychology and law, and hospital administration are also available to students who wish to work in policy engagement, legal consultation, or health administration positions.

Part Three: The ADP Practicum as a Crucible
for the Fordham Model

Field experience is an essential core element of applied developmental psychology education and enables students to extend their skills and understanding of development in context to the practical challenges of real-world settings (Rebok & Miller-Sostek, 1996). Fordham's Applied

Developmental Psychology Practicum is a two-semester course for advanced students that provides them with an opportunity to work as consultants in applied settings, collaborating with community stakeholders in the translation of research into application and application into research (Fisher, Murray, et al., 1993).

Practicum Goals

The goals of the ADP Practicum are multileveled: (1) to offer Fordham's communities-of-interest a mechanism for sustained university-community partnerships; (2) to provide co-learning opportunities for students and community stakeholders; (3) to work with institutional staff to identify their needs and help foster the continued evolution of the institution's mission; and (4) to test and strengthen students' self-definitions as applied developmental psychologists.

Sustaining University-Community Partnerships

The practicum should broaden and deepen the positive relationships Fordham has with the communities of people and institutions in the Bronx, other boroughs of New York City and surrounding areas, and sensitize students to their concerns. Students enter communities to experience firsthand the realities and problems faced by those serving the developmental needs of individuals and families. By sharing ideas and information with community leaders, site administrators, and staff, they are given the opportunity to provide and enhance services to community institutions—hospitals, clinics, schools, nursing homes, women's shelters, and child development centers—through the administration of developmental assessments, design of intervention programs, and the evaluation of service outcomes. Evidence that the practicum has strengthened relationships is indicated by the eager "demands" of participating institutions that they receive a graduate student year after year. In addition, the continued flow of students into these practicum sites allows for sustained program implementation and growth that would not otherwise be available if the joint activities were conducted on the basis of time-limited grant support.

While we try to maintain an ongoing relationship with all the practica sites, in different years we have different needs, and sites experience changing situations. Occasionally some sites are not utilized or are lost due to changes in their staffing, expiration of research projects or funding, or leaves of absences; however, at the same time, new sites are explored and utilized to meet the needs and interests of our students. This cycle of change serves two purposes: It allows for greater diversity in opportunities for field experiences, constantly enriching the scope of ADP and our program; and it allows us to customize the field experiences to meet the specialized interests of individual graduate students. The fact that this is an ongoing cycle has enabled our ADP specialty to have sustained relationships with many communities in the greater New York City area.

Opportunities for Co-Learning

At the second level, engagement in community practica increases students' understanding of their activities in relation to the ecology of community institutions, and broadens community perspectives about applied developmental psychology as a profession that complements the activities of other disciplinary professions that serve the same populations. A critical aspect of applied developmental work includes steeping oneself in the culture of the institution in which one works. This means understanding both the philosophical mission of the institution and practical limitations of fulfilling that mission. The practicum provides students the opportunity to learn how to ask questions about institutional policies, staffing, and economic resources that enable productive joint decision making about what type of research and/or interventions are not only desirable, but possible. Students also learn how to communicate the role the applied developmental psychologist can play in the everyday functioning of the institution and communities it serves.

Ideally, co-learning should lead to joint projects that integrate developmental theory and scientific inquiry into the process of fulfilling institutional missions. For example, one student incorporated the study of nurses' moral reasoning and performance at her hospital-based practicum site into the articulation and implementation of programs designed to enhance staff self-esteem, motivation, and service. This work is soundly situated in the theoretical and empirical work on institutional cultures (Higgins, 1995; Higgins-D'Alessandro & Hamilton, 1996; Koys & DeCotiis, 1991; Moos, 1974), and nursing roles (Nokes, 1984), but goes beyond them by ascertaining how the subordinate role of nurses in some hospital cultures and their more collegial role in others differentially affects their moral reasoning, their judgments about the extent of their moral responsibilities on the job, and their actual job performance. Ongoing involvement of this hospital as a site for the Fordham ADP practicum will facilitate the design and implementation of programs to enhance the ethical training of nurses and other health-care professionals, which will move beyond mere education to the application of ethics in practice (Erlen, 1994; Levine-Ariff, 1989).

Helping Institutions Identify Evolving Needs and Goals
The third level of ADP practicum goals focuses on how an applied developmental psychologist who is sensitive to the culture of an institution can help develop institutional policies that will better meet the needs of staff, administrators, and clients. The opportunity to work with stakeholders to facilitate their mission and to enhance their services is illustrated by students' practica experiences at a specific site over two consecutive years. The agency serves children and families who are at risk due to involvement with drugs. Because this agency provides child-care for mothers while they receive drug treatment and therapies, the ADP practicum student saw the opportunity to both more actively intervene with the youngsters and to enhance the child-care providers sense of their professional responsibilities and potential. She designed and taught a course for the child-care providers on child development. The evaluation of this program indicated that the child-care workers not only had increased their knowledge of children, but felt more responsible and able to enhance the experiences of the children in their care. The increasing success of the on-site child-care center led the agency staff to request that their own children be admitted. In the following year, another ADP practicum student designed and conducted a formal needs assessment of agency staff child-care needs and submitted a detailed report to the agency director. The student's assessment and report were important components of his overall feasibility study to expand the institution's mission to provide day care for children of both staff and clients.

Student Identity Development
We believe it is crucial in the early stages of the development of the field of applied developmental psychology that students graduating from an ADP program be clear in their professional self-definition and the scope and boundaries of their competencies. Applied developmental psychology practicum sites place students in contact with professionals from a large variety of disciplines. Since the field placements are in hospitals, clinics, agencies, and schools, the on-site supervisors are sometimes professionals in other fields such as education, psychiatry, pediatrics, social work, or clinical psychology. While the students generally feel positive about their supervision, we encourage them to define and articulate the

ADP perspective, both what it is and how it differs from other disciplinary perspectives.

Students must also be able to see opportunities for an ADP perspective and to persuade other professionals of its usefulness. Some of the Fordham practicum students are placed in research institutes for their field experience. One very successful placement site over several years has been The Lighthouse for the Blind, described previously. Several practicum students have worked on large multiyear research studies to answer questions about the extent to which vision impairments and disabilities are functionally maladaptive for people, especially the elderly. The students have conducted assessments, analyzed multiyear, multisite, multimeasurement data sets, and written major components of grant proposals. They have learned concretely about the outcomes research must produce to actually influence policy or determine services for people in need.

Structure of the Practicum Experience

The practicum experience is two-pronged: work and research at the field site and participation in a weekly seminar. The Fordham faculty and the on-site supervisors meet at least twice yearly to discuss the needs and goals of the site, potential and actual students and their activities, and how the two will interface. Students spend two hundred hours (one day per week for thirty weeks) at their field-placement sites, with the time fairly equally divided between work for the site, including case conferences, and work on their own research. In addition, students attend relevant seminars and colloquia offered at their sites. They should receive one hour weekly supervision and at this point in our development, about half of the students do so. Currently all students receive at least one-half hour weekly on-site supervision on average.

A primary focus of the seminar is the students' research projects. A research project designed by each student utilizes the site, is responsive to its needs and goals, and is carried out with the facilitation of the site supervisor; however it is evaluated by the faculty supervisors and the seminar of peers at each step in the research. Students collect data from the site, either archival or current, conduct primary or secondary data analyses, and write research articles of publishable quality.

Metal is heated in a crucible to test it, and in a similar way, the practica research projects test the students' mettle. Practica sites serve as crucibles because they are not perfect. They are neither model programs nor are they engaged in all the best practices. They are research and service agencies and institutions that must produce results daily and care for their clients immediately and in the best ways possible with the means available. We feel, and the students have confirmed, that the educational value of their experiences at the sites is proportional to the problems and constraints that they have seen their supervisors work through and overcome in delivering services and doing research, as well as those the students have had to work out in the course of their own research projects. These experiences seem to mark the critical beginning of turning graduate students into seasoned professionals.

The secondary focus is on developing students' professional self-definitions through their preparation of curriculum vitae, learning to screen and respond to job/position advertisements, and in performing writing exercises to articulate in "lay-person's" terms their theoretical orientations and methodological expertise in research and evaluation for presentation to agency administrators, funding bodies, and audiences of other professionals. Thus, we prepare students not only to respond to opportunities at their practica sites, but also to be able to seize opportunities to shape policy, intervention, and training in the human services in their internships and later careers.

Ethics in the Practicum

The third focus of the seminar is ethics. Every student has had questions about the ethicality of practices at their placement sites; most have been questions of role responsibilities, sometimes of their own responsibilities. Other questions about ethics in research have generally been concerned with the extent to which participants have actually understood their rights due to their ages, level of mental functioning, or due to the procedures of data collection. Discussions of the objectivity and ethicality involved when research is conducted on site by staff who are both service providers and researchers have been productive. Our students learn that ethical issues are part of the woof and warp of institutions and of the web of relationships between institutions.

Supervisors at the ADP practicum sites see the graduate students' work with them as an important way in which researchers and the university give back to the community. They want to continue to be involved not only because of the services the students perform but also because they are convinced that research designed and conducted within the practicum framework really does support and inform their efforts to serve their communities.

Internships: The Fourth-Year Experience

Some of the ADP graduate students choose to work in paid internships during the fourth, and occasionally fifth, year of their Ph.D. program, while others hold adjunct teaching positions at the same time as they propose and complete the dissertation. Internships are the newest component of the Fordham ADP specialty and are not yet official offerings or requirements; however, it seems worthy to note the range of internships in which thirteen of the students are currently engaged. Eleven positions provide at least two hours of weekly supervision by a Ph.D. psychologist, which meets licensing requirements in New York State. Five students hold research internships; two on a project that provides license-eligible weekly supervision and three that do not. Six students are employed full-time and seven students half-time. Six internships focus on working with infants, toddlers, and children with their parents, two involve working with adults and elderly, and five engage students in work with adolescents as well as children and parents. Seven students work primarily with people belonging to ethnic minorities, mostly Hispanic, and the rest work with ethnically diverse populations. One intern conducts research with elderly populations in a state agency for the explicit purpose of informing and guiding social policymakers. Five students working with young children conduct assessments and make decisions that directly inform state foster care and child welfare agencies; many of the children assessed by these students are abuse victims. Three of these five students conduct parenting classes for parents of children placed in foster care who seek to have their children returned. The results of a survey sent to the thirteen interning students indicate that the Fordham ADP program prepared them well. On the basis of their recommendations we are planning additional specialized courses and training in assessment of special populations, such as the severely developmentally delayed and retarded.

Summary: Using Models of Best Practices to Create the Reality of "Good Enough" Practices

University-community partnerships whose goal is to foster individual and family development through serving and enhancing communities and their institutions are always complex; and at the same time, each is unique. Thus, these partners recognize that no single best practice exists for relating research to practice nor for creating and evaluating interventions to test or develop theories. Perhaps there are no best practices, even in many different forms. In the Fordham ADP model we have transformed the idea of best practices into a Weberian ideal-type, which means that best practices can provide standards for, and insights into, the goals and reasons for our collaboration with communities. As ideal-types, best practices inform our goal of creating scientists-professionals who understand that research, assessment, and program development and evaluation must have both scientific and social validity.

More importantly, this conceptualization of best practices has made room in our thinking for the idea of "good enough" practices, following Winnicott's (1965) notion of the "good enough" mother or parent. "Good enough" practices are the actual research projects, programs, and evaluations carried out in real-world settings that embody at least the relevant minimal and necessary qualities and components to adequately address issues of scientific validity (e.g., generalizability and replicability) and issues of social validity (e.g., cultural sensitivity and relevance, and instrument appropriateness). Although no one project can exemplify a best-practice model, all projects can, and should, be "good enough." Moreover, assuring the relevant minimal and necessary scientific and social validity in each situation or project, "good enough" practices will also embody the ethical stance inherent in the goals of applied developmental psychology as we have discussed throughout this chapter.

Opportunities for students to explicitly examine how best practices inform "good enough" practices are in the practica and internship experiences. The practica and internship settings—for example, hospitals, schools, day-care centers, and nursing homes—broaden and test students' understanding. They must utilize knowledge and ethical principles learned throughout the coursework and earlier supervised research experiences. Practical experiences quickly lead students to questions of "What is good enough?" In the real world of fiscal constraints, conflicting priorities of institutions, poor participant compliance, etc., students must be able to answer those questions with sound judgment. Sound judgment is, first, developing several best practice alternatives that are grounded in developmental psychology knowledge base and methodological expertise, and second, using them together with the knowledge of a site's particularities and contexts to, third, design the most optimal research or application program, one that is "good enough."

A measure of the success of these ideas is that the practica site supervisors see the graduate students' work with them as an important way in which researchers and the university give back to the community. The supervisors want continued involvement of their sites and themselves because they are convinced that research designed and conducted within the "best practices/good enough practices" framework really does support and inform their efforts to serve their communities-of-interest. A measure of the distance we still must go is highlighted by our continuing work to develop a complete licensure-eligible internship and academic program and to place a steady stream of graduating professionals into research, administrative, managerial, consultative, and policy-making positions in private and public institutions and agencies. Our Ph.D. graduates who work in these kind of positions, and those who work in traditional academic settings, all define themselves as applied developmental psychologists, pioneers in an emerging field. Because diverse communities-of-interest in the university and in the larger community have helped to shape and drive the development of the ADP specialty, we will continue to look to them for insight and criticism as the program matures.

We have argued in this chapter that applied developmental psychology is a new configuration of knowledge and skills defined by its practical purpose; that is, to bring to bear the best psychological knowledge and tools available to help individuals and families live full lives by understanding, assessing, and ameliorating individual and familial problems within the contexts of communities and institutions and to understand and change society's constraints as they currently impede those goals. We hope that this chapter—describing the Fordham Applied Developmental Psychology specialty, its mission, goals, and curriculum—contributes to defining applied developmental psychology as a field, to explaining its perspective, strengths, and boundaries, and to clarifying its relationship with other professions dedicated to bettering the human condition.

References

American Psychological Association. (1987). Model act for state licensure of psychologists. *American Psychologist, 42,* 696–703.

———. (1992) Ethical standards of psychologists and code of conduct. *American Psychologist 47* (12), 1597–1611.

Baltes, P. B., Reese, H. W., & Lipsitt, L. P. (1980). Life-span developmental psychology. *Annual Review of Psychology, 31,* 65–110.

Bronfenbrenner, U. (1977). Toward an experimental ecology of human development. *American Psychologist, 32,* 513–531.

Erlen, J. A. (1994). Ethical dilemmas in the high-risk nursery: Wilderness experiences. *Journal of Pediatric Nursing, 9* (1), 21–26.

Fisher, C. B. (1993). Integrating science and ethics in research with high-risk children and youth. *SRCD Social Policy Report, 7,* 1–27.

———. (1994). Reporting and referring research participants: Ethical challenges for investigators studying children and youth. *Ethics and Behavior, 4,* 87–96.

Fisher, C. B. & Brennan, M. (1992). Application and ethics in developmental psychology. In D. Featherman, R. M. Lerner, & M. Perlmutter (Eds.), *Life-span development and behavior* (Vol. 11, pp. 189–219). Hillsdale, NJ: Lawrence Erlbaum Associates.

Fisher, C. B. & Fyrberg, D. (1994). Participant partners: College students weigh the costs and benefits of deceptive research. *American Psychologist. 49,* 417–427.

Fisher, C. B., Higgins-D'Alessandro, A., Rau, J. M., Kuther, T. L., & Belanger, S. (1996). Referring and reporting research participants at risk: Views from urban adolescents. *Child Development, 67,* 2086–2100.

Fisher, C. B. & Koocher, G. (1990). To be or not to be? Accreditation and credentialing in applied developmental psychology. *Journal of Applied Developmental Psychology, 11,* 381–394.

Fisher, C. B. & Lerner, R. M. (1994). Foundations of applied developmental psychology. In C. B. Fisher & R. M. Lerner (Eds.), *Applied developmental psychology.* (pp. 3–22). New York: McGraw-Hill.

Fisher, C. B. & Murray, J. P. (1996). Applied developmental science comes of age. In C. B. Fisher, J. P. Murray, & I. E. Sigel (Eds.), *Applied developmental science: Graduate training for diverse disciplines and educational settings* (pp. 1–22). Norwood, NJ: Ablex.

Fisher, C. B., Murray, J. P., Dill, J. R., Hagen, J. W., Hogan, M. J., Lerner, R. M., Rebok, G. W., Sigel, I. E., Sostek, A. M., Smyer, M. A., Spencer, M. B. & Wilcox, B. (1993). The national conference on graduate education in the applications of developmental science across the life span. *Journal of Applied Developmental Psychology, 14,* 1–10.

Fisher, C. B., Rau, J. M. & Colapietro, E. (1993). Models of graduate education in applied developmental science: The Fordham University doctoral specialization in applied developmental psychology. *Journal of Applied Development Psychology, 14,* 289–301.

Fisher, C. B. & Rosendahl, S. A. (1990). Psychological risks and remedies of research participation. In C. B. Fisher & W. W. Tryon (Eds.), *Ethics in applied developmental psychology: emerging issues in an emerging field* (pp. 43–60). Norwood, NJ: Ablex.

Fisher, C. B. & Tryon, W. W. (1988). Ethical issues in the research and practice of applied developmental psychology. *Journal of Applied Developmental Psychology, 9,* 27–39.

————. (1990). Emerging ethical issues in an emerging field. In C. B. Fisher & W. W. Tryon (Eds.), *Ethics in applied developmental psychology: emerging issues in an emerging field* (pp. 1–15). Norwood, NJ: Ablex.

Groark, C. J. & McCall, R. B. (1996). Building successful university-community human service agency collaborations. In C. B. Fisher, J. P. Murray, & I. E. Sigel (Eds.), *Applied developmental science: Graduate training for diverse disciplines and educational settings* (pp. 237–252). Norwood, NJ: Ablex.

Hagen, J. W. (1996). Historical and current reasons for graduate education in applied developmental science. In C.B. Fisher, J.P. Murray, & I. E. Sigel (Eds.), *Applied developmental science: Graduate training for diverse disciplines and educational settings* (pp. 41–52). Norwood, NJ: Ablex.

Higgins, A. (1995). Teaching as moral activity: Listening to teachers in Russia and the United States. *Journal of Moral Education, 24* (2), 143–158.

Higgins-D'Alessandro, A. & Hamilton, M. G. (1996). Understanding minority groups' views of college climate as the basis for interventions. Paper presented at the 25th Anniversary Conference of the *Journal of Moral Education,* Lancaster, England, July, 1996.

Hispanic Research Center. (1994). *Report of Activities: 1977–1994.* New York: Author.

Horowitz, F. D., & O'Brien, M. (1989). In the interest of the nation: A reflective essay on the state of our knowledge and challenges before us. *American Psychologist, 44,* 441–445.

Koocher, G. P. (1990). Practicing applied developmental psychology: Playing the game you can't win. In C. B. Fisher & W. W. Tryon (Eds.), *Ethics in applied developmental psychology: Emerging issues in an emerging field* (pp. 215–224). Norwood, NJ: Ablex.

Koys, D. J. & DeCotiis, T. A. (1991). Inductive measures of psychological climate. *Human Relations, 44,* (3), 265–285.

Kuther, T. (1996). Doctoral training in applied developmental psychology: Matching graduate education to student needs and career opportunities. In C. B. Fisher, J. P. Murray, & I. E. Sigel (Eds.), *Applied developmental science: Graduate training for diverse disciplines and educational settings* (pp. 53–74). Norwood, NJ: Ablex.

Lerner, R. M. (1984). *On the nature of human plasticity.* New York: Cambridge University Press.

————. (1986). *Concepts and theories of human development*, 2nd ed. New York: Random House. (Originally published by Addison-Wesley, 1976.)

————. (1995). *America's youth in crisis: Challenges and options for programs and policies*. Thousand Oaks, CA: Sage.

Lerner, R. M., Abrams, L. A., Hoopfer, M. M., Miller, J. R., Patterson, A. T. & Votruba, J. C. (1996). Training applied developmental scientists for community outreach. In C.B. Fisher, J.P. Murray, & I. E. Sigel (Eds.), *Applied developmental science: Graduate training for diverse disciplines and educational settings* (pp. 163–188). Norwood, NJ: Ablex.

Lerner, R. M. & Fisher, C. B. (1994). From applied developmental psychology to applied developmental science: Community coalitions and collaborative careers. In C. B. Fisher & R. M. Lerner (Eds.), *Applied developmental psychology* (pp. 503–522). New York: McGraw-Hill.

Lerner, R. M., Miller, J. R., Knott, J. H., Corey, K. E., Bynum, T. S., Hoopfer, L. C., McKinney, M. H., Abrams, L. A., Hula, R. C., & Terry, P. A. (1994). Integrating scholarship and outreach in human development research, policy, and service: A developmental contextual perspective. In D. L. Featherman, R. M. Lerner, and M. Perlmutter (Eds.), *Life-span development and behavior* (Vol. 12, 249–273). Hillsdale, NJ: LEA.

Levine-Ariff, J. (1989). Institutional ethics committees: A survey of children's hospitals. *Issues in Comprehensive Pediatric Nursing, 12*, 447–461.

Liss, M. (1994). State and federal laws governing reporting for researchers. *Ethics and Behavior, 4*, 133–146.

McCall, R. B. (1996). The concept and practice of education, research, and public service in university psychology departments. *American Psychologist, 51*, 379–388.

Melton, G. B., Levine, R. J., Koocher, G. P., Rosenthal, R. & Thompson, W. C. (1988). Community consultation in socially sensitive research: Lessons from clinical trials of treatments for AIDS. *American Psychologist, 43*, 573–581.

Moos, R. (1974). *The social climate scales: A user's guide*, 2nd ed. Palo Alto, CA: Consulting Psychologists Press.

Morrison, F. J., Lord, C., & Keating, D. P. (1984). Applied developmental psychology. In F. J. Morrison, C. Lord, & D. P. Keating (Eds.), *Applied developmental psychology* (Vol. 1, pp. 4–20). New York: Academic Press.

Nokes, K. (1984). The relationship between moral reasoning, the relationship dimension of the social climate of the work environment and perception of realistic moral behavior among registered professional nurses. (Doctoral dissertation, New York University, 1984).

Power, F. C., Higgins, A. & Kohlberg, L. (1989). *Lawrence Kohlberg's approach to moral education*. New York: Columbia University Press.

Rebok, G. W. & Sostek, A. M. (1996). Field experiences in applied developmental science. In C. B. Fisher, J. P. Murray, & I. E. Sigel (Eds.), *Applied developmental science: Graduate training for diverse disciplines and educational settings* (pp. 221–238). Norwood, NJ: Ablex.

Scarr, S. (1990). Ethical dilemmas in recent research: A personal saga. In C. B. Fisher & W. W. Tryon (Eds.), *Ethics in applied developmental psychology: emerging issues in an emerging field* (Vol. 4, pp. 29–42). Norwood, NJ: Ablex.

Sigel, I. E. (1985). Parental belief systems: The psychological consequences for children. Hillsdale, NJ: Lawrence Erlbaum Associates.

Talley, R. C. & Short, R. J. (1996). Social reforms and the future of school practice: Implications for American psychology. *Professional Psychology: Research and Practice, 27*, 5–13.

Tryon, W. W. (1990). Predictive parallels between clinical and applied developmental psychology. In C.B. Fisher & W.W. Tryon (Eds.), *Ethics in applied developmental psychology: Emerging issues in an emerging field* (pp. 203–214). Norwood, NJ: Ablex.

Winnicott, D. W. (1965). *The maturational process and the facilitating environment*. New York: International Universities Press.

Youniss, J. (1990). Cultural forces leading to scientific developmental psychology. In C.B. Fisher & W.W. Tryon (Eds.), *Ethics in applied developmental psychology: emerging issues in an emerging field* (pp. 285–302). Norwood, NJ: Ablex.

Chapter 9
The Children, Youth, and Family Consortium
A University of Minnesota/Community Partnership

Martha Farrell Erickson and Richard A. Weinberg
University of Minnesota

In a time of careful scrutiny of public spending, public universities—which absorb a large portion of state educational resources—are challenged more than ever before to be accountable. Often driven by a land-grant mission, universities are under the microscope to demonstrate efficient deployment of resources in addressing educational needs and applying research to practice for the benefit of their constituents. The ivory tower is tilting under a vigorous press to eliminate program redundancy, pursue new target audiences, widen the scope of extension teaching and adult education, retool professionals for the changing job market, and promote outreach activities that address community needs (Weinberg, Fishhaut, Moore, & Plaisance, 1990).

Institutions of higher learning also feel the pressures that stem from a society in turmoil. Children, youth, and families in Minnesota, not unlike those in other states, face enormous challenges at the brink of the twenty-first century: economic distress, isolation, violence, substance abuse, teenage pregnancy, inadequate health care, and strained educational and human-service systems. These problems will not wait. The price of delay is too heavy by any measure, from the unforgivable loss of human capital to the staggering costs of future remediation. The University of Minnesota, with its wealth of knowledge and resources on children, youth, and family issues, has a strong obligation to understand and respond to these needs and challenges.

It is in this context that the Children, Youth, and Family Consortium at the University of Minnesota was created. Founded in November 1991,

This chapter was adapted from a published article by Weinberg, R. A. & Erickson, M. F. (1996). Minnesota's Children, Youth and Family Consortium: A University-Community Collaboration, *Journal of Research on Adolescence*, 6 (1), 37–53. For additional information about the Children, Youth, and Family Consortium, please write to Ms. Judith Kahn, University of Minnesota, 12 McNeal Hall, 1985 Buford Avenue, St. Paul, MN 55108.

the Consortium reflects the growing commitment of faculty and community professionals to nurture a far-reaching, cross-disciplinary, community-based effort to address the pressing needs of Minnesota's children, youth, and families. Although still (and ever) evolving, the Consortium provides a model of a public university as a vital and dynamic force for the well-being of children and the strengthening of families and communities. And, on a broader level, it is an example of systems change that could apply to other topics and disciplines as well.

In this chapter we present a case study of the Consortium, an innovation that has evolved in the current sociopolitical climate but that is rooted in the unique traditions and context of the University of Minnesota. The growth and direction of the Consortium have been guided by particular circumstances and events unique to the setting and its stakeholders. Here we highlight the early history of the Consortium, set out the guiding principles and mission that fuel its development, summarize the first five years of its activities, and discuss some of the hurdles that have been confronted during this formative period.

Setting the Stage

As a land-grant institution, the University of Minnesota already had established by 1991 a legacy of cooperation in addressing children, youth, and family issues by connecting related activities within the University and forging links with the community. These included:

- cross-departmental centers, institutes, and an extension service with particular goals and constituents in mind, funded through a wide range of internal and external sources;
- professional training programs with multidisciplinary foci;
- collaboratives of faculty and community people for the pursuit of research, teaching, and service-outreach;
- formal and informal communication networks among University and community groups.

Furthermore, the University had earned a solid reputation, within the state of Minnesota and nationally, for top-quality research and teaching in child- and family-focused fields.

These achievements notwithstanding, our efforts seldom had been coordinated or leveraged in a way to maximize their impact. As a fundamental example, the University had no inventory of its own personnel and research

and outreach activities in the area of children, youth, and families—
a serious obstacle to internal and external synergism. We were driven by
an appreciation of the problems and ideas about how to solve some of
them. Collectively, we were aware that we know much more than we used
or applied; we had to begin to translate that interdisciplinary knowledge
into action that would have true impact on the lives of Minnesota's children and youth.

We were guided also by the fact that a university can do little in isolation. The best hope for impact is through partnership with individuals
and agencies in the community who know the crises first-hand and who
may be piloting innovation. Collaborative effort is no longer a choice—it
is a necessity. This consortium, unlike some past efforts, could be neither
paternalistic nor unilateral. A clear acknowledgment of the authority of
both the University and the community would be integral to planning
and guiding the Consortium's development. It would be imperative that
both worlds be fully invested in this effort to ensure its success.

We were also aware that we had an unprecedented window of opportunity to take advantage of heightened public interest and more open pock-
ets in the area of children, youth, and families. But the window would not
be open forever. As Anthony Downs (1972) wisely cautioned over twenty
years ago, public attention rarely focuses on one domestic issue for very
long, even if it involves a problem of crucial importance to society. Typically, problems leap into prominence, remain there for a short time, then—
even though unresolved—fade from the center of attention. Because that
kind of focused public scrutiny and the political pressure it can engender
are essential to the implementation of change, the climate of concern about
children, youth, and families made the timing for a University-community consortium ideal.

The Retreat

A concerned and impassioned group of faculty and community representatives set the stage for this initiative, determined not to do simply a better
job at what they had already undertaken but to try a new and different
strategy. Building on the legacy of cooperation between town and gown
established over time, a steering committee hosted a one-and-a-half-day
planning retreat in late 1990, with thirty-nine faculty and eleven community representatives participating. In early fall, Twin Cities campus
deans and chancellors on other campuses had been asked to nominate
University candidates; steering committee members had recommended

community candidates. Participants were selected on the basis of fair and balanced representation of gender, area of expertise, and ethnicity.

A set of broad questions guided the agenda for the retreat:

- Have the University's research, teaching, and service activities to date really made a difference in the lives of Minnesota's children, youth, and families?
- Are we effectively marshaling the considerable expertise and resources of the University and community in setting agendas for meeting the needs of those populations?
- Have we been proactive as well as reactive in guiding the course of our efforts?
- Do we even know the key players within the University and community, and do we create sufficient opportunities for them to share perspectives and to participate in joint ventures?

Guiding Principles and Mission

The outcome of this highly productive retreat was a set of guiding principles to provide direction to the development of the consortium:

1. The press for an all-University/community collaboration to improve the lives of Minnesota's children, youth, and families originates in a social/economic/political zeitgeist that has raised our collective consciousness, irrespective of our individual disciplines.
2. There is a great need for a forum that links University and community personnel interested in children, youth, and families. Such a forum would create a much-needed symbiosis, nourishing the work of community practitioners and enriching the work of academic researchers.
3. The current state of tension between the University and community agencies cannot be ignored. Problems seem to stem from the two parties' diverging missions and culture types: The University is a deliberative culture where knowledge is generated and disseminated, while community agencies are action-oriented providers of direct service. To be effective, this consortium must be grounded in the principle of reciprocity and mutual respect between the community and University.
4. The consortium idea reflects the need for an organizing/coordinating mechanism among the many University units active in the area of children, youth, and families. It does not imply the need for another

such unit. The consortium is best thought of as a *process* not a structure. (Note that once established, the consortium subsequently was described by some as an "attitude" or even an "essence.") A consortium should create a culture, an environment that empowers faculty and community professionals to work more effectively on behalf of children, youth, and families.

5. This consortium should attempt to develop a matrix of concerns about children, youth, and families throughout the state. Information sharing and synergism should be encouraged not only at the intra-University level, but at community and state levels as well, so that all those working for improvements understand each other's programs and are supportive whenever possible. For example, at the University level, this would mean connecting the child health activities of the pediatrics department with research and policy initiatives in the Institute of Child Development, the Department of Family Social Science, and the Institute on Community Integration, and linking all those units to the dissemination efforts of others such as the Minnesota Extension Service and the Center for Early Education and Development.

6. The intent of this consortium is to be inclusive rather than exclusive. Membership should be open to all individuals and agencies with interest in the well-being of children, youth, and families. The strength of this network will depend on the multidisciplinary, intersectional (community, University), ethnically diverse character of its membership.

7. This effort to launch a cooperative, multidisciplinary attack on a range of critical societal problems is congruent with the University's growing emphases on maximizing efficiency, cross-departmental planning, and responsiveness to state needs. Our proposal seeks to better coordinate existing resources for optimal effectiveness.

In November 1991, the Consortium turned on its lights and telephones and set out to pursue its mission, as defined at the planning retreat:

. . . to bring together the varied competencies of the University of Minnesota and the vital resources of Minnesota's communities to enhance the ability of individuals and organizations to address critical health, education, and social policy concerns in ways that improve the well-being of Minnesota children, youth, and families.

The Start-Up

Guided by a motivational statement made at the end of the planning Retreat to "Get going fast! Don't lose the momentum!" we moved into action to establish a structure and begin our work:

1. We expanded the existing faculty Steering Committee to include community representation from greater Minnesota as well as the metropolitan Twin Cities area. The committee would report to the president of the University.
2. We established a Consortium office, *separate from any existing University unit*, and easily accessible for individuals from the community.
3. We established a nominal staff structure to include a part-time coordinator (subsequently upgraded to director), secretary, and other staff to oversee and coordinate Consortium activities and to staff the Steering Committee.
4. We actively promoted Consortium participation for University and community professionals interested in the well-being of children, youth, and families (CYF).
5. We established regular meetings of the expanded Steering Committee and more frequent meetings of the Executive Committee, a subset of the larger group committed to working closely with staff until the Consortium was solidly established.
6. We also established work groups to bring people together face-to-face on a regular basis to pursue common goals that enhance their own work and serve the needs of young people, families, and the professionals who work with them. Each work group was cofacilitated by a University person and a professional from the community at large. The groups functioned in an autonomous, self-directed way with support and assistance from Consortium staff. Groups were expected to form, transform, end, and reform as necessary, remaining dynamic and responsive to the changing needs and challenges around CYF issues.

Five Years Later: Where Is the Consortium Today?

Since its inception, the Consortium has been the catalyst for exciting collaboration across a wide range of CYF issues. Through symposia, publications, ongoing work groups, innovative use of technology, partnership with grassroots community initiatives, and collaborative grant seeking, the Consortium has taken its place as a central agent in bringing about meaningful change for Minnesota communities and ensuring that the University of Minnesota is an active partner in the process. More than twenty-three academic departments and units, twenty University centers, and the Minnesota Extension Service are joining efforts and pooling resources. The Consortium Advisory Council (formerly Steering Committee) is more broadly representative—and more actively involved in Consortium activities—than ever before. In addition, a Deans Policy Group meets quarterly to ensure investment and participation across all relevant colleges.

Most importantly, the Consortium is fulfilling a moral and ethical responsibility to "give away" information and put our knowledge to work on behalf of children, youth, and their families. Furthermore, we are listening constantly to the larger Minnesota community (and, increasingly, communities across the nation), working to see that our teaching and research agenda are informed by community wisdom.

The accomplishments and ongoing activities of the Consortium can be profiled best according to the three facets of the University's land-grant mission: instruction, research, and outreach. (Note that in reality those three facets are intricately interwoven and activities rarely fall solely into one category.) While special events and short-term projects (e.g., conferences and symposia, an annual holiday book drive [Food for Thought], and public-awareness campaigns) should be part of the Consortium in order to ensure visibility and bring people together around current issues, *our primary intent is to focus our energy and resources toward systems change.*

Instruction

From the early planning stages of the Consortium, we have heard from community representatives that universities send too many professionals into the field who are not prepared to function in a cross-disciplinary world. Although we have given lip service to ideas of cross-disciplinary education and we recognize that the situations facing professionals demand it, educational practice has continued to be centered largely within isolated departments and disciplines. Furthermore, CYF issues demand that *all* citizens—not only the usual CYF professionals—share responsibility for the well-being of children and families. Yet, university programs often do little to prepare students to assume that responsibility, nor do we prepare our CYF professional students to work effectively with the broader citizenry in addressing CYF needs. No longer can disciplines educate in parallel with other disciplines on interrelated issues. In addition, we cannot afford to ignore broad community expertise in developing practitioners and community leaders into the year 2000.

With this in mind, the Consortium has been the nexus of planning for several major cross-disciplinary instructional initiatives:

- A series of noncredit seminars on raising safe, healthy children, offered through the Compleat Scholar program for University employees and students. The seminars have been facilitated *jointly* by University and community experts.
- A descriptive directory of CYF course offerings at the University, available as a part of the Consortium Electronic Clearinghouse (described in a later section of this chapter).
- Development of a new extension program to educate and certify CYF workers, in partnership with Early Childhood Studies through Continuing Education and Extension.
- Implementation of interdisciplinary training in adolescent development as a part of the Adolescent Health Partnership. (This partnership, which also encompasses research and outreach activities, is described in some detail in Weinberg & Erickson, 1996.)
- Internships for graduate and undergraduate students providing unique cross-disciplinary, community-linked, learning opportunities.
- An initiative funded by the Minnesota Higher Education Coordinating Board that focuses on transdisciplinary professional education in service to children and families. This project includes:
  1. development of an all-university graduate-level seminar designed to enhance the collaborative professional competencies of students from diverse disciplines;
  2. establishment of a work group aimed at reconciling the unique, narrow, specialized credentialing requirements of individual disciplines by examining barriers to licensing and credentialing of professionals, and identifying next steps toward the goal of inclusive, transdisciplinary educational and credentialing requirements.
- Establishment of a University-funded interdepartmental task force to improve coordination of course offerings and training among various University units providing education in mental-health practice.

Research

In a time of limited resources, departments and units with similar purposes too often compete against each other rather than join forces. The

Consortium is playing a central role, both within the University and between the University and the community at large, in organizing people around ideas, leveraging resources, and aggressively pursuing new outside funding for research that addresses real community issues. Much of the Consortium's effort in the area of research is driven by what the community tells us they want from the University: Research that addresses their pressing issues, with findings shared promptly in a way that is understandable and useful. Throughout the community we also hear a cry for the University to ensure that its students in CYF programs enter the field of practice with a solid understanding of how to conduct evaluation research. And, facing increasing pressure from funders and the general public to demonstrate the effectiveness of their programs, CYF service providers are calling on the University to provide ongoing training and technical assistance to professionals already in the field. In the domain of research our accomplishments thus far include:

- Partnership in Kids Count with the Children's Defense Fund, Congregations Concerned for Children, and the Minnesota Extension Service. Data from Kids Count are available on the Consortium Electronic Clearinghouse to facilitate research on the status and well-being of children throughout Minnesota.
- Identification of factors that facilitate or hinder University-community collaborative research, and successful efforts to eliminate some of the barriers to such collaboration (e.g., library privileges for community research collaborators).
- A major conference on evaluating CYF programs, jointly sponsored with the Minnesota Chapter of the American Evaluation Association, followed by an ongoing series of skill-building workshops on evaluation strategies.
- Creation of an evaluation research section on the Consortium Electronic Clearinghouse (described later).
- Formation of the Adolescent Health Partnership (mentioned earlier under "Instruction"), which designs and implements creative, interdisciplinary evaluations of community interventions and proposed youth policies at the national, state, and local level.
- Matching faculty and graduate students for paid or volunteer consultation on evaluation initiatives at community agencies (e.g., Washburn Child Guidance Center, St. David's School, and the Hennepin County Children's Mental Health Initiative).

- Coordination of a major evaluation and research project with the Institute on Community Integration as part of the Minneapolis Area Learning Readiness Initiative.
- For the U.S. Department of Health and Human Services, preparation of a synthesis of research on fathering, leading to the development of a theoretical framework to guide DHHS in their efforts to encourage father involvement and responsibility. This synthesis is informed by our work with father support leaders in Minnesota, and by a national network of practitioners and researchers working on fatherhood issues. The work is an outgrowth of our involvement in Vice President Gore's annual family policy conferences, as described below under our outreach activities.
- Participation in a national network of researchers coordinated by the National Center on Fathers and Families at the University of Pennsylvania, with a goal of creating an extensive research library on fathering and identifying new areas of practical fatherhood research to pursue collaboratively.

Outreach

At a time when relations between the University and Minnesota's communities often have been strained at best, the outreach efforts of the Consortium are especially critical. In close partnership with the Minnesota Extension Service, the Consortium makes the University more user-friendly and ensures that the vital knowledge of the University is put to work effectively in communities around the state. We view this as the area in which we have brought about the greatest change in the five years since the Consortium was founded.

In a relatively brief time we have achieved high visibility in the community. We have established a public identity as a "place" where people can connect with others and can find access to resources about children, youth, and families. We have accomplished that largely by reaching out to community organizations as they plan their own efforts to address the needs of children and families. We have demonstrated that we are not trying to claim credit or ownership, but to support and facilitate, helping to make sure that efforts are grounded in the latest research on what really matters for young people and their families. Outreach activities have included:

- Publishing a quarterly newsletter, "Community Connections," that goes to over 9,000 people and is designed to present information on CYF programs around the state and to enhance connections and collaborations among people within the University and throughout Minnesota. The newsletter includes substantive articles about work in progress; a calendar of relevant University and community events; summaries of Consortium work-group activities; and a "Connection Corner" column that allows readers to seek program volunteers, information and materials, or colleagues with whom to collaborate or exchange information.

- Coordinating the first Minnesota Children's Summit, which brought together 250 leaders from throughout the state for a research-based, action-oriented dialogue about what we know about supporting the healthy development of children, youth, and families.

- Producing a forty-minute video of highlights of the Children's Summit, with accompanying study guide, to serve as a springboard for discussion and action at the local community level.

- Developing and disseminating a set of guiding principles to help parents, professionals, and policymakers determine if their decisions take into account the basic needs and rights of children.

- Supporting grassroots public awareness and community education initiatives, including "The Village Project" in Washington County, the "Kids—Handle with Care" project in Goodhue County, and the statewide "Turn Off the Violence" campaign.

- Linking the University with broad community initiatives, including the Children's Initiative, Minneapolis's Neighborhood Revitalization Project, the United Way's Vision Councils, "Success by Six," and St. Paul's Safe Cities Initiative.

- Working with various organizations around the state to develop a coordinated effort to provide parenting education and support for parents of school-age and adolescent children. As one major step in this initiative, we have implemented the Homework Project, which documents existing resources for parents of children of all ages and promotes these resources through a printed catalogue and an online directory.

- Coordinating the "University in the Community Project," which brought University faculty and administrators face-to-face with people in diverse communities around the state to listen to community concerns and let citizens know how the University can be a resource to them.

- Implementing the "Community Connectors Institute," funded by the McKnight Foundation, which brought together a diverse, interdisciplinary cohort group from each of three Minnesota communities for an innovative process of education and problem solving.

- "Giving away" information to the media, including a parenting column in small-town newspapers throughout the upper Midwest, a weekly radio feature on forty Minnesota stations, and a weekly television feature on the Twin Cities NBC affiliate.

- In partnership with the *Star Tribune* newspaper and WCCO-TV, presenting a series of four photojournalistic reports entitled "Seeds of Violence or Seeds of Promise." These clear and compelling reports, and the accompanying TV news features and newspaper commentaries, are designed to educate the public about risk and resiliency in children, to let people know how they can make a difference in the lives of children in their families and communities, and to point them to helpful resources.

- Promoting the "Safe Team" campaign, a joint effort with KMSP-TV and the Minnesota Department of Children, Families, and Learning, to teach and encourage nonviolent conflict resolution among school-age children.

- Building relationships beyond Minnesota, working with colleague organizations such as the Applied Developmental Science Consortium (which includes Michigan State University, Fordham University, Pennsylvania State University, University of Nebraska, and Johns Hopkins University). This group of universities, primarily land-grant institutions, has been exploring ways to collaborate in the translation and application of developmental knowledge to societal problems.

- Hosting "Family Re-Union," an annual national conference moderated in Nashville by Vice President and Mrs. Gore, bringing together each year one thousand researchers, program leaders, and policymakers to explore critical issues in family policy. These conferences have addressed "The Role of Men in Children's Lives," "Media and the Family," and "Work and Family," and have informed ongoing action plans both in Minnesota and on a national level.

- As an outgrowth of Family Re-Union III, coordinating the development of "Father to Father," a national movement to "Unite fathers for their children and mobilize communities for fathers and their families." As a part of this national effort, we also have worked with Minnesota leaders in the father support movement to sustain an ongoing practitioner network and stimulate new community support for Minnesota fathers.

- As an outgrowth of Family Re-Union IV (Media and the Family), working with the Office of the Attorney General of Minnesota and the Minnesota Medical Association to lead a three-pronged campaign to promote more positive use of media for the sake of children. The three strands of activity include media literacy training for parents and classroom teachers; a corporate responsibility campaign aimed at advertisers and leaders in the media industry; and the grassroots "Turn Off the Violence" campaign.

- Launching "Seeds of Promise," a University-wide outreach effort to address the needs of Twin Cities urban children and youth. Organized around the conceptual framework of the importance of caring adults in the life of a child, this new initiative integrates research, teaching, and service activities with a focus on the urban communities in which the University of Minnesota is located. We are reaching beyond the usual CYF departments and units at the University to include students, faculty, staff, and alumnae from all departments in this major effort to respond to the Twin Cities communities' call for us to: (1) Make our research relevant and useful in addressing the needs of urban youth; (2) help evaluate the effectiveness of programs that aim to strengthen the connection of children and youth with caring adults in their families and neighborhoods; and (3) "roll up our sleeves" and work alongside other community members in reaching out to urban children and families. With a small planning grant from the Danforth Foundation, this initiative is just getting underway, but already it has sparked the interest and commitment of many University citizens outside the usual CYF circle.

The Consortium Electronic Clearinghouse (CEC)

Certainly, there are many Consortium activities that serve purposes across all three functions of the land-grant mission. One such bridging activity that deserves special recognition is CEC (we say "seek"). The original plan for the Consortium included a goal of creating an extended "rolodex" of people and programs that deal with CYF issues. This was one of the first activities that we pursued when the Consortium offices opened. We soon recognized the need—and the potential—for something much larger than the "rolodex" as originally envisioned. We discovered that within the University was the technology and the know-how to create a user-friendly system by which professionals and the general public might acquire current information about children, youth, and families. Thus, in partnership with the Minnesota Extension Service, we began to develop CEC, an Internet web site, which includes the original concept and much more.

We also discovered that many organizations within and outside of the university had similar visions, but none had taken significant action in realizing their plans. Consequently, we played a catalytic role in bringing together representatives of those groups and figuring out how we could achieve our goals efficiently and effectively together. As a result, CEC now houses data from Kids Count (a Children's Defense Fund/Congregations Concerned for Children project), serves as the gateway of information exchange on adoption issues (AdoptInfo), facilitates a wide range of work on fathering (FatherNet, created in conjunction with Family Re-Union III), and links users to multiple resources on media and the family (MediaForum, created as an outgrowth of Family Re-Union IV). Beyond these and other specialized resource centers, CEC manages and updates a wide range of general informational resources on a variety of CYF topics, including many newsletters and small publications that otherwise would reach very limited audiences. And, in cases where quality resources already exist on-line, CEC points to those sites to ensure a "seamless" experience for the user.

Consortium staff often make presentations about CEC at professional conferences and community events, and they provide free or low-cost training tailored to the needs of specific agencies so that professionals and lay people can take advantage of this rich electronic resource. CEC is the major tool by which we facilitate information exchange and connect people with needed resources. Thanks to a remarkably dedicated CEC advisory board, whose community and University members bring strong content knowledge, technical expertise, and an understanding of information management, CEC is perhaps our clearest example of a real synergistic partnership. To date, thousands of individuals have accessed CEC. Our intent is to continue to harness resources to create real order and value on the electronic information highway, for the well-being of children, youth, and families.

Barriers to Change

In five years the Consortium has made substantial progress in accomplishing its mission, but we know that we still have a long way to go. In particular, we are working hard to:

1. increase the level of involvement and commitment of stakeholders within the University such that the synergy made possible through the Consortium becomes a way of doing daily business;

2. broaden the base of involvement within the University, reaching beyond the usual CYF units to engage the entire University community in working toward the well-being of Minnesota's citizens ("Seeds of Promise" is a significant step toward this goal);

3. increase and strengthen our connections with professionals from outside the metropolitan area to ensure that the Consortium works for the benefit of all Minnesotans;

4. reach out to other Minnesota institutions of higher learning to build a rich network of cross-disciplinary educational experiences for pre- and in-service professionals in CYF-related fields.

As with all of our Consortium activities, the results of these efforts will be evaluated in terms of their "value-added" uniqueness and centrality to the mission of a land-grant university.

We would be remiss if we created a Pollyanna image that there have been no obstacles to establishing the Consortium. Resistance to change is not uncommon where traditional paradigms and the status quo are challenged. Our experience is not unlike what others have encountered in attempting to modify the way the academy goes about its work (e.g., Lawson & Hooper-Briar, 1994). The most critical barriers that the Consortium continually confronts include:

Distrust of the University
The community often looks on the University with considerable mistrust. A number of explanations seem to account for this climate of tension:

- *Perceptions of University arrogance, egocentrism, and paternalism.* "The University takes, but it doesn't give back." The University often uses community sources for research but seldom shares the results of that research with these sources.
- *Difficult access:* The complex structure of the University is confusing to outsiders; physical barriers to visitors, especially parking, are often insurmountable.
- *Poor communication:* The University's goals and purposes in research are not clearly explained to community collaborators.
- *Lack of acknowledgment that the University and the community are dif-*

ferent cultures exploring unique missions: The University generates and disseminates knowledge and often addresses long-term solutions to long-term problems, but the community provides direct service and often must provide prompt intervention with short-term results.

The University Reward System

The University historically appears to penalize faculty who excel in service and community-outreach activities by not weighting those accomplishments equally with research and teaching in promotion and tenure decisions, salary merit increases, and other aspects of faculty career development. Furthermore, interdepartmental collaboration appears to be a disincentive when an individual faculty member's "independent" scholarly contributions are reviewed. This model must be modified if effective cooperative ventures are to be supported.

Turfdom Among the Disciplines

Unfortunately, intellectual and professional "territorialism" pervade the academy and the professions that serve the needs of children, youth, and families (Lerner & Fisher, 1994). We have recognized that the disciplines that typically have defined practice in the area of CYF do not necessarily provide the most effective paradigm for education and service in today's world. New ways of preparing and supporting professionals who serve those populations must be explored. The time is right to identify the common knowledge and competencies that cut across disciplines, to tear down (or at least cut windows in) the walls that separate disciplines, and to educate and serve in a way that is driven by the needs of children, youth, and families rather than by departmental or disciplinary labels.

Funding Issues

The work of the Consortium is not peripheral, not some "extra" that has been added onto a core of traditional activities pursued by the University. And yet initially, in terms of financial support, the Consortium was treated in some ways as an "extra." Operating on a bare-bones budget, the Consortium relied largely on the goodwill of staff and committee members who worked well beyond compensation. We knew that to fulfill our vision and mission, we must have a more realistic, stable financial base. Fortunately, the passion underlying the development of the Consortium was shared by members of central administration who shape the University's budget. But ironically, at a time of retrenchment and reallocation, funds provided to the Consortium are likely drawn away from the constituent departments and units the Consortium hopes to bring together. The generation of external support from foundations and other funding sources requires that the Consortium have a secure and adequate institutional funding base. While our general operational funding is more generous and stable than it was initially, we still sustain our momentum with more heart than dollars.

Conclusions: Achieving the Vision

We believe the Children Youth, and Family Consortium at the University of Minnesota is: (1) an effective prototype of how land-grant institutions can create linkages among disciplines to accomplish shared goals for meeting the needs of our nation's children, youth, families, and communities, and (2) a dynamic, reciprocal model for connecting a university with its communities.

As universities reassess, redefine, and restructure, the Consortium provides an innovative and practical example of systems change for community good. We hope that the financial, psychological, and emotional resources will continue to be sufficient to sustain and nurture this exciting collaboration and outreach enterprise.

References

Downs, A. (1972). Up and down with ecology: The issue-attention cycle. *The Public Interest, 29*, 38–50.

Lawson, H. A. & Hooper-Briar, K. (1994). *Expanding partnerships: Involving colleges and universities in interprofessional collaboration and service integration.* Oxford, OH: The Danforth Foundation and the Institute for Educational Renewal at Miami University.

Lerner, R. M., & Fisher, C. M. (1994). From applied developmental psychology to applied developmental services: Community coalition and collaborative careers. In C. B. Fisher & R. M. Lerner, (Eds.), *Applied Developmental Psychology.* New York: McGraw-Hill.

Weinberg, R. A. & Erickson, M. F. (1996). Minnesota's children, youth, and family consortium: A university-community collaboration. *Journal of Research on Adolescence, 61*, 37–53.

Weinberg, R. A., Fishhaut, E. H., Moore, S. G., & Plaisance, C. (1990, December). The Center for Early Education and Development: "Giving away" child psychology. *American Psychologist, 45* (12), 1325–1328.

Chapter 10
Challenges of University-Community Outreach to Traditional Research Universities
The University of Pittsburgh Office of Child Development Experience

Robert B. McCall, Christina J. Groark,
Mark S. Strauss, and Carl N. Johnson
University of Pittsburgh

In the mid-1980s, the University of Pittsburgh, as part of its bicentennial celebration, convened 120 faculty, administrators, policymakers, industrialists, philanthropists, and community leaders to explore how the University and community could work collaboratively to improve the quality of life in the Pittsburgh region in six domains (e.g., human services, economic development, etc.). In five of the six domains, independent panels suggested that a unit be established, jointly supported by the University and the community, which would be a point of contact between these constituencies and would facilitate university-community collaborations that would address problems of mutual interest.

Simultaneously, but quite independently of this massive strategic planning, two junior faculty members, one in the Department of Psychology (M.S.S.) and one in the Program of Child Development/Child Care of the School of Social Work (C.N.J.), observed that there were numerous faculty members who had interests in children, youth, and families, but who were scattered across different schools and departments and rarely had any contact with each other. Moreover, the gulf between University faculty and community human-service providers and policymakers was even wider than that separating faculty from different disciplines and schools. As a consequence, they organized an interdisciplinary group of faculty members to plan a unit similar to that which

Portions of this paper were supported by an Urban Community Services Program grant P252A20082 from the U. S. Department of Education and by the Howard Heinz Endowment.

the large University-community planning group ultimately recommended.

The purpose of this new unit was to promote interdisciplinary training and research as well as to facilitate university-community collaborations that would contribute to the welfare of children, youth, and families in the Pittsburgh area. The organizers persuaded the University to join with two local foundations, the Howard Heinz Endowment and the Buhl Foundation, to jointly sponsor the unit, which was made administratively independent of the University's departments and schools. The organizers and funders then hired a director (R.B.M.) who in turn hired an associate (C.J.G.), who eventually became codirector, plus an administrative secretary, and the University of Pittsburgh Office of Child Development was born in 1986.

In many respects, the organizers of the strategic-planning process as well as the creators of the Office of Child Development were more prescient than they knew, antedating the more recent clarion calls for university-community collaborations in general (Bok, 1992; Boyer, 1990, 1994; Johnson & Bell, 1995; Lynton & Elman, 1987; Millard, 1991), in science (Byerly & Pielke, 1995), and in specific disciplines (Lerner et al., 1994; Lerner, Miller, & Ostrom, 1995; McCall, 1996). Consequently, the Office of Child Development was one of the first modern interdisciplinary units designed to facilitate collaborative education, research, and human-service projects for children and families in a large research-oriented university. Since its inauguration, the Office has evolved on a learn-by-doing basis, and today it has a decade of experience forging interdisciplinary, applied, university-community collaborations pertaining to children, youth, and families.

In this paper, we present a brief description of the current version of the Office of Child Development, henceforth simply called "the Office," and we refer readers to other papers for more details on the Office's procedures and projects (McCall, Groark, Strauss, & Johnson, 1995) and on its methods of promoting university-community collaborations (Groark & McCall, 1996, 1993; McCall, 1990a, 1990b; McCall, Green, Strauss, & Groark, in press).

The Nature of the Office of Child Development

The concept and activities of the Office of Child Development have changed over the ten years of its existence, but the "partnership" concept of mutual responsibility and benefit among collaborators has been an enduring theme.

The Original Concept

Purpose

The original concept was simple. The Office was to stimulate, promote, and facilitate interdisciplinary training, research, and university-community collaborations to solve applied problems of mutual interest pertaining to children, youth, and families. From the beginning, the Office was conceived as a partnership between the University and the two sponsoring foundations. Initially, this "partnership" was primarily financial—that is, the University and the foundations were to share the core costs of the Office.

Core Program

The Office was to operate a set of basic activities for the benefit of its faculty and community constituencies designed to give the Office identity, to give prominence to children and families as a focal activity on the campus and in the community, to bring University and community professionals together, and to provide an atmosphere in which interdisciplinary and collaborative projects could be fostered. This core program of activities included:

- publishing a newsletter and special reports that summarized research-based information about a given applied problem;
- distributing notices of Requests for Proposals to the Office's faculty and community constituencies;
- sponsoring interdisciplinary and applied colloquia, workshops, conferences, and discussion-luncheons;
- providing a variety of support services and technical assistance to faculty, agencies, and policymakers;
- sponsoring self-help networks and interdisciplinary study groups;
- assembling and publishing health, education, and welfare data on children and families for metropolitan areas and counties in the state and providing specific data to constituencies upon request;
- publishing a variety of directories of personnel and services, internship opportunities, etc.

These core activities were available to all interested faculty, students, community agency professionals, policymakers, and funders. There are approximately seven hundred faculty and research associates at the University interested in children, youth, and families; five hundred sixty-five agencies that provide services to families in the local Pittsburgh area; dozens of policymakers and funders; and approximately 5,000 professional and interested individuals.

Special Projects

These core activities, while intrinsically valuable and useful, also were seen as a means to fostering specific projects of a collaborative nature that would be separately funded and live and die on the basis of that specific funding. Since the Office was to be a facilitative unit, the ultimate criteria for the Office was the number, nature, and size of the special collaborative projects it fostered.

Changes in Concept

Two major evolutionary changes have occurred in the way the Office operates.

The Office as Facilitator

First, as originally conceived, the Office was to be primarily a facilitator of collaborative projects that other people ultimately would own and operate. For example, the Office might bring together a small set of faculty members with diverse expertise, coordinate their meetings to define a particular collaborative research or training project, oversee the coordination of the application, and then turn the project over to the collaborative group and its self-selected project directors once the project was funded. Although not much thought was given to the issue, initially it was not anticipated that the Office would operate, manage, or perform such projects with its own employees. Instead, it was presumed that Office staff would be facilitators of what would eventually become other people's projects, and then the Office would facilitate the next collaborative project.

While the Office does act in a purely facilitative role, many of the initial collaborative groups the Office facilitated requested that the Office manage the operation of the project itself, not just its formation and grant application. In retrospect, the rationale seems obvious and clear: If a collaborative group needs an independent convener and manager to create and plan the project and orchestrate its grant application, it is also likely to need that independent manager to administer the collaboration once the project is funded and there are real financial and administrative decisions to make. As a result, the Office began to manage projects, although it still refrains from delivering services or conducting research and training with its own staff if existing agencies and faculty are available to do it.

This operating principle was further qualified when the Office received an Urban Community Services Program grant from the U.S. Department of Education to conduct program evaluations and policy studies for agencies and policymakers in the area. In this case, it hired such specialists to conduct these projects, although the Office continues to be deferential to faculty and community professionals and agencies who are able and available to perform evaluation and policy studies. In short, while the Office now uses its own employees to conduct some projects, it tries not to compete with members of its own constituencies, whose support and participation it may need for the next collaborative project.

The Office as Partner

The second change that evolved over the course of the Office's development consisted of an expansion of the meaning of the concept that the Office was a university-community "partnership." Originally, this idea simply applied to the fact that the University and the community contributed to the basic operational expense of the Office. However, over the years, the Office has developed a true operational as well as financial partnership with local funders, policymakers, and agencies, which has substantially changed the way the Office operates.

A "partnership" implies that the partners each have substantial influence over and responsibility for the way projects are conceived, funded, and operated, which is a very different set of procedures than academics (and some community professionals) are typically trained for and operate under (see McCall et al., in press). For example, rather than the Office writing a detailed proposal for a project that it alone conceives, and submitting it to a funder who then either approves or disapproves funding for the project, discussions between the Office and funders may be initiated by either party, projects are planned together, an application for funding may or may not be written, the funders and participating agencies may be active participants in the operation of the project, projects may be governed by a community board, results may or may not be publicly available or published, etc. Such a partnership also means that funders call and ask the Office to perform a given project, sometimes on very short notice and with nearly impossible deadlines (e.g., "write this grant application on behalf of the County in the next week"). By the same token, funders frequently respond to the need for local matches for projects that the Office initiates, and they may rally support in the community for funding and operating a project.

Mission and Operation

The current mission of the Office and its operating principles are summarized in tables 10.1 and 10.2. These have been discussed in more detail elsewhere (McCall et al., 1995).

While most of these principles are essentially inherent in the concept of the Office as a facilitative, interdisciplinary, and applied unit that forges partnerships, some principles were elective and other such units could choose alternative approaches. For example, the Office conducts activities that are relevant to policy but it does not engage in direct or partisan political advocacy. Further, the Office is largely a structure and a facility that is responsive and without a specific proactive content agenda (see below), and the Office has no formal membership.

Growth

Fiscal Growth

The Office has been remarkably successful in facilitating, planning, implementing, funding, operating, and managing collaborative projects. In its first ten years, for example, the Office has received approximately $40 million in grants (including some awarded but not yet paid contingent upon congressional allocations). An additional $40 million has been

---

Table 10.1. Purposes of the University of Pittsburgh Office of Child Development

- To foster a supportive and facilitative atmosphere within which interdisciplinary programs pertaining to children, youth, and families may be conceived, nurtured, implemented, and managed.
- To promote interdisciplinary research and educational programs, especially of an applied nature, within the university for undergraduate and graduate students and professionals seeking continuing education.
- To stimulate, plan, and sometimes manage interdisciplinary and multi-institutional collaborative research, policy, and human-service demonstration and evaluation programs involving university faculty and community human service professionals.
- To coordinate, conduct, and produce background information, needs assessments, white papers, and other research and professional services for policymakers.
- To provide a wide range of interdisciplinary program evaluation services and technical assistance to human-service agencies, funders, and policymakers.
- To communicate research and professional information on children, youth, and families to those individuals who can use that information, including academics, service professionals, policymakers, parents, and citizens.

Table 10.2. Principles of Operation of the Office of Child Development

- The Office emphasizes **interdisciplinary and collaborative** projects among faculty, human-service agencies, community groups, and policymakers. Projects that are the rightful province of a single discipline or do not require substantial collaboration are typically not pursued.
- Collaborative projects are viewed as **partnerships that must be mutually beneficial** to participants, each of whom shares responsibility and control over the project and contributes a necessary, but not sufficient, component of it.
- The Office emphasizes projects that pertain to the **University of Pittsburgh and Western Pennsylvania,** but it also conducts interuniversity collaborations and **regional, state, and national** projects.
- The Office exists primarily to facilitate, coordinate, and **help others** to attain goals that they are unlikely to achieve without collaboration. It supports, rather than supplants, the work of other faculty and community professionals who have an interest in children, youth, and families
- The Office has **no formal membership,** and it attempts to serve all relevant faculty, human-service agencies, and policymakers.
- While the Office does initiate projects of its own creation and design, it tends to be **responsive and flexible** to changing needs, policies, personnel, and funding opportunities. The Office does not have a focused content mission or specific planned agenda; instead the Office consists of a structure and capabilities that are mobilized, often rapidly, to meet the changing needs of its constituency.
- The Office **does not charge or exact "quid pro quo" benefits** from collaborative groups it organizes for special projects, and it will serve such consortia whether or not it is the primary grant recipient. In fact, the Office prefers other groups ultimately to own and operate collaborative projects that the Office has stimulated, planned, helped to fund, or implemented. However, it will maintain a continuing presence if necessary and if separately funded.
- The Office **prefers not to operate direct human services,** but it does coordinate services and perform case-management functions.
- The Office operates as an **independent, credible, unbiased, and balanced source** of information, administrative management, program evaluation, and policy analyses rather than as an advocate for specific pieces of legislation or policy, partisan issues, or particular strategies of social change.

awarded to other agencies. In these cases, the Office managed the grant application, operated the planning and implementation year that was then approved and funded, or administered the project (e.g., the Office is given a subcontract to manage the project, but the remainder of the funds are given directly to the collaborators). Finally, a facilitative unit provides faculty and service agencies with technical assistance in crafting their own grant applications and in giving seed money that eventually produces a grant. Such activities have resulted in approximately $20 million in additional funds to other faculty and agencies in the region. This means that the Office has played a major role in generating $100 million in new projects in the region in ten years. McCall et al. (1995) have discussed the factors that they believe have contributed to this growth.

It should be noted that, in contrast to residential research centers that house or count among their members numerous faculty who usually apply for funds alone and operate their own projects, the Office now has the equivalent of 1.5 full-time equivalent faculty members and 4.5 full-time equivalent doctorates. We believe this shows the leveraging power of an investment in a university-community facilitative unit, both in terms of the amount of grant support returned on the external investment in the general costs of the program (roughly fifty dollars for every dollar spent), and in terms of the return on faculty investment.

Table 10.3 presents a few of the special projects fostered by the Office in the domains of interdisciplinary education, interdisciplinary research, collaborative human-service demonstration programs, program evaluation, and policy studies. In addition to the core program of general services, these special projects "define" the current nature of the Office. But if the past is a guide to the future, the mission, operating principles, and special projects are likely to continue to evolve with changing political, social, and financial circumstances.

Intangible Growth

While dollars are easily counted, documented, and communicated, intangible correlates of growth may be more important. We believe, and survey results support (McCall et al., 1995), that the successful operation of the core program and special projects has:

- helped to create a collective identity for children, youth, and families in the University and community;
- established trust and confidence between the Office and its faculty and community partners;
- created a better climate of mutual understanding, communication, and respect in which interdisciplinary and university-community partnerships can more easily be forged and operated;
- contributed positively to the image of the University in the local community and in the halls of the state legislature and its agencies.

Table 10.3. Selected Special Projects of the University of Pittsburgh Office of Child Development

Interdisciplinary Education

- Funded and codirected one of ten **Child Abuse and Neglect Training Grants** in the country;
- Funded and codirects one of five original **Interdisciplinary Child Welfare Training Grants** in the country;
- Operates a two-semester **Interdisciplinary Proseminar on Applied Issues of Children, Youth, and Families** for advanced undergraduates and graduate students as well as community service professionals.

Interdisciplinary Research

- Convened and seeded researchers from Penn State and the University of Pittsburgh who are conducting one of nine studies in the country on the **NICHD Study of Early Child Care**, tracing the antecedents and consequences of different early childhood experiences.
- Seeded and stimulated a collaboration of researchers within the University and the community to study **Antecedents of Development in Infants from Low-Income Families.**

University-Community Human Services Collaborations

- Operates one of the twenty-four original national sites of the **Comprehensive Child Development Program** for high-risk children from birth to six years of age.
- Created and operated the **Alliance for Infants**, which provided case-managed services to disabled and high-risk infants and families and those potentially needing early intervention services.
- Coordinated **A Better Start**, a statewide program to bring pre- and perinatal services to hard-to-reach, at-risk women.
- Operated one of sixteen **Drug and Alcohol Prevention Task Forces for Runaway and Homeless Youth**, a federal program providing education and prevention services.
- Organized the grant application and supervised the planning year for the **Pittsburgh Healthy Start Program**, a federal project to prevent infant mortality.
- Manages the **Partnerships for Family Support**, a set of three community-empowered family support programs in Pittsburgh.
- Operates one of fifteen **Early Head Start** programs and research and evaluation projects.

Program Evaluation

- Operates one of the seventeen original **Urban Community Services Programs** of the federal Department of Education, which provides a variety of program evaluation services and policy studies for numerous local agencies and policymakers.
- Conducts the data analyses for the evaluation of the local site of the **Comprehensive Child Development Program.**
- Designed and conducts the evaluation of the **Partnerships for Family Support** in Pittsburgh.

Table 10.3 continued next page.

Table 10.3 continued.

- Designed and conducts the evaluation of **First Steps,** a home-visiting program for all infants and their parents in four Pittsburgh neighborhoods.
- Conducts the evaluation of **Project Beacon,** which promotes prereading skills in three- to five-year-old children.

Policy Studies

- Publishes collaboratively with the Pennsylvania Partnerships for Children an annual *Kids Count Fact Book,* a county-by-county presentation of health, education, welfare, economic, and mental-health indices for Pennsylvania's children and families.
- Publishes *Overcoming the Odds,* a report that designates geographic areas in Allegheny County in which children and families are at greatest risk, summarizes services, and identifies service gaps.
- Conducted the **Statewide Needs Assessment of Early Childhood Services in Pennsylvania,** a comprehensive report of literature and three statewide surveys conducted for the State Board of Education.
- Wrote the Human Services section of Pittsburgh's successful application to become a federal **Empowerment Zone.**
- Performed the **Statewide Needs Assessment for Family Support, Family Preservation, and Home Visiting Services** for the state Department of Welfare.
- Defined the concept, assessed existing services and needs, and offered a strategic plan for **After-School Safe Places** in the county.
- Operates **Starting Points,** a project that creates a knowledge-based model for managing transitions in political power in a way that promotes ongoing, nonpartisan commitment to children and families.

These intangibles are now leading to new roles for the Office that were not possible earlier in our history. For example, rather than simply funding, implementing, and managing collaborative projects that local and state policymakers conceived, the Office is increasingly being asked to conduct needs assessments and plan area-wide, integrated approaches to general problems (e.g., family-support services, program evaluation, after-school safe places). Further, the university is beginning to look to the Office as a disciplinarily neutral representative of the diverse faculty, departments, and schools concerned with children, youth, and families to coordinate the study of interdisciplinary initiatives as the first step in university strategic planning in this domain.

Growing Pains

Growth, while often an indicator of success, is not uniformly positive, or at least, it requires continuous administrative management. For example:

- the Office's personnel growth (to as many as eighty-five) has outstripped the university's ability to provide space, so the Office has two on-campus sites provided by the university and two off-campus sites paid for by special project funds;

- intraoffice administrative procedures and communications must be expanded and become more formalized to prevent things falling through the cracks and employees from losing a sense of organizational identity;

- as funders and policymakers increasingly come to the Office with new projects, the Office must be vigilant not to step on the turf of its constituents;

- the Office must guard against cannibalizing its major staff members by having them fully committed to operating special projects so that they have no time to respond to or create new initiatives;

- special project funds alone will never be able to cover all the costs of the core program or ensure that a staff of experienced professionals will be continuously and dependably available, so the Office must constantly search for core funding of an ever-increasing amount to cover the diversity of services and capabilities that the faculty and community have come to expect from the Office.

Challenges Posed by University-Community Partnerships

What follows is a discussion of several challenges to university-community facilitating units and traditional research universities if the goal espoused by this volume is to be achieved. Change is always difficult, because it may threaten entrenched, highly invested values and methods of operation. At the same time, the benefits of change may seem uncertain. In the face of the current financial difficulties facing universities, some university administrators favor marshaling new energy to pursue the tried and true, while others take the external challenge as a stimulus for transforming the university to be more consonant with the contemporary demands of society. The latter course will require substantial modifications in the way we teach, conduct research, and relate to the community (McCall, 1996), and such changes will produce uncertainty, require new values, and demand new operational procedures. Based upon our experience attempting to promote university-community collaborations through the Office of Child Development, we describe some of these challenges below.

Universities Should Take the Lead in University-Community Collaborations

We believe that being involved in university-community partnerships is appropriate and beneficial for universities, they should take the lead in creating such partnerships, and units that promote these collaborations should be housed in universities rather than in the community.

Proper Role for Universities

Although the press for universities to renew their contracts with society seems more urgent now, critics have frequently challenged whether this is the proper role for universities (e.g., Whiting, 1968). Others (e.g., Corson, 1968; McCall, 1996) argue that it is proper for a university to collaborate with society to solve its problems, and that universities have several attributes that make them especially suitable for this role.

For one thing, universities have physical resources and prestige that permit them not only to contribute but to take a leadership role. Second, universities have a tradition of studying such problems more so than do government, religious groups, private enterprise, foundations, and other institutions. Third, faculty tend to be more independent and objective, or, at least, they tend to be unbought if not unbiased. Fourth, universities can contribute a tradition of scholarship that emphasizes examining the evidence of the past and focusing that evidence around creating new solutions. Fifth, universities value the intellectual freedom that is necessary for a creative and comprehensive examination of social issues and alternatives.

These several characteristics focus on the university as an independent, unaligned, convener of collaborative groups that has a clear identity and prestige that supports its potential leadership contribution. But we (McCall, 1996) and others (e.g., Perkins, 1966) believe that there should be limits to the university's role. Specifically, while universities and their faculties are revisionists in their thinking, they should not implement those revisions in society. Other institutions, such as government, business, foundations, and religious groups, have as their main purposes managing society, producing and distributing products and services, and implementing changes. "Partnerships" imply a division of labor, with each partner contributing its knowledge, perspectives, and expertise to the collaborative enterprise. Academics should bring resources, prestige, scholarship, education, and ideas to the table, but other institutions should use their skills, resources, and experience to manage or implement changes in society.

Further, we believe that universities that implement change threaten their traditional role. Specifically, implementing changes implies a vested interest, and such a vested interest would dilute the university's valuable potential contribution as an independent organizer of collaborative groups, a provider of a free range of creative options, and the evaluator of the implemented solution.

While some university administrators may agree with the general principles stated above, they may balk at the particulars. For example, some university administrators may wonder why the university should be managing, say, a collaborative human-service demonstration project in which all of the services are delivered by community agencies. What does this have to do with academics?

For one thing, creating and managing a new human-service demonstration project in the community would seem to be a very appropriate activity for a faculty member in the schools of social work or education, so, in principle, such an activity is not tangential to typical faculty projects. The demonstration project hires service agencies, rather than graduate students, because service agencies are licensed to provide such services, are experienced at it, and confer on the demonstration an ecological validity that could not be achieved in a university "lab program" or school, for example. Further, because it is a demonstration program, it is likely to be evaluated, and the evaluators may be university faculty. Traditionally, many demonstration intervention programs in certain fields (e.g., early intervention and early childhood education) were designed, conducted, and evaluated by faculty; but it is equally important to evaluate how service programs are (or will be) actually conducted when funded and operated in and by the community, not by universities. Finally, having the university manage the demonstration may help the university bring its expertise indirectly to the project, by providing it with literature reviews of what works, improving the monitoring system used by management to guide the project's operation, and insisting on an appropriate evaluation that may be conducted by faculty.

Take the Initiative

We believe universities should take the initiative to reach out to society. While both the academic community and society have contributed to the gulf between them, we believe many universities have been more aggressive about distancing themselves from society in the past and are currently in greater need of restoring a mutually beneficial relationship with society.

At least in such cases, it seems fitting that the university make the initial overture.

What may be shocking to some universities, however, is the possible skepticism and outright resistance of society to their initiative. Depending upon the nature of the past town-gown relationship, a university bid to create a partnership may be greeted with, "Why are you doing this? What is in this for you? What are you going to take from this venture?" In the past, some universities have not seriously partnered with the community. Instead, they viewed their relationship as consisting either of giving information to the community and expecting it to adopt their suggestions, or of using the community to provide a living laboratory for their faculty's scholarship. In each case the benefits are one-sided, plus the first can create the impression of academic arrogance, and the second, of mercantilism. Consequently, some universities will need to take special steps to assuage these fears and to understand and act as a true partner in such collaborations from the beginning.

Locate the Unit in the University
The unit responsible for promoting and managing university-community collaborations could be located in the community (in government, in a foundation, as a free-standing unit) or in the university. Because universities are accustomed to controlling every aspect of their activities, it may never have occurred to a university that a unit in which it is a major player might not be housed within its organizational structure.

But from the community's standpoint, there may be several disadvantages to having such a unit located in the university. If the community distrusts the university, perceives it as arrogant, and worries that it will attempt to dominate and control the collaboration, locating the unit in the university may symbolize, and perhaps contribute to fulfilling, all of these fears. Moreover, the university is likely to be a large bureaucracy, and as such it imposes bureaucratic encumbrances on letting contracts, hiring staff, grant management services, and accounting for funds—functions that the community requires but may perform at much faster speeds than do many universities.

Conversely, we believe that such a unit should be located in the university. For one thing, the university can function as an unaligned, independent manager of collaborations. But to do so, the unit should not be administratively housed within any school or department and should be directed by both academics and community personnel (see below).

Second, the university brings some measure of prestige to the collaboration, which may be especially useful when applying for external funds to support a collaborative project. Although the community may criticize "those eggheads" at the university for being obfuscatory and arrogant, at least some community-service agency directors, legislators, and funding officers nevertheless regard the university as an honest and dependable entity and faculty as respectable sources of knowledge and expertise. In such cases, applications for funding may be viewed more favorably when the university is the lead organization. Of course, other funders may perceive the university as relatively rich and a bureaucratic nightmare and faculty as irrelevant. They are likely to view applications from the university less favorably than those from the community.

Finally, the university is an established institution, and while it may function slowly and sometimes with what seems like unnecessary bureaucracy, it is set up to let contracts, account for funds, provide legal services if necessary, loan money (i.e., set up an account and permit spending upon notification but not necessarily payment of a grant award), provide publicity, arrange for space, contribute computer and Internet services, and provide a library. It is also an established legal entity, and funders feel comfortable having it handle their money.

Manage a Partnership with a Partnership

A unit devoted to forging university-community partnerships should be codirected by a representative from academics and from the community.

A partnership means that all the partners have rights and responsibilities and each plays a necessary but not sufficient role in an activity that none could accomplish without the others. It seems reasonable, then, that the unit promoting such partnerships also should be administered by a university-community partnership, for example, codirectors, one representing academics and the other the community.

Such a codirectorship has more than symbolic value. The university and community have very different values, methods of operation, criteria for success, goals, and reward systems (Groark & McCall, 1993, 1996), and it helps for the administrators of the university-community unit themselves to live this collaboration inside the unit. In a real sense, each codirector represents a major party to every collaboration, and each needs to learn and understand the differences between academics and community professionals.

In addition, the codirectors are responsible for recruiting the support and participation of academic and the community professionals, respectively, and having both an academic and a community codirector, each of whom is a respected and trusted representative of his or her respective constituency, helps enormously to break down skepticism, establish trust and confidence, and bring crucial players to the table from the beginning.

But such an administrative marriage will not be easy, especially for the codirector who represents the community if the unit is housed in the university (the reverse might be true if the unit were located in the community). The community codirector is likely to be viewed as having different status within the university than the academic codirector, who presumably comes to the position with substantial traditional academic credits (which, incidentally, may or may not be directly relevant to this new task). While it is assumed that the community codirector has similar credits on the community's value system, he or she may not be appreciated by the university to the same extent, because such credits are likely not valued as much by the academy. Further, the natural and reasonable practice for the codirectors to have a division of labor in which the community codirector tends to deal with the community and the academic codirector with the university inadvertently can maintain the perception of inequality. Therefore, both codirectors should insist on being present at major meetings with university and community leaders to convey that they are indeed codirectors of equal status and that the unit itself always represents a university-community partnership.

The Unit Needs Core Funding

While it seems obvious that such a unit needs core funding to support its basic operation, a facilitative unit is different from a research center or agency and has a special need for core funding. Unfortunately, core funding is difficult to obtain, even by units that otherwise raise millions of dollars in special project funds. In the case of the Office of Child Development, "core funding" pays for the core program of activities described above and underwrites the salaries of major staff people.

Both universities and communities have difficulty with core funding. Many university centers are simply administrative collections of faculty members, whose salaries are paid by schools and departments and who raise funds to support their own scholarly activities. Such a unit does not need much additional core support. Other university units, such as large research centers, do have their own buildings and pay for support staff and portions of faculty salaries, but it is assumed (and often monitored) that the grants obtained by those faculty members will offset such costs through direct and indirect allocations. From the community's standpoint, most private service agencies need but never receive core support—they may live from year to year on allocations from the city, county, or foundations. Why should this university-community unit be any different?

A case must be made to both the university and the community that such a unit *is* different. For one thing, forging collaborations takes time and energy. It needs full-time nurturance by highly respected senior individuals—we have rarely seen it flower when the principle organizers are part-time or are junior faculty or professionals. Second, forging collaborative groups is an activity that cannot be reimbursed retrospectively by a special project grant obtained to support the resulting activity. Furthermore, not all planned collaborative projects come to fruition. Third, such a unit is likely to sponsor a variety of core activities (see above) that help create an identity, a point of contact, and an atmosphere and facility within which collaborations can be fostered and nurtured. Such activities require personnel and nonpersonnel support. Fourth, the unit should not compete for grants with its faculty and community constituencies, so it may have a more limited set of funding opportunities to pursue than might otherwise be the case.

Finally, such a unit may well become a regional resource that provides management services, helps faculty and community professionals and policymakers write grants, conducts needs assessments and policy studies, performs program evaluations, and does a variety of other activities that often must be executed on exceedingly short notice and require competent, experienced personnel. The salaries for such personnel must be underwritten by some form of core support so that they have a modicum of security and so that portions of their time that are not allocated to specific project grants can be supported by the core. For example, Requests for Proposals for collaborative services, in contrast to most research RFPs, may allow only three to four weeks in which to submit an application, and this time may be shortened by political and administrative processes in the community and university. Similarly, needs assessments and program evaluations may need to start immediately. Consequently, there literally may not be the three to five or more weeks required to hire new personnel to write grants or execute the project. Not only must a cadre of staff be maintained to conduct these activities, they must be able to be reassigned to projects on a moment's notice. Therefore, some level of core support of a dependable nature is required, preferably with mechanisms that allow the unit to draw on support as needed but to save that support and carry it over from year to year when it is not.

The Implications of True Partnerships

Academics are not accustomed to partnerships. Traditional scholastic training emphasizes the total control and responsibility of the scholar for identifying and defining the question, applying for money, executing the project, analyzing the results, drawing the conclusions, writing the paper, and publishing it (McCall et al., in press). Academics do not even collaborate with each other very often, let alone collaborate with community agencies, policymakers, and funders in a true partnership in which each collaborator potentially has an equal say about each major aspect of a project. Similarly, university administrators, who may have been professionally born, raised, and rewarded within the traditional academic system, similarly may be unaccustomed to the administrative implications of a true university-community partnership.

Fundamentally, such partnerships are a bit like a marriage, not of two, but of many people. The problem, perhaps especially for academics, is sharing control, of giving up some hallowed principle of scientific rigor or management authority to obtain an end that is valued and that could not be obtained otherwise. Like a marriage, it is the day-to-day living together that is difficult, and one must be prepared to compromise, to give up some things, and to have a commitment to making the collaboration work in the face of the inevitable frustrations, unintended insults, and compromises that will likely occur.

Scholarly Rigor

Disciplines differ in their scholastic standards and the extent to which those standards accommodate to working in society. Social workers and educators, for example, have long been accustomed to the demands and limitations that working in the community may require, whereas many psychologists are not. In the latter case, the training and experience of many psychologists in performing a research project is completely different from that which will be required when working in the community. This is true even when performing a program evaluation of a community-based intervention or service, one of the more traditional academic activities that a university-community collaborative unit might foster. The details of these differences are discussed extensively in McCall et al. (in press). Basically, the academic must share some control over nearly every aspect of the project, and the criterion must be to obtain the best available, rather than the scientifically ideal, information.

Partnerships with Funders

Many of the activities, including the core operation of the university-community unit, are likely to be funded by community foundations and local and state governmental agencies and policymakers. Not only do such funders often operate differently from federal granting agencies, but the very nature of a university-community collaborative unit invites them to be a major player at every stage. For example, they may want to approve the choice of the directors of the unit, and later they may suggest particular projects and which people or agencies should be involved and/or which should not. They may design a project themselves and then call the unit to implement it. A project may be crafted on the telephone, and a check arrives in the mail to support it without an application. Or funds may be added to an existing grant for this special activity without any serious written description of what is to be done with them. Both of these situations are troubling to bureaucrats who are responsible for monitoring compliance with grant and contract agreements. Another problem for the unit may be that some projects desired by local policymakers and funders are not what the unit would like or has time to do. But because the funders cooperate in providing local matching money for some federal projects and because they support the core program, it is not in the unit's best interest to refuse.

In addition, the manner in which community funding is decided and the speed that may be expected are very different from typical investigator-initiated federal research funding. Grant applications may not be sent out by funders for review by "experts"; decisions may be made by a foundation project officer alone (subject to Board approval). Applications submitted by community agencies to support services are often surprising to academics. They may contain unsupported claims for the potential benefits of such services; some provide little rationale for why a particular service should achieve a particular result; the actual services to be delivered may be described in much less detail than academics expect; and, except for the agency director, the personnel who will enact the program may not be named. Instead, local funders often sit on many advisory boards, meet regularly with each other and with agency directors, and know the agencies and personnel that they fund. They are aware that particular models of services and generic service strategies are less important than the people who deliver them, so it makes perfect sense to base funding decisions on personal knowledge of a given agency and its personnel.

On that basis, a university-community collaborative agency needs to take steps to develop relationships with local policymakers and funders, place them on an advisory board to the unit, discuss potential projects with them, and work collaboratively with them on projects of their initiation as well as those created by the university. Indeed, one possible role for the university-community collaborative unit is to act, formally or informally, as a resource center for policymakers and funders, in which the unit provides background information for funding and policy decisions, brokers program evaluations between funders and service programs, and conducts needs assessments (see Bickel, 1995, for a description of one such relationship).

The major implication of a partnership arrangement with local funders and policymakers is that the university and its faculty participants will lose some degree of independence and control. University administrators may balk at giving a funder a say in hiring a university employee, dictating the terms of a project, constantly being at the table when the project is designed and implemented, and possibly changing its work scope after the contract has been let. But in part, this is what a partnership with community agencies and policymakers implies. At the same time, while community services and policy making are often conducted in a crisis, seat-of-the-pants manner, no one, policymaker or faculty member, seriously believes this is the best or desired style. Universities and faculty are information-driven, contemplative, analytic, conceptual, and planful by professional nature, and while they must understand the different circumstances under which agencies and policymakers operate, they can and should contribute these dispositions to the system of services and the policy planning process.

The Various Roles the Unit Plays in a Project

The university-community unit may play a great variety of different roles from one project to the next. For example, it may manage the grant application but not be part of the project once it is funded; the money may go to community agencies directly, which in turn subcontract with the university-community unit for management services; all of the money may come to the unit, but most of it is subcontracted to a variety of community agencies; or the unit may be asked to manage a planning and implementation year, but then have little role in the project thereafter. Viewed from the perspective of traditional university research administration, the unit may be criticized for raising a great deal of money, most of which goes out the door to other agencies. Further, the unit could be exceedingly successful as a facilitator of grants for other people, including faculty, but those sums do not show up on the unit's bottom line in the university's cost-benefit accounting system.

The unit and the university need to understand that the activities of such an enterprise are likely to be administratively, scholastically, and financially different and more complicated than those of a traditional research center, for example, and the parties need to agree on what types of services the university will provide and what the performance criteria will be for the unit. Otherwise the unit is likely to be perceived as a thorn in the side of the administration and the university bureaucracy. There is no substitute for a "patron senior administrator" who understands these needs and issues, who is committed to the unit and its function, and who will support the unit politically.

The Financial and Administrative Demands Will Be Difficult

Partnerships, by definition, mean that two or more parties will play important roles in a given project, and thus they are likely to share funds provided by grants and contracts. Therefore, funded projects are likely to have more and more complicated subcontracts with institutions outside the university than is typically the case for traditional research grants. In short, instead of hiring graduate students to be the assistants for a project, community agencies are likely to deliver the interventions and services as well as collect evaluation data (see McCall et al., in press). In contrast to graduate students, however, agencies need contracts and grant payments, and they need them fast, because many are not able to float the project a loan for two to six months while the university prepares such contracts in advance of the first subcontract payment. Further, when a graduate student does not perform well, it is relatively easy to "transfer" him or her to a teaching assistantship or other means of support. But when an agency does not perform, a funded contract must be broken, raising legal, financial, and political issues of potentially substantial proportions.

One solution to the need for having contracts issued rapidly so that initial payments can be made promptly is to generate a stock contract with options that are selected to tailor the contract to each particular circumstance. The Office of Child Development maintains a stock contract for conducting program evaluations with community agencies that covers major issues of ownership of data, confidentiality arrangements, right to publicize results, right to make scholarly presentations and publications, payment schedules, deliverables, recourse, etc. The generic contract has been approved in advance by the university legal counsel and the Office of Research, so that all that needs to be done is to select the appropriate options in consultation with the contractor. The university can approve the contract in one to two days. A similar standard contract may be used by the county, which could be examined once by the university, tailored to meet university needs, and then only the particulars specified and approved at the time of letting the contract.

Another issue that partnerships may create is the requirement by county agencies that employees funded by the county conform to the county's personnel system, including pay scales and benefit programs. This requirement can exist even though the county gives a contract to the university, which in turn hires the staff as its employees. Merging the pay scales and benefit programs of two independently created personnel systems can be challenging at best. For example, what happens when the county gives raises or pays year-end bonuses, but the university does not? And what happens when the unit wants to hire a former community member at the same position classification and with a higher salary than the university employee who will be his or her supervisor?

These problems may not be unique, but solving them requires an understanding and commitment by the university that these issues are likely to be more frequently encountered by such a university-community endeavor. They will take more than the usual relationships between the unit and the university administration to solve, and it helps if they are expected early on as inherent in the enterprise.

An Uncertain Agenda

In the extreme, the university-community unit may have no specific programmic agenda. Instead, it may have a general mission and principles of operation (see tables 10.1 and 10.2), it offers a structure and a process that can be used for any particular project, and it operates predominately in a responsive, rather than a proactive, mode. The rationale may be that the unit provides personnel, support services, and administrative and management capabilities that stand ready when a university-community need is identified, institutions and other individuals are available to do the job, and funds can be applied for or are in hand. When these three criteria are met, the unit acts. Such an approach guarantees the appropriateness and timeliness of the unit's activities and provides it with the flexibility that may be necessary to survive and flourish during the changing priorities and funding patterns likely to characterize the next few years.

But while we readily accept such a mode of operation in the university's office of research, the library, and the computer center, academics typically demand an agenda and an excruciatingly detailed plan of activities covering several years from its academic units and faculty. Both the university and the community may be willing to set up such a unit, but they want to know in advance what it is actually going to do, not what it has the promise of doing. Even after nearly ten years of operation and a track record of substantial proportions, the university administrators and even some ardent community supporters of the Office of Child Development do not really understand this responsive operational approach.

In part, this criticism also represents a failure to completely understand the partnership concept and the way the community often operates. First, collaborative projects have the participants identify and define the project as well as fund and operate it. It would be presumptuous and antithetical to the partnership philosophy for the unit to have an agenda that is not planned collaboratively. Second, while it is possible, even desirable, for the unit to lead strategic-planning groups that do collaboratively identify an agenda and a strategic plan, much of what happens in community human services and policy making is not so planful. Programs often represent a response to a crisis, a response to state or federal regulations or funding initiatives, or a response to a given political initiative. The community, in short, is often less planful than academics have traditionally been and than it should be, because they work in a system in which other individuals and institutions play a greater role in determining the activities that transpire. Nevertheless, the problem for the unit is selling itself to funders, especially initially, when it cannot necessarily specify the main projects that it will undertake in the course of three to five years. To say that the unit will "facilitate university-community collaborative projects" is often not sufficient without being able to specify what those projects will be. The unit needs one or more initial projects that will attract core funding, and then it can try to "go with the flow."

The Unit Will Challenge Traditional Academic Values and Performance Criteria
Publications
The traditional academic value system rewards faculty for conducting scholarly activities that produce highly generalizable results (i.e., basic research)

that are communicated to other academic colleagues in scholarly, refereed journals. It is unlikely, however, that such activities will be the primary products of a university-community collaborative unit, because the nature of the scholarly and other activities of the unit is likely to be more applied than basic; the results of its activities are more likely to be specific to particular agencies, programs, and localities than to produce generalizable principles; and the audience for its products and services is likely to include agency directors and governing boards, local funders and policymakers, and even the media and parents.

For example, the Office of Child Development issues a written report, publishes a paper, or makes a professional presentation every week on the average, but few of these represent publications in traditional refereed journals. Instead, Office staff conduct needs assessments and policy studies for state and county governments and local funders; write special reports and briefing papers that are published in a newsletter and that are sent to legislators, service professionals, and funders in the area; conduct evaluations of service programs that produce reports that go to the agency and sometimes their funders; produce and distribute a *Kids Count* compilation of health, education, and welfare indicators for the metropolitan regions and counties of the state; and are the sources or authors of articles in local newspapers or for stories on the electronic media. Staff do publish in scholarly books and journals, but this represents a small segment of our productivity and only one of our intended audiences.

The university administration, including most of the relevant deans, must accept that the nature of the products of such a unit and the audiences to which they are directed will be different and much broader than the traditional academic value system dictates (McCall, 1996). In many respects, however, this is the new scholarship for different and expanded audiences, and many administrators recognize this is the direction of the future. But while the support of top-level administrators is crucial, it may not be sufficient to motivate junior faculty to participate in the unit. Departmental-level tenure review committees consist of individuals who have track records of accomplishment on the traditional criteria, and they may be slow to embrace new audiences, different communication modalities, and diverse criteria of excellence and utility.

Critics may assume that the products of the unit are of less quality and contribute less to knowledge than traditional academic scholarly articles (McCall, 1996). Even within academic publishing, applied research is frequently assumed to be of less scholastic quality than basic research, so it is not unreasonable to suppose that traditional academics will assume that reports to the State Department of Welfare, evaluations of specific service programs, literature reviews of four printed pages written for service professionals or the media, or an op-ed newspaper piece are of less academic quality.

Some products may not be distributed or even published. Program evaluations, for example, may be contracted for by the service agency, which understandably wants to own and control the report, lest it be negative and threaten the very existence of the agency. Federal government agencies conducting large demonstration projects may embargo publication of local analyses of data until the national evaluation is reported to Congress.

We, of course, do not agree that such products are necessarily of inferior quality (McCall, 1996). Reports can be as rigorous and scholarly as basic research, and they should be so because they may have more influence than traditional scholarly reports. For example, our special reports and newspaper articles are read by more people and our reports to policymakers have a greater influence on the funding and quality of services than a career's worth of academic publishing.

Nonrefereed publications can be of high quality, but they may not be, and few people will know. So the unit should take steps to deal with the quality and influence issues by having its products reviewed by an external committee, perhaps including faculty at the university or from across the county as well as representatives of the community and other constituencies of the unit, who can judge their quality and utility. Perhaps "valid" or "portfolio assessments" should come to higher as well as to primary and secondary education.

Indirect Costs

Indirect costs, often part of the "benefits" universities use to assess the cost-benefit of their units, can be another source of friction between the unit and traditional academic administrators. Many local foundations, state and county governments, and other typical funders of projects that a university-community unit is likely to manage will not pay the full federally audited indirect-cost rate of the university. Indeed, many such funders will pay no indirect costs at all. The Office of Child Development, for example, has a $5.1 million annual budget, but the indirect payments generated by these grants and contracts amount to only 5% of the total. The university may decide on this basis that the unit is a losing proposition and that the university simply cannot afford it.

While a case can be made for such a proposition, an argument can also be forged that the unit's indirect cost revenue should be compared to its actual cost to the university rather than as a percentage of its grant and contract income. It may be that the amount of indirect cost dollars (not its rate) is sufficient to pay for the university's investment of salaries, space, research accounting and administration, and other indirect services that the unit actually uses. Further, more than most university units, such a university-community center might join the university in searching for new ways to cover indirect costs. For example, community agencies may not really understand that their projects actually use substantial fiscal and administrative services that are real costs to the university and should be paid out of project grants. In addition, human-service funders may pay no indirect costs but be accustomed to paying for space rental, furniture, utilities, and accounting and legal services, for example, as direct costs. The university and such funders may need to consider an arrangement for the funder to be able to make "direct-cost payments" for what the university usually considers "indirect-cost items."

Finally, not every university tub will be able to float on its own bottom, and a university-community facilitative unit might be viewed as being more similar to a decentralized office of research or university computer center than to a typical academic research center. In addition, some disciplines simply do not have access to funds that pay full indirect costs, and university administrators must decide on the purpose of the university, what units are necessary to attain that purpose, and how to pay for them.

Training Programs

The university-community unit may promote interdisciplinary applied training programs, and such training regimens may bring their own challenges to the academic status quo (McCall et al., in press). For example, professionals destined to work in human services and in early-childhood services should probably be trained substantially in social work, early education, public health, clinical psychology, elementary pediatrics, nonprofit management, law, *and* special education. If such an interdisciplinary curriculum were indeed designed, such students may be the best educated and most prepared to deal with the diverse facets of their subsequent employment. At the same time, they may not be employable unless they have satisfied the requirements to be credentialed in social work, education, etc. While certificate programs can be constructed to provide interdisciplinary educational experiences without challenging current degree and credentialing systems, students may be required to attend more courses and take longer to graduate than is typical, precisely at a historical time in which many students cannot afford more education.

Again, administrators must be prepared to deal with innovations in curricula and credentialing, but their support alone may not be sufficient. Individual faculty members may resist having to teach and prepare for new courses and new student audiences, and they may have marked disciplinary prejudices about their own students receiving substantial training in other disciplines that they regard as "academically inferior." However, as indicated above, the Office's core program has helped to create a climate that is conducive to fostering interdisciplinary training programs, and the Office has operated such programs and courses for eight years.

Conclusion

We suspect that university-community outreach or partnerships are a wave of the future. But no convoy of change travels a smooth road; there will be bumps and challenges. Nevertheless, the university and community need each other—universities must revise their contract with society and broaden the audiences for their educational and scholarly activities (McCall, 1996), and communities need to be more planful, informed, and creative in their services and policies for children and families and monitor such services to make them more effective and efficient. Together, as true partners, these and many more goals can be attained that will contribute to the welfare of children, youth, and families in ways that otherwise would not be possible.

References

Bickel, W. E. (1995). Why foundations use evaluation: The case of a private foundation-university evaluation partnership. Unpublished manuscript, University of Pittsburgh.

Bok, D. (1992). Reclaiming the public trust. *Change*, 13–19.

Boyer, E. L. (1990). *Scholarship reconsidered*. Princeton, NJ: The Carnegie Foundation for the Advancement of Teaching.

———. (1994, March 9). Creating the new American college (Point of View column). *The Chronicle of Higher Education* (p. A48).

Byerly, R. Jr., & Piekle, R. A. Jr. (1995). The changing ecology of United States science. *Science, 269*, 1531–1532.

Corson, J. J. (1968). Public service and higher education: Compatibility or conflict? In C. G. Dobbins and C. Lee (Eds.), *Whose goals for American higher education?* (pp. 83–90). Washington, DC: American Council on Education.

Groark, C. J., & McCall, R. B. (1993, Spring). Building mutually beneficial collaborations between researchers and community service professionals. *Newsletter of the Society for Research in Child Development*, 6–14.

———. (1996). Building successful university-community human service agency collaborations. In C. B. Fisher, J. P. Murray, and I. E. Sigel (Eds.), *Applied developmental science: Graduate training for diverse disciplines and educational settings*. Norwood, NJ: Ablex.

Johnson, D. M., & Bell, D. A., (Eds.). (1995). *Metropolitan universities: An emerging trend in American higher education.* Denton, TX: University of North Texas Press.

Lerner, R. M., Miller, J. R., Knott, J. H., Corey, K. E., Bynum, T. S., Hoopfer, L. C., McKinney, M. H., Abrams, L. A., Hula, R. C., & Terry, P. A. (1994). Integrating scholarship and outreach in human development research, policy, and service: A developmental contextual perspective. In D. L. Featherman, R. M. Lerner, & M. Perlmutter (Eds.), *Life-span development and behavior* (Vol. 12, pp. 249–273). Hillsdale, NJ: Erlbaum.

Lerner, R. M., Miller, J. R., & Ostrom, C. W. (1995, Spring). Integrative knowledge, accountability, access, and the American university of the twenty-first century: A family and consumer sciences vision of the future of higher education. *Kappa Omicron Nu FORUM, 8* (1), 11–27.

Lynton, E. A., & Elman, S. E. (1987). *New priorities for the university: Meeting society's needs for applied knowledge and competent individuals.* San Francisco: Jossey-Bass.

McCall, R. B. (1990a, Spring). The University of Pittsburgh Office of Child Development: An experiment in interdisciplinary, applied, and policy programming. *Newsletter of the Society for Research in Child Development,* 14–15.

———. (1990b). Promoting interdisciplinary and faculty-service professional relations. *American Psychologist, 45,* 1319–1324.

———. (1995). Birds of a feather: Administrative choices and issues in creating a specialized applied, multidisciplinary, developmental unit. In C. B. Fisher, J. P. Murray, and I. E. Sigel (Eds.), *Applied developmental science: Graduate training for diverse disciplines and educational settings.* Norwood, NJ: Ablex.

———. (1996). The concept and practice of education, research, and public service in university psychology departments. *American Psychologist, 16,* 609–628.

McCall, R. B., Green, B. L., Strauss, M. S., & Groark, C. J. (in press). Issues in community-based research and program evaluation. In I. E. Sigel and K. A. Renninger (Eds.), *Handbook of child psychology, Vol. 4* (5th ed.). New York: Wiley.

McCall, R. B., Groark. C. J., Strauss, M. S., & Johnson, C. J. (1995). An experiment in promoting interdisciplinary applied human development: The University of Pittsburgh model. *Journal of Applied Developmental Psychology, 16,* 593–612.

Millard, R. M. (1991). *Today's myths and tomorrow's realities: Overcoming obstacles to academic leadership in the twenty-first century.* San Francisco: Jossey-Bass.

Perkins, J. A. (1966). *The university in transition.* Princeton, NJ: Princeton University Press.

Whiting, A. N. (1968). A proposal for colleges of applied sciences and public service. In C. G. Dobbins and C. Lee (Eds.), *Whose goals for American higher education?* (pp. 94–97). Washington, DC: American Council on Education.

Chapter 11
Making University and Community Collaborations Work

Christine M. Todd   *Aaron T. Ebata*
University of Georgia   *University of Illinois at Urbana-Champaign*

Robert Hughes, Jr.
The Ohio State University

By any measure, American higher education is under attack. Colleges and universities are being criticized for inattention to teaching, overemphasis on research that is perceived to be irrelevant and costly, and a failure to address the pressing needs of local communities (Grossman & Leroux, 1996). In reaction to these attacks, institutions of higher learning are re-examining their missions. Undergraduate teaching is being emphasized and there are attempts to "reconnect" institutions of higher learning with the general public through increased attention to outreach (Aiken & Faulkner, 1995; Boyer, 1990).

Despite the rhetoric evident within higher education, real change within many institutions has been slow. The lack of progress, especially in developing outreach activities, stems in part from how faculty are trained and rewarded. The first step toward developing an academy more responsive to the concerns of local citizens must therefore be a reconceptualization of the meaning of scholarship to include outreach activities and the development of new methods for evaluating outreach scholarship (Bonnen, 1986; Boyer, 1990; Lerner et al., 1994).

Equally important, however, is understanding the nature of the collaborative process itself. Collaborations can take many forms and are affected both by the context in which the collaboration exists and the process skills evident among the collaborators (Bergstrom, Clark, Hogue, Perkins, & Slinski, 1995). The purpose of this paper is to articulate some of the factors we have found to be particularly important to consider in

Projects discussed in this paper were funded by grants from the W. K. Kellogg Foundation and the Agricultural Experiment Station, College of Agricultural, Consumer and Environmental Sciences, University of Illinois at Urbana-Champaign, Project # IL-60-0307.

developing university-community collaborations. We begin by briefly describing some of the outreach activities that have been undertaken by the Department of Human and Community Development at the University of Illinois. Next we present an ecological model of collaboration that highlights the complexity of university-community partnerships and we consider the effect of selected contextual and process variables in developing outreach initiatives. We end with a discussion of some of the benefits and challenges resulting from university-community partnerships.

Outreach Initiatives at the University of Illinois

As a land-grant institution, the University of Illinois has responsibility to uphold the three-fold mission of land-grant universities: teaching, research, and public service. While public service activities are an important part of many University departments, some of the most visible outreach programs of the University are provided by the Cooperative Extension Service, which is comprised of extension faculty and field staff aligned with each department in the College of Agricultural, Consumer, and Environmental Sciences.

Faculty within the Department of Human and Community Development have primarily resident or extension appointments. Faculty with extension appointments have as their major responsibility conducting outreach activities, typically directed toward children, youth, families, professionals, and communities. Extension faculty also develop a program of applied research, and contribute to the teaching mission by advising graduate students, supervising student internships, and occasionally teaching university courses. Faculty with resident appointments contribute primarily to the on-campus teaching mission and conduct basic and applied research. Many of the resident faculty have applied interests and therefore also contribute to the outreach mission of the university by offering inservice opportunities for extension field staff, supervising student internships, conducting applied research in local communities, and providing the results of their basic and applied research to the general public. Thus, most faculty contribute to all three missions of the department, at least to some extent.

Extension activities take many different forms. Some are done through collaborations between extension faculty and local, regional, state, or national agencies and organizations. The majority of Extension activities, however, are conducted by teams of faculty and Extension field staff (academic professionals with primarily masters' degrees who are housed in county and regional offices). The teams are organized around broad themes in human functioning (e.g., family life, youth development, youth risk prevention, family and consumer economics, nutrition and wellness), community and economic development (e.g., community leadership and volunteerism, small-business management), agriculture (e.g., animal systems, crop systems), and the environment (e.g., natural resource management).

Every four years, Extension field staff, working in cooperation with local volunteer Extension councils, conduct thorough needs assessments to determine the issues of concern in each Illinois county. Extension faculty contribute to this process by providing local councils with overviews of state and national trends and research updates on relevant issues. Based on the results of the local needs assessments, four-year plans of work are developed at the local, regional, and state levels to address issues of primary concern to Illinois citizens.

Although it is not possible to convey the full range of public service activities undertaken by the Department of Human and Community Development, it is useful to present three major initiatives that have been conducted.

Child Care Impact Project

The Child Care Impact project represents a ten-year collaboration involving University faculty and Extension field staff with over twenty local and state agencies concerned with child care. The purpose of this collaboration has been to develop an integrated child-care system and improve the availability, accessibility, and quality of child care in Illinois. Toward this end, faculty and Extension field staff aligned with the Department of Human and Community Development have: (1) developed training materials and curricula and provided professional development courses and workshops for over 5,000 Illinois child-care providers; (2) conducted school-age child-care needs assessments (Riley, 1992) involving over 10,000 families in eighty-two schools, leading to the establishment of new school-age child-care programs; and (3) collaborated in the development of a statewide child-care resource and referral service, which in 1995 maintained a database of 13,345 child-care businesses with capacity for 286,000 Illinois children, assisted 36,613 parents in locating care, provided training to child-care professionals (with over 29,500 training contacts in one year), issued reports on child-care supply to local employers and agencies, and recruited 1,334 new child-care businesses in areas of need. Faculty also provided training and technical assistance to electronically connect the child-care agencies throughout the state via the Internet and to help the child-care resource and referral system analyze child-care supply and demand issues.

Illinois Youth and Family Project

The Illinois Youth and Families Project, which is based on the Teen Assessment Program developed by Small (1995a, 1996), involves collaborations among faculty, students, and Extension field staff from the university and representatives from local communities who are interested in identifying and addressing local youth concerns. Extension field staff serve as liaisons between the University and schools, agencies, or coalitions interested in identifying community concerns related to youth. University faculty and students work with Extension field staff to define the issues, often through conducting a community survey. Graduate students and faculty at the University provide technical support in developing the survey instrument, analyzing the data, and communicating the results to the community via a technical report. Then, the data provided by the survey are used by the local community group to develop a plan of action to address specific concerns. At this point, the involvement of campus-level faculty and students ends, but Extension field staff continue as part of the local community committee to facilitate implementation of the plan of action. This basic procedure has been utilized in a number of Illinois communities to better understand and address the needs of youth. For example, the process was used to identify the needs of youth and families whose homes were destroyed by the midwest flood of 1993 (Ebata, 1995).

The Nation of Tomorrow

The Nation of Tomorrow was a five-year collaborative project between the Chicago and Urbana-Champaign campuses of the University and four schools in inner-city Chicago neighborhoods (Nucci et al., 1990). The initiative was funded by a $3.6 million dollar grant from the W. K. Kellogg Foundation. The project, which involved the Colleges of Education, Nursing, and Social Work at the Chicago campus, and units now in the Department of Human and Community Development on the Urbana-Champaign campus, was developed to improve the educational achievement, health, and social skills of inner-city youth attending one elementary school in each of four high-risk Chicago communities. In recognition of the ecological perspective guiding the project, an attempt was made to affect youth development not only directly, but also indirectly, through programming efforts directed toward parents, child-care professionals, teachers, and community agencies. Extension faculty in the Department of Human and Community Development were responsible for coordinating the "Family Ties" component of the project, which focused on parent education, child-care, and youth activities in each of the four communities. These faculty worked in collaboration with a local extension educator, who supervised a staff of eight to ten paraprofessionals who were based in the school in each community. These paraprofessional staff worked with staff from other components of the project, the schools, and community agency personnel and volunteers to develop and implement specific activities.

Our experiences in these and other outreach initiatives have led us to believe that university-community collaborations are essential to the future of higher education. However, such collaborations are also difficult and require special skills. In our journey from basic researchers to applied scholars and community collaborators, we have learned a great deal about what it takes to promote effective university-community collaborations. In the next section, we reflect on our experiences and outline factors that have fostered or hindered effective university-community partnerships.

An Ecological Framework for Collaboration

Although we tend to think of collaborations as interactions between individuals, in fact, collaborations actually represent the interplay between systems. This perspective parallels recent shifts in the literature on leadership away from an emphasis on "heroic" forms of leadership, which typically focus on the leadership characteristics of individuals, to a "postheroic" vision of leadership as a group-level function that can be shared by many individuals and institutions (Sandmann & Vandenberg, 1995).

Figure 11.1 illustrates a contextual model of a simple university-community collaboration, derived from Bronfenbrenner's ecological framework (1979, 1986) and Lerner's theory of developmental contextualism (Lerner & Kauffman, 1985; Lerner et al., 1994). This model represents a collaboration between a single faculty member and one representative from the community. An example of such a collaboration would be a partnership between a faculty member and a teacher to develop a parent involvement program for the school. These individuals also are affected by the immediate environments in which each works—a university department for most faculty members, and a school for most teachers. At the next level, the department is influenced by its larger institutional climate and the school is influenced by its membership in a school district. The uni-

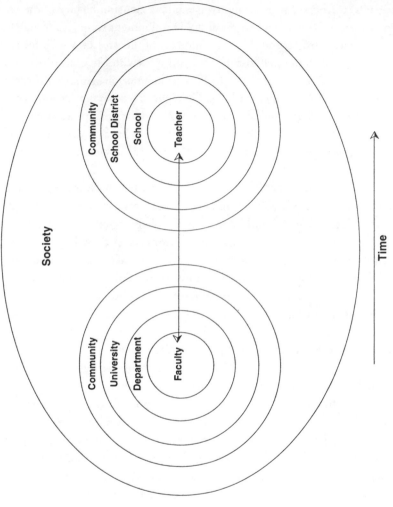

Figure 11.1. A model for collaboration between two systems.

versity as a whole and the school system are, in turn, influenced by the communities in which they reside, which may or may not be the same. Lastly, each of these systems is influenced by the values, beliefs, and social trends in the society at large.

There are three critical aspects of this contextual model of collaboration: (1) the number of systems involved in the collaboration; (2) the level(s) within each system that are involved; and (3) the effect of time on the collaborative process.

Number of Systems Involved

As outlined in figure 11.1, the most basic collaboration would involve interplay between only two systems. In our experience, however, university-community collaborations typically must involve many more systems in order to address the complexity of problems facing children, youth and families. As the number of systems involved in the partnership increases, so does the complexity of developing a shared vision and maintaining communication between the various systems. Each system will approach issues in a different way and may prefer slightly different goals or methods for achieving those goals (Kagan & Neville, 1993). This is one reason why collaborations involving multiple systems require so much time (McHale et al., 1996).

Involvement of Levels within Systems

Collaborations also can involve individuals from many different levels within each of the systems that contribute to the partnership. Involving individuals from multiple levels within each system is critical when the goal of the collaboration is to change entire systems. For example, institutionalizing a parent involvement program within a school district is likely to require the efforts not only of teachers, but also principals and the school district. However, since individuals at various levels may have different goals for the project or hold different criteria for success, it can also take longer to create a shared vision when multiple levels are represented.

It is essential to include stakeholders from those levels within organizations that have a direct investment in achieving the specific goals of the collaboration. For example, if the goal is to effect change within a particular school, the collaboration should include individuals and groups that are invested in and able to promote change within that particular site (e.g., parents, students, school staff and administrators, and representatives from the school district and agencies with investment in that *particular* school).

In contrast, if the goal is to effect change at the community level, one must draw together individuals with interests in and the ability to effect community-wide change (e.g., school superintendents, city government officials, and agency members with community-wide authority).

We have been part of several collaborations that have failed because the collaborators did not agree on the level at which the intervention should occur. For example, we have found it very difficult to effect community-level changes working from within a site-based program, such as a single school. Site-level collaborators tend to be primarily invested in the needs of the particular children and families that they serve. They sometimes perceive attempts to work at a community-wide level as taking resources away from their site and clientele. In contrast, individuals with community-wide interests are seldom content with programs focused on a single site, since they are primarily interested in community-wide changes. Likewise, some participants in community-university collaborations may be interested in increasing the university system's responsiveness to the community. Achieving this goal is likely to require the involvement of university administrators, who control both resources and the reward structure for outreach initiatives. It is important that collaborators carefully define the level at which change is desired and include stakeholders in the collaboration who are able to effect change at that level.

The Effect of Time

Collaborations occur over time and are affected by both historical events and events that occur during the collaboration process. Prior experience with the institutions represented in the collaboration may facilitate or hinder development of the collaboration. For example, in the Nation of Tomorrow project, inner-city residents initially held negative perceptions of the University as an institution that continually took knowledge from the community through its programs of research without giving anything back in return. These views slowed our early outreach efforts in these communities.

Collaborations are also affected by the passing of time—both in terms of the changing contexts in which each system exists and the experiences of the individual players in the collaboration itself. For example, our work on the Child Care Impact project has been facilitated over time by the increasing centrality of public service to the University mission and by the development of standardized contractual agreements between the University and state agencies. The collaboration has also grown easier over time as we have identified the unique strengths and resources of individuals and agencies and developed greater levels of trust among the partners. In contrast, public-policy changes at the federal level are causing stress in the project as the partners attempt to understand how their own organizations will be affected by welfare reform.

University-community collaborations are more likely to succeed when faculty and administrators understand the degree of complexity involved in particular outreach initiatives. Understanding the collaboration structure increases the likelihood that all relevant systems and appropriate levels within those systems will be included in the partnership, thus increasing the likelihood of a successful outcome. Moreover, careful consideration of the complexity involved will allow faculty to develop realistic time frames for each project and to consider what types of scholarly products are likely at each stage in the process. Finally, when the collaboration is not providing the intended results, understanding the structure can provide useful insights into how the collaboration may need to be modified to be more effective, and the time frame that might be involved for such modification to occur.

Factors Affecting University-Community Collaborations

Bergstrom et al. (1995) have suggested that collaborations are affected by the contexts in which the collaboration occurs and by process factors that depend on the knowledge and skills of the individuals in the partnership. In this section we discuss some of the contextual and process factors that uniquely affect university-community collaborations.

The Influence of Context

By considering the collaborative process within an ecological framework, it is clear that many different contexts can influence this process. In this section we highlight some of the contextual factors within the university and within communities that affect the long-term success of university-community collaborations.

University Context

Administrative Support. University-community collaborations are influenced by the institutional climate and resource base of the college or university involved. Strong administrative support is essential for developing successful collaborations. Department administrators set the tone for what is valued in their unit and they control resources, including the reward structure. It is therefore essential that academic units with outreach responsibilities be headed by scholars who understand how to nurture and evaluate outreach initiatives. Beginning faculty need a clear job description and guidelines for what constitutes good outreach scholarship. Some faculty may also need assistance in selecting appropriate outreach initiatives and identifying colleagues within the university and at other institutions who can serve as mentors. Becoming integrated into a national and international network of applied scholars is essential both for growth as a scholar and for achieving tenure and promotion. Providing adequate administrative support to outreach initiatives can be a challenge for departments that also have active basic research and teaching programs. To insure sufficient attention to outreach, the Department of Human and Community Development has created a departmental committee on outreach and has recommended the establishment of an Associate Head for Outreach.

Administrators at the university level also have a great effect on the willingness and ability of faculty to address pressing societal issues. Our own work at Illinois has been facilitated by recent actions of campus-level administrators. For example, "a commitment to outreach and partnerships" is included as one of seven priorities outlined in the strategic plan for our campus by the chancellor and provost (Aiken & Faulkner, 1995). The "Partnership Illinois Council" has been established to facilitate outreach initiatives throughout the university and encourage strong ties with our external constituencies. In addition, a document has been developed for faculty that outlines how to plan, document, and evaluate public-service activities in preparation for promotion and tenure (University of Illinois, 1993). Such actions by university leaders send a strong message to faculty and constituents alike that university-community collaborations will be valued and rewarded.

Institutional Infrastructure. Universities must also develop the infrastructure to support university-community collaborations. Just as there are enrollment procedures, a registration office, and classrooms to support teaching and laboratories, contract offices, and support staff to facilitate research, there need to personnel, budget procedures, and a physical infrastructure to support outreach activities. In our experience, most research universities provide insufficient institutional support for outreach initiatives. Space often is limited or inappropriate. For example, outreach activities may need field offices in community locations rather than on a central campus. Budget procedures are sometimes overly complex, and policies on how money can be spent may not be flexible enough to accommodate the needs of outreach initiatives. Personnel policies also can create difficulties for outreach projects. For example, standard job classifications may not include skills critical to the success of an outreach project, such as being bilingual.

On a positive note, the technological capacity of the University of Illinois has greatly enhanced our ability to conduct university-community collaborations. The teleconferencing system maintained and centrally funded by the Cooperative Extension Service enables faculty to hold planning meetings with partners anywhere in the country, and also has been used extensively for distance education. In addition, Extension offices throughout the state have been connected to the campus via the Internet, further increasing the link between the University and local communities. Currently, the University is working with local phone companies and organizations to increase Internet access in rural and inner-city areas and to train agency personnel and the general public on accessing the Internet. In addition, many units of the university provide educational resources to the general public via the World Wide Web.

The overall commitment of a university to outreach initiatives and the infrastructure of the university contribute greatly to the initiation and success of university-community partnerships. As McCall suggests, our constituents are interested in prompt follow-through and timely completion of projects (McCall, Groark, Strauss, & Johnson, 1995). This is only possible in a university climate that values public service and provides the resources needed to conduct effective collaborations.

Community Context
Just as the faculty are affected by the politics and institutional support systems within which they operate, citizens, professionals, and agencies operating in the community are affected by their context. Again there are many different factors that influence the ease with which university-community collaborations can be done. Those who are involved in university-community partnerships would do well to read the community development literature for insights on how community-level variables might affect the collaborative process (e.g., Flora & Flora, 1993; Putnam, 1993).

Community Resources and Cohesion. Like universities, communities have various amounts and types of resources. Community resources include the human, financial, technical and physical infrastructure that is available. Moreover, one must not only assess the number of resources available, but also the degree to which the community is able to link these resources, which Flora and Flora (1993) have termed "entrepreneurial social infrastructure." Partnerships will be more difficult with communities lacking in entrepreneurial social infrastructure because there tends to be a lower density of relationships, greater feelings of mistrust toward outsiders, and less equitable utilization of resources (Flora & Flora, 1993; Hughes & Todd, 1995). The concept of entrepreneurial social infrastructure helped us understand why we were able to develop partnerships more easily in some low-income communities than others, despite the fact that all were lacking in resources (Hughes & Todd, 1995).

Organizational Climate. When work is being conducted with professionals in the community, their institutional system will also affect them. Community organizations, agencies, and government bodies each have rules, procedures, and practices that may either facilitate or inhibit collaboration. For example, the philosophy held by the agency, the degree of hierarchy present, and the extent to which the agency already has formed partnerships with other groups in the community can make it easier or harder to develop partnerships (Price & Lorion, 1989).

The contexts in which collaboration occurs—within both the university and the community—will greatly affect the ease with which university-community partnerships can be undertaken. Although we have used the term "collaboration" generically, in fact, there are different degrees of collaboration possible (Bergstrom et al., 1995). Universities must carefully consider what level of interaction is appropriate given the context of both the university and the community. We must be careful not to avoid partnerships with those communities with which it is "difficult" to work. Often, these are the communities most in need of partners. Rather, we should consider what level of collaboration *is* possible in such a context and recognize that effecting change in such communities will occur at a much slower rate than in other communities. It is also important to realize that it is often problems within the university structure, not the community structure, that impede the ability to develop partnerships.

Process Factors That Influence
Community-University Collaborations

There is substantial literature describing process factors that affect collaborations (see Bergstrom et al., 1995, for a synthesis of this literature). In this section we focus on some unique processes that have special significance for university community collaborations—the role of faculty, developing a shared vision for projects, and long-term sustainability of projects.

Faculty Roles in Participation

Collaborations work best when the partners involved share a similar vision of how to work together. Our experiences have led us to believe that faculty tend to work in one of three modes in university-community collaborations: faculty as consultants, faculty as equal partners, and faculty as learners. Individual faculty may be more or less comfortable with each of these roles. It is essential that faculty adopt the role that works best for them and then seek collaborators who will accept that role.

Faculty as Consultants. Although most action-oriented research models advocate an egalitarian relationship between faculty and communities (Small, 1995b), we continue to believe there is a role for faculty as experts in outreach projects. There are some issues about which faculty know a great deal. When this is the case, it would be foolish for local communities to "rediscover" knowledge that is already available. Moreover, in our experience, some communities are not ready for egalitarian partnerships, which typically involve long-term negotiations to create a shared vision. Some communities have identified a specific need, believe the faculty member can meet that need, and simply want what the faculty member has to offer. In such cases, community members are satisfied with being the recipient of what the faculty member has to offer.

When faculty have a "mature" program—one that draws from a well-developed theoretical and empirical base and which has been pilot-tested in diverse contexts—they should seek community partners who are interested in adopting the program. The role of the faculty member in such collaborations is primarily that of consultant. Although some modifica-tions may be required to adapt the program to each local context, it is unlikely that major revisions will be made by the community.

The Illinois Youth and Families Project has been involved in consultative relationships that were initiated by community groups. In one example, a network of schools, businesses, agencies, and organizations concerned about youth issues in a small city requested assistance in conducting an analysis of a youth survey on substance use, gang involvement, and perceptions of risks and opportunities for youth in the community. The relationship was "brokered" by a local University of Illinois extension educator who played a prominent role in the network. The bulk of the project was assigned to a graduate student interested in social policy as a way of learning how to analyze data and communicate results that would be useful for policymakers. After the report was submitted, our involvement was completed. The relationship enhanced the reputation of the university by demonstrating our commitment to the local community, offered an opportunity for training students, and provided the community with useful data for better understanding the unique issues facing youth in their community.

Collaborations based on the "faculty as consultant" model require a careful matching of what the faculty member has to offer with what a particular community wants. This type of collaboration is most likely to result in data that are applicable to basic research questions as well as meeting local needs, since the faculty member often retains a high degree of control over the situation and a fairly standardized procedure may be used across communities. While we agree that this type of collaboration is less likely to result in massive, system-level changes within the community or the university, such collaborations can meet specific local needs and also can promote positive feelings toward the university. These experiences may also develop the necessary groundwork for more complex roles for faculty in the community and help the faculty member develop the appropriate skills for working effectively in the community. This type of collaboration can also be appropriate with communities lacking in entrepreneurial social infrastructure, as long as what the faculty member has to offer fits closely with what the community wants.

Faculty as Partners. There are situations in which universities and local communities each have information that can be integrated to produce a more advanced understanding of an issue or more effective solutions to a problem. This model is closer to the action-research model outlined by Small (1995b), since both the faculty member and local community members serve as experts. The faculty member typically brings her or his expertise of the research literature while local community members serve as experts concerning the local context.

The development of the school-age child-care training videos, as part of the Child Care Impact project, represents such a partnership. One of the challenges facing the child-care field in the late 1980s was the lack of appropriate training materials for child-care professionals working with school-age children. Most university courses on child-care focused on caring for preschool-age children. The basic dilemma facing universities was that we did not have a model of high-quality school-age child-care, given the newness of the field. For example, the criteria for developmentally appropriate practice developed by the National Association for the Education of Young Children pertained only to infants through age eight years (National Association for the Education of Young Children, 1987).

Faced with this dilemma, the Illinois Department of Children and Family Services partnered with faculty from the Department of Human and Community Development to develop a series of videotapes for use in training school-age child-care providers (Todd, 1990, 1991, 1992). University faculty met with school-age child-care providers to develop the framework for the videotapes. Faculty provided their research-based knowledge of middle childhood and child-care. School-age child-care professionals provided their understanding of effective school-age child-care practice. This information allowed faculty to interpret general developmental principles within a school-age child-care context. For example, the child-care staff were able to articulate how separation anxiety was manifested in school-age children. Similarly, they raised issues that were more difficult for children to negotiate in a school-age child-care program than at home, such as how to negotiate multiple friendships when all of the friends are constantly together and how to manage to be "alone" in an environment where licensing regulations require children to be in sight at all times. While the collaboration required time and energy by both parties, the partnership resulted in the development of much higher quality training materials than would have been developed by either group on their own.

To adopt a partnership model, faculty must be willing to view their collaborators as equals in the creative process and be willing to invest the time and energy needed to integrate the knowledge of the various partners. In addition to meeting a specific need, this level of collaboration is likely to result in transformation of both the research literature and local practice. In our experience, such collaborations work best with communities high in entrepreneurial social infrastructure. We agree with Douglas Nelson, executive director of the Annie E. Casey Foundation, that not all communities or universities are ready for this partnership approach (Annie E. Casey, 1995). University members must also realize that true partnerships result in a situation in which university participants are not always in charge. Moreover, in the best collaborations, it will be difficult to determine what unique contribution the university provided. In our experience, highly effective collaborations transcend the individual groups that comprise the partnership. It is the synergy between the groups, rather than the contribution of any one group, that is responsible for the outcomes. One challenge for studying collaborations is how to measure this latent variable. A second challenge relates to authorship on products produced by collaborations. Promotion and tenure committees traditionally have placed high value on single-authored papers and first-author status. Moreover, publishers tend to prefer a limited number of authors. These practices are difficult for collaborations involving distributed leadership. In highly effective collaborations, both credit and blame are shared equally by all partners. Consistent with this philosophy, all partners typically are included on publications, often in alphabetical order.

Faculty as Learners. In the previous two models, faculty typically work from a strong research base and have specific contributions to make toward the solution of a complex problem. In contrast, some collaborations are formed to address highly complex problems to which there is no immediate solution. Our experiences with the Nation of Tomorrow project in inner-city Chicago represent this type of collaboration. Although there was an extensive research literature on working with limited-resource audiences, we were ill-prepared for the complexity of the issues. In retrospect, we had a very incomplete understanding of the many forces affecting urban families and, despite our best intentions, we held many stereotypes about low-income families, people of color, and inner-city neighborhoods. Faculty involved in this type of collaboration need to recognize that they have some knowledge that may be useful, but that they have much to learn as well. In addition, faculty must be very careful about what outcomes they promise to the community and funders. In this type of project it is highly unlikely that conditions at the local level will improve substantially in the short term (Annie E. Casey Foundation, 1995). Often, faculty and the university must make a long-term commitment (perhaps ten years) to the activity in order to see significant, sustained changes in the community.

Initially, the most important outcomes of the project are likely to be the transformations that occur in the individuals and institutions participating in the project, rather than the target audience to whom the program is directed. For example, the Nation of Tomorrow project resulted in a significant transformation in our approach to outreach and the way we train students. The project helped us understand the limits of current parent-education models, gave us a deeper appreciation of the unique cultures of African-American and Latino families, and taught us to better recognize instances of institutional racism and classism. The project also helped us to understand what needs to change in universities to do effective outreach, and provided insights in how to sustain university-community collaborations long-term (see section on sustainability issues, below).

Potentially, all three faculty roles can be effective. The key to success is a careful matching of what faculty and universities have to offer with the specific needs of the local community. When universities fail to meet the expectations of local communities, it is likely that the collaboration will be viewed as a failure by all involved.

Creating a Shared Vision

Universities and communities tend to approach outreach initiatives in different ways and also tend to hold different criteria for success (McHale et al., 1996; Rappaport, 1981; Small, 1995b). It is essential that universities become more flexible in their approach to science and respect the right of local communities to have differing goals, methods, and criteria for success. It is also important for communities to understand the perspective of the university. It is through the interplay between the differing cultures, or world views, of universities and communities that truly innovative solutions to problems are identified.

A typical university approach to outreach is to study the situation, read the relevant research literature, and develop an impact model of how various factors influence one another. In contrast, communities are more likely to develop a plan of action based on current local practice, implement the plan, and then revise the plan based on the resulting outcome. Thus, universities draw on research while local communities often rely on practice as the basis for program development.

Failure to recognize the importance of each approach can lead to frustrations on the part of both the university and the community. Community members often are frustrated by the long planning process proposed by universities. From the university perspective, the community's "implement, then modify" approach appears unscholarly. It is important to note, however, that each method can *potentially* achieve the stated goals of the project. The two approaches are simply different means to achieve the same ends. Combining the two approaches, however, is seen as preferable by action researchers (Small, 1995b), who believe that both knowledge of general laws and specific information about a local situation are needed to develop an appropriate response to a particular problem.

There also tend to be different ways in which universities and communities determine the success or failure of a collaboration. These differing criteria can result in opposite conclusions about the success of the project. Consistent with the continued adherence to principles of logical positivism within many universities (Small, 1995b), academics tend to rely heavily on statistical and methodological criteria to determine the success of a project (Coie et al., 1993). As a result, university faculty and administrators are seldom satisfied with the outcome of an outreach initiative unless change is evident in a statistically significant number of people, and it can be demonstrated with random assignment and control groups that this change is due to the treatment provided, using instruments for which acceptable levels of reliability and validity have been demonstrated empirically (Schumm, 1990).

In contrast, local community members are more likely to rely on their personal experiences. They judge the success of a project in terms of whether they personally saw improvements sufficient to offset the perceived cost of the program. In other words, they are concerned primarily with the issue of face validity (Schumm, 1990). Local community members often argue that the cost of verifying the results statistically requires excessive amounts of funding for data collection and analysis activities that would be better spent on program activities. Their simpler criterion—"Are things getting better from my perspective?"—seems to be a more cost-effective method for determining success in their view. Community residents have a valid point. Universities should carefully consider which projects warrant expensive, scientifically elegant designs (Small, 1990), and must be ready to explain how the community, as well as science, will benefit from these data.

All collaborations, however, should engage stakeholders in identifying specific objectives that must be met in order to consider the project a success (Price & Lorion, 1989). Most collaborations form to achieve long-term, vague goals, such as improving family life or helping youth become productive citizens. Stakeholders must develop a shared vision of the specific changes that must occur to know that they are making progress toward these goals. We agree, however, with the conclusions of evaluators at the Annie E. Casey Foundation that the goals and objectives for complex collaborative projects may need to be revised frequently as the causes and potential solutions to problems are better understood (Annie E. Casey Foundation, 1995).

Sustainability Issues
As we work with local groups to develop university-community collaborations, we have come to expect a certain pattern. The first meeting tends to

be stressful, at least for us. Often, we must sit through a litany of complaints about the university. Many of these complaints center around a view of the university as an ivory tower with faculty who storm into a community, make a lot of promises, provide some short-term resources, collect a lot of data, and then leave—taking everything with them. The wonderful projects stop. Not much has changed (Lorion & Saltzman, 1993).

If universities are serious about developing partnerships with communities, we must do a better job of sustaining efforts at the local level. Over the years, we have identified three strategies that can help to insure that our outreach efforts will be sustained. First, it is important to design programs that can be sustained with the resources available in local communities. Creating a flagship program is a disservice to a community that has only row-boat resources to sustain the program. Second, requiring that communities match the resources provided by the university, either with real dollars or in-kind contributions, will reduce the level of outside funding that must be replaced when the project ends. Third, user fees can be an important source of ongoing revenue. Even in low-income communities there is some capacity for residents to pay for services. Moreover, there may be public funding available for those who cannot. However, user fees must be charged from the outset, not implemented at the end of the project. People seldom want to pay for what they originally got for free. If grant funds are available to cover initial program costs, user fees can be put into a community-controlled interest-bearing account and will provide a nice cushion for the community when the university withdraws from the project. Universities must become more sensitive to sustainability issues, both to enhance the image of universities in local communities and to truly effect long-term change in society.

Benefits and Challenges

The land-grant system represents a partnership between educational institutions and the people. At critical points in U.S. history, people in local communities sent a clear message to the academy that change was required. Change was forthcoming in every case, resulting in institutions of higher learning that were better able to meet the current challenges and future needs of our nation.

The Morrill Acts of 1862 and 1890 strengthened the teaching mission of the university by broadening the curriculum to include subjects of practical interest and by making higher education potentially accessible to all. This change helped to institutionalize the concepts of democracy and equality during the early evolution of our country. The Hatch Act of 1887 and the Smith-Lever Act of 1914 established the land-grant system's commitment to outreach by making applied research and extension activities an important part of the land-grant mission. From this effort emerged a strong agricultural system, one that fed the world and supported the burgeoning of the population and increasing urbanization. The focus on basic research that emerged during and after World War II contributed to the national defense mission of the nation and set the stage for the shift from an agricultural and industrial nation to a world leader in technology and information systems (Anderson, 1976; Boyer, 1990; Neyland, 1990; Virginia Agricultural Extension Service, 1959; West Virginia University, 1963).

Once again, the people are demanding change in the academy in order to better address current problems and move our nation forward. Earlier societal crises led to the establishment of teaching, outreach, and research as three important missions of the land-grant system. However, each mission evolved in isolation from the other and each was viewed as more important than the others at certain points in history. Today, the issues facing not only America but the world—expanding populations in a time of declining resources, living in an increasingly diverse and global society, the aging of the population and the alienation of our youth—require the full resources of the academy. The new challenge before us is to give equal attention to and fully integrate the teaching, research, and outreach missions of the academy. Why should we take on this task? What challenges do we face?

In our experience, the benefits of integrating research, teaching, and outreach far outweigh the challenges. First, we can point to important changes in the fabric of society that have resulted from our efforts. For example, as a result of contributing to the Child Care Impact project, thousands of Illinois children, families, and small-business owners have a stronger child-care system—one that will be better able than some to weather the coming storms created by welfare reform.

Second, our involvement in university-community partnerships has improved the quality of instruction provided to our students. Our lectures are no longer dull recountings of our discipline, but rather filled with examples of real people and real communities that illustrate the abstract concepts we are trying to communicate. Our ability to help students integrate knowledge across disciplines has been enhanced. Our deeper understanding of diversity—in all its forms—has helped us to critically evaluate the appropriateness of research findings for subgroups of the population and also has contributed to the creation of a more diverse student and faculty population.

Finally, our involvement in university-community collaborations has strengthened our ability to conduct high-quality research. Doors normally closed to basic researchers are open to us. Moreover, the cost of collecting data is greatly reduced since many communities contribute time and funds for data collection in order to meet their own needs. Our involvement in collaborations has also contributed greatly to theory development and our ability to form increasingly complex models of human functioning. Finally, like McCall et al. (1995), we have been highly successful in generating external funding for applied projects.

There are, however, a number of challenges still before us. First, the academy must evolve into a system that can effectively respond to the increasing diversity of our society. Our traditional adherence to one viewpoint—whether it be the importance of classical studies or dogged adherence to logical positivism—must be replaced by a commitment to multiple approaches and multiple viewpoints. Within academia, there is no longer one reality of the world. We need a multiplicity of approaches to address the complexity of problems before us and the multiplicity of contexts in which people now reside. To achieve this goal, we must reevaluate how we teach students. More than ever, we need students who are broadly educated, who are exposed to many different populations, contexts, and methods of inquiry during their training, and who can integrate research and practice to address critical social issues.

The Department of Human and Community Development has attempted to achieve these goals in part by incorporating training in application into its teaching program at both the undergraduate and graduate level. At both levels, advanced students can take capstone courses that provide training in program development and implementation, evaluation, and public policy. In addition, students can elect to gain actual experience in application through internships with agencies. At the graduate level, there is a formal applied concentration within the Ph.D. program. Students in the applied concentration complete the same requirements as all Ph.D. students, taking two to three courses in application as electives. In addition to completing a research-based dissertation, students in the applied concentration also complete two internships. In the first internship, students gain specific skills by working in an applied setting. In the second internship, students utilize their training in application to actually develop and direct an outreach initiative.

The inclusion of an applied emphasis in the teaching program allows both undergraduate and graduate students to be actively involved in Extension and outreach activities. External funding obtained for outreach activities also serves as an important source for graduate assistantships and student employment opportunities. Students at both the undergraduate and graduate levels who have participated in outreach activities indicate that they feel better prepared to enter the workforce and have developed valuable professional networks as a result of their experiences.

Second, the academy must design new criteria for evaluating outreach scholarship and must reward those who meet these criteria. Consistent with the view that there are multiple realities, the outcomes of university-community collaborations must be evaluated from multiple perspectives— from the view of scholars and from the viewpoint of the community (Ebata, 1996). The best outreach initiatives will receive high ratings by each group. Applied efforts that satisfy the scholarly community but result in negative feelings and no lasting change at the local level represent poor scholarship. Applied efforts that make local residents happy but do not draw from or contribute to research and practice also represent poor scholarship. There is good applied scholarship and there is bad applied scholarship. We must develop criteria that better distinguish between the two and improve the reward structure for those who do it well. To this end, we must provide forums in which students, faculty, and administrators involved in outreach can share their thoughts and move the field along.

Finally, we must give careful attention to helping faculty learn how to balance the demands of participating in all of the three-fold land-grant mission. Simply requiring faculty to add one more responsibility to their current load is unlikely to increase the number of high-quality outreach activities. In a time of declining resources, how do we encourage faculty to contribute to all *three* missions and still maintain quality? Boyer (1990) has proposed that faculty be encouraged to focus more heavily on certain forms of scholarship at different points in their career. There is much merit to this approach. Junior faculty would not be overwhelmed by multiple demands. Senior faculty, who sometimes become disengaged when the job becomes routine, can be presented with new challenges. Each of the three missions will get adequate support and recognition. Moreover, all faculty will develop a better appreciation for and be better able to evaluate each form of scholarship.

The challenge is before us. Our country has survived past crises because of the willingness of its people to demand change from the academy. The land-grant colleges and universities have endured because of their willingness to change in response to these demands. History suggests that we should welcome and embrace the challenge of developing effective university and community collaborations.

References

Aiken, M. & Faulkner, L .R. (1995). *A framework for the future: A strategic plan for the University of Illinois at Urbana-Champaign.* Urbana: University of Illinois at Urbana-Champaign.

Anderson, G. L. (Ed.). (1976). *Land-grant universities and their continuing challenge.* East Lansing, MI: Michigan State University Press.

Annie E. Casey Foundation. (1995). *The path of most resistance: Reflections on lessons learned from New Futures.* (Annie E. Casey Foundation, 701 St. Paul Street, Baltimore, MD 21202).

Bergstrom, A., Clark, R., Hogue, T., Perkins, D., & Slinski, M. (1995). *Collaboration Framework: Addressing community capacity.* Columbus, OH. UCDA Cooperative State Research, Education, and Extension Service National Network for Collaboration.

Bonnen, J. T. (1986). A century of science in agriculture: Lessons for social policy. *American Journal of Agricultural Economics 68,* 1065–1080.

Boyer, E. L. (1990). *Scholarship reconsidered: Priorities of the professoriate.* Princeton, NJ: The Carnegie Foundation for the Advancement of Teaching.

Bronfenbrenner, U. (1979). *The ecology of human development: Experiments by nature and design.* Cambridge: Harvard University Press.

———. (1986). Ecology of the family as a context for human development: Research perspectives. *Developmental Psychology, 22,* 723–742.

Coie, J. D., Watt, N. F., West, S. G., Hawkins, J. D., Asarnow, J. R., Markman, H. J., Ramey, S. L., Shure, M. B., & Long, B. (1993). The science of prevention: A conceptual framework and some directions for a national research program. *American Psychologist, 48,* 1013–1022.

Ebata, A. T. (1995). Community-based action research and adolescent development. In L. J. Crockett & A. C. Crouter (Eds.), *Pathways through adolescence: Individual development in relation to social contents* (pp. 235–242). Mahwah, NJ: Erlbaum.

———. (1996). Making university-community collaborations work: Challenges for institutions and individuals. *Journal of Research on Adolescents, 6,* 71–79.

Flora, C. B., & Flora, J. L. (1993). Entrepreneurial social infrastructure: A necessary ingredient. *Annals of the American Academy of Political and Social Sciences, 529,* 48–58.

Grossman, R. & Leroux, C. (1996, January 28). Research grants actually add to tuition costs, study claims. *Chicago Tribune,* pp. 1, 19.

Hughes, R., Jr., & Todd, C. M. (1995). *Assessing community in the design of family support services for low-income families.* Unpublished manuscript.

Kagan, S. L. & Neville, P. R. (1993). Family support and school-linked services. *Family Resource Coalition Report, 12,* 1–3.

Lerner, R. M. & Kauffman, M. B. (1985). The concept of development in contextualism. *Developmental Review, 5,* 309–333.

Lerner, R. M., Miller, J .R., Knott, J. H., Corey, K. E., Bynum, T .S., Hoopfer, L .C., McKinney, M. H., Abrams, L. A., Hula, R. C., and Terry, P. A. (1994). Integrating scholarship and outreach in human development research, policy, and service: a developmental contextual perspective. In D. L. Featherman, R. M. Lerner, & M. Perlmutter (Eds.), *Life-span development and behavior* (Vol. 12, pp. 249–273). Hillsdale, NJ: Erlbaum.

Lorion, R. P. & Salzman, W. (1993). Children's exposure to community violence: Following a path from concern to research to action. *Psychiatry, 56,* 55–65.

McCall, R. B., Groark, C. J., Strauss, M. S., & Johnson, C. N. (1995). An experiment promoting interdisciplinary applied human development: The University of Pittsburgh model. *Journal of Applied Developmental Psychology, 16*, 593–612.

McHale, S. M., Crouter, A. C., Fennelly, K., Tomascik, C. A., Updegraff, K. A., Graham, J. E., Baker, A. E., Dreisbach, L., Ferry, N., Manlove, E. E., McGroder, S. M., Mulkeen, P., & Obeidallah, P. (1996). Community-based interventions for young adolescents: The Penn State PRIDE Project. *Journal of Research in Adolescence, 6*, 1–7.

National Association for the Education of Young Children. (1987). *Developmentally appropriate practice in early childhood programs serving children from birth through age 8.* Washington, DC: Author.

Neyland, L. W. (1990). *Historically black land-grant institutions and the development of agriculture and home economics: 1890–1990.* Tallahassee: Florida A&M University Foundation.

Nucci, L., Hughes, R., Todd, C. M., Gast, G. G., Smylie, M. A., & McElmurry, B. J. (1990, Spring/Summer). The "Nation of Tomorrow": A land-grant university experiment. *Illinois Research,* 6–8.

Price, R. H. & Lorion, R. P. (1989). Prevention programming as organizational reinvention: From research to implementation. In D. Shaffer, I. Philips, & N. B. Enzer (Eds.), *Prevention of mental disorders, alcohol and other drug use in children and adolescents* (Prevention Monograph #2, DHHS Publication No. ADM 89–1646, pp. 97–123). Rockville, MD: Office of Substance Abuse Prevention and American Academy of Child and Adolescent Psychiatry.

Putnam, R. D. (1993). The prosperous community: Social capital and public life. *The American Prospect, 13*, 35–42.

Rappaport, J. (1981). In praise of paradox: A social policy of empowerment over prevention. *American Journal of Community Psychology, 15*, 121–148.

Riley, D. (1992). *School-age child care project manual: The SACC Community Assessment and Development Project.* Madison: University of Wisconsin Center for Action on the Family.

Sandmann, L. R. & Vandenberg, L. (1995). A framework for 21st century leadership. *Journal of Extension, 6.* Available from: joe-ed@joe-org.

Schumm, W. R. (1990). Evolution of the family field: Measurement principles and techniques. In J. Touliatos, B. F. Perlmutter, & M. A. Straus (Eds.), *Handbook of family measurement techniques.* Newbury Park, CA: Sage.

Small, S. A. (1990). Some issues regarding the evaluation of family life education programs. *Family Relations, 39*, 132–135.

———. (1995a). Enhancing contexts of adolescent development: The role of community-based action research. In W. Crockett & A. C. Crouter (Eds.), *Pathways through adolescence: Individual development in relation to social contexts.* Mahwah, NJ: Erlbaum.

———. (1995b). Action-oriented research. *Journal of Marriage and the Family, 57*, 941–955.

———. (1996). Collaborative community-based research on adolescents: Using research for community change. *Journal of Research on Adolescents, 6*, 9–22.

Todd, C. M. (1990). *School-age child care: Meeting developmental needs.* Urbana: University of Illinois Cooperative Extension Service, Videotape, 33 minutes.

———. (1991). *School-age child care: Guidance and discipline.* Urbana: University of Illinois Cooperative Extension Service, Videotape, 43 minutes.

———. (1992). *School-age child care: Activity planning.* Urbana: University of Illinois Cooperative Extension Service, Videotape, 38 minutes.

University of Illinois at Urbana-Champaign. (1993). *A faculty guide for relating public service to the promotion and tenure review process.* Urbana: Author.

Virginia Agricultural Extension Service. (1959). *Hearings, report, and debate: Smith-Lever Act of 1914: U.S. House of Representatives.* Blacksburg: Author.

West Virginia University. (1963). *The development of the land-grant colleges and universities and their influence on the economic and social life of the people.* Morgantown: West Virginia University.

Chapter 12
Toward a Scholarship
of Relevance
Lessons from a Land-Grant University

Stephen A. Small and Karen Bogenschneider
University of Wisconsin-Madison

In recent years, publicly supported universities have come under increasing criticism from a variety of sources, including legislators, parents of students, business leaders, and taxpayers (see also Todd, Ebata, & Hughes, this volume). Although some of this criticism results from such issues as athletic department scandals, the alleged disappearance of faculty from the classroom, and questions of political correctness, we believe a primary reason for criticism stems from the fact that many universities and their faculties are out of step with the needs of citizens who are increasingly concerned about the complex and problematic world in which they live.

We argue that this problem stems from narrowing definitions of scholarship and university function and a straying from the guiding mission of universities. We believe the solution can be found, at least in part, by examining history and rediscovering the land-grant roots upon which many publicly supported universities were founded.

This chapter is divided into four parts. In the first section, we provide a brief history of the land-grant university in the United States and examine what history can tell us about making universities more relevant to the needs of the public. Next, building on the work of Boyer (1990), we explore various definitions of family scholarship and discuss the need for broadening our conception. In the third section of this chapter, we provide concrete illustrations of how family scholars at one land-grant university have begun developing outreach efforts that meet the rigorous scholarly expectations of academia while also being relevant to the needs of the public. Finally, we draw implications for how the land-grant university can once again become a place of relevance where scholarship is developed to help meet the needs of the state's citizens.

History of State Land-Grant Universities

In the mid-nineteenth century, as America expanded to the west, a shift in the aims of higher education began to occur (McDowell, 1988). Whereas the college of colonial America was largely focused on building character and preparing the next generation of leaders for civic and religious life (Boyer, 1990), the opening up of new western frontiers led to a need for farmers and families who possessed practical skills and knowledge about farming and home life.

The Morrill Act of 1862 (later called the Land Grant College Act) was one of the first official recognitions of the need for higher education to pursue knowledge that was practical and widely useful. This historic legislation gave federal land to each state, with proceeds from the sale of this land going to support higher education and establish agricultural universities (Caldwell, 1976; Eddy, 1956). In contrast to colleges and universities prior to this time, the land-grant university was explicitly anti-elitist and highly democratic (Caldwell, 1976; McDowell, 1988). According to Caldwell (1976), the establishment of land-grant colleges reflected

the practical view that knowledge should be applied to improve the human condition . . . the growing belief that man could in fact better his lot and "make progress," and the American commitment to democratic goals of opportunity for the common man, "the industrial classes," and open-ended mobility. (p. 13)

McDowell (1988) pointed out three ways the land-grant college was intended to be a new model of American higher education. First, land-grant colleges were meant to be colleges of the people. That is, they were to provide formal instruction in the classroom to ordinary people, many of whom were children of farmers. Second, the knowledge base of the college was to be made available to all people. Even those who were not formal students in the classroom were to benefit from the growing scientific knowledge base. Third, land-grant colleges were to make all human endeavors legitimate topics for scientific investigation and scholarship. Prior to the establishment of the land-grant college, scholarship had been confined largely to history, the arts and letters, theology, law, and medicine. These changes helped democratize the nature of higher education and broaden what was considered legitimate scholarship. In addition to basic research, scholarship was to provide scientific insights and answers to people's problems as they occurred in the community, on the farm, and in the home.

The Hatch Act of 1887 further supported this trend in higher education by providing federal funds to create university-sponsored agricultural experiment stations. The primary aim of these experiment stations was to create local knowledge for the farmer (Caldwell, 1976). They were based on the idea that university scholarship was an important democratic function that could and should serve the common good of the people.

The final link in this new practical approach to scholarship in higher education was established with the passing of the Smith-Lever Act in 1914 (Rogers, 1989). This federal legislation established the Cooperative Extension Service in each state. Although land-grant universities were teaching about and conducting research on issues of practical importance to farmers and other citizens, much of this knowledge was not reaching the people who could benefit from it. With the addition of Cooperative Extension, a system was established that could both create practical knowledge on issues of local importance and distribute it to citizens of the state. The establishment of county-based faculty who could disseminate this knowledge directly to the citizens who needed it was critical to making the system complete.

The people of the state would benefit from the new land-grant system not only by having their children educated in its classrooms, but by having their emerging concerns and problems addressed by the scholars of the university. The addition of Cooperative Extension with its local agents also helped democratize the scholarly agenda of university researchers by giving citizens some influence over the research focus (McDowell, 1988).

Although land-grant universities were designed to be "people's colleges" that educated the common person and addressed the practical problems of a state's citizens, in recent years most have strayed from their original mission (see Harkavy, this volume). Several factors account for this gradual drift, but two seem particularly noteworthy. First, the reduction of state funding for land-grant universities has meant that faculty look to private and federal grants to support their work. This change in funding has resulted in numerous special interests exerting an influence on the university scholarly agenda. The concerns of the state's citizens (and their representatives) are now only one among many competing interests. A second related trend is the narrowing of what it means to be a scholar. According to a growing number of critics, in the past forty years American universities have moved into a period where basic research has come to dominate universities to the exclusion of teaching, service, practice, and application (Boyer, 1990, 1994; Lynton & Elman, 1987).

Perhaps what is most surprising is that these trends have affected not only major private research universities, but also state-supported land-grant institutions. This narrowing of what is considered legitimate scholarship has meant faculty are less likely to engage in and to be rewarded for performing important scholarly activities other than basic research. Consequently, land-grant universities have become decreasingly involved in the types of applied research and outreach functions upon which they were founded and which remain, at least in principle, an integral part of their mission.

Broadening the Definition of Scholarship

In response to this increasingly narrow definition of scholarship and university function, Ernest Boyer of the Carnegie Foundation for the Advancement of Teaching published a seminal report on the meaning of scholarship (Boyer, 1990). The report's discussion of the nature of scholarship provided insight into how publicly supported universities and their faculty members could once again become relevant to the needs and concerns of citizens.

Boyer (1990) identified four overlapping types of scholarship that closely correspond to the primary functions that should be served by university faculty. The four types of scholarship are highly relevant to faculty who consider themselves human development or family scholars. According to Boyer, all four types are legitimate and should be equally valued.

The first type of scholarship discussed by Boyer (1990), and the one most familiar to researchers, is the *scholarship of discovery*. This is generally what is referred to as basic research. When done well, it contributes to the body of human knowledge and the understanding of the human condition.

The second type of scholarship identified by Boyer (1990) is the *scholarship of teaching*. According to Boyer, this type of scholarship assumes that the work of the scholar becomes consequential only if it is communicated to and understood by others. Teaching as scholarship means not only transmitting knowledge, but transforming and extending it as well. Scholarly teachers are stretched in new and creative ways through their preparation for classes and interaction with students.

A third type of scholarship is what Boyer (1990) terms the *scholarship of integration*. This involves the need for scholars to interpret and provide meaning to isolated facts and put them into perspective. Integration involves identifying meaningful patterns and trends in existing research. Making connections across studies and disciplines and placing studies in a larger context help illuminate data in new and different ways and thereby expands the field of knowledge.

The scholarship of integration also includes interpretation. This involves summarizing and integrating existing research in ways that give it meaning and coherence for a particular audience such as families. Such efforts are more critical than ever given the high level of specialization in academia and the proliferation of data in the current information age. Winnowing out what is important and putting it together in ways that are useful for particular audiences is becoming an increasingly important role for scholars.

According to Boyer (1990), those engaged in the scholarship of discovery are concerned with "What is to be known? What is yet to be found?" whereas those engaged in the scholarship of integration ask, "What do the findings mean?"

The final category of scholarship identified by Boyer (1990) is the *scholarship of application*. Those engaged in this type of scholarship are concerned with how knowledge can be applied to important human problems. In other words, how can knowledge be helpful to individuals, families, communities, and society?

The scholarship of application is not unidirectional. It does not assume that knowledge is first "discovered" and then "applied." The process is more dynamic and reciprocal. New knowledge and a better understanding of knowledge can arise out of the very act of application. Such a perspective posits that social problems themselves can define an agenda for scholarly investigation (Boyer, 1990). In the scholarship of application, research, theory, and practice interact, each informing the others. The scholarship of application is based on the belief that for knowledge to be meaningful it must be used.

Of the four types of scholarship identified by Boyer (1990), the scholarship of discovery—that is, basic research—is clearly the type land-grant universities today handle best. We believe they do only a fair job of the scholarship of teaching because universities tend to transmit most of their knowledge only to people who come to learn within their classrooms. We think universities are doing the poorest job of addressing the last two types of scholarship—integration and application. As faculty have become more specialized, their research is less apt to be informed by new discoveries in fields outside their discipline. And as faculty have become more isolated, they have become increasingly out of touch with society and the needs of families.

A final concern is that in addition to being unequally valued and performed, these four types of scholarship have been increasingly treated as separate and distinct forms of professional activity (Votruba, 1992).

Scholarship responsibilities have become rigidly divided among different faculty and staff at the university. For example, at most land-grant universities, resident faculty are responsible primarily for conducting research and doing some classroom teaching. Increasingly, teaching assistants and short-term lecturers are doing the undergraduate classroom teaching as faculty buy out their teaching with research grants. State-level Extension specialists are primarily responsible for integrating, translating, and conveying scientific knowledge to professionals and county Extension faculty. County Extension agents are largely responsible for applying this knowledge to practical problems in the field.

Unfortunately, a number of problems have resulted from the segregation of various types of scholarship. They include: (1) the increasing number of research studies that are scientifically rigorous but socially irrelevant because research faculty are isolated from the knowledge needs of practitioners, policymakers, and the public; (2) relevant research findings that sit on the shelf because research scholars lack the skills or incentive to translate and communicate these findings to those who could benefit from them; (3) simplistic solutions offered to address complex problems because Extension specialists or other knowledge disseminators fail to conduct critical, integrative reviews of the relevant scientific literature; and (4) practitioners who fail to draw on state-of-the-art scientific knowledge because they are unaware of it, do not know where to find it, or do not know how to interpret it.

In our opinion, for universities to remain viable and relevant a more inclusive view of what it means to be a scholar and a university is needed. We must recognize that in addition to basic research, scholarship must include synthesis, application, and teaching, and that these are all legitimate, even necessary, functions for universities and their faculty members. This inclusiveness is even more critical for the land-grant university because it has a social responsibility and historical mandate to address the practical problems and needs of its state's citizens.

Models of Scholarship and Relevance at the University of Wisconsin-Madison

In this section we will provide examples of how we have attempted to implement a broader view of scholarship around issues relevant to youth and families while also working toward making the university more responsive to the needs of people. We hope these illustrations of how a scholarship of relevance has evolved at the University of Wisconsin are helpful to other scholars who are committed to improving the lives of families, youth, and children, but who also must negotiate the expectations of academia.

Teen Assessment Project

During the past ten years, there has been increasing concern about the problems faced by contemporary adolescents and what these problems may mean for their well-being and the future of society (see Dryfoos, 1990; Hamburg, 1992; Lerner, 1995). Although the available evidence indicates that many of the problems facing contemporary adoescents are not restricted to any one geographical location, socioeconomic class, or ethnic-racial group, it has been our experience that parents and local policymakers often believe that these issues are not relevant in their own community or to their own youth. There is a tendency to perceive such problems as early teen sexual activity, drug use, sexual violence, and gang activity as problems that only occur elsewhere or with other people's children. As a result of this commonly held perception it is often difficult to get citizens to recognize, much less to work to ameliorate, the problems and challenges facing their young people.

In response to this situation and the need for communities to have detailed, research-based information about local adolescents, we developed a program of research and dissemination known as the Teen Assessment Project or TAP. It is based on a model of research and knowledge dissemination that involves collaboration between the university and members of a community (for more information, see Small, 1996; Small and Hug, 1990; Riley, 1996). We work collaboratively with communities to help them conduct their own research on the needs and problems faced by local adolescents and their families. The roots of this approach can be found in the action and participatory research programs carried out by a number of community and organizational psychologists (e.g., Argyris, Putnam, & Smith, 1985; Elden & Chisholm, 1993; Price & Polister, 1980; Rappaport, 1990) and in Bronfenbrenner's (1979, 1989) ecological model of human development. The aims of the collaborative research approach are two-fold: to address the practical concerns of local citizens and to contribute to the body of social science knowledge.

TAP provides communities with localized research-based knowledge by administering a survey to local adolescents that "taps in" to the adolescents' behavior and concerns and the processes that can affect them. This information is then made available to local citizens who can begin to solve the problems the survey reveals. TAP empowers parents, policymakers, and youth-serving task forces and organizations with localized research-based information on which to develop community-based strategies that support adolescent development.

At the local level, the project is facilitated by a county Cooperative Extension family-living educator or 4-H/youth-development educator. Working with a local steering committee of community leaders, we design a survey reflecting the needs and concerns facing adolescents and their families. The steering committee of local policymakers, educators, social-service professionals, students, and other concerned community members works collaboratively with the researchers to identify the most important research questions and knowledge needs, and to plan how and when to administer the survey. Although each survey is unique, the typical questionnaire covers a range of issues relevant to adolescent health and development such as sexuality, drug use, mental health, family and peer relations, perceptions of school and community, academic achievement, and future aspirations. Adolescents are administered a self-report questionnaire through the schools. The data are analyzed by researchers at the University and then returned to the community to be disseminated and acted upon. Some of the ways the data are shared are written reports, community forums and press conferences, press releases, and presentations to government, civic, professional, and parent groups. A series of newsletters, featuring major findings of the survey, are also sent to parents of the surveyed teens.

In addition to this project being an example of applied research that directly addresses the needs of citizens, it illustrates other aspects of an expanded vision of scholarship. First, it moves the educational process beyond the walls of the University by sharing recent, relevant scientific knowledge with local citizens. Second, it teaches about the value of the research process and provides community leaders with skills needed to conduct their own research on issues that might emerge in the future. Although the primary audience for the findings is local citizens, the data generated also have relevance to the broader scholarly community and have contributed to our scientific knowledge base. Numerous scientific papers based on data collected via these community surveys have been published in scholarly journals (e.g., Small & Kerns, 1993; Small & Luster, 1994). Third, the project has contributed to more traditional undergraduate and graduate education. Many students have worked on the project and written their master's theses and doctoral dissertations from the data generated. In sum, we believe the TAP program is a good example of how land-grant universities can both meet the immediate needs of its state's citizens and address the broader scholarly agenda of academia.

Wisconsin Youth Futures

What is most notable about this next project is that its impetus came, not from the University, but from local citizens whose satisfaction with TAP led them to approach the University and request that we work with them to ensure TAP research findings were translated into concrete programs and policies to benefit youth and their families. Responding to this request required a more explicit focus on the scholarships of teaching, integration, and application. A cross-institution, multidisciplinary task force was formed to analyze theoretical frameworks for conceptualizing prevention programming, to synthesize current research on risk and protective processes associated with youth development; and to review research dissemination methodologies, age-appropriate prevention strategies, and model prevention programs. This year-long process resulted in Wisconsin Youth Futures, a prevention program in which the University teams up with communities to build coalitions that develop comprehensive programs and policies to support youth and families. Since our pilot effort in the fall of 1990, we have collaborated with our county Cooperative Extension partners in family living, 4-H/youth development, community development, and agriculture to establish twenty-two coalitions in Wisconsin communities and neighborhoods, ranging from a small agricultural community of less than seven hundred people to a twelve-block inner-city neighborhood.

The purpose of these coalitions is to build community support for youth, and develop comprehensive action plans for preventing specific youth problems such as alcohol and tobacco use, prejudice and intolerance, violence, gang involvement, and depression. These coalitions typically include thirty to thirty-five individuals; about one-third of these are youth and the remainder are judges, school officials (superintendents, principals, and teachers), law-enforcement personnel, presidents of parent/teacher associations, clergy, business leaders, local government officials, representatives of community service clubs, and parents. During five or six meetings, coalition members identify the most critical local youth issues using local TAP data and their knowledge of the community. With the help of Extension specialists and county faculty, they learn about the latest research on adolescent development, risk and protective processes, characteristics of effective prevention programs, and success stories from other communities. Armed with community inventories that we've developed based on current research on specific youth problems, the coalition assesses which community resources and supports for youth are in place and which are missing. Using this information, members develop a multidimensional action plan targeted toward the gaps that exist locally. County Extension faculty and staff work with local volunteers to implement the plan.

These coalitions have influenced known risk and protective processes through such comprehensive prevention strategies as reducing the supply of alcohol, providing parent education and family support, and establishing meaningful roles to help youth connect to the community. For example, in one community, anyone who sells alcohol to a minor is now required to appear in court so that judges can detect repeat offenders and enforce penalties more uniformly than could arresting officers. Half the parents of all high-school students in another community joined a parent network and pledged that parties in their home would be chaperoned and alcohol-free. Judges now suspend driver's licenses for underage drinking violations in one community, but reduce the penalties if parents get involved in the treatment. Older teens in one school taught tobacco refusal skills to every sixth grader in the district. (For a more detailed description of the theoretical framework, methodology, and results, see Bogenschneider, 1996b).

In our work with these coalitions, it has become even more apparent how the research and knowledge of the University can benefit those outside the University and, conversely, how the knowledge, skills, and resources present in the community can benefit the mission of the University (for other examples, see Todd, Ebata, & Hughes, this volume). Extension specialists working with county-based Cooperative Extension faculty bring theoretical frameworks for conceptualizing prevention strategies, expertise on youth development and prevention programming, the technical know-how to conduct local research on youth problems, and experience in applying this research and knowledge to solving real problems. By building on this research base, citizens have been strategic in their planning and implementation, moving beyond stereotypes of what youth need and focusing instead on community responses with the greatest potential payoff. Citizens bring an intimate knowledge of the community and the energy and commitment it takes to apply this knowledge in ways that are consistent with local values and priorities.

In times of dwindling faculty and staff at universities, volunteers in our first eighteen sites have donated over 80,000 hours of time in less than five years. In times when resources to higher education are shrinking, Wisconsin Youth Futures has generated over $1,073,000 of cash or in-kind services at the local level and almost $600,000 at the state level. In times of increasing skepticism about the relevance of universities, the program has generated a form of positive public relations that is often difficult to elicit. For example, surveys of youth and adult volunteers from five sites showed the majority of respondents had personally recommended this university-affiliated program to another adult or teen in the community. Finally, in times when the mission of the University is being criticized, this outreach project provided the impetus for still another project that meets the needs of the people and is a legitimate topic for scientific inquiry.

Tapping Into Parenting (TIP) Survey

Most Youth Futures coalition members recognized the important role parents play in youth development; yet they did not know if parents were aware of their teenager's involvement in such risky behaviors as drinking and early sexual activity, and were often uncertain about parents' views on how involved the community and other organizations should be in prevention efforts. Furthermore, coalition members told us that parents often felt isolated; that is, they do not talk with other parents or know how other parents handle issues such as curfews, dating, and drinking. In response, Youth Futures coalitions asked us to help them conduct formal surveys of parents to collect information parents in earlier years gathered more informally. The project that emerged is known by the acronym TIP, or the Tapping Into Parents survey, and involves surveying local parents about their worries and concerns, perceptions regarding their adolescent children, their parenting practices, and perceptions of the school and community.

TIP is a survey of parents of sixth to twelfth graders, which, like TAP, is developed in consultation with parents and community leaders and conducted in collaboration with county extension agents. The results of this survey are fed back to parents and other members of the community through community reports, newsletters, news releases, and community forums. TIP has proven to be a powerful way to educate parents and other community members about local concerns and to motivate them to action. For example, TIP and TAP findings have been disseminated to parents through a series of parent education newsletters. Compared to nonreaders, parents who read the newsletters monitored their teens more closely, were more available and responsive, and engaged in more frequent discussions of risky behaviors with their teens (Bogenschneider &

Stone, 1997). Also, results from one recent TIP study found that whereas only 13% of mothers and 12% of fathers felt there was even a slight possibility their child uses alcohol (Bogenschneider & Raffaelli, 1995), over half the teens reported using alcohol at least once a month. The value of findings like these to citizens seems clear: Mobilizing parents around youth issues can be difficult if they are unaware that their child's development is being compromised by involvement in potentially risky behaviors. Incorporating data from local surveys regarding teen alcohol use into parent education newsletters was associated with increased parental awareness of adolescent alcohol use (Bogenschneider & Stone, 1997).

The value of this research to the University is also clear. Like the TAP program, TIP introduces graduate students to relevant scholarship and helps demonstrate the role the University can play in moving research beyond the walls of academia. In addition, the scientific papers beginning to emerge from this fledgling project can advance scholarly understanding of adolescent development and parent-teen relations (e.g., Bogenschneider & Raffaelli, 1995; Bogenschneider & Stone, 1997; Bogenschneider, Wu, & Raffaelli, 1996; Bogenschneider, Wu, Raffaelli, & Tsay, 1996; Stone & Bogenschneider, 1996), while having immediate and important educational and policy implications for the communities where the research was conducted.

As we worked with communities helping them conduct research and establish prevention coalitions, it became apparent to us that children, youth, and families were affected not only by what was happening within their community but also by the larger political environment. Clearly, public policy shapes the contexts in which families live and, thus, shapes human development as surely as the other professional endeavors we have described. Based on this rationale, a fourth outreach project was developed, Wisconsin Family Impact Seminars.

Wisconsin Family Impact Seminars

Calls for a family focus in policy making have come from many sources, including federal agencies (United States Department of Education Office of Educational Research and Improvement, 1991), national commissions (Committee for Economic Development, 1987; National Commission on America's Urban Families, 1993; National Commission on Children, 1991), and professional organizations whose members work with families (Council of Chief State School Officers, 1989; National Commission on Child Welfare and Family Preservation, 1990). Yet in Wisconsin, state and local policymakers have not always had ready access to the growing body of research about families, nor the staff or time to research all the relevant data on the complex issues that confront them. The information and analyses on family issues available to them from lobbyists, diverse interest groups, and special constituencies were often biased, fragmented, and even inaccurate. Too often, policy debate on complex issues was restricted to dialogue within institutional settings—among officials within the same agency, among academics, among practitioners, and among legislators. Even though in Wisconsin, the Madison campus of the University of Wisconsin, state agencies, and the legislature are within walking distance of each other, little cross-fertilization of perspectives occurred.

Although many university scholars claim to be interested in how their research can inform public policy, it was our experience that this connection was made all too infrequently. We believed that injecting research into the policymaking process was another legitimate role for scholars (see Bogenschneider, 1995) and an especially appropriate function for a state university that views its mission as improving the condition of its state's citizens.

Research, the hallmark of the university, can perform several important functions in family policy. For example, research can help policymakers identify social problems or refute contentions that a problem exists. Research can provide direction for family policy by identifying factors that contribute to social problems and identifying which of these factors are amenable to government intervention. Evaluation research can help policymakers assess whether programs and policies meet their stated outcomes. Family impact analysis can ascertain whether the program goals may be counterproductive by producing negative consequences for families, sometimes in unintended ways.

In contrast to most other institutions, the university is well positioned to provide research-based knowledge to policymakers. In addition to having ready access to current research based knowledge, the university is often perceived as being relatively unbiased. Even when working on controversial issues, university scholars can help maintain their objectivity and nonpartisanship by clarifying the potential consequences of a range of policy alternatives and refraining from advocating for a particular political position.

Disseminating research to policymakers requires a broad definition of scholarship with a heavy emphasis on teaching, synthesis, and application. With the assistance of a diverse cross-institutional advisory committee, we developed Wisconsin Family Impact Seminars, a continuing series of seminars and in-depth briefing reports designed to provide state-of-the-art research and theory on current family issues for state policymakers, representatives of state agencies, University and Extension faculty, representatives of the governor's office, staff members of legislative support bureaus, and practitioners. The goals of Wisconsin Family Impact Seminars are: (1) to analyze the consequences an issue, policy, or program has for family well-being; (2) to clarify the potential consequences of various policy alternatives; (3) to illustrate how policy making might benefit by taking into account the central role of the family in addressing social problems; and (4) to promote family well-being as one criterion for policy making, just as economic and environmental considerations have become standard fare in policy debate.

Since 1993, two-hour forums have been held twice a year on such topics as government's role in competent parenting, juvenile crime, teenage pregnancy, and welfare reform. The seminars provide objective, unbiased information and do not advocate for particular policy alternatives. Panelists include university researchers, policy analysts, and service providers. About one-third of the time is allocated for participants to discuss policy options and identify where common ground exists. Each seminar is accompanied by an in-depth briefing report that synthesizes the latest research on the topic and summarizes policy options from across the political spectrum.

The seminars have been so well received that the state assembly has delayed its starting time one hour so that state representatives can attend the seminar. The objective, nonpartisan focus of the seminar is evidenced by the financial support of two foundations with vastly different political perspectives and by the attendance of 675 participants from all political persuasions including 58 different legislators and 70 legislative offices. In telephone interviews with twenty-one state legislators and four legislative aides who attended one seminar, we asked them to compare the usefulness of the seminars with other information sources. Information from constituents was rated as the most useful; information obtained at Family Impact Seminars was rated the second most useful, ahead of newsletters, other print material, and lobbyists. One state representative reported that information from the welfare-reform seminar helped him decide how to vote on an upcoming welfare-reform issue. Another state legislator reported that the prevention seminar helped him formulate an opinion on a cigarette excise tax pending in the state budget. One participant wrote that information from the juvenile crime seminar helped develop a statewide juvenile justice plan that directed where federal funding should be spent (for further discussion of the program and its impacts, see Bogenschneider, 1995).

Evidence is emerging that we are also reaching our goal of establishing ongoing linkages with the state legislature that extend beyond the seminars. Following one seminar, we arranged thirteen personal appointments for our speakers with state policymakers including the governor, the secretary of Health and Family Services, the co-chair of Joint Finance, and several state legislators. For example, a faculty member who presented at the first seminar was appointed to the Governor's Commission on Families and Children and now links the Commission with university faculty who have expertise on family issues. Legislators or their aides increasingly ask the seminar coordinator for research on family issues or for the names of university scholars with expertise in a particular area. As with our other outreach projects, the linkages have been bidirectional, with state policymakers also influencing the research agenda at the University. In response to a request the coordinator received from a state legislator, one faculty member is now conducting an evaluation of the effectiveness of a teenage-pregnancy prevention program.

Implications

In this chapter we have argued that some of the recent criticism directed toward public universities may be justified. From a historical perspective, definitions of scholarship have narrowed in recent years. At the same time, land-grant universities have strayed from their guiding mission of generating and applying knowledge in ways that can improve the human condition and address the challenges currently faced by children, youth, families, and communities. Building on Boyer's (1990) definitions of scholarship, we have tried to provide some concrete illustrations of how a more inclusive definition of scholarship has been operationalized through our work at the University of Wisconsin-Madison.

In this final section, we briefly reiterate the lessons that can be learned from our experience developing outreach programs at a land-grant university. Then we discuss some implications of our work for university administrators, faculty, funders, and others.

Scholarship Can Be Relevant

We hope our descriptions of TAP, TIP, Youth Futures, and Family Impact Seminars provide convincing examples of how land-grant universities can once again be places of relevance where scholarship is pursued not only for the benefit of science, but also for the benefit of the people of the state. We think the progression of outreach programs in Wisconsin, beginning with community research and expanding to prevention coalitions and seminars for state policymakers, demonstrates how the demand for relevant scholarship grows when universities are able to successfully bridge the gap between research and action. Not only is relevant scholarship consistent with the mission upon which land-grant universities were founded, but relevant scholarship is also essential if land-grant universities are to regain the respect they once held as "people's colleges" that addressed the practical concerns of their state's citizens. Scholars who continue to conduct studies with little regard for the information needs of policymakers, practitioners, or citizens, or for the implications of their findings for policy or practice (Cohen & Ooms, 1993; Grob, 1992; Small 1992) reduce the likelihood that findings will be used in ways that better the human condition, thereby calling into question the relevance of scholarship and jeopardizing public support for universities.

Relevance Can Be Scholarly

Bronfenbrenner (1977) has argued that the need for relevance does not obviate the need for rigor. In fact, we contend that it is even more important that relevant research meet the highest academic standards because these outreach projects are not merely published in journals read by other academics, but are actually implemented in communities and state legislatures where they can actually make a difference in people's lives (Bogenschneider, 1996a). Perhaps the most compelling evidence that relevant scholarship can meet the high scholarly expectations of academia is that each of the outreach projects cited in this paper and many described throughout this book have been published in refereed journals or presented at scholarly meetings.

These conclusions have many implications for universities, scholars, and funders. We will mention only a few with the intent of initiating dialogue about the university's responsibility for relevant scholarship. Based on our experience, we believe universities can take immediate steps to encourage more relevant scholarship. First, the reward structure of universities must explicitly affirm that outreach is not an optional responsibility of faculty, fulfilled only after meeting the requirements of research and campus teaching (for similar arguments, see Erickson & Weinberg, this volume; Todd, Ebata, & Hughes, this volume). Just as universities expect applied scholars to demonstrate their ability to conduct rigorous scientific research, universities should expect research scholars to demonstrate the relevance of their research and their competence in performing outreach.

Second, the tenure and reward system needs to acknowledge and take into account that relevant scholarship is time-consuming. For example, relevant scholarship often entails developing a prevention program or seminar series, implementing the program, allowing time for the program to demonstrate its effectiveness, and then evaluating its impact. Conceivably, there can be a mismatch between the time it takes to develop and evaluate some applied outreach projects and the six-year tenure clock.

Third, universities need to provide the same recognition to scholarship directed outside academia as that directed toward academic peers (for a similar argument, see McCall, Groark, Strauss, & Johnson, this volume). As an example, the intent and purpose in writing for policymakers or practitioners is markedly different than synthesizing this same body of literature for academic peers. Whereas many outlets exist for publishing articles directed toward academic peers, few outlets currently exist for papers directed toward policymakers or practitioners.

We believe universities can be changed from within by faculty who actively seek out opportunities for relevant scholarship and who recognize that the scholarships of integration and application may require that they gain skills to improve their effectiveness in this domain just as they actively seek out skills to improve their effectiveness as researchers and teachers. In their departments, faculty can support the work of applied scholars, treating them not as second-class citizens, but as colleagues who share in the important work of the university (see also McCall et al., this volume). As reviewers, faculty can demand that scholarly papers identify the relevance of the findings for those outside academia.

We believe universities can also be changed from the outside. As public resources directed to universities continue to decline, universities will continue to seek outside sources of funding. Funders can play an important role in promoting relevant scholarship at universities by requiring that grant applications address both the issue of rigor ("How certain can we be that this program will meet its expected outcomes or that the data generated will be adequate to answer the questions being asked?") and relevance ("To whom or for what are these activities or findings important?").

The Morrill Act of the mid-nineteenth century is considered historic legislation because it revamped the mission of higher education to include the pursuit of knowledge that was practical and widely useful. As we approach the dawn of the new millennium, universities are again faced with historic decisions about the future role of higher education. It is our hope that the university will once again become a place of relevance where various forms of scholarship are valued and pursued and where addressing the problems of society are central to the university's mission.

References

Argyris, C., Putnam, R., & Smith, D. (1985). *Action science*. San Francisco: Jossey-Bass.

Bogenschneider, K. (1995). Roles for professionals in building family policy: A case study of state family impact seminars. *Family Relations, 44*, 5–12.

———. (1996a). Applied research: Caught between relevance and rigor. Invited address for the Applied Research Symposium, Society for Research on Adolescence, Boston, MA.

———. (1996b). An ecological risk/protective theory for building prevention programs, policies, and community capacity to support youth. *Family Relations, 45*, 127–128.

Bogenschneider, K., & Raffaelli, M. (1995). *Other teens drink, but not my kid: Family and community influences on adolescent alcohol use*. Manuscript presented at the annual meeting of the National Council on Family Relations, Portland, OR.

Bogenschneider, K., & Stone, M., (1997). Delivering parent education to low and high risk parents of adolescents via age-paced newsletters. *Family Relations, 46*, 123–134.

Bogenschneider, K., Wu, M. Y., & Raffaelli, M. (1996). *Parent influences on adolescent peer orientation and substance use: The interface of parenting practices and values*. Unpublished manuscript.

Bogenschneider, K., Wu, M. Y., Raffaelli, M., & Tsay, J. C. (1996). *Other teens drink, but not my kid: Does parental awareness of adolescent alcohol use influence parent's responsiveness and adolescent's risky behaviors?* Manuscript submitted for publication.

Boyer, E. (1990). *Scholarship reconsidered: Priorities of the professoriate*. Princeton, NJ: Princeton University Press.

Boyer, E. (1994, March 9). Creating the new American college. *The Chronicle of Higher Education*, A48.

Bronfenbrenner, U. (1977). Toward an experimental ecology of human development. *American Psychologist, 32*, 513–531.

———. (1979). *The ecology of human development*. Cambridge, MA: Harvard University Press.

———. (1989). Ecological systems theory. *Annals of child development, 6*, 187–249.

Caldwell, J. T. (1976). What a document . . . that land-grant act! In C. A. Vines and M. A. Anderson (Eds.), *Heritage/Horizons: Extension's commitment to people,* (pp. 12–16). Madison, WI: Journal of Extension.

Centers for Disease Control (1991). Premarital sexual experience among adolescent women, United States, 1979–1988. *Morbidity and Mortality Weekly Report, 39*, 929.

———. (1992). Sexual behavior among high school students. *Morbidity and Mortality Weekly Report, 40*, 885–888.

Cohen, E., & Ooms, T. (1993). *Data integration and evaluation: Essential components of family-centered systems reform*. Washington, DC: The Family Impact Seminar.

Committee for Economic Development. (1987). *Children in need: Investment strategies for the educationally disadvantaged*. Washington, DC: Author.

Council of Chief State School Officers. (1989). *Family support, education, and involvement*. Washington, DC: Author.

Dryfoos, J. G. (1990). *Adolescents at risk: Prevalence and prevention*. New York: Oxford University.

Eddy, E. D. (1956). *Colleges for our land and time: The land-grant idea in American education*. New York: Harper Brothers.

Elden, M., & Chisholm, R. P. (1993). Emerging varieties of action research: Introduction to the special issue. *Human Relations, 46*, 121–142.

Erickson, M. F., & Weinberg, R. A. (this volume). The Children, Youth, and Family Consortium: A University of Minnesota/community partnership. In R. M. Lerner & L. A. Simon (Eds.), *University-community collaborations for the twenty-first century: Outreach scholarship for youth and families.* New York: Garland.

Grob, G. (1992). How policy is made and how evaluators can affect it. *Evaluation Practice, 13,* 175–183.

Hamburg, D. A. (1992). *Today's children: Creating a future for a generation in crisis.* New York: Time Books.

Harkavy, I. (this volume). Organizational innovation and the creation of the new American university: The University of Pennsylvania's Center for Community Partnerships as a developing case study. In R. M. Lerner & L. A. Simon (Eds.), *University-community collaborations for the twenty-first century: Outreach scholarship for youth and families.* New York: Garland.

Irwin, C. E., Bundis, C. D., Brodt, S. E., Bennett, J. A., & Rodriguez, R. Q. (1991). *The health of America's youth: Current trends in health status and utilization of health services.* San Francisco: University of California at San Francisco.

Lerner, R. M. (1995). *America's youth in crisis: Challenges and options for programs and policies.* Thousand Oaks, CA: Sage.

Lynton, E. A., & Elman, S. E. (1987). *New priorities for the university.* San Francisco: Jossey-Bass

McCall, R. B., Groark, C. J., Strauss, M. S., & Johnson, C. N. (this volume). Challenges of university-community outreach to traditional research universities: The University of Pittsburgh Office of Child Development experience. In R. M. Lerner & L. A. Simon (Eds.), *University-community collaborations for the twenty-first century: Outreach scholarship for youth and families.* New York: Garland.

McDowell, G. R. (1988). Land-grant colleges of agriculture: Renegotiating or abandoning a social contract. *Choices, 3,* 18–23.

National Commission on America's Urban Families. (1993). *Families first.* Washington, DC: Author.

National Commission on Child Welfare and Family Preservation. (1990). *A commitment to change.* Washington, DC: American Public Welfare Association.

National Commission on Children. (1991). *Beyond rhetoric: A new American agenda for children and families.* Washington, DC: Author.

Price, R., & Polister, P. (1980). *Evaluation and action in the social environment.* New York: Academic Press.

Rappaport, J. (1990). Research methods and the empowerment social agenda. In P. Tolan, C. Chertok, F. Keys, & L. Jason (Eds.), *Researching community psychology: Issues of theory and methods* (pp. 51–63). Washington, DC: American Psychological Association.

Riley, S. (1996, August). Using local research to change 100 communities for children and families. Award address given at the 104th convention of the American Psychological Association, Toronto, Canada.

Rogers, E. M. (1989). The intellectual foundation and history of the agricultural extension model. *Knowledge: Creation, Diffusion, Utilization, 9,* 492–510.

Small, S. A. (1992, November). *The relevance of research and the research of relevance.* Paper presented at the annual meeting of the National Council on Family Relations, Orlando, FL.

———. (1995). Enhancing contexts of adolescent development: The role of community-based action research. In L. Crockett & A. Crouter (Eds.), *Pathways through adolescence: Individual development in relation to social contexts* (pp. 211–234). Hillsdale, NJ: Lawrence Erlbaum.

———. (1996). Collaborative, community-based research on adolescents: Using research for community change. *Journal of Research on Adolescence, 6,* 9–22.

Small, S. A. & Hug, B. (1990). The Teen Assessment Project: Tapping into the needs and concerns of local youth. *Journal of Extension,* Spring, 27–29.

Small, S. A., & Kerns, D. (1993). Unwanted sexual activity among peers during early and middle adolescence: Incidence and risk factors. *Journal of Marriage and the Family, 55,* 941–952.

Small, S. A., & Luster, T. (1994). An ecological, risk-factor approach to adolescent sexual activity. *Journal of Marriage and the Family, 56,* 181–192.

Todd, C. M., Ebata, A. T., & Hughes, R. Jr. (this volume). Making university and community collaborations work. In R. M. Lerner & L. A. Simon (Eds.), *University-community collaborations for the twenty-first century: Outreach scholarship for youth and families.* New York: Garland.

United States Department of Education Office of Educational Research and Improvement. (1991). *Policy perspectives: Parental involvement in education* (Publication No. PIP 91–983). Washington, DC: U.S. Government Printing Office.

Votruba, J. C. (1992). Promoting the extension of knowledge in service to society. *Metropolitan Universities, 3,* 72–80.

Chapter 13
Organizational Innovation and the Creation of the New American University

The University of Pennsylvania's Center for
Community Partnerships as a Case Study in Progress

Ira Harkavy
University of Pennsylvania

Introduction

The problems of the American city have increasingly become the problems of the urban college and university. Urban higher educational institutions cannot escape from the issues of poverty, crime, and physical deterioration that are at their gates. The choice is to return to the mythic image of the university on the hill, and suffer for it, or to become engaged in an effective and proactive fashion. No urban university has developed *the* model for working effectively with its environment. A number of excellent experiments and being undertaken, but they all represent partial attempts that do not mobilize the broad range of university resources and expertise.

Partial attempts simply will not do for either the university or society. A full-hearted and full-minded effort is needed—one that defines the problem of the city as the strategic problem for the American urban university. Ernest Boyer's (1994) extraordinarily influential call for creating the "New American College" has relevance here. Deploring the "crisis in our public schools" and desperate condition of "our cities," Boyer challenged American higher educators to change radically their priorities and act effectively to meet their civic and societal responsibilities: "Do colleges really believe they can ignore social pathologies that surround schools and erode the educational foundations of our nation?" Specifically, Boyer called for creating a "New American College . . . [that takes] special pride in its capacity to connect thought to action, theory to practice. . . . The New American College, as a connected institution, would be committed to improving, in a very intentional way, the human condition." (Boyer, 1994, p. A48)

Calling for creating the New American College is one thing, creating it is something else indeed. To put it mildly, it is very hard to do.

Since World War I, a strong tradition developed that separated scholarly research from the goal of improving the human condition in the here and now. Disconnection from, rather then connection to, society became the operational style of the vast majority of America's colleges and universities.[1]

After 1945, of course, higher education did connect. It connected, however, to distant, not local, problems. The Cold War became the defining issue that led to the development of the vast American "university system." Propelled by fear of and competition with the Soviet Union, American politicians, with significant support from the American public, unquestionably accepted higher education's requests for increased aid and support. The collapse of the Berlin Wall in 1989 and the breakup of the Soviet Union in 1991 signaled the end of the "Cold War University." Long ignored internal problems, including those Boyer identifies, could be ignored no longer. Over forty-five years of looking outward had its costs as unresolved domestic problems developed into unresolved, highly visible crises.[2]

But crises alone will not undo a nearly one-hundred-year history of universities' functioning as if they were in, but not of, their communities. Moreover, ignoring pressing societal problems was accompanied by a fragmentation of mission that separated service from research and teaching, and spurred the development of self-contained, self-referential disciplinary "communities," making effective engagement all the more difficult.[3]

Tradition and fragmentation are certainly significant barriers to creating connected institutions. An additional barrier, however, may be even more formidable. A fundamental contradiction exists in the structure of the American research university itself, a contradiction built in at its very creation. Daniel Coit Gilman, the founder of Johns Hopkins and central architect of the nineteenth-century research university, claimed that one of his proudest accomplishments was "a school of science grafted on one of the oldest and most conservative classical colleges" (Gilman 1898/1969, p. iii). Although referring specifically to the merger of the Sheffield Scientific School with Yale College, Gilman felt that this achievement exemplified his contribution to American higher education.

As a product of a merger of the German research university and the American college, the American research university was bound to develop severe tensions and contradictions from a joining of two markedly different entities. The research university was dedicated to specialized scholarship, and the university provided service through specialized inquiry and studies. For the American college, on the other hand, general education, character building, and civic education were the central purposes. The college provided service to society by cultivating in young people, to use Benjamin Franklin's phrase, "an *Inclination* join'd with an *Ability* to serve" (Franklin, 1907, p. 396; *Franklin's italics*). The research university has, of course, dominated this merger, creating an ethos and culture that rewards specialized study rather than more general scholarship and the education of the next generation for moral, civic, and intellectual leadership.

Given structural contradictions, nearly a century of increasing specialization, fragmentation of knowledge, and separation of scholarship from direct and immediate service to the city and society, what can be done to reinvent higher educational institutions? To put it another way, what steps can be taken to help universities and colleges become connected institutions, exemplifying Boyer's vision of a New American College in practice? To achieve Boyer's vision, we might begin by building on John Dewey's theory of instrumental intelligence and his identification of the central problem affecting modern society.

A Deweyan Approach

According to Dewey (1910), *genuine* learning only occurs when human beings focus their attention, energies, and abilities on solving *genuine* "dilemmas" and "perplexities." Other mental "activity" fails to produce reflection and intellectual progress. As John E. Smith (1993) has written about Dewey's theory of instrumental intelligence: "Reflective thought is an active response to the challenge of the environment" (Smith, 1993, p. 124). In 1910, Dewey spelled out the basis of his real-world, problem-driven, problem-solving theory of instrumental intelligence as follows:

Thinking begins in what may fairly be called a forked-road *situation, a situation which is ambiguous, which presents a dilemma, which proposes alternatives. As long as our activity slides smoothly along from one thing to another, or as long as we permit our imagination to entertain fancies at pleasure, there is no call for reflection. Difficulty or obstruction in the way of reaching a belief brings us, however, to a pause. . . .*

Demand for the solution of a perplexity is the steadying and guiding factor in the entire process of reflection. . . . *a question to be answered, an ambiguity to be resolved, sets up an end and holds the current of ideas to a definite channel. . . . (emphasis added)*

[In summary]. . . the origin of thinking is some perplexity, confusion, or doubt: Thinking is not a case of spontaneous combustion; it does not occur just on "general principles." There is something specific which occasions and involves it. (Dewey, 1910, pp. 11–12).

Employing Dewey's theory of instrumental intelligence takes us only so far in solving our problem. An infinite number of perplexities and dilemmas exist for universities to focus upon. Which problem or set of problems are significant, basic, and strategic enough to lead to societal as well as intellectual progress? In 1927, in *The Public and Its Problems*, Dewey unequivocally identified the existence of "neighborly community" as indispensable for a well-functioning democratic society: "There is no substitute for the vitality and depth of close and direct intercourse and attachment. . . . Democracy must begin at home, and its home is the neighborly community." In that same book, he also noted that creating a genuinely democratic community is "in the first instance an intellectual problem." (Dewey, 1927, pp. 147, 213) Sixty-nine years later, we still do not know how to create democratic neighborly communities. Events in Bosnia, the states of the former Soviet Union, South Africa, France, Germany, Northern Ireland, etc., indicate that this very practical and core theoretical problem of the social sciences is more than an American dilemma.

It is within the American city that the need for communities rooted in face-to-face relationships and exemplifying humanistic universal values is most acute. The problem of *how* to create these communities is, moreover, the strategic problem of our time. As such, it is the problem most likely to advance the university's primary mission of producing and transmitting knowledge to advance human welfare.

The particular strategic real-world and intellectual problem Penn (as well as other urban universities) faces is how to overcome the deep, pervasive, interrelated problems affecting the people in its local environment. This concrete, immediate, practical and theoretical problem, needless to say, requires creative interdisciplinary interaction. Penn and the other comprehensive research universities encompass the broad range of human knowledge needed to solve the complex, comprehensive, and interconnected problems found in the city. The Center for Community Partnerships is Penn's primary vehicle for bringing that broad range of human knowledge to bear, so that West Philadelphia (Penn's local geographic community), Philadelphia, the University itself, and society benefit.[4]

The Center for Community Partnership

The Center is based on three core propositions:

1. Penn's future and the future of West Philadelphia/Philadelphia are intertwined.
2. Penn can make a significant contribution to improving the quality of life in West Philadelphia/Philadelphia.
3. Penn can enhance its overall mission of advancing and transmitting knowledge by helping to improve the quality of life in West Philadelphia/Philadelphia.

The first proposition, it would seem, is self-evident. Safety, cleanliness of the area, and attractiveness of the physical setting contribute not only to a general campus ambiance, but also to the recruitment and retention of faculty, students, and staff. The deterioration of the city and of West Philadelphia has a direct impact on Penn's ability to enhance its position as a leading international university. As studies by the Center have indicated, West Philadelphia has declined precipitously since 1980.

West Philadelphia's severe urban crisis is evident in population decline, increases in poverty, crime, violence, physical deterioration, and the poor performance of the schools, among other quality-of-life indicators. For example, the population of West Philadelphia has been decreasing since 1960. The numbers are as follows: 1960—301,742; 1970—275,611; 1980—232,979; 1990—219,705 (Bureau of the Census, 1960–1990). From 1989 to 1993, the number of West Philadelphia residents receiving some form of public assistance increased by approximately 25% (Philadelphia City Planning Commission, 1994). Crime increased 10% from 1983 to 1993 in the neighborhoods surrounding the University (University of Pennsylvania, 1994). A study of the Mantua/Parkside/Mill Creek area of West Philadelphia (population 68,000) shows the prevalence of violence in the area: between 1987 and 1990 there were 172 violence-related deaths, 60% of which involved guns; 94% of area males in their twenties made at least one emergency-room visit (Schwarz et al., 1994). Physical deterioration in the area surrounding the University is well-documented in neighborhood plans prepared by local community-based organizations in partnership with the Center for Community Partnerships, (1994, 1995). Finally, ranked by performance on national standardized tests for reading and mathematics, four public elementary schools proximate to the University ranked 107th, 130th, and

160th out of 171 elementary schools in Philadelphia (School District of Philadelphia, 1994). For Penn to advance significantly requires that West Philadelphia be transformed from an urban environment that has become increasingly dangerous and alienating into a reasonably safe, attractive (in all respects), cosmopolitan urban community.

This proposition does not take us terribly far. It can be argued that conditions are indeed deteriorating—but that nothing can be done to reverse them. Put another way, this argument views deterioration as an irreversible phenomenon, a phenomenon beyond our control that at best can be delayed or dealt with on a purely cosmetic basis. A similar and somewhat less pessimistic scenario is that the deterioration can be reversed, but that Penn as an institution can do little to improve conditions. In this interpretation, the University is, in effect, completely dependent upon the actions of others—government at all levels and corporations, for example—for any significant improvements to occur in the quality of life in West Philadelphia/Philadelphia.

The Center is founded upon a very different notion—a notion that Penn can lead the way toward revitalizing West Philadelphia/Philadelphia. Its leadership role derives from its status as an international research university with extraordinary intellectual resources, its position as the most prestigious institution in the city, as well as the city's largest private employer. Appropriately organized and directed, Penn's range of resources can serve as *the* catalytic agent for galvanizing other institutions, as well as government itself, in concerted efforts to improve the quality of life in West Philadelphia/Philadelphia. The Center has already taken a lead in initiating a number of projects based on this assumption. These projects include the development of a city-wide higher-education coalition, the Philadelphia Higher Education Network for Neighborhood Development (PHENND); an action seminar on "Urban Universities and the Reconstruction of American Cities, 1945–2000; How Universities are Affected by, and Actively Affect, Their Off-Campus Environments: Penn-West Philadelphia as a Strategic Case Study of Institutional Policy and Action," comprised of senior Penn administration, faculty members from across the University, and community leaders; and a West Philadelphia coalition of institutions, governmental agencies, community groups and businesses (organized with the West Philadelphia Partnership) that is developing plans for a business corridor bordering the University.

As stated, the arguments presented thus far are largely defensive. That is, they are based on the assumption that Penn is faced with a severe problem in its locality (which it is) and that something must be done to solve that problem (which it must). There is, however, an additional line of argument: Enormous intellectual benefits for the University can accrue from a proactive strategy to improve West Philadelphia/Philadelphia. In fact, the Center's guiding assumption is that significant advances in teaching and research will occur by focusing on the strategic problems of the city. Faculty and students will be increasingly able to put their ideals and theories into practice and test those ideals and theories as they work to solve important intellectual and real-world problems. Undergraduates will be able to learn and contribute to society simultaneously. Their academic work will engage them with the central dilemmas of our time as they focus their intellectual energy, skill, and idealism on helping to make West Philadelphia and the city better places to live and work.

Based on the assumptions outlined above, the Center was founded in 1992 to achieve the following objectives: improve the internal coordination and collaboration of all University-wide community-service programs; create new and effective partnerships between the University and the community; encourage new and creative initiatives linking Penn and the community; and strengthen a national network of institutions of higher education committed to engagement with their local communities. The Center is an outgrowth of the Penn Program for Public Service, which was created in 1989 to replace and expand the Office of Community-Oriented Policy Studies in the School of Arts and Sciences.[5]

The Center's director reports to both Penn's vice president for government, community, and public affairs and the provost (the university's chief academic officer). Through the Center, the University currently engages in three types of activities:

- academically based community service;
- direct traditional service;
- community and economic development.

The following discussion highlights the work of the Center in these three key areas.

Academically Based Community Service

Academically based community service may be defined as service rooted in and intrinsically tied to teaching and/or research. It encompasses problem-oriented research and teaching, as well as service learning emphasizing student and faculty reflection on the service experience. In Penn's case, the primary location for the service is its community of West Philadelphia.

Much of the Center's work has focused on the public school as the educational and neighborhood institution that can, if effectively transformed, serve as the concrete vehicle of community change and innovation. The Center has helped to create university-assisted community schools that function as the centers of education, services, engagement, and activity within specified geographic areas. With its community and school collaborators, the Center has developed significant service-learning programs that engage young people in creative work designed to advance skills and abilities through service to their school, families, and community. Penn students and faculty are also engaged in service learning that requires the development and application of knowledge to solve problems as well as active and serious reflection on the service experience and its impacts. This Deweyan approach might be termed "learning by community problem solving and real-world reflective doing."

The mediating structure for on-site delivery of academic resources is the West Philadelphia Improvement Corps (WEPIC), a school-based school and community revitalization program founded in 1985. WEPIC's goal is to produce comprehensive, university-assisted community schools that serve, educate, and activate all members of the community, revitalizing the curriculum through a community-oriented, real-world problem-solving approach. WEPIC seeks to help develop schools that are open year-round, functioning simultaneously as the core building for the community and as its educational and service-delivery hub.

Specifically, the Center's academically based community-service activities include the following:

1. Develops and supports undergraduate and graduate seminars, courses, and research projects. By academic year 1996–1997, approximately forty-five courses were offered that supported Penn's work in West Philadelphia.

2. Coordinates internships for students to engage intensively in work in the community, especially in the public schools. Of particular note are the following:
    *   *Pennsylvania Service Scholars,* a statewide higher education AmeriCorps program funded by the Corporation for National Service. Full-time students, these nineteen Penn undergraduates work part-time over a period of three years in local public schools.[6]

- *Public Service Summer Internship Program,* a project that supports twelve undergraduates during the summer to take a research seminar with the Center's director and conduct a six-week summer institute for incoming sixth graders at a local middle school.
- *Undergraduate Social Science Initiative,* a program funded by the Ford Foundation designed to enhance undergraduate social-science teaching (sixteen courses created to date) expand undergraduate academic internships linked to work in the public schools (fifty-eight to date), and support interdisciplinary action research seminars for faculty and graduate students.
- *Program to Link Intellectual Resources and Community Needs,* a new program funded by the W. K. Kellogg Foundation that develops academically based community service in cultural and community studies, environmental studies, and nutrition. In 1996–1997 the program supported fifteen undergraduate students working as academic interns; it also supported course development and seminars designed to integrate action research into the university curriculum.

3. Coordinates the National WEPIC Replication Project, a three-year grant from the DeWitt Wallace-Reader's Digest Fund to replicate WEPIC's university-assisted community school model at three universities (Miami University of Ohio, University of Kentucky-Lexington Campus, and the University of Alabama at Birmingham). The project is also developing a national network of colleagues interested in this work through a journal (*Universities and Community Schools*), a newsletter, an on-line database, and a series of national conferences.

Direct Traditional Service

Here there is a coordination with the Penn Volunteers in Public Service (Penn's staff and alumni service organization) of various service projects, including a mentoring program for twenty-one middle-school students, a postsecondary scholarship program for twelve high-school students from West Philadelphia who have actively served their communities and achieved academically, and annual drives to fill community needs.

In addition, in this category there is a coordination with the Program for Student-Community Involvement (PSCI), Penn's student volunteer center, of an extensive service program initiated by undergraduates. In turn, the Center works closely with the Community Service Living/Learning Project, a residential program for students committed to community service. In 1995–1996, the twenty-four residents of the project devoted their activities to work with WEPIC, Penn's university-assisted community school partnership. Finally, here we work with Penn's Facilities Management Department to coordinate Operation Fresh Start, in which members of that department, together with student, faculty, staff, and community volunteers, work on the physical improvement of local public schools.

Community and Economic Development

Here we act to coordinate work-based learning programs in which students from a local middle school are mentored at Penn's Medical Center and high-school students serve as interns in various Penn publication departments and as paid apprentices in the Medical Center. In addition, we work in coordination with local community associations and the West Philadelphia Partnership, a mediating, nonprofit organization composed of institutions (including Penn), businesses, and community organizations, on community planning projects that have produced the following:

1. City funding for capital improvements of a major business corridor along the university's western boundary. A business owners association has been formed to oversee the project.
2. Strategic plans for housing and commercial revitalization of two West Philadelphia communities, Walnut Hill and Spruce Hill.

Moreover, we work with Penn's Purchasing Department to create opportunities for minority and female employment and business ownership in West Philadelphia through minority purchasing contracts. As a direct result of the Buy West Philadelphia Program, Penn's purchasing from West Philadelphia suppliers increased from $2.1 million in 1987 to $15 million in 1994. In 1995, Penn signed an additional $2.8 million in minority purchasing contracts. Furthermore, we work on developing (with Penn's Office of Data Communication and Computing Services and the West Philadelphia Partnership) a highly accessible West Philadelphia data and information system. A web site on West Philadelphia and the Center has been established. The Center also coordinates Internet training, involving software and technical support for approximately five hundred West Philadelphia teachers. Finally, we provide (with Penn's Human Resources Department) training and technical assistance to the West Philadelphia Partnership's Job Network and Referral Center, helping to implement a

Hire West Philadelphia strategy at Penn and other institutions in West Philadelphia.

Conclusion

The above programs illustrate the Center's multidimensional, integrated focus on solving a practical, real-world problem—the problem of the American city. It is a problem of such interrelated complexity that no single component of the university can solve it by itself. The Center is an organizational innovation responsible for mobilizing the broad range of university resources to help Penn better fulfill its mission and to help create a better West Philadelphia/Philadelphia. The Center also helps to form partnerships with other institutions (including public schools, businesses, not-for-profits, community organizations, unions, churches, and governmental agencies) that will facilitate ongoing interorganizational cooperation, learning, and improvement.

The Center is only one of a number of such organizational innovations throughout the American academy that are part of a movement toward creating the New American College that Ernest Boyer envisioned. Three recent examples include: the University of Illinois at Chicago's "Great Cities" program, created in 1993 as an additional unit within the Office of the Chancellor; the State University of New York at Buffalo's "Vice President for Public Service and Urban Affairs," created in 1992; and "Campus Compact," created in 1985 as an organization of college presidents dedicated to advancing community service and citizenship (it has expanded from thirteen member institutions in 1985 to over 520 in 1995). These examples illustrate a movement that needs to be encouraged and supported. The state of our society, particularly the crisis of the American city, are testimony that the self-contained, isolated university will no longer do. Community problem-solving, civic colleges and universities are needed as never before for achieving sustained intellectual and societal progress.

At a national conference on "The University and the City" held at the University of Pennsylvania in June 1993, William R. Greiner, president of the State University of New York at Buffalo, described how universities might proceed toward becoming civic institutions:

If every research-intensive university in this country commits itself to changing a small portion of events in its own community, if every urban and metropolitan research university commits itself to addressing needs in its own city, then,

*in the total of all our acts on behalf of our neighbors and our mutual future,
we will be a massive and unparalleled force for the good of our people and our
country. (Greiner, 1994, p. 15)*

The "Greiner strategy" holds enormous promise for taking us from where
we are to where we have to go.

The Center for Community Partnerships is playing a leading role in
helping Penn to become a model urban university for the twenty-first century, a "research university that [fully] commits itself to addressing needs
in its own city" (Greiner, 1994, p. 15) in order to advance knowledge and
human welfare. Although building on over a decade of experience, the
Center was created approximately five years ago. To help Penn become a
model urban university will require significant "organizational learning"
and doing on our part.[7] Reports from the field will be ongoing.

Notes

1.   For discussion of these trends, see Ira Harkavy and John L. Puckett, "Toward Effective
     University–Public School Partnerships: An Analysis of a Contemporary Model," *Teachers
     College Record* 92 (1991): 556–581; and "Lessons from Hull House for the Contempo-
     rary Urban University," *Social Service Review* 68 (1994): 301–321.
2.   A discussion of the impacts of the end of the Cold War on the American university can
     be found in Lee Benson and Ira Harkavy, "School and Community in the Global Soci-
     ety: A Neo-Deweyan Theory of Community Problem-Solving Schools and Cosmopoli-
     tan Neighborly Communities." *Universities and Community Schools* 5 (1/2) (1997)
     16–71.
3.   For a more extended discussion, see Harkavy and Puckett, "Toward Effective Univer-
     sity-Public School Partnerships," *Teachers College Record* 91 (4): 558–560; and Ira
     Harkavy, "The University and Social Sciences in the Social Order: An Historical Over-
     view and 'Where Do We Go from Here?'" *Virginia Social Science Journal* 27 (1992):
     1–8, 17–19.
4.   My understanding of John Dewey's writings and their implications for the work of the
     Center for Community Partnerships have been advanced significantly by Lee Benson.
     I am indebted to him for illustrating how Dewey's theory of instrumental intelligence
     could be extraordinarily useful to our efforts in West Philadelphia. See Lee Benson and
     Ira Harkavy, "Progressing beyond the Welfare State: A Neo-Deweyan Strategy; Univer-
     sity-Assisted, Staff-Controlled and Managed, Community-Centered Schools as Compre-
     hensive Community Centers to Help Construct and Organize Hardworking, Cohesive,
     Caring, Cosmopolitan Communities in a Democratic Welfare Society," *Universities and
     Community Schools* 2 (1/2) (1991): 1–25.
5.   For more details on this development, see Lee Benson and Ira Harkavy, "Progressing
     beyond the Welfare State: A Neo-Deweyan Strategy," *Universities and Community
     Schools* 2 (1/2): 12–23.
6.   AmeriCorps is the central program in President Clinton's effort to develop and ex-
     tend national service. The Corporation for National Service is the federal administra-
     tive entity responsible for AmeriCorps and other national and community-service
     programs.
7.   A discussion of the complex process of organizational learning can be found in William F.
     Whyte, ed., *Participatory Action Research*. Newbury Park, CA: Sage, 1991, 237–241.

References

Benson, L. and Harkavy, I. (1991). Progressing beyond the welfare state: A neo-Deweyan strategy; University-assisted, staff-controlled and managed, community-centered schools as comprehensive community centers to help construct and organize hardworking, cohesive, caring, cosmopolitan communities in a democratic welfare society. *Universities and Community Schools 2* (1/2), 1–25.

———. (1997). School and community in the global society: A neo-Deweyan theory of community problem-solving schools and cosmopolitan neighborly communities. *Universities and Community Schools 5* (1/2), 16–71.

Boyer, E. (March 9, 1994). Creating the new American college. *Chronicle of Higher Education,* A48.

Bureau of the Census (1960–1990). *Census of Population and Housing.* Washington, U.S. Department of Commerce.

Center for Community Partnerships. (1994). *Walnut Hill strategic neighborhood plan.* Philadelphia: University of Pennsylvania.

———. (1995). *Spruce Hill community renewal plan.* Philadelphia: University of Pennsylvania.

Dewey, J. (1910). *How we think.* New York: D.C. Heath.

———. (1927/1954). *The public and its problems.* Denver, CO: Allan Swallow.

Franklin, B. (1907). *The Writings of Benjamin Franklin* (ed. A. Smyth, Vol. 2). New York: Macmillan.

Gilman, D. (1898/1969). *University problems in the United States.* New York: Garett.

Greiner, W. (1994). In the total of all these acts: "How can American universities address the urban agenda?" *Universities and Community Schools 4* (1/2), 12–15.

Harkavy, I. (1992). The university and the social sciences in the social order: An historical overview and "Where do we go from here?" *Virginia Social Science Journal 27,* 1–25.

Harkavy, I. and Puckett, J. (1991). Toward effective university-public school partnerships: An analysis of a contemporary model. *Teachers College Record 91* (4), 556–581.

———. (1994). Lessons from Hull House for the contemporary urban university. *Social Science Review, 68* (3), 301–321.

Philadelphia City Planning Commission. (1994). The plan for West Philadelphia. Philadelphia: Philadelphia City Planning Commission.

School District of Philadelphia. (1994). *School profiles.* Philadelphia: School District of Philadelphia.

Schwarz, D., Grisso, J., Miles, J., Wishner, A., and Sutton, R. (1994). A longitudinal study of injury morbidity in an African-American population. *Journal of the American Medical Association, 271,* 755–760.

Smith, J. (1993). *The spirit of American philosophy.* Albany, NY: State University of New York Press.

University of Pennsylvania. (1994). Safety is everyone's right, everyone's responsibility, let's form a partnership. Unpublished manuscript. Philadelphia: University of Pennsylvania Division of Public Safety.

Whyte, W. (Ed.). (1991). *Participatory action research.* Newbury Park, CA: Sage.

Chapter 14
The Young Spartan Program
A Bridge between the Ivory Tower and the Community

Joanne G. Keith, Daniel F. Perkins,* Joy C. Greer,
Karen McKnight Casey, and Theresa M. Ferrari

Michigan State University
*University of Florida

> Our troubled planet can no longer afford the luxury of pursuits con-
> fined to an ivory tower. Scholarship has to prove its worth, not on its
> own terms, but by service to the nation and the world.
> (Handlin, cited in Boyer, 1994, p. A48)

With the movement from the industrial era to the postindustrial information age, Western societies are experiencing substantial paradigm shifts.
The dramatic economic, political, and technological changes occurring at
all levels of society impact human capital development. Universities are
not immune to these changes; in fact, they face the challenges of preparing
students to be competent and successful for this ever-changing future (Levitz
& Noel, 1995; Marcos, Edens, & Goldsmith, 1993). Scholars suggest
that the success of a college graduate will be measured not by the hierarchical management paradigm of the industrial period, but by a collaborative, pluralistic, consensus-driven framework that characterizes the postindustrial society (Boyer, 1994; Snyder, 1996).

Given these changes, we need to design specific learning opportunities to address the discrepancy between the world of the twenty-first century and the world inside the university's "ivory tower." Research supports
the contention that many students need more than lectures and library
research; they also need active learning opportunities (Gardner, 1983; Kolb,
1984; Perkins & Miller, 1994). Lectures and library research characterize
a *teaching* institution, whereas, "hands-on" activities and experiential education are the marks of a *learning* institution (Barr & Tagg, 1995). The
teaching paradigm asserts that the university's responsibility is to provide
instruction and transfer knowledge. In contrast, in the learning paradigm
universities are responsible for producing learning and sharing this
responsibiliy with students. Therefore, the role of the "new" university is

to "create environments and experiences that bring students to discover and construct knowledge for themselves, to make students members of communities of learners that make discoveries and solve problems" (Barr & Tagg, 1995, p. 15).

Increasingly, university faculty have embraced a learning paradigm; the process of incorporating active learning practices into their teaching has transformed their curricula. Service learning (i.e., community-based experiential learning combined with reflection) is one such learning strategy appropriate for university students. However, some universities and faculty find it difficult to engage students in service learning (Boyer, 1994). The process may be easier when the university has an investment, or stake, in the communities where its students serve. Official university-community partnerships provide a means for developing active learning opportunities that provide a "real-life" training ground for university students. Moreover, "academically-based community service focused on improving the quality of life in the local community [can benefit the university through] the integration of research, teaching, and service" (Harkavy & Puckett, 1994, p. 300; see also, Harkavy, this volume).

Many individuals and groups recommend working together to form strong problem-solving collaborative relationships to improve the present status and future well-being of children and the communities in which they live (Benard, 1991; Carnegie Council on Adolescent Development, 1992, 1995; Dryfoos, 1990, 1994; Ellison & Barbour, 1992; Hamburg, 1992; Hodgkinson, 1989; Hogue et al., 1995; Kagan, 1989; Keith, Covey, & Perkins, 1996; Keith, Knox, Perkins, & Blackman, 1995; Keith & Perkins, 1995; Keith et al., 1993; Lerner, 1993, 1995; National Commission on Children, 1991; Schorr, 1988; W. T. Grant Foundation, 1988). As part of this trend, universities are rediscovering the mission and practice of working in partnership with the community to address societal concerns (Harkavy, this volume; Harkavy & Puckett, 1994).

Collaboration implies the development of a reciprocal relationship, a co-learning partnership: It is not the university "doing to" the community, but "doing with." However, the traditional context of the university does not encourage cooperative and collaborative efforts (Small, 1995). Thus, the movement of universities toward partnerships with communities has challenged the traditional university institution.

The purpose of this chapter is to describe both a theoretical framework and an applied context for university-community collaboration. We present a rationale that supports strong university-community partnerships because they are crucial to the learning and development of university students. Specifically, through a case study of a kindergarten–fifth grade, university, and community partnership, we will explore the roles that have evolved for administration, faculty, and students in support of an active learning paradigm. The case study highlights models for outreach involvement that facilitate professional and individual development for university students. Finally, we will identify practical principles and their application concerning the case study of the educational partnership.

The Young Spartan Program: An Overview

The Young Spartan Program[1] is a broad-based collaborative effort designed to engage the community for the enhancement of educational outcomes for elementary and higher education students. The principal partners in this effort are from a metropolitan area that includes the capital city of a large industrial state, Lansing, Michigan, with a population of approximately 150,000. Partners include: (a) Six elementary schools in Lansing, a public school district with more than 20,000 students in kindergarten through twelfth grade; (b) Michigan State University, a land-grant, research-intensive university with more than 40,000 students enrolled in more than seventy major areas of study; (c) state government (Jobs Commission); and (d) the Lansing Regional Chamber of Commerce. The shared vision of this collaborative body is increased academic achievement and career awareness for elementary and higher education students. The relevance of the community as a "learning laboratory" for the university students helps to create bridges linking the ivory tower with the "real world." Indeed, the "real world" becomes *now* and not something distant and off in the future. Thus, learning is not separate from the community; rather, it is an integral part of active problem solving.

To reach the above noted objectives, the Young Spartan Program creates opportunities for elementary school students to experience the community and its members as educators in a reciprocal exchange. For example, elementary students often come to the university for planned learning experiences. Likewise, university faculty, staff, students, retirees, and other community members go to the school sites and share their expertise in a variety of ways. During the course of the 1995–1996 academic year, approximately 100 such learning experiences were implemented with the six elementary schools through the Young Spartan Program. Each week an average of just over 140 Michigan State undergraduates participated in some manner in the education of the elementary students. Over fifty different campus units, both academic and nonacademic, were involved in a variety of ways. The breadth of the campus units involved in this outreach is illustrated by figure 14.1. The scope of the approach and content for this programming is outlined in the project models described below. In addition, the Young Spartan Resource Guide (1994) highlights many campus-based resources as educational opportunities for elementary-aged children.

Although the primary focus of this project is developing elementary students and providing leadership and service opportunities for university students, the benefits extend to other participants, including community volunteers and businesses, teachers and principals, university staff, and faculty (Young Spartan Program, 1995). For this chapter, we will focus upon the roles that have evolved for administration, faculty, and students in support of an active learning paradigm. The case study highlights models for outreach involvement that facilitate professional and individual development for university students. Finally, we will identify practical principles and their application concerning the case study of the educational partnership.

The Young Spartan Program as a Problem-Solving Collaboration: Human Ecological Theory in Action

Human ecological theory is particularly well suited to the study of *relationships* in a variety of social environments; thus, it can be used to understand the dynamics of the university-community relationship. This theory provides a framework for analyzing existing settings and how to enhance their capacity as a developmental influence (Garbarino, 1982). Research has provided support for using ecological theory in designing programs and in policy formulation (Bubolz & Sontag, 1993; Lerner, 1995). Therefore, the Young Spartan Program, as a collaborative effort, "is an ecological approach to community problem solving" (Perkins, Ferrari, Covey, & Keith, 1994, p. 41).

Bronfenbrenner (1979, 1986) proposed an ecological model consisting of multiple levels of the environment. These levels capture the interaction and uniqueness of individuals, institutions, and communities (a detailed description of this model as it pertains to community-based programs can be found in Perkins et al., 1994). The basic premise of this model is that there are connections between and among the different levels of the environment. Moreover, these connections can be described as a web of interpersonal relationships, activities, and roles. Individuals engage in these

Figure 14.1. Young Spartan Program.

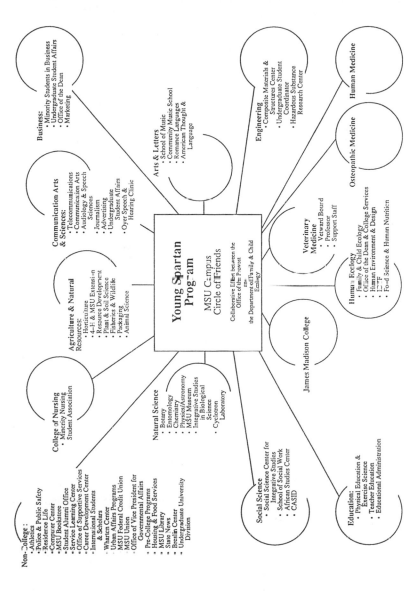

Young Spartan Program

MSU Campus Circle of Friends

Collaborative Effort between the Office of the Provost and the Department of Family & Child Ecology

Non-College:
• Athletics
• Police & Public Safety
• Residence Life
• Computer Center
• MSU Bookstore
• Student Alumni Office
• Service Learning Center
• Office of Supportive Services
• Career Development Center
• International Students & Scholars
• Wharton Center
• Urban Affairs Programs
• MSU Federal Credit Union
• MSU Union
• Office of Vice President for Governmental Affairs
• Pre-College Programs
• Housing & Food Services
• MSU Library
• State News
• Breslin Center
• Undergraduate University Division

Business:
• Minority Students in Business
• Undergraduate Student Affairs
• Office of the Dean
• Marketing

Communication Arts & Sciences:
• Telecommunications
• Communication Arts
• Audiology & Speech Sciences
• Journalism
• Advertising
• Undergraduate Student Affairs
• Oyer Speech & Hearing Clinic

Arts & Letters
• School of Music
• Community Music School
• Romance Languages
• American Thought & Language

Engineering
• Composite Materials & Structures Center
• Undergraduate Student Coordinator
• Hazardous Substance Research Center

Human Medicine

Osteopathic Medicine

Veterinary Medicine
• Verward Bourd
• Professor
• Support Staff

Human Ecology
• Family & Child Ecology
• Office of the Dean & College Services
• Human Environment & Design
• LCT
• Food Science & Human Nutrition

James Madison College

Education:
• Physical Education & Exercise Science
• Teacher Education
• Educational Administration

Social Science
• Social Science Center for Integrative Studies
• School of Social Work
• African Studies Center
• CASID

Natural Science
• Botany
• Entomology
• Chemistry
• Physics/Astronomy
• MSU Museum
• Integrative Studies in Biological Science
• Cyclotron Laboratory

Agriculture & Natural Resources:
• Horticulture
• 4-H & MSU Extension
• Resource Development
• Plant & Soil Science
• Fisheries & Wildlife
• Packaging
• Animal Science

College of Nursing
Minority Nursing Student Association

connections at the many different levels of the environment. The stronger, more positive, and more diverse the links and connections among the levels, the more beneficial they will be as an influence on an individual's development (Bronfenbrenner and Morris, in press; Garbarino, 1982). In other words, a web that is tightly woven will decrease an individual's chance of slipping through it.

Therefore, we think the connections among settings is the core function of a collaboration from an ecological perspective. For example, university faculty and school-district administrators may work together to create an institutional partnership, and their actions make it possible for university students and elementary students to engage in shared learning experiences. The partnership represents a complex array of linkages and connections between different levels of the environment that are involved (e.g., university administration, university faculty, students, principals, teachers, elementary students, and other community partners). Ultimately, university-community educational partnerships should strive to create strong connections and linkages for the education of elementary and university students. Service learning is one approach to providing opportunities to create linkages and connections in students' educational experiences.

Utilizing Service Learning to Create Learning Institutions

Although often interchanged, community service and service learning are distinctly different (Perkins & Miller, 1994). The focus of community service is the activity, such as university students volunteering in the community. Service learning, however, formally or informally integrates an individual's community involvement with the individual's studied (i.e., scholarly) reflection about the activity and its meaning. An individual enhances his or her learning during such reflection time. This reflection can be formal, such as being integrated into the classroom or course work agenda, or informal, such as students' keeping journals on their own. Thus, reflection about the service activity and its relationship to learning is what distinguishes service learning from community service. Service learning benefits students in several ways: (a) it aids in the development of citizenship and character; (b) it aids in the integration of youth into adult society; and (c) it is an effective way to promote active, integrative, and involved learning (Keith, 1994; Perkins & Miller, 1994). Service learning theory *applies* principles of experiential education and *connects* the university and community systems. These benefits provide a rationale for promoting service learning in the higher-education setting as a teaching strategy to help foster students' development.

Students often act as the bridge that connects the university to the community. Indeed, the effective involvement of students in outreach can simultaneously meet the needs of the individual student, the university, and the community. Service learning in colleges and universities can enhance the educational experience of students by providing applications of theory and learning in community settings. Thus, the student moves beyond the classroom and into the community. Specifically, students involved in service learning activities have shown improved academic standing and increased awareness about community needs (Perkins & Miller, 1994). In addition, students show an improved conceptual and practical understanding of course material (Markus, Howard, & King, 1993) and change their attitudes concerning the people they assist and their ability to make a difference (Giles & Eyler, 1994; Kraft & Krug, 1994; Markus, Howard, & King, 1993). Students involved with service learning also report a higher level of commitment to service and display an orientation for leadership (Battistoni, 1994).

More than providing learning opportunities for students, the university leads by its example. A university that supports service in the community serves as a role model of civic responsibility for students (Harkavy & Puckett, 1994). Participation in service learning leads to the development of what we want students to value: (a) service in achieving public good; (b) community development and empowerment; (c) reciprocal learning; and (d) social and civic responsibility (Edens, 1994).

Finally, it is important to note that service learning is an applied learning technique that embodies the ecological perspective. Service learning connects the learner to "real-world" systems that provide opportunities for him or her to apply knowledge. Service learning is the vehicle through which learners and other participants engage in a variety of activities, interpersonal relationships, and roles. For example, a noon-hour math club links the service-learning student in the role of facilitator and teacher with a child and the child's school setting. If that facilitator becomes intensely involved, *stronger* connective opportunities for the facilitator with the child, the club as a whole, and the child's classroom teacher are often realized. As we have stressed, the stronger, more positive, and more diverse the links among settings, the more beneficial is the influence on an individual's life (Bronfenbrenner & Morris, in press; Garbarino, 1982). As shown in this example, then, a service-learning experience may benefit both the one who is teaching and the one who is taught.

One model of service learning proposes that students enter community service and progress through five phases that result in learning (Delve, Mintz, & Stewart, 1990). The first phase, *exploration,* is characterized by student eagerness and openness to new opportunities. Their understanding is framed by student motivation to "do good." The *clarification* phase is marked by students deciding what issues their service and efforts will address. Students' world views begin to change in the *realization* phase, when they see the realities for the people they serve and the impact of their contribution. Student commitment to the people or cause they serve becomes consistent and frequent during this stage. Furthermore, the student can recognize the different cultures, subcultures, and political climate within the target population and the service organization. Students' ability to integrate the experience and use it to address larger, more complex issues is evidenced in the *activation* phase. Finally, in the *integration* phase, the students are able to integrate fully the lessons learned from community service into their lifestyle. Ideally, a student commits to a lifetime of social responsibility and advocating for social justice. The Young Spartan Program provides opportunities for faculty, staff, retirees, and students to engage in service activities that foster social responsibility and enhance learning.

The Young Spartan Program: Structural and Functional Features

In maintaining a commitment to the goals of the project, members of the university community have taken leadership at varying levels of the academic system—central and departmental administration; faculty, staff, and retirees; and students. Participants at each level have played primary roles in the development and continuation of the partnership. The university's roles, especially those of the undergraduate students, have not been reported elsewhere and are the focus of this chapter. Because roles are a basic component of the system, we will identify the major administrative, faculty, and student roles. We will place particular emphasis upon the roles of students, because it is through those roles that they develop the activities and interpersonal relationships that bring the Young Spartan Program to life.

The Roles of Administrative Personnel

Research suggests that institutional factors and faculty factors contribute to the failure or success of universities in embracing outreach projects that involve service learning or experiential education (Ziegler, 1987). Traditionally, the communication between the university and the community has been inadequate. Faculty members divide the time they spend in outreach among varying tasks (Ziegler, 1987). Time needed to carry out community outreach is extensive and unpredictable. There are few institutional supports and rewards for faculty to engage students in service (Boyer, 1994; Checkoway, 1991). The tenure and promotion process usually does not include outreach or service learning as criteria for consideration. Universities have finite resources available to support the needs of the community, and faculty may perceive the university as unable or unwilling to provide the resources needed to offer quality service options (Checkoway, 1991).

The university administration of the Young Spartan Program has addressed these very concerns. The program's concept was developed in response to a community request and was initiated by and with the support of the university's president and provost. The project is viewed as a collaborative effort between central administration and the department/college of the faculty member taking leadership responsibility. Further, the university made a substantial financial commitment to the program with an initial eighteen months invested in the partnership development, followed by five additional years of declining budget support. The budget includes faculty, staff, and student support. Moreover, the administration has given the project a lot of latitude and time to develop partner relationships. Many outcomes have been successful and are described in this chapter. Other outcomes have been challenging and time-consuming; examples have occurred most notably in relation to previous negative university–school-district relationships, delays in action by offices in contracts and grants, the university's high overhead costs for contracts, and lack of a teacher's contract in the school district. In such cases the administration allowed for success and also failures.

The Roles of Faculty, Staff, and Retirees
Faculty, staff, and retirees have been involved in many different ways—as consultants, mentors, hosts of university-sponsored learning experiences, directors of service-learning opportunities for students, and advisors to program administrators. Three roles evolved that have been critical to program maintenance and continuity: program coordinator, academic outreach specialist, and professor emeritus.

Program Coordinator
A tenured professor with considerable community development and outreach experience was asked to take the leadership for the project. She

was given an operating budget and the authority to make decisions about the partnership. Her primary responsibilities are to direct the university's role in the partnership, including conceptualizing the project, building and maintaining relationships with the other partners, and evaluating the direction of the partnership. A faculty member in this position has given the program access to working with school-district central administration along with school principals and teachers. It has also given access to other community partnerships and a resulting expansion of the ideas as the partnership evolves. Having the assignment out of the office of the provost has given the program credibility in the university community when working to establish relationships with other faculty and staff; having the work carried out through a department has given the opportunity to develop the program as outreach scholarship from an academic unit.

Academic Outreach Specialist

Although initially the primary motivation for the project was increased achievement for elementary students, the university clearly needed to place priority on the development of its own students. When selecting students to participate in the outreach experiences, the importance of choosing students from a wide range of backgrounds emerged as an important goal. Initially, competent students—both undergraduate and graduate—served as student supervisors. However, it soon became apparent that a staff person was necessary to ensure program continuity. An academic outreach specialist, who was well acquainted with both university programs and public-school curriculum, was hired to be responsible for placement and supervision of the university students. The specialist is essential for assuring the quality of the service-learning experience by the higher-education students.

Professor Emeritus

The ties of the university extend beyond current faculty and staff to retirees. Retirees' roles have included traditional roles such as facilitating lunchtime programs, sharing expertise as a guest lecturer, tutoring students, and chaperoning events. However, one professor emeritus from the College of Education has gone well beyond these traditional roles and has served as a primary steering-committee member, program advisor, and university-student advisor. Perhaps his most significant role has been to connect the university partnership to extensive state and national educational networks.

He views his role as "redefining retirement and the viability of retirees." To the program staff, he has become affectionately known as "the wisdom" of the program.

The Roles of University Students

A key component to the successful implementation of the Young Spartan Program is the involvement of university students in the delivery of service. Students not only serve to enlarge the personnel base available to the participating elementary schools but, more important, students have an increased array of service-learning opportunities available to them. These opportunities transcend academic majors and career paths, affording placements not contingent on a major in education, but instead related to a specific area of interest or career exploration.

Each year more than 300 university students, with an average of approximately 140 per week, from more than fifty academic and nonacademic units (e.g., centers and institutes) within the university participate in the Young Spartan Program. Six to ten of these students take extensive leadership responsibility for programs as student coordinators. The service-delivery models that have emerged from working with Michigan State University students in the Young Spartan Program fall into five categories: (1) Single-Event Involvement; (2) Multiple-Events Involvement; (3) Focused Content Area; (4) Course-Related Assignment; and (5) Coordination.

All five models provide a range of opportunities for university students to have an active involvement in outreach, provide service, connect to the surrounding community, explore options beneficial to their individual growth, and gain experience. Each model affords an involvement opportunity for university students; however, the level of student investment, the level of structured learning, and the level of time involvement vary depending on the model (see table 14.1). Student investment refers to the degree to which a student is committed to and responsible for the outreach experience, including its planning and implementation. A student with high investment takes ownership of the project, whereas a student with a low investment is fulfilling a responsibility planned largely by someone else. The level of structured learning takes into account the opportunity provided for purposeful learning and reflection by the university student. This dimension illustrates the difference between community outreach and service learning. Lastly, the amount of time commitment required by students differs among the models. Both Single- and Multiple-Event models require less student investment and structured learning than the Focused-Content, Course-Related, and Coordination models. Indeed, we would argue that the learning from a short-term outreach activity (e.g., Single-Event Involvement) is not as rich as from a formalized service learning project (e.g., Course-Related Assignment and Coordination). However, we believe that the short-term service-learning activity significantly contributes to a student's learning. Descriptions of these models are presented below to allow for replication by others (within a university, a business, or a community organization).

Program Models

1. Single-Event Involvement

In the Single-Event Involvement model, the student volunteers for a specified, one-time event that occurs in or outside the elementary school. University students are recruited through residence halls, fraternities, sororities, and curriculum-related clubs to serve as chaperons and small-group or site facilitators. This model provides opportunities to engage in service within a short, specified period; to interact with younger students; to gain documentable experience; and to achieve a sense of personal satisfaction for helping. In addition, those students who serve as a site facilitator, (e.g., the history major who guides ten-year-olds through an exhibit at the university museum, or an animal science major who hosts a trip through the university farms), are given a vehicle in which to put "ivory tower" learning into action within a limited time and in a structured setting. Involvement in a single event exposes the student to the idea that any individual can help facilitate learning. This corresponds to the *exploration* phase of the service learning model described earlier. Yet the student is not committed to or responsible for the program's success and no formalized method of reflection is provided.

2. Multiple-Events Involvement

As with the Single-Event model, the Multiple-Events model offers students the opportunity to engage in service within the elementary schools in specific events predetermined by the program. Students volunteer at least twice by engaging in activities such as chaperoning field trips, facilitating track and field days, judging contests, or becoming "extra hands" during creative projects. They may accompany a fifth-grade visit to the Cyclotron one month, monitor a school spelling bee at a different school the next, and finish the semester by helping to staff other program or promotional events. The university student is exposed to the idea that

Table 14.1. Project Models of University Student Involvement in the Young Spartan Program.

Project Model	Examples	Student Investment	Structured Learning	Time Involvement
Single Event	Chaperon field trip; judge contests; be "extra hands."	Low	Low	Low
Multiple Event	Do more than one single event.	Low	Low	Low-Medium
Focused Content Area	In-school or after-school clubs: create K–5 math, science, computer, or media clubs.	High	Low	Varies
	Co-implemented lessons that fit K–5 curriculum. University horticulture club teaches 1st & 2nd graders about plants.	High	Low	Varies
	Academic-based contests: Students facilitate elementary career contest.	High	Low	Varies
	Tutoring and Mentoring: Students tutor elementary students in academic subjects. Mentors help children with behavior problems.	High	Low	Varies
Course-Related Assignment	Class assignment in Integrated Social Studies and Integrated Studies in Biological Sciences (e.g., students taking a course on diversity learn about the cultures of the elementary school while helping young students with science).	High	High	High
	Field experience: Duties similar to focused content model.	High	High	Varies
Coordinator of Educational Experiences	Assess needs; facilitate volunteer involvement; provide leadership to educational experiences involving community members.	High	High	High

engaging in service can aid the learning process and expands his or her résumé with a variety of experiences. These experiences bring the student to the *exploration* phase and possibly the *clarification* phase of service learning. While the student feels appreciated and necessary, the short-term nature of the student's involvement makes it unlikely that attachment to a particular class or school and ownership of a project will develop.

3. Focused Content Area

The Focused Content Area allows the student to increase initiative and self-directed involvement. While the idea for the project or volunteer placement may originate with a school, a teacher, or the program, the accomplishment becomes a joint venture and student investment is relatively high. Concentrating on a specific subject area, this model allows for active university-student participation over an extended period. However, the opportunities for structured learning are low. We provide four illustrations of the Focused Content Area model: in-school and after-school clubs; co-implemented curriculum units; academic-based contests; and tutoring and mentoring programs.

In-School and After-School Clubs

Elementary-school clubs provide informal and nonthreatening learning settings that address a specific subject matter or theme. University students develop one-hour modules carried out over a period of six to eight weeks during a specified portion of the day. The modules require the student to be responsible not only for the subject matter, but also for creating a structure that shares the material at an age-appropriate level. University-student leadership in clubs has allowed kindergarten through fifth-grade students to hone math skills through games and group activities, to learn computer literacy while creating a slide presentation, to experience chemistry through cooking, and to explore careers in the media industry while learning video production. This involvement allows university students to make a substantial level of commitment to elementary-school students in an area that is of particular interest to them.

Co-Implemented Curriculum Units

Similar to the club example, university students design and execute a learning module focused on a specific content area; however, the lesson is integrated into the grade-level curriculum. In partnership with the classroom teacher, university students work by themselves, in pairs or in small groups, to apply the content of their academic major by providing hands-on instruction for the elementary students. For example, undergraduates majoring in horticulture, who also participate in the on-campus student Horticulture Club, teamed with first- and second-grade teachers to teach the prescribed school-district Life Science curriculum. Weekly for six weeks, horticulture students take primary-grade students step-by-step through the plant growth process by having them raise plants from seeds. During the modules, the teams of university students become the actual instructors. Although few, if any, of these university students are destined to become classroom teachers, they have a keen interest in sharing their knowledge and love of plants.

Academic-Based Contest

During the course of the academic year, elementary schools are sometimes offered the option of participating in community-, government-, or business-sponsored contests. The contest usually highlights a specific subject matter or theme, such as spelling and geography "bees," a spacesuit-design contest, or a career-based speech contest. Often, schoolteachers and principals see the educational and growth potential of these contests, but do not have the time or personnel to give the endeavors adequate attention. Thus, university students with interests that complement the subject or thematic unit can become the staff for these contests. The university student takes leadership of a limited-duration project that focuses on his or her developing area of expertise. While the format and outcomes of the contest are dictated by the rules of the sponsoring entity, the methods of preparation, motivation, and additional recognition are not. Ideally, the university student can show initiative and creativity in those aspects while organizing the contest according to the dictated rules and regulations of the sponsor. The university student, then, takes the written prescription for the contest and translates it into activities designed to help the elementary student research, prepare, and practice for the competition. Moreover, students take responsibility for the structure and execution of the contest.

Tutoring and Mentoring Programs

One-to-one involvement programs offer the university student more intense, direct contact than the other Focused Content Area models. Tutoring allows the university student to take a single academic subject and assist a younger student who is struggling to grasp the ideas. While the area of study is dictated by the child's classroom performance and a request of the teacher, the university student has the opportunity to assist in devising strategies and to influence directly the child's learning. Success is measured in small ways, through understanding of a particular story, an improved grade on a spelling test, or correct completion of an assignment in long division. The elementary student benefits from sustained one-to-one interaction, while the university student becomes a distinct stakeholder in the child's success. Because many tutors are education majors, the process allows them to become actual teachers on a small, but intense scale.

University-student mentors work to impact and motivate those students whose behaviors have become disruptive. Through one-to-one interaction, the mentors provide a sounding board and a consistent force for the child. The mentor may use tutoring as a vehicle to build a trusting relationship with the child, because the child who needs mentoring often demonstrates low academic achievement. The mentors' interpersonal skills are crucial to the process; consequently, university students seeking a mentoring experience are most often social science or human ecology majors. The notable exception is those students who choose to become a mentor because their own elementary or middle school experiences were difficult, but who now feel that they have achieved success by being at the university. These students believe that through direct, sustained involvement with children who are struggling as they once did, their life experience can motivate another child to persevere.

In summary, students in Focused Content Area projects show a higher level of investment, consistent with the *realization* of service learning. The students' sense of leadership and ownership grows beyond that of students involved only in the Single-Event and Multiple-Events models. The clubs become "our" clubs and the elementary-school students become "my" students. Despite changes in their leadership, on-campus clubs have maintained interaction with the children of the Young Spartan Program over time. The activities described as Focused Content Area models may provide "real-world" experience through the coordination and execution of a program, but structured learning is not systematically facilitated for all university-student volunteers.

4. Course-Related Assignment

University students who participate in the Course-Related Assignment model fall into three categories: (1) those who work to fulfill field-experience course requirements for the College of Education and for the College of Social Science; (2) those who participate to fulfill experiential requirements for the behavioral sciences; and (3) those who volunteer for a course service option not dependent on any major or academic discipline. The latter example is the most nontraditional placement-for-credit option. A course grade or credit gives the student a motivation for working the specified number of hours and, more important, the time to reflect upon the experience to extract personal meaning. The appropriate matching of the student to the placement, and the student's inherent desire to gain from and contribute to the experience give the university student the opportunity to take pride in and ownership of the assignment.

Those university students who take part in the Course-Related Assignment model for credit in education and behavioral science courses often carry out responsibilities and activities outlined in the Focused Content Area model. That is, they work within the elementary schools facilitating clubs and curriculum units, implementing contest and incentive programs, and serving as tutors and mentors. In addition, many students, particularly education majors, choose to work as a classroom assistant. In this role, the university student has the opportunity to pair with the classroom teacher for one-half day per week, and to become part of the instructional team in a variety of subject areas. The university student, often a first- or second-year student, is given the chance early in his or her academic career to try an intended profession firsthand. The success of this format is illustrated by the comment by a freshman: "Now I *know* this is what I want to do!" A further indication of success is that this student continued to work with the classroom teacher although the specified time required for course credit had ended. In addition, the student initiated a lunchtime art club at the school, which allowed her to focus on her primary area of interest. This club not only served a need for this university student and the elementary children, but served as a recruitment tool for additional university students. Through the "mini-teaching" experience as a classroom assistant, university students have a chance to see firsthand if their goal matches reality, rather than having to wait until they are totally committed to the education major. The structured learning allows the student to progress through the *activation* and *integration* phases of service learning.

The most ambitious endeavor to date involves one section of the course, Integrative Studies in Social Science: Diversity in the United States. Students enrolled in the course have a social contract option of volunteering at an elementary school near campus. Each semester sixty to seventy-five of the 450 university students elect the option, and become facilitators for small groups of elementary students completing hands-on science and technology assignments. The experience becomes that of parallel learning: University students enhance the elementary students' science education through small-group interaction and assisting in completing their projects, and they observe diversity firsthand in a multicultural, lower-socioeconomic setting. As part of the course requirements, university students keep journals noting their experiences with the children and their subsequent feelings. Reflection sessions are scheduled apart from the regular lecture time. The culminating activities are a science/technology field trip for both university and elementary students, and attendance by the elementary students at one of the regularly scheduled university course lectures. During this class period, a selected group of elementary students gives a presentation to the entire class of 450 university students.

5. Student Coordinators

The role of student coordinator provides the most intense level of undergraduate involvement in the Young Spartan Program. It is another means for students to experience the *activation* and *integration* phases of service learning. There is a student coordinator based in each of the partnership's six elementary schools working twelve to fifteen hours per week. Placing them directly in the school allows them to serve as the liaison between their school and program resources. The coordinator works with the principal and teachers to identify school curriculum enrichment and career exploration needs that can be met within program parameters. Coordinator responsibilities within the schools include, but are not limited to: arranging for classroom speakers and school assemblies; scheduling field trips; organizing noon-hour and after-school clubs; and facilitating volunteer and parent involvement.

As with all Young Spartan Program student placements, students self-select the role of coordinator. However, there is an application process in place for the coordinator position. They represent a range of academic majors of different cultural and socioeconomic backgrounds and are attracted to the position because of the responsibility it offers, the supervision it provides, and the interaction with children it affords. Once in place, coordinators often find the position to be more challenging than they had anticipated, finding that the ways of doing business in the university, as well as other aspects of the university (e.g., its institutional culture), are very different from those of their elementary school. They need to communicate and team with a wide range of school personnel, organize and prioritize their time, create programs from a mere spark of an idea, and assume project leadership. At times, they are given the responsibility, but not necessarily the authority, to provide leadership in the school setting. However, they often find the rewards to be greater than the challenges.

In the performance of their role, the students are expected to be personable, organized, self-motivated and disciplined, respectful of diversity, and to exhibit leadership and management skills. These are attributes that lead a student to be hired into the coordinator position; however, these attributes are those that, due to their age and lack of experience, are still developing and can be inconsistent. To enhance the students' potential, supervision and reflection sessions are integrated into the experience. An "academic outreach specialist" devotes approximately fifteen hours per week to work with student coordinators. She provides program orientation, an introduction to service-learning concepts and program planning, weekly group informational and reflection sessions, individual consultations, and systematic performance evaluation and goal setting. Students set goals concerning communication, organization, teamwork, leadership, creativity, workplace etiquette, and knowledge of program concepts. In the program's first year, students wrote project summary papers that incorporated program preparation, implementation, and evaluation experiences; these papers became the basis for the "Coordinators' Orientation Manual." In the current model, students use project experiences as the base for building a career-based Life-Work Portfolio (National Occupational Information Coordinating Committee, 1995). Similar to the performance evaluation, portfolio development challenges the students to assess their individual values, strengths, and weaknesses; their learning styles; and their choice of academic major and career paths within the context of their Young Spartan position. The academic outreach specialist encourages the coordinators to work with school personnel to assess school needs, and subsequently to develop and carry out a school project or program that is related to their academic major. Through all these processes, they learn to accept both credit for their accomplishments and responsibility for lack of success. A clear sense of ownership emerges as is evidenced as student coordinators make reference to "my school," "my speech contest," "my math club," and "my girl's group." Program ideas grow out of collaboration, but the student coordinators hold them as their own.

The coordinator's role gives students an opportunity to make decisions about their career paths based on their experiences and to develop a world view that values social responsibility. Two high-achieving coordinators entered the university system with a clear vision of their futures as lawyers. One student, attending the university's honors college, has applied and been accepted to the College of Education. The other student has not fully abandoned law, but has decided to first pursue a degree in

Family and Child Ecology to prepare for a career in child-advocacy law. These students have directly related their experiences as coordinators to their occupational choices. Furthermore, they have noted that their potential contribution to child welfare far exceeds their original vision of becoming a lawyer.

Model Summary

We have presented five models of student involvement: Single Event, Multiple Events, Focused Content Area, Course-Related Assignment, and Coordinator. We described each of the models with specific examples of student activities. The models vary according to the amount of student investment, time commitment, and opportunity for structured learning. The event models typically do not require much time or structured learning, nor is program success contingent upon student investment. However, the remaining models do elicit more student investment and also more time and structured learning. The most intense of these models, from a program point of view, is that of student coordinator. The schools serve as a "real-world" training ground for developing the knowledge, skills, and attitudes necessary to succeed in the coming century. The students focus on professional growth and development in a system that values and depends on their participation.

We have provided a detailed description of the models to encourage others to use them. These models can be adapted and replicated by many units of the university community including professional organizations, departments, colleges, retirees, and special programs. Furthermore, involvement can and should extend beyond the university to include local businesses, government units, and civic organizations. *The involvement of other collaborators increases the linkages and connections that serve to strengthen the development of students, children, youth, and families.*

Reflections on the Role of the University
in a Community and Educational Partnership

This chapter began with the proposition that collaborations are an ecological approach to problem solving within the community. We described the roles of one segment of the educational collaboration—the university, through the participation of administrators, faculty, staff, retirees, and students. Moreover, we argued that it is the creation of strong connections and linkages that ultimately support partnership development for the increased academic achievement of students. We conclude, then, with reflections on principles that we have found imperative to follow if we are to provide learning environments for university students as they participate in community-based service learning.

Principle 1: Partnership progress requires maintaining the focus on students at both the university and elementary levels.

While this principle may seem obvious, in practice it is not easily done. The personal agendas of adults in both the university and public schools are important, but the academic achievement and development of students must be paramount. Opportunities such as authorship of publications, travel opportunities for professional improvement, or personal recognition are valuable and necessary for professionals. However the primary objective for all institutions involved must be student achievement and growth. As partners we must frequently remind ourselves of this principle.

Principle 2: Partnership progress requires an understanding of and ability to work within the varying contexts of partners.

Each partner comes to the collaboration from a unique organization that has its own beliefs, goals, and accepted ways of working. In addition, within the units of each partner there are wide variations in the organizational culture, for example, each school has its own climate that is different from the other schools (a similar situation exists within university departments). Students' understanding of various organizational cultures is essential for their own success.

In a partnership, the balance of shared responsibilities between the community and the university is difficult. On the one hand, the schools may look to the university for the "answers" and want the work done for and not with them. At the same time, schools may not really trust that the "ivory tower understands the real world" or that students are capable of carrying out professional roles. Conversely the university may be accustomed to working in the mode of "advice giving" and directing, and may find it difficult to be co-learners with the partnership members. We have found this dialectical tension to be ongoing and never fully resolved.

Changing contexts internal to the university or to the public schools may also impact the work of the students in community outreach. We cite two examples that have impacted directly upon the student learning experiences. In recent years with downsizing, faculty workloads are shifting as they take on added responsibilities. Therefore, finding the time needed to provide support to the student has become increasingly difficult. The public schools provide the second example. This past year the teachers in our community have been working without a contract. Teachers have been advised not to work outside the contract time limits; this has created an environment that makes it very difficult for partners to work effectively and to involve teachers in after-school meetings.

Principle 3: Partnership success requires creating and sustaining trusting relationships between and within institutions.

Building trusting relationships is time-consuming, uncertain, and under-valued, but it is perhaps the most essential skill in building partnerships. Given the large time investment, we have attempted consistently to docu-ment the progress of the relationships within this partnership (see Keith et al., 1995). Clearly, every person is not willing to collaborate. This is espe-cially true for individuals whose primary agenda, however worthwhile, is their own advancement and not the goals of the students' development. We also found this true of people who may have stagnated in their careers and were less open to new ideas. Another serious, but important factor is the ordinary, seemingly insignificant, remarks that devalue the work of another person. Assisting the student's understanding of these partnership dimensions and development of strategies for working with many adults requires ongoing monitoring and support on the part of the university faculty involved in the partnership.

Principle 4: Partnership success requires a "safety net" of support for university students involved in outreach learning.

Student success in communities is wonderful when it happens. Sometimes the school principals have become advocates for the viability of the stu-dent coordinator's role in their elementary school. Moreover, some of the elementary-school principals have become trusted mentors who are cru-cial to the student successfully maneuvering the public-school culture and developing a sense of mastery. Conversely, the lack of a student's success, for whatever reason, is very difficult when it occurs. Thus, it is crucial to build on the learning experience that has occurred, and to transform it into a positive experience.

University students engaged in outreach often face situations that are uncomfortable, foreign, and even perhaps beyond their developmental level. Community members may have stereotypes about students and their perfor-mance based upon countless reasons—such as cultural stereotypes, imma-turity, and even reality. The belief by community members that young people can perform valuable and meaningful functions cannot be assumed. Such an orientation has to be built with care, and monitored consistently as a part of the relationship strategies.

Two of the models we presented—the Coordinator model, and the Course-Related Assignment model—have built-in support from university staff. All students who participate in this program have several points of contact with the academic outreach specialist. She is accessible to the students and respectful of them. In addition, university staff, including the provost, department chairperson, project faculty and retirees, all recognize student well-being as the central focus, and accept an additional role of student support as an integral component to the programs' success. This support may be made manifest by an arranged face-to-face group meeting, verbal or written commendation, participation in reflection sessions, availability for appointments, or simply informal greetings when passing in the hall.

Principle 5: Partnership success requires respect for community-based experiential learning as a valuable contribution to the university's mission and a valuable learning/teaching strategy.

We have encountered faculty who, one-on-one, are eager to participate in the program by engaging their students in outreach. However, there are colleges and departments that neither place a high priority on outreach nor see it as a potentially rich resource for student learning. Moreover, the success of faculty associated with these units is measured not by their contribution to the community but, rather, by their contribution to scholarly publications, research, and teaching. In contrast, some departments not only encourage community involvement, but embrace it. As such, faculty are recognized for their contributions not only to academic publications, but also to community-outreach publications and teaching.

For faculty to value an outreach model there has to be a pedagogical foundation. Faculty involved in the Young Spartan Program use theories of service learning and experiential education as the scholarly foundation for their work. We suggest administrators work with those faculty who see the value of experiential community learning and support their efforts with human and financial resources. The more pleasant the experience for all parties the larger the potential impact upon society. A series of small successes and the occasional big success make the program and the use of this type of learning more likely to be accepted by resistant faculty.

Conclusion

The work of university partnerships is expanding rapidly as an approach to reduce fragmentation of community relationships and to build social and intellectual capital on behalf of children and youth (Albert & Wilbur, 1995). The Young Spartan Program is one such effort, and this chapter has described part of this effort, focusing upon the roles of the university and, in particular, the role of university students.

We hope that through the sharing of these roles and our observations, other partnerships will be aided in their quest to contribute to students' learning through outreach experiences. Although successes and challenges are met daily, the compelling reasons for our continued involvement in this program are summarized by these words:

Our institutions of higher learning might certainly take heed, not only by encouraging students to do . . . service, but by helping them stop and mull over . . . what they have heard and seen. This is the purpose, after all, of colleges and universities—to help one generation after another grow intellectually and morally through study and the self-scrutiny such study can sometimes prompt. (Coles, 1993, p. 148)

Notes

The authors thank Charles Blackman, Professor Emertius, Michigan State University for his review of this chapter and continuous support of this project.

1. The name "Young Spartan" was selected because the Spartan of Greek mythology is the university mascot and students and alumni are known as Spartans. The children participating in the program were viewed as "young" Spartans to emphasize the role of education in their lives.

References

Albert, L., & Wilbur, F. (Eds.) (1995). *Linking America's Schools and Colleges*. Jaffrey, NH: Anker Publishing

Barr, R. B., & Tagg. J. (1995, November). From teaching to learning: A new paradigm for undergraduate education. *Change*, 13–25.

Battistoni, R. M. (1994, September). Education for democracy: Service learning and pedagogical reform in higher education. Paper presented at the American Political Science Association, New York.

Benard, B. (1991). *Fostering resiliency in kids: Protective factors in the family, school, and community*. Portland, OR: Northwest Regional Educational Laboratory, Western Regional Center for Drug-Free Schools and Communities, Far West Laboratory.

Boyer, E. (1994). Creating the new American college. *Chronicle of Higher Education, 40*, A48.

Bronfenbrenner, U. (1979). *The ecology of human development: Experiments by nature and design*. New York: Cambridge University Press.

———. (1986). Ecology of the family as a context for human development: Research perspectives. *Developmental Psychology, 22*, 723–742.

Bronfenbrenner, U. & Morris, P. A. (in press). The ecology of developmental processes. In

R. M. Lerner (Ed.), *Theoretical models of human development* (Volume 1, *The handbook of child psychology*. Editor-in-Chief: W. Damon). NY: Wiley.

Bubolz, M. M., & Sontag, M.S. (1993). Human ecology theory. In P. G. Boss, W. J. Doherty, R. LaRossa, W. R. Schumm, & S. K. Steinmetz (Eds.), *Sourcebook of family theory and methods* (pp. 419–448). New York: Plenum.

Carnegie Council on Adolescent Development. (1992). *A matter of time: Risk and opportunity in the nonschool hours.* New York: Carnegie Corporation.

———. (1995). *Great transitions: Preparing adolescents for a new century.* New York: Carnegie Corporation.

Checkoway, B. (1991). Unanswered questions about public service in the public research university. *Journal of Planning Literature, 5,* 219–224.

Coles, R. (1993) The call of service: *A witness to idealism.* Boston: Houghton Mifflin.

Delve, C. I., Mintz, S.D., & Stewart G. M. (1990). Promoting values development through community service: A design. In C. I., Delve, S. D., Mintz, & G. M., Stewart (Eds.), *Community Service as values education* (pp. 7–29). San Francisco: Jossey-Bass.

Dryfoos, J. G. (1990). *Adolescents at risk: Prevalence and prevention.* New York: Oxford University Press.

———. (1994). *Full-service schools: A revolution in health and social services for children youth and families.* San Francisco: Jossey-Bass.

Edens, M. (1994). Community-linked learning: The role of the service-learning center. Unpublished manuscript. East Lansing: Michigan State University Service-Learning Center.

Ellison, C., & Barbour, N. (1992). Changing child care systems through collaborative efforts: Challenges for the 1990s. *Child & Youth Care Forum, 21,* 299–316.

Garbarino, J. (1982). *Children and families in the social environment.* New York: Aldine.

Gardner, H. (1983). *Frames of Mind.* New York: Basic Books.

Giles, D. E., & Eyler, J. (1994). Impact of a college community service laboratory on students' personal, social and cognitive outcomes. *Journal of Adolescence, 17,* 327–339.

Hamburg, D. A. (1992). *Today's children: Creating a future for a generation in crisis.* New York: Times Books.

Harkavy, I., & Puckett, J. (1994). Lessons from Hull House for the contemporary urban university. *Social Service Review, 8,* 299–321.

Hodgkinson, H. L. (1989). *The same client: The demographics of education and service delivery systems.* Washington, DC: Institute for Educational Leadership.

Hogue, T., Perkins, D., Clark, R., Bergstrom, A, & Slinski, M. (1995). *Collaboration framework: Addressing community capacity.* Columbus: Ohio State University.

Kagan, S. L. (1989). The care and education of America's young children: At the brink of a paradigm shift? In F. J. Machiarola & A. Gartner (Eds.), *Caring for America's children* (pp. 70–83). New York: Academy of Political Science.

Keith, N. (1994, Fall). Educating tomorrow's citizens through service learning. *National Society for Experiential Education Quarterly,* 12–26.

Keith, J. G., Covey, M. A., Perkins, D. F. (1996). *Building and maintaining community coalitions on behalf of children, youth and families: The roles of religious institutions* (Research Report 543). East Lansing: Michigan State University Agricultural Experiment Station.

Keith, J. G., Knox, A., Perkins, D. F., & Blackman, C. (1995). *Building an educational collaboration on behalf of children, youth and families* (Research Report No. 539). East Lansing: Michigan State University Agricultural Experiment Station.

Keith, J. G., & Perkins, D.F. (1995). *13,000 Adolescents speak: A profile of Michigan youth.* East Lansing: Institute for Children, Youth, and Families.

Keith, J. G., Perkins, D.F., Zhou, Z., Zongqing, Z., Clifford, M. A., Gilmore, B., & Townsend, M. Z. (1993). *Building and maintaining community coalitions on behalf of children, youth and families* (Research Report 529). East Lansing: Michigan State University Agricultural Experiment Station.

Kolb, D. A. (1984). *Experiential learning: Experience as the source of learning and development.* Englewood Cliffs, NJ: Prentice Hall.

Kraft, R., & Krug, J. (1994). Review of research and evaluation on service learning in public and

higher education. In R. Kraft and M. Swander (Eds.), *Building community: Service learning in the academic disciplines* (199–213). Denver: Colorado Campus Compact.

Lerner, R. M. (1993). Investment in youth: The role of home economics in enhancing the life chances of America's children. *AHEA Monograph Series, 1*, 9–34.

———. (1995). *America's youth in crisis: Challenges and options for programs and policies.* Thousand Oak, CA: Sage.

Levitz, R., & Noel, L. (1995, July). *The earth-shaking but quiet revolution in retention management.* Noel & Levitz Occasional Paper. USA Enterprises.

Marcos, F., Edens, M., & Goldsmith, P. (1993). Transferable skills and competencies for the workplace 2000. Unpublished paper. East Lansing: Michigan State University Service-Learning Center.

Markus, G.B., Howard, J., & King, D. (1993). Integrating community service and classroom instruction enhances learning: Results from an experiment. *Educational Evaluation and Policy Analysis, 15*, 410–419.

National Commission on Children. (1991). *Beyond rhetoric: A new American agenda for children and families.* Washington, DC: Author.

National Occupational Information Coordinating Committee. (1995). *Guide to the life work portfolio.* Washington, DC: Career Development Training Institute.

Perkins, D. F., Ferrari, T. M., Covey, M., & Keith, J. (1994, Spring). Getting dinosaurs to dance: Community collaborations as applications of ecological theory. *Home Economics FORUM, 7*, 39–47.

Perkins, D. F., & Miller, J. (1994). Why community service and service learning? Providing rationale and research. *Democracy and Education, 9*, 11–16.

Schorr, L. B. (1988). *Within our reach: Breaking the cycle of disadvantage.* New York: Doubleday.

Small, S. A. (1995). Action-oriented research: Models and methods. *Journal of Marriage and the Family, 57*, 941–955.

Snyder, D. P. (1996). The revolution in the workplace: What's happening to our jobs? *Futurist, 30*, 8–13.

Young Spartan Program (1994). *Resource guide.* East Lansing: Michigan State University.

———. (1995). Annual Report. East Lansing: Michigan State University.

William T. Grant Foundation Commission on Work, Family, and Citizenship. (1988). *The forgotten half: Pathways to success for America's youth and young families.* Washington, DC: William T. Grant Foundation.

Ziegler, J. M. (1987). Experiential learning and the purpose of a college education. *Human Ecology Forum: A Cornell University Magazine, 16*, 2–5.

Chapter 15
Promoting the Health
of Maryland's Adolescents
The Center for Adolescent Health
at the Johns Hopkins University

Cheryl S. Alexander and Madlyn C. Morreale
The Johns Hopkins University

Young people growing up in contemporary America face a host of health-related issues that potentially diminish their lives and futures. Alcohol and other drug use, violence, unsafe sexual practices, and psychological distress not only take a toll on adolescents, but many of the behaviors initiated during the teenage years impact on the incidence of chronic illness in adulthood. For example, despite warnings by the Surgeon General and public attacks on the tobacco industry, nearly one in five high-school seniors are regular smokers (Bachman, Johnston, & O'Malley, 1994). These percentages have been virtually unchanged over the past decade. Lung cancer, emphysema, coronary heart diseases, all major causes of death for adults, have their roots in the behaviors and lifestyle choices made during adolescence (U.S. Centers for Disease Control and Prevention [CDC], 1994). As the Carnegie Council on Adolescent Development notes in its final report, *Great Transitions: Preparing Adolescents for a New Century*, adolescence is "the last phase of the life span in which social institutions have reasonably ready access to the entire population so the potential for constructive influence and for improving adolescents' life chances is great," (Carnegie Council on Adolescent Development, 1995).

In order to enhance the health of adolescents, it is necessary to bridge traditional gaps between the world of academic health research and the worlds in which adolescents are embedded: families, schools, and communities. Schools of public health, accustomed to addressing prevention issues such as immunization, prenatal care, infectious diseases, environmental health, and screening for disabilities, are natural partners with communities for health promotion and disease prevention activities. But when partnerships between communities and health institutions involve adolescents, sensitive behaviors, such as teenage sexual practices or illegal or antisocial behaviors, challenge collaborative processes. The academic agenda to advance scientific knowledge about adolescent health and development often conflicts with school, family and community views of appropriate adolescent behavior, family rights, community self-determination, and the adolescent's own right of privacy.

Moreover, solutions to the health problems of adolescents are not simple but require a multifaceted, multidisciplinary approach that integrates the work of scholars across divergent divisions within the health institutions of a university. Faculties from schools of medicine, nursing, public health, social work, pharmacy, and dentistry bring unique expertise to the prevention of adolescent health problems. Too often collaborations among the faculty of varying health professions are tenuous and short lived. They tend to be project specific, grant dependent, and lack the sustainability necessary for making substantive changes in the lives of young people.

Academic-community collaborations that advance scientific knowledge and assist communities to intervene effectively in the health and well-being of their youth require an organizational infrastructure that both acknowledges the divergent views and needs of academic institutions and communities and provides the tangible linkages needed for health professionals, public health practitioners, community leaders, and academic scholars to work together on high-priority adolescent health issues. Such an organizational structure exists at the Johns Hopkins School of Hygiene and Public Health through the Center for Adolescent Health Promotion and Disease Prevention, or Center for Adolescent Health.

The Center for Adolescent Health is one of 14 prevention research centers funded by the CDC. The Prevention Research Center Program, which began in 1986 with a congressional appropriation of $1.3 million and three centers, has grown to more than $8 million and 14 centers by 1996. The mission of the program is to improve the health of the public by forming partnerships between academic health institutions, governments, and local communities in order to conduct applied research and demonstration projects that address major public health issues. Centers apply knowledge regarding health promotion and disease prevention through community-based interventions, evaluation of programs and policies, information dissemination, and training for public health professionals in applied prevention research. Core funding is provided by CDC to assist academic centers in addressing key population health issues at a time when the credibility of health institutions and their ability to impact on the health of the public is being questioned. Core funding also is used to support the organizational structure of a center, to provide resources for student training, pilot or seed funding for innovative faculty research, and support for community-based educational activities.

As part of a collaborative agreement, CDC centers partner with various divisions of the National Center for Chronic Disease Prevention and Health Promotion of CDC to conduct "Special Interest Projects," and projects of mutual interest. Topics range from policy research on environmental health issues to the development of research methods for school-based health studies. Each prevention research center selects a theme and a population around which to organize its applied research program. For the Johns Hopkins University (JHU) School of Hygiene and Public Health, the theme is adolescent health and the focus of our research is adolescents residing in urban and rural communities in Maryland.

Background about the Center for Adolescent Health Promotion and Disease Prevention

Established in 1993, the mission of the Center for Adolescent Health is to promote healthy behaviors in adolescents and reduce their risk of disease through an integrated program of research, training, policy and information dissemination, and community service. Our work addresses four key areas: transitions that serve as opportunities for health promotion interventions (e.g., transitions from elementary to middle school); modifications of risk-taking behaviors; interventions that engage families, schools, and communities; and academic-community partnerships that enhance the delivery of health services to adolescents.

The Center for Adolescent Health is administratively housed within the Department of Maternal and Child Health at the Johns Hopkins School of Hygiene and Public Health. Center faculty are drawn from a wide range of academic disciplines representing the Johns Hopkins Schools of Hygiene and Public Health, Medicine and Nursing, the University of Maryland School of Medicine, the Baltimore City Health Department, and Salisbury State University (SSU) on Maryland's Eastern Shore.

In order to include both rural as well as urban adolescents as the focus of our research and community activities, the Center established a contractual agreement to collaborate with Salisbury State University, a regional state university located on the Eastern Shore. Central to this collaboration is the belief that local universities understand best the needs of their constituencies, and have the credibility necessary to conduct community-based preventive interventions with youth.

At JHU, all faculty who affiliate with the Center for Adolescent Health have primary academic appointments in departments within the schools of Hygiene and Public Health, Medicine, and Nursing. Accordingly, faculty have a variety of responsibilities and engage in myriad activities that are critical to their home department or division, but may be external to the mission of the Center. On average, faculty tend to provide between 70% and 80% of their salary support through external funding sources (i.e., research grants and contracts). By having infrastructure support as well an attractive physical setting for research activities (several row houses off campus), the Center has been able to attract and engage faculty in adolescent-health research.

In addition to providing staff organizational support (i.e., project director, administrative secretary, and data analyst), core funds have been used to develop opportunities for new partnerships with state and local health departments, schools, community-based organizations, and policymakers. These funds allow the Center to dedicate faculty, staff, and student resources to activities that are identified as priorities for these local partners. For example, the Center has supported faculty and student involvement in the evaluation of a community-based teenage-pregnancy prevention program and in the development, implementation, and evaluation of a school-based health-center intervention to decrease aggressive behaviors in middle-school students. These small joint projects are not typically funded through traditional research grants nor through university funds, yet their value in promoting academic "outreach" and in building sustained community partnerships with university health institutions is immeasurable. Furthermore, these discretionary dollars can be leveraged in pursuit of other private and public funding sources. In the past year, for example, a small grant from the Center to a faculty member for a school nutrition study was complemented with funding from the Bureau of Maternal and Child Health within the Health Resources and Services Administration and the Maryland State Department of Health and Mental Hygiene. In a sense, CDC's core support to the Center has served to reinforce the importance of integrating applied research with "service" to the mission of the School of Hygiene and Public Health.

The majority of the Center's activities are coordinated through a steering committee, which has responsibility for setting the agenda of the Center, determining allocations of core funding, and evaluating productivity as relevant to a set of annual goals and objectives. The steering committee comprises the Center directors at JHU and SSU, the project director, and three faculty with heavy investments in Center activities.

The Center uses a "working group" model to facilitate faculty collaboration. The intent of the "working group" is to engage students and faculty in scholarship related to crosscutting areas of adolescent health. While the number and priorities of the working groups have changed over the past four years, the model seems to be an effective way of fostering multidisciplinary work. The Center currently has two working groups dedicated to information dissemination and research methodology. Each group is comprised of faculty, students, and staff with diverse disciplinary training. Working groups are product oriented and set their own objectives and timetables for endpoints.

The mission of the Policy and Information Dissemination Work Group is to help the Center to provide targeted information, education, and communication about issues related to adolescent health to a variety of audiences. These include service providers, policymakers, researchers, and the general public. Products associated with this group include: seminars, workshops, and teleconferences for students and other professionals; a community fair that provided information about local programs and services for young adolescents and their families; "policy news briefs" that describe national and state legislation and polices related to children and adolescents; "issue briefs" that summarize major findings from research; and newsletters about Center projects and activities. Members represent the fields of health policy, mass communication, and nursing.

The Methods and Measurement Work Group has grappled with research design, measurement, and analytic issues plaguing adolescent-health research in community settings. The Group, consisting of faculty from sociology, statistics, epidemiology, behavioral science, and health economics, has applied several statistical models to an examination of adolescent child-bearing and school drop out. By integrating the expertise of multiple scholars, this exercise has resulted in an expanded analytic knowledge base that can be applied to other adolescent-health behaviors. The working group is now pursuing the writing of an edited volume on research methods for use in community-based adolescent-health interventions.

Collaborations and Partnerships with Communities

The Center's "links" with others in the public health and youth-service communities are established through a variety of mechanisms, ranging from building on existing relationships that individual faculty, staff, and students have with these organizations, to responding to requests from entities previously unknown to the Center. Most importantly, the Center's advisory committees have played a critical role in our ability to establish, develop, and sustain relationships with local partners.

Working with Advisory Boards

From a philosophical as well as a practical perspective, it has been important to involve young people as integral parts of the life and activities of the Center. An understanding of the problems facing adolescents and their families and the potential strategies for addressing them can only come from an active cooperative engagement of youth with Center faculty and staff. In the second year of its existence, the Center established a Youth Advisory Committee (YAC) comprised of adolescents who live in Baltimore City and who range from thirteen to eighteen years of age. The YAC contributes to the vitality and productivity of the Center in a variety of ways. YAC members help faculty, students, and staff plan community activities, review pilot instruments for researchers, assist with recruitment of study participants, formulate research questions, and provide insights regarding the perspectives of adolescents growing up in urban environments.

The Youth Advisory Committee has also enhanced the ability of the Center to understand the concerns and priorities of urban adolescents through a grant funded by a local community organization. Just four months after the YAC was established, members submitted a proposal to a foundation that was interested in funding projects developed and implemented by youth that addressed local community problems. Their proposal, subsequently funded, allowed them to invite twenty-five Baltimore City youth on a weekend-long, leadership-development retreat.

As part of the nomination process (juried by the YAC), adolescents were asked to identify the most important problems facing the city, and strategies they would undertake to solve those problems. During the retreat, youth participated in a variety of outdoor activities designed to help participants build trust and learn group decision-making and leadership skills. In addition, YAC members led workshops to help participants identify and begin to solve local priorities. Adult participants from the Center assumed supportive roles, facilitating the organization but not the content of youth-run activities. The YAC leadership retreat represents a paradigm shift from a collaborative model that is adult developed with youth advisement, to one in which youth assume the defining roles with adults providing the scientific and technical expertise. This shift is reflected in the major outcome of the retreat: the establishment of a city-wide youth-developed and run council, "YAWS" (Young Adults Working for Success).

The Center has two community advisory boards, representing the distinct perspectives of Baltimore City and our rural partners on Maryland's Eastern Shore. The two boards operate independently and with different types of memberships. On the Eastern Shore, the Community Advisory Board is comprised of officials from local departments of health, education, and social services. These individuals meet regularly with the center director at SSU on a variety of issues that are broader than the Center's agenda. In these rural communities where there are only a few key health, education, and social service leaders, these individuals are burdened with demands to serve on many advisory boards, community groups, and local commissions. Thus, the model of limited formal advisory board meetings, but increased contact through informal mechanisms, seems to be effective.

The Community Advisory Board (CAB) in Baltimore has experienced fundamental changes over the past three years. Initially consisting of fifteen representatives of public and private agencies and organizations, the CAB met yearly with Center faculty, students, and staff to review the progress of specific projects and to chart directions for future collaborations. The annual "dog and pony show" advisory meeting was less than satisfying for either the Center or CAB members. In its third year, Center faculty, staff, and students engaged in a series of discussions about the importance and role of the Community Advisory Board. These meetings directly addressed the diversity of our definitions of "community" and challenged us to develop a consensus about our "constituencies" and how best to foster partnerships that would provide meaningful direction to the research, training, and information-dissemination activities of the Center.

The results of the Center's discussions were twofold. First, it was decided that the expertise of our original "community advisory board," which consisted primarily of individuals representing state and local health departments and other governmental agencies, would best be tapped through the development of specific collaborative projects. Second, the remaining board members were reconfigured to explicitly include representation from local community-based and youth-serving organizations. The resulting board is smaller but more actively engaged with the Center. The small size has allowed group members to get to know each other and has enhanced the ability of Center faculty and staff to work closely with individual members between quarterly meetings. Membership on the board expanded in 1997, but does not exceed ten members.

Just as the Center has continued to explore the potential mechanisms for enhancing the perspective of community and youth in our work, faculty have also reflected on the unique contributions that an academic center can make to the benefit of its partners. Although it is perhaps too early to list the full range of collaborative opportunities available to the Center, it appears that linkages initiated by community organizations are often related to requests for technical assistance with evaluation, needs assessment, or training. Those initiated by Center faculty and staff tend to focus on the development of applied research studies and information dissemination.

Collaboration with Local Partners
Program Evaluation

As foundations and government agencies become increasingly interested in both funding community-based interventions and requiring evidence to support the impact of programs on adolescents and their families, program evaluation appears to create a natural link for academic-community collaboration. There are, however, significant challenges to designing evaluations of intervention programs that meet academic criteria for scientific rigor and at the same time are feasible within the real-world constraints of communities. Field trials of an intervention with random assignment, considered the "gold standard" of research, are often unrealistic or are perceived as objectionable by community partners (Hollister & Hill, 1995). Academics may recognize the limitations of traditional design and measurement methods, but may be reluctant to explore new methods for fear of risking sanctions from the scientific communities that recognize and fund their research. Moreover, while funders of programs may be "bottom-line" oriented, that is, requiring that programs demonstrate significant impact in the most cost-effective manner, a priority of community agencies may be that evaluation benefit practitioners. Community organizations are concerned about the quality of the programming they offer and how to target their efforts to groups most likely to benefit from their programs (Hollister & Hill, 1995).

In our ongoing collaborative work with local organizations, Center faculty have identified several strategies to facilitate evaluation linkages that are mutually beneficial to academic and community partners. One strategy has been to offer formal as well as informal education to community organizations regarding the role of evaluation in program implementation, what evaluation can and cannot do for a program, the kinds of resources that are required to answer various questions, the time line necessary, and the commitment required to ensure that quality data is obtained. These types of questions served as the basis of the opening session at the Center's "Best Practices in Adolescent Health," a one-day training workshop for fifty participants from health departments, social service and educational agencies, and youth-serving organizations (i.e., YWCA) for Baltimore City and the Eastern Shore. The intent of the conference was to present prevention models in the areas of adolescent violence, unintended injuries, and substance use that had demonstrated efficacy, and to discuss why these models appear to work. As part of the discussion, issues of design, outcome identification and measurement, implementation or process evaluation, and analytic strategies were raised and commented on by various community stakeholders. The dialogue between community practitioners and Center faculty initiated at this workshop represents a first step toward assessing the realities of evaluating community-based adolescent interventions, including the need to balance stakeholders' needs for timely information with academics' requirements for scientific rigor and replicability.

A second strategy has been to invest faculty time and Center resources in project development with community partners prior to funding opportunities. In this instance, trust, communication, and respect have a chance to develop, conflicting expectations and priorities among the parties can be resolved, issues of power and control can be negotiated, and the criteria for determining success can be made explicit before the pressures of funding drives decision making. For example, Center faculty have worked with the Baltimore City Health Department on the implementation of a computerized school-based clinic data system to address clinic staff questions about utilization of clinic services and billings to third-party payers. During the course of working together, health-department staff and Center faculty identified several key outcome indicators that clinic staff felt should be impacted by school-based clinical services. The result has been a recently funded proposal to a state agency for a multi-year evaluation of twenty-three school based health clinics in Baltimore City and Baltimore County. Because the health department sees the practical significance of evaluation for the organization and delivery of school-based health services, faculty have been able to build into the design and implementation of the evaluation appropriate control groups, data-monitoring and quality-control procedures, and mutivariate analytic procedures for data analysis.

A third strategy has been to involve students in joint evaluations of programs that will benefit the community partner while providing valuable training and experience for the student, but whose benefit to a faculty member is questionable in terms of the academic reward system. Included in this category would be small descriptive evaluations, and those that are labor intensive but whose findings are not likely to make a unique contribution to the published literature. For example, Center faculty responded to a local health department's request to assess the impact of a policy change involving the administration of discretionary medications by school nurses. The data had not been collected with a systematic evaluation in mind. It was likely that the evaluation would raise more questions than it could answer. Nonetheless, it appeared to be an excellent training opportunity for graduate students to apply health information and data analytic skills gleaned from course work to a real-world application. Faculty and two second-year master's degree students met with health department and school personnel to identify the questions to be addressed in the evaluation, determine the sampling plan, and identify measurable outcomes, timetable, and budget. After the initial design and analysis decisions were made, the students implemented the sampling design, abstracted school health records, entered data, conducted the analyses, and assisted in writing the final report. This practicum experience provided valuable lessons for the students in the craft of evaluation research with minimal time investment of faculty.

Policy Impact

To have a significant impact on the health of adolescents, academic-community collaborations must effect systems change at local and state levels. This means that administration of academic health institutions must sanction and reward faculty involvement in state advisory boards, local commissions, and policy-setting committees and that faculty must view advisory activities as integral to the development of their academic careers. Many faculty, including those in schools of public health, do not envision themselves as agents of change or fashioners of public policy. Yet when invited to the table, academic researchers have the potential to influence program priorities through legislative processes. At a time when government agencies at state and local levels are being diminished by reorganization and downsizing, there is a pressing need for policies and programs that make maximum use of scarce resources. University faculty have the expertise necessary to provide policymakers with data on which to base programmatic decisions. For example, at the Center for Adolescent Health, faculty involvement on several statewide advisory groups was influential in retaining support for school-based health services for poor youth through legislative changes of the Maryland Medicaid system.

Center members have produced several policy-related documents. *The Health of Maryland's Adolescents*, a data sourcebook displaying mortality, morbidity, social and educational indicators for adolescents, is a policy-oriented publication produced by Center faculty and students in collaboration with the Maryland State Department of Health and Mental Hygiene. Over eight hundred copies of the sourcebook have been distributed to local health departments, schools, social service agencies, libraries, and juvenile justice agencies across the state. Several county health departments have reported that they are utilizing information from *The Health of Maryland's Adolescents* to set local priorities for adolescent-health initiatives.

At regional and national levels, the Center has collaborated with the JHU Child and Adolescent Health Policy Center to produce a policy brief on school-based health centers. This brief uses a framework of primary care to assess the components of health services delivered within school settings. Nearly 2,000 copies of the policy brief have been distributed to state and local health departments, MCH directors, federal agencies, legislators, and national organizations. As a vehicle for informing policymakers, this form of information dissemination has the potential to influence policy and programs at multiple levels of government.

On Maryland's Eastern Shore, Center faculty from Salisbury State University have collaborated with three county health departments and a tertiary hospital to produce a Tri-County Health Needs Assessment. This population-based survey of the health needs of residents in the three counties includes a lengthy section on adolescents. The assessment will serve as the planning document for the regionalization of health resources and for the development of new programs and services. In all the examples above, Center faculty have influenced adolescent health policy by utilizing research expertise to assist public agencies in defining key adolescent health indicators and by assuming the leadership role for the assembly, analyses, presentation, and interpretation of data.

Community Service

The Center's service mission is fulfilled through both initiating activities and contributing to those convened by other organizations. For example, our community fair and our annual essay and art-work contests have helped the Center establish relationships with local schools and youth-serving organizations, while showcasing the resources and talents of our communities. Similarly, the Center has been asked to assist community partners with their own service agendas by providing speakers, student and faculty assistance with programs and events, and even coordinating the development of an AmeriCorps grant, the Partnership for Adolescents on the Lower Shore (PALS).

The PALS project employs eighteen AmeriCorps participants to work with twelve agencies, including schools, health departments, social-service agencies and other nonprofit organizations that provide services to adolescents in rural, Eastern Shore Maryland. The responsibilities of the AmeriCorps members range from tutoring and mentoring, to improving the life skills of pregnant and parenting teens, and training adolescents with conflict-negotiation skills. One AmeriCorps participant was assigned to the Center to work with the School of Nursing (at Salisbury State University) on a variety of health-related projects. In addition, the Center Director at SSU serves as one of the project directors and was instrumental in developing two adolescent health courses that are provided as part of the training for the AmeriCorps participants.

Collaboration with Other Academic Partners
The Center directly benefits from opportunities to collaborate with other academic colleagues who share our interests in policy and information dissemination and collaborative research with communities. For example, faculty from the Center have collaborated with colleagues at the JHU Child and Adolescent Health Policy Center to produce a variety of information dissemination products, including *Policy News Briefs*, timely reports of national and state legislation and policies affecting children, youth, and families, and the previously mentioned policy/research monograph about the potential of school health centers to meet the primary care needs of adolescents. Center faculty have collaborated with faculty from the Maternal and Child Community Health Science Consortium, funded by the Bureau of Maternal and Child Health, and the JHU Center for Injury Research and Policy, funded by the CDC, to sponsor the "Best Practices in Adolescent Health" workshop. Most recently, faculty have collaborated with colleagues from the JHU schools of Medicine and Nursing on a project to enhance the ability of academic faculty to participate in the prevention and treatment of alcohol, tobacco, and other drugs, within their own clinical settings and in collaboration with partners in community-based and managed-care organizations serving East Baltimore.

This model of cross-center collaboration within a university holds considerable promise for making significant strides in improving the health and well being of vulnerable population groups, such as adolescents. Centers tend to develop their own web of community partners, some who overlap with other centers but many who do not. Collaboration between centers extends the scope and diversity of potential community partners for any one center by building on a system of established relationships and networks. Given that the development of academic-community partnerships is time and labor intensive, the ability of a center to readily access other community collaborators increases the likelihood that universities and communities can respond rapidly to funding opportunities. Through joint ventures, centers can pool resources to address a more comprehensive research agenda than is possible by a single center. For example, in the area of school health, the Center for Adolescent Health and the Maternal and Child Community Health Science Consortium have shared personnel costs associated with implementation of a database system for school-based health centers. The system, when in place, will yield a rich data source on the health needs, behaviors, and health care utilization patterns of middle and high school students in Baltimore City. This investment in data system development was not financially feasible for either center but, by combining resources, both centers and their health department partners will benefit from a database that can be used to address relevant research and programmatic questions.

The Center has also developed collaborations across universities. The partnership with Salisbury State University has allowed us to expand our scope of research to include rural youth. Additionally, the Best Practices conference utilized the community advisory boards in both locales to help identify and prioritize topics for the conference presenters. Some core support is provided to the faculty of SSU to engage in evaluations of locally relevant programs and to engage in community outreach.

Challenges and Opportunities
Achieving Balance between Funding Diversity and Mission
Centers located in academic institutions with a high reliance on external sources of research funding frequently struggle with balancing the need for diversified funding with a desire to maintain a clear focus on promoting the health of a specific population. Since the majority of the faculty who affiliate with the Center for Adolescent Health are also involved in research activities that do not address adolescents, the steering committee

regularly assesses the extent to which the Center should broaden its theme to include research on conditions that affect younger children or adult populations. This temptation is especially strong, for despite the pressing health and social issues facing young people, the numbers of research and training grants dedicated to adolescent health are limited. Additionally, these grants tend to be funded categorically (i.e., teen pregnancy prevention) rather than comprehensively, and often lack flexibility to utilize funds in ways that build community collaboration.

A major challenge is how to maintain programmatic and research integrity while at the same time developing a diversified portfolio of funders that will underwrite support of the Center's organizational infrastructure and community outreach functions. At present, the Center's core funding comes from a single source, CDC, making it highly vulnerable to changes in government policies and funding priorities. One strategy, recently taken, has been to spread the administrative costs of the Center over a variety of grants and contracts. In order for this strategy to be effective over the long term, it will be necessary to have a constant stream of funded projects, each covering a fraction of administrative, student, and faculty support. Another approach is to develop academic-community collaborations within distinct geographically defined communities. Here the intent is to pull together a variety of projects within the same community under a single administrative umbrella, and at the same time, provide an integrated information base on a well-defined population of adolescents.

Conceptual Models of Health Promotion versus Disease Prevention

While espousing health promotion as an objective of public health research, funders still gravitate to disease prevention studies that use epidemiologic risk/deficit models in explaining adolescent health behaviors. For example, studies of teenage pregnancy often highlight the influence of poverty, female-headed–household status, and welfare dependence on risks for early childbearing (Alan Guttmacher Institute, 1994). Poor urban communities, weary of having their youth characterized as high risk, are reluctant to enter into partnerships with academic institutions that they view as potentially exploitative and whose study findings they believe are irrelevant. Knowing that poverty is a risk factor for adolescent childbearing does little to inform community-based pregnancy prevention programs in economically disadvantaged neighborhoods. The use of resilience/resource models in researching adolescent health issues in urban settings is a relatively new phenomenon. Measures of competence or resilience are less familiar to the public health research community but more acceptable and relevant to urban communities. The challenge is how best to apportion resources to development of these competence-based models of adolescent health and how to secure funding support for their application in community settings.

Balancing the Agendas of Academic and Community Partners

As a center within a school of public health, we are well positioned to promote systems change related to health promotion and disease prevention. These issues give us "entree" through their immediate relevance to community needs. A challenge for the Center for Adolescent Health is how to set priorities for investment of resources that balance the competing agendas of the public health field and community partners.

These competing agendas manifest themselves in a variety of trade-offs, including at least three that have emerged from the Center's work to date: the desire of academics to conduct carefully controlled research and evaluation versus the community's desire to maximize the use of grant funds for service delivery; the desire of academics to conduct innovative, crosscutting research, versus the community's desire to implement already proven interventions; and, the desire of both academics and communities to respond to "Request For Proposals," versus the need for both parties to negotiate about the actual content, focus, and conduct of research.

The Center for Adolescent Health's mission to generate and apply new knowledge to health problems of communities is shared by other divisions within the health institutions. In the past, public health academics developed research proposals and then attempted to "sell" them to communities. Community collaboration was but an euphemism for community cooperation. Academic-community models for the twenty-first century will require that community involvement begin at the initiation of the research process and continue through all phases of study design, implementation, analyses, interpretation, and utilization of findings.

A challenge for adolescent health centers such as ours is how best to engage communities in the adolescent research enterprise, particularly around sensitive topics. Topics perceived as too sensitive for study by community members, such as adolescent sexual behaviors, may be viewed by public health researchers as very important, particularly in locales where rates of sexually transmitted diseases or teen births are high. In addition to topic sensitivity, the intentions of public health researchers are often met with distrust in urban communities where there is a long-standing history of poor communication between universities and the communities that surround them. One strategy is to view the academic as a co-learner; that is, part of a team that includes both university faculty and community members. This approach gives recognition to the unique knowledge that community participants bring to the team as well as the technical expertise that faculty bring.

A team approach may also help diffuse sensitivity of particular topics by directly involving community participants in the formulation of the questions and the design of the approaches to address them. For example, as part of our research on HIV high-risk behaviors among out-of-school youth, Center faculty have organized an executive committee comprised of faculty, students, and representatives from each of the youth-serving organizations who have agreed to participate with the intervention. The role of this committee will be to formulate the study questions as they pertain to the development of interventions for youth in shelters, to determine how the intervention will be implemented and tailored to meet site needs, devise instruments, determine methods of data collection including quality-control measures, and share analyses of findings in a timely manner. This model of participatory research has been used successfully in evaluating community initiatives in distressed neighborhoods in Detroit (Sarri & Sarri, 1992), and has been elaborated in the DICE model for community-collaborative research (Ostrom, Lerner, & Freel, 1995). Participatory research models are not without their limitations. They tend to be highly labor and resource intensive and require a significant commitment by all team members for community change. Nonetheless, this mode of research is likely to be successful in sustaining intervention effects in communities.

The Center has sought to articulate a long-term strategy that acknowledges and balances the multiple and sometimes competing agendas of our community partners. In its ideal, the strategy begins with a careful assessment of how opportunities relate to the Center's mission and priorities; the short-term and long-term potential of establishing mutually beneficial and sustainable partnerships; and the ability of Center faculty, staff, and students to respond to the specific requirements of requests for assistance. In reality, however, our ability to collaborate is often constrained by a "competing demands" paradigm that contrasts interesting opportunities against short timetables, quick deadlines, and the Center's limited resources, particularly the ability of existing faculty and staff to assume new responsibilities.

As mentioned previously, the Center relies on the active participation of our community and youth advisory boards to help guide the development and implementation of our work. We have also invited two members of the Baltimore City Health Department to serve on our core faculty, to provide an important perspective about the city's most pressing adolescent-health priorities. In addition, the Center's ability to respond to locally defined needs has been enhanced by the support of our academic institution, especially the school's allocation of space and the Center's "home" Department of Maternal and Child Health, which has allowed us to hire one tenure-track and two nontenure-track faculty members within the past year. These three faculty members have full-time appointments in the department, with a significant proportion of their time spent on Center research and activities. Equally important to the multidisciplinary goals of the Center, chairs from other academic departments within the schools of Hygiene and Public Health, Medicine, and Nursing have allowed their faculty to participate in Center activities, even though we support little to none of their salaries.

Integrating Academic-Community Collaboration in Public Health Graduate Education

In response to the call to "reinvent public health," schools of public health have increased their efforts to integrate education and practice (Sommer, 1996; Sorenson & Bialek, 1991). One implication of the reorganization of graduate education for adolescent health is to critically examine the adequacy of prevailing public health models for addressing the health needs of youth and their families. The inclusion of models that emphasize resilience and competence along with the traditional risk/deficit models alters public health research training in fundamental ways. Courses on adolescent development, family processes, and community development would be added to public health curricula to complement course work in epidemiology, biostatistics, infectious diseases, environmental health, and health policy.

In addition to changes in course requirements, graduate students in public health need direct exposure to the diversity of families and organizations within inner-city communities in order to appreciate the strengths inherent in urban settings. By engaging graduate students in work with advisory boards and youth-serving organizations, models of community collaboration will be more fully integrated into public health research and practice.

Faculty can also benefit from direct exposure to public health issues facing adolescents, their families, and communities. Although the degree of exposure would vary among faculty, all members of a research team including statisticians and computer analysts need to see the faces that are represented by the numbers generated from a study. Moreover, their ability to interpret findings is only strengthened by their knowledge of community context.

Conclusion: Visions for the Future

In assessing our directions for the future, the faculty, students, and staff at the Center for Adolescent Health have identified five major elements of our strategic plan to develop and sustain partnerships with youth and communities.

1. Academic health centers, including schools of public health, must learn to integrate youth and community perspectives into their efforts to assess the needs and priorities of adolescents and their families in urban and rural communities. The credibility of their agenda and work will depend on systematic efforts to undertake research, policy, service, and training initiatives that assist local schools, organizations, and officials to enhance the health of families and communities. Therefore, decisions about how academic health centers select their advisory board members, how they work with those boards, and how they select their partners for collaboration must be part of a routine assessment of their mission and definition of community.

2. Academic health centers must nurture the generation and elaboration of new knowledge relevant to the public health problems of communities by providing a forum in which creative and multidisciplinary scholarship can thrive. Universities can advance the mission of centers by rewarding faculty who engage in community-collaborative applied research through the academic promotion system and by funding innovative ideas that push the boundaries of traditional public health adolescent research. Centers should use discretionary funds to encourage faculty to explore new research topics, develop new methodologies, and link with other faculty across departments and divisions within the university.

3. Academic health centers must continue to develop the capacity of faculty and students to apply and disseminate new knowledge through a "product-oriented approach" that is tailored to audiences that do

not traditionally subscribe to academic journals and public health publications. For some projects, this work will involve a "translation" of "what we know" to the press, policymakers, and directors of local programs. For other projects, however, new products and activities must be developed that are specifically designed for professionals in community-based and youth-serving organizations.

4. University faculty, staff, and students must actively seek out opportunities to assist local, state, and national officials to develop public policy that promotes adolescent health and the role of prevention in youth and community development. This goal can be accomplished, in part, through efforts related to information dissemination, but will also require increased participation in governmental advisory boards, task forces, needs assessment, and planning efforts.

5. Centers should foster the integration of graduate education with public health practice by providing practicum opportunities for students with youth-serving agencies, on state and local advisory boards, and apprenticeships on applied research studies. Center faculty can contribute to the socialization of new adolescent-health researchers by integrating models of community collaboration, youth competence, and resilience into their classes, seminars, and independent reading courses.

Today's adolescents are facing a host of health problems that cannot be easily addressed through the traditional medical care system. The leading causes of death and disability for youth have shifted from infectious agents to behaviors that have immediate and long-term consequences for the health and well-being of young people. Centers in academic health institutions must work in concert with youth, families, schools, and communities to develop comprehensive community-based strategies that help adolescents make healthy transitions into adulthood.

References

The Alan Guttmacher Institute. (1994). *Sex and America's teenagers*. New York: The Alan Guttmacher Institute.

Bachman, J. G., Johnston, L. D., & O'Malley, P. M. (1994). *Monitoring the future: Questionnaire responses from the nation's high school seniors, 1992*. Ann Arbor: Institute for Social Research, University of Michigan.

Carnegie Council on Adolescent Development. (1995). *Great transitions: Preparing adolescents for a new century*. New York: Carnegie Corporation of New York.

Hollister, R., & Hill, J. (1995). Problems in evaluations of community-wide initiatives. In J. P. Connel, A. C. Kubisch, L. B. Schoor, & C. Weiss (Eds.), *New approaches to evaluating community initiatives: Concepts, methods, and context* (pp. 127–172). New York: Aspen Institute.

Ostrom, C., Lerner, R., & Freel, M. (1995). Building the capacity of youth and families through university-community collaborations: The Development-In-Context Evaluation (DICE) model. *Journal of Adolescent Research, 10* (4), 422–448.

Sarri, R., & Sarri, C. (1992). Organization and community change through participatory action research. *Administration in Social Work, 16*, 99–122.

Sommer, A. (1996). Whither public health? *Public Health Reports, 110*, 657–661.

Sorenson, A., & Bialek, R. (1991). *The public health faculty/agency forum: Linking graduate education and practice.* Gainesville: University Press of Florida.

U.S. Centers for Disease Control and Prevention. (1994). *Preventing tobacco use among young people: A report of the Surgeon General.* Atlanta: National Center for Chronic Disease Prevention and Health Promotion, Office on Smoking and Health.

Chapter 16
Changing the Culture of the University to Engage in Outreach Scholarship[1]

Mary Brabeck, John Cawthorne, Marilyn Cochran-Smith, Nancy Gaspard, Carol Hurd Green, Maureen Kenny, Rosemary Krawczyk, Claire Lowery, M. Brinton Lykes, Alan D. Minuskin, Jean Mooney, Catherine J. Ross, John Savage, Michael Smyer, Avi Soifer, Elizabeth Sparks, Robbie Tourse, Robert M. Turillo, Sandra Waddock, Mary Walsh, and Nancy Zollers[2]

Boston College

Describing university–public-school collaborations, Fullan and Steigelbauer wrote, "University partnerships, if they are to work, are a new way of life, not just another project. In the process, the culture of the school and the culture of the university change and begin to overlap in organic ways" (1991, p. 323). At Boston College (BC), over thirty faculty and administrators, across five professional schools and the College of Arts and Sciences, have been engaged since 1992 in intense, deliberate efforts to change the culture of the university. We are developing new relationships among departments and schools, between faculty and administrators, and among Boston College communities, schools, and agencies.

We are engaged in three overlapping and integrated efforts. The first is an educational effort. Drawing on the knowledge bases of diverse professions and disciplines, we are designing curricula that will prepare professionals to work more effectively with children, families, and communities. We are training future professionals in an interprofessional[3] service-delivery model and documenting the results of our curriculum revisions. Second, we are engaged in a community outreach effort that focuses primarily on local schools, but also clinics, hospitals, and community agencies. In partnership, we are developing effective strategies (also termed "integrated services") for prevention and intervention that will improve the lives of children, families, and communities. Our third effort is scholarship. We are building collaborative, co-learning research agendas to engage in outreach scholarship (Lerner, 1995a; Lykes, 1989). Through leadership in our respective fields, we hope to demonstrably improve the lives of children, families, and communities in ways that *they* deem valuable. In documenting our efforts, we are adding to the scholarship on collaborations emerging within each of our respective fields.

To tell the BC story about changing the university culture, a key step to succeeding in our efforts to improve the lives of children, families, and communities, we provide a short description of BC's history and culture. We then describe the work developing out of the experience of each school and across our professions and disciplines. Finally, we present our organizational model, offer some reflections on our successes and failures, and provide our thoughts about the future.

The BC Context

Boston College is a Jesuit university, founded in 1863 to provide a Catholic, liberal-arts education. Boston College's Jesuit identity is reflected in its commitment to the application of knowledge to solve human problems, and the preparation of students "to serve others" in the tradition of Catholic social justice teaching. The University's stated commitment to social justice provides the shared value system that is essential for collaboration among the diverse schools and departments on campus to address the needs of children and families in today's society. We are trying to interrupt ways in which many professionals maintain distance from those needs.

BC has a long-standing commitment to the action-knowledge link, and an institutional identity marked by an obligation to serve others. At the undergraduate level, engagement in service to others is seen in the large numbers of students who volunteer to work during their four years on campus, or join the Jesuit Volunteer Corps following graduation. The Pulse program, begun in 1970, is one of the oldest service-learning programs in the country (Byrne, 1995). In Pulse, students combine academic work in theology and philosophy courses with reflection on the volunteer service in which they are engaged.

Concerned about the decreasing number of men entering the Jesuit order, and the potential threat this poses for the Catholic identity of Boston College (Marsden, 1994), Boston College faculty and professional staff recently have been engaged in a discussion of what it means to be a Jesuit university. This has led to extensive discussions about service, values, and the responsibilities of a Catholic and Jesuit university to society. The discourse at BC fostered through these conversations reflects a receptivity to the efforts underway to employ the resources of the university to improve the lives of children, families, and communities.

Our language of commitment must now be transformed into committed action; that is the role of our partnerships with schools, families, and communities.

Boston College has grown from an undergraduate college to a complex university. Yet it retained its name, Boston College, evincing an uninterrupted commitment to undergraduate liberal-arts education. Strong independent disciplines have developed within a departmental structure. At the same time, BC has engaged in cross-disciplinary faculty collaborations through a number of interdisciplinary undergraduate minors, particularly those that foster group identity and cultural studies: Black Studies, Women's Studies, Latin American Studies, Irish Studies, the Faith, Peace, and Justice program, etc. However, the culture, structure and reward system of BC, like many universities, supports competition among and between departments. While faculty have experience with interdisciplinary collaborative work, particularly around curriculum efforts, there is a tension among departments that must compete for resources and must retain independence and autonomy in accounting for productivity. History and organizational structures have made interdisciplinary collaboration difficult on campus; our challenge (and opportunity) is to create a culture that encourages cross-unit collaboration.

The University's reputation for excellence in graduate education has grown steadily. In recent years the schools of Law, Nursing, Education, and Social Work have ranked among the top graduate programs in the country (*U.S. News and World Report*). The rankings were obtained largely through the faculty and student scholarship and sponsored project expenditures, which in 1994–1995 totaled $22.4 million. However, scholarship at Boston College is balanced by the obligation to be engaged in work that serves others. While basic research is pursued, scholarship "in the real world" is encouraged, particularly among the professional schools. Faculty and administrators speak of preparing "contemplative activists" by joining reflection and action, the "thinking and doing." These dual commitments are realized through what Lerner (Lerner et al., 1994) calls "outreach scholarship" and what Boyer (1990) calls the "scholarship of application." Such scholarship develops knowledge (what universities are expected to do) that is *useful* to the community. Outreach scholarship requires a two-way relationship with the community to make certain that the research questions are relevant, and that the knowledge is valid, useful, and used. Thus, collaborative efforts to improve the lives of children, families, and communities began at BC with a culture that values service scholarship. In this regard, Boston College has a climate conducive to creating what Boyer (1994) called the "new American college."

Three other realities of Boston College set the context for our work. First, the administrative structure at BC historically has been centralized with the academic vice president and his associate vice presidents playing key roles in decision making. Centralized fiscal management has resulted in an increased endowment growing from $4.3 million in 1970 to one that in 1996 exceeded $500 million, thirty-fourth among American universities. Higher-administration support is critical to the success of any individual effort, and essential for a cross-campus endeavor, such as our interprofessional work.

Second, we are a relatively small university with about 600 full-time faculty; we award approximately 2,300 undergraduate degrees and 1,400 graduate and professional degrees each year. Frequently, faculty members know at least one person in each department on campus; during lunch the academic vice president is likely to choose an empty chair at any table in the faculty dining room, and the other chairs are likely to be occupied by faculty from different disciplines. There is a sense of community at Boston College, and the higher administration fosters it by frequent references to the "BC family." Our size and administrative centralization reinforce that effort.

Third, part of our campus is physically located in Boston contiguous to the borough of Allston-Brighton, an economically depressed and ethnically diverse urban area. University-community tensions were heightened three years ago, when BC expanded its football stadium against the will of some local members of the community. Confrontational meetings and newspaper headlines voiced the needs of the neighborhood and the responsibility of the University to its neighbor. One tangible result was the establishment of the BC Neighborhood Center, which attempts to work with the community to identify needs and find ways to address them. Thus, while the higher administration has recently initiated efforts to build university-community collaborations, recent and ancient histories have resulted in a need to raise the level of trust in order for outreach scholarship to succeed and the community and university to reap the benefit. In the fall of 1995, the Department of Education of the Urban League moved into the BC School of Education. The Urban League historically had been committed to university-community partnerships and the potential for joining their efforts with ours is a reason for optimism.

The Higher Administration's Supportive Mission Statement

Each institution's history and mission shapes its particular approaches to outreach scholarship. Boston College's interprofessional, integrated-services initiatives developed out of a history of collaboration among faculty colleagues across several schools. Equally important is the university's mission and overall priorities. During the 1994–1995 and 1995–1996 academic years, Boston College undertook a strategic-planning process. We faced a presidential transition for the first time in twenty-four years and the University was in strong fiscal health. Our board of trustees and our outgoing president agreed that the time was right to reassess our progress and set goals for the next decade. Faculty members, administrators, and staff members were involved in an eighteen-month process designed to develop consensus regarding the mission and goals of the University. The resulting statement described the distinctive contributions that Boston College might make to society, including, "producing nationally and internationally significant research that advances insight and understanding, thereby both enriching culture and addressing important societal needs . . . " Throughout the planning process, the University's mission was linked to specific goals; these goals provide an institutional home for outreach scholarship efforts and several goals focus on interdisciplinary collaboration. For example, one relevant goal is, "Initiate a small number of multidisciplinary policy, research and service centers dedicated to scholarship that benefits society, enriches culture or addresses important social issues." The recently established Boston College Center for Child, Family, and Community Partnerships, which will continue and will expand the work described here, is one instance of the implementation of this goal.

Senior administrators (the president, executive vice president, academic vice president, and deans) were centrally involved in developing the mission statement, and the academic affairs committee of the Board was engaged in review and consultation on both substance and process. Eventually, after the campus community reviews the draft, the entire board of trustees will consider and approve the plan. Central support and university-wide consensus form an important and effective context for the faculty and student collaborations with Allston-Brighton, and reflect broad institutional encouragement for our work.

Challenges and Barriers

Since 1992 we have been organizing and maintaining a monthly faculty seminar on interprofessional collaboration. With grant money (see note

1) we have instituted a brown-bag series; brought to campus national and local speakers with expertise in interprofessional collaborations; revised aspects of professional preparation programs, most extensively the teacher education curriculum; and created faculty and student work teams who regularly go to schools and community agencies. These efforts are described more fully in later sections of this paper.

We are a typical university faculty, steeped in traditions that create barriers to working together. Most of us are white and upper middle class, and our homogeneous and limited experience can blind us to the needs and the resources of the complex communities with which we are claiming partnership. This challenge is heightened by the fact that we are working primarily in Boston public schools that lack a geographical identity. Because of court-ordered desegregation, Boston students are bused to schools throughout Boston. Lacking a community school, we have had difficulty defining "the community" with whom we are in partnership.

Within our disciplines/professions we have encountered challenges of different language (one colleague says "client," one says "patient," one says "student"—we wonder if we are talking about the same person); professional identities and hierarchies (Who owns the problem? Whose definition of the problem prevails?); and ethical codes (Who can break confidentiality, when and to whom?). Within the university we face the structural challenges outlined by Lerner and Simon in the opening chapter of this volume, of the relentless tenure clock and reward system, and of inflexible class scheduling.

There are also significant barriers to the work within each of us. Each of us was educated in a model of autonomy and independence that militates against collaboration. We have the normal dose of fear of exposure, loss of control, and the unknown. We suffer the typical symptoms of laziness (How long does it take to drive there?) and a hierarchical understanding of town/gown issues (Who are the experts?). Our concerns are shared by the school community, which has a history of disappointment with universities and a distrust and anger toward faculty who are paternalistic, communicate distrust, and usually leave the community after a short stay. The school professionals, family members, and community leaders with whom we have good relationships also lack time for collaboration with universities and, in an increasingly overstressed situation, many have high levels of burnout and diminished hope.

Our biggest challenge has been to learn to trust each other. Over and over we learn the lesson that if we can keep our focus on our goals, on our mutual commitment to do work that makes some difference in the lives of children, families, and communities, we can make progress. When we are distracted by ownership issues, personal fears, and turf claims, everyone loses. It is difficult to acknowledge that essential expertise to do the work resides outside of the university campus and the credit for the work is not in any individual. We are learning that we can accomplish much if we share the credit; when getting individual recognition for the work becomes the goal, collaboration is impossible.

Writing this chapter collaboratively has allowed us to "tell our story" both individually and collectively. The sections that follow describe contributions of each university unit; sections have been read and rewritten by many of us. There are overlaps in our stories and no one unit's (or person's) contributions would be the same without collaboration across the schools and departments and with the schools. Furthermore, no single section that follows tells the whole BC story. This chapter symbolically represents and is an organic (emergent) example of what we are learning: Our whole is qualitatively better than the sum of our parts.

The Work Begins: BC "Origin Stories"

Within the context of our history and values, discussions took place about interprofessional collaborations to improve how we educate students. It is noteworthy that these discussions occurred in different parts of the campus, among a variety of faculty groups, and within the group of deans, at roughly the same time. Our different "origin stories" indicate that this work has multiple mothers and fathers. These stories are important in a couple of ways. They tell us that the work developed synergistically in different groups in different parts of the campus; some of us had been doing this work individually for some years. Our stories reveal a broad base and diverse contributions. Origin stories also reveal different visions and goals we have for the work, and these hold some tensions and potential conflicts as well as sources of new learning for each of us.

School of Education (SOE) Beginnings

Because the School of Education prepares people for both education and applied psychology, there has been an ongoing discussion about how these professions might better work together. In 1993 the School of Education obtained a Comprehensive Health Education Grant from the Commonwealth of Massachusetts to implement one aspect of educational reforms (health education) in the teacher preparation and school counseling curricula. The state money brought in speakers to educate us about health issues for children and youth: drugs, alcohol, teen pregnancy, violence. We began to read about reform movements, "integrated services," "integrated social systems," and "full-service schools" (Carnegie Foundation, 1990; Dryfoos, 1994). We extended invitations to members of other professional schools to join the discussions, developed a brochure announcing our efforts and collaboration, got participants involved on an e-mail list, and began to build a resource library that now houses a significant collection of books, professional journals, and media about interprofessional collaborations, integrated services, and university-community outreach (Boston College Initiative, 1996). We upgraded from brown-bag to pizza lunches ("If you feed them, they will come") and we wrote grant proposals. The proposal writing made the collaboration concrete. It also led us to realize the importance of joining with other professional schools on campus in order to be competitive in the grants. We dreamt about starting a charter school and launching a journal that would bring the different professions together in scholarship.

Our efforts complemented the Boston College teacher-education faculty's earlier revision of the teacher-education curriculum. The curriculum is premised on the assumption that children do not learn, and teachers do not teach, in a vacuum. Learners and teachers construct meaning out of the life contexts in which they find themselves. For teachers and students in urban schools, these contexts encompass the negative realities of poverty, ill health, violence, and racism, as well as the positive influences of family, culture, and community. The teacher-preparation curriculum addressed the needs of the "whole child" and could embrace a partnership among education, health, human service, and legal professions to meet those needs. We knew that like students and teachers, professionals construct problems differently. The social worker, teacher, psychologist, lawyer, and health provider each understand the child from a slightly different perspective. While each profession sees problems and solutions slightly differently, a complete solution must be informed by multiple perspectives.

Most training models hinge on the assumption that there is an agreed-upon and codified body of knowledge that can be transmitted to professionals. In the case of teachers, outside experts are assumed to have the "right" skills and knowledge (Cochran-Smith & Lytle, 1991; Hargreaves & Fullan, 1992). However, there is mounting criticism that these training models are inadequate to the major tasks of teaching and school reform

(Little & McLaughlin, 1994), particularly in urban areas where the student population is culturally diverse and primarily poor, the teaching force is culturally homogeneous and middle class, and social and economic conditions provide diminishing opportunities for employment and social mobility.

Much of the work that explores the cultures of schools and the nature of teachers' work and workplaces (Hargreaves & Fullan, 1992; Little & McLaughlin, 1994) points to the fact that what is needed in professional development are opportunities for aspiring professionals to explore and question their own and others' interpretations, ideologies, and practices through inquiry, reflection, and joint work. For example, the most promising professional-development practices are those that provide opportunities for teachers to identify, reconsider, bolster, or alter classroom beliefs and practices that support or undermine their own students' learning opportunities and life chances (Cochran-Smith & Lytle, 1993).

The education and applied psychology faculty in SOE reached out to faculty in the other professional schools to further revise the teacher-preparation curriculum by integrating the knowledge bases of other professions that serve urban children and families. Faculty from law, nursing, social work, and psychology on the Boston College campus joined teacher-education faculty in a working group to articulate the issues involved in supporting the academic development of urban schoolchildren. With endorsement from each school's dean and the higher administration, we articulated an interprofessional, integrated services program, called Project IntServ. This work was funded by the U.S. Office of Education Fund for the Improvement of Secondary Education (FIPSE).

The goal of Project IntServ (an integrated model of professionals who work "in service" to learners) is to prepare current and future teachers to work in partnership with families and health/human-service professionals to address the multiple needs of children who face multiple barriers to learning. To accomplish this, the Boston College faculty from across the professional schools work with the staff and parents from the Boston public schools to articulate new pedagogy, knowledge, and perspectives to assist future teachers in identifying, addressing, and preventing the complex educational, social, psychological, and health needs of today's children. We are achieving these goals by modifying the teacher-education course curriculum to include relevant portions of the knowledge bases from the other professions. BC faculty are participating in interprofessional teams in the Student Support Team Meetings in our partner schools and agencies, and interprofessional practicum/internship teams of students are placed and supervised in our partner schools and community agencies.

The first of these efforts led to a significant and unanticipated learning experience for all of the faculty involved in the project (Mooney, Brabeck, Cawthorne, Sparks & Walsh, 1996). We had assumed that the faculty within each profession could inform the teacher-education faculty about which portions of their respective knowledge bases would be important for teachers to learn. Law faculty, we thought, would be able to tell us what teachers should ideally know about legal aspects of schools and teaching, and similarly for faculty in nursing, social work, and psychology. However, after months of trying, the BC faculty could only generate meager lists of obvious areas of knowledge, e.g., social work suggested "child abuse," law focused on "special-needs advocacy," and psychology highlighted "childhood depression." It was extremely difficult for us as university faculty to take the perspective of practicing teachers and identify knowledge that would be of use to new teachers. Our frustration in this task was short-lived. We met with a group of teachers, principals, health professionals, and parents from the local school and community and asked them to tell us what teachers needed to know about legal, health, social, and psychological issues of children and families. In contrast to the limited accounts we received from the academic professionals, the practitioners and parents provided us with rich and detailed descriptions of the knowledge bases of each profession that ought to be included in our teacher-education curricula (Mooney, Sparks & Walsh, in press). As academic professionals, we had learned a powerful lesson about the necessity of university-community partnerships in this work.

While we expanded our teacher-education curriculum to include the issues parents and practitioners identified as important, we also drew from the literature on teacher-education. Although working from different empirical and conceptual research, the teacher-education literature reinforces the notion that teachers and other professionals who work with children in urban and increasingly diverse contexts must learn to link in new ways to families and communities (Dryfoos, 1994). We have incorporated ways to build on the cultural and linguistic resources that children bring to school with them; and we are learning to consciously avoid situations where school professionals serve as a wedge between children and their families (Delpit, 1995; Meier, 1995). School professionals' conceptions of culture, their knowledge of cultures different from their own, and their images of schools and classrooms have enormous influences on the ways they construct and act upon "differences" in schooling: differences between and among teachers; differences with other service providers; and differences among the students they teach, their families, and communities. The concept of culture is not captured in lists of "the characteristics" of groups of "others," a practice that may in and of itself bolster rather than interrupt stereotypes (Cazden & Mehan, 1989; Villegas, 1991). Applied to schools and schooling, a broad concept of culture allows professionals to realize that classrooms are not neutral sites for the transmission of information but are instead culturally and socially constructed contexts with deeply interactive, embedded, and political layers of meaning (Cazden & Mehan, 1989; Cochran-Smith, 1995). To learn the meanings of any given culture requires partnerships with parents and community members.

Preparing teachers to recognize and address the multiple needs of their students also requires that we teach them about interprofessional collaboration in school settings. However, as academic professionals who had spent much of our working lives in university schools or departments that isolated us from faculty in other professions, we needed to learn how to collaborate with each other in real-world contexts. Consequently, interprofessional teams of faculty spent an entire year working at the elbows of the interprofessional Student Support Teams in our partner schools, and meeting regularly to reflect on what we were learning.

Professionals tend to have a narrow view of what teachers in the schools need, and we are no exception. For example, when we began working in schools, the psychologists understood that teachers "need to be listened to, heard and acknowledged," and the nurses understood teachers needed "reassurance that there was medical backup," particularly for their special-needs students. As our work continues, we are seeing that the needs of teachers are like all professionals: complex, multiple, and best addressed in partnerships. Both the University and the schools are benefiting from our collaborative work. Schools are receiving additional resources and teachers are included in planning sessions that will deploy resources to meet the overwhelming needs of students. The responsibility to deliver these services and conduct the follow-through is shared and teachers are relieved of the burden of knowing about, but not being able to respond to, complex problems of children and youth that impede their ability to learn. This is a "benefit" that should be key in reducing the probability of burnout.

Our collaborative efforts through IntServ have given us new understandings, particularly regarding the ways that we think about professional education. Interprofessional collaboration and integrated services requires a rethinking of professional roles, identities, and power structures within each individual profession. Faculty who were socialized into professions that emphasized boundaries, territoriality, and competition for resources must socialize a new generation of professionals to think differently. Helping students to make those changes has its own challenges. Students, for example, may seek professional training to gain feelings of expertise, legitimacy, and status within their profession, as well as access to financial rewards. Interprofessional collaboration requires that a professional be able to recognize and value the contributions of other professionals to the welfare of children and families—sometimes above the contributions of one's own profession and one's own personal gain.

Collaboration also generates anxiety among our students, who seek a cloak of expert status to compensate for limited experience and confidence. When resources to meet child and family needs are scarce or insufficient (as they almost always are), choices have to be made. For example, a mental-health professional trained in a collaborative and ecological perspective may recognize that tutoring for the child, respite child care to relieve parental stress, or funding for nutritional lunches may be more critical to the psychological well-being of the child and family than mental-health services such as psychotherapy or even psychoeducational intervention (Brabeck, Walsh, Kenny, & Comilang, in press). When professionals view children and families as experts in articulating their own needs, professionals may find themselves delivering services that seem mundane in comparison with traditional roles. They may also discover that a "nonprofessional" or community person can better or more easily provide the service. In addition, as government cuts and stringent managed-care guidelines reduce mental-health funding, professionals who advocate for alternative services for the benefit of the child may be forfeiting billable hours for the agency or personal income from a private practice. Finding ways to help students overcome the natural inclinations of professional territoriality and competition for resources is another challenge we face in training for interprofessional collaboration. These challenges requires that university faculty take the risk to become role models of this changed professional role and manage the same concerns with which our students struggle.

Graduate School of Social Work (GSSW):
First Collaboration in Joint Supervision

The profession of social work historically has been committed to serving the needs of children, youth, and families. Faculty in Boston College's

Graduate School of Social Work for fifty years have bridged the theory-practice gap by educating students for the profession and by doing the scholarship needed to inform the field of social work. Collaboration between the schools of Social Work and Education, both concerned with the lives of children and youth, seemed a natural. In late fall 1993, the dean of the Graduate School of Social Work approached the dean of the School of Education with an idea for collaboration: Fordham University's National Center for Social Work and Education Collaboration on behalf of the DeWitt Wallace-Reader's Digest Fund had issued a call for proposals. Faculty were called in, pages were written, papers were signed and in 1994, Boston College's Schools of Social Work and Education were awarded funding for a two-year project.

Following recommendations of Comer (1987), Sarason (1994), and Dryfoos (1994), faculty designed curricula to train interns from education and social work to work collaboratively within the school setting. We wanted to better enhance learning through working with children and their families, and to teach students from the two graduate schools the importance of collaborative integrated public-school service. DeWitt Wallace-Reader's Digest funded our efforts to increase awareness across the university of the need for interprofessional collaborative curriculum reform, and to provide regional leadership on interprofessional collaboration. University awareness was heightened through the monthly lunch sessions, which extended beyond the agenda of the SOE lunches to include issues that confront social workers and educators in public-school settings. The series became a forum for faculty from the professional schools to come together around shared interests. Through our monthly discussions we gained insight into a possible educational and practice paradigm shift, from professional isolation (Soler & Shauffer, 1993) to professional collaboration. (Comer, 1987; Dryfoos, 1994; Lerner, 1995a, 1995b)

We implemented monthly project-coordination meetings to keep the collaborative effort focused and ensure integration and coordination of ideas and project planning. We clarified roles: the principal investigators, project directors, education and social-work supervisors, and project coordinator. Supervisors bridged the professions by providing profession-specific supervision, meeting with each other to coordinate joint collaborative projects students carried out in the schools. Supervisors were also the weekly administrative contact from the University with the participating public schools and were also involved in the public schools' coordinating teams' meetings. The project coordinator was responsible for the daily administrative tasks and activities from the three program levels of the project and ensured that the various project foci were implemented effectively and efficiently.

We held annual joint retreats for university and community project participants to reflect on the nature of the challenge facing schools (Delpit, 1995; Dryfoos, 1990; Knitzer, Steinberg, & Fleisch, 1991) and the need for more effective connections to professional services. Grant participants, principals, teachers, student support coordinators, and parents offered critical information for carrying out public-school programs and grant activities. We developed and implemented a team taught, social-work–education graduate course on the impact of psychosocial issues on learning and the need for integrating educational, health, and social services in the effort to support children and their families. The course provided the opportunity for school-based professionals and graduate students from both disciplines to think, discuss, and reflect in a collaborative manner. In this course we attempted to overcome the social workers' minimal interest in schools (Costin, 1981), and students' resistance to collaboration between educators and social workers. We developed a brochure to recruit social work and education graduate students (and faculty) to become involved in this partnership in schools; we highlighted collaborative placement opportunities in school settings and the knowledge and service possibilities available in such collaborations. We were educating ourselves and our university about the benefits of this work and overcoming strong stereotypes about working in schools. We spread the word at regional and national conferences and produced a videotape of the social-work–education model at Boston College. We began a jointly edited (social work and education) book on our experience of interprofessional collaboration (Tourse & Mooney, in press).

Our DeWitt Wallace-Reader's Digest grant story is one of two professions learning concretely to work in partnership: social workers, historically committed to addressing individual socioemotional and human survival needs, and teachers, historically committed to learning, dissemination of knowledge, and development of problem-solving skills. In the past, these two professions worked in a parallel manner—side by side, but seldom together. The DeWitt Wallace grant committed these two professional schools at BC to establishing joint training experiences for graduate students. Through their efforts to develop a joint course on the "Impact of Psychosocial Issues on Learning," social work and education faculty struggled to learn each other's language, theoretical frameworks, research bases, and foci of intervention. For example, both the holistic (education) and ecological (social work) perspectives are important frameworks for understanding individuals (Costin, 1981; Germain, 1991; Germain & Gitterman, 1986). Social Work and Education use different words to convey the same purpose—to hold a complex and contextualized understanding of the person served within the teaching and helping professions.

Graduate students, placed in collaborative internship/practicum experiences in local schools, struggled to figure out how to collaborate with one another. In joint sessions with supervisors from each profession, student teachers shared their hesitancy to welcome social workers into "my classroom" and student social workers revealed their reluctance to expand their repertoire of interventions beyond individual psychotherapy. The students brought different foci and expertise: The education students were familiar with the culture of schools and could quickly identify the power structure, the network of services already in place, and the demands of the regular classroom. Social-work students understood the critical role of family, community, and culture in children's school achievement and knew how to access noneducational systems on behalf of children and families.

After joint classroom observations, participation in Student Support Team meetings and problem-solving discussions with classroom teachers about the needs of individual children, students began some creative and collaborative projects. Teachers, supervisors, and faculty responded to the needs they observed in their respective schools. For example, one team started a "rap" group for middle-school boys diagnosed as having attention deficits with hyperactivity and experiencing a great deal of difficulty with impulse control in the classroom. This very lively and challenging group of eight worked hard to develop better attending behaviors and appropriate social skills for group interaction. The same social work/education student team, observed that fifth graders in the elementary school were terrified at the prospect of entering the middle school the following fall. The team worked with the social-work/education students at the middle school to make a videotape of life in the middle school. They hosted a tour of the middle school and held a very frank discussion of issues such as homework, school buses, lockers, cafeteria fare, weapons, violence, and detention. As the university students focused on collaborative projects to respond to the broad-based needs of the children, students in each profession slowly grew to appreciate the perspective and goals of the other. In some cases, this appreciation came to be a mutual dependence, which was noticed in its absence when their next placement or job the following semester did not involve a cross-professional partnership. As one alumna of the program reported, "While I like my new job, I find it much more difficult to be a teacher without a social work partner."

Another social work/education team designed a social-skills curriculum with a particular focus on friendship, which they implemented within the regular first-grade class. Within the class there were four children with serious social/emotional problems receiving intensive individual therapy by the full-time psychotherapist or the social work intern. The goals of increased social competence and self-esteem were enhanced within the classroom through direct instruction in the behaviors that facilitate positive peer interaction. Through the year the social work/education teams progressed from a focus on individual needs and interventions to understanding individuals within group experiences and designing group interventions.

Although we could anticipate some of the organizational issues associated with an interprofessional effort to prepare social workers and teachers, we can identify the clear advantages of joint training. The collaborative model enlarges the sphere of influence of the social worker through active participation in classrooms and provision of opportunities for direct input into the everyday life of the school. By being part of the school support team and gaining entry into the classroom, students were able to supervise interventions firsthand and to recognize recommendations that were unrealistic or missed the mark altogether. They could also recognize that individual therapy has more power when connected to the real world of the classroom where new perspectives on the part of children can effect more appropriate behavior and ultimately greater achievement. By the end of the year the students also began to appreciate the unique value of working with groups, particularly at the middle-school level.

There are also many personal benefits to the collaborative model of field work. The usual insecurities of being a practicum student in a school are far less unsettling when one is part of a pair. Interpretation of interactions with children, parents, teachers, administrators, etc., is easier when two people react to, and reflect on, the experience. The mutual support and reflective practice seems to bring students to greater understanding of the problems children present and the options for resolving them. It also gave the students an awareness of the need to connect other professionals to the schools. Once they came to appreciate what can be accomplished by a team, they wanted to know why more students from the professions that touch children's lives were not with them.

One of the most important lessons learned by the student interns involved the importance, and difficulty, of communication. The need to build trust and establish communication was a difficult skill to learn but essential to working successfully in schools or social service agencies. Recognition of the unit of analysis of each profession—for a teacher a class of twenty-five students, for social workers the individual client or family—helped each profession to make sense of the responses of the other profession. As an example, social workers came to understand why it can be difficult to convey the value of mental health interventions to a teacher when only one or two students might benefit. Social work students learned about the need to respect the territory of the classroom and to develop strategies for negotiating partnerships. Education students learned to develop a collaborative model of intervention and to reach outside their classrooms for help

The social work-education collaboration provided us an opportunity for implementing interprofessional collaboration in two graduate programs. While there had been many joint efforts across various schools (e.g., multidisciplinary courses, joint-degree programs), this project involved university faculty modeling interprofessional collaboration in a real-world setting. Students did more than learn the ways of two distinct professions; they experienced the collaborative process in practicum/internship placements and supervision. Faculty contributed more than the perspectives of their professions as they reflected together on the process and possibilities of collaboration. Such reflection however, did not come easily. The social work–education collaboration has not yet been institutionalized, although discussions about how to accomplish this are underway. The DeWitt Wallace-Reader's Digest project was the first such funded project at the University and the project served as a prototype that demonstrated interprofessional collaboration can work.

The School of Nursing (SON) Joins

Faculty in the School of Nursing entered into the interprofessional collaboration efforts through the Allston-Brighton Coalition for a Healthy Boston and their contacts with the community's hospitals where students had clinical placements. The Healthy-Boston subcommittee on school-linked services, funded by the Massachusetts Department of Education, is working to enhance family-school relationships in the Allston-Brighton community. This group helped identify the health needs of the community, and BC nursing faculty joined with the Boston College Neighborhood Center to address these needs.

Thus, nursing came first through the involvement with the community, including two local hospitals and a neighborhood health center. Nursing faculty brought these relationships "to the table" during early discussions held in the School of Education. Nursing students were doing clinical work with school nurses in other communities, and the common goal of working for the well-being of students in school settings kindled a commitment to collaboration with other faculty and students in schools.

SON faculty admit that the early discussions had more questions than answers. ("What," one of these faculty recalls thinking, "am I doing here with all these Education people?") The fears have been answered through our joint efforts to place more nursing students with other professionals-in-training in school settings, to interest more students in pursuing nursing careers in schools, and to work with community leaders for a healthier community.

The Law School's Beginnings

At the same time that the SOE faculty in psychology and teacher education were beginning a collaborative effort, the law school dean as well as faculty engaged in child and family law invited SOE faculty to informal discussions of what they accurately perceived to be our mutual interests in addressing the needs of children and families. The law faculty viewed interprofessional collaborative work as important to their efforts both to prepare new lawyers and to address the needs of children and families in today's society.

The Law School's primary clinical program, the Boston College Legal Assistance Bureau (LAB), was an early effort at interprofessional collaboration, and has been located in the economically depressed community of Waltham since 1968. Employing a teaching-hospital model,[4] LAB was established to provide access to justice in civil matters for the economically poorest members of the community[5] while instilling in law students both strong legal skills and high professional values. Originally students learned that professional values involved the way lawyers should conduct themselves in relationships with clients, other lawyers, and representatives of the legal system. Gradually, students came to recognize and appreciate the constellation of influences that caused chronically poor legal health. Racism, sexism, and other systemic barriers to economic and social advancement were seen as forces that would keep clients' lives troubled, legally and otherwise, despite the good legal work LAB student attorneys performed for them.

To enhance student and faculty understanding of, and ability to address, the cyclical and systemic underpinnings of clients' problems, LAB began to teach students a more holistic approach to working with clients. In the late 1970s, the Boston College Legal Assistance Bureau was among the first law-school clinical programs in the country to include on its professional staff a full-time, clinical social worker. The social worker's role was two-fold. First, to contribute to the education of law students by helping them see a different professional perspective on problems their clients faced. Specifically, the social worker helped students define what lawyers are able to do and appreciate the services and support available from other helping professionals. The second major role of the social worker was to enrich and expedite the program's ability to make intelligent, constructive referrals for clients to sister agencies from which they would receive the services they needed.

While there were interesting and enriching results of this early experiment in collaborative learning and service provision, the absence of a well-considered and tested theory of interprofessional education caused a fragmentation that the LAB faculty could not process in a constructive enough way. The legacy of that experiment, however, was that the role of the social worker in the education of law students has expanded to include three additional components. First, over the past ten years the social worker has helped the law school clinical faculty to better understand the supervision process, and to enhance their clinical supervision skills. Second, she has enriched students' lawyer skills in the interpersonal areas of client interviewing and counseling. Finally, while not doing clinical work with students, she has been available to help them understand and appropriately channel their own thoughts and feelings about the work they were doing and the transformations they were undergoing.

In 1993, the Law School's criminal defense clinical program[6] followed LAB's example and began to employ a clinical social worker on a part-time basis. The social worker's role has not expanded or become as integrated into the criminal programs as it has at LAB. However, the effort to instill in students a broader and more specific knowledge of what other professional do was motivated by the recognition that professional isolation is ultimately detrimental to the advancement of clients' legal positions and overall improvement of their daily lives.

We made plans for a clinic that would both train students and provide legal services to families, and had lofty ideas about how we could meet their needs. Discussions were quickly underway about developing an

Interprofessional Assessment/Referral Center in the community for children and families with complex needs. It was anticipated that such a center could serve as a training facility for graduate students in all of the professional schools on campus. However, exploratory conversations with some
neighborhood agencies indicated that these agencies felt no need for such
a center since they did well at assessing and referring needs. They did
indicate that they were short on sites and strategies for intervention. Simultaneously, the university was securing a site in the same neighborhood
for a Boston College Neighborhood Center, which the university hoped
would house some services for neighborhood residents. Because
interprofessional collaboration was still in the "infancy stage," some of the
professional schools chose to offer specialized services at this Center in the
traditional single-profession modality, for example, Law School set up an
Immigration Law Service.

Boston College Law School has long held a place of national prominence in the field of family law, dating at least to the deanship of Father
Robert Drinan, who also served as chair of the American Bar Association's
Section of Family Law. In order to help facilitate collaboration on children's
issues across professional school lines, the Law School initiated the first
interdisciplinary appointment at Boston College: Catherine Ross joined
the faculty for a two-year visit in 1994, with appointments in Law, the
School of Education, and History. As vice chair of the American Bar
Association's Working Group on the Unmet Legal Needs of Children, she
was the principal author of the American Bar Association's (1993)
groundbreaking report, *America's Children at Risk: A National Agenda for
Legal Action.* Among other things, that report called for collaboration among
the professions on behalf of children *before* the children become involved
with the justice system. The report also recommended the development of
additional curricula to train law students to serve the needs of child clients.

History and law faculty joined together for an interdisciplinary colloquium on child abuse, and we sponsored a major public lecture on
"America's Children at Risk." These events helped to launch a monthly
faculty seminar for members of all of the professional schools interested in
bringing an integrated approach to children's problems. That seminar, which
has come to be called "The Barat House seminar" because it was located in
Barat House on the Law School campus, has met regularly since 1994. We
have used a case-method approach to learn to talk across our professions
and disciplines. The Barat House seminar gave us a working group to
generate the conceptual basis for interprofessional collaborations, and the

impetus for our early discussions about our desire to build a center or institute that would help to support our work.

Through the Law School we offered our first cross-listed courses for students in law, education, psychology, nursing and social work, as well as American studies, sociology, and history. In 1995–1996, the Law School received a small grant to support a practicum on children's rights, jointly taught by another law professor and a nationally renowned child advocate. This intensive course immersed students in interdisciplinary materials about children and their rights, developmental issues relevant to optimizing healthy development, and clinical projects ranging from a "legal advice" table in local schools to investigation of major legal problems such as illegal detentions of adolescents in adult facilities.

The Law School also sponsored a number of colloquia and conferences that showcased interprofessional work at Boston College. For example, in December 1994 we joined with Harvard Law School to cosponsor a national conference on juvenile justice. Several members of the integrated services faculty spoke at the conference, and many attended. Through the Law School we held a one-day retreat on professional ethics and responsibility to children and families that drew together a multiprofessional, multidisciplinary group of faculty to examine the different ethical frames we use in making decisions. Thus, projects in and through the Law School extend our partnerships in curricula, school-based work, and professional development.

The College of Arts and Sciences (A & S)

Gradually faculty in the College of Arts and Sciences are learning about the work across the campus. Those who study the history of childhood, the sociology of families, the discourse of media, or the popular literature of youth, are beginning to see a role for themselves in the work we are doing. Their scholarship, critique, and analysis has been featured at colloquia and our pizza lunch series. The interdisciplinary majors, housed in Arts and Sciences, can inform our struggle to learn how to be partners in collaboration. However, these links are in the early stages of formation and will need to be extended and strengthened.

The Institute for Religious Education and Pastoral Ministry, a unit within A & S that prepares professionals, joined the effort early. The Institute, a division of the theology department, offers graduate degrees in theology that prepare students as religious educators, pastoral counselors, social workers, and pastoral ministers in the church. Contemporary concerns over a cultural ethos that portrays today's religious practice as less communitarian and more individualistic led faculty in the Institute to seek partnerships in addressing the ways in which ministers and religious educators can work with the professions that provide services to children and families in today's complex society.

The Institute has directed our discussions toward an integrated model of *advocacy*. We are moving away from the individualized, ad hoc approach of disciplines, to a shared vision and action strategies. In our Barat House conversations, the emerging voices and insights of the interprofessional faculty uncover the possibilities that exist for churches as they pursue a less private and more actively public presence through their ministries. We are beginning the first stage of a field internship opportunity for Institute graduate students. They are working with other student interns in education, nursing, and social work in the Allston-Brighton school district. The Institute students build bridges and develop strategies for networking communities of faith in activities that can further a collaborative model of care and action that serves children and families.

Working beyond the traditional dialogues within academic departments and schools has fostered new understandings and new ways of collaborating beyond the current "single service" model of care providers. It has provided both the space and opportunity to envision possibilities for models of service that will both strengthen and enhance the "communal" over the "private" in today's society.

The Carroll School of Management (CSOM) Is Recruited

As we listened to people with whom we were working in Allston-Brighton, we quickly became aware that the structural needs of the community are very much tied to employment and business opportunities. Our work could be strengthened by involvement of BC faculty who had expertise in that area. We learned that a School of Management faculty member had written a book about the role of business in public education (Waddock, 1995), and we sought her out. She brought not only an understanding of the issues we were feeling our way into, but also a conceptualization of the systemic changes we were undertaking on the BC campus and, as well, other CSOM colleagues who shared a commitment to applying their scholarship to serve communities.

Two issues made it difficult for faculty in the School of Management to see their work as relevant to the interprofessional level. First, we had focused the work on children, youth, and families; their emphasis is com-

munity. We needed to draw a larger circle to describe the work in a way
that they fit. Second, the word "interprofessional" was problematic. Some
faculty questioned whether management is a profession, and whether they
have a voice in an interprofessional discussion. We learned that faculty in
the College of Arts and Sciences had a similar question and learned to use
language like "interdisciplinary" to be more inclusive.

All of our work in curriculum development, professional training,
outreach scholarship, and service delivery, is based on the assumption that
effective service is provided in collaboration, rather than through a "top
down" expert-to-needy delivery system. Our collaborative model is inherently an asset-based (as compared to a deficit-based) approach to communities. The CSOM faculty brought new ways of thinking about the model
of partnership we are building, helped us think critically about the systems we were creating, and joined us to systematically examine the changes
in the culture of the University needed for outreach scholarship. A description of our University collaborative model follows.

The Boston College Model for Child, Family,
and Community Partnerships

Most professional education and professional service delivery during the
twentieth century has occurred within a context of what management experts Preston and Post (1975) called a "collateral-systems model." In a
collateral-systems model, two or more systems perform their transforma-
tive or service functions as if they were substantially independent of each
other. They operate in an exchange relationship with each other. Thus,
professional schools, such as education, social work, law, management,
and nursing, have evolved their own distinctive curricula, specialties, paradigms, ethical codes, and languages without specific reference or even much
knowledge of what is happening within other professions. The educational
process that follows from a collateral-systems model emphasizes strong
analytical and functional skills and only later, almost as an afterthought,
provides any kind of integration for students. It is obvious that many businesses, schools, social-service agencies, and other societal enterprises have
been operating under a similar set of assumptions, that is, that they can
perform their own activities and functions independently of any others.

However, as management systems experts and theoretical physicists
(Capra, 1983) recognize, it is not easy to separate either individuals or
institutions into independent entities because their activities are inherently bound together. Despite our tendency toward atomistic thinking

and fragmentation, many societal problems do not neatly break into functions or disciplines. The problems of community, family, education, health care, legal services, management, and social services are all intermingled. Being intermingled, they cannot be broken down into separable elements if they are to be properly resolved, or new problems will crop up elsewhere as unintended consequences (Senge, 1991). Thus, educators, psychologists, lawyers, social workers, managers, and nurses must learn ways to work together. Nationally, increasing numbers of professionals are recognizing that the focus for school reform, a major thrust of the Republican Bush and the Democratic Clinton administrations, will occur from successfully addressing the myriad social issues, as well as health and academic issues, with which children are faced (Comer, 1987; Huston, McLoyd & García Coll, 1994; Sarason, 1994; Walsh, 1992).

Sandra Waddock (1996) described our alternative model as a "collaborative-systems" model. In collaborative systems, individuals and communities exist within a macrosystem as conceptually separable subsystems, but ones inherently influencing each other as well as their own larger context. No system within the macrosystem, in this view, can be seen as truly independent of the other systems, since all are bound together in the macrosystem (Bronfenbrenner, 1974; Lerner et al., 1994).

In higher education, a collaborative-systems approach requires considerable innovative thinking to help both universities and the professionals they educate develop broader approaches to working in their professions. It is unlikely that professions will give up their distinctive specialties. However, our experience at Boston College suggests that changes are both necessary and possible if a more collaborative orientation is assumed among professional schools themselves. Only then can one expect to foster collaboration among service providers, as well as between the University and its communities.

The collaborative-systems approach emerging at BC takes place at multiple levels: among the professional schools themselves in the education of new professionals; between the University and the schools where we are trying to work in mutually supportive and respectful partnerships; and in the schools with respect to actual service delivery. It is not fully developed, and few major structural changes have occurred. There is, however, increased recognition that the development of a professional for the twenty-first century demands a new perspective that orients the student holistically both prior to specialization as well as within that specialization. (Figure 16.1 provides an illustration of the BC collaborative-systems model.)

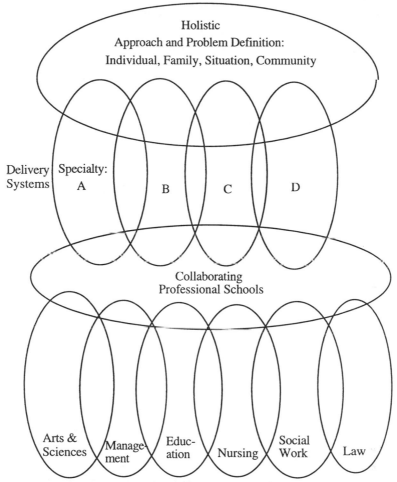

Source: S. Waddock and the Boston College Center for Child, Family, and Community Partnerships, 1996.

Figure 16.1. The Boston College Collaborative-Systems Model.

Our model assumes interdependence among individuals, organizations, and even whole systems. As we extend our work beyond schools to the larger community, it will require breaking down the artificial barriers constructed by each specialization and asking, *with* the school, family, or community, what services are needed and how can they best be delivered. In our ongoing Barat House seminar we have learned that focusing on a specific case involving real people diminishes our differences and focuses attention on what we all share: a commitment to figuring out a better way for people and their communities. The Boston College interprofessional partnership for children, families, and communities is based on the recognition that individual and societal problems cannot be reduced to the categories defined by traditional disciplines and professions. Effective prevention, intervention, and policy require an intersection and integration of the knowledge bases and modes of service delivery from a number of professions and in collaboration with the "recipients" of services.

Our collaborative-systems model acknowledges the need for specialization but *within the context* of a holistic and ecological conception of the situation (Bronfenbrenner, 1974). In order for our overlapping areas to coexist, we have begun to learn each other's language (the systems language of management; the medical language of nursing; the individualistic language of education and psychology, etc.), examine each others' professional codes of ethics (the circumstances under which confidentiality can be broken, the different perspectives on paternalism, etc.), and even the style manuals of other professional journals (American Psychological Association [APA], Modern Language Association [MLA], Science, etc.).

Boston College is not unique in recognizing that shortcomings of our current segregated and segmented professions. Interprofessional collaboration represents what appears to be a paradigm shift for a number of professions and disciplines, one involving new ways of relating to one another and to society (Boston College Initiative, 1995). However, professionals are currently not trained in an interprofessional model; our work at BC is directed at moving professional training in this direction.

Reflections on Failures, Work That Remains

As our title suggests, our major focus in this chapter has been on changing the culture of the University to prepare ourselves and our students for integrated and collaborative work. However, since our early meetings there have been tensions within our group surrounding the timing of and strategies for expanding our links to the communities of Boston. Initial discussions included a debate about which neighborhood(s) in Boston would be the primary base for our activities. There were those who suggested that we explore criteria for selecting neighborhoods and favored neighborhoods known to have the least access to resources, particularly to University-community partnerships. However broader institutional ties, local politics, and the proximity of Allston-Brighton dictated the neighborhood of primary affiliation and a totally open discussion of differences around these issues never took place. Our subcommittee, formed to explore community ties, spent time at local Allston-Brighton meetings and getting to know neighbors at the local level, on the street, in our neighborhoods. However, liaisons being formed with the schools, urgings from the higher administration to begin our work in our local neighborhood, and the commitment of a number of leaders in the group to work through existing schools, won out over the considerably slower, grassroots process of working with community leaders that was urged by some.

We have learned several critical lessons from these experiences. First, and most importantly, there is not one community but many, even within the same narrow strip of streets surrounding Boston College that fall within Allston-Brighton. In our work to date we have related primarily to school communities. Schools have been targeted as central to the community; yet the history of Boston's schools, particularly in the past twenty years, suggests that they are peculiar proxies for networking with local community folks. This is because parents often live long distances from the schools to which their children are bused, and after-school/weekend programs for students that might bring parents into a closer partnership (Dryfoos, 1994) with schools are rare.

Second, when one institution seeks to develop relations with "the community" it often seeks some representative force that claims such an identity and formal ties are established. Such has been the case with our work, which has been deeply shaped both by Boston College's commitments within the greater Boston area and by existing ties to existing institutions, particularly schools.

In contrast a more community-based participatory strategy demands different kinds of time, energy, and commitment. It begins with getting to know the diversity of communities and neighborhoods within Allston-Brighton. It moves out from there to design a model for working with residents to clarify their needs. It then seeks to match resources from these communities and the University in developing strategies for meeting those needs. Notwithstanding their multiple strengths and gifts, university professors and their students are not in the best position to work collaboratively and in a participatory fashion from the ground up. The short span of time in which most students are at the University, the reward systems for faculty, and other factors militate against such collaboration. Foundations and funding organizations are, typically, even further from this reality, seeking to support short-term interventions that produce immediate results. Yet the problems faced by most communities are long-term and resist quick fixes. Thus, a more participatory strategy may only be workable, as it is emerging within our ranks, as a small effort on the parts of some who are committed to this way of building collaboration. Perhaps this "mini-effort" will contribute to the larger institutional ties forged within our programs to date.

We have learned that both grassroots involvement of the community and faculty (bottom up) and administrative participation (top down) are needed to do this work. Our institutional mission and values provide a context essential for our ongoing commitment to the work. However, we know that it will take a cultural sea-change to accomplish our goals. Time will tell if our sustained efforts will be integrated into the broader fabric of Boston College and become, as Fullan and Steigelbauer wrote (1991, p. 323), "a new way of life, not just another project."

Notes

1. The work described here has been funded by the Massachusetts Department of Education, the DeWitt-Wallace Reader's Digest Foundation through the National Center for Social Work and Education Collaboration at Fordham University, the U.S. Office of Education (Fund for the Improvement of Post-Secondary Education; Patricia Roberts Harris Grant), and Philip Morris Companies, Inc.
2. The first author took responsibility for coordinating this collaborative writing effort and editing the manuscript. Contributors are listed in alphabetical order. The academic fields of the coauthors follow here: Mary Brabeck, dean, School of Education; John Cawthorne, Urban League, Department of Education, SOE; Marilyn Cochran-Smith, teacher education; Nancy Gaspard, nursing; Carol Hurd Green, associate dean, arts and sciences; Maureen Kenny, psychology in education; Rosemary Krawczyk, nursing; Claire Lowery, pastoral ministry; M. Brinton Lykes, psychology in education; Alan D. Minuskin, law school; Jean Mooney, teacher education; Catherine J. Ross, law, education, history; John Savage, teacher education; Avi Soifer, dean, law school; Michael Smyer, associate vice president research/dean, graduate arts and sciences; Elizabeth Sparks, psychology in education; Robbie Tourse, social work; Robert M. Turillo, social worker, community contact; Sandra Waddock, management; Mary Walsh, psychology in education; Nancy Zollers, teacher education). Correspondence regarding this paper may be sent to Boston College Center for Child, Family and Community Partnerships, Chestnut Hill, MA 02167.
3. To date our work has involved primarily faculty in the professional schools, and thus we characterize it as "interprofessional." Increasingly, however, faculty in the College of Arts and Sciences have become involved in the work, and our language is changing to include that fact. We are becoming more "interdisciplinary."
4. Students in the advanced stage of their legal education, supervised by experienced, full-time clinical faculty served clients who either walked in or were referred by other clients or community poverty agencies in family law (divorce, separation, child custody, child visitation, child support, and abuse prevention), eviction defense, discrimination in housing and employment, and public benefits (appeals of the denial of applications for food stamps, Medicaid, Aid to Families with Dependent Children, Supplemental Security Income, and Social Security Disability, and unemployment compensation) cases.
5. LAB's client population was limited to people whose income fell below 125% of the federally established poverty line.
6. Entitled "Criminal Process—Defense," students were assigned by courts to advise and represent criminal defendants who were deemed unable to afford lawyers.

References

American Bar Association. (1993). *America's Children at Risk: A National Agenda for Legal Action*. Chicago, IL: Author.

Boston College Initiative for Child, Family and Community Partnerships. (1995). Professional association statements on interprofessional collaboration. Available from Boston College Center for Child, Family and Community Partnerships, Campion Hall, Chestnut Hill, MA 02167.

———. (1996). *Interprofessional Collaboration/ Integrated Services: Annotated Bibliography*. Available from Boston College Center for Child, Family and Community Partnerships, Campion Hall, Chestnut Hill, MA 02167.

Boyer, E. (1990). *Scholarship reconsidered: Priorities of the professoriate*. Princeton, NJ: The Carnegie Foundation for the Advancement of Teaching.

———. (1994, March). Creating the new American college. *The Chronicle of Higher Education*, p. A48.

Brabeck, M., Walsh, M., Kenny, M., & Comilang, K. (in press). Interprofessional collaboration for children and families: Opportunities for counseling psychology in the twenty-first century. *The Counseling Psychologist*.

Bronfenbrenner, U. (1974). Developmental research, public policy, and the ecology of childhood. *Child Development, 45*, 1–5.

Byrne, P. (1995). Paradigms of justice and love. *Conversations*. St. Louis: National Center on Jesuit Higher Education.

Carnegie Foundation. (1990). *Turning points: Preparing American youth for the twenty-first century*. (Report of the Task Force of Education of Young Adolescents). New York: Author.

Capra, F. (1983). *The turning point: Science, society, and the rising culture*. New York: Bantam Books.

Cazden, C., & Mohan, H. (1989). Principles from sociology and anthropology: Context, code, classroom, and culture. In M. Reynolds (Ed.), *Knowledge base for the beginning teacher*, (pp. 47–57). Oxford: Pergamon Press.

Cochran-Smith, M. (1995). Color blindness and basket making are not the answers: Confronting the dilemmas of race, culture and language diversity in teacher education. *American Educational Research Journal, 32* (3), 593–522.

Cochran-Smith, M., & Lytle, S. (1991). Teacher research as a way of knowing. *Harvard Educational Review, 62* (4), 447–474.

———. (1993). *Inside/outside: Teacher research and knowledge*. New York: Teachers College Press.

Comer, J. (1987). New Haven's school-community connection. *Educational Leadership, 44* (6), 13–16.

Costin, L. B. (1981). School social work as specialized practice. *Social Work, 26*, 26–43.

Delpit, L. (1995). *Other people's children: Cultural conflict in the classroom*. New York: The New Press.

Dryfoos, J. G. (1990). *Adolescents at risk: Prevalence and prevention*. New York: Oxford University.

———. (1994). *Full service schools: A revolution in health and social services of children youth and families*. San Francisco: Jossey-Bass.

Fullan, M. G., & Steigelbauer, S. (1991). *The new meaning of educational change*. New York: Teachers College Press.

Germain, C. B. (1991). *Human behavior in the social environment: An ecological view*. New York: Columbia University Press.

Germain, C. B. & Gitterman, A. (1986). *The life model of social work practice revisited*. In F. J. Turner (Ed.), Social work treatment (3rd ed.) (pp. 618–644). New York: The Free Press.

Hargreaves, A., & Fullan, M. G. (Eds.). (1992). *Understanding teacher development*. New York: Teachers College Press.

Huston, A. C., McLoyd, V. C., & García Coll, C. T. (1994). Children and poverty: Issues in contemporary research. *Child Development, 65*, 275–282.

Knitzer, J., Steinberg, Z., & Fleisch, B. (1991). Schools, children's mental health, and the advocacy challenge. *Journal of Clinical Child Psychology, 20* (1), 102–222.

Lerner, R. M. (1995a). *America's youth in crisis: Challenges and options for programs and policies.* Thousand Oaks, CA: Sage.

———. (1995b). Features and principles of effective youth programs: Promoting positive youth development through the integrative vision of family and consumer sciences. *Journal of Family and Consumer Sciences, 87* (4), 16–21.

Lerner, R. M., Miller, J. R., Knot, J. H., K. E. Corey, Bynum, T. S., Hooper, L. C., McKinney, M. H., Abrams, L. A., Hula, R. C., & Terry, P. A. (1994). Integrating scholarship and outreach in human development research, policy, and service: A developmental contextual perspective. In D. L. Featherman, R. M. Lerner, & M. Perlmutter (Eds.), *Life-span developmental behavior,* (Vol. 12). Hillsdale, NJ: Erlbaum.

Little, J. W., & McLaughlin, M. W. (1994). *Teachers' work: Individuals, colleagues and contexts.* New York: Teachers College Press.

Lykes, M. B. (1989). Dialogue with Guatemalan Indian women: Critical perspectives on constructing collaborative research. In R. Unger (Ed.) *Representations: Social constructions of gender* (pp. 167–185). Amityville, NY: Baywood.

Marsden, G. M. (1994). *The soul of the American university: From Protestant establishment to established nonbelief.* New York: Oxford University Press.

Meier, D. (1995). *The power of their ideas: Lessons for America from a small school in Harlem.* Boston: Beacon Press.

Mooney, J., Brabeck, M., Cawthorne, J., Sparks, E., & Walsh, M. (1996). *Preparing teachers to meet the needs of children and youth: An interprofessional model.* Paper presented at the 48th Annual Meeting of the American Association of Colleges of Teacher Education, Chicago.

Mooney, J., Sparks, E., & Walsh, M. (in press). *New knowledge bases for teacher education curriculum:* Boston College, Chestnut Hill, MA 02167.

Preston, L. E., & Post, J. E. (1975). *Private management and public policy: The principle of public responsibility.* Englewood Cliffs, NJ: Prentice-Hall.

Sarason, S. (1994). *Parental involvement and the political principle: Why the existing governance structure of schools should be abolished.* San Francisco: Jossey-Bass.

Senge, P. M. (1991). *The fifth discipline: The art and practice of the learning organization.* New York: Doubleday.

Soler, M. & Shauffer, C. (1993). Fighting fragmentation: Coordination of services for children and families. *Education and Urban Society, 25,* 129–140.

Tourse, R., & Mooney, J. (in press). *Social work and education: A collaborative model.*

Villegas, A. M. (1991). Culturally responsive pedagogy for the 1990s and beyond, (*Trends and Issues Paper No. 6*). Washington, DC: ERIC Clearinghouse on Teacher Education.

Waddock, S. (1995). *Not by schools alone: Sharing responsibility for America's education reform.* Westport CT: Praeger.

———. (1996). *An emerging model of integrated services and interprofessional collaboration: Working together for community welfare.* Paper presented at the Academy of Management annual meeting.

Walsh, M. E. (1992). *Moving to nowhere: Children's stories of homelessness.* New York: Auburn House.

Section III

Perspectives from Community Stakeholders

Chapter 17
Boldness for Our Times
Mobilizing University Expertise to Meet Youth Needs

Russell G. Mawby
W. K. Kellogg Foundation

Great emergencies and crises show us how much greater our vital resources are than we had supposed.
—*William James to W. Lutoslawski, May 6, 1906*

The dictionary defines "crisis" as an unstable or crucial time or state of affairs whose outcome will make a decisive difference for better or worse. Crisis, viewed creatively, is opportunity. Moments of crisis demand action, and at such times, daring or novel solutions to vexing problems are more readily acceptable. Leaders and their institutions must be opportunistic in capitalizing on the moment to accomplish significant goals.

In the theme of this book, two crises seem to converge. One is a crisis in higher education, with colleges and universities experiencing a lessening of confidence, and an erosion of credibility on the part of the public, with a consequent diminishing of support. With growing pressures in the allocation of limited resources, decision makers conclude that the academy is isolated from the realities of the day and is unresponsive to societal needs; thus, resources are directed elsewhere in seeking solutions to complex problems. In response, throughout higher education, in boards of governance, administrative structures, and faculty cohorts, questions are being asked and solutions are being sought to redress the role of our institutions of higher education in serving society's goals. The outreach dimension of the university, elaborating the teaching and research missions through linking the intellectual resources of the academy with communities and their needs in mutually beneficial relationships, is a focal point of such discussions. While some would argue that this is not a matter of crisis proportion—and this is certainly true for certain institutions in relation to specific issues—more would agree that this is a facet of university life deserving of greater attention and action.

A second crisis in America concerns our children and youth. Experts and knowledgeable observers describe in detail the problems that confront and confound America's youth. Studies by scholars and reports by distinguished commissions serve notice that our way of life is endangered by shortcomings of the rising generations. The magnitude and complexities of this situation will challenge the best minds and talents that can be mobilized. Certainly the society that has created and sustained our colleges and universities is justified in expecting them to be responsible and responsive in addressing this threat and need. Strengthening the outreach dimension of the universities' public-service mission through building university-community collaborations to serve America's youth and families is a credible response.

University Outreach: An Historical Overview

To anticipate the future, we must understand the past. Those of us concerned with higher education and with youth are the beneficiaries of those who have gone before. The successes of the past reflect the efforts of pioneers in each generation, individuals of remarkable vision, energy, and boldness who identified specific concerns and addressed them creatively and effectively.

The spirit of public service, of which outreach activities are a vital component, is the oldest tradition of institutions of higher education in this country. When the universities of Georgia and North Carolina were created over two hundred years ago as our country was being formed, when George Washington advanced his plan for a national university, when Thomas Jefferson sat at Monticello watching through his spyglass the growth of his beloved University of Virginia, the central intent of all the founders was to set higher learning within a public context. In their view, collegiate study should be guided by the principles of the Constitution, by democracy and independence, by ability and ambition, and not by religion or heredity. The new nation needed an abundant supply of leaders to serve its various needs. Access to education should be open to all who could benefit from it. The curriculum should include practical and contemporary subjects as well as theoretical and classical ones. Research, or the creation of new knowledge, was not a clearly articulated role for these institutions, though the records show frequent references to experimentation and demonstration. Such were the aspirations of our pioneers.

These ambitious goals were too broad for the new little state colleges to achieve. Sixty years after the first cluster of them was founded and again thirty years after that, Congress created two waves of land-grant institutions, each one intended to bring the benefits of higher education to a sector of the population hitherto denied it, a new part of the public. It is useful to remind ourselves of the language in the act, which was signed into law by President Lincoln on July 2, 1862. Each state that accepted the benefits of this first land-grant act was obligated to provide: "at least one college where the leading object shall be, without excluding other scientific and classical studies and including military tactics, to teach such branches of learning as are related to agriculture and the mechanical arts . . . in order to promote the liberal and practical education of the industrial classes in the several pursuits and professions in life. . . ."

For these eighteenth- and nineteenth-century pioneers, public service meant essentially the instruction on campus of young, white, free men, sixteen to twenty-two years of age. The enlargement of the clientele even within that age group was not to come until much later and after much strife.

It took one hundred years for research to become a formal part of public higher education. The National Association of State Universities and Land-Grant Colleges was founded in 1887 by the same group of leaders who were fighting to persuade Congress to support scientific agricultural research in these colleges, through passage of the Hatch Act. In those days, the eyes of the general state universities were just beginning to be dazzled by the accomplishments and scholarly study at the German universities. But in our country, research did not take its place as an established public-university function until well into the twentieth century.

Public service, as a clear-cut separate principle distinguishing it from the service of the public interest through collegiate programs of teaching and research, entered the American university about a quarter century after research did. Seaman Knapp, one of the distinguished leaders of public higher education, wrote the Hatch Act supporting research, which was passed in 1887. In 1914, Knapp's pioneering work in agricultural extension was established nationally by the Smith-Lever Act. Meanwhile the movement for general university extension, which began at Cambridge and Oxford universities in England in the 1870s, swept through the American public colleges in the early part of the twentieth century.

The term "public service" has come to evoke many images; it is better understood by citing familiar examples than by defining a core idea. When we mention public service, we think of the Cooperative Extension Service, general extension, lifelong learning, community development, continuing education, distance learning, and other aspects of our vision of a learning society. President Van Hise of the University of Wisconsin established the spirit of university public service early in this century in his oft-quoted comment that the boundaries of Wisconsin's campus were the borders of the state. Such leaders provided the endorsement and example of outreach scholarship that is receiving revised attention in academe today.

The leaders of these institutions a century ago provided remarkable breadth of vision and scope in carrying out their responsibilities. While the central preoccupation of deans of agriculture and their associates was with the application of scientific principles and concepts of management in farming, they became increasingly concerned with broad issues impacting upon the quality of life of farm families and rural communities. Thus, in the early days of the twentieth century, they moved decisively and boldly to address issues related to home and family, schooling, and community life, focusing scholarly attention on three major influences in human development—family, community, and schools.

To enhance the quality of farm living, they created departments of home economics, studying and teaching concepts of family living, home improvement, nutrition, parenting and child development, and home management, with programs of research, teaching, and outreach to address the quality of home and family-living circumstances on the farm.

To address their concern with schooling, they created departments of rural education to improve the curriculum and pedagogy of the one-room country schoolhouse. It became generally recognized that the classic curriculum did not prepare farm girls to be effective farm wives and mothers or farm boys to be successful farmers and agribusinessmen. Thus the colleges, through their extension services, established "Boys and Girls Club Work" to relate formal education to farm living and as a technique to inject innovations in both agriculture and homemaking. Early publications of Boys and Girls Club Work in Michigan stated their first purpose to be "to strengthen the schools at their weakest point." These clubs, which originally depended upon schoolteachers for leadership, but which quickly and effectively involved community volunteers as well, taught girls concepts and skills of homemaking, and taught boys concepts and techniques of farming, with projects based upon principles of "learning by doing." This dramatic initiative has evolved into the 4-H Club movement, based on educational principles that have proven to be adaptable to youngsters in urban as well as rural settings.

To address issues of community life, departments of rural sociology were created. Programs of study and action focused upon such issues as community infrastructure, public health, organization for problem solving, and leadership.

These bold moves were dramatically effective and earned broad public support and involvement. Now, with the passage of time and as universities have grown in scale and comprehensiveness, emphases have changed. In colleges of agriculture, for example, the central emphasis is upon agriculture per se, with a heavy production orientation but with some concentration upon management and marketing. Concern for broader issues of farm living, rural education, rural community life, including health care and all the rest, has been shifted elsewhere within the university, where contemporary issues may or may not be effectively addressed. Increasingly, attention has been focused upon knowledge disciplines and professional concentration, with research exalted. In colleges of agriculture and throughout the university, this has resulted in superb specialization, but with difficulties in integrating the specialties and relating them to the larger issues of changing socioeconomic and political circumstances and needs.

As public universities have grown and matured, the triumvirate of their mission—teaching, research, and public service/outreach—has become generally accepted, at least in rhetoric. In this process, however, two clearly identifiable tendencies have occurred. First, *teaching* has become narrowly defined, referring generally to that which occurs in a classroom or laboratory setting, usually on campus, with students enrolled in courses for credit leading to credentials. The vast array of other teaching carried out by university faculty in less formal settings and structures is lumped ignominiously into public service. Nontraditional patterns of teaching, often with nontraditional students in nontraditional settings, are thus relegated to a position of lesser status.

Second, the *research* mission of the university, though the latest entrant on the scene in some respects, has become omnipotent. Professors who neither teach nor directly address attention to public concerns are exalted. Publication is essential to faculty success. Basic research is preeminent, while those research efforts described as "applied" are viewed with less acclaim. Thus, in the academic life of public institutions today, research represents the ultimate exercise, with teaching—especially at the undergraduate level—seen as a mandated duty, and public service an obligation too often accepted with reluctance.

Decisions about public service—what to do or not do, when to begin and when to end, whether to persevere or concede—must, like all other university decisions, be made in each specific case in terms of all the relevant facts and values. But after eighty years of full-scale experience, the major lesson we have learned about university-based public service/outreach is that it is best conceived as dynamic and creative teaching and research carried out in the full dimensions of the human lifespan and the broad range of human association both on and off campus.

The relative imbalance of teaching, research, and public service/outreach within the university and in its relationships with the larger society must be addressed if continuing public support is to be warranted. The benefits of superb specialization in various fields of concentration are awesome and must continue to be encouraged and rewarded. At the same time, it is increasingly apparent that none of the comprehensive issues confronting society can be addressed effectively by any one specialty. Leadership must be exercised in mobilizing and integrating the expertise and talent of various fields of study in addressing significant societal concerns. It is to this end that the outreach dimension of the university is concentrated. The academy's response to its institutional crisis in serving the society that created and sustains it must be dramatic, comprehensive, and focused. Time is of the essence.

America's Youth in Crisis

Our attention turns now to the second crisis, the problems confronting and confounding America's children and youth. In the last decade, scholars have produced studies that describe the status of children and youth, with grim statistics and vivid detail proving their case. Panels of thoughtful observers have issued reports with thoughtful analyses documenting the looming "crisis of youth" and with recommended courses of action to avoid creation of a "permanent underclass" of the young. Such reports serve notice that the futures of too many young people are dismal and that our way of life is in fact endangered.

These reports have done a service by identifying the very real and critical problems of many youth. Yet we need to recognize that even the grim statistics of failure so often cited can be inverted to tell a tale of success. While shortcomings cannot be denied, most female teenagers do not become pregnant, most teenagers do not regularly get drunk or use drugs, and most eighth graders go on to graduate from high school. While special attention still must be given to troubled youth, such concern should not warp our perspective in addressing the needs of young people. Emphasis should be given to positive approaches that enhance the opportunities and circumstances that influence *all* youth through their developmental years. It is to this end that the superb knowledge resources from through-out the university should be mobilized and integrated more effectively.

This positive focus underscores the need to recognize the vital role of the various influences in the process of growing up. While many elements come to bear, the following three have special importance: Family, schools, and community. In relation to each, opportunities for university-community collaboration are apparent.

Family

The family is the basic unit of human society. It is in the family that the next generation is created and nurtured. The goal should be to have every baby born into a loving and caring environment, with at least one adult who loves, cares, encourages, and nurtures. Experience would suggest that most adults who are unproductive in society—chronically unemployed, perpetually on welfare, dependent on the state or others for support, in-carcerated, unsuccessful in fulfilling society's expectations for adults in being self-supporting, contributing members of society—are a product of inad-equate home and family situations, particularly in the early months of life. Persuasive evidence stresses the importance of the first hours, days, weeks, and months in positive early-childhood development. Yet our society has institutionalized a pattern of education that does not serve all youngsters until they reach age five. Thus responsibility for positive influence in early development rests essentially with the family.

In earlier days this may have been adequate. But the traditional Ameri-can family is now nearly extinct. In 1955, 60% of American youngsters lived in a home with a working father, a housewife mother, and one or more school-age siblings. Now, two generations later, that number has dropped dramatically, to perhaps 5%. More mothers, by economic neces-sity or career choice, are working away from home.

The trade-off may be consequential. Some studies suggest that full-time, nonparental out-of-home child care commencing at an early age leads to social and personal problems later in life. Some experts believe that such children are more likely to be uncooperative, unpopular, have poorer study skills, lower grades, and diminished self-esteem. Other stud-ies conclude that away-from-home day care for infants, conducted by quali-fied child development staff, can be very effective. It is regrettable that, in general, our society has been unresponsive in dealing with the significant consequences of changing family patterns and circumstances.

Skillful parenting is absolutely essential in early-childhood development. By definition, all first-time parents are amateurs. Many mothers and fathers are remarkably successful in parenting, a result of self-initiated study, intuition and commitment, or experience gained in their childhood family. Where parenting is ineffective or even negative in nature, the child may suffer consequences that are virtually irreversible.

Professionals concentrating on human development and family issues have been relatively unimaginative and uncreative in developing programs to prepare youngsters and young adults to become effective parents. Concepts and principles of human development could be infused into the educational experiences of the elementary and secondary years, perhaps concentrating particularly in the upper grades as the assumption of adult roles and responsibilities approaches. During pregnancy, opportunities should be universally available for soon-to-be mothers and fathers to prepare for their parenting roles. Recognizing the importance of home and family to productivity of employees, employers should be encouraged to provide parenting training and counseling services.

Too often family professionals concentrate upon dealing with failures, stepping in only after the family unit is distressed. While such corrective services are vitally important, greater effort should be concentrated on prevention and constructive initiatives to enhance success.

Our society licenses hairdressers and plumbers, with specific requirements and criteria. Yet we impose no conditions or qualifications for parenthood. While it seems unlikely that this issue could be addressed legislatively, expectations for parents should be elevated and opportunities to prepare oneself to be successful in the privileged role of parenthood should be abundantly available and easily accessible. Intervention when family failure in child development is evident should be immediate and consequential.

In terms of human welfare, society must provide support and safety nets of various kinds. But in the final analysis, if the human condition is to be enhanced for the individual and family, a decent job is an essential ingredient.

Similarly, in child development, there is simply no substitute for a loving, nurturing home and family environment. The marvelous intellectual resources of the university from a broad range of intellectual specialization and organizational entities must be mobilized to that end.

Schools

Education in the United States has a very rich and successful history. Until recently the envy and the model for the world, our educational system has provided knowledge and skills for the masses while encouraging the individual creativity that has enabled this country to produce more Nobel prizewinners than any other nation in the world.

The first public-education initiative that had a nationwide impact was the Northwest Ordinance of 1787, which dedicated land in each county of the upper-midwest states for support of education. This commitment provided the opportunity for every child in then-rural America to experience an education, initially at least through what we now call the elementary phase. While one-room country schools quickly became a tradition throughout the countryside, it was not until nearly fifty years later that the model for the structure and control of our educational system was developed.

In 1837, Horace Mann, while serving as president of the Massachusetts state senate, was chiefly responsible for the enactment of the bill creating the state board of education. Prior to the creation of this state board, there had been two opposing factions seeking to change the deficient public schools of Massachusetts. One faction supported the establishment of academies; the other, the reformation of education by establishing a central authority. Mann led the charge vigorously for the reformers amidst the attack of those who opposed the creation of the state system.

Once the Massachusetts State Board of Education was established, Horace Mann was selected as its first secretary. Mann accepted this responsibility at considerable financial sacrifice and with little authority. The Board could neither form nor administer schools; its function was to collect and disseminate information. With this limited mandate, the success of the state board was directly attributable to the personality and persuasiveness of its secretary. Armed with only the power of his intellect and his salesmanship, Horace Mann established the concept of public meetings for education, a county teacher-training institute, and the publication of *The Common Sense Journal* to influence the educational conditions in Massachusetts and elsewhere, which occupy a commanding position in the history of education. His seventh report, printed in 1843 after a five-month study tour of Europe, drew attack from schoolmasters in Boston. The report praised European schools and their methods of instruction, particularly the use of the "word method" in teaching reading and the abolition of corporal punishment in Germany. These new ideas seemed ridiculous to most Massachusetts schoolmasters and controversy over Mann's leadership ensued. Horace Mann boldly stood his ground in support of his futuristic concepts.

Horace Mann was a visionary educational leader in his time. His dedication to the improvement of education was a stimulus to progress in the Massachusetts education system, making it the prototype for all the states. Mann's impact on education made his era arguably a most influential period in America's education history.

The years since then are replete with other educational innovators, pioneers, and visionaries. While few have had the pervasive impact of the authors of the Northwest Ordinance two centuries ago and Horace Mann a half century later, all have demonstrated a boldness appropriate to their time.

In recent years reform initiatives have aimed at raising America's level of achievement in fields as diverse as education and product manufacturing. Yet in this period marked by impressive progress on many fronts, America continues to be plagued by the realization that too many of its young are failing to mature into responsible, competent, and contributing young adults.

In seeking at least a partial explanation, it becomes apparent that three of the basic institutions of society for socializing its next generation—the family, the school, and the local community—are falling short of fulfilling their historic roles. The school system—the most structured and clearly identifiable of the three—is most often assigned the blame.

In no field has reform been more stridently recommended and more ambitiously implemented than in our schools that provide precollegiate education. Nearly a dozen major reports have indicted the school systems of our nation for their outdated teaching methods, inflexibility, and poor record of success. Yet the various prescriptions advanced by the reformers—be they "new kind of teacher" approaches, mandated curricula, or improved organizational models—have not, in most cases, brought about substantial improvement.

To give proper perspective, while there is much that is disturbing and indeed deplorable, there is still much in our public educational system in this country about which we can be very proud. No other society has made a longer, broader, more pervasive commitment to provide educational opportunities for its young, with multiple options and alternatives. And while we continue to struggle with the standards of serving better the needs of each individual, and we despair when any individual is not well served or fails to achieve his or her potential, our schools do a remarkably good job with most young people. And despite all the criticism and despair, two truths remain. First, education is still the way by which a society progresses. And second, education is still the way to a better life for the individual. Education should be broadly defined, not limited to courses, credits, and credentials. Rather, we should think of education as teaching and learning in the broadest conceptual framework, in school and out, from early childhood throughout life.

Our system of public education is a creature of our institutions of higher learning. In fact, colleges and universities command a monopolistic hold on its structure and operation. Teachers and administrators must be graduates of accredited institutions of higher learning. The accreditation of K–12 institutions is dominated by patterns of higher learning, with college-admission requirements and criteria a controlling concern. Recognizing both the merits and the shortcomings of that which exists, the higher-educational intellectual establishment should once again be pioneers, mobilizing its resources from throughout the institution—not just its college of education—to move forward in research, teaching, and public service/outreach with vision, competence, courage, and boldness to strengthen public schooling. Three broad foci deserve particular attention.

First, universities and schools should join forces in addressing the complex influences in the developmental processes of the young, from prebirth through adolescence to young adulthood. It has been suggested earlier that three of the basic institutions of society need attention—the family, the schools, the local community. University-trained educators at the community level generally show concern for only one—the school. The interrelationships of these three institutions, however, are inevitable and consequential. While schools cannot be expected to do everything, community-based educators, though having primary responsibility for the formalities of the K–12 process, cannot disassociate themselves from the other two. Youngsters who enter school are a product of their environment, and the home/family and local community are of such importance in shaping young lives that they can no longer be ignored by community educators, nor can their consequences be fully countermanded after the child enters kindergarten.

A pervasive concern in school administration is a preoccupation with systems management and detail. In the pressures and busyness of their days, administrators too often drift away from the basic concepts and principles of education, to become preoccupied with the management of the highly complex and sophisticated systems they have created. Time is occupied with the manipulating of bus transportation schedules, managing millage votes, scraping together funds for building maintenance, putting out the fires of the moment. While all such issues and more must be dealt with, the essential mission of this entire enterprise should remain the center of focus and preoccupation.

Quite obviously, schools should not assume responsibility for everything that influences and shapes the education or development of the young, from prebirth through young adulthood. However, as professional educators and recognized leaders in the community, school leaders should provide the intellectual and conceptual framework, the visionary leadership, the catalytic influence in ensuring comprehensive attention at the community level on the myriad influences that impact the lives of youngsters. Community educators must be concerned with homes and families and parenting, with housing and neighborhoods, with the services provided by government and nonprofit agencies, with nonschool opportunities and alternatives in the young lives for whom schools have a stewardship responsibility. While the central attention of school personnel must continue to be upon the institutional structures and systems for which they are responsible, as professional educators their purview must be broader and deeper and greater. Universities, in their pre-service preparation, in-service continuing education, and outreach relationships must prepare and collaborate with schools in fulfilling their broad mission.

A second consideration relates to components of the school system that have been institutionalized over time, and that need review in light of changing circumstances and knowledge. One example is the school year designed for an agrarian society, with school convening in early fall and ending in late spring to accommodate the workforce needs of farm families. Evidence is clear that the three-month break is simply too long for knowledge and skill retention; a maximum interlude of five to six weeks would be more appropriate. The 180-day school year was also established to accommodate farm labor needs. Now, in light of prolonged adolescence, burgeoning body of knowledge, changed economic and social patterns, and advancing maturation rates, it would seem wise to devote 220–230 days each year to formal schooling.

Additionally, the system should do a far better job in relating the activities and responsibilities of school to the rest of the student's day and week and year. Obviously the pattern should be quite different for elementary than for middle school or high school. Through legal restrictions and technology change, most teenagers are denied the satisfaction of a decent job before or after school or on weekends or during vacation periods. Most of the teenagers in the country are turned out on the streets in the hot months of summer with few alternatives for constructive engagement. There should be greater opportunities for the young to be constructive contributors to self, family, community, society, both for pay and as volunteers, as well as to be the recipients or beneficiaries of the actions of others.

A further structural component requiring thoughtful reconsideration is the concept of "the school day." Despite changing patterns of family life and in society, school continues to start fairly early in the morning and end early to mid-afternoon. This schedule was also designed for the agrarian society that created it. Now, as an instrument of society to serve the needs of the young and their families, every school building should be open from at least 6:00 A.M. until 10:00 P.M. This is not to suggest that classes should be scheduled throughout that time frame, although particularly at the high-school level there could be far more flexibility than is characteristic today. Rather, society through its schools should provide a safe haven and a constructive environment for youngsters of working parents. A single working parent should be able to deliver a daughter or son to school at an early hour on the way to work, assured that the child has a safe haven, perhaps for breakfast, perhaps for homework or computer activities or library study or physical activities—a warm, secure, caring, nurturing environment. And after school the "latchkey kid" problem would again be avoided by having alternative activities and opportunities available in the school as a community haven. Volunteers and paraprofessionals can provide much of the educational and supervised activity or the simple monitoring necessary. The school, instead of being an inaccessible enclave isolated from the full scope of life's needs, would become a central, catalytic element in neighborhood life.

Rethinking the static elements of the school year and the school day could have dramatic impact on the whole concept of school in the life of the individual student, the family, the community, and the system. It provides exciting alternatives for interaction between educational activities of the school and life as it is lived by individual students of all ages—interaction between school and work; interaction between school and volunteerism; and, interaction between the classroom and the recreation ground, the streets, parks, museums, cultural programs, and nonschool influences on development. The concern is not simply one of better use of the massive investment society has made in bricks and mortar and equipment, but the infusion of education in a quite different way in the lives of students and their families and the society of which they are a part.

Universities in their pre- and in-service as well as outreach activities should mobilize expertise from a broad range of disciplines in reconceptualizing the school to serve contemporary circumstances and needs.

A third area for concentration relates to basing the school curriculum and structure on now-known knowledge regarding child/youth development. Much of the current pattern was put in place before research and specialization had produced volumes of factual information about the human development process. It is apparent in reviewing the elementary-secondary system that it does not serve in the best ways possible the developmental needs of individuals and age groups.

A first concern of course relates to the period of development to which we now refer as preschool. As emphasized earlier, society needs to more systematically address the developmental needs of infants, from prebirth through the first thirty-six months of life. Then, for ages four and five, something of a formal educational experience outside the home should be provided, in constructive day-care settings with purposeful schedules. Skills and learning should be appropriate to the age, not pushing to younger and younger levels tasks that may be stressful. Children need time to play, to socialize, to have fun.

Once formal schooling begins, the importance of the elementary years should be recognized. As a local school-board member, I was perplexed in the budgeting process. In frustration, I would ask administrators, "Why have you educators set up a system that forces us as board members to make the wrong decisions? When resources are limited, we always take away from the elementary grades—increase class size, eliminate special activities in reading, music, the arts, remedial resources—so that we keep our high school accredited so that our graduates can go to accredited colleges and universities. Yet, all of the behavioral research I read emphasizes the importance of the elementary years in shaping and building the future. If educators really believe their research, they would accredit the elementary schools—and let the rest of the system build from a solid beginning."

While every year is important, the elementary-school years seem to be particularly crucial in developing self-image, peer relationships, attitudes, and patterns of learning. If a youngster has a miserable experience with a poor teacher in the second or third grade, the consequences are enduring. It is very difficult to overcome bad results of early schooling.

In later years, high school for example, with greater maturity and several teachers each day, a student can cope with a poor teacher. But in an early grade, during the formative student years, with one teacher monopolizing each day and setting the total pattern of learning expectation, and patterns and feelings of failure or success, the impact—positive and negative—is permanent. In most school systems, with emphasis on specialization and credentials, elementary teachers tend to be underpaid, underappreciated, and underrecognized as professionals.

School structure for the middle grades is generally not clear-cut, though new patterns are being implemented in schools throughout the country. The definition of what the middle-grades schools should be and do is not yet clear. Part of the lack of precision relates to the absence of experience during the schooling of most adults, those who are educators and those who are parents. Most people have an idea of what an elementary or high school should be and do—usually based on their own experiences. But the middle grades are not easy to characterize. Should they be patterned after the high school—or should they be an extension of the elementary years—or something unique and distinct, designed for the early-adolescent learner?

Part of the confusion has to do with the nature of young adolescents' development. Rapid and uneven growth, acquisition of secondary sex characteristics, and new ways of relating to friends and family are just some of the changes these young people experience—at different rates and with varying degrees of ease and angst. The concept of middle-grades education is just taking shape and needs the thoughtful input of university expertise in its planning and implementation.

Finally, the high-school years provide for the transition from adolescence to young adulthood, from the world of schooling to the world of work or higher education. While some high schools have implemented marvelous innovations, most continue with patterns and protocols designed for an earlier age. Probably the approach to the high-school years should be akin to that which was practiced in colleges two or three decades ago. While there needs to be structure and discipline enough to guide the learner, there needs to be flexibility and variety enough to nurture creativity and assumption of adultlike roles and responsibilities. Again, expertise from throughout the university—from disciplines and professional cohorts not typically involved—should be mobilized to reinvigorate this high-school setting and its trappings.

Throughout the formal schooling years, from kindergarten through graduation, the lockstep pattern of assessment and promotion should be rethought. Perhaps the elementary grades should not move wholly and automatically from grade one to grade two and on, with a change in teacher each year. The experience of the one- and two-room country school, with students of varying ages studying separately and together through multiple years, has merit as well as disadvantage. Creativity would suggest more flexibility, sensitivity to individual qualities and needs, and relaxation of arbitrariness in facilitating the learning process. Much of the responsibility for such details should be delegated to the professionals—principals and teachers—in each building, rather than imposing mandated patterns from above.

As universities have become specialized and elaborately structured, the responsibility for higher education's role in K–12 schooling has been concentrated in colleges of education. If our schools are to benefit maximally from the rich intellectual resources of the academy, this pattern must be changed. The university at large must become engaged, working collaboratively in new ways in pre-service, in-service, and outreach initiatives. To do less will be to fall short of what society has a legitimate right to expect.

Community

The community at large, of which families and neighborhoods and schools are a part, is a third major influence in youth development. A vast array of government agencies and their programs, plus nonprofit organizations, institutions and their services and activities, provide challenging, enriching, and rewarding opportunities and encouragement for youngsters of all ages. Usually public (tax-supported) and nonprofit (voluntary) organizations collaborate in fulfilling their varied missions. While the services of government are essential, in the community where life is lived, much of the character and quality of life is a contribution of the nonprofit, independent, voluntary sector—a plethora of initiatives in health, recreation, culture, education, enrichment.

In this regard, two aspects of child/youth development deserve mention. First, when America was a predominantly agrarian nation, children performed tasks from a very early age that made a real contribution to the family's livelihood. Children were an economic asset. In the mainly urban and suburban America of today, youth are economic liabilities. Today's suburban child may have some chores, but most are not crucial to the family's well-being. Ways need to be found to offer youth opportunities for personal-skills development and character building—ways to boost self-esteem, to be contributors to as well as beneficiaries of their families and the larger society.

Second, the period of dependency for youth has been extended, often into their mid- or late-twenties. As the age of puberty is shortened and youngsters are physically and mentally more ready and able to perform adultlike roles, the time frame of training to take one's place in adult society has been lengthened. Caught in the conflict of earlier maturation and prolonged dependency, many youth are endangered by a sense of aimlessness and anomie.

Youth need chances to contribute to their society—opportunities to work and serve both as employees and as volunteers. Both experiences can be motivating and rewarding. In this way—becoming givers as well as takers—youth can move beyond the fences of dependency. Far greater opportunities for such growth need to be provided.

Conventional wisdom might suggest that the problems of youth are too overwhelming, too complex, too persistent, and too expensive to solve. Such an aura of intractability could destroy public support for youth programs. That is why the message of Lisbeth B. Schorr in her book, *Within Our Reach: Breaking the Cycle of Disadvantage*, is so important:

It is a strange and tragic paradox that confidence in our collective ability to alter the destinies of vulnerable children has hit bottom just as scientific understanding of the processes of human development and the rich evidence of success in helping such children has reached a new high. (Schorr, 1988, p. xvii)

Schorr describes the enigma. Theoretically, society knows how to design the effective school, how to deliver high-quality prenatal care, and how to effectively intervene to repair dysfunctional families. We *know* much better than we *do*. As Schorr points out: ". . . in the last two decades we have accumulated a critical mass of information that totally transforms the nation's capacity to improve outcomes for vulnerable children. . . . But many administrators, academics, practitioners, and public policy analysts are not aware of the newly emerging insights, especially from outside their own fields." (1988, p. xix)

Ironically, the very specialization so helpful in *acquiring* knowledge often hinders its *use*. The problems affecting youth are usually multifaceted and interconnected. They cut across boundaries of disciplines, professions, interests, and services. In a word, they are complex. A pregnant teenager, for instance, may be alone, unemployed, and thinking of leaving school. She may also be on drugs, and leaning toward suicide. Such a person could benefit from the combined skills of a guidance counselor, an expert on substance abuse, an employment skills trainer and a psychologist; treatment by just one would not likely prove successful. While the individual is a whole, the delivery systems are fragmented.

While this example may be extreme and may imply a negative focus, its point is more basic. The challenge for us all is to harness the incredible knowledge resources that specialists have created, and blend them into forward-looking action programs that address all facets of youth problems. Some of that groundwork is being laid by government, by foundations, by service agencies, and by other concerned groups. Our universities should be catalysts and leaders in assuring that it happens.

One way the Kellogg Foundation is addressing the challenge is through its Kellogg Youth Initiatives Partnership (KYIP). The program has been launched in three diverse Michigan communities: Calhoun County, a rural area of farms and small towns; a designated section of center-city Detroit; and two counties in the state's Upper Peninsula, a sparsely populated area with a limited resource base.

The program involves a partnership between the Foundation and the communities to develop new and innovative programs. It mobilizes community residents to work simultaneously to improve conditions in home and family, church and neighborhood, schools and youth-serving organizations, and public and private agencies; it calls on a wide array of professionals and volunteers to support these efforts.

Clearly, the Foundation does not have answers to the problems these communities face. However, some valuable lessons from past programming activities have been applied to the KYIP. Based on experience, the Foundation is convinced that the following three qualities undergird any successful program for youth:

1. *Comprehensiveness.* Children's lives are intertwined with the differing elements in their environment: Home and family, church and neighborhood, schools, and youth-serving organizations. The elements are inseparable and distinct at the same time. A program that affects only the child's school life but is meant to achieve answers to complex self-identity, self-worth issues is unlikely to have much effect, because it leaves the home and neighborhood untouched. It seems obvious and imperative that any initiative must encompass all of the problem, not just a facet of it.

2. *Collaboration within the Community.* Youth problems do not exist in a vacuum. They pervade communities and profoundly affect their residents. Unilateral approaches to solutions usually are not adequate. Rather, the interests and resources of various entities—home and family, agencies

and organizations—must be mobilized to work in concert. Collaboration within the community is essential.

3. *Continuity.* The problems of youth evolved over a span of years; it is unlikely they can be solved overnight. Sufficient time must be allowed for a community to build collaborative, comprehensive, workable programs. A generation of young people may grow to maturity before the program models are fully developed, and the Foundation's commitment to assist is vital across that long view.

The KYIP combines those three key qualities. The first individual project planned under the partnership—and the only one actually spearheaded by the Foundation—was the Kellogg Youth Development Seminars (KYDS). A group of thirty to fifty residents from each local community was selected for a two-year series of seminars on topics relating to youth. Participants included professionals and volunteers who were developing, administering, and conducting activities that constituted or influenced the developmental years. High-school students were included to represent area youth. These people (as well as selected individuals who were not formally a part of KYDS) spearheaded initial KYIP activities. The seminar series continues, developing new cadres of community participants.

These groups of local leaders—mobilized by their concern, energized by the seminars—are devising solutions to many of the primary problems of youth in their communities. They do so on a continuum, representing or ensuring both comprehensiveness and collaboration. The Foundation's role is supportive with advice and financial assistance, thus doing what Mr. Kellogg admonished nearly seventy years ago: Helping people to help themselves.

The inclusion of youth as participants in KYDS illustrates, too, the Foundation's conviction that young people are assets, not liabilities. All are involved, not merely the "untroubled" young; many programs have proved that "troubled" children are highly effective in helping each other.

In setting forth its plans, the Foundation stated in its 1988 Annual Report:

In developing and implementing the Kellogg Youth Initiatives Partnership, we have opted not to give way to despair. Though we feel we cannot afford to ignore our troubled youth, nothing less than a modification of social expecta-

tions and structures is sought. We no longer expect that the provision of reme-
dial programs for at-risk youth will be adequate to solve the problems of the
young. An unprecedented pattern of social changes makes it incumbent on our
society that we try to motivate every child through the provision of challenges
and opportunities. Even the majority of youth who are not at risk of failure
can benefit from being pushed and stretched, both intellectually and physically.

This agenda for change is ambitious. It is imperative. It is doable. The
family must have support in childrearing. Schools must become more respon-
sive to the needs of families and children. People must join together to foster a
sense of community in their towns and neighborhoods. At the same time, higher
education must become more proactive in training future leaders. The business
community must take on an even greater role of leadership in advocacy for
youth. And higher education and the business community must form partner-
ships with communities, government, and other institutions, to help spark the
necessary changes.

We already know much about what is required to produce successful out-
comes for young people—good parenting is the key to raising good children—
one caring adult, serving as a role model over an extended period, can be the
difference between success and failure for children—teenagers benefit when
they volunteer to help others—youth need to belong to a group or groups—
youngsters need success to develop positive self-concepts.

When considering America's youth, experience dictates that it would be
wise to chart a course somewhere between Cassandra and Pollyanna. Histori-
ans remind us that virtually every generation in every nation has despaired of
its "younger generation." Yet we know that the youth of the past usually proved
equal to the test.

"Our country's history is replete with crises that have been met and over-
come by the young, and with fewer resources and less knowledge than Ameri-
can children now have at their disposal. Our coda may properly come from
Ralph Waldo Emerson, who wrote:

> *So nigh is grandeur to our dust,*
> *So near is God to man,*
> *When Duty whispers low, thou must*
> *The youth replies, I can.*

Conclusion

William James reminded us that ". . . crises show us how much greater our
vital resources are than we had supposed." The convergence of two crises

in contemporary American society provides unusual opportunity for constructive response.

The first crisis lies in higher education, with a need for institutions of higher learning to demonstrate a commitment and a capacity to serve the needs of society in creative and vigorous ways. Outreach scholarship, linking the intellectual resources of institutions of higher education with communities and their needs in mutually beneficial ways, represents a remarkable opportunity to revitalize the internal workings of the institution and its programs of research and teaching while contributing invaluably to the betterment of society.

The second crisis—the multiplicity of problems confronting and confounding America's youth—provides the venue for this enhanced outreach initiative, building on higher education's oldest tradition of public service. America simply must do a better job of preparing its coming generations for the responsibilities they will assume and the lives they will lead. The richness of the intellectual resources of higher education must be mobilized to this end.

Mrs. Frances Hesselbein, while the renowned president and CEO of the Girl Scouts of America, addressed a group of nonprofit leaders in Michigan. Mrs. Hesselbein asked this group of professional and volunteer leaders to reexamine their mission—their reason for being. She advised them to ask themselves three main questions: "What is your business?" "Who are your customers?" and "Who are your funders?" This can provide a beneficial exercise for institutions of higher education today.

Mrs. Hesselbein also reminded, "We must work on sloughing off yesterday's accomplishments for tomorrow's challenges." This statement becomes particularly intriguing as we discuss the critical points of education's history. Without question, *today* is the critical point in the history of education. Unless we slough off yesterday's accomplishments and accept tomorrow's challenges, our entire country and its institutions will falter. There are no simple or short-term answers.

Society today is the beneficiary of the leaders of generations past—individuals of vision, expertise, courage, conviction, venturesomeness, boldness. Concerned leaders now must so act that, fifty years hence, astute observers will note that these leaders were the cadre that engineered the evolution of education, dramatically responding to the challenges of this era. The challenge is to respond, as did Horace Mann, Seaman Knapp, and others in their day, with the *boldness* that these times demand.

References

Lerner, R. M. & Simon, L. A. K., (Eds.) (1995, October). *Creating the new outreach university for America's youth and families: Building university-community collaborations for the twenty-first century.* Prospectus. Michigan State University.

Lerner, R. M. (1995, Winter). Features and principles of effective youth programs: Promoting positive youth development through the integrative vision of family and consumer sciences. *Journal of Family and Consumer Sciences 87,* (4), 16–21.

Mawby, R. G. (1987, November). Public Service address at the 100th Annual Meeting of the National Association of State Universities and Land-Grant Colleges, Washington, DC.

———. (1988). Changing the Focus on Youth. Chairman's Message, Annual Report, W. K. Kellogg Foundation, Battle Creek, MI.

———. (1990, February). Boldness for Our Time. Address at the Horace Mann League Luncheon, San Francisco.

Sandmann, L. R. (Ed.) (1996, April). *Fulfilling higher education's covenant with society: The emerging outreach agenda.* Report of Capstone Symposium of the W. K. Kellogg Foundation-MSU Lifelong Education Grant. Michigan State University.

Schorr, L. B. (1989). *Within our reach: Breaking the cycle of disadvantage.* New York: Anchor.

W. K. Kellogg Foundation. (1996, January). *Middle Start Facts.* (Vol. 1, No. 1). Battle Creek, MI: Author.

Chapter 18
Furthering Community Youth Development

Richard J. Sauer
National 4-H Council

Introduction

America's land-grant universities are undergoing self-assessments and a refocus of their missions, especially relative to their future "outreach" role. They have begun to recognize the need to more effectively integrate their teaching, research, and service, connecting knowledge to addressing the critical needs of America's communities. And they are also learning that they must approach this community work with the community and its citizens being full partners in needs assessment and in the design, implementation, and evaluation of the results of programs addressing these needs. In the process, these universities could once again build a value not unlike they had among many citizens during the early and middle parts of the twentieth century, when our country was much more rural and agrarian.

As part of this struggle, university boards, presidents, and other officers are questioning the appropriate mission for their state's Cooperative Extension Service or equivalent (part of the Cooperative Extension System, or simply "Extension") and the best use of its considerable, though sometimes declining, public resources. Extension, as a national system, seems undecided about its focus, including whether or not its broader programming for children, youth, and families is a legitimate and integral part of its future; there is considerable variance of emphasis from state to state, especially in terms of whether or not to give major priority to urban and other nonagricultural populations, via what some critics and others who resist change call "social" programs. At the same time, Extension's more innovative local (county) staff are often moving away from the traditional "knowledge expert" role to one of being community conveners and facilitators, leading the development of community-wide collaborations that are implementing the integration of youth development and community development into "community youth development" (which is a process of youth and adults working in partnership to create the preferred social, physical, civic, economic, and environmental conditions in their community, resulting in the healthy development of its young people). And this holistic, community-focused work is increasingly being resourced by private and nontraditional pubic funding sources.

The current outreach status and impact of land-grant universities can be enhanced considerably, and these universities can play an increasingly more vital role in contributing to the solution of problems faced by the increasingly diverse citizens of our nation, if the Cooperative Extension System were to create and actualize a very different vision for the twenty-first century—getting out of the box in which it did operate so effectively for much of its past.

Community-focused youth-development efforts are critical to the future health of our communities. And these efforts will be most effective and have the most rapid and sustaining positive impact on youth, families, and communities if youth are valued and involved as true partners (Lerner, 1995).

Our land-grant university faculty and staff and the rest of us involved in community youth development must recognize and value multiple funding sources, some very unfamiliar to us in the past, and treat them as active, engaged partners rather than passive providers who pay our bills. We must respect not only their investments of resources but their ideas and needs.

A Vision for the Cooperative Extension System

My vision for the Cooperative Extension System of the twenty-first century is that of an adaptive educational organization, supported by a broad diversity of public and private financial resources, highly valued by individuals, families, and communities as being critical for the community's citizens to both make a living and live a quality life, and with great internal flexibility and the ability to respond quickly in focusing and redirecting its resources to current or anticipated future societal issues and problems. The issues and problems will be identified by the people, at the local level; this will empower these citizens and build their capacity for leadership. In connecting knowledge to the needs of people, Extension will be seen as the premier organization providing educational programs, from prenatal to adulthood, and lifelong, in the context of family and community. It will be a key convener, collaboration-builder or partner, more often than the acknowledged knowledge expert, in facilitating knowledge-based community solutions to local problems and issues. And it will organize itself to function in a "chaordic" (Hock, 1995) model, instead of the hierarchical command-and-control model of the past.

One assumption that some would make for this vision to be actualized is that Extension disconnect from the U.S. Department of Agriculture at the federal level—or at least from such a heavy, unilateral dependence on this one federal agency. There is still need for an agricultural extension organization, but continuing to shoehorn a legitimate and growing-broader need into the banner of agriculture and the specific needs of farmers may be stifling the institution, making any move towards the above vision an impossibility, except perhaps in a few isolated local situations and even fewer states. Maintaining the paradigm may also be doing a disservice to farmers, as their issues often do not receive the dedicated and sharp focus they need. And it may be constraining the broad resources of the land-grant universities from being brought to bear on community needs in a collaborative way.

Alternatively, the Cooperative Extension System could refocus entirely on agriculture and agribusiness, and the land-grant and urban universities could develop a new outreach model to serve other human and community needs. Politics and changing public sentiment suggest that either of the two alternatives are likely to evolve from the status quo.

Youth as Partners in Community Youth Development

America's communities are on a roller coaster—in the wrong direction—regarding the positive development of their youth as well as the capacity of these communities to assure their future health and viability (Lerner, 1995). We must reverse a national trend of devaluing, punishing, separating, disenfranchising, and alienating our young people. And critical issues affecting both youth and their communities are coming at them at an increasing pace.

The full engagement of youth—all youth—in addressing their issues as well as the community's issues can reverse this roller coaster and be a major catalyst to the quality and pace of positive community development. Further, dramatically different and more inclusive processes must be used to develop these self-sustaining, learning communities. And we must scale up from successful model systems to build effective capacity in large numbers of communities—work that land-grant universities with a broad, integrated community-collaborative outreach commitment can and should do.

Land-grant universities could and should lead the interconnection and integration of the learnings and practices of the youth development field with those of the community development field into a holistic approach called "community youth development." Via this approach, each community will be prepared to provide better support for its young people—their development, their academic achievement, and their community participation; young people will have the skills as facilitative leaders to engage community dialogue and issue resolution, while acquiring critical life skills; each community will benefit from the stronger, sustained engagement of young people in the resolution of key issues; and the community will become the method/focus of the engagement, and thus, the developmental tool/process, on an ongoing basis. Finally, the communities become ongoing laboratories for university research and sources of the universities' future students and scholars.

Every young person in a community must have access to a complete bank of developmental assets to be an engaged community citizen and become a resilient, contributing adult. Developing a critical mass of youth in each community with access to these assets and teaching them facilitative action and other civic-process skills creates for the community a human resource that could massively accelerate the pace of community development and catalyze positive change. Youth are impatient, and they do not carry the baggage and barriers that adults harbor.

Why is it so important to be inclusive and engage and involve *all* youth? It's important so that communities will be inclusive, viable, and liveable. All youth have value and all have ideas and solutions to offer. All youth are potential leaders in their own lives, their family, and their community. All youth can benefit. And our civil society and nation are at risk, requiring that we learn how to work together—with all different segments, including ages, integrated, with cross-society access—if we are to preserve our visioned societal outcomes. Finally, for community youth development to work, strategically, the community must believe it is for all youth— or it will not happen.

Youth feel they can make a real difference in addressing their issues, which are often the community's issues as well, by working in partnership with adults in their communities—if only adults would respect and value them and give them a chance. They want to and can be part of the solution, rather than be labeled as the problem. They can literally intervene in their own development.

Our communities and our nation need to hear the voice of youth, speaking out about the actions they are taking to solve critical issues in their lives and communities. There are voices from all other age groups in our society and, yes, there are many speaking out for youth or on behalf of youth. But where is the voice of youth?

Resourcing Community Youth Development

It is obvious that land-grant universities are becoming "less public" in terms of the percent of the budget from public sources. Even at the state level, they are often now more appropriately described as "state-assisted" rather than "state-supported." And Extension's public funding is shrinking in real-dollar terms and has been for some time. Thus, any real growth in the outreach capability and impact of land-grant universities in community youth development is going to be resourced by private (and perhaps nontraditional or redirected public) dollars—nationally, statewide, and locally. The potential for local resources especially should not be overlooked, as local prospective funders are closest to the community's issues—which are their issues as well.

The monopolistic control of knowledge by higher education institutions, accompanied by a public perception that these institutions are a special source of wisdom and favored places to enter for learning, is on the verge of major erosion (see also chapter 1 by Lerner and Simon, this volume). The "boundary acid" is the new communications technologies—and as soon as some universities will allow access to their accreditation remotely, universities are in for a very rough ride. Classrooms will be empty and sustaining large numbers of tenured faculty positions will no longer be possible. The marketplace will finally play a major role in the vitality and success of academic programs, including research and extension education, and any legitimate and valued role in community youth development.

While there are a growing number of youth, family, and community development professionals in Extension who understand this situation, Extension staff in general are not very skillful or successful in acquiring private resources, compared to research faculty or nonprofit organizations whose very livelihood depends on the success. (There are, of course, some wonderful exceptions.)

Why is this so? First, the need/incentive was not there until fairly recently (public funding was fairly easy to obtain and sustain). Second, the issues of credibility and objectivity are often raised as a defense for refusing private resources, or not pursuing this kind of funding more aggressively ("We can't let dollars drive programs!" or "We must be objective and not allow ourselves to be influenced by the agendas of private businesses!" are often-heard exclamations when one confronts Extension faculty with the need to seek alternative funding sources).

Extension staff could perhaps afford the luxury of this somewhat arrogant stance if there were sufficient recurring public funds, but even public funding sources (bodies of elected officials) are now demanding a new accountability and relevance, and the old backroom lobbying is less and less effective.

And all funding sources, both public and private, demand a role in the design, implementation, and evaluation of the proposed research or education project. This demand literally sends shivers up the spines of many university faculty—that someone on the outside, not credentialed in their disciplinary wisdom, should have a say in what they do or what value it might have. Unless Extension faculty, including 4-H/youth development, family living, and community development specialists and agents, are willing to enter true partnerships with funders, acknowledging that the funders have as much say as they do in the co-creation of a response to an issue of mutual interest, they will have fewer and fewer resources to support their education-driven social action for changing and saving kids' lives.

Also, while it is important to make sure that children, youth, and family Extension programs are undergirded by sound research, that is generally not the most critical factor in the eyes of potential funders—it surely is not with the ones we work with. Thus, university faculty must overcome an arrogance growing out of the bill of goods we (that is, the Cooperative Extension System) have sold ourselves over the years—to the point that it has become one of our sacred articles of faith in land-grant universities. That is, we have argued for the *uniqueness* of our Extension programs, being research based, compared to other agencies and organizations that provide education programs for children, youth, and families. This research base is only partially true, and perhaps less true for 4-H/ youth-development than for family living; but in both cases, it is less so than for agricultural Extension programming. I say this having been director of a state agricultural experiment station that invests more in children, youth, and family research than almost any other in the U.S., and still seeing the amount far short of what would be close to the relative need or fair share, and having been a university vice president responsible for both Extension and research, where I saw all too many youth and family programs not based on research findings—neither ours nor anyone else's.

The research is out there, but often not in land-grant universities and often not heavily accessed by many of the 4-H/youth-development staff.

In my experience, the most critical research, in the eyes of funders, is documentation and evaluation research—to document what you did and how you did it *and* to show that what you tried worked and is worth funding again—whether or not your initial effort was based on "sound research." Further, private-sector funders do not generally want to fund basic research, or even applied research to develop the youth development experience or other Extension educational programs. Increasingly, they are saying the research has been done, or it must have been done, and they want to support your best idea for an action program, coupled with a community-focused, research-based evaluation to show whether or not it worked. At the same time, if you simply argue that they should support programs like 4-H that have been around a long time and that we know work—"Just look at the wonderful kids coming out of it"—that is not enough.

There has been a dramatic shift in funding in the past two decades, especially over the past seven to ten years, in our work of resourcing 4-H/youth development programs: from entitlement and 4-H alumni in key roles as corporate CEO's who make phone calls to other CEO's; to enlightened self-interest, involving contribution departments; to proven value, involving very focused professionals investing "their" resources around corporate strategies, with the expectation of measurable return. The same shift has occurred in public funding: from backroom confabs with legislative and congressional committee chairs (coupled perhaps with a campaign contribution, private favor, or public recognition) to lobbying the whole committee with visits, letter writing, and phone calls, to being challenged with questions of impact and value (just consider the Government Performance Review, or its equivalent in various states).

While every corporation and foundation is different, and I could relate many stories from the past year alone, we are finding these common threads among private sector funding prospects:

1. They want to fund *innovation* aligned with their corporate strategies and priorities;
2. they want *community benefit*, often in their headquarters city and/or in other cities or regions that are major facility sites or markets for them;
3. they often want to be actively involved in *co-creating* what they fund;
4. they demand *accountability*, via mutually agreed upon outcomes and a satisfactory, defined way to measure them;

5. they usually will not commit funds for more than *one year at a time;*
6. they value especially those innovative initiatives that reach *underserved youth and families in high-risk or poverty situations;* and
7. they prefer that we/4-H *collaborate or partner* with other organizations to carry out the initiatives they fund.

Land-grant universities have an enormous opportunity (and, some would say, responsibility) to strengthen their integration and focus to be of greater benefit to America's communities. It will require different ways of doing business, fully engaging the citizens in the process of a co-learning partnership. It will require paradigm shifts in these academic institutions. It will need to be funded by new, nontraditional partners and their resources. And a transformed Cooperative Extension System could play a key leadership role in bringing broad and effective outreach into a balance to positively impact community issues in more substantial ways.

Will it happen? I am curious enough to stick around and find out, as the next several years unfold. And our nonprofit organization will do what we can to seed, catalyze, and support serious efforts in this direction. Perhaps we can someday assure that each community will have available the maximum number of positive youth development assets for its youth and families, and the resulting strengthened human resources will create and sustain a new level of positive community change, so that all youth will have hope for a positive future.

References

Hock, D. W. (1995). The chaordic organization: Out of control and into order. *World Business Academy Perspectives, 9* (1), 5–18.

Lerner, R. M. (1995). *America's youth in crisis: Challenges and options for programs and policies.* Thousand Oaks, CA: Sage.

Chapter 19
The Common Pursuits of Modern Philanthropy and the Proposed Outreach University
Enhancing Research and Education

Lonnie R. Sherrod
William T. Grant Foundation

Introduction

This volume explores the creation of outreach universities, characterized by university-community collaborations. The objectives of this new vision of the land-grant university for the twenty-first century are to empower communities and to enrich and revitalize institutions of higher education. This development is timely for several reasons: the increasing number and severity of problems faced by contemporary communities (in this volume, the devastating consequences for children and youth are highlighted); a heightened interest in most social science fields for using research information to address these social problems; a perceived stagnation in American universities, resulting at least in part from their isolation from the communities in which they reside; and a new concern in many fields of research, particularly the social-behavioral sciences, for the contextual and relational nature of scientific knowledge.

The history of the modern university in this country is closely linked with that of philanthropy and the social behavioral sciences. To understand fully the implications for education and research of the university model being proposed in this volume, it is helpful to review this history briefly. Several detailed reviews are available elsewhere (e.g., Cahan, 1986; Katz & Katz, 1981; Prewitt, 1995); as a result, the following overview is intentionally simplistic, serving in large part to highlight the important role of philanthropy in the history of behavioral research and the research university—a role it should continue to play in the proposed reinvention of the university.

Historical Considerations around the Turn of the Century

At the turn of the nineteenth century, social-economic conditions in this country prevailed similar to those of the present day. Industrialization and urban expansion fueled waves of international immigration and increased urban poverty, particularly for children. In this context, our views of childhood changed. Philanthropy as we now know it emerged, and the social-behavioral sciences grew and gained a stronghold in the university.

Changing Attitudes toward Children

Due to the deteriorating situation of children, a heightened concern for their well-being arose in the last half of the nineteenth century, just as is occurring in the present context. Child-labor laws, juvenile-justice laws, and laws to prevent cruelty to children were all passed in the late 1800s. In fact, society's attitudes toward children were transformed. A variety of factors other than concern for children contributed to this change: reduction in labor's needs for child workers, an increase in the skills and hence in the preparation needed for work, and a changing population structure as people were living longer. The magnitude of this change in society's view of childhood is illustrated by pointing out that the law to prevent cruelty to animals was passed before the law to prevent cruelty to children. In fact, this time has been characterized as representing a change from viewing children as "economic assets" (for their families) to recognizing them as "emotionally priceless" economic liabilities (Zelizer, 1985; see also chapter 18).

Social work oriented to children followed soon after the change in society's views of childhood; the settlement houses and U.S. Children's Bureau are illustrative. This new humane concern for children fueled the emergence of research on children and on child development. Early in the twentieth century, the Child Study Movement was given a boost by the work of G. Stanley Hall, and the Child Guidance Movement was fueled by private philanthropic support (from the Commonwealth Foundation among others) and by the growth of social work; each contributed to formation of the field of child-developmental research in the U.S. The establishment of six university centers to study children (funded by the Laura Spelman Rockefeller Memorial Fund) in the late 1920s led to the development of the National Research Council Committee on Child Development. That committee was the immediate forerunner of the Society for Research in Child Development (SRCD), which is currently the premier professional association of child-development researchers, with an international, interdisciplinary membership over 5,000 (Cahan, 1986).

The Origins of Philanthropy

The industrialization of the early twentieth century, in addition to contributing to a new view of children and their place in society, also created numerous self-made men committed to using their business skills as well as their accumulated wealth to heal some of the emerging social ills. These new philanthropists, such as Carnegie and Rockefeller, began their work in the context of a variety of charities and relief organizations. They saw these charities as providing temporary relief by treating symptoms; their goal, however, was to cure the core causes of social problems—to accomplish social change. This attitude arose in the private sector at a time when government was not involved in social welfare and reform. Hence, there was a clear role for the privately funded philanthropies. And several of the U.S.'s largest and most influential foundations today arose early in this century: Russell Sage Foundation in 1907, the Carnegie Corporation in 1911, the Rockefeller Foundation in 1913, and the Commonwealth Fund in 1918. As general-purpose foundations, their objective was to advance public welfare, but science was seen as a means to that goal. Research in the social sciences, with its clear distinction between cause and effect, provided a strategy for approaching the solution of social ills, by identifying core causes of problems that could then be addressed, as opposed to alleviating symptoms or temporarily providing relief (Cahan, 1986; Katz & Katz, 1981). Although most of these new foundations did not provide substantial support directly for science, the appreciation of science as a tool provided a funding context that fueled the growth of the social behavioral sciences and the universities in which they became housed.

The Growth of the Social-Behavioral Sciences

The social sciences were already gaining importance by the mid-1800s, but the following seventy-five years witnessed substantial growth and diversification as well as increasing ties with the university. The American Social Sciences Association was formed in 1865. In fact, five core social sciences already existed by the Civil War, which proved to be a time that greatly influenced their subsequent development. Four formed graduate departments and published journals in the late 1800s, and the first discipline-specific professional associations (in economics and in psychology) emerged before the end of the nineteenth century (Prewitt, 1995). Universities, which had served mainly to educate elite males, also expanded after the Civil War. A science curriculum supplemented their religion-based education, and graduate training was introduced. The German uni-

versity model spread (Greenwood, 1995). Research became the key to pro-
fessionalism in the existing social science fields, and universities provided
fertile ground for this research basis to flourish and grow (Prewitt, 1995).

By the time that philanthropy entered the scene early in the twentieth
century, the research-based social science disciplines and the university
were already wed (Prewitt, 1995). Philanthropy, however, played an important role in the growth, expansion, and differentiation of the social
sciences. The importance of the Laura Spelman Rockefeller Memorial Fund
and the Commonwealth Fund in nourishing child-development research
has already been noted. The Laura Spelman Rockefeller Memorial Fund
also initially contributed to the support of the Social Science Research
Council, an interdisciplinary research planning organization incorporated in 1924 to advance the social sciences. The early years of the council's
history include several Research Planning Committees of relevance to
studies of human development: The Family (1928–1932), Interracial
Relations (1925–1930), and Personality and Culture (1930–1940)
(Sibley, 1974). The Council continues to play an important role in the
development of the social/behavioral sciences in this country as well as
internationally.

The founding of the William T. Grant Foundation in 1936 can provide an example of the role philanthropy played in establishing the social
behavioral sciences, particularly for studies of children and youth. Mr.
Grant built a chain of "dry goods" stores, selling miscellaneous household
wares at economical prices. His first store opened in 1906, and when he
retired in 1966, there were over a thousand stores across the country. Mr.
Grant was particularly interested in his employees, many of whom were
young people whose lives were compromised by a variety of social, emotional, or health problems. He wanted his foundation to focus on "the
study of man." By this time, foundations had made important progress in
the medical and health sciences (in funding research on the causes, treatment, and prevention of numerous physical ailments such as typhoid, yel-
low fever, and hookworm, for example) and in macrolevel studies relating
to social reform (for example, working for world peace following World
War I). Mr. Grant, however, wanted his foundation to fund research that
would ". . . help children develop what is in them" in order to live up to
their full potential (Cahan, 1986). He also wanted the Grant Foundation
to focus on prevention of problems rather than adopting a patchwork
approach to solving current problems, as the charities of that time seemed
to be doing. He recognized that even the brightest and most successful

individuals could be at risk. Furthermore, he thought it equally important to understand developmental successes and failures (Cahan, 1986; B. A. Hamburg, 1992). Mr. Grant established his foundation to contribute to the development of a science of human development; and in so doing, he, like several others (e.g., Frederick Gates, John D. Rockefeller's early consultant, and Beardsley Ruml, who headed the Laura Spelman Rockefeller Memorial Fund [Prewitt, 1995]), carried the trend of his philanthropic contemporaries one step further, to directly fund social-behavioral science inquiry that could then be used to address social and individual problems. The William T. Grant Foundation follows that mission to this day. The U.S. Federal agencies that support research on human development—for example, the National Science Foundation and the National Institutes of Health—originated around midcentury, too late to contribute to the early development of these fields.

In summary, the point of this brief historical overview is to demonstrate how interconnected was the growth of the university, social-behavioral science research, and philanthropy early in this century. In many ways, the outreach university being proposed for the twenty-first century in this volume represents renewed, not new, concern for the deteriorating conditions of children and for using university-based science as a tool to improve the well-being of children and youth. Comparable social-historical factors in the present are leading to the choice of solutions similar to those used earlier in the century.

Philanthropy has a role to play in this renewed concern, just as it made a critical contribution to comparable efforts early in the century. Philanthropy and the proposed outreach university pursue similar goals. Hence, it is reasonable that a partnership may increase the effectiveness of either alone. Departing from its early history, philanthropy has become increasingly separated from university-based research in the last half of the century, as each field has expanded and as government at all levels has assumed a greater role in education and research. The outreach university can enhance its contributions to research and education as well as to the promotion of the well-being of youth by including private philanthropy as a partner in its attempts to reinvent the modern university and enhance research and education. In the remainder of the paper I discuss the expansion of philanthropy and of education across the past few decades, and describe how the outreach university, by combining forces with philanthropy, can address some of the challenges created by these expansions.

The Growth of Philanthropy in the United States

As was true a century ago, the globalization of market economies and the emergence of new technologies in communication and information processing have again fueled economic growth, which has driven an increase in philanthropy in this country in recent decades. Private foundations by their nature are affluent, so they benefit from the same domestic economic policies that benefit business and affluent citizens. The tax laws in the U.S. create an incentive for individual charity and are an important factor in accounting for the growth of philanthropy in the U.S. relative to other parts of the world.

The last few decades have, in fact, been characterized by substantial growth both in the size of existing foundations, even after controlling for inflation, and in the number and types of foundations in the U.S. The number of private foundations in the U.S. has nearly doubled since the mid-1970s, and the total assets of these foundations have doubled even after considering the impact of inflation. The largest decade of growth was in the 1980s (28%), reflecting the economic boom of that decade, followed by the 1950s (22%) (Heimann, 1973; Renz & Lawrence, 1993). Since the 1960s, foundations have been required by federal law to pay out a minimum percentage of their assets, currently 5%. Thus, as foundation resources grow so does their potential impact.

In addition to growing in absolute numbers and assets, foundations in the U.S. have become increasingly diverse. Four major types of foundations currently exist in the U.S. All of the foundations I have so far mentioned, including Grant, are *independent foundations*. They are intended to be self-perpetuating. They have a substantial endowment. The interest earned on this corpus supports programs and projects, according to the mission established by the founder. Most major independent foundations are governed by boards of directors who are largely independent of the founding family or corporate entity. There are three other types of foundations. Some foundations may be direct arms of the families or corporations that established them. In these cases, they function collaboratively with the founding family members or corporate boards. These are designed as *family* or *corporate foundations*. *Community foundations* have also arisen to serve the needs of specific communities. These foundations both receive contributions and dispense grant support. They are typically mandated to support only local programs—to contribute to the well-being of a designated community area, typically city, county, or state. The final type of foundation is the *operating foundation*. Regardless of source of endowment or funding, these foundations actually develop and run the projects that they fund.

These three "other" types of foundations have represented a substantial portion of the growth in the last decades. These newer types of foundations are now funding as much as, and in some areas more than, independent foundations. Predictions are that local philanthropic activities, such as community foundations, will represent the most intense area of future philanthropic activity (Hall, 1988; Nason, 1989). For example, there has been a proliferation of health foundations as nonprofit hospitals have been converted to for-profit status as a consequence of the rise of managed care (Young, 1996).

The newer expansion of philanthropy has contributed little to the growth or development of the social sciences across the past couple of decades, in contrast to the role of philanthropy earlier in the century. Currently, only 2–5% of both dollars and number of grants goes directly to science/technology or to social science. Corporate and community foundations are less likely to fund social science—and although they do fund relevant other categories (specifically education and human services), these do not tend to be research based (Renz & Lawrence, 1993).

The latter-day growth of philanthropy in the U.S. has not been guided by the notion that propelled it during its origins earlier in the century: that science offers a useful means of addressing social problems. Foundations have, however, continued to search for ways of increasing their effectiveness in addressing social problems. With increasing frequency, social programs have been funded that adopt comprehensive approaches to problem solving rather than target specific issues. Collaborations of community constituencies have been encouraged or required. Community-wide initiatives have been developed. Collaborations of foundations have developed to share resources and wisdom. That is, a range of new strategies and targets has been sought by philanthropy in an effort to increase its effectiveness. Research has not, however, generally been seen to be very helpful in enhancing effectiveness, except in looking to evaluation research methods to *demonstrate* effectiveness.

There are several possible explanations for the increasing separation of science support and philanthropy, for the departure from the historical trends that characterized the early development of both fields. The first is the increased role of government, particularly at the federal level. There are now several governmental agencies whose primary mission is the support of research. Examples such as the National Science Foundation need not be described because they are all familiar to the readers of this volume. However, government at all levels, local as well as federal, has assumed a major role in *all* areas of philanthropic endeavors. In response to government's entry into social welfare efforts, philanthropy has redefined its role, to identify a niche that distinguishes its efforts from those of government. Private funding gets things started with the idea that effective undertakings will then be sustained by government funding. This is perhaps a questionable expectation, particularly in these days when government is downsizing; but that is another topic. The point is that governmental support for research does not fully explain philanthropy's abandonment of science as a tool in attempting social change, because government has also increased its role in other areas, such as social welfare, where philanthropic activity has not decreased.

A second factor may be a perception that social conditions have deteriorated, particularly for children and families. As the urgency of social problems increases, research can come to be viewed as an unaffordable luxury. The opening chapter in this volume describes the social condition of many children in this country. Children may be worse off than they were a few decades ago, and they certainly merit our help, but they do not live in poorer conditions than they did a century ago. In fact, recognizing society's views of children during the late nineteenth century (before child-labor and juvenile-justice laws were enacted), one may even argue that today's children enjoy a more privileged position. Nonetheless, at that time, philanthropists recognized that research is not a luxury; research of varied types was recognized to be necessary to the success of society. In fact, as social conditions worsen, research becomes more important in order to insure that resources aimed at improving social welfare are used wisely. Thus, this factor also cannot fully explain the separation of philanthropy and science.

Another factor may be that the social sciences have not lived up to their promise of usefulness. Prewitt (1995) emphasizes the importance of objectivity in the early development of the social sciences and refers to the potential of the social-behavioral sciences to serve as the "systematic social intelligence" of society. Advocacy and neutrality (or objectivity) have been viewed to conflict, but social-science research integrates them by imparting objectivity to strategies aimed at the betterment of society. Knowledge rather than ideology determines the choice of solutions to social problems. It is this view of science that appealed to the early philanthropists and that needs to be reintegrated into modern reform efforts. Some in philanthropy, perhaps especially in its newer forms, see wisdom, knowledge, or intelligence to reside in experience that is more firmly grounded in the "real world" than seems to be true for science. There are those who view science as relegated to universities, which have become increasingly isolated from the communities in which they reside; the knowledge housed in universities is not viewed to relate to the problems addressed in the real world, outside the academy. And some philanthropists and others oriented to promoting the social good have developed their own forms of wisdom and knowledge based on experience.

The outreach university has the potential to confront these views and to reaffirm the place of social science as the "systematic social intelligence" of society (Prewitt, 1995). It brings research out of the academy and demonstrates its usefulness in multiple ways. It educates and helps as well as generating new knowledge. It has the potential to rebuild the partnership among philanthropy, science, education, and social reform.

The Expansion of Education in the U.S.

Research and education are different sides of the same coin. At higher levels of education—collegiate and postgraduate—the relationship between different forms of learning are made explicit. Research is generating (or learning) entirely new information; whereas "education" typically consists of learning information that already exists—that has been generated through research. The process of that learning should ideally mirror the process involved in generating new information. It should be research based. Thus, education provides another vehicle as does philanthropy for reaffirming the place of science as the systematic intelligence of society. Also like philanthropy, education—both mass public precollegiate education and postsecondary higher education—has expanded during the twentieth century, to a larger proportion of the population and to a larger portion of the life course.

Public precollegiate education has become the main endeavor of children. That represents a change from a single-digit percent of the youth population that attended school at the end of the previous century, to more than 80% by 1950. Having reached a ceiling in terms of percent attending school, since 1950 the absolute numbers attending precollegiate schools have increased as the population has grown. As a result, the size of schools has increased, and schools have served to segregate children increasingly by age, as middle schools split off from high schools. Originally established in part to minimize the separation of the social classes, in recent decades segregation by social class has increased in public schools and segregation by race has also again increased, despite the civil rights movement of the 1960s. The time children spend in schools has also increased at both ends of the age distribution, extending downward into toddlerhood and upward well into young adulthood in the form of postgraduate study. Schools have become the major social institution serving children and youth, and as other institutions such as the family and the church have changed or declined in influence, schools have been asked to do more and more for children (Dryfoos, 1994). In some cases, institutions such as schools, families, and the media have come to offer competing messages to children (Cremin, 1990).

Similarly, higher education has grown. The biggest increase has been since World War II, both in numbers of individuals attending some form of college, and in the diversity of types of postsecondary educational experiences available (Greenwood, 1995). Colleges and universities now number over 3,400 and their expenditures comprise about 2.8% of the gross national product. Half of the youth population now attends some type of college for some portion of time, but only about a quarter actually acquire a degree in four years (Clotfelter and Rothschild, 1993) although many youth simply "stop-out," returning to obtain a degree in six–ten years. Furthermore, despite an increase in the proportion of the population that believes education is important to life success, public confidence in higher education is decreasing (Greenwood, 1995). The gap in earnings between high school and college graduates has increased in recent years, yet undergraduates are not particularly proficient at estimating returns from higher education (Manski, 1993), so their decisions about education are not necessarily always in their best interests.

This expansion of education has not been based on the developmental needs of children and youth and has not kept pace with the evolving needs of a rapidly changing society. As a result, the current system neither fulfills its function in training individuals to be productive members of society nor accommodates to the developmental needs of a growing child. Like philanthropy, education has not maintained sufficient grounding in research on child and youth development. However, educational reform, particularly at the precollegiate level, has been an area of substantial philanthropic activity during the past decade. The outreach university enjoys a particularly strategic position for undertaking educational reform, at collegiate as well as precollegiate levels, and for strengthening connections to research. Here then is another opportunity for the outreach university to pursue an effective partnership with philanthropy.

Opportunities for the Outreach University

The outreach university inherently addresses both faces of the coin representing research and education. By extending its outreach to the community and to social reform efforts, it creates the potential for science and learning to once again partner with philanthropy so as to reaffirm the role of the social/behavioral sciences as the "systematic social intelligence" of society. By doing so, it also can increase its society-wide impact by reinventing education at all levels—not just the collegiate and postgraduate—by extending its educational outreach beyond its own traditional students, and by reviewing the place of education in the human life course.

Enhancing Research

The new vision of the outreach university pursues four accomplishments that will build greater connections between private philanthropy, research, and universities. It preserves a belief in the importance of basic research while using the tools of science to address immediate problems, particularly in promoting a revised outlook on evaluation research. It concerns itself directly with the dissemination of research, demonstrating its usefulness in addressing social problems. And it recognizes that varied constituencies, not just the academic community, have useful contributions to make to science policy.

Preserving Basic Research

The outreach university blurs the distinction between basic and applied research. All research is potentially applicable to social problems. Research differs in the time frame of that application and in the source of the research question, but neither factor undermines relevance to social problems. Research typically labeled "applied" has immediate relevance but can also yield basic knowledge, whereas "basic" research may become relevant in unexpected ways and on an unpredictable timetable as new social problems arise. The purpose of basic knowledge is to have some information "on the shelves" to retrieve as needed to address newly emerging social issues. The outreach university recognizes that social problems change faster than does our ability to generate useful information. As a result, it is essential to have research-based knowledge available that can be used to deal with new social problems or to guide research directly focused on those problems (Lerner et al., 1994; Prewitt, 1980).

The use of research on self-efficacy and self-esteem is one example. Research on these personal attributes provides important weapons to promote behavior changes aimed at reducing risk for HIV infection (Bandura, 1992). Yet no one expected that this research tradition would prove useful in this way, because AIDS was not an epidemic at the time the research developed. On the other hand, research on a variety of existing youth problems (e.g. early-adolescent sexuality and pregnancy, substance-abuse prevention, reducing school dropout) have produced important information on adolescent development as well as addressing the particular problems of young people (Feldman & Elliot, 1990). Research is learning, and learning needs to be part of social action, just as action should be triggered by the learning process.

A New Outlook on Evaluation Research

Evaluations of social programs and interventions are one explicit form of directly "applied" research. O'Connor (1995) describes the history of evaluation research in this country since its origins around midcentury. Early efforts in particular emphasized a "black box" approach, stemming from the social experimentation paradigm prevalent then. To some extent, this paradigm persists, and parallels a drug-testing model. Individuals are randomly assigned to groups, then one group receives an intervention, and selected outcomes are measured in the two groups. If there is a statistically significant group difference, it is safe to attribute causality to the one difference between the groups—the intervention. The standard experimental paradigm applies.

The problem is that interventions are not drugs. They are more complex in multivariate ways, and many factors other than the intervention affect the group outcomes. It is also not clear that random assignment can serve to obtain comparable groups in the contexts in which most social interventions are launched; and, often, random assignment is simply not possible in certain interventions (Hollister and Hill, 1995). In these cases, it may be more informative to ask what percentage of the variation in selected outcomes is accounted for by selected variables of the intervention. Most of what we know about youth development is based on quasiexperimental, correlational, or descriptive analyses. Children are not, for example, randomly assigned to good and bad parents; yet we attribute considerable importance to these nonexperimental analyses of what constitutes effective parenting practices for children. Similar analytical strategies may prove useful in examining which variables of program participation relate to which participants outcomes, and to what extent.

At the same time, many interventions are not set up as experiments and are not set up to accomplish much learning. They are established to heal, to help, to promote the well-being of their recipients. Recent philanthropic efforts offer numerous examples. Yet all such interventions are based on models of change. The intervention is designed to include certain components thought to affect certain outcomes in the form of youth development or community change. In these cases, it is important to identify these implicit theories of change, because the intervention and research on it then becomes a test of that "theory of change" (Connell, Aber, & Walker, 1995; Lerner et al., 1994; Price, 1987). That is, the evaluation then becomes theory-based research, contributing to knowledge about the phenomena addressed by the intervention, as well as offering information on the effectiveness of a particular social program or policy. A logical extension of this position is to view interventions for youth as natural contexts for studying development, and thus as important opportunities to contribute to our basic knowledge about developmental process (Sherrod, 1995).

The outreach university is a perfect vehicle for promoting a new outlook on evaluation that both recognizes the potential for learning in all social change efforts, and, at the same time, offers an array of tools other than the standard experimental paradigm for learning about the role of the intervention in the lives of the recipients. Philanthropy has important lessons to share with the outreach university in this regard, and university-based research has valuable expertise to aid philanthropy in promoting the social welfare. In this regard, collaborations between universities, national independent foundations, and locally based community foundations could be particularly effective. Science, however, offers an objectivity that is not inherent in this more grounded knowledge, which is vulnerable to accusations of ideological bias.

Science-Based Dissemination

The outreach university also recognizes that the scientific community must take some responsibility for disseminating its findings to the public and to policymakers, for demonstrating the relevance of its work, and even for using that work to improve the general social good, as the early philanthropists wanted to do. For students of human development, science-based dissemination is especially important, because it increases the chances that developmental issues are considered when policies are made for children, youth, and families.

Too often policies are determined not by individuals' developmental needs, but by political considerations, together with social and institutional needs. The growth of mass public schooling in the U.S. is one historical example where social-economic rather than developmental considerations have disproportionately driven the formation of a major social institution for children: The Carnegie Council's report, *Turning Points* (1989) describes the problems that the growth of one component of public education, the middle schools, has created for young adolescents. The separation of middle schools, devoted to grades six through eight, from elementary and high schools requires that children move to a new school and experience a sometimes bewildering variety of changes in peer groups and academic routine at a time that they are also experiencing the equally confusing changes of puberty. That is, the characteristics of this school structure in the U.S. conflict with the developmental needs of this age period; the growth of schools has been driven by factors such as overall population growth and the needs of labor rather than by the developmental needs of children and youth. Private funders such as Grant, Carnegie, and MacArthur attempt to represent young people in bringing developmental issues to the public agendas for children and youth; the *Turning Points* report provides one such example. The new vision of the outreach university offers an important opportunity for the scientific community to increase its role by joining with philanthropy in such dissemination efforts.

Setting Science Policy

Perhaps the most important achievement of the new collaborative university is that the scientific community recognizes that communication between the policy or service or philanthropic communities and researchers should be bidirectional. That is, science has information to share with the policy and service communities. However, those individuals who serve children and youth in direct service as well as in public service or who use philanthropy to improve the public well-being also have questions to ask and lessons to share with the scientific community. That is, they too are an expert system (Lerner et al., 1994).

In summary, the reinvented outreach university, by collaborating with philanthropy of various types, can bring current research knowledge and methods to efforts at social improvement and can use the knowledge inherent in communities and in philanthropy to contribute to the research agendas of universities. It can preserve basic research in expectation of future needs as new social problems arise, and it can structure current efforts at social change by philanthropy (as well as government and others) to insure that they contribute to our learning.

Opportunities for Educational Outreach

The outreach university can integrate research and learning at all levels of education. It can contribute to educational reform at the precollegiate level by partnering with schools in the communities it serves, it can foster needed reforms in education at the collegiate level, it can help students of all levels become lifelong learners, and it can serve communities by expanding its access beyond the traditional college student.

Increasing the Educational Attainment of All Precollegiate Students

Considerable public and private philanthropic attention has been devoted to precollegiate educational reform. For example, a lack of support for making the transition from high school to work has been identified (William T. Grant Foundation, 1988), and a variety of approaches, for example, apprenticeships, have been proposed to assist that half of the population that does not attend college (Hamilton, 1990, 1994). While mechanisms to link school and work are needed, the precollegiate educational experience should *not* be tracked or dichotomized into the college and noncollege bound. Entry into the current, high-skills workforce after high school requires the same educational preparation as college (Berryman & Bailey, 1992). Concomitantly, college-bound students need some of the applied learning experiences that were previously reserved for those youth preparing to enter the workforce after graduation from high school. Experience in real-world settings not only grounds students' learning so as to enhance its meaningfulness, but also contributes to the acquisition of problem-solving, critical-thinking, communication, and other social skills, and benefits academic skills and classroom-based performance (Gardner, 1991; Hamburg, 1994; Resnick, 1987, 1990).

The outreach university can join with philanthropy to further the efforts at reform at all levels of precollegiate education in order to guarantee a high level of learning for all students. It can, for example, provide effective and meaningful educational experiences for high-school students, particularly those from disadvantaged communities. Advanced academic courses can be created, or admission to select introductory college courses allowed. That is, the transition from high school to college or the workplace can be aided by programs developed by the university for high-school students. This provides one relatively easy form of outreach to communities that directly aids youth and is fully consistent with universities' general mission. Additionally, the outreach universities can provide important applied-learning experiences for high-school students. Apprenticeships in research labs, in university-based hospital settings, in university museums, in development or administrative offices are one vehicle. Additionally, involvement in community-based programs, through the efforts of the new outreach university, provides ideal applied settings for service learning experiences, for contact with evaluation research, and for civic participation. Families and communities are as important to youth as schools (Howe, 1993), so such experiences aid learning and provide a vehicle for youth to become engaged in productive activities, thereby reducing their marginality to society (Petersen & Mortimer, 1994).

Collegiate Educational Reform

The array of skills and competencies needed by today's citizens includes not just knowledge in typical academic subjects such as reading, writing, and arithmetic—the traditional three Rs. Three new Rs are needed: reasoning, responsibility, and relationships (Hamburg, 1994; Gardner, 1991). The distinction between progressive and traditional approaches to education is no longer useful. Creative, child- and youth-centered methods of instruction are needed that are grounded in real-world experiences, but structured methods of promoting a high level of basic skills are also required (Gardner, 1989). Such a view is needed at both the precollegiate and collegiate levels of education.

While philanthropy has attended to precollegiate school reform, there has been less attention to collegiate education. The outreach university, however, provides a logical and effective vehicle for approaching educational reform at the collegiate level. Whether college students aim for postgraduate professional education or plan to enter the workforce, the level of skills and knowledge cover the same broad range as that addressed by precollegiate educational reform efforts—that is, the six Rs, not just the traditional three. Colleges have done no better job than secondary schools in attending to the new three Rs (particularly responsibility and relationships); yet college may be a particularly opportune time for such psychosocial development to occur. Furthermore, liberal-arts graduates have no easier time making the transition to work than do high school graduates, and many enter the workforce underemployed because they do not possess the type of skills and competencies needed in the current workplace.

As a result, their departure from their family's home may be increasingly delayed, and their assumption of productive adult roles thwarted (Sherrod, Haggerty, & Featherman, 1993). The outreach university has the potential to connect its students to the real world in a way that contributes to decision making about careers and sets them on a track to meaningful employment. In fact, college students need some of the applied-learning experiences previously reserved for those youth who did not attend college; the outreach to communities pursued by the new vision of the university provides an ideal vehicle for providing educationally meaningful applied experiences to its students throughout their college careers.

Contributing to Lifelong Learning

Given the rapidly changing nature of today's work environments, students must learn to learn; they must become lifelong learners. It is no longer effective, even possible, if we are to maintain the nation's international competitiveness, to invest all our educational resources in the early years of the life course. Adult education, work-based training, and a variety of other educational strategies are needed to keep citizens up-to-date in their skills and knowledge.

Outreach universities can provide these types of opportunities for lifelong learning for America's citizens. Many schools are already offering a range of adult-education courses, but there is a need to move beyond an ad hoc approach oriented to hobbies, career changes, or providing opportunities to update one's training only in a few fields (such as education and health care) that reward continuing study. If it is no longer fruitful to center all of our educational investment in the early years, it becomes important to alternate periods of education and productive civic involvement early in the life course, even during childhood. Providing avenues for productive engagement in society early in life can aid learning and decrease youth's feelings of marginality. The outreach university has an important role to play in facilitating early civic and work involvement and in promoting lifelong learning. Universities may collaborate with schools to provide opportunities for youth's productive activities and with businesses to generate learning opportunities for employees in a variety of fields.

Extending Access to the University

Of particular relevance to the outreach universities and central to many current philanthropic efforts are programs to assist disadvantaged individuals increase their capacity for economic self-sufficiency. Numerous studies involving thousands of individuals in a variety of programs across many states have demonstrated that governmental and other programs to move people from welfare to work increase the earnings of the recipients and lower costs associated with welfare, but cannot end welfare dependency permanently or eliminate poverty. More is needed than social programming. One important form of outreach for the university is to increase its population receiving educational services, beyond that half of the young-adult population that now attends college, beyond the traditional students. Welfare recipients, low-income workers, and unemployed youth are worthwhile targets for the outreach university.

For example, recipients of Aid to Families with Dependent Children (AFDC) have already begun to take advantage of the opportunity to further their educations. Close to half of this population have GEDs or highschool diplomas and are, therefore, eligible for higher education. A number of institutions (mostly community colleges) have already begun to develop special programs adapted to meet the needs of nontraditional or reentry students. However, the Family Support Act of 1988 and the associated Jobs Opportunities and Basic Skills (JOBS) programs greatly expand the possibilities (Kates, 1995). Here, then, is another opportunity for the outreach university, particularly as much decision making about welfare policy is returned to the states; it is an opportunity where effective collaboration with philanthropy is indicated.

Research has already begun to document how institutions of higher education can assist nontraditional students such as AFDC recipients. A nationwide survey of seventy-six colleges and universities and of JOBS policies in thirty-two states identifies the special needs of these students who require flexibility and new forms of support from the policies of JOBS programs and the institutions of higher education. Institutional, program, and policy or legislative change is required if the potential benefit, particularly to the student, is to be realized (Kates, 1995). Nonetheless, research has already demonstrated the benefits to the recipient of taking advantage of education, in terms of increasing earnings and decreasing welfare dependency. Of particular note is that AFDC mothers report benefits to children through the mother's increased self-esteem and other family members' expanded vision of opportunities for themselves (Gittell & Moore, 1990; Kates, 1995).

Conclusion

In summary, the outreach university has an important potential role to play in reinventing education for the twenty-first century at both the precollegiate and collegiate levels. Attending to the developmental appropriateness of educational strategies so as to contribute to a high level of attainment for all persons, incorporating applied learning into curricula at all levels, and reaching a fuller representation of the population across a fuller portion of the life course are examples of promising and needed strategies. Private philanthropy has already begun to pursue a variety of strategies for educational reform at the precollegiate level. Outreach universities, by partnering with philanthropy in its various forms, can bring a different level of expertise to such efforts and can improve collegiate education at the same time.

The outreach university proposed in this volume carries considerable potential for enhancing research on children and youth and for revising and reforming education for the full populace throughout the life course. To maximize its impact, the outreach university should reestablish the ties between philanthropy, education, and research.

This collaboration will not be easy to foster. Each partner is large and complex. One role, for example, that the university can play in regard to philanthropy is to serve as a bridge between the different forms of philanthropy. Local, community foundations frequently struggle with mission and program focus; they can benefit from the work of the national, independent foundations. The outreach university, with its interests in community development as well as research and education, is a strategic force for facilitating such collaboration within philanthropy (Young, 1996). Additionally, forging ties between precollegiate and collegiate education in ways other than tracking young people for college will be challenging; the university's outreach to communities, including local schools, provides a potential mechanism. And the research community is large and diverse, but is almost wholly represented by universities, making the outreach university a forceful vehicle for accomplishing change in the research enterprise and for increasing its visibility and usefulness in addressing community problems.

In short, the outreach university promises potential new forms of teaching and of scholarship, and by partnering with philanthropy, can also impact the face of charitable giving in this country.

Acknowledgments

I wish to thank Sharon Brewster for her help in preparing this manuscript and Michael Fultz, University of Wisconsin; Beatrix Hamburg and Linda Newman, William T. Grant Foundation; and Kathryn Young, Commonwealth Fund, for reading and offering much useful feedback on an earlier version.

References

Bandura, A. (1992). A social cognitive approach to the exercise of control over AIDS infection. In R. J. Diclemente (Ed.), *Adolescents and AIDS: A Generation in Jeopardy.* Newbury Park, CA: Sage.

Berryman, S. E., & Bailey, T. R. (1992). *The double helix of education and the economy.* New York: Teachers College, Columbia University.

Cahan, E. D. (1986). *William T. Grant Foundation: The first fifty years, 1936–1986.* New York: William T. Grant Foundation.

Carnegie Council on Adolescent Development. (1989). *Turning points: Preparing American youth for the twenty-first century.* New York: Carnegie Corporation of New York.

Clotfelter, C., & Rothschild, M. (Eds.). (1993). *Studies of supply and demand in higher education.* Chicago: The University of Chicago Press.

Connell, J., Aber, J.L., & Walker, G. (1995). How do urban communities affect youth? Using social science research to inform the design and evaluation of comprehensive community initiatives. In J. Connell, A. Kubisch, L. Schorr, & C. Weiss (Eds.), *New approaches to evaluating community initiatives: Concepts, methods, and contexts.* Washington, DC: The Aspen Institute.

Cremin, L. (1990). *Popular education and its discontents.* New York: Harper & Row.

Dryfoos, J. (1994). *Full-service schools: A revolution in health and social services for children, youth, and families.* San Francisco: Jossey-Bass.

Feldman, S. S., & Elliott, G. R. (1990). *At the threshold: The developing adolescent.* Cambridge, MA: Harvard University Press.

Gardner, H. (1989). *To open minds: Chinese clues to the dilemma of contemporary education.* New York: Basic Books.

———. (1991). *The unschooled mind: How children think and how schools should teach.* New York: Basic Books.

Gittell, M., & Moore, J. (1990). *From welfare to independence: The college option.* New York: Ford Foundation.

Greenwood, M. R. C. (1995). Societal expectations from research universities and the higher education system. In C. Kumar & N. Patel (Eds.), *Reinventing the research university.* Los Angeles: Regents of the University of California.

Hall, P. D. (1988). Private philanthropy and public policy: A historical appraisal. In R. Payton, M. Novak, B. O'Connell, and P. Hall (Eds.), *Philanthropy Four Views.* New Brunswick, NJ: Transaction Books.

Hamburg, B.A. (1992). President's Report. *William T. Grant Foundation Annual Report.* New York: William T. Grant Foundation.

———. (1993). President's report. New futures for "The Forgotten Half": Realizing unused potential for learning and productivity. William T. Grant Foundation Annual Report. New York: William T. Grant Foundation.

———. (1994). President's report. Education for a changed America: The need for stronger basics and an additional "3Rs" Reasoning, responsibility, and relationships. *William T. Grant Foundation annual report.* New York: William T. Grant Foundation.

Hamburg, D.A. (1992). *Today's children: Creating a future for a generation in crisis.* New York: Time Books.

Hamilton, S. (1990). *Apprenticeship for adulthood: Preparing youth for the future.* New York, NY: The Free Press.

———. (1994). Social Roles for youth: Interventions in unemployment. In A.C. Petersen & J. Mortimer (Eds.), *Youth unemployment and society.* New York: Cambridge University Press.

Heimann, F. (Ed.). (1973). *The future of foundations.* Englewood Cliffs, NJ: Prentice-Hall.

Hollister, R., & Hill, J. (1995). Problems in the evaluation of community-wide initiatives. In J. Connell, A. Kubisch, L. Schorr, & C. Weiss (Eds.), *New approaches to evaluating community initiatives: Concepts, methods, and contexts.* Washington, DC: The Aspen Institute.

Howe II, H. (1993). *Thinking about Our Kids.* New York: The Free Press.

Kates, E. (1995). Escaping poverty: The promise of higher education. *Social Policy Report. 9*, (1). SRCD.

Katz, B. & Katz, S. (1981). The American private philanthropic foundation and the public sphere, 1890–1930. *Minerva, 19*, 236–269.

Lerner, R. M. (1995). *America's youth in crisis: Challenges and options for programs and policies*. Thousand Oaks, CA: Sage.

Lerner, R. M., Miller, J. R., Knott, J. H., Corey, K. E., Bynum, T. S., Hoopfer, L. C., McKinney, M. H., Abrams, L. A., Hula, R. C., & Terry, P. A. (1994) Integrating scholarship and outreach in human development research, policy, and service: A developmental contextual perspective. In Featherman, D. L., Lerner, R. M. & Perlmutter, M. (Eds.), *Life-span development and behavior, Vol. 12* (249–273). Hillsdale, NJ: Erlbaum.

Manski, C. F. (1993). Adolescent econometricians: How do youth infer the returns to schooling? In C. Clotfelter & M. Rothschild (Eds.), *Studies of supply and demand in higher education*. Chicago: University of Chicago Press.

Nason, J. (1989). *Foundation trusteeship: Service in the public interest*. New York: The Foundation Center.

O'Connor, A. (1995). Evaluating comprehensive community initiatives: A view from history. In J. Connell, A. Kubisch, L. Schorr, & C. Weiss (Eds.), *New approaches to evaluating community initiatives: Concepts, methods, and contexts*. Washington, DC: The Aspen Institute.

Petersen, A. C., & Mortimer, J. T. (Eds.), (1994). *Youth unemployment and society*. New York: Cambridge University Press.

Prewitt, K. (1980). The council and the usefulness of the social sciences. *Annual report of the president, 1979–1980*. New York: Social Science Research Council.

———. (1995). *Social sciences and private philanthropy: The quest for social relevance*. Essays on Philanthropy, No 15. Series on foundations and their role in American life. Indiana University Center on Philanthropy.

Price, R. H. (1987). Linking intervention research and risk factor research. In A. Steinberg & M. M. Silverman (Eds.), *Preventing Mental Disorders: A Research Perspective* (DHHS Publication No. ADM 87–1492). Washington, DC: U.S. Government Printing Office.

Renz, L., & Lawrence, S. (1993). *Foundation giving: Yearbook of facts and figures on private, corporate and community foundations*. New York: The Foundation Center.

Resnick, L. B. (1987). *Education and learning to think*. Washington, DC: National Academic Press.

———. (1990). Literacy in school and out. *Daedalus, 119* (2), 169–185.

Sherrod, L. (1995, June). *Policy options for investing in youth*. Paper presented at American Association of Family and Consumer Sciences Research and Policy Agenda Conference: Investment in Youth. Roanoke, VA.

Sherrod, L., Haggerty, R. J., & Featherman, D. L. (1993). Introduction: Late Adolescence and the Transition to Adulthood. Special Issue, *Journal of Research on Adolescence, 3* (3), 217–226.

Sibley, E. (1974). *Social Science Research Council: The first fifty years*. New York: SSRC.

William T. Grant Foundation Commission on Work, Family & Citizenship. (1988). *The forgotten half: Pathways to success for America's youth and young families*. New York: William T. Grant Foundation.

Young, K. (1996). Personal communication in response to an earlier draft of the paper.

Zelizer, V. A. (1985). *Pricing the priceless child: The changing social value of children*. New York: Basic Books, Inc.

Chapter 20
The Fermilab Program for Science and Mathematics Education of Youth

Marjorie G. Bardeen and Leon M. Lederman
Fermi National Accelerator Laboratory

Introduction

Why would a university—in Fermilab's case, a national research laboratory—want to get involved in community education outreach? Beyond the genuine satisfaction many volunteers get from participating in community activities and interacting with youth, there is an underlying need for preservation and diversification of the cadre of scientists. Scientists who rely increasingly on public support of their research need to raise the level of public scientific literacy and convince the public that investment in science is in society's best interests. Scientists need to inspire a new generation of scientists and, given the changing population demographics, they need to diversify that next generation. In order to stimulate the natural curiosity of students traditionally underrepresented in science and technology, efforts to encourage a life-long interest in science must begin at the youngest levels. Whether these students become practicing scientists or scientifically savvy citizens, their support will be needed to maintain American leadership in science. Therefore, scientists have a vested interest in joining the efforts to help communities provide both formal and informal science programs for their youth.

Most national laboratories have large open spaces, lecture halls, staffs, and resources to serve as informal education centers. If one adds the accident of a felicitous environment and zeal in high places, then the potential is enormous. Probably no national laboratory is endowed with as many of these attributes as Fermilab, a 6,800-acre site of the world's most powerful particle accelerators and a restored prairie located in the densely populated suburbs of Chicago. With over forty high schools, sixty-four middle schools, and two hundred and fifty elementary schools just within DuPage and Kane counties, where Fermilab is located, the response to Fermilab's outreach efforts has been instantaneous and enormous.

From the Fermilab education outreach experience we can identify four critical issues related to the creation of university/community collaboratives: institutional commitment, institutional approach, point of interaction, and participants. The most crucial issue is institutional commitment. The university commitment need not begin with the president, but it must eventually have the president's whole-hearted, unstinting, enthusiastic support. Top administration must give visible support to community programs; reward staff participation, especially in job-performance assessment; sanction use of university services for outreach activities; and use its influence with other sectors to enlist and sustain their participation. Beginning an outreach program may mean that institutional priorities are reordered.

Following closely behind institutional commitment is the need to begin a collaboration as a partnership among equal entities. When linking university talent to solve local problems, it is always best if the initiative comes from outside the university. University initiatives are usually driven by someone's "great idea." The proper attitude is one of equally excitable participants ready to argue and refine an idea on the basis of collegial partnership.

How, then, can a university implement an outreach mission beyond one of the obvious first steps, bringing leaders together for initial planning? Before taking that step, a small staff of community members with previous experience and credibility in the program areas of interest should be assembled. This can ensure that the university's main point of contact will support and nurture leadership among the community members. Whether or not this staff is organized as an office is not as important as their empowerment to be the bridge between the university and the community. Success or failure of the entire partnership may very well depend on the care with which these individuals are chosen.

A final issue is getting the right people involved, often as volunteers. Many may wish to participate, but some may not have the human-relations skills to work with community programs, particularly if they are used to being "experts." The idea of equal partnership must permeate the outreach university at all levels. Support should be available to those individuals who choose to become involved, and in some cases staff should be prepared to replace individuals who are not effective.

Science Education Needs

Every graduating high-school student of the twenty-first century must be ready and equipped to participate in and shape a society confronted with accelerating scientific advances, careers and jobs based on those advances, and increasingly wondrous technologies that impact our daily lives. While the dashboard of today's automobiles contain more computer power than Apollo 13, the classroom of today is all too often the same as one hundred years ago. Our world is changing so dramatically that the workers of thirty years ago would be overwhelmed by today's job requirements. Meanwhile our industries cry out about the lack of adequately trained workers. Schools must respond to this challenge with new approaches that provide the student with a solid knowledge base, develop the critical-thinking skills, and prepare the student to keep on learning.

The project to map the human genome could not have been imagined thirty years ago; yet today it is in full swing, and tomorrow it will be the source of new jobs in health care, medicine, and agriculture. How will today's high-school education prepare students to learn the new fields that will derive from mapping the humane genome? Scientific understanding and habits of mind are essential to reaching these goals.

Our nation's success in the twenty-first century requires that our citizens be scientifically literate and savvy. Our leaders, our parents, and our workers need to:

- be responsive to accelerating change;
- work together to find measured yet creative solutions to problems that are today unimaginable;
- anticipate the impacts of our actions;
- communicate effectively;
- maintain the balance and viability of our society and our ecology.

As a nation we now have the challenge to ensure that all America's children have the opportunity to learn and understand science, mathematics, and technology at the higher levels defined by national standards. We can no longer permit or afford to have the fundamental tools of educational, economic, and social viability accessible to only some students. The long-term sustainability of the "American Dream"—equal access to opportunities for success—is dependent on a dual commitment to equity and quality.

This new challenge has higher stakes, a shorter timeline, and involves all students. By the turn of the century it is essential we have in place a science-education program that addresses the needs of students as future workers and citizens. What should this new science-education program be? Loucks-Horsley et al. (1990) and the National Center for Improving

Science Education (1991) both present a vision and model for science education that has been termed "constructivist science." The reports stress that students must experience in-depth engagement and that by doing so they develop content knowledge and scientific habits of mind. The National Center for Improving Science Education report (1991) is a synthesis of the significant reports issued since 1980 regarding the status of science education.

How can educators turn kids on to science? The answer lies in helping children engage in experiences that require them to use scientific knowledge and processes as tools as they make sense of their experiences. This solution demands that the science classroom be transformed into an inquiry-based culture—a community of explorers—where curiosity, creativity, and questioning are valued, where resources and opportunities are made readily available, and where students can "work" like scientists engaged in the process of collective sensemaking. Critical thought develops in this culture as new ideas are encouraged and where all of them—from the teacher, students, and textbook—are subjected to review and analysis by the scientific community of students. Children will come away from these experiences with the ability to use scientific knowledge to describe, explain, predict, and control their world. (p. 2)

Science Education Issues

How do we put this new science-education program in place? The first step toward change is for schools and districts to place a high priority on science education. Although many national initiatives place much emphasis on science, The 1990 Science Report Card prepared by the National Center for Education Statistics (Jones et al., 1992) reports that science is given a relatively lower priority than mathematics, reading and writing. Only 45% of schools give science a priority for grade four, 40% for grade eight, and 35% for grade twelve. "The same low priority surfaced in a recent Gallup Poll on attitudes toward public schools, which showed that the national education goal emphasizing science and mathematics learning"(Elam et al., 1991)—by the year 2000, American students will be first in the world in mathematics and science achievement—"received the public's lowest priority ranking among the six national education goals adopted by the President and governors." (*Educating America*, 1991).

National standards call for a comprehensive change in the way science is taught and learned. Schools must become "learning organizations" where "people continually expand their capacity to create the results they truly desire, where new and expansive patterns of thinking are nurtured, where collective aspiration is set free, and where people are continually learning how to learn together" (Senge, 1990). Transforming schools will require major change throughout the educational system, in areas such as governance, management, curriculum, instruction, assessment, access to educational technology, and teacher preparation and enhancement. Organizations like the American Association for the Advancement of Science, Benchmarks for Science Literacy, and the National Research Council, National Science Education Standards, provide the frameworks; local communities translate these broad guidelines into specific programs to achieve their education goals.

Even as communities begin this exercise, they are under tremendous pressure from impatient constituents—the public, Congress, and state legislatures. They have heard enough, they want to see change, mostly in the form of improved test scores, *now*. But change is a slow, continual process and often yields few immediate results. And the focus of the current reform is not so much improved paper-and-pencil test scores as it is lasting knowledge and understanding. Change is occurring in suburban schools, where it is considered easy because these schools are often among our most successful. Change is occurring in rural schools and in our largest urban systems. In order to truly succeed, we must succeed everywhere.

What will it take? Think of the enormous effort necessary to change the way science is taught in the Chicago Public Schools. About 17,000 Chicago elementary-school teachers must teach science, and most of them are essentially untrained to do so; each year about 2,000 new teachers enter the system. Over 60% of Chicago students live in poverty, with all the attendant problems of single-parent families, inadequate housing, and crime-ridden neighborhoods; 30% are nonnative English speaking. Chicago has some 540 school buildings, many of them in need of extensive repairs and/or remodeling. The Chicago Public Schools have had five superintendents in the last ten years; the Illinois State Legislature has made major changes in the CPS school governance three times in the same ten years and has implemented major state reforms that also require change for CPS. Chicago's declining financial resources provide annual budget crises. It is a minor miracle that some exceptionally good schools overcome these formidable obstacles. But our future depends on this being the rule rather than the exception.

Restructuring science education calls for a systemic approach. There are few exemplars to guide comprehensive change in school systems, and few of the current education leadership, lay or professional, understand how to manage the change process. This task is bigger than the schools themselves, and we cannot expect them to work in isolation. Clearly, outside partners must raise the level of awareness and contribute to and support the needed change by sharing resources, expertise, and technology. Among these partners are colleges and universities, research institutions, and business and industry that, through outreach programs, provide resources and support to schools. In Chicago, many museums, universities, businesses, and foundations conduct effective interventions. One example is the partnership of Fermilab, Argonne National Laboratory, and many universities that created an academy to provide extensive and continued training to elementary-school teachers of the Chicago Public Schools. The Teachers Academy for Mathematics and Science in Chicago could not have been started without Fermilab participation and leadership derived from its long experience as a partner in science-education outreach initiatives.

The Fermilab Experience

A U.S. Department of Energy national laboratory, Fermi National Accelerator Laboratory operates the world's highest energy particle accelerator, the Tevatron. More than 2,500 scientists from laboratories, colleges, and universities worldwide have carried out research at Fermilab to explore the invisible world within the atom. The current staff of 2,132 employees includes 614 scientists and engineers and 479 technicians who work at the 6,800-acre site thirty miles west of Chicago.

As part of its basic commitment to science, Fermilab pioneered education-outreach activities that engage young people as apprentice scientists and assist communities in providing exciting science activities that demonstrate sound scientific process and present content in line with current scientific knowledge. Fermilab began by offering educational tours for high-school students and teachers in 1972. When Leon M. Lederman became laboratory director in 1979, educational opportunities at the precollege level were expanded. Fermilab offered programs in response to regional needs to sustain young people's interest in science and mathematics, to encourage young people to pursue careers in science and engineering, to revitalize the skills of current science teachers, and to maintain interest in the teaching of science as a career.

In 1979, Fermilab funds could not be spent on precollege education programs, so with Dr. Lederman's encouragement, a not-for-profit corporation, Friends of Fermilab, was established under the leadership of Stanka Jovanovic and Marjorie G. Bardeen to facilitate the formation of partnerships among Fermilab, school districts, and public and private funding agencies.

Friends of Fermilab operates under a "Memorandum of Understanding" with Fermilab and, in partnership with Fermilab and area educators, designs and conducts programs to enhance the teaching and learning of science and mathematics at the precollege level. Since its incorporation in 1983, Friends of Fermilab has raised over $2,856,000 from public and private sources, including the U.S. Department of Energy, the National Science Foundation, the state of Illinois, and various private foundations and individuals. Friends of Fermilab has sponsored more than fifty programs; most are still offered today. The corporation is governed by a board of directors composed of Fermilab staff members, civic, business, and education leaders, and is supported by approximately two hundred regular members who represent a cross section of the community, including teachers and businessmen, scientists, and school administrators.

After new federal legislation was passed in 1989, Fermilab established the Education Office to provide needed infrastructure to handle the day-to-day operations of the precollege outreach programs. The current staff of nine includes a manager, three education specialists, and support staff. On-call docents assist classes who visit the Lab. Friends of Fermilab continues to seek grants to support specific programs.

Fermilab has developed a successful format for program development and implementation that allows schools to tap the resources of a national research facility. The format includes two key components: conducting a needs assessment and establishing a program committee. Program development is guided by recommendations from an appropriate needs assessment conducted with educators, community leaders, Fermilab scientists, and representatives of Friends of Fermilab. A typical needs-assessment workshop includes around twenty participants, lasts three to four hours and covers a major program type or a new age group. It is important for Fermilab to listen to the education needs as perceived by the people who teach the students and employ the graduates. National laboratory staff are not necessarily experts in precollege education. However, when they understand what the local priorities for improving science and mathematics education are, they can assess the laboratory resources and determine ways to work in partnership with educators to promote change.

We cannot overemphasize the importance of these needs assessments. All too often faculty from research institutions, colleges, or universities go to schools with all the answers. "We know if you do it this way, your problems will be solved." Outreach programs must be collaborative and the partners on an equal footing if the programs are to succeed.

After the needs assessment is completed, a program committee, composed of local educators (master teachers, department chairmen, or instructional administrators) and a Fermilab scientist, evaluates the results of the needs assessment and makes program recommendations to the manager of the Fermilab Education Office. Based on those recommendations, education office staff prepare proposals for the U.S. Department of Energy or for Friends of Fermilab to seek funds from other public and private sources. Wherever possible, program budgets include stipends for classroom teachers who are paid for their time either as staff or as participants. For the most part, Fermilab technical staff serve as volunteers.

When funds are available, with the advice of the program committee, the manager hires staff, usually master teachers, to conduct the program. The staff is responsible for such tasks as program announcement, curriculum development, participant selection, instructor selection, follow-up activities, evaluation, program reports, and dissemination.

Strengths of this program-development model include:

- developing ownership of the programs among teachers by involving them from the beginning;
- giving teachers leadership roles recognized both by their peers and research scientists;
- establishing continuing communication channels between researchers and teachers;
- utilizing expertise from various groups—teachers, science-education specialists, scientists—with minimum interference with their regular job;
- integrating national laboratory education programs with existing local programs.

The Leon M. Lederman Science Education Center is the centerpiece for precollege education at Fermilab. The Center houses an exciting set of interactive exhibits called "Quarks to Quasars" a teacher resource center, a technology classroom, and a science laboratory. Visitors can discover the fascinating world of quarks and quasars using intriguing hands-on activities and multimedia kiosks to explore some of today's most amazing ideas and exciting scientific tools. In the Teacher Resource Center, staff help teachers, students, and parents find instructional materials, gain awareness of the Internet, and connect with scientists. In the Technology Classroom, students and teachers can use the Internet and receive Internet training, explore science with multimedia, and collect, analyze, and share data on computers. In the Center's laboratory, students and teachers classify specimens from the Fermilab prairie and conduct a variety of experiments related to prairie field work and to physics.

Fermilab education programs are developed within a framework that takes into account national education goals and standards, the mission of Fermilab, the appropriate use of its facilities, and the talents and interests of its personnel. Programs for higher grade levels are inaugurated first. At a given level, programs begin by bringing students and their parents or teachers to Fermilab in order to establish an awareness of the laboratory and the role it can play in education. Programs are offered in the following areas: Student Incentives and Opportunities, Teacher Preparation and Enhancement, Systemic Reform and Resource Center, and Public Awareness and Scientific Literacy.

Student Incentives and Opportunities

These are structured opportunities to reinforce classroom instruction, enhance scientific literacy, participate in research, and develop career awareness.

High school research programs offer experiences to high-school students who have the background to join either a physics research or technical group. Two programs, the Department of Energy High School Science Student Honors Research Program in Particle Physics and Target: Science and Engineering, enhance the research experience with seminars or classroom work on a related science project. DOE Honors is a two-week research program for gifted high-school students. The program includes lectures by Fermilab staff physicists, lab tours, and tutorial sessions as well as hands-on experiences. Students come from the fifty states, the District of Columbia, Puerto Rico, and six foreign countries. Target is a six-week program for twenty-five minority participants, the majority from Chicago schools, who work side-by-side with a scientific, engineering, or technical mentor at Fermilab. In the afternoons the students attend classes and receive assistance in the preparation of an individual or group research project, which is generally based on some aspect of the morning work.

"Saturday Morning Physics" introduces selected high-school students to topics in modern physics. Three times each school year, a series of ten lectures is conducted at Fermilab. One hundred students from area high schools are selected by their schools to participate in each series. Lectures on topics such as "Accelerators and Detectors," "Special Theory of Relativity," "Leptons and Hadrons," and "Cosmology" are delivered by Fermilab physicists. The program also includes lab tours, demonstrations of equipment and instruments, and tutorial sessions led by physicists to discuss in-depth the material presented in the lectures.

Explorer Scouts provides a planned program of career interest exposure that brings eleventh and twelfth graders together with professional adults. The program assists young people define future career goals.

Guided tours introduce high-school science classes to high-energy physics research and give them an opportunity to see the extent of the facilities involved. Physics teachers receive an informational packet to use in the classroom, and their students may also visit the Quarks to Quasars exhibits described below.

Midlevel and Elementary Programs: Groups of teachers have developed instructional materials that make the Fermilab reconstructed prairie accessible to intermediate and midlevel classes. Teachers attend a credit-bearing workshop that provides familiarity with Fermilab field-study sites, pertinent background information, and student and teacher materials. After attending the workshop, teachers incorporate the activities into their curriculum and may schedule a prairie experience for their class at Fermilab.

"From Beneath the Ashes" extends the educational impact of a videotape by the same name that's part of "The New Explorers" public-television series. Students learn about the prairie from an interdisciplinary approach. "Particles and Prairies" gives students a unique opportunity to be scientists by doing research that provides meaningful data for researchers and by collaborating with students from other schools in ongoing research. Teachers may purchase a kit of curriculum-related materials. The instructional materials include an optional award-winning videodisc with thirty-seven segments and ten slide collections covering four aspects of the Fermilab prairie: its history, restoration, ecology, and its use as a research site. A barcode guide and software with activities and databases of plants and birds comes with the videodisc.

Several programs introduce students to the world of particle physics. Instructional materials enable students to discover relationships for themselves through activity-based investigation. While the activities are simple, they represent ways that particle physicists gather direct evidence and think about the unseen world of subatomic particles. The purpose of these materials, however, is not to instill directly the language and concepts of particle physics—some of this may happen—but to provide an experience of science to broaden and enrich attitudes and develop an appreciation for physics and the world of national laboratories. Credit-bearing workshops are held to familiarize teachers with the materials.

"Beauty and Charm at Fermilab" emphasizes simple hands-on experiments that portray concepts such as "How Small Is Small" and "How to Measure What We Cannot See." The instructional kit includes materials for classroom experiments, a manual outlining the curriculum, and audiovisual materials to supplement the curriculum. After completion of the classroom unit, the teachers may accompany their students to visit Fermilab working areas and the Lederman Science Center and meet with a Fermilab physicist.

The "Quarks to Quasars" collection includes more than twenty hands-on demonstration experiments to develop an understanding of the operations and experiments that take place in the Fermilab accelerator and detector halls. The collection of experiments allows students to explore Fermilab from four perspectives: accelerators, detectors, collisions and scattering experiments, and the structure of matter.

In "Hands-on Science," teachers become familiar with basic principles used in Fermilab research through demonstration experiments of the Lederman Science Center and interactive classroom activities. The classroom activities use a collection of traveling demonstration experiments available on loan to schools. Teachers are able to offer their students a depth of insight and involvement with science that cannot be matched in most regular classroom programs.

Teacher Preparation and Enhancement

Structured programs are offered for teachers to learn science, participate in research and internships, develop instructional materials, and experience what educational research and best practice demonstrate will build an effective classroom program and contribute to student learning.

Fermilab has offered summer research appointments to secondary teachers since 1983. Projects range from testing polymers to evaluating phototubes and developing software. A first-hand experience in the laboratory can translate into enhanced teaching strategies and new instructional materials for teachers who may never have worked in a research environment. The Fermilab Teacher Fellowship Program provides a year-long research experience. Fellows are required to develop educational materials related to their experience at Fermilab.

Institutes and workshops offer opportunities to enhance teachers' backgrounds in basic science, model successful teaching strategies, and present new instructional materials. The Topics in Modern Physics Summer Institute is designed to update high-school physics courses by improving teachers' content knowledge and augmenting the curriculum. The three-week institute includes a particle physics science immersion experience with associated background seminars on modern physics, site tours of accelerator and experimental areas, and laboratory sessions where participants try out classroom materials. Participants receive the *Topics in Modern Physics Teacher Resource Book* and other materials. During the institute, participants develop curriculum implementation and dissemination plans. Physics mini-courses consist of lectures by Fermilab physicists or physicists affiliated with Fermilab and demonstrations by master physics teachers. Teams make presentations across the country upon request. Special presentations and translated materials have been prepared for Latin American audiences. Fermilab hosts topical symposia recommended by and organized with master teachers. Topics have included fractals and conceptual physics.

One of the most effective spin-offs of Fermilab institutes are teacher-support networks. High-school physics, biology, and chemistry teachers and midlevel science and mathematics teachers meet on a monthly basis during the school year to share successful teaching strategies and instructional materials. A corps of dedicated teachers keeps the networks alive, and Fermilab supports the newsletters.

Leadership Institute Integrating Internet, Instruction and Curriculum (LInC) is a course for teacher-leaders who commit to providing in-service to other educators on how to integrate Internet resources into the curriculum. The training includes relevant topics such as identifying effective teaching strategies for using telecommunications; learning how to find and access Internet resources; and publishing documents on the Internet. Participants collect Internet curriculum materials and select existing exemplary telecomputing instructional units as they design, develop, and implement a project using Internet tools. In addition, the participants, as school/district leadership teams, develop a plan to in-service other educators.

Preservice Education Interns is a program that serves education and/ or science majors from community colleges or four-year institutions who serve as docents, explainers, or teacher assistants in programs offered through the Fermilab Education Office. These programs may include Particles and Prairies, Quarks to Quasars, and Beauty and Charm. Interns may earn college credit for their efforts by enrolling in approved courses from a number of area institutions.

Systemic Reform and Resource Center

Services and resource materials are available to educators, schools, and school districts seeking assistance in systemic reform efforts to develop and improve their science programs and resource collections.

In the Teacher Resource Center, educators have access to curriculum materials, books, multimedia, educational supply catalogs, periodicals, and newsletters. The collection also includes reports on science and mathematics education, standards, assessment, equity, and other topics. Visitors have access to and can receive assistance with electronic bulletin boards and Internet resources. TRC services include outreach resource and Internet awareness workshops, consultation assistance, a periodical holding list, bibliographies, and telephone reference. A U.S. Department of Education Eisenhower National Clearinghouse Demonstration Site for the North Central Region is located in the TRC.

A variety of classroom materials has been developed in conjunction with or to enhance Fermilab education programs. Videotapes, posters, and instructional materials are available at nominal costs. Instructional materials relate to the following programs: "Beauty and Charm," "From Beneath the Ashes," "Particles and Prairies," and "Topics in Modern Physics."

A quarterly newsletter, *sciencelines*, is provided free of charge to educators: *sciencelines* includes articles about Fermilab, Fermilab scientists and outside resources, media reviews, student activity sheets, workshop and program information, and lists of reasonably priced or free materials available to teachers. Fermilab has developed *Resources for the Science Classroom*, a database listing over 150 opportunities for educators to enhance the teaching of science. The database, which includes federal, state, local, not-for-profit and corporate programs, tours, materials, and people resources in northeastern Illinois, is available as a printed directory at no charge.

The Fermilab Education Office plays a coordinating role in the "Technology Forum" for the area school districts by providing vision, leadership, and structure; working with local/regional network service providers and users to create an integrated plan based on school needs and available resources; facilitating preparation of collaborative grant proposals; serving as a focal point and broker of ideas; and collaborating on pilot classroom and curriculum projects.

Fermilab has established partnerships with two area schools. The Lab collaborates with a school district to provide in-service opportunities for teachers and science experiences for students, particularly those underrepresented in science, engineering, and technology.

Public Awareness and Scientific Literacy

Programs in this category offer opportunities for families and the public to enhance general interest in and knowledge of science and for staff to assist public libraries and systems in the interest of improving the scientific literacy of their patrons.

Fermilab offers Science Adventure classes for children and families during the summer months of June, July, and August. Experienced teachers offer classes that cover a variety of science and mathematics topics.

Fermilab engineers have developed a "Cryogenic Show" of liquid nitrogen demonstrations for teachers and students of all ages. Presentations are given at schools, for youth groups, and in conjunction with other science activities.

In addition to these programs offered by the laboratory, Fermilab and Friends of Fermilab have conducted design workshops for three of Dr. Lederman's special initiatives. The Illinois Mathematics and Science Academy, founded in August 1986, is a three-year, public, residential high school for talented and gifted students from throughout the state of Illinois. The Teachers Academy for Mathematics and Science, founded in September 1990, is an institution dedicated to reforming mathematics and science teaching in Chicago public schools. The American Renaissance in Science Education is a new initiative to develop a three-year inverted high-school science sequence with a ninth-grade course that is largely conceptual physics, a tenth-grade course that is largely chemistry, and an eleventh-grade course that is largely biology.

Conclusion

In 1983 it was not at all clear that a national research facility was an appropriate partner in major science-education reform initiatives. Teachers and students have given us the answer: "Yes!" Precollege education programs work at Fermilab because it is not business as usual. Teachers come to the world-class high-energy physics research laboratory for a unique opportunity to witness science conducted at the frontiers of human understanding and to learn from leading research scientists. Students have an experience in science that broadens and enriches their attitudes and develops their appreciation for science. Students see, perhaps for the first time, what the world of science is really like, and they like what they see.

From Fermilab's experience it is also clear that an institution like Fermilab is an appropriate partner only when the laboratory staff is willing to put communities and schools in a leadership position: listening to their needs before looking to see what resources may assist in meeting those needs, inviting teachers to develop solutions rather than offering prepackaged programs. Whether it is designing a four-week summer institute, writing an instructional unit, establishing a collection of science materials, or developing an informal science program, teachers working together with scientists have always been the key to success. Fermilab cannot make change, but Fermilab can be an important catalyst supporting and nurturing change efforts of our education community.

References

Bush, G. *America 2000: An education strategy.* Washington, DC: U.S. Department of Education.

Educating America: State strategies for achieving the national education goals. (1991). Washington, DC: National Governors' Association.

Elam, S. M., Rose, L. C. & Gallup, A. M. (1991). "The twenty-third Gallup poll of the public's attitudes toward the public schools," *Phi Delta Kappan, 73,* (1), pp. 41–56.

The high stakes of high school science (1991). Andover, MA: The National Center for Improving Science Education, The Network, Inc.

Jones, L. R., Mullis, I. V. S., Raizen, S. A., Weiss, I. R., & Weston, E. A. (March 1992). *The 1990 Science Report Card: NAEP's Assessment of Fourth, Eighth, and Twelfth Graders.* Washington, DC: National Center for Education Statistics.

Loucks-Horsley, S., Kapitan, R., Carlson, M. D., Kuerbis, P. J., Clark, R. C., Melle, G. M., Sachse, T. P. & Walton, E. (1990). *Elementary school science for the 90's.* The National Center for Improving Science Education, The Network, Inc.

Senge, Peter M. (1990). *The fifth discipline: The art and practice of the learning organizations.* New York: Doubleday.

Chapter 21

"One Foot in the Library and One Foot in the Street"

Strategies for Investing in University-Community Collaboration

Jane Quinn
Program Director, DeWitt Wallace-Reader's Digest Fund

Introduction

Around the turn of the twentieth century, Jane Addams advised her colleagues that in order to be effective as social workers they should keep "one foot in the library and one foot in the street." This notion of the interdependence of theory and practice is as relevant today as it was one hundred years ago.

As America begins the countdown toward the twenty-first century, we face stark reminders of the same conditions that confronted Addams and the other leaders of the Progressive Era—rising numbers of children and families living in poverty; rising numbers of immigrants, both legal and illegal, coming into the nation's cities; and rising demands on the community's social institutions that are designed to support, nurture, serve, and protect children and families. The task of strengthening these institutions is enormous, and its success depends on focused application of the best available knowledge. It is not a task for the "library" or the "street" acting alone. What can be and is being done to bring the two together?

For the DeWitt Wallace-Reader's Digest Fund (the Fund), one of the nation's largest private grantmaking foundations, universities and community institutions are key partners in furthering the Fund's mission—to foster fundamental improvement in the quality of educational and career-development opportunities for all school-age youth, and to increase access to these improved services for young people in low-income communities. This chapter will describe the portion of the Fund's grantmaking that involves university-community collaboration, emphasizing the rationale for supporting these partnerships and the centrality of such grantmaking to the accomplishment of the Fund's mission.

The Fund's Grantmaking Priorities and Approach

In 1987, following the deaths of DeWitt Wallace and his wife, Lila Acheson Wallace, the Fund began a transformation from a small family foundation to a major national grantmaker. With approximately a billion dollars in assets and annual grant payments of $40 to $50 million, the Fund today ranks number nineteen in size among the nation's largest private foundations. Since 1990, the Fund has invested more than $300 million in programs designed to benefit American youth. This grantmaking is organized into three major categories:

- improving services to children and youth in elementary and secondary schools;
- improving services to children and youth in community-based organizations;
- improving services to children and youth through school-community collaboration.

Although the Fund's mission is related to youth, nearly half of its grants have focused on adults—teachers, school counselors, youth workers, and parents. The Fund firmly believes that investing in the adults who work with young people on a daily basis is one of the best ways to improve services. This belief is so central to the Fund's work that it represents one of seven of the Fund's grantmaking principles. These principles are the underlying beliefs, values, and philosophy that guide the translation of the Fund's mission into specific grantmaking across its program areas.

1. Education and career development are lifelong processes that are most effective when they involve active engagement in meaningful pursuits and build on the learner's strengths and current knowledge.
2. Education and career development occur in a wide range of settings, including schools, families, community institutions, and the workplace.
3. Career development is a component of the education process that connects school to work and prepares young people for productive adulthood.
4. Youth are best served when programs to educate and guide them are coordinated and complementary.
5. Increasing young people's access to high-quality services requires community institutions to be more inclusive in their outreach and be more responsive to the diverse needs of today's youth.

6. Improving the quality of services for young people requires investments in the adults who work with and on behalf of youth in schools and community organizations.

7. Fundamental improvement in services for youth requires work on several levels of a problem at the same time, combining investments in direct service with complementary efforts to educate leaders in both the public and private sectors.

In crafting these principles, the Fund's staff and board drew on the best available knowledge from both research and practice. And in applying these principles, the Fund seeks to make choices that are consistent with this stated philosophy.

The Fund's programmatic approach, then, is to improve services for young people, using an institutional framework of schools, community-based organizations, and school-community collaboration. For maximum impact, its grantmaking approach is to award large multi-year grants to selected organizations with national or substantial regional reach. Often this grantmaking is organized around Fund-initiated projects—for example, Library Power, a $40 million effort involving twenty communities across the country to restore and revitalize public elementary and middle schools libraries. In other instances, the Fund will award a cluster of grants for programs that have similar goals but diverse activities and delivery systems. An example is comprehensive school restructuring and reform, which represents $30 million in grants organized around four specific strategies for improving K–12 public education. In contrast to Library Power, in which the grants were made to local education funds to support similar work at each site (physical refurbishing of school libraries, collections development and staff development), the Fund's school reform work currently supports fifteen different grantees ranging from the National Board for Professional Teaching Standards to the Community Training and Assistance Center.

University-Community Connections
and the Fund's Grantmaking

Of the Fund's 230 current grants, fifty-six are to colleges and universities. These grants, totaling over $46 million, represent investments in teacher recruitment and preparation (pre-service education), teacher development (in-service education), professional development of school counselors (pre- and in-service), comprehensive school restructuring and reform, staff development of youth workers and child-care professionals, career exploration and preparation, school-to-college transition, school/family partnership, extended-service schools, and interprofessional preparation and development (of teachers, social workers, and others). Ten additional grants have been awarded to university-affiliated not-for-profit organizations (such as the Coalition of Essential Schools at Brown University and the School-Age Child Care Project at the Wellesley College Center for Research on Women). The following description, organized around the Fund's current grantmaking framework, presents a sample of these grants and a flavor of the whole.

Program Area I: Improving Services to Children and Youth in Elementary and Secondary Schools

Over the past six years, the Fund allocated more than half—approximately 57% (or $180 million of the total $318 million)—of its grant dollars to school-based and school-related work, much of it involving universities in partnerships with public schools.

Teacher Recruitment and Preparation

Since 1989, the Fund has awarded over $40 million in grants to forty-five colleges and universities nationwide through its "Pathways to Teaching Careers Program." The goal of this program is to increase the number of highly qualified teachers, particularly minorities, working in America's public schools. The program provides scholarships and other support services to individuals interested in public school teaching careers, and it also invests in institutions that support teaching as a profession. This latter investment includes providing resources to colleges and universities to restructure and update course offerings to meet the needs of today's teachers, as well as supporting organizations that promote the teaching profession. Through the Pathways to Teaching Careers Program, the Fund directly supports the education of over 2,000 adults who are preparing to become public school teachers. These adults are drawn from specific target groups: noncertified teachers and paraprofessionals working in the public schools that partner with Pathways university grantees; and second-career populations, including returned Peace Corps volunteers. In an effort to work further up "the pipeline," other components of the Pathways to Teaching Careers Program encourage liberal-arts majors in undergraduate schools to consider teaching, and introduce middle and high-school students to basic concepts about career development and to teaching as a possible career choice. A team of evaluators from the Urban Institute and the Educational Testing Service is assessing the impact of this multi-year effort that is designed to address the serious demographic mismatch between the composition of the student body and the teaching force in most of America's urban communities. (Approximately 13% of all current teachers are persons of color, while nearly one-third of their students are of color.)

Another well-documented mismatch is being addressed through a Fund grant to John Goodlad and his colleagues at the Institute for Educational Inquiry (of the University of Washington)—the skills mismatch between those taught in most schools of education and what's actually needed in today's public school classrooms. Based on Goodlad's earlier research (Goodlad, 1990), his Fund-supported work is providing Incentive Awards in Teacher Education, so selected schools and colleges of education can replace their existing teacher preparation programs with fundamentally redesigned ones. The goal of the project is to create a core group of teacher preparation programs that can serve as models for effective teacher education in the United States. Just as doctors are trained in teaching hospitals, Goodlad argues for the establishment of teacher-preparation programs that emphasize the clinical training of teachers in partnership with schools. In 1991 Goodlad formed the National Network for Educational Renewal, a consortium of twenty-three schools and colleges of education that have committed themselves to his teacher preparation principles.

Teacher Development

Because so many of today's teachers were prepared for yesterday's classrooms and schools, the Fund has invested over $25 million since 1990 in programs designed to upgrade the skills and knowledge of working teachers. One of these first grants went to the Yale-New Haven Teachers Institute, a nationally recognized partnership between an elite university and its neighboring public schools. The Fund provided a challenge grant to help the Institute build an endowment that would ensure its ongoing interaction with the New Haven school system. Through the Institute, Yale faculty members and schoolteachers work together in collegial relationships. Each participating public school teacher becomes an Institute fellow and prepares a curriculum unit to be taught during the following academic year. In the spirit of partnership, teachers have primary responsibility for identifying the subjects the Institute addresses. Program evaluations have shown that the Institute experience has increased teachers' preparation in their disciplines, raised their morale, heightened their expectations for their students, encouraged them to remain in teaching in New Haven, and has, in turn, enhanced student performance.

A grant to the Bread Loaf School of English at Middlebury College underwrites the work of the Bread Loaf Rural Teacher Network, which provides intensive summer institutes and year-round follow-up for rural teachers of English from six target states. One of the program's most popular services is BreadNet, an electronic mail network that allows participating teachers (many of whom work in remote locations) to share best practices with one another and with Bread Loaf staff.

The Fund has been a key supporter of the National Writing Project, an excellent example of university-community collaboration. As the nation's largest teacher development network, the project now comprises over 150 sites across the country. Most sites are based on college campuses and are largely self-sufficient. Some funding is provided by the national organization and by host campuses, but the bulk of support comes from local funders and from contracts with local school districts to supply teacher development services. The basic NWP model includes a four- or five-week invitational summer institute that involves teachers in writing, examining their own writing processes, and assessing the implications for their students. Upon returning to their classrooms, these teachers are able to use writing across the curriculum and to engage their students in both active and reflective writing experiences. The Fund's current grant will enable the National Writing Project to work intensively with eighteen of its affiliated sites to improve the quality and quantity of services to teachers of low-income children.

The Fund's newest teacher development work is an initiative called "Students at the Center." The initiative is designed to increase the capacity of urban teachers in selected sites to teach in student-centered ways that promote problem solving, higher-order thinking, and critical analysis among their students. The development work is being carried out by consortia of local teacher development organizations in partnership with local public-school systems. Many of these teacher development organizations are university-based. To measure the effectiveness of the program, the Fund has selected a team of researchers from Stanford University to evaluate the four-and-one-half-year program.

Professional Development of School Counselors
In 1991, the Fund commissioned a national study on the state of school guidance and counseling services in America. This study, which was sub-

sequently published by the College Board, called for fundamental changes in the school guidance and counseling field (Hart and Jacobi, 1992). These changes include how counselors are trained in universities, what they do in their jobs, and how they define their roles in relation to other members of the school and local community. The Fund then developed a grantmaking program to implement these recommendations, which are consistent with (and draw on) the work of other national commissions.

The Fund's initial grant to upgrade the skills of school guidance counselors supported the College Board's Equity 2000 program. Launched in 1991, the program is designed to train math teachers and school guidance counselors to encourage poor and/or minority students to take academic subjects that will prepare them to enter and succeed in college. In its initial five-year demonstration phase, the project worked as a partnership between the College Board, fourteen schools districts in six sites, and selected universities in those sites. The participating universities offered inservice training to teachers and counselors and educational enrichment opportunities (such as Saturday Academies, mentors, and campus orientation visits) for middle and high-school students. The program reached more than 500,000 public-school students in approximately 700 schools during its pilot phase, and is now expanding to new sites. The Fund has contributed approximately $9 million to Equity 2000 since 1991.

While Equity 2000 focuses on helping students prepare for college, a program spearheaded by Kansas State University prepares counselors to help students who do not plan to attend four-year colleges. Research has shown that most counselors spend little time with this group of students—the group aptly named "the forgotten half" (William T. Grant Commission, 1988). The Fund's $3.3 million grant is allowing KSU, together with the American School Counselor Association and the American College Testing Program, to work with counselors in thirteen states. These counselors are trained to gather and provide information to students about accredited postsecondary vocational-technical education programs. Known as "Counseling for High Skills," this program is being evaluated by a team of researchers from MPR Associates in Berkeley, California.

The Fund's most recent grant in this program area is to the American Association for Higher Education to plan an initiative that will support selected universities in their efforts to produce fundamental change in the professional preparation of school guidance counselors who serve students in poor urban and rural communities. Over the next three or four years, the Fund expects to make grants to up to six universities that can serve as models for upgrading counselor preparation programs around the following key components:

- placing greater emphasis on academic and career counseling and less on mental-health counseling;
- training counselors to focus more on student potential and less on perceived deficits;
- emphasizing skills for reaching and serving children most in need of academic and career counseling (i.e., children in low-income rural and urban communities);
- training counselors to serve as coordinators of services rather than as primary or sole providers.

Comprehensive School Restructuring and Reform

The Fund supports a select group of organizations that are leading national efforts to reform and restructure schools to make teaching and learning more effective. The major thrust of these activities is to improve schools so that teaching and learning focus on problem solving, critical analysis, and higher-order thinking skills. Many universities are involved in this difficult and important work, and the Fund supports several university-based efforts, including the Coalition of Essential Schools, based at Brown University, and the National Center for Restructuring Education, Schools, and Teaching, based at Columbia University's Teachers College.

The Coalition of Essential Schools is a national network of high schools committed to nine common principles developed by Professor Theodore Sizer. The network has grown substantially over the past several years and now includes over 700 high schools that are working to restructure their instructional programs for students. The Fund's support has helped the Coalition establish regional centers that provide direct assistance to local schools. In addition, Fund support has underwritten portions of the Coalition's *School Change Study*, which is developing and disseminating research-based materials about specific school improvement strategies, based on case studies of reform efforts in specific Coalition high schools.

The National Center for Restructuring Education, Schools, and Teaching at Teachers College, Columbia University, seeks to increase the ability of people working in schools to implement and sustain educational improvements. Led by Linda Darling-Hammond and Ann Lieberman, the Center was established in 1990 with Fund support. Since that time, it has produced more than twenty well-regarded publications on school reform;

hosted several national conferences involving thousands of educators; and established solid working relationships with fifty-seven affiliate organizations representing schoolteachers and administrators, teacher-trainers, researchers, policymakers, parents, and community organizations from around the country.

The grants described in this program area involve universities in a variety of broad, mission-consistent activities: building and applying knowledge; preparing and developing professionals; generating and allocating resources. While some universities ignore or actively shun their public-school neighbors, those cited here as well as in other chapters of this volume are demonstrating the value of building solid working relationships with their counterparts at the elementary and secondary levels—relationships that provide real-world settings for the development, testing, and replication of university-generated ideas.

Program Area II: Improving Services to Children and Youth in Community-Based Organizations

American youth spend large amounts of time outside of school, given the relatively short school day (six to seven hours, on average) and school year (180 days) in this country (Carnegie Council on Adolescent Development, 1992). An increasing number of universities have begun to recognize the value of the nonschool hours in promoting positive youth development and the role of community-based organizations in helping young people to structure that time and use it productively. This work brings some of these universities into the Fund's second overall program area—Improving Services to Children and Youth in Community-Based Organizations. Since 1990, about 25% of the Fund's total grantmaking was devoted to this area, which includes youth-serving organizations (such as Boys and Girls Clubs, Scouts, 4-H, and the YMCA), school-age child care, and informal education that takes place in science centers and youth museums.

Staff Development in Youth-Serving Organizations

The Fund's single largest program in this area is its support of professional development of youth workers, which accounted for $44 million during this six-year period. These investments were designed to address the well-documented gaps in the preparation of youth workers (Carnegie Council on Adolescent Development, 1991). Grants have underwritten a wide variety of efforts, including training to strengthen youth workers' skills, initiatives to recruit minority staff, and establishment of consensus within the field about the competencies needed by all youth workers. Universities were involved as partners in several of these grants. For example, through the Fund's grant to the National 4-H Council and its myriad connections to the land-grant college system, the University of Kentucky developed program materials on diversity and the University of Arizona developed a curriculum to improve academic preparation of county Extension agents who work with youth. Springfield College joined with the YMCA of the USA to strengthen its staff development training for youthworkers. And Jewish Community Centers of North America worked with the Mandel Center for Nonprofit Management (of Case Western Reserve University) to evaluate its youth development training programs. In addition, the Chapin Hall Center for Children at the University of Chicago recently completed a strategic analysis for the Fund of its overall grantmaking in this area and is now working with the Fund to disseminate the findings of that analysis, which revealed that the Fund's leadership and financial investment in the recruitment and development of youth workers has made a significant impact in a very short period of time (Ogletree et al., 1995).

School-Age Child Care

In its support of school-age child-care services, the Fund is working in a partnership with the School-Age Child Care Project at the Wellesley College Center for Research on Women. For the past fifteen years, the SACC project has produced the most significant and consistent research on the needs of America's youth for high-quality care during the nonschool hours—needs that include safety, structure, satisfying peer and adult relationships, and constructive, enriching activities (Seligson and Fink, 1989). The Fund's school-age child-care initiative, known as MOST (Making the Most of Out-of-School Time), used that research to identify selected communities that were willing to develop comprehensive systems for school-age care. Grants to three communities (Boston, Chicago, and Seattle) are underwriting the work of consortia of school-age child-care providers, schools, and resource and referral agencies that are working to upgrade the quality and quantity of before- and after-school services for young people ages five through fourteen. In addition, through partnerships with local two- and four-year institutions of higher education, these consortia will improve the skills of school-age child-care providers through training and professional development.

These partnerships stand as exemplars of productive university-community connections but they represent exceptions rather than the rule and, as such, they point to an area of significant untapped potential. The Fund, in its efforts to help practice catch up with theory, hopes to foster additional partnerships between universities and community-based organizations in its future grantmaking.

Program Area III: Improving Services to Children and Youth through School-Community Collaboration

The Fund invested about 18% of its grantmaking resources (approximately $58 million) over the past six years in a variety of programs that deliberately join schools and community institutions. These programs focus on career exploration and preparation, school-to-college transition, parental involvement in children's education, extended-service schools, and interprofessional preparation and development. Universities are involved in this work in several ways, from direct sponsors to evaluators.

Career Exploration and Preparation

Although most of the Fund's grantees in this program area are community-based organizations, many of these groups are working with university-based researchers as program evaluators. For example, faculty from Brandeis University's Center for Human Resources are evaluating several Fund-supported programs, including the Walks of Life career-preparation program developed by the Greater New York Hospital Foundation. Another Fund grantee, YouthBuild, worked with an evaluation team from MIT and Harvard University to assess its program's effectiveness.

School-to-College Transition

For reasons that include social conscience and enlightened self-interest, many universities are concerned about the well-documented disparities in college-going rates between minority and majority youth and between lower-income and higher-income youth. The Fund supports a variety of programs designed to increase the quality and quantity of services that promote high school completion and college-going among minority and economically disadvantaged youth. Several of these programs are sponsored by universities.

The Puente Project of the University of California seeks to promote college attendance among a population that is at very high risk of dropping out of high school—Mexican American and Latino students. The project uses a combination of approaches—mentoring, academic preparation, counseling, and field trips to colleges and workplaces—to encourage college-going among this population. Drawing on the resources of Mexican American and Latino communities located throughout California, the program will involve 2,000 high school students and their families over four years. An additional 6,000 students will be involved through after-school Puente clubs. The Fund's four-year $2 million grant is allowing the University to develop, refine, and evaluate this research-based program prototype. If the program is successful, it will provide a model for other programs seeking to involve communities in increasing the college enrollment rate of minority youth.

In New York City, LaGuardia Community College and Hunter College have teamed up with the Middle College High School Network—a group of fourteen high schools for at-risk students located on community college campuses throughout the United States—to strengthen the academic program at these high schools and to bolster the links between the high schools and the community colleges. Fund support underwrote a planning grant and is now underwriting the implementation phase of this national program that is incorporating the methods and materials of the American Social History Project developed by faculty at Hunter College.

School/Family Partnership

Despite strong research evidence that parental involvement can enhance students' achievement in school, many schools do an extremely poor job of involving parents in meaningful ways, and some schools actively discourage such involvement (Fruchter et al., 1992). Since 1993, the Fund has awarded grants to nine national and regional organizations that are seeking to develop innovative ways to engage low-income parents in supporting, monitoring, and advocating for their own children's education. One such grant, to Boston's Suffolk University, trains facilitators from community-based programs to conduct workshops with low-income parents. Called "The Right Question Project," this effort enables parents (many of whom have only recently moved to the United States from other countries) to learn about their children's education and to communicate effectively with teachers and school administrators. The results of this intervention are being documented and assessed by a third-party evaluator as part of the Fund's grant.

Extended-Service Schools

These schools are partnerships between public schools and nonprofit organizations or universities that offer children and their families education, career development, recreation, and human services at school sites, both during and beyond the regular school day. The Fund made its first grant in this relatively new program area (approved by the Fund's board of directors in late 1994) to the University of Pennsylvania to replicate and adapt the West Philadelphia Improvement Corps, an extended-service school program model, in three other locations around the country. The WEPIC model, which operates in twelve Philadelphia public schools, is a year-round program that offers educational, recreational, cultural, and community service activities to young people and their families both during the regular school day and during the nonschool hours. The three adaptation sites selected by the University of Pennsylvania team are: Miami University of Ohio with the Cincinnati Public Schools; the University of Kentucky with the Lexington Public Schools; and the University of Alabama with the Birmingham Public Schools. The Fund's three-year $1 million grant provides direct financial support to each of the replication sites as well as support for national technical assistance and information dissemination. For example, the University of Pennsylvania hosts visits to its partner schools from other universities, coordinates an annual national conference on university–public schools partnerships, and maintains an active on-line database on university-community collaboration.

Interprofessional Preparation and Development

Since 1990, the Fund has invested nearly $6 million in grants to prepare teachers, social workers, and other youth-serving professionals to work as effective collaborators on behalf of children and families in public school settings.

A 1992 grant to Fordham University established the National Center for Social Work and Education Collaboration, which is working with nine partner universities around the country in a targeted effort to change the way teachers and social workers are educated at the pre-service level. Two major emphases of this four-year experiment are to involve these professional schools in meaningful relationships with area public school systems and in effective collaborative relationships with one another. For many of these professionals, the interaction afforded by this project has helped teachers and social workers learn firsthand about how members of the other discipline are prepared to work with children and their families as well as about how each discipline's expertise can complement the other's.

A second grant in this program area went to the American Association of Colleges for Teacher Education, which worked with four of its member universities to develop and refine models of professional preparation that involve teachers in collaborative working relationships with health care and social service providers in public school settings. AACTE has promoted these models among its network of member colleges through publications and conferences.

Conclusion

Outreach universities have been important partners with the DeWitt Wallace-Reader's Digest Fund in its first seven years as a national grantmaker. These universities have generated and applied knowledge about how to improve services for young people and their families, often against tremendous odds. While the most obvious of these odds are the difficult circumstances in which many American children and families live, there are barriers internal to universities that must be overcome as well.

The Fund has had an opportunity to witness the struggle in many universities as they have worked to redefine incentives and rewards for faculty and to redefine their relationships with surrounding communities and with other community institutions. We've observed the culture clash that can occur as public schools try to accommodate themselves to universities' calendars or as community-based organizations try to convey their sense of urgency about youth problems to their university partners. From our vantage point, these struggles have paid off, as these universities have learned—and modeled for others—that the "street" outside the university is very much a two-way thoroughfare, a path on which universities both give and receive.

References

Carnegie Council on Adolescent Development. (1991). *Report on the consultation on professional development of youth workers.* New York: Carnegie Corporation of New York.
———. (1992). *A matter of time: Risk and opportunity in the nonschool hours.* New York: Carnegie Corporation of New York.
Fruchter, N., Galletta, A., & White, J. L. *New directions in parent involvement.* (1992). Washington, DC: Academy for Educational Development.
Goodlad, J. I. (1990). *Teachers for our nation's schools.* San Francisco: Jossey-Bass Publishers.
Hart, P. and Jacobi, M. (1992). *From gatekeeper to advocate: Transforming the role of the school counselor.* New York: The College Board.
Ogletree, R., Garg, S., Robb, S., & Brown, P. (1995). *Strategic analysis of the DeWitt Wallace-Reader's Digest Fund's grantmaking in support of the recruitment and development of youth workers.* Chicago: Chapin Hall Center for Children.

Seligson, M. & Fink, D. (1989). *No time to waste: An action agenda for school-age child care.* Wellesley, MA: School-Age Child Care Project, Wellesley College Center for Research on Women.

William T. Grant Commission on Work, Family and Citizenship. (1988). *The forgotten half: Pathways to success for America's youth and young families.* New York: William T. Grant Foundation.

Chapter 22
Partnership in Action
The Governor's Clergy Summit in the City of Detroit

John Engler and Connie Binsfeld
State of Michigan

"Unless the Lord builds the house, its builders labor in vain." That famous line from Psalm 128 was one of the key themes in the 1995 State of the State address to the people of Michigan.

The underlying premise of the administration's message was simple. A large state government such as Michigan's has tremendous fiscal and human resources. But big government programs, by themselves, cannot solve all or even most of today's social problems. They certainly have not—and cannot—solve the majority of social problems encountered in a city like Detroit. But that should not be cause for despair. There are creative ways to deal more effectively with society's many intransigent problems. One way is for the public sector to tap into perhaps the richest vein of knowledge, service, and trust in our cities—our religious institutions.

Religious leaders and Good Samaritans in neighborhood churches, synagogues, and mosques have always been at the forefront of efforts to improve the human condition. In Detroit alone, there are some 1,600 congregations. The people in these congregations know things that bureaucrats, social workers, and other public servants do not. Religious leaders and churchgoers can identify and anticipate many of the problems that arise in their communities: the unmarried teen who has become pregnant, the toddler that is not getting vaccinations in a timely manner, the student who is at risk of dropping out of school, the young man who is tempted to join a gang, the worker who has been laid off, and the shut-in who is not receiving proper care. To religious leaders and churchgoers, these are not mere statistics in a database, but real people in need of help.

Besides churches, there is another institution that has played an historically important role in serving the community, albeit more indirectly. Michigan's fifteen public colleges and universities, like religious institutions, are concentrations of knowledge and service. Not only have our institutions of higher education taken the lead in admitting young people from disadvantaged backgrounds; they have frequently reached a helping hand out to the broken communities of which they are a part. Urban campuses are thus uniquely positioned to establish what might be called "university enterprise zones,"[1] in which they identify problems, develop strategies to fix what's broken, and equip people to renew and rebuild their communities from within.

All three sectors—religious, academic, government—bring tremendous resources to our communities in need. Working together in partnership, these centers of faith, learning, and public authority can achieve much more than any one sector can alone.

The need for partnership was the rationale behind the Governor's Clergy Summit, convened on October 17, 1995. It was no accident that the summit was held on the campus of one of Michigan's premier state institutions of higher education, Wayne State University, in the heart of Detroit. The purpose of the summit was to bring together religious leaders, academics, and public servants, as they represent three of the most powerful, service-oriented institutions in our society.

Interestingly, the very word "clergy" suggests the logic for holding such a summit on a university campus. "Clergy" is derived from the Latin *clericus*, which in the Middle Ages referred to both the educated and religious classes of society. So the 1995 Clergy Summit continued a long, if not entirely unbroken, tradition in the West.

Does such a summit, which encourages religious institutions to form partnerships with government, undermine the principle of church-state separation? Not at all. Cooperation between government entities and the social, educational, and medical services of faith-based organizations does not violate the First Amendment. The original intent of America's founders was to bar the establishment by the federal government of a state-approved religion; it was not to bar religion from the operations of the state.

Pulitzer Prize–winning columnist William Raspberry has elaborated on this point. It is a mistake, he believes, to interpret the First Amendment to mean that government should "reduce the influence of faith in the ordinary affairs of society. Indeed, the evidence points the other way." Our society simply cannot afford to have government get in the way of faith-based programs. "America," he writes, "has some devastatingly difficult problems, and the eradication of faith isn't making them better." (Raspberry, 1994)

Unfortunately, debate encourages procrastination, and procrastination remains one of our biggest enemies. There are elderly citizens who need our help and young people we cannot let slip through the cracks. We are reminded of an anecdote about the Devil, who was concerned that the number of souls coming down into hell seemed to be falling off. So he called a meeting with three of his most wicked lieutenants and asked for their advice. One said he had been busy trying to convince people that there was no heaven, but without much success. The second said he had been busy trying to convince people that there was no hell, again without much success. The third said, "Look, I know how to fill this place from wall to wall. Don't waste your time telling people there's no heaven or hell; tell them there's no hurry!"

Given the gravity of the problems we face, our society cannot afford to procrastinate. Children may be only 30% of our population, but they are 100% of our future. An entire generation is growing up without the possibility of achieving, much less dreaming, the American dream. With a determination to act decisively, however, we can do much good, and we can do it in a hurry. Many of our cabinet members attended the Clergy Summit, and they apprised the audience of the specific resources that state government could mobilize immediately—in transportation and vaccination, in health care and child care, in jobs and job training. We want to bring these state resources to our most desperate neighborhoods in a spirit of partnership, and work with the talent and leadership that fills our congregations.

And what leadership was present! We were heartened to look out at the audience and see so many examples of personal courage and commitment to the city of Detroit. Day after day, these men and women give all of their heart. There was Reverend Perkins and his Greater Christ American Baptist Church on Iroquois, doing so much for young people on the East Side. There was Reverend Spann and the Church of the Messiah on East Grand Boulevard, helping to develop high-quality, affordable housing. There was Reverend Adams of Hartford Avenue Baptist at Seven Mile and the Lodge, strengthening the economic and business base of the city. There was Reverend Cross from Rosedale Park Independent Baptist Church, situated on Schoolcraft and Evergreen, also ministering to young people. There was Reverend Edwards of Joy of Jesus in Ravendale, providing much-needed services in child care, parenting skills, and entrepreneurship.

We were also impressed by the cross section of denominations represented at the Clergy Summit. There were Catholic, Protestant, Muslim, and Jewish religious leaders—all in the same room—because they know that a house divided cannot stand. And we know that faith will provide a firm foundation for Detroit's renaissance. As King David said three thousand years ago, "The things which are impossible with men are possible with God."

We realize that there are those who are skeptical of a partnership between state government in Lansing and the city of Detroit. But our shared responsibility does far more to unite us than any differences do to divide us. Too many people want to look back and talk about yesterday. We want to look forward and talk about tomorrow.

There's an old maxim in politics: Don't let the best be the enemy of the good. We cannot wait for that perfect day when the state and the city see eye-to-eye on every issue. There are men, women, and children in Detroit who are hurting and desperately in need of help. We said it was time to roll up our sleeves and work in partnership—the clergy, academics, and the state, side by side—because together we can help the needy much better than if we go it alone.

There are numerous concrete ways in which we can unite our talents and work in partnership. After all, this partnership will not survive, much less thrive, on a few platitudes and vague promises, but on concrete action and results. To get to the point where we can see the fruit of our efforts, we need first to make sure that we know the scope of the city's problems and exactly where they occur.

This is where Michigan universities can play a key role. The University of Michigan, Michigan State University, Wayne State University, and others can add significantly to our knowledge base. For example, we know that children make up about 30% of Detroit's population. To put that number in perspective, consider this: If you counted just the 300,000 children of Detroit—if you removed every adult in the city and left the children behind—Detroit would still be the largest city in the state, by far.

Perhaps more importantly, we know that almost half the city's children, a little over 46%, are living in poverty. If the poor children of Detroit constituted a Michigan city by themselves, that city would be the fourth largest in the state—nearly tied with the city of Flint in size. These children are the first and foremost reason we convened the Clergy Summit. They need not just intervention; they need faith-based intervention. They need not just a home; they need a mom and a dad at home.

Moreover, our poorest children desperately need immunization. They desperately need to be able to attend safe schools. And as they grow up and get close to graduation, they need world-class academic preparation, first-rate job training, and a way to get to the jobs that are going begging right now. In short, they need a foundation of rock and not of sand to succeed in life.

But there are obstacles, chief among them, the "index," or serious, crimes committed in the city. Index crimes are murder, rape, robbery, larceny, burglary, arson, and aggravated assault. Police reports indicate that every four minutes there is a serious crime committed in Detroit.

Often the victims of crime are society's most vulnerable citizens—the elderly. About 12%—one in every eight Detroiters—is sixty-five years of age or older, and a number of them are poor. As we know only too well, when older people are poor, they do not go to Florida. They age in place—and that often means they require services in the home, which is preferable to institutionalization.

This is just a sampling of the data we have. Our colleges and universities have an important role to play in gathering and interpreting the data. They can give us a good idea of the challenges we face, and where they are. Now, what do we do with our knowledge base? What can we do to meet the challenges head on and improve the lives of people in these disadvantaged neighborhoods?

To answer this question, it is important to know something about the State of Michigan's presence in the city of Detroit, in particular the offices of our Family Independence Agency (FIA). As most of the clergy at the summit knew, the state has more FIA offices per capita in Detroit than any other place in the state. FIA sends more than $3 billion to Wayne County each year, and the bulk of that to Detroit, so Lansing has a presence—but a limited presence when compared to religious institutions in the city.

Examine a map showing the location of Detroit's churches, and you will understand why the Governor's office convened the Detroit Clergy Summit. There are some 1,600 church buildings and congregations within the city. Compare that with the handful of FIA offices. The juxtaposition of these two images is striking. It shows why the clergy summit was so important and why we have been stressing the need to form a partnership between those two sectors, and why we need to strengthen those two sectors with the knowledge infrastructure our universities provide.

Examination of the map of Detroit's churches reveals two important things. First, there are churches in every part of the city. You cannot go many blocks without encountering a church and all that it represents—

namely, the compassion, trust, and moral leadership that are needed to raise up our neediest citizens and put them on their feet. William Raspberry put it well when he said:

I am struck by a growing sense that America's major failings aren't political or economic but moral, and by the discovery that the most successful social programs are driven by moral or religious values. Show me a program that helps people change their lives, and I'll show you one with a strong spiritual element. (Raspberry, 1994)

Raspberry admirably summarizes why the state needs to be in partnership with the clergy.

The second important point about Detroit's churches is the way they cluster—on Seven Mile, on Gratiot, on Grand River, and in numerous other neighborhoods. The way many of these churches are grouped together to form a critical mass suggests one way of attacking the problems in any given neighborhood. It is the old solution known as division of labor. Take any cluster of churches and their collective talent. One church might focus on picking up, cleaning up, and fixing up the neighborhood. Another might patrol the streets to make sure our young people are not just wandering around with nothing to do and looking for trouble. Another might offer recreational opportunities to these kids. Another might specialize in rebuilding houses. Another might offer job training and interview skills. Another might be able to set up high-quality day care. Still another might give remedial training to students so they can go from the back to the front of the class.

The possibilities are limited only by our imagination, dedication, and energy. These 1,600 congregations and the men and women who lead them are Detroit's greatest resource. They are oases of help and hope.

But there is no reason why the churches have to go it alone. Working in partnership with the state could help both our sectors provide services to the city's neediest citizens. Consider, for example, the children. Most pastors probably know every baby born in their congregation personally, and they probably know most of the children in their neighborhood. Despite the fact that we are spending one million dollars a year to immunize at-risk children, despite the fact that we even had the National Guard come into the city and help immunize kids, Michigan recently made national headlines for having the worst immunization rates in the nation.[2] That is unacceptable. With 1,600 churches in the city, there is no reason why any baby should go without immunization. Religious leaders can help identify who these children are, and they can urge mothers and fathers, grandmothers and grandfathers, to take them to a nearby health clinic. They can be more effective than any government bureaucrat. Better yet, they can have the health clinic come to their church, and nurses will immunize the kids there.

Whether it's the very young or the very old, the very poor or the very ill, the people in need are neighbors to many of these churches. These people usually trust religious leaders and look to them for guidance. Pastors help the disadvantaged get the help they need, but are they utilizing existing state resources to the fullest extent possible? There are numerous services the state of Michigan already performs in Detroit. Collectively, these services add up to billions of dollars that Lansing sends to the city each year, so the problem is not too little money. The problem is that the residents of this city are not getting enough for their money. Clergy working in partnership with the state could change that—right now.

Before concluding, it is useful to focus on an area that is called the "Fellowship District," and that the Reverend James Perkins calls "Redemptive Turf." It is an area of some thirty blocks on the east side of Detroit, and it is one of the most depressed areas of the city. Reverend Perkins has spearheaded an awesome collaborative effort with the Urban Affairs Department at Michigan State University to inventory the area. He also offers a creative model for how clusters of churches can form the critical mass necessary to tackle the problems in any given neighborhood. Reverend Perkins is president of a cluster of twenty-three congregations known as the Detroit East Side Coalition of Churches, which is in its second year of existence.

With an army of workers, Reverend Perkins has detailed all the assets and liabilities in this area—the vacancies and vacant lots, the commercial and residential properties, some of the characteristics of the people who live there. With maps he has produced a striking visual image of the area's strengths and weaknesses. These maps offer a powerful tool for the way our partnership should work—a clergy-academic-government partnership that helps focus the state's resources within the city at those points where they are most needed.

Reverend Perkins knows an incredible amount about his "turf," but for any area of the city, there are basic questions that need to be answered so that we can apply existing state laws and marshall existing resources.

Working together, the clergy, academic leaders, and public servants can find out:

- How many children are not getting immunized?
- How many elderly residents are shut-ins?
- How many people are living in houses without heat in winter?
- How many abandoned houses could be fixed up?
- How much crime is committed in the neighborhood?
- How many sites are polluted and need to be cleaned up?
- How many children are dropping out of school?
- How many graduates can find jobs—and what kind of jobs are they?
- What's the unemployment rate in this area?
- What's the public transportation in the area?

There are many other questions. To a government bureaucrat in Lansing, the answers are just statistics, but to those at the ground level, they are real people with real faces and with real lives. And if we are going to resurrect a city like Detroit, it is going to be by helping one life at a time. It starts with the individual, then spreads to the family, then encompasses the neighborhood, then gathers up the whole community.

Again, the state cannot do it alone, any more than any single sector can do it working alone. In fact, if you look at how many state offices are in the "Fellowship District"—Reverend Perkins's "Redemptive Turf"— you will see that it is a blank map. Compare that to the many churches. The churches are a great resource, oases of help and hope that can assist the state in mobilizing resources where they are needed.

So many of the people living in this area would benefit from faith-based intervention. The goal of the state in this partnership is not to supplant any of the existing resources currently offered—by the city, the Urban League, or other community-based organizations that are making a difference—but to augment and complement what is already there.

The Clergy Summit convened because there is work to be done— moral work, physical work, hard work. But this is hard work with a difference: It is work of the heart, a loving heart. That is essential, because love never asks how much *must* we do, but how much *can* we do. Those who attended were united by a common vision and a common mission: It is nothing less than the revival of our cities, family by family, block by block, neighborhood by neighborhood.

Note

1.   The term "university enterprise zones" was developed by former University of Michigan President James Duderstadt.

2.   Michigan's immunization rate has improved dramatically since this chapter was first submitted. Based on 1996 rates, Michigan is virtually at the national average, improving faster than any other state.

References

Fagan, P. F. (1996, January 25). Why religion matters: The impact of religious practice on social stability. *Heritage Foundation Backgrounder* (pp. 5, 24).

Raspberry, W. (1994, June 14). Eradicating faith has its dark side. *Lansing State Journal*, op. ed.

Section IV

Conclusions

Chapter 23
Directions for the American Outreach University in the Twenty-First Century

Richard M. Lerner　　*Lou Anna K. Simon*
Boston College　　　*Michigan State University*

The focus of this book has been on presenting examples of university-community collaborations aimed at promoting the life chances of America's youth and families. Predicated on the establishment and elaboration of partnerships involving co-learning among community members and universities, the outreach pursued within these collaborations has altered in salutary ways both the higher-educational institutions and the communities engaged in these partnerships.

The chapters in this volume provide, then, rich illustrations of the ways in which a university may contribute to usefully addressing the problems of contemporary human life, perhaps especially those confronting the children, youth, and families of America's diverse communities. The examples provided by the university and community leaders represented in this volume indicate that a systems change, one directed to the creation of outreach universities, has the potential to improve the vitality of America's universities through changing the prior "paradigm" for universities' work in communities, a past approach that clearly has been insufficient, at least as gauged by the burgeoning problems of America's children, adolescents, and families (Huston, 1991; Lerner, 1995; Lerner & Fisher, 1994; Lerner, Terry, McKinney, & Abrams, 1994; McKinney, Abrams, Terry, & Lerner, 1994).

As illustrated by the programs of outreach scholarship described in this volume, the new paradigm for university-community collaboration offers a vision of outreach scholarship that involves the integration of two cultures: the campus/faculty culture and the community culture. To address the problems of contemporary children, youth, and families, universities and their faculties seek legitimacy in both cultures (cf. Boyer, 1994). Indeed, as exemplified by the programs described in this volume, effective outreach institutions create bridges to bring the campus and the community together into productive, co-learning collaborations, partnerships producing mutually valued outreach scholarship.

Thus, as reported in this book, to promote outreach scholarship requires input from both the faculty and community cultures. Outreach scholarship compels collaboration. It necessitates co-learning.

We have seen that from the perspective of the campus, outreach scholarship must be multidisciplinary, given that the problems faced by communities are multifaceted and thus cut across the boundaries of any one disciplinary specialization. But in addition, it appears critical that such scholarship also simultaneously and synthetically try to be "multicultural"— in several senses of the word: Such scholarship must link the cultures of different professions; the cultures of different disciplines, departments, and colleges; the culture of the Cooperative Extension Service, of the Agricultural Experimental Station, or of other analogous community-oriented research or educational units; and the diverse cultures within the spectrum of communities that are constituted by the children and families served by the university.

Scholarship derived from such multicultural competence represents a new vision for the knowledge functions of a university, one that promises to embody the way in which a university can best position itself in the next century to respond to the multifaceted problems of the people it serves. To provide an overview of this vision it is useful to discuss the components of figure 23.1.

The Campus Context

As shown in the top half of figure 23.1, outreach scholarship requires: (1) a change in campus culture, (2) faculty and graduate-student capacity building, and (3) the development of research-outreach theory and methodology.

Campus culture. Schein defines organizational culture as:

. . . a pattern of basic assumptions that a given group has invented, discovered or developed in learning to cope with its problems of external adaptation and internal integration, and that has worked well enough to be considered valid, and therefore, to be taught to new members as the correct way to perceive, think, and feel in relation to those problems. (Schein, 1992: 12)

The campus culture provides meaning and context for faculty. It holds people together and provides both an individual and collective sense of

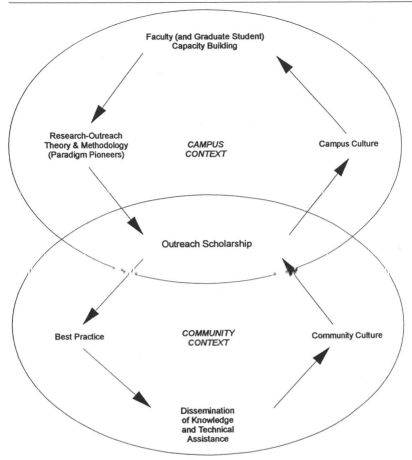

Figure 23.1. Changes in the campus and community context promoted by the creation of university-community collaborative, outreach scholarship.

purpose. Perhaps most importantly, the campus culture defines the nature of reality for those who are part of the culture.

The traditional campus culture—with its overemphasis on research for the sake of research—has placed universities in trouble. Indeed, as noted by the Pew Higher Education Research Program:

> *The message is that whatever their claims to a special calling, these institutions are no different, no better, no longer exempt from public scrutiny and caricature. . . . The practical consequence is that institutions of higher education can expect less of the public purse and more of public intervention. (PHERP, 1991)*

Moreover, in 1992, the Pew Higher Education Research Program noted that:

Those who hold their breath are likely to turn blue before higher education again feels secure in its claim to public support and trust. . . . Already there has been a steady and marked decline in the proportion of financial support that state legislatures provide their colleges and universities. . . . States tend to increasingly regard higher education as a mature industry, and the monies they accord to colleges and universities have become a prime source of "flexible" funds capable of redirection without adverse political consequence. (PHERP, 1992)

In this climate, a university must realize that it cannot take a business-as-usual approach (Boyer, 1994). As noted by several of the authors in this volume, a key to the success of any attempt at instituting a revised approach to the activities of the university rests on changing the campus culture. However, to discuss how such culture change may be fostered it is important to look at the two other components in the top half of figure 23.1.

Faculty capacity building. As exemplified by several of the programs described in this volume, institutions that effectively promote outreach scholarship build the capacity of faculty (and graduate students) to see the world as a "system." The inculcation of this perspective may require helping faculty see beyond their disciplinary-based perspectives and aiding them in understanding the changing interrelations among levels of organization that comprise human systems. Using a systems perspective will allow a linkage among outreach scholarship, graduate education and, as well, undergraduate service-learning experiences—systemic associations found in several of the university programs described in this volume.

Integrating theory and methodology. In order to address adequately the serious problems faced by today's children, adolescents, and families, multidisciplinary research must involve more than just assembling researchers from different disciplines. Such an approach typically results in a simple layering of investigations and publications—project faculty from each discipline approach the topic with their own theory and method, and report their findings separately or in an edited collection of articles (Lerner, 1995).

Pursuing this traditional paradigm has built the scholarly careers of numerous generations of faculty. However, this paradigm is not adequate for meeting the needs of the youth and families of our communities. What is required is a pioneering effort to formulate a new paradigm promoting an integrative or, even better, a "fused" and multicultural (in the above senses) approach to research.

The variables that various disciplines typically study, and the models that they develop to interrelate those variables, are all comingled in the day-to-day situations of real life. This systemic connection has been integrated in various systems conceptions of human behavior and development, for instance, "developmental contextualism" (Lerner, 1986, 1991, 1995, 1996) or the "applied developmental science" perspective (Fisher et al., 1993; Fisher & Lerner, 1994). Only through building such integrated models, ones that focus on the combined interactions of systems studied by different disciplines, will the heretofore disconnected insights of those different disciplines develop into a useful, synthetic theory guiding the development of innovative and useful outreach programs. The point is not simply the obvious one that the world is complex; rather it is that the fusing of distinct approaches requires building systemic, integrated, and dynamic models and methods.

To enable high-quality outreach scholarship derived from this systems perspective to be pursued productively requires innovative methodology. Such methods must be able to garner evidence that is both scientifically rigorous and persuasive to the faculty culture and that is relevant and compelling to the communities with whom we collaborate. As a consequence of such a systems perspective, the methodology that is promoted will be multivariate, longitudinal (developmental), and change-sensitive. In other words, the systems perspective to be pursued will be, by necessity, a *developmental* systems perspective (Ford & Lerner, 1992; Lerner, 1996).

There is one important implication for the conduct of university outreach that follows from this approach to methodology. Because of these methodological choices and, in particular, the commitment to the longitudinal approach, one must be involved in communities over a long period of time. Certainly, this view was expressed clearly in the chapters in this volume from community partners, and in particular those writing from the perspective of the foundation world. This temporal commitment means, substantively, that activities associated with outreach scholarship will avoid the "hit and run" character of many prior attempts at action research, applied research, and demonstration projects.

We do not see as scientifically or ethically defensible scholarship that parachutes into a community and fails to grapple with (1) the long-term outcome of individual and family changes, (2) the status of the capacity of the community to sustain programmatic changes once the demonstration period has ended, or (3) the unintended consequences or new insights that arise during the period.

Campus culture change. As many of the authors in this volume point out, to understand and effect these pioneering efforts requires a major qualitative change in the current culture of America's campuses (Boyer, 1994). However, it is clear from the reports in this volume that the involvement of faculty in such cultural change is no small task. Indeed, because there are still only a relatively few faculty at any institution involved with the type of multicultural integration we have described, one of the major activities within an outreach university is the building of teams of colleagues that exemplify the integrations that are embodied in the above-noted concept of campus cultural change. With this team, it is possible to begin to institutionalize and extend the diffusion of these innovations.

To this end, we believe that the cycle in the top part of figure 23.1 is synthetically reinforcing: Outreach scholarship changes the campus culture, which, in turn, leads to increases in the capacity of faculty and graduate students to conduct outreach scholarship, which leads to pioneering efforts to enhance theory and methodology.

As suggested by the reports of university outreach programs found in this volume, both the quality and quantity of outreach scholarship increases as a consequence of these efforts. As well, the catalyzing of outreach scholarship facilitates efforts to collaborate within communities. At this point, then, it is useful to review the bottom half of figure 23.1.

The Community Context

As shown in the bottom half of figure 23.1, outreach scholarship generates a knowledge base about best practice; and the knowledge base is disseminated through activities such as training, demonstration projects, consultation, needs assessment, and technical assistance. These activities generate positive outcomes in the community, such that there is an increased likelihood that it will turn to the university for further collaborations involving outreach scholarship.

This process of community collaboration captures a sense of community that is at least as broad as the diverse settings and constituencies that influence the lives of children, adolescents, and families. Thus, included in this sense of community are geographical units (e.g., neighborhoods and municipalities), institutional units (e.g., school districts and service agencies), and governmental actors (e.g., elected and appointed officials). As well, and as emphasized repeatedly in this book, this process of community collaboration rests on co-learning: Members of the campus and the community contexts need to learn about each other's culture in order for productive and effective outreach scholarship to result.

Thus, as noted in several of the community-based chapters in this volume, commitment to scholarship predicated on co-learning, creates, from the perspective of the community, a different type of academic research institution. Whereas other research institutions see the community as a laboratory, a co-learning conception sees the community as a classroom in which both the university and community learn. As such, involvement with communities is one of comingled destinies. Each partner's success is interdependent with that of the other partner.

As described in this volume, this mutuality means that campus and community become competent about the mores, values, and practices of each other's culture. Indeed, unless such cultural competence is developed, neither co-learning nor effective scholarly and community outcomes can be achieved.

It is here, then, in the establishment of effective systems of co-learning, that university units specialized to integrate outreach scholarship throughout the fabric of the institution, for example, the Cooperative Extension Service or institutes bridging research and outreach, can play a vital role in the enhancement of integrating the cultures of campus and community. For example, as part of both communities, cooperative extension colleagues can enhance and facilitate within each setting understanding of the meaning and value systems of the other setting. However, whether conducted by extension or other analogous units (e.g., institutes/ centers or service-learning programs), we have seen that enactment of this role is crucial in the design, implementation, and evaluation of effective community-based programs for children and youth.

Research and outreach collaborations and the development of effective community-based programs for children and youth. Developmental systems ideas stress that the problems facing the youth of America require an integrated set of activities by the members of our nation's research and extension communities (Lerner, 1995; Lerner & Miller, 1993). As emphasized in the scholarship of Dryfoos (1990), Hamburg (1992), Little (1993), and Schorr (1988), numerous programs have been empirically shown to be able to "break the cycle of disadvantage" (Schorr, 1988) and to prevent some of the sequelae of persistent and pervasive child and adolescent poverty (Dryfoos, 1990).

Yet despite the presence of such evaluation data, many of these demonstrably effective programs have not been sustained (Schorr, 1988). Even fewer have been replicated. The problems of sustainability and replicability are interrelated, and the potentially integrated role of members of the research and outreach components (e.g., Cooperative Extension Service) of universities and youth and family program workers in communities arises in connection to this interrelation.

Effective programs for youth have often not been sustained because members of the community within which the program is embedded do not have the capacity to themselves continue to conduct the program (Lerner, 1995; Lerner, Ostrom, & Freel, 1995; Ostrom, Lerner, & Freel, 1995; Weiss & Greene, 1992). With no attempt to empower the youth or other members of the community to sustain the program over the long term, any salutary outcomes of the program are likely to "fade out." Thus, what needs to be ascertained is how—for a specific program in a particular community—can such capacity be developed? More specifically, what needs to be asked is:

- How can the members of a given community, and particularly the youth who are involved in the program, be provided with the leadership abilities to sustain the program after the term of the demonstration project (or grant) has ended?
- What set of developmental skills, and what array of community, political, and economic leadership abilities, need to be inculcated in these youth in order to enhance their capacity and, as a result, that of their community?

Research and outreach go hand-in-hand in what are clearly youth-development endeavors. Once researchers provide answers to these questions, either new programs and/or adjuncts to existing programs need to be devised in order to turn these answers into changed outcomes, that is, into increased leadership capacity, for the youth of a specific community. Furthermore, the capacity-building programs or program supplements need to be evaluated for their effectiveness. Knowledge about, and programs for, one community need to be calibrated for applicability to (i.e., replicability in) any other community. As a consequence, the partnership among research, outreach, and community needs to encompass understanding of, and programs for, both sustaining effective efforts in any one community and replicating such efforts in other communities (cf. Lerner,

1993, 1995; Lerner & Miller, 1993). A partnership that creates such products is generating exemplary outreach scholarship. However, as seen in this volume, from a community perspective, such scholarship is not an end in itself.

From replication to building "best practice." As is clear from the views provided in the community-based chapters in this volume, from the perspective of the members of a community, the value of such outreach scholarship is that it results in knowledge of the *best practices* available to them for policies, policy implementation, and program design and delivery in their neighborhoods. As noted by Washington:

> *Dozens of effective strategies have been used across the country to address the needs of youth and families. Yet in all areas of social development there is the temptation to start over again rather than build on efforts already underway and proven successful. . . . The time has come to focus on less glamorous, self-aggrandizing aspects of program development. Instead, professional communities need to cooperate more to leverage their collective investments and establish comprehensive, coordinated policies and practices that work efficiently and effectively. . . .*
>
> *To avoid the temptation of starting over again, better systems for documenting what has been done and providing a clearinghouse for the information are needed. In addition, there is a need for development of a reporting and rating system for social development efforts that would help successful models that have been developed locally to be highlighted and shared nationally.*
>
> *University faculty, through their research and evaluation activities, can give important leadership to helping design appropriate techniques to learn and transfer information about "what works." (Washington, 1992)*

The sort of information called for by Washington would include programs that have been developed, implemented, and evaluated all over the world (cf. Little, 1993). This information may allow public policymakers, community organizers, researchers, and others to better use their money and time developing or replicating features of successful programs. Many people within these groups know there are programs that succeed in improving the life chances of America's children, adolescents, and families. As emphasized eloquently and often by Edelman (1993) and by Little (1993), we have a good deal of the knowledge and the skills needed to design and deliver programs that ameliorate undesirable behaviors, that prevent the occurrence of problems, and that enhance the abilities and life opportunities for the diverse youth and families across our nation (see also, Hamburg & Takanishi, 1996; Lerner, 1995).

Simply, there are ways that we can construct the contexts of youth that enhance their development across the life span, that do not squander their human capital. Indeed, many of these programs, and the policies and values that legitimate and promote them, have been identified by Hamburg (1992), by Schorr (1988), and by Dryfoos (1990, 1994). However, despite the proven successes of selected programs—often documented through the results of rigorous evaluations—these programs are neither sufficiently sustained nor adequately replicated. A failure to replicate, or more primarily to disseminate the details of successful programs so that replication can be attempted, means that practitioners in different communities must "reinvent the wheel." Best practice cannot be identified if replication does not exist. More primarily, however, even when a community finds that a program works, it is often not sustained because there is a lack of community-based capacity to generate requisite leadership, infrastructure, and funds (Schorr, 1988).

The need exists, then, to catalog information about what works in specific communities in regard to preventive, enhancing, or ameliorative programs for children, adolescents, and families. Of course, "best practice" is an ideal that can only be approached, especially given the fact that particular instances of individual and ecological relations may not generalize precisely to different individual or contextual conditions (Lerner, 1986, 1995). Thus, work here is more readily characterized as the pursuing of "better practice." Nevertheless, we need to disseminate best (or at least, better) practice information in order to inform communities and policymakers about the sorts of programs that may work and about how programs that have been sustained have managed to achieve this end. Moreover, dissemination is required to increase the capacity of the community to itself sustain activities beyond the period of university collaboration.

Dissemination of knowledge. As illustrated by the programs discussed in this volume, to translate research-outreach collaborations into community-based programs that are marked by the capacity of the people of the community to themselves sustain the programs, research-outreach teams must be proactive about disseminating knowledge, for example, by providing technical assistance or conducting evaluations or demonstration projects. Simply, this approach not only helps to extend and sustain identified best practices but it also assists in building the capacities of community collaborators. As co-learning members of a culturally competent community-collaboration, colleagues involved in outreach scholarship initiate the delivery, to the community, of knowledge about and skills for enhancing the lives of children, youth, and families.

As made clear by the authors in this book, the knowledge valued and sought by the community-university partnership must be usable and used. As a consequence, dissemination involves ascertaining the relevance of knowledge and assuring accessibility to it.

This view of knowledge utilization underscores the need for a sustained commitment to a campus-community partnership. As seen in this volume, when such partnerships are successful, they build the understanding of universities as a potential part of a confederation of community members; they are partnerships that bring to the "collaborative table" knowledge-based assets. In this way, the community can also be proactive in approaching the university.

These approaches help further attempts by outreach scholarship colleagues to learn with the broader community the means to refine the outreach scholarship being pursued; to further the inculcation of best practices that meet the specific needs of the community; and that, as a consequence, help to further merge the cultures of the campus and the community.

Community culture. If the university's efforts at pioneering a new paradigm for outreach scholarship are effective in the community, then the community will alter the way it views its problems, the policy choices it pursues, the programs to which it subscribes and, perhaps superordinately, the university-based resources it perceives it can access for making these changes. In other words, if community culture change occurs, then the view of the role of the university will also change.

These alterations are a key goal of pursuing outreach scholarship. A hope is that legislative and community leaders will recognize that funds expended on the university-community relationship constitute a productive investment, one that has a tangible return in regard to the issues and problems they define as crucial. This volume provides some evidence that such changes in perception are occurring.

As Little (1993) believes, if such systems change is useful in one community context, then it may be possible to create economies of scale: Building better practices in one setting may teach us how to extend our efforts to other settings, to other parts of the ecology of human development. As a consequence, the developmental approach to co-learning and to community collaboration may help facilitate the development of systems thinking among policymakers, program professionals, volunteers, and the children and families involved in the outreach scholarship collaboration.

To some extent, the chapters in this volume may contribute to such systems thinking and to systems change as well. Indeed, the programs reported in this book should help persuade university and community teams that it is possible to pursue successfully collaborative youth-development efforts. By together learning how to build the capacity of the youth of our communities to take leadership in sustaining effective prevention and enhancement programs, such university-community partnerships can aid American universities in making substantial contributions to ending the destruction of our nation's youth. Indeed, such collaborations can help move beyond just the deterrence of problems; these collaborations can help build better lives for the children and youth of our nation (Pittman & Zeldin, 1994).

However, to better achieve these goals, academic policies that currently inhibit university-community collaborations will need to be revised if universities are to be institutions involved in the solution of the problems of our nation's youth and families. It is important to specify, then, the academic policy innovations that need to be introduced in order to allow outreach scholarship to continue to build and to sustain effective programs for the youth of our nation.

Promoting Academic Policy Change Enabling the Growth and Viability of Community-Collaborative Universities

American universities cannot become effective parts of the solution to the problems besetting our nation's youth until increased numbers of faculty members and community members begin to work collaboratively, both among themselves and with the broader communities they serve. To bring faculty into this collaboration will not only require the cultural changes discussed above. As stressed in several chapters in this volume, in addition, and possibly primarily, the reward systems of American universities will have to be altered (Boyer, 1990, 1994; Lerner et al., 1994; Votruba, 1992, 1996). Indeed, we have seen across the chapters in this book several authors noting that incentives will need to be created to provide an exciting and attractive basis for the reorientation of the work of established scholars and for the reward of a career in outreach scholarship among junior faculty.

Moreover, educators in each of the disciplines involved in the study of human behavior and development should be presented with a vision for beginning to train their students differently (see too Birkel, Lerner, &

Smyer, 1989; Fisher et al., 1993). Indeed, in our view, an appreciation of systematic change, context, and human relationships should be the cornerstone of future graduate education. Furthermore, several authors in this volume stress that undergraduates should be involved, for instance, through service learning opportunities (that are made a core part of their educational experience), in the faculty and graduate-student programs of outreach scholarship. In this way, community service and community collaboration will become a part of the fabric of the academic life of all members of the university.

In short, to create such systems change in the academy, it appears we must: reward system changes that promote multidimensional excellence (e.g., focus on unit versus faculty member assessments of performance in outreach); pursue graduate training that creates outreach scholars for the twenty-first century; and promote undergraduate service learning, thus making education relevant to community needs. These emphases are central points stressed in the growing attention being paid among scholarly societies and universities to the importance of training in applied developmental science for future scholars and professionals in fields associated with human development and education (Fisher & Lerner, 1994; Fisher et al., 1993).

Furthermore, it is crucial that university merit, tenure, and promotion committees evaluating faculty engaged in outreach scholarship must be urged to begin to consider the relative value of multidisciplinary collaborative, and hence multiauthored, publications, in comparison to within-discipline, single-authored products, and as well, those publications in outlets that fall outside the boundaries of those traditionally seen as "prime" within a given discipline. Academic policy discussion must also involve the nature of the reception given by university review committees to the sort of contextual and collaborative research associated with developmental-systems approaches to outreach scholarship. The issue to be debated here is, first, can we train future cohorts of outreach scholars to engage productively in the multidisciplinary, multiprofessional, and community collaborations requisite for advancing understanding of the basic process of development (Lerner, 1995) and for producing knowledge of applied significance to the community? Second, can we *not* reward and value these new scholars (e.g., tenure and promote them) for successfully doing these two, integrated tasks?

If we follow a systems orientation that leads to the synthesis of research and outreach, then it would seem that we must devise means to assign value to, and reward, an array of collaborative, multidisciplinary, and multiprofessional activities (Votruba, 1992, 1996), ones disseminated (e.g., published, presented, or archived) in both traditional and nontraditional ways. Similarly, if we are to take seriously the need for change-oriented (and hence longitudinal), multilevel (and hence multivariate), and multidisciplinary research, we must recognize the need to educate government agencies and private foundations about the time and financial resources that should be given to such collaborative activities (McLoyd, 1994). As suggested by discussions in this volume, such recognition is certainly represented in these portions of the community.

Simply, American universities must do more than provide a model for the integration of multiple academic disciplines and multiple professional activities with the community. They must embrace fully—by rewarding behavior consistent with—the ideal of multidimensional excellence, that is, of high-quality contributions across the breadth of the academic missions of research, teaching, and outreach. In other words, if universities are to significantly advance the integration of research and outreach for the diverse children, adolescents, and families of America's communities, sustained efforts must be made to build and maintain—through a revised academic reward system—a new, community-collaborative scholarly agenda.

As exemplified by the university- and community-based programs described in the chapters in this volume, the key elements that allow a community-collaborative university initiative to succeed involve: (1) a precise and stakeholder-valued substantive focus; (2) an up-front and broad buy-in by the university administration; (3) a strategic plan for the involvement of a critical mass of high-quality faculty; (4) a system of evaluation and accountability; (5) a true collaboration, based on co-learning and partnership, with the community; and (6) the maintenance of a means to keep all stakeholders invested in the success of the program.

However, in attending to the concerns that will attract and maintain the collaboration of the diverse, individual stakeholders involved in university-community partnerships, a potential pitfall exists. We must be certain that we do not fall into a reductionism that distributes resources in a manner that, while affording individual participation, loses sight of the molar, or emergent, need to create an integrated community-wide system promoting the positive development of youth and families. We must not let the recruitment of individual stakeholders, be they people, groups, or institutions, detract from the concerted, system-wide support of youth and families.

Simply, the whole must be more than the sum of its parts. The spirit and exchanges of true collaboration must take precedence over a focus on the role or assets of only one part of the partnership—be it the university or the community. Certainly, however, the creation of such a systemic focus on collaboration is not easily accomplished.

Challenges to the Creation of Collaborative Systems

The chapters in this book underscore the presence of common issues involved in building outreach universities, for example, the need to establish co-learning between universities and communities and changing the faculty reward system to promote outreach scholarship. At the same time, however, the routes that have been taken to address these issues vary across the universities and community organizations represented in the volume. This variation suggests that there is not likely to be a single path universities may follow to become outreach institutions (e.g., see Votruba, 1996). For instance, at some universities, outreach scholarship pertinent to youth and families may be focused in a center or institute having a university-wide mandate to represent the institution's contributions to this area; alternatively, at other universities, a corporate commitment to children and families may be actualized by having such outreach scholarship exist as a theme of multiple units. The system that fits best a particular institution must be developed in the context of that university's culture, the culture of the community with which it partners, and the joint, or emergent, culture that is produced by the collaboration.

However, and in light of our view that the collaboration—whatever its form or constituent parts—must put the benefits to youth and families above the benefits to individual partners, a commitment to developing and sustaining a strong collaboration must take precedence over strengthening the collaborating units per se. The creation of such selflessness is a daunting task, given "human nature" and, we believe, will lead to necessary changes in programs pursued by university-community collaborators.

For example, a program involved in a given university-community collaboration may enhance the parenting skills of a young woman. While such an outcome is highly significant, to sustain the collaboration, it should be coupled with attempts to strengthen the system that produced the program. In this case, we would suggest that actions should be taken to make the young woman more than a recipient of aid. She should be empowered to become part of the partnership that produced the program, that makes decisions about the program's further development, that enacts the program, and that in fact governs the continued functioning of the partnership.

This empowerment will mean that the originators of the partnership, and of the program in question, will constantly have to share power and resources with a new, growing set of collaborators. Such devolution of individual "ownership," or—conversely—ownership by an empowered and increasingly broader community of full partners, means that the collective system will be strengthened. Recipients of programs become, in this vision, responsible for sharing their learning, their abilities, and ultimately their power. The participants of programs become assets of a strengthened collective.

We believe this sort of expanding collaborative system is a logical outcome of the approach to outreach scholarship evidenced across the contributions to this volume. However, it is not an inevitable one. The institutions that are involved in the initiation of the university-community collaborations exemplified in this book—including foundations, government, NGOs, as well as higher-education institutions—will need to include, as part of the culture change that is requisite to build real partnerships, a commitment to sharing ownership with individuals who first enter the system more as recipients than as owners of programs. However, unless such a culture change occurs university-community collaborations will not be able to adequately redress the breadth and depth of problems facing America's youth and families. Unless our programs create greater human capital—community "assets" that are empowered to "give back" to the community, to strengthen its resources, and to establish an ethos balancing the caring aspects of (and arguments for) entitlement programs with the responsibility to be an active agent in producing a better life for self, family, and community—all the resources available to universities, foundations, governments, and other major institutions of society will not be sufficient to diminish the risks associated with the increasing challenge faced by today's youth and families.

The best way to begin to create this empowered, collaborative system is to involve youth and family program recipients in the design and implementation of future actions in their communities. We need to understand their vision and learn their idealogy and values. Such participation is a critical first step in empowerment and in actualizing the resources—the human capital—represented by the individuals in our communities (Lerner, 1995; Lerner, Ostrom, & Freel, 1995; Ostrom, Lerner, & Freel, 1995). In the end, it is people working together that will matter in the lives of our nation's youth and families. Their empowerment must involve not just the power to decide but, critically, the responsibility—through modeling and teaching—to help others. In this sense it not only takes an entire village to raise a child; more than this, the whole village must be involved as partners if we are to create a system enabling sustained actions promoting positive youth and family development.

Participation in the creation and maintenance of such a developmentally empowering partnership is the key challenge facing American universities as our nation approaches the next millennium (Boyer, 1994). And this is the path upon which we, as scholars, educators, youth-serving professionals, volunteers, and, most basically, citizens, must embark. Indeed, as we noted in the opening chapter in this volume, the stakes are high, not only for universities but, more important, for an American society faced with the loss of much of the human capital represented by its children, youth, and families.

Conclusion

Ultimately, all citizens—whether working in universities or not—must continue to educate themselves about the best means available to promote enhanced life chances among *all* of America's youth and families, but especially among those whose potentials for positive contributions to our nation are most in danger of being wasted (Lerner, 1993, 1995). The expertise of university faculty, students, and outreach colleagues can provide much of this information, but only if developed in partnership with strong, empowered communities. Policies promoting such coalitions must be an integral component of a national youth and family development policy aimed at creating caring communities having the capacity to nurture the healthy development of our children and families.

However, we cannot wait for the enactment of such policies before we launch, on a national scale, the sorts of collaborative programs discussed in this book. Rather, we must adopt the strategy of broadening such programs to create a *zeitgeist* for the formulation of such policies. And, most important, universities must lead the way in promoting such systems change.

"Business as usual" in our universities and in our communities has failed American youth and families, and will continue to fail America unless such systems change occurs. If we value the future of our nation, we cannot afford to let this failure occur. We need to form community-wide collaborations among all institutions. If universities are not part of these collaborations, we predict they will not be viable entities in twenty years.

Indeed, when we take off our hats as academics and put on our hats as citizens, we do not see it as feasible or desirable to support institutions that do not contribute to allowing our children and families to have a decent chance in life.

Accordingly, it seems apt to close with a quote from another time and another place, said for another reason, but appropriate here: "If you're not part of the solution, then you're part of the problem" (Cleaver, 1967). Let's not be part of the problem. Let's be part of the solution. Let us work together to save our children, to save our families and communities, and— superordinately—to save America.

References

Birkel, R., Lerner, R. M., & Smyer, M. A. (1989). Applied developmental psychology as an implementation of a life-span view of human development. *Journal of Applied Developmental Psychology, 10,* 425–445.

Boyer, E. L. (1990). *Scholarship reconsidered: Priorities of the professoriate.* Princeton, NJ: The Carnegie Foundation for the Advancement of Teaching.

———. (1994, March 9). Creating the new American college. (Point of View column). *The Chronicle of Higher Education* (p. A48).

Cleaver, E. (1967). *Soul on ice.* New York: McGraw-Hill.

Dryfoos, J. G. (1990). *Adolescents at risk: Prevalence and prevention.* New York: Oxford University.

———. (1994). *Full service schools: A revolution in health and social services of children, youth and families.* San Francisco: Jossey-Bass.

Edelman, M. W. (1993). *Leave no child behind: Mobilizing families and communities for America's children.* Washington, DC: Children's Defense Fund.

Fisher, C. B., & Lerner, R. M. (Eds.). (1994). *Applied developmental psychology.* New York: McGraw-Hill.

Fisher, C. B., Murray, J. P., Dill, J. R., Hagen, J. W., Hogan, M. J., Lerner, R. M., Rebok, G. W., Sigel, I., Sostek, A. M., Smyer, M. A., Spencer, M. B., & Wilcox, B. (1993). The national conference on graduate education in the applications of developmental science across the life span. *Journal of Applied Developmental Psychology, 14,* 1–10.

Ford, D. L., & Lerner, R. M. (1992). *Developmental systems theory: An integrative approach.* Newbury Park, CA: Sage.

Hamburg, D. A. (1992). *Today's children: Creating a future for a generation in crisis.* New York: Time Books.

Hamburg, D. A., & Takanishi, R. (1996). Great transitions: Preparing American youth for the twenty-first century—The role of research. *Journal of Research on Adolescence, 6* (4), 379–396.

Huston, A. C. (Ed.). (1991). *Children in poverty: Child development and public policy.* Cambridge: Cambridge University Press.

Lerner, R. M. (1986). *Concepts and theories of human development* (2nd ed.). New York: Random House.

———. (1991). Changing organism-context relations as the basic process of development: A developmental-contextual perspective. *Developmental Psychology, 27,* 27–32.

———. (1993). Investment in youth: The role of home economics in enhancing the life chances of America's children. AHEA *Monograph Series, 1,* 5–34.

———. (1995). *America's youth in crisis: Challenges and options for programs and policies.* Thousand Oaks, CA: Sage.

———. (1996). Creating caring communities: Building university-community partnerships to enhance youth and family development. *Conversations,* [newsletter of the National Center for Social Work and Education Collaboration, Fordham University, Bronx, NY] *3* (1–2), pp. 8–12.

Lerner, R. M., & Fisher, C. B. (1994). From applied developmental psychology to applied developmental science: Community coalitions and collaborative careers. In C. B. Fisher & R. M. Lerner (Eds.), *Applied developmental psychology* (pp. 505–522). New York: McGraw-Hill.

Lerner, R. M., & Miller, J. R. (1993). Integrating human development research and intervention for America's children: The Michigan State University model. *Journal of Applied Developmental Psychology, 14*, 347–364.

Lerner, R. M., Ostrom, C. W., & Freel, M. A. (1995). Promoting positive youth and community development through outreach scholarship: Comments on Zeldin and Peterson. *Journal of Adolescent Research, 10*, 486–502.

Lerner, R. M., Terry, P. A., McKinney, M. H., & Abrams, L. A. (1994). Addressing child poverty within the context of a community-collaborative university: Comments on Fabes, Martin, and Smith (1994) and McLoyd (1994). *Family and Consumer Sciences Research Journal, 23*, 67–75.

Little, R. R. (1993, March). *What's working for today's youth: The issues, the programs, and the learnings.* Paper presented at an ICYF Fellows Colloquium, Michigan State University, East Lansing.

McKinney, M., Abrams, L. A., Terry, P. A., & Lerner, R. M. (1994). Child development research and the poor children of America: A call for a developmental contextual approach to research and outreach. *Family and Consumer Sciences Research Journal, 23*, 26–42.

McLoyd, V. C. (1994). Research in the service of poor and ethnic/racial minority children: A moral imperative. *Family and Consumer Sciences Research Journal, 23*, 56–66.

Ostrom, C. W., Lerner, R. M., & Freel, M. A. (1995). Building the capacity of youth and families through university-community collaborations: The development-in-context evaluation (DICE) model. *Journal of Adolescent Research, 10*, 427–448.

Pew Higher Education Research Program (1991). *Policy Perspectives, 3* (4), 1–8A.

———. (1992). *Policy Perspectives, 4* (3), 1–8A.

Pittman, K. J., & Zeldin, S. (1994). From deterrence to development: Shifting the focus of youth programs for African-American males. In R. B. Mincy (Ed.), *Nurturing young black males: Challenges to agencies, programs, and social policy* (pp. 45–55). Washington, DC: The Urban Institute Press.

Schein, E. H. (1992). *Organizational culture and leadership.* San Francisco: Jossey-Bass.

Schorr, L. B. (1988). *Within our reach: Breaking the cycle of disadvantage.* New York: Doubleday.

Votruba, J. C. (1992). Promoting the extension of knowledge in service to society. *Metropolitan Universities, 3* (3), 72–80.

———. (1996). Strengthening the university's alignment with society: Challenges and strategies. Journal of *Public Service & Outreach, 1* (1), 29–36.

Washington, V. (1992). Leadership for children in the twenty-first century: Professors, public policy, and philanthropy. Institute for Children, Youth, and Families: Fellow's Lecture. East Lansing: Michigan State University.

Weiss, H. B., & Greene, J. C. (1992). An empowerment partnership for family support and education programs and evaluations. *Family Science Review, 5*, 131–148.

Contributors

Cheryl S. Alexander is a professor at the Johns Hopkins School of Hygiene and Public Health, with appointments in the departments of Maternal and Child Health, Health Policy and Management, and in the School of Nursing. She is the director and principal investigator of the Center for Adolescent Health Promotion and Disease Prevention. Dr. Alexander is an active member of the American Public Health Association, the Society for Research in Adolescence, the Association for Teachers of Maternal and Child Health and is a fellow of the American Academy of Nursing. She is also a member of the editorial board of the *Journal of Research on Adolescence*. Dr. Alexander's research interests include gender differences in health problem behaviors and the influence of community context on adolescent behaviors. Dr. Alexander holds a Masters of Arts in Child Psychiatric Nursing, a Masters of Public Health degree, and a Ph.D. in Behavioral Sciences.

Marjorie G. Bardeen is manager of the Fermi National Accelerator Laboratory (Fermilab) Education Office that offers staff development programs for precollege teachers, inquiry-based science programs for students and a public science program for families. Also, Bardeen is president of Friends of Fermilab (FFLA), a not-for-profit corporation whose purpose is to support the conduct of precollege education programs at Fermilab in Batavia, Illinois. Bardeen has over thirty years of experience in precollege education as a parent volunteer, classroom teacher, school board member and program administrator. She has served as a community volunteer in a number of programs for youth. She was the FFLA vice president for programs from 1983 to 1993. Bardeen has served on the board of trustees, College of DuPage and was its chair from 1990 to 1992, and she has served on the Glenbard Township High School District #87 Board of Education from 1979 to 1985, and was its president from 1980 to 1985.

Lionel J. Beaulieu is Director of the Southern Rural Development Center at Mississippi State University. Prior to that, he was professor of rural sociology in the Department of Family, Youth and Community Sciences and director of the Florida Inter-University Center at the University of Florida. He came to the University of Florida in 1977 after completing his Ph.D. degree in Sociology at Purdue University. As part of his activities in the Florida Cooperative Extension Service, Dr. Beaulieu has devoted his energies to community and rural development initiatives, particularly community leadership development, public policy education, and workforce preparation. In his research activities, Dr. Beaulieu has focused on the human resource problems facing many rural areas of the country. He is the author of *The Rural South in Crisis: Challenges for the Future* (1988), a volume that examines the social and economic problems that confront many rural areas of the South. His latest edited book, *Investing in People: The Human Capital Needs of Rural America,* offers a comprehensive examination of the quality and capacity of rural America's human capital resources. Dr. Beaulieu teaches courses on community and social research methods as part of University of Florida's Human Resource Development undergraduate program.

Connie Binsfeld, Lieutenant Governor of Michigan, was elected with Governor John Engler on the Republican ticket in November 1990. Prior to becoming Lt. Governor, Binsfeld served four terms in the State House of Representatives (1974–1982). She was elected Assistant Republican Leader in 1979 and 1981. In 1982 Binsfeld was elected to her first term in the Michigan Senate, where she served from 1983 to 1990. During her first year as a senator, she was elected assistant majority leader. In April 1991 she was selected by Governor Engler to chair the Binsfeld Special Commission on Adoption. In January 1994 Binsfeld was appointed chair of the Michigan International Year of the Family's year-long observance, which led to the creation of the Chance at Childhood Foundation. In July 1995 the Governor appointed her chair of the Children's Commission. Binsfeld received her bachelor's in secondary education from Siena Heights College and pursued graduate study at Wayne State University. Before entering the political arena, she was a social studies teacher.

Karen Bogenschneider is an associate professor of Child and Family Studies at the University of Wisconsin-Madison and a family policy specialist for University of Wisconsin Extension-Cooperative Extension. She worked directly with families for fourteen years as a county Extension Family Living Agent before receiving her doctoral degree in 1990. Dr. Bogenschneider is Coordinator of Wisconsin Family Impact Seminars, a continuing series of seminars designed to bring a family focus to policymaking. She also served for seven years as the director of Wisconsin Youth Futures, a community prevention program operating in twenty-two Wisconsin communities. She is principal investigator of the Tapping into Parent (TIP) Survey, a community-based research program which aims to improve parenting and build local support for youth and families. Her research focuses primarily on adolescent development and how it is influenced by the social ecology—specifically the family, peer, work, and community settings.

James T. Bonnen is professor of agricultural economics at Michigan State University. He received his Ph.D. in economics from Harvard University. Dr. Bonnen was elected President of the American Agricultural Economics Association in 1975 and made a Fellow of that association in 1978. In 1981 he received the American Statistical Association's Washington Statistical Society's "Julius Shiskin Award for Outstanding Achievement in Economic Statistics." In 1984 he was elected a Fellow of the American Statistical Association and also of the American Association for the Advancement of Science in 1992. He is the author of numerous articles focusing on agricultural policy, development, and trade. He is currently conducting a study on "The Future of the Land Grant Idea."

Mary Brabeck is the dean of the School of Education and a professor in the Counseling, Developmental Psychology, and Research Methods Department at Boston College. She received her Ph.D. from the University of Minnesota in Educational Psychology. She is a fellow of Division 35 (Psychology of Women) and is the author of over fifty journal articles, book chapters, and books on intellectual and ethical development, the intersection of culture and gender, and professional ethics, including: *Who Cares? Theory, Research, and Educational Implications of an Ethic of Care* (Praeger Press).

Carol A. Cartwright is the tenth president of Kent State University. She has served as chair of the Board of the American Association for Higher Education. She currently serves on the board of directors of the National Association of State Universities and Land-Grant Colleges and chairs the association's Commission on Outreach and Technology Transfer. Dr. Cartwright chaired the Technology in Education committee which designed a statewide master plan for incorporating technology in education in Ohio. In addition, she serves on the NCAA Council and the newly formed Board of Directors of the NCAA. Before coming to Kent State University in 1991, she served as vice chancellor for Academic Affairs at the University of California at Davis, and as dean for Undergraduate Programs and Vice Provost of the Pennsylvania State University. Her doctorate and master's degrees are from the University of Pittsburgh and her bachelor's degree is from the University of Wisconsin at Whitewater. Both of her alma maters have recognized her achievements with Distinguished Alumni honors. Dr. Cartwright has authored numerous refereed publications including research reports and articles as well as popular articles and book chapters. She has also authored or co-authored fifteen books, including *Educating Special Learners* (in its fourth edition) and *Child Care Administration.*

Karen McKnight Casey currently serves as academic outreach specialist for the Young Spartan Program. In this capacity she works with the partnership as the primary linkage between the human and programmic resources of Michigan State University and the needs of the participating elementary schools, with primary focus being on orchestrating experiential learning opportunities for both university and elementary school students. Casey brings to this position a unique background consisting of a degree in social work from MSU, and professional work experience in college residential and academic student affairs, development and implementation of community service programs engaging and servicing elementary school students, and volunteer management for youth and adults. In addition, she has been an involved parent in two of the partnership schools, having served as a PTA board member in both.

John E. Cawthorne has served as the vice president of the National Urban League's Education Division, which was housed at Boston College. He is currently assistant dean, School of Education, Boston College, and senior research associate in the Center for the Study of Testing, Evaluation, and Educational Policy at Boston College. He began his career in teaching immediately after graduating from Harvard in 1964, when he ran a federal program for primary students in Washington, DC. Subsequently, he was principal of the Lower School of the Massachusetts Experimental School System; and director of Chapter I for the Massachusetts Department of Correction, where he was responsible for all educational programs for twenty-year-olds and under in the Commonwealth's prisons and jails.

Marilyn Cochran-Smith received her Ph.D. in Language Education from the University of Pennsylvania. She is currently a professor of education and the director of programs in Teacher Education at Boston College. Her current research focuses on teacher education, particularly how prospective teachers learn to teach and how they continue to do so over their careers. She also studies and teaches about teacher research, a form of practitioner inquiry and a nationwide professionalization movement in teaching and teacher education. She has numerous publications, including *Inside/Outside: Teacher Research and Knowledge,* winner of the 1995 American Association of Colleges of Teacher Education Award for Excellence in Professional Writing in Teacher and Teacher Education.

Mary Beth Crowe is administrative project associate in the Office of the President at Penn State where she frequently writes on issues in higher education. She previously was involved in continuing education needs assessment and program development at Penn State, and also has worked in applied educational research settings. She holds master's and Ph.D. degrees in educational psychology from Northwestern University and a bachelor's degree in psychology and education from Washington University in St. Louis.

Aaron T. Ebata is an associate professor of Human Development and director of Graduate Programs in the Department of Human and Community Development at the University of Illinois at Urbana-Champaign. Dr. Ebata also has an appointment as an extension specialist with the University of Illinois Cooperative Extension Service. A former elementary school and preschool teacher, Dr. Ebata received his Ph.D. in human development and family studies in 1987 from the Pennsylvania State University, and completed a research fellowship at Stanford University before joining the faculty of the University of Illinois in 1990. Dr. Ebata is currently involved in research on the effects of natural disasters on adolescents and families, in outreach efforts focused on helping rural families cope with the aftermath of disasters, and in efforts to apply technological innovations to education and prevention.

John Engler was first elected to office in 1970 at the age of twenty-two, becoming, at that time, the youngest state representative in state history. In 1990 he was elected Michigan's forty-sixth governor. Under Governor Engler's leadership, taxes have been cut twenty-one times, saving Michigan taxpayers more than $1.5 billion in 1996. Since he took office, both families and job providers have saved more than $3.6 billion and per capita income growth has been the fastest in America. At the same time, the deficit was eliminated by cutting spending and the state's Rainy Day Fund recently topped $1 billion for the first time in history. Michigan presently leads the nation in welfare reform. More than 30% of welfare recipients in Michigan are working and earning a paycheck—almost four times the national average. In addition, the state welfare caseload has dropped by 20% to the lowest level in more than two decades. He was selected by his fellow governors to serve as chairman of the Republican Governors Association, the Council of Great Lakes Governors and the National Education Goals Panel. Engler earned a bachelor's degree in Agricultural Economics from Michigan State University and a law degree from the Thomas M. Cooley Law School.

Martha Farrell Erickson is the director of the Children, Youth, and Family Consortium at the University of Minnesota. Since 1987 Dr. Erickson also has been coordinator of Project STEEP, a longitudinal study of the effectiveness of preventive intervention with high-risk mothers and infants, at the University of Minnesota. Dr. Erickson has taught a variety of courses on early development, assessment, and family-focused intervention at the University of Minnesota and was co-developer of the core curriculum for the Child Abuse Prevention Studies program in the School of Social Work. Dr. Erickson consults and speaks on these same topics throughout the United States and abroad. She is author of many journal articles, book chapters, and a forthcoming book on early intervention. Earlier in her career Dr. Erickson worked as a school psychologist and special educator in both school and hospital settings and served two terms as president of the Minnesota School Psychologists Association.

Theresa M. Ferrari is a Ph.D. candidate in the Department of Family and Child Ecology at Michigan State University. She received her master's degree from Michigan State University in 1979 and a bachelor's in Home Economics Education in 1977 from the State University of New York– College at Oneonta. While completing her doctoral degree at Michigan

State, she assists with the Young Spartan Program and 4-H programs, working with teachers to develop school-to-work initiatives and designing a 4-H workforce preparation curriculum for elementary-age students. Prior to returning to Michigan State University, she was a county-based extension educator with the University of Maine Cooperative Extension. She designed innovative educational programs for school-age children, teens, child care providers, and 4-H leaders, including *Reaching Out for Teen Awareness: A Model for Education Through Interactive Theater*, now part of the National 4-H Juried Curriculum. Her current teaching, research, and outreach efforts focus on school-age children and issues of workforce preparation.

Celia B. Fisher, professor and director of Fordham University's Doctoral Specialization in Applied Developmental Psychology, received her Ph.D. in experimental psychology from the Graduate Faculty of the New School for Social Research in 1978. Chair of the National Task Force on Applied Developmental Science and a former member of the American Psychological Association's (APA) Ethics Committee, Dr. Fisher has served as chair of the New York State Board for licensure in Psychology, and chair of the Society for Research in Child Development's (SRCD) Committee for Ethical Conduct in Child Development Research, among other committees. Dr. Fisher is the author of numerous scholarly articles on child and adolescent development, ethnic minority development, graduate training in applied developmental psychology, and on professional and scientific ethics, as well as co-editor of a number of books primarily dealing with applied developmental psychology. She is a founding co-editor of the journal *Applied Developmental Science*, served as book review editor for the *Journal of Applied Developmental Psychology* and is on the editorial board for the *Journal of Research on Adolescence.*

Nancy Gaspard is an associate professor in the School of Nursing at Boston College. She received her Ph.D. in Public Health from the University of California, Los Angeles. Her current areas of interest and practice are community health nursing. Her research interests focus on the preparation of students for interprofessional practice in urban communities. She has been a faculty leader in connecting the University with the local community.

Joy C. Greer received her master's degree from the University of North Carolina at Greensboro from the department of Human Development and Family Studies. Presently, she is a Ph.D. candidate in Family and Child Ecology at Michigan State University. Greer regards herself as a family and child generalist based on her current projects: infant assessment, adolescent development, work-family stressors, program evaluation, and faculty implementation of service learning.

Christina J. Groark is co-director (with Dr. Robert B. McCall) of the University of Pittsburgh Office of Child Development (OCD) and director of the OCD Central Program. Dr. Groark is the principal investigator for several collaborative programs working on behalf of children and families, such as the Alliance for Infants, Early Head Start, Partnerships for Family Support, A Better Start, and the Starting Points Program. Dr. Groark is also the author of many articles and book chapters in the areas of university-community collaborations, international youth services, and early interventions. Dr. Groark has been a staff person or consultant to many institutions such as ARC/Allegheny, Allegheny County MH/MR, Valley Community Services, Community Human Services Corp., Allegheny County Health Department, Allegheny General Hospital, Allegheny-Singer Research Institute, the City Council of St. Petersburg in Russia, Howard Heinz Endowment, the Pittsburgh Foundation, the Jewish Healthcare Foundation, and the National Early Childhood Technical Assistance System.

Mimi G. Hamilton is a doctoral candidate in Developmental Psychology at Fordham University. She received a masters in education from Fairfield University. She served as program co-chair for the twenty-first annual conference of the Association for Moral Education, co-sponsored by Fordham University in 1995. She has conducted research on moral and racial climate across college campuses and is co-editing a collection of conference papers from the AME conference, "International Dialogue: Discussing Morality for the Twenty-First Century." Presently she is completing her dissertation on the relationship between leadership style and moral climate in the middle-school classroom and teaches courses in statistics, research design and methodology, and personality.

Ira Harkavy is associate vice president and director of the Center for Community Partnerships at the University of Pennsylvania. He teaches in the departments of history, urban studies, and city and regional planning, and is executive editor of *Universities and Community Schools.* Harkavy recently served as assistant to the president, director of the Penn Program for Public Service, vice dean of the School of Arts and Sciences, and executive director of the Program for Assessing and Revitalizing the Social Sciences also at the University of Pennsylvania. He is currently a consultant to the U.S. Department of Housing and Urban Development and its Office of University Partnerships. Harkavy received his doctorate in history from the University of Pennsylvania in 1979. His research has focused on school and community revitalization in Philadelphia and other cities. In recent years, he has written on how to involve universities effectively in democratic partnerships with local public schools and their communities. The West Philadelphia Improvement Corps (WEPIC), a partnership linking the University of Pennsylvania and the West Philadelphia community, emerged from seminars and research projects he directs with other colleagues at the University.

Ann Higgins-D'Alessandro is an associate professor in the Department of Psychology, Fordham University. Educated in Human Development and Family Studies at Pennsylvania State University, Higgins-D'Alessandro received her Ph.D. in 1979. She was founder and past-president of the Association for Moral Education (AME) and is currently a board member there. In 1995 she was program chair of the AME's twenty-first annual conference, the organization's second international conference with participants from all continents and over twenty countries. Before coming to Fordham in 1989, she was a senior researcher at the Center for Moral Development and Education at the Harvard Graduate School of Education, working with Lawrence Kohlberg. Higgins-D'Alessandro co-authored *Lawrence Kohlberg's Approach to Moral Education* and has written many scholarly articles and chapters on adolescent moral development as well as school and college moral cultures, developing instruments assessing both. She has published several studies on the influence of the workplace climate on moral development and action.

Robert Hughes, Jr. is an associate professor and extension specialist in the Department of Family Relations and Human Development at the Ohio State University. Hughes received his Ph.D. from the University of Texas at Austin in 1980. Prior to joining the faculty of OSU he was a member of the faculty at the University of Illinois at Urbana-Champaign from 1982 to 1994. Dr. Hughes has developed and evaluated preventive programs designed for families dealing with difficult life situations. He has conducted research about how families obtain and utilize informal social support to manage stressful life transitions.

Carol Hurd-Green is the associate dean in the College of Arts and Sciences and an adjunct associate professor in the English Department at Boston College. She received her Ph.D. in American Studies from George Washington University. She teaches courses in American Studies, American Literature, and Women's Studies, and has published several books on American women and American women writers.

Carl N. Johnson received his Ph.D. in child psychology from the Institute of Child Development, University of Minnesota, with a focus on cognitive development. He began and continues his career with an appointment in an applied, professional Program in Child Development and Child Care at the University of Pittsburgh. He co-founded the Office of Child Development at the University of Pittsburgh with Mark Strauss. Dr. Johnson spends most of his time teaching in his applied program, serving as a core member of the developmental faculty in psychology, and pursuing his research on children's concepts of mind, magic and religion. In addition to journal publications, Carl co-authored a book with Nancy Curry, *Beyond Self-Esteem,* published by the NAEYC. He is currently editing a book with Karl Rosegren and Paul Harris, *Imagining the Impossible: The Development of Scientific, Magical and Religious Thinking in Contemporary Society,* to be published by Cambridge University Press.

Joanne G. Keith is a professor in the Department of Family and Child Ecology at Michigan State University. Her academic responsibilities include research, teaching, and outreach related to child/youth development and family systems. She is the faculty director of the Young Spartan Program, a K–12 community partnership with Michigan State University, Lansing Public School District, the State of Michigan and the Lansing Regional Chamber of Commerce. Additional areas of expertise include: demographic trends related to children, youth and families; community collaborations on behalf of children, youth and their families; and youth and families from an international perspective.

Maureen Kenny is an associate professor and director of training in the Counseling Psychology Program at Boston College. She completed an M.Ed. from Teachers College, Columbia, and Ph.D. in 1985 from the

University of Pennsylvania. Dr. Kenny's research interests include adolescent-parent attachments, psychosocial factors contributing to adolescent gender differences in depressive symptoms, and the development of integrated models of service delivery for adolescents and families.

Rosemary Krawczyk received her Ph.D. in Higher Education from Boston College. She is currently an associate professor in the School of Nursing at Boston College. Her research addresses the development of moral judgment in nursing students.

Leon M. Lederman is director emeritus of the Fermi National Accelerator Laboratory in Batavia, Illinois, having been director from 1979 to 1989. He is Pritzker Professor of Science at the Illinois Institute of Technology. He was professor of physics at Columbia University from 1958 to 1989 and the Frank L. Sulzberger Professor of Physics at the University of Chicago from 1989 to 1991. Dr. Lederman's research has spanned four decades and includes many remarkable achievements. In 1956 Dr. Lederman and his team from Columbia University discovered the long-lived neutral K-meson (kaon) particle. In 1961 Dr. Lederman and his group discovered the muon neutrino, which provided the first proof that there was more than one type of neutrino, for which he received the Nobel Prize in Physics in 1988. In 1977 he and his collaborators discovered evidence for a new elementary particle called the "bottom quark." He has initiated over fifteen programs introducing topics in modern physics to high school students, elementary school teachers, and college teachers. He was chairman of the board and past president of the American Association for the Advancement of Science (1991–1993). He is a member of the National Academy of Sciences. Among his numerous awards are the National Medal of Science (1965), the Wolf Prize in Physics (1983) and the Nobel Prize.

Richard M. Lerner (Volume Editor) is the Anita L. Brennan Professor of Education at Boston College and the director of the Boston College Center for Child, Family, and Community Partnerships. A developmental psychologist, during the 1994–1995 academic year he held the Tyner Eminent Scholar Chair in the Human Sciences at Florida State University. He is the author or editor of many books and scholarly articles, including his 1995 book, *America's Youth in Crisis: Challenges and Options for Programs and Policies.* Lerner is known for his theory of and research about relations between life-span human development and contextual or ecological change.

He is the founding editor of the *Journal of Research on Adolescence* and of the new journal, *Applied Developmental Science*.

Claire Lowery is currently the director of the Institute of Religious Education and Pastoral Ministry and an adjunct associate professor of Theology and Pastoral Ministry. She received her Masters of Divinity and Doctorate of Ministry from the Andover Newton Theological School. The focus of her research has been the interdisciplinary use of theology and psychology in the ministry of pastoral care and counseling.

M. Brinton Lykes, professor in the Developmental and Educational Psychology Program at Boston College, has worked since 1986 in the development of community-based psychological assistance programs in contexts of war and state-sponsored violence throughout Latin America. She received her Ph.D. in Social-Community Psychology from Boston College. Her research explores alternative conceptions of the self and the importance of culture and indigenous practices in the lives of women and child survivors and the dilemmas encountered in multicultural, engendered participatory action research.

C. Peter Magrath assumed the presidency of the National Association of State Universities and Land-Grant Colleges (NASULGC) in 1992. A political scientist with a Ph.D. degree from Cornell University, he served as president of the University of Missouri System from 1985 to 1991. Previously he was president of the University of Minnesota from 1974 to 1984. Before that, Dr. Magrath headed the State University of New York at Binghamton from 1972 to 1974. Between 1968 and 1972, Dr. Magrath held faculty and administrative posts at the University of Nebraska, Lincoln. He began his academic career at Brown University, where he rose from instructor to professor of political science from 1961 to 1968, as well as serving as associate dean. An author of numerous books, monographs, and articles on American Constitutional Law and history, higher education, and international affairs, he has been active on many national higher-education commissions, task forces, and committees.

Russell G. Mawby is Chairman Emeritus of the W. K. Kellogg Foundation of Battle Creek, Michigan. After thirty years on the Foundation staff, he retired in 1995, having served from 1970 through 1995 as the Foundation's chief executive officer. Prior to joining the Foundation,

Mawby served on the faculty at Michigan State University, including nine years as assistant director of the Cooperative Extension Service of the University, with responsibilities for 4-H youth programs. With degrees from Michigan State and Purdue Universities, Mawby currently serves on the boards of Starr Commonwealth Schools in Albion, Michigan, serving troubled youth and their families; Michigan's Children, a youth advocacy group; Calhoun County (Michigan) Communities in Schools, integrating child/family services into the school setting; Michigan Nonprofit Association; Council of Michigan Foundations; the Michigan 4-H Foundation; and is a Fellow of the Institute for Children, Youth and Families at Michigan State University.

Robert B. McCall is co-director (with Dr. Christina J. Groark) of the University of Pittsburgh Office of Child Development, co-director (with Dr. Mark S. Strauss) of its Policy and Evaluation Project, and professor of psychology. Dr. McCall is the author of hundreds of books and articles for both scholarly and general audiences in the areas of infant mental behavior, development changes in general mental performance, the prediction of later IQ, developmental research design and analysis, parenting and child development, science communication through the media, and university-community partnerships. He is an action editor for *Child Development,* covering the areas of applied research, program evaluation, policy studies, and research methodology; he has been a consulting editor for a number of leading developmental journals; and he was a contributing editor, monthly columnist, and feature writer for *Parents* magazine.

Peggy S. Meszaros is senior vice president, provost, and professor of Family and Child Development at Virginia Polytechnic Institute and State University. As provost since 1995, she is the university's chief academic officer responsible for all instruction, research, and outreach of the institution. Dr. Meszaros was department head at Hood College from 1973 to 1977 when she joined the Maryland State Department of Education as State Supervisor of Home Economics. In 1979 she was named associate dean of Home Economics Cooperative Extension at Oklahoma State University and in 1983 became Director of Academic Affairs. In 1985 she joined the University of Kentucky as dean of the College of Human Environmental Sciences and in 1993 she became dean of the College of Human Resources at Virginia Tech. A family social scientist, Dr. Meszaros received a Ph.D. in 1977 from the University of Maryland, College Park.

She is the author of more than eighty scholarly articles and chapters and one book.

Alan D. Minuskin is a clinical professor in the Boston College School of Law. He received his J.D. from the New England School of Law. He has been a practicing attorney for twenty years and is a member of state and federal bars in Massachusetts and New Jersey. He teaches courses in lawyering process and pretrial litigation. His research interests focus on lawyer incivility and clinical supervision models across disciplines. He is committed to the interprofessional collaboration model as a way in which legal and mental health professionals discuss and co-handle clients' problems in a holistic way, with the focus on improving the clients' quality of life, rather than simply solving the legal or situational problem.

Judy Jolley Mohraz became the ninth president of Goucher College in 1994. Dr. Mohraz holds bachelor's and master's degrees from Baylor University and a Ph.D. from the University of Illinois at Urbana-Champaign, where she was a University of Illinois Fellow. She spent most of her academic and administrative career at Southern Methodist University (SMU) in Dallas. She first went to SMU in 1974 as an assistant professor in history, became coordinator of the Women's Studies Program in 1977, was promoted in 1980 to associate professor of history and in 1988 was named associate provost for student academic affairs. At SMU, Dr. Mohraz was twice selected as Outstanding Professor, Outstanding Administrator and Outstanding Woman of SMU. She has authored a book on urban education and minority students in the early twentieth century, as well as numerous articles and reviews on the history of education and women in America. Her other community service activities have focused on issues related to quality child care. Currently she sits on the boards of the Independent College Fund of Maryland, the Maryland Committee for Children and the Baltimore Equitable Society.

Jean Mooney is an associate professor in the Department of Curriculum, Administration and Special Education at Boston College. She received her Ph.D. from Boston College. Her research interests focus on developing the pedagogy of diversity for regular classroom settings and creating an integrated services model for urban schools. She has collaborated extensively with the Graduate School of Social Work at Boston College to design joint training experiences for students in the Schools of Education and

Social Work. She is currently editing a book on social work–education collaborations.

Madlyn C. Morreale is an instructor at the Johns Hopkins University School of Hygiene and Public Health, with appointments in the departments of Maternal and Child Health and Health Policy and Management. She is the community planning and policy coordinator for the Center for Adolescent Health Promotion and Disease Prevention at Johns Hopkins, a Prevention Research Center funded by the U.S. Centers for Disease Control and Prevention. Morreale's interests include access to care for youth in high-risk situations, HIV/AIDS policy, the effects of health system reform on adolescents and vulnerable populations, the participation and perspective of youth and community members in the work of academia, and the translation of academic findings for policy makers and other professionals. Prior to joining the faculty at Johns Hopkins, Ms. Morreale was a professional staff member of the Select Committee on Children, Youth, and Families in the U.S. House of Representatives. She is co-chair of the Maryland AIDS Legislative Committee.

Ann K. Mullis earned a Ph.D. in Child Development from Iowa State University. She serves as coordinator of the Florida State University Family Institute and associate director of the Florida Inter-University Center. She teaches courses in infant and preschool development and programming. Her research involves child and adolescent development in the context of parent-child relations. She has published on this topic in numerous scholarly and professional journals. Dr. Mullis has worked with the Cooperative Extension System in Florida and North Dakota in the areas of youth at risk and parenting issues. She has received support for her research and project activities from a wide variety of sources, including the Agricultural Experiment Stations of Florida and North Dakota, U.S. Department of Health and Human Services, Bush Foundation, and the Otto Bremer Foundation. Dr. Mullis has served on faculties of the University of Florida, North Dakota State University, California State University-Chico, and Idaho State University. She serves as a representative for the Council for Early Childhood Professional Recognition, and as a validator in the accreditation program of the National Academy of Early Childhood Programs.

Ronald L. Mullis received his Ph.D. from Iowa State University in Child Development. He is currently a professor of Family and Child Sciences, director of the Early Childhood Development Project, and acting director of the Family Research and Policy Program at Florida State University. He teaches courses in child and adolescent development at both the graduate and undergraduate level. Dr. Mullis researches adolescent development with particular attention to the influence of family and community on adolescent educational aspirations and career decision-making. He has published numerous scholarly articles on this topic in professional journals and proceedings of international and national meetings. Dr. Mullis has served in several offices of the North Dakota Council on Family Relations. He serves as a consultant for national and regional Head Start and for the National Association for the Education of Young Children.

Daniel F. Perkins is an assistant professor of family, youth, and community sciences at the University of Florida. A human ecologist, Dr. Perkins received a Ph.D. in 1995 from Michigan State University. Currently, he is examining factors related to positive youth development and youth engagement in risky behaviors. In addition, he has published several research reports on his evaluation of collaborative efforts on behalf of children, youth, and families. He is an advisory board member to the National Network for Collaboration. This national effort is funded as part of the Children, Youth and Families at Risk Initiative of the Cooperative State Research, Education and Extension Service, United States Department of Agriculture.

Jane Quinn joined the DeWitt Wallace-Reader's Digest Fund as program director in January 1993. She is responsible for program development, day-to-day administration and grantmaking activities. Quinn came to the Fund from the Carnegie Council on Adolescent Development, Washington, DC, where she directed a three-year study of youth development programs and services in the United States, and was principal author of a national report (*A Matter of Time: Risk and Opportunity in the Nonschool Hours*) on that subject. Quinn served from 1981 to 1990 as director of program services for Girls Clubs of America in New York. In prior years, she had held positions in Washington, DC, at the D.C. Health Department and the Center for Population Options. In addition, she was a caseworker for the Juvenile Protective Association of Chicago, and Family Counseling Center, Catholic Charities of Buffalo, NY. Quinn received a master's degree from the University of Chicago School of Social Service Administration in 1969 and a bachelor's degree in economics from the

College of New Rochelle in 1966. She is the author of numerous articles on youth issues, and has served on the boards of many youth and social service organizations.

Catherine Ross received her Ph.D. in History from Yale University, and her J.D. from Yale Law School. She was a visiting professor at Boston College from 1993 to 1996. She is currently a faculty member at the George Washington Law School. Her areas of interest in history include history of family and childhood, U.S. constitutional history, history of the welfare state, and legal history. Her areas of interest in law include family law, the power of the state, intellectual property, law and medicine, and discrimination. She is currently the vice chair for the American Bar Association Steering Committee on the Unmet Legal Needs of Children and Families, a member of the American Bar Association's Section of Litigation Task Force on Children, and the author of *America's Children at Risk: A National Agenda for Legal Action* (1993, American Bar Association).

Richard J. Sauer is president and chief executive officer of National 4-H Council. A biologist and entomologist by professional training, Dr. Sauer has degrees from St. John's University in Collegeville, Minnesota, the University of Michigan and North Dakota State University, the latter a Ph.D. earned in 1967. Prior to joining National 4-H Council, Dr. Sauer spent over eight years at the University of Minnesota as Director of the Agricultural Experiment Station, with the last five-and-a-half years as vice president for Agriculture, Forestry and Home Economics. From March 1988 until January 1989, he was interim president of the University. Before going to the University of Minnesota in 1980, Dr. Sauer was on the faculty at Kansas State University for four years and Michigan State University for eight years. He worked in a variety of faculty, administrative and leadership roles in these land-grant universities, and in 1989 redirected his career to youth development and nonprofit leadership.

John Savage is currently a professor in the Curriculum, Administration, and Special Education Department at Boston College. He received his Ed.D. from Boston University in 1966. His research interest focuses on literacy instruction. He is the author of numerous journal articles and books. His most recent book is *Using Literature to Teach Reading* (Brown & Benchmark).

Lonnie R. Sherrod, a development psychologist, is executive vice president of the William T. Grant Foundation. Before joining the Foundation, he was assistant dean of the Graduate Faculty, New School for Social Research, and he has also been on the staff of the Social Science Research Council. He received his Ph.D. in psychology from Yale University in 1978, a master's in biology from the University of Rochester in 1974, and a bachelor's from Duke University in 1972. His research interests have focused on social cognitive development during infancy and adolescence. Recent publications include *Stress, Risk, and Resilience During Childhood and Adolescence* coedited with Robert Haggerty, Norman Garmezy, and Michael Rutter and published by Cambridge University Press, and *Late Adolescence and the Transition to Adulthood,* a special issue of the *Journal of Research on Adolescence.* He is on the editorial boards of several journals including *Applied Developmental Science, International Journal of Behavior Development,* and *Human Nature.*

Lou Anna K. Simon (Volume Editor) is provost and vice president for academic affairs at Michigan State University and a professor of educational administration. She served as interim provost beginning September 1992. Dr. Simon has a long history of experience in academic administration. She was assistant provost for General Academic Administration in the Provost's Office at MSU from 1981 through 1987. She joined the Office of Institutional Research, now the Office of Planning and Budgets, in 1970 as a graduate assistant. She became an assistant professor in that office in 1974 and was named assistant director in 1977. In 1978, she was named an associate professor and an assistant to the president for Affirmative Action Programs.

Stephen A. Small is professor and chair in the Department of Child and Family Studies at the University of Wisconsin-Madison and Extension Human Development and Family Relations Specialist for the University of Wisconsin-Extension, Cooperative Extension Service. He received a Ph.D. in developmental psychology from the Department of Human Development and Family Studies at Cornell University in 1985. Dr. Small's current work focuses on using the tools of social science to help policymakers, professionals, community leaders and other citizens address community problems. For the past eight years he has conducted the Teen Assessment Project, a community-based action research program aimed at helping communities better understand and address the problems facing adolescents. Dr. Small is currently completing a book entitled *Bridging the Gap Between Research and Action,* which is aimed at helping social science scholars make their work more relevant to policy and practice. He is on the editorial board of the *Journal of Marriage and the Family* and serves as an editorial reviewer for the *American Journal of Community Psychology, Family Relations, Journal of Research on Adolescence* and *Child Development.*

Michael Smyer is the dean of the Graduate School of Arts and Sciences and associate vice president for Research at Boston College. He received his Ph.D. in psychology from Duke University. He is a past president of Division 20 (Adult Development and Aging) and Section 2 (clinical gerontology) of Division 12 (Clinical) of the American Psychological Association. His research focuses on the design, implementation, and evaluation of health-related interventions for older adults. Among his recent publications are two edited volumes: *Mental Health and Aging* (1993, Springer) and *Older Adults' Decision-making and the Law* (with K. W. Schaie & M. B. Kapp) (1996, Springer).

Avi Soifer is the dean of the Boston College School of Law. He received his J.D. from Yale Law School. He has published over forty articles, book chapters, and other writings, including the book entitled *Law and the Company We Keep* (1995, Harvard University Press). He is currently the vice chair of the Massachusetts Supreme Judicial Court Task Force on Judicial Education, commissioner of the American Bar Association's Commission on College and University legal studies, and he serves on the steering committee for the United States First Circuit Court of Appeals Task Force on Gender, Race, and Ethnic Bias.

Graham B. Spanier is president of the Pennsylvania State University where he also holds academic appointments as professor of human development and family studies, professor of sociology, and professor of family and community medicine. He previously served as chancellor of the University of Nebraska Lincoln, provost and vice president for academic affairs at Oregon State University, vice provost for undergraduate studies at the State University of New York at Stony Brook, and in three administrative positions in Penn State's College of Human Development where he was a faculty member from 1973 to 1982. Dr. Spanier has more than one hundred scholarly publications, including ten books. He is a family sociologist, demographer, and marriage and family therapist. He earned his Ph.D.

in sociology from Northwestern University, where he was a Woodrow Wilson Fellow, and his bachelor's and master's degrees from Iowa State University. He has served in several positions of national leadership in higher education, including the Board of Presidents of the Commission on Information Technology of the National Association of State Universities and Land Grant Colleges, the Commission on Women of the American Council on Education, the NCAA President's Commission, and the Joint Commission on Accountability Reporting.

Elizabeth Sparks is currently an assistant professor in the Department of Counseling, Developmental Psychology, and Research Methods at Boston College. Dr. Sparks received her Ph.D. in Counseling Psychology from Boston College. Her research interests include: youth and violence, training issues in multicultural counseling, and culture-specific interventions with at-risk youth. Her clinical practice is directed towards survivors of physical and/or sexual abuse.

Mark S. Strauss is a faculty member and former chair of the Department of Psychology at the University of Pittsburgh. His primary research is infant cognitive development. In 1986 he co-founded the Office of Child Development at the University of Pittsburgh with Carl Johnson. The Office functions as a facilitator for educational, research, and service programs at the University and between the University and the community.

Christine M. Todd is currently associate dean for Outreach in the College of Family and Consumer Sciences at the University of Georgia. In this position she facilitates the outreach activities of the College. Prior to joining the University of Georgia, Dr. Todd was associate professor and extension specialist in the Department of Human and Community Development at the University of Illinois at Urbana-Champaign. She also served as faculty director of the Child Care Resource Service, an outreach program of the Department of Human and Community Development that addresses the child-care needs of parents, child-care professionals, employers, and communities in east-central Illinois. A developmental psychologist, Dr. Todd received her doctorate from the Institute of Child Development at the University of Minnesota in 1985. She conducts research on child-care stability, parental selection of child care, and prevention programming for children, youth, and families living in high-risk environments.

Robbie Tourse received her Masters in Social Work from Simmons College, and her Ph.D. in Higher Education from the Boston College School of Education. She is currently the director of field experience and a clinical adjunct assistant professor in the Graduate School of Social Work at Boston College. She just completed work as co-principal investigator on a DeWitt Wallace Reader's Digest grant that focused on social work and education collaboration in public schools.

Robert Turillo is a practicing social worker and currently serving as an intensive case manager at Massachusetts Behavioral Health Partnership in Boston. He received his Masters in Social Work from Boston University. He has directed numerous programs for at-risk adolescents. His clinical interest focuses on the mental health dimensions of substance abuse and delinquency.

Sandra Waddock received her M.B.A./D.B.A. from Boston University. She is currently an associate professor in the Operations and Strategic Management Department of the Carroll School of Management at Boston College. Dr. Waddock has published one book and thirty articles. Her current areas of interest include corporate social performance and public/private collaboration. Her book, *Not By Schools Alone: Sharing America's Education Reform,* was recently released (1995, Praeger). At Boston College Dr. Waddock teaches courses on strategic management and social issues in management.

Mary Walsh is a professor in the Department of Counseling, Developmental Psychology, and Research Methods at Boston College. She received her Ph.D. in clinical-developmental psychology from Clark University. Her research focuses on the intersection of developmental psychology and clinical practice, and addresses the delivery of integrated services in urban schools, developmental conceptions of illness, and the psychosocial impact of homelessness. Her book, *Moving to Nowhere,* (1992, Praeger Press), examines the impact of homelessness on the development of children and families.

Carol Weinberg is the Coordinator of Community Service and a lecturer in Education and Women's Studies at Goucher College. She is one of the original members of the Shriver Center Higher Education Consortium funded by the Corporation for National Service. Dr. Weinberg holds a

Ph.D. in Curriculum and Instruction from Michigan State University, a M.Ed. in Counseling from the Graduate School of Education at the University of Pennsylvania, and a B.A. in Psychology from Harpur College (SUNY Binghamton). She was the Associate Dean for Student Affairs at Smith College from 1986 to 1991 and the Associate Dean of Students and Director of Residential Living at Goucher College from 1978 to 1986. She has also taught Educational Psychology at Towson State University and the University of Delaware. Dr. Weinberg is the author of *The Complete Handbook for College Women: Making the Most of Your College Experience* (1994) and *The Transition Guide for College Juniors and Seniors: How to Prepare for the Future* (1996), both published by New York University Press.

Richard A. Weinberg, the Birkmaier Professor of Educational Leadership, is a professor of child psychology and adjunct professor of psychology and educational psychology at the University of Minnesota-Twin Cities where he is also director of the Institute of Child Development. For many years he directed the School Psychology Training Program, one of the first doctoral programs in the U.S. to receive accreditation from the American Psychological Association. He also helped create the Center for Early Education and Development which he directed until June 1994, and has served as chair of the Advisory Council for the University of Minnesota Children, Youth, and Family Consortium. He has co-authored or edited several books including a child development textbook and a volume on observing young children in early childhood settings. He has served on the professional advisory board of *Baby Talk Magazine,* and is former associate editor of *Contemporary Psychology.* Weinberg currently chairs a national advisory board for a TV series for parents (being developed by PBS) and is an editor of the journal, *Applied Developmental Science.*

Nancy Zollers received her Ph.D. in Special Education from Syracuse University and is currently an assistant professor in the Department of Curriculum, Administration and Special Education at Boston College. Her current areas of interest include disability, integrated services, and models of inclusion. Her field-based research on inclusion of special needs of children in regular education settings is conducted in Boston Public Schools.

Name Index

Subject Index